TOPICS IN MICROECONOMICS

INDUSTRIAL ORGANIZATION, AUCTIONS, AND INCENTIVES

ELMAR WOLFSTETTER

Humboldt University at Berlin

CAMBRIDGE
UNIVERSITY PRESS

PUBLISHED BY THE PRESS SYNDICATE OF THE UNIVERSITY OF CAMBRIDGE
The Pitt Building, Trumpington Street, Cambridge, United Kingdom

CAMBRIDGE UNIVERSITY PRESS
The Edinburgh Building, Cambridge CB2 2RU, UK
40 West 20th Street, New York, NY 10011-4211, USA
477 Williamstown Road, Port Melbourne, VIC 3207, Australia
Ruiz de Alarcón 13, 28014 Madrid, Spain
Dock House, The Waterfront, Cape Town 8001, South Africa

http://www.cambridge.org

First published 1999
Reprinted 2002

Typeset in Times Roman 11/14 pt. in LaTeX 2_ε [TB]

*A catalog record for this book is available from
the British Library.*

Library of Congress Cataloging-in-Publication Data
Wolfstetter, Elmar, 1945–
Topics in microeconomics : industrial organization, auctions, and
incentives / Elmar Wolfstetter.
p.   cm.
ISBN 0-521-64228-0 (hb). – ISBN 0-521-64534-4 (pbk)
1. Microeconomics.   2. Competition, Imperfect.   3. Industrial
organization.   I. Title.
HB172.W673   1999
338.5 – dc21   99-11535
                              CIP
ISBN 0 521 64228 0 hardback
ISBN 0 521 64534 4 paperback

Transferred to digital printing 2003

This text in microeconomics focuses on the strategic analysis of markets under imperfect competition, incomplete information, and incentives.

Part I of the book covers imperfect competition, from monopoly and regulation to the strategic analysis of oligopolistic markets. Part II explains the analytics of risk, stochastic dominance, and risk aversion, supplemented with a variety of applications from different areas in economics. Part III focuses on markets and incentives under incomplete information, including a comprehensive introduction to the theory of auctions, which plays an important role in modern economics.

Each chapter introduces the core issues in an accessible yet rigorous fashion, and then investigates specialized themes. An attempt is made to develop a coherent story, with self-contained explanations and proofs. The only prerequisites are a basic knowledge of calculus and probability, and familiarity with intermediate undergraduate microeconomics.

The text can be used as a textbook in courses on microeconomics, theoretical industrial organization, and information and incentives for senior undergraduate or first-year graduate students.

Elmar Wolfstetter is Professor of Economics at Humboldt University, Berlin. He has taught at the State University of New York, Buffalo (1974–82) and the Free University of Berlin (1982–92), and held visiting appointments at King's College, Cambridge University, at the Universities of Copenhagen, Bern, and Pittsburgh, and at the Hebrew University, Jerusalem. The author of two other books and numerous articles in professional journals, including the *Economic Journal*, *Oxford Economic Papers*, and the *RAND Journal of Economics*, Professor Wolfstetter is Associate Editor of the *European Economic Review*, a Council Member of the Verein f. Socialpolitik (German Economic Association), and Editor of the *Journal of Institutional and Theoretical Economics*.

Contents

Preface   *page* xiii
Acknowledgments   xvii

I Imperfect Competition   **1**

1 Monopoly   3
  1.1   Introduction   3
  1.2   Cournot Monopoly – Weak Monopoly   5
      1.2.1   Cournot Point   5
      1.2.2   Deadweight Loss of Monopoly   14
      1.2.3   Social Loss of Monopoly and Rent Seeking   16
      1.2.4   Monopoly and Innovation   17
      1.2.5   Monopoly and Product Quality   21
  1.3   Price-Discriminating or Strong Monopoly   22
      1.3.1   First-Degree Price Discrimination 23
      1.3.2   Second-Degree Price Discrimination 24
      1.3.3   Third-Degree Price Discrimination 24
      1.3.4   Limits of Price Discrimination   26
  1.4   Hidden Information and Price Discrimination   26
      1.4.1   Solution of the Restricted Program 29
      1.4.2   The Optimal Sales Plan   30
      1.4.3   Why it Pays to "Distort" Efficiency   31
      1.4.4   Sorting, Bunching, and Exclusion   32
  1.5   Price Discrimination and Public Goods*   34
  1.6   Intertemporal Price Discrimination   36
      1.6.1   Durable-Goods Monopoly   37
      1.6.2   Time-Inconsistency Problem   39
      1.6.3   Optimal Time-Consistent Price Discrimination   40
      1.6.4   Coase Conjecture   42
      1.6.5   An Example Where the Coase Conjecture Fails*   42
  1.7   Bilateral Monopoly and Bargaining*   43
      1.7.1   A Finite-Horizon Bargaining Game   44
      1.7.2   Infinite-Horizon Bargaining   45

	1.8	Digression: The Case Against Microsoft	49
	1.9	Concluding Remarks	50
	1.10	Bibliographic Notes	50

2 Regulation of Monopoly — 52

	2.1	Introduction	52
	2.2	Positive Theory: The Averch–Johnson Effect*	53
		2.2.1 Assumptions	53
		2.2.2 Effects of Regulation	54
		2.2.3 Relation to Cost Minimization	55
		2.2.4 Welfare Implication	56
	2.3	Normative Theory: Two Almost Perfect Regulations	57
		2.3.1 The Total Surplus Subsidy Mechanism	57
		2.3.2 The Incremental Surplus Subsidy (ISS) Mechanism	58
	2.4	Bibliographic Notes	63

3 Oligopoly and Industrial Organization — 65

	3.1	Introduction	65
		3.1.1 Game-Theoretic Foundations	65
		3.1.2 Historical Note	67
	3.2	Three Perspectives	67
		3.2.1 The Three Market Games	68
		3.2.2 Cournot Competition	70
		3.2.3 Bertrand Competition	72
		3.2.4 Stackelberg Competition	74
		3.2.5 Welfare Ranking	77
		3.2.6 The Dual of Cournot Duopoly	77
		3.2.7 Discussion	78
	3.3	More on Stackelberg Competition	79
		3.3.1 Criticism and Extensions	79
		3.3.2 Managerial Incentives as Commitment Mechanism	80
		3.3.3 Commitment and Observability	85
	3.4	More on Cournot Competition	89
		3.4.1 Existence and Uniqueness	89
		3.4.2 Digression: A Prescription for Leviathan*	95
		3.4.3 What Does a Cournot Equilibrium Maximize?*	97
		3.4.4 What If Suppliers Form a Cartel?	98
		3.4.5 Selten's "Four Are Few and Six Are Many"	100
		3.4.6 Are Mergers Profitable?	102
		3.4.7 The Welfare Loss of Cournot Oligopoly	104
		3.4.8 A Corrective Tax	105
		3.4.9 The Generalized ISS Regulatory Mechanism*	106
		3.4.10 Entry*	107
		3.4.11 Exit*	111

3.5		More on Bertrand Competition	116
	3.5.1	Capacity-Constrained Price Competition: An Example	117
	3.5.2	An Alternative Rationing Rule	122
	3.5.3	Generalizations	124
3.6		A Defense of Cournot Competition*	125
	3.6.1	Benchmark Cournot Equilibrium	125
	3.6.2	The Price-Competition Subgame	126
	3.6.3	Equilibrium of the Overall Game	130
	3.6.4	Excess Capacity and Collusion	131
	3.6.5	Discussion	131
3.7		Bibliographic Notes	132

II Risk, Stochastic Dominance, and Risk Aversion **133**

4		Stochastic Dominance: Theory	135
	4.1	Introduction	135
	4.2	Assumptions and Definitions	136
	4.3	First-Order Stochastic Dominance (FSD)	136
	4.3.1	Main Results	137
	4.3.2	FSD and the "Stochastically Larger" Relationship*	138
	4.3.3	Relationship to Other Stochastic Orderings	139
	4.4	Second-Order Stochastic Dominance	140
	4.4.1	Main Results	141
	4.4.2	SSD and the "Stochastically More Risky" Relationship*	142
	4.5	An Invariance Property*	143
	4.6	Ranking Transformations of Random Variables*	144
	4.7	Comparative Statics of Risk	145
	4.7.1	Framework	145
	4.7.2	Key Issue	145
	4.7.3	Summary Table	148
	4.8	Bibliographic Notes	148

5		Stochastic Dominance: Applications	149
	5.1	Introduction	149
	5.2	Portfolio Selection I	149
	5.3	The Competitive Firm under Price Uncertainty	150
	5.4	Labor Supply	152
	5.5	Entry in Cournot Oligopoly	153
	5.6	Auctions	155
	5.7	Portfolio Selection II*	155
	5.8	Income Inequality*	157
	5.9	Supplement: Variance-Minimizing Portfolios*	159
	5.9.1	Portfolios	160
	5.9.2	Conjectures	160
	5.9.3	Outlook	160

		5.9.4	Assumptions	161
		5.9.5	A Lemma That Clears the Road	161
		5.9.6	Main Result	162
		5.9.7	Summary	163
		5.9.8	Discussion	163
	5.10	Bibliographic Notes		163

6 Risk Aversion — 165

	6.1	Introduction		165
	6.2	Absolute and Relative Risk Aversion		165
		6.2.1	Pratt's Theorem	166
		6.2.2	An Incomplete-Insurance Puzzle	167
	6.3	Strong Absolute Risk Aversion*		168
		6.3.1	Ross's Theorem	169
		6.3.2	A Portfolio Selection Puzzle	170
	6.4	Wealth-Dependent Risk Aversion*		171
	6.5	Bibliographic Notes		172

III   Incomplete Information and Incentives — **173**

7 Matching: The Marriage Problem* — 175

	7.1	Introduction		175
	7.2	Notation and Basic Assumptions		175
	7.3	Stable Two-Sided Matchings		176
	7.4	Who Benefits from Which Procedure?		178
	7.5	Strategic Issues		179
		7.5.1	Two Impossibility Results	179
		7.5.2	Stable Matchings?	180
	7.6	Bibliographic Notes		181

8 Auctions — 182

	8.1	Introduction		182
		8.1.1	Information Problem	182
		8.1.2	Basic Assumptions	182
		8.1.3	Cournot-Monopoly Approach	183
		8.1.4	Auctions – What, Where, and Why	184
		8.1.5	Popular Auctions	185
		8.1.6	Early History of Auctions	186
	8.2	The Basics of Private-Value Auctions		186
		8.2.1	Some Basic Results on Dutch and English Auctions	186
		8.2.2	Revenue Equivalence	187
		8.2.3	Solution of Some Auction Games – Assuming Uniformly Distributed Valuations	188
		8.2.4	An Alternative Solution Procedure*	195
		8.2.5	General Solution of Symmetric Auction Games	196
		8.2.6	Vickrey Auction as a Clarke–Groves Mechanism*	202

8.3	Robustness*	203
	8.3.1 Introducing Numbers Uncertainty	204
	8.3.2 Discrete Valuations	204
	8.3.3 Removing Bidders' Risk Neutrality	205
	8.3.4 Removing Independence: Correlated Beliefs	205
	8.3.5 Removing Symmetry	206
	8.3.6 Multiunit Auctions	207
	8.3.7 Split-Award Auctions	208
	8.3.8 Repeated Auctions	208
8.4	Auction Rings	209
8.5	Optimal Auctions	211
	8.5.1 A Simplified Approach	212
	8.5.2 The Mechanism-Design Approach	214
	8.5.3 Secret Reservation Price?	221
	8.5.4 Optimal Auctions with Stochastic Entry*	222
8.6	Common-Value Auctions and the Winner's Curse	225
	8.6.1 An Example: The Wallet Auction	225
	8.6.2 Some General Results	226
8.7	Affiliated Values*	229
	8.7.1 Private and Common Value Generalized	229
	8.7.2 Stochastic Similarity: Affiliation	230
	8.7.3 Generalized Solution of the Vickrey Auction	230
	8.7.4 Linkage Principle	232
	8.7.5 Why the English Auction Benefits the Seller	233
	8.7.6 Limits of the Linkage Principle	234
8.8	Further Applications*	235
	8.8.1 Auctions and Oligopoly	235
	8.8.2 Natural-Gas and Electric Power Auctions	238
	8.8.3 Treasury-Bill Auctions	239
8.9	Bibliographic Notes	241
8.10	Appendix: Second-Order Conditions (Pseudoconcavity)	241
9	**Hidden Information and Adverse Selection**	243
9.1	Introduction	243
9.2	Adverse Selection	243
	9.2.1 The Market for Lemons	244
	9.2.2 Adverse Selection in Labor Markets	245
9.3	Positive Selection: Too Many Professors?	248
	9.3.1 Assumptions	248
	9.3.2 Occupational Choice	249
	9.3.3 Positive vs. Adverse Selection	249
	9.3.4 Subgame-Perfect Equilibrium	250
	9.3.5 A Corrective Tax	250
9.4	Adverse Selection and Rationing	251

	9.5	Adverse Selection and Screening	252
		9.5.1 Screening in Insurance Markets	253
		9.5.2 Screening in Labor and Credit Markets	258
		9.5.3 Alternative Equilibrium Concepts	258
		9.5.4 Limits of Screening	259
	9.6	Screening without Competition*	259
		9.6.1 Price Discrimination with a Continuum of Types	259
		9.6.2 Implementation by Nonlinear Pricing	265
	9.7	Bibliographic Notes	266
10	**Hidden Information and Signaling**	267
	10.1	Introduction	267
	10.2	The Education Game	268
		10.2.1 Rules of the Game	268
		10.2.2 Payoff Functions	269
		10.2.3 Subgame	269
		10.2.4 Sequential Equilibrium	269
	10.3	Equilibrium – Embarrassment of Riches	270
	10.4	Equilibrium Selection: Intuitive Criterion*	272
		10.4.1 The Criterion When Type 2 Is Rare	273
		10.4.2 The Criterion When Type 1 Is Rare	274
	10.5	Screening vs. Signaling	275
	10.6	Bibliographic Notes	276
11	**Hidden Action and Moral Hazard**	278
	11.1	Introduction	278
	11.2	Risk Aversion and Incentives	279
		11.2.1 A Simple Model	279
		11.2.2 Generalization	285
	11.3	Limited Liability and Incentives	288
		11.3.1 A Simple Model	289
		11.3.2 Generalization	291
		11.3.3 Monitoring and Incentives*	294
	11.4	Renegotiation Problem	297
	11.5	Bibliographic Notes	299
	11.6	Appendix	300
12	**Rank-Order Tournaments**	302
	12.1	Introduction	302
	12.2	A Simple Model	302
		12.2.1 First Best Effort and Wage	303
		12.2.2 Tournament Game	304
	12.3	Tournaments under Risk Neutrality	304
		12.3.1 Tournament Subgame	304
		12.3.2 Equilibrium Prizes	305

	12.3.3 Two Illustrations	306
	12.3.4 Discussion	307
12.4	Tournaments under Common Shocks	307
12.5	Bibliographic Notes	308

IV Technical Supplements **309**

A Nonlinear Optimization: The Classical Approach 311
   A.1 Introduction 311
   A.2 Unconstrained Optimization 311
   A.3 Equality-Constrained Optimization 314
   A.4 Digression: Quadratic Forms 317

B Inequality-Constrained Optimization 320
   B.1 Introduction 320
   B.2 The Problem 320
   B.3 First-Order Necessary Conditions 321
   B.4 Second-Order Conditions 323

C Convexity and Generalizations 324
   C.1 Introduction 324
   C.2 Convex Sets 324
   C.3 Convex Functions 325
   C.4 Strongly Convex Functions 327
   C.5 Convexity and Global Extreme Values 328
   C.6 Generalized Convexity: Quasiconvexity 329
   C.7 Convexity Properties of Composite Functions 333
   C.8 Convexifiable Quasiconvex Programs 336

D From Expected Values to Order Statistics 339
   D.1 Introduction 339
   D.2 Expected Value 339
   D.3 Variance, Covariance, and Correlation 340
   D.4 Rules to Remember 340
      D.4.1 Expected Value 340
      D.4.2 Variance, Covariance, Correlation 341
      D.4.3 Expected Utility 342
      D.4.4 Transformations of Random Variables 343
      D.4.5 Order Statistics 344
   D.5 Proofs 345

Bibliography 351
Index 365

Preface

Purpose

The book is designed as a main textbook in *advanced undergraduate* courses on *microeconomics, information economics,* and *industrial organization* or as a supplementary textbook in the first-year *graduate course* on *microeconomic theory.*

The book distinguishes itself from other textbooks in that it focuses on an in-depth treatment of a few core topics, rather than on a complete self-contained overview of the entire field of microeconomics.

Another distinct feature is that the book breaks with tradition and completely ignores the standard competitive analysis, and instead focuses on the more modern themes of imperfect competition, uncertainty and incomplete information, auctions, and incentives.

Prerequisites

The core sections of the book should be accessible to students with a working knowledge of intermediate microeconomics. Mathematical prerequisites are at an introductory/intermediate level, though openness towards mathematical thinking is essential. Given these prerequisites, a good part of the book should be well suited as a main textbook in advanced microeconomics, industrial organization, or information economics.

In an advanced *undergraduate* class one would make a selection from the core material and stay away from supplementary and more demanding topics marked "*". The variety of issues leaves the instructor with a wide range of choices. Of course, in a *graduate* class one should include the starred sections, which are a substantial part of the book, depending upon the instructor's interests in the selection of topics.

By making different selections, the book can be used as textbook in *microeconomics* or in courses with an emphasis on *industrial organization, information economics, applications of game theory,* or *auctions and incentives.* THE book is also of potential interest to students and researchers who want to study certain topics independently, as an introduction to their research.

Outline of the Book

Chapter 1 (Monopoly) is ideally suited for the first sessions of the micro sequence because it starts with intermediate-level material that can be skimmed through quickly, and then gradually turns to more advanced topics and methods such as a simple version of the incomplete-information theory of price discrimination, the durable-goods monopoly problem, and bargaining. I usually start out the micro sequence with this material because students find it accessible from their undergraduate background and appealing to economic common sense.

Chapter 2 (Regulation of Monopoly) is a more specialized topic that one would not necessarily treat in the micro sequence. However, the sections on normative theories of regulation should be considered for inclusion because they offer a nice and simple introduction to the modern mechanism design approach.

Chapter 3 (Oligopoly and Industrial Organization) contains some core micro sequence material plus a great deal of supplementary material for use in a specialized course on industrial organization. In the micro sequence I use only the first two sections plus Section 3.5. However, in a course that emphasizes industrial organization one would cover also cover in detail Sections 3.3 and 3.6.

Chapters 4, 5, and 6 (Risk, Stochastic Dominance, and Risk Aversion) introduce basic concepts and results of stochastic dominance rankings of probability distributions and present the theory of comparative statics of risk. This material is useful in many decision problems under uncertainty, though some of details may be too involved for a standard micro sequence.

The exposition of the basic theory is followed by a sample of fully worked-out applications of the comparative statics of risk, drawn form various areas in economics – from portfolio selection to labor supply, entry in oligopolistic markets, auctions, and the ranking of income distributions.

In the micro sequence I usually go over most of Chapter 4, then select two or three applications from Chapter 5, and cover the core sections (without "*") of Chapter 6. In a course on information economics, I cover Chapter 6 in full detail.

Chapter 7 (Matching: The Marriage Problem) opens the detailed coverage of incomplete information. The topic is two-sided matching of the members of two distinct groups, and the focus is on marriage.

In a standard micro sequence one will probably not use this material, and some people may find its inclusion a bit extravagant. However, in my own teaching I tend to use this brief chapter as "warm-up" material, ideally after a semester break. The topic is somewhat entertaining, and although the exposition is not loaded with technicalities, it has rigor and beauty.

Chapter 8 (Auctions) gives a comprehensive introduction to auction theory and surveys a great deal of the auction literature.[1] Auctions are increasingly important

---

[1] This chapter is an extended version of my survey, Wolfstetter (1996).

as a market mechanism, and auction theory is an ideal topic to exercise many of the tools and tricks of modern economic theory. This is why I strongly recommend it for inclusion in the micro sequence.

Many of the competing texts do not cover auctions at all or in sufficient detail. Of course, in the micro sequence one should not cover the entire chapter. One should use Sections 8.1–8.4 and 8.6, and leave the other material for a more specialized course.

Chapter 9 (Hidden Information and Averse Selection) surveys adverse-selection models and elaborates some standard applications, from insurance to labor, credit, price discrimination, and education. Most of the material is at a fairly elementary level, except the analysis of price discrimination. The latter generalizes the two-type model of hidden information and second-degree price discrimination in Chapter 1 to a continuum of types.

In the micro sequence I usually go quickly over the basic material, and then spend time exercising more advanced techniques using the example of price discrimination with a continuum of customer types.

Chapter 10 (Hidden Information and Signaling) surveys signaling models, using the famous education game, shows how signaling games are plagued by multiplicity-of-equilibria problems, and evaluates various proposed equilibrium refinements. Again, in the micro sequence I cover all core sections of this chapter.

Chapter 11 (Hidden Action and Moral Hazard) gives an introduction to the principal–agent problem and its various ramifications. Two basic models are distinguished: the *risk-vs.-incentives* model and the *limited-liability* model. The simplicity of the latter makes it a good framework for the analysis of the interrelationship between optimal contracts and optimal monitoring. Attention is also paid to the renegotiation problem and possible solutions to the disturbing lack of renegotiation-proofness of standard optimal contracts.

Nowadays, most micro courses include some coverage of the principal-agent problem. In an advanced undergraduate course one would probably only use the two-state, two-efforts models, whereas in a graduate course one should cover at least one of the generalizations, and possibly the analysis of optimal monitoring.

Chapter 12 (Rank-Order Tournaments) explains and debates incentive systems that are based on relative performance measures. This introduces the reader into the important area of principal–agent relationships between one principal and *many* agents.

Technical Supplements The book comes with several *technical supplements* (appendixes) that review basic concepts and results of *nonlinear optimization theory* (Appendixes A and B), *convexity and generalizations* (Appendix C), and *expected values and order statistics* (Appendix C). The emphasis is on basic concepts and results, mostly without proofs. These surveys should be useful for the working economist, even though the material is not required for the other parts of the book.

Most graduate programs have specialized math courses and assign one of the many excellent textbooks on optimization theory. The technical supplements included here are by no means a substitute for such a text.

Complementary Texts   In recent years many good texts were published that one might combine with the present book. When I teach the graduate micro sequence, industrial organization, applied game theory, and auctions and incentives, I also assign parts of Fudenberg and Tirole (1991), Varian (1992), Kreps (1990), Tirole (1989), Milgrom and Roberts (1992), and Mas–Colell, Whinston, and Green (1995).

Why No Competitive Analysis?   I close with a word of explanation for the absence of competitive analysis in this text. Over the years of teaching the micro sequence I found myself putting less and less emphasis on the relatively uninspiring competitive analysis, which is well covered in Varian (1992) and in other texts. This reflects not just my own preferences, but a general shift of emphasis in research. This fact, combined with the availability of good texts on competitive analysis, made me decide to put together a micro text that excludes competitive analysis altogether.

Acknowledgments

During the years that elapsed between the conception of the book and its final completion, many people helped me with encouragement, pointing out errors, and making detailed recommendations.

Several chapter were tested on graduate and advanced undergraduate students at the departments of economics at the Free University of Berlin, the University of Bern, and the Humboldt University at Berlin. This gave me the opportunity to test and revise the material repeatedly. I am very grateful to my students for their criticism and suggestions. Part of my work on this book was supported by the *Deutsche Forschungsgemeinschaft*, SFB 373 ("Quantifikation und Simulation Ökonomischer Prozesse"), Humboldt-Universität zu Berlin.

Many people contributed useful comments and suggestions at various stages. In particular, I would like to mention Brigitte Adolph, Gerard van den Berg, Fan Cuihong, Ulrich Dorazelski, Uwe Dulleck, Walter Elberfeld, Veronika Grimm, Roman Inderst, Thomas Jeitschko, Dorothea Kübler, Michael Landsberger, Carlos Lenz, Peter Lutz, Steven Matthews, Georg Meran, Dieter Nautz, Jörg Oechssler, Aloys Prinz, and Manfred Stadler.

I am especially grateful to Murray Brown, András Löffler, Marc Dudey, John Kagel, John Riley, and the four anonymous referees for detailed written comments that led to major improvements. András Löffler made such detailed suggestions concerning the technical supplements that I no longer feel solely responsible for their content.

I also acknowledge the support of Getachew Bekele, Dietmar Fischer, David de Gijsel, Brit Großkopf, and Andreas Stiehler, who prepared the diagrams and contributed to the index. And I am grateful to Anne Bussmann, Regine Hallmann, and Sandra Uzman for weeding out errors in grammar and typography.

I am greatly indebted to the Cambridge University Press team, in particular to Joseph Fineman for his most careful copyediting, with perceptions quite beyond what I could offer, and to my most supportive editor, Scott Parris.

The typescript was typeset by the author using Aleksander Simonic's marvelous WinEdt together with the Y&Y–TeX implementation of LaTeX, and the diagrams were made with PiCTeX.

Of course I appreciate being notified of errata. E-mail can be sent to: elmar. wolfstetter@rz.hu-berlin.de. Exercises to accompany each chapter of the book can be downloaded from: http://www.wiwi.hu-berlin.de/wt1/topics.

Part I

Imperfect Competition

1

Monopoly

The best of all monopoly profits is a quiet life.
Sir John Hicks

1.1 Introduction

In this chapter we analyze the supply and pricing decisions of a pure, single-product monopolist facing a large number of price-taking buyers. We take the firm's choice of product as given and assume that consumers know all about product characteristics and quality. Moreover, we assume that the monopolist's market is sufficiently self-contained to allow us to neglect the strategic interdependency between markets. The strategic interdependency between markets is the subject matter of the theory of oligopoly with product differentiation.

Monopolies do exist. In the early days of photocopying, Rank Xerox was the exclusive supplier – some still use "xeroxing" as a synonym for "photocopying." Postal and rail services are (or have been) monopolized (things are changing fast in these sectors), and so are public utilities (gas and electricity) and computer operating systems, to name just a few. One can even find inconspicuous products that are subject to monopolization. For example, in Germany matches were exclusively supplied by a single Swedish supplier who had acquired a monopoly license from the German government during World War I, when the German government was hard pressed for foreign currencies. Similarly, gambling licenses are often issued by states to raise revenue. Moreover, there are many local monopolies, like the single hardware store in a small community, the bus line exclusively served by Greyhound, or the flight route, say from Ithaca to New York City, served by a single airline.

As these examples suggest, monopolization has a lot to do with the size of a market, but also with licensing, patent protection, and regulation – supported by law. If entry into a monopolized market is not prohibited, a monopoly has little chance to survive unless the market is too small to support more than one firm. Monopoly profits attract new entrants. And even if entry is prohibited, eventually patent rights expire, or rival firms spend resources to develop similar products and technologies or even to gain political influence to raid the monopoly license. Therefore, a monopoly is always temporary unless it is continuously renewed through innovations, patents, or political lobbying.

Monopolies – Weak and Strong A monopolist has exclusive control of a market. But to what extent a monopoly is actually turned into a fat profit depends upon several factors, in particular:

- the possibility of price discrimination,
- the closeness to competing markets,
- the ability to make credible commitments.

A *strong* monopolist has full control over his choice of price function. He can set linear or nonlinear prices, he can even charge different prices to different buyers. In other words, the strong monopolist can use all his imagination to design sophisticated pricing schemes to pocket the entire gain from trade, restricted only by consumers' willingness to pay. No one will ever doubt the credibility of his announced pricing policy.

In contrast, the *weak* monopolist is restricted to linear prices.[1] He cannot even price-discriminate between consumers.

Monopolists come in all shades, between the extremes of weak and strong. For example, a monopolist may be constrained to set linear prices, but he may be able to price-discriminate between some well-identified groups of consumers. Or a monopolist may be restricted to set a menu of nonlinear prices, like the ones you are offered by your long-distance telephone company and your public utilities suppliers.

In the following pages you will learn more about these and other variations of the monopoly theme. We will not only analyze the monopolist's decision problem under various pricing constraints, but also attempt to explain what gives rise to these constraints from basic assumptions on technology, transaction costs, and information structures.

We begin with the simplest analysis of the weak monopoly, also known as *Cournot monopoly*, in homage to the French economist Antoine Augustin Cournot (1801–1877), who laid the foundations for the mathematical analysis of non-competitive markets. Most of this analysis should be familiar from your under-graduate training. Therefore, you may quickly skim through these first pages, except where we cover the relationship between rent seeking and the social loss of monopoly, the durable-goods monopoly problem, and the analysis of regulatory mechanisms.

Finally, keep in mind that there are really two opposite ways to model pure monopoly. The most common approach – exclusively adopted in this chapter – describes the monopolist as facing a given market demand function and ignores potential actions and reactions by the suppliers of related products. The other, opposite approach faces the strategic interdependency of markets head on and views monopolist pricing as an application of the theory of oligopoly with product

---

[1] A price function $\mathcal{P}$ is called linear if it has the form $\mathcal{P}(x) := px$, where $p > 0$ is the unit price.

differentiation. While we stick, in this chapter, to the conventional approach, you should nevertheless keep in mind that there are many examples where oligopoly theory gives the best clues to the monopolist's decisions.[2]

1.2 Cournot Monopoly – Weak Monopoly

We begin with the weak or Cournot monopolist who can only set a linear price function that applies equally to all customers. The demand function, defined on the unit price p, is denoted by $X(p)$, and the cost function, defined on output x, by $C(x)$. Both $X(p)$ and $C(x)$ are twice continuously differentiable; also, $X(p)$ is strict monotone decreasing, and $C(x)$ strict monotone increasing. The inverse demand function, defined on total sales x, exists (due to the monotonicity of $X(p)$) and is denoted by $P(x)$. The rule underlying this notation is that capital letters like X and P denote functions, whereas the corresponding lowercase letters x and p denote supply and unit price.

In a nutshell, the Cournot monopolist views the market demand function as his menu of price–quantity choices from which he picks that pair that maximizes his profit. We will now characterize the optimal choice.

At the outset, notice that there are two ways to state the monopolist's decision problem: one, in terms of the demand function:

$$\max_{p,x} \quad px - C(x), \quad \text{s.t.} \quad X(p) - x \geq 0, \quad p, x \geq 0,$$

and the other in terms of the *inverse* demand function:

$$\max_{p,x} \quad px - C(x), \quad \text{s.t.} \quad P(x) - p \geq 0, \quad p, x \geq 0.$$

Obviously, the two are equivalent. Therefore, the choice is exclusively one of convenience. We choose the latter. Also, notice that the constraint is binding (the monopolist would forgo profits if he did sell a given quantity below the price customers are willing to pay). Therefore, the monopolist's decision problem can be reduced to the unconstrained program:

$$\max_{x \geq 0} \quad \pi(x) := R(x) - C(x), \tag{1.1}$$

where R denotes the revenue function:

$$R(x) := P(x)x. \tag{1.2}$$

1.2.1 Cournot Point

Suppose, for the time being, that X and C are continuously differentiable on $\mathbb{R}_+$, that revenue $R(x)$ is bounded, and that profit is strictly concave.[3] Then the decision

---

[2] Of course, also the opposite may hold, where standard monopoly theory gives the best clues to oligopolistic pricing. This is the case when reaction functions are horizontal.

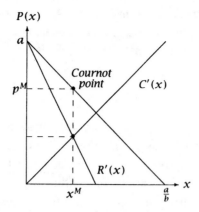

Figure 1.1. Cournot Point.

problem is well behaved, and we know that there exists a unique solution that can be found by solving the Kuhn–Tucker conditions:[4]

$$\pi'(x) := R'(x) - C'(x) \le 0 \quad \text{and} \quad x\pi'(x) = 0, \quad x \ge 0. \tag{1.3}$$

In principle, one may have a corner solution ($x = 0$). But if $P(0) - C'(0) > 0$, an interior solution is assured, which is characterized by the familiar condition of equality between marginal revenue and marginal cost, $R'(x) = C'(x)$. Denote the solution by x^M, $p^M := P(x^M)$. The graph of the solution is called the *Cournot point* and illustrated in Figure 1.1.

Example 1.1 Suppose $P(x) := a - bx, a, b > 0$, and $C(x) := \frac{1}{2}x^2, x \in [0, a/b]$. Then profit is a strictly concave function of output, $\pi(x) := ax - bx^2 - \frac{1}{2}x^2$. From the Kuhn–Tucker condition one obtains

$$0 = \pi'(x) = a - 2bx - x. \tag{1.4}$$

Therefore, the Cournot point is ($x^M = a/(1 + 2b)$, $p^M = a(1 + b)/(1 + 2b)$), and the maximum (or indirect) profit function is $\pi^*(a, b) := a^2/(2(1 + 2b))$.

Obviously, the monopolist's optimal price exceeds the marginal cost. But by how much? The answer depends upon how strongly demand responds to price. If demand is fairly inelastic, the monopolist has a lot of leeway; he can charge a high markup without suffering much loss of demand. But if demand responds very strongly to a price hike, the best the monopolist can do is to stay close to marginal cost pricing. This suggests a strong link between monopoly power and the price responsiveness of demand.

---

[3] Concavity of the revenue and convexity of the cost function – at least one of them strict – are sufficient, but not necessary.

[4] In case you are unsure about this, prove the following: 1) strong concavity implies strict concavity; 2) if a solution exists, strict concavity implies uniqueness; 3) the Weierstrass theorem implies the existence of a solution (you have to ask: is the feasible set closed and bounded?); 4) the Kuhn–Tucker theorem implies that every solution solves the Kuhn–Tucker conditions, and vice versa. Consult Appendixes C and D.

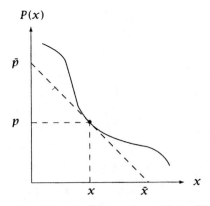

Figure 1.2. Relationship between Marginal Revenue and Price Elasticity $|\varepsilon| = p/(\bar{p} - p)$, $R'(x) = p - (\bar{p} - p)$.

The conventional measure of price responsiveness of demand is the *price elasticity of demand:*

$$\varepsilon(p) := X'(p)\frac{p}{X(p)}. \tag{1.5}$$

We now use this measure to give a precise statement of the conjectured explanation of monopoly power.

As you probably recall from undergraduate micro, marginal revenue is linked to the price elasticity of demand as follows (see also Figure 1.2):[5]

$$R'(x) = P'(x)x + P(x)$$

$$= P(x)\left[1 + P'(x)\frac{x}{P(x)}\right]$$

$$= P(x)\left[1 + \frac{x}{X'(P(x))P(x)}\right]$$

$$= P(x)\left[1 + \frac{1}{\varepsilon(P(x))}\right]$$

$$= P(x)\left[\frac{1 + \varepsilon(P(x))}{\varepsilon(P(x))}\right]. \tag{1.6}$$

Therefore, marginal revenue is positive if and only if demand responsiveness is high, in the sense that the price elasticity of demand is less than -1.

Using this relationship together with the Kuhn–Tucker condition (1.3) for an interior solution, one obtains the following optimal *markup rule:*

$$P(x) = \frac{\varepsilon(P(x))}{1 + \varepsilon(P(x))}C'(x). \tag{1.7}$$

[5] Note, by the definition of the inverse one has $P(X(p)) \equiv p$; hence, $P'(X(p))X'(p) \equiv 1$.

Another frequently used variation of this form is the *Lerner index* of monopolization:

$$\frac{P(x) - C'(x)}{P(x)} = \frac{1}{-\varepsilon(P(x))}. \tag{1.8}$$

These convenient forms should also remind you that the Cournot point always occurs where the price elasticity of demand is less than minus one, that is, where an increase in output raises revenue.

Monopoly and Markup Pricing

In the applied literature on industrial organization it is claimed that monopolistic firms often stick to a rigid markup pricing rule. This practice is sometimes cited as contradicting basic principles of microeconomics. Notice, however, that (1.7) is consistent with a constant markup. All it takes is a constant elasticity demand function and constant marginal cost.

Another issue in this literature concerns the problem of measurement. Usually, one has no reliable data on firms' cost functions. So how can one ever measure even such a simple thing as the Lerner index? As in other applications, a lot of ingenuity is called for to get around this lack of data.

A nice example for this kind of ingenuity can be found in Peter Temin's study of the German steel cartel in imperial Germany prior to World War I (see Temin (1976)). He noticed that the cartel sold steel also on the competitive world market. Temin concluded that the world-market price, properly converted using the then current exchange rate, should be a good estimate of the steel cartel's marginal cost. And he proceeded to use this estimate to compute the Lerner index. Make sure you understand the economic reasoning behind this trick.

Monopoly and Cost-Push Inflation

In economic policy debates it is sometimes claimed that monopolists contribute to the spiraling of cost-push inflation because – unlike competitive firms – monopolists apply a markup factor greater than 1. To discuss this assertion, it may be useful if you plot the markup factor $\varepsilon/(1 + \varepsilon)$ for all $\varepsilon < -1$. Notice that it is always greater than 1, increasing in ε, and approaching 1 as ε goes to minus infinity and infinity as ε approaches -1.

Software Pirates and Copy Protection

As a brief digression, consider a slightly unusual Cournot monopoly: the software house that faces competition from illegal copies and in response contemplates introducing copy protection.

Legally, the copying of software is theft. Nevertheless, it is widespread, even among otherwise law-abiding citizens. Software houses complain that illegal copies rob them of the fruits of their labor and pose a major threat to the industry.

Suppose copy protection is available at negligible cost. Should the monopolist apply it, and if so, how many copies should he permit? A copy-protected program can only be copied $N \geq 0$ times, and copies cannot be copied again. Therefore, each original copy can be made into $N + 1$ *user copies*.

To discuss the optimal copy protection, we assume that there is a perfect secondary market for illegal copies. For simplicity, users are taken to be indifferent between legal and illegal user copies, and marginal costs of copying are taken to be constant.

Given these admittedly extreme assumptions, the software market is only feasible with some copy protection. Without it, each original copy would be copied again and again until the price equaled the marginal cost of copying. Anticipating this, no customer would be willing to pay more than the marginal cost of copying, and the software producer would go out of business because he knew that he could never recoup the fixed cost of software development.

An obvious solution is full copy protection ($N = 0$) combined with the Cournot point (p^M, x^M). However, this is not the only solution. Indeed, the software producer can be "generous" and permit any number of copies between 0 and $x^M - 1$ without any loss in profit. All he needs to do is to make sure that N does not exceed $x^M - 1$ and that the price is linked to the number of permitted copies in such a way that each original copy is priced at $N + 1$ times the Cournot equilibrium price, $(N + 1)p^M$.

Given this pricing-plus-copy-protection rule, each customer anticipates that the price per user copy will be equal to the Cournot equilibrium price p^M; exactly $x^M/(N + 1)$ original copies are sold; each original copy is copied N times; exactly x^M user copies are supplied; and profits and consumer surplus are the same as under full copy protection.

At this point you may object that only few software houses have introduced copy protection;[6] nevertheless, the industry is thriving. So what is missing in our story?

One important point is that copy protection is costly, yet offers only temporary protection. Sooner or later, the code will be broken; there are far too many skilled "hackers" to make it last. Another important point is that illegal copies are often imperfect substitutes, for example because handbooks come in odd sizes (not easily fit for photocopying) or because illegal copies may be contaminated with computer viruses. Instead of adding complicated copy protection devices, the monopolist may actually plant his own virus-contaminated copies in the second-hand market. Alas, computer viruses are probably the best copy protection.

Leviathan, Hyperinflation, and the Cournot Point

We have said that monopoly has a lot to do with monopoly licensing, granted and enforced by the legislator. Of course, governments are particularly inclined to grant such licenses to their own bodies. This suggests that some of the best applications of the theory of monopoly should be found in the public sector of the economy.

A nice example that you may also come across in macroeconomics concerns the *inflation tax* theory of inflation and its application to the economic history of hyperinflations. A simple three-ingredient macro model will explain this link (the classic reference is Cagan (1956)).

---

[6] Lotus is one of the few large software houses that rely on copy protection.

1. The government has a monopoly in printing money, and it can coerce the public to use it by declaring it *fiat money*. Consider a government that finances all its real expenditures G by running the printing press. Let p be the price index, let M^S be the stock of high-powered money, and suppose there are no demand deposits. Then the government's budget constraint is

$$pG = \Delta M^S \qquad \text{(budget constraint)}. \qquad (1.9)$$

2. Suppose the demand for real money balances M^d/p is a monotone decreasing and continuously differentiable function of the rate of inflation[7] $\hat{p}$,

$$\frac{M^d}{p} = \phi(\hat{p}) \qquad \text{(demand for money)}. \qquad (1.10)$$

3. Assume the simple quantity theory of inflation,

$$\hat{p} := \frac{\Delta p}{p} = \frac{\Delta M^S}{M^S} = \frac{\Delta M^d}{M^d} \qquad \text{(quantity theory of money)}. \qquad (1.11)$$

Putting all three pieces together, it follows that the real expenditures that can be financed by running the printing press are a function of the rate of inflation:

$$G(\hat{p}) = \hat{p}\phi(\hat{p}). \qquad (1.12)$$

The government has the exclusive right to issue money, and it can force people to accept this money in exchange for goods and services (this is the origin of the term "fiat money"). However, even though it can set the speed of the printing press, the real expenditures that it can finance in this manner are severely limited. Therefore, the inflation tax is only a limited substitute for conventional taxes.

To determine these limits, simply compute the Cournot-point rate of inflation $\hat{p}^M$, defined as the maximizer of $G(\hat{p})$ over $\hat{p}$. Since the government's maximization problem is equivalent to that of a Cournot monopolist subject to zero marginal costs, it follows immediately that real government expenditures reach a maximum at that rate of inflation where the elasticity of the demand for real money balances ε is equal to -1:

$$\varepsilon(\hat{p}) := \phi'(\hat{p})\frac{\hat{p}}{\phi(\hat{p})} = -1. \qquad (1.13)$$

Of course, this revenue-maximizing rate of inflation imposes a deadweight loss upon society, just like any other Cournot monopoly. The socially optimal rate of inflation is obviously equal to zero. However, alternative methods of taxation tend to impose their own deadweight loss, in addition to often high costs of collecting taxes. Keeping these considerations in mind, it may very well be that some inflation is optimal, depending upon tax morale and other institutional issues. Different countries with their different institutions may very well have different optimal inflation rates. Incidentally, these considerations are the background of current discussions on optimal currency areas.

---

[7] In macroeconomics it is often assumed that the demand for real money balances is a strict monotone decreasing function of the nominal interest rate. The latter is usually strongly correlated with the rate of inflation.

Table 1.1. *German hyperinflation 1923*

Month		Exchange rate, monthly average (Mark/$)
January	1921	64
January	1922	191
January	1923	17,972
July	1923	353,412
August	1923	4,620,455
September	1923	98,860,000
October	1923	25,260,208,000
November	1923	4,200,000,000,000

Source: Stolper (1964).

Another interesting application of the inflation tax concerns the theory of hyper-inflations, like the one in Weimar Germany in 1923 (or most recently in Serbia, after the breakup of Yugoslavia). There, a government was in desperate need for funds, due to a fatal combination of events, from the exorbitantly high demands for reparations imposed by the Versailles treaty (aggravated by the French occupation of the Ruhr area in 1923) to a parliament torn between cooperation and conflict. Unable to finance its expenditures to any significant degree by explicit taxes, the government took recourse to the printing press. But the faster it set its speed, the fewer real expenditures it could finance in this manner. The result was a rapidly exploding rate of inflation, reflected in the catastrophic devaluation of the mark relative to the dollar reported in Table 1.1, and a complete breakdown of government financing.[8]

Some Comparative Statics

How does the Cournot point change if marginal cost or demand function shift? As always, such questions are meaningful only if uniqueness of the Cournot point is assumed. This is one reason why comparative statics is always pursued in a framework of relatively strong assumptions.

As an example, suppose C is a continuously differentiable function of a cost parameter α in such a way that higher α represents higher marginal costs: $C_{x\alpha}''(x, \alpha) > 0$. Also assume that the profit function is *strongly* concave in output and that the Cournot point is an interior solution.[9] Then, the optimal output is a differentiable function of α, described by the function $x^*(\alpha)$. And we can pursue comparative statics using calculus.

We now show that the monopolist's supply is strict monotone decreasing in α: $x^{*'}(\alpha) < 0$. For this purpose, insert the solution function $x^*(\alpha)$ into the Kuhn–

---

[8] At one point, the Reichsbank employed 300 paper manufacturers and 2,000 printing presses, day and night.

[9] Recall that *strong concavity* is strict concavity plus the requirement that the determinant of the Hessian matrix of the profit function (which is here simply the second derivative of this function) does not vanish. Strong concavity is always invoked if one wants to make sure that the solution functions are differentiable in the exogenous parameter, which is a prerequisite for the calculus approach to comparative statics.

Tucker condition (1.3), and one obtains the identity

$$\pi'_x(x^*(\alpha), \alpha) := R'(x^*(\alpha)) - C'_x(x^*(\alpha), \alpha) \equiv 0. \qquad (1.14)$$

Differentiating it with respect to α gives, after a bit of rearranging,

$$x^{*'}(\alpha) = \frac{-\pi''_{x\alpha}(x^*(\alpha), \alpha)}{\pi''_{xx}(x^*(\alpha), \alpha)} = \frac{C''_{x\alpha}(x^*(\alpha), \alpha)}{R''(x^*(\alpha)) - C''_{xx}(x^*(\alpha), \alpha)} < 0. \qquad (1.15)$$

This proves that the monopolist's optimal supply is strictly monotone decreasing in the marginal cost parameter, as asserted.

Two Technical Problems

We close the analysis of the Cournot point with two slightly technical problems. The first one concerns the existence of the Cournot point in the face of plausible discontinuities of demand or cost functions. The second explains how you should proceed if the profit function is not strictly concave. If you are in full control of your undergraduate micro, you may skip this exposition and move directly to Section 8.8.2.

An Existence Puzzle Suppose demand is unit elastic ($\varepsilon = -1$ for all $x > 0$), and the cost function is strictly convex with positive profits at some outputs. Then the profit function is strictly concave. Yet, the monopolist's decision problem has no solution.

The explanation is very simple. First, notice that revenue is constant for all positive x whereas cost is strictly increasing. Therefore, profit goes up as x is reduced (less output means higher profit), except if x is reduced all the way down to $x = 0$. Second, notice that there is no smallest positive rational number (there is no smallest positive output). Combine both observations, and it follows that there is no profit-maximizing choice of x. So which of our assumptions has failed?

As you check the assumptions one by one, you will see that almost all of them are satisfied. The only exception is the continuity of the revenue function, which is violated at precisely one point ($x = 0$).[10] This seemingly minor deviation changes it all.

The discontinuity of the demand function at $x = 0$ is something that one would not like to rule out. For example, applied economists often work with constant elasticity demand functions, all of which share this discontinuity property.

Another frequently encountered discontinuity that should not be excluded concerns the cost function. Recall, costs are usually decomposed into fixed and variable, where fixed costs are defined as $\lim_{x \to 0} C(x)$. Some fixed costs are *reversible* (or quasifixed), and some are irreversible or *sunk*. Whenever some fixed costs are reversible, one has $C(0) < \lim_{x \to 0} C(x)$, so that the cost function has a discontinuity at $x = 0$. In the face of it there is always a reasonable chance that the corner point $x = 0$ may be optimal. Therefore, watch out for a corner solution.

So, what shall you do if the demand or the cost function has such a discontinuity, and how can one assure existence of the Cournot point even in these cases? As in

---

[10] This discontinuity rules out the application of the Weierstrass theorem, which was invoked in the proof of existence of the Cournot point sketched in footnote 4.

other applications, a safe procedure is to break up the search for a solution into three steps: 1) search for a solution in the restricted domain $\mathbb{R}_{++}$ (an interior solution); 2) evaluate profit at the corner point $x = 0$; 3) choose the solution (either corner or interior) with the highest profit.

Since this procedure is cumbersome, one would of course like to know in which case existence of an interior solution is guaranteed so that the procedure can be stopped after round 1). A simple and often used sufficient condition is the following:

$$\lim_{x \to 0}[R'(x) - C'(x)] > 0, \qquad \lim_{x \to \infty}[R'(x) - C'(x)] < 0. \qquad (1.16)$$

Make sure that you understand why this condition is indeed sufficient.

Example 1.2 Suppose the demand function has a constant elasticity $\varepsilon < -1$. Then it must have the form $X(p) = ap^\varepsilon$ (show this), so that the inverse demand function is $P(x) = (x/a)^{1/\varepsilon}$. Twice differentiate the revenue function $R(x) := P(x)x$, and you see that the revenue function is strictly concave. Now add the assumption that the cost function is convex and that condition (1.16) holds. Then the Cournot point has a unique interior solution.

The Cournot Point without Concavity Let us get another technical problem out of the way: characterizing the Cournot point if the profit function is not strictly concave. Concavity, as a local property, assures that a stationary point is indeed a maximum, and strict concavity, as a global property, assures uniqueness. But concavity is far too strong a requirement.

A popular weaker requirement is quasiconcavity. But, as a global property, quasiconcavity is often difficult to confirm or reject. As in other optimization problems, if a maximization problem is not concave (that is, if either the objective function is not concave or the constraint set is not convex), it is often a better procedure to look for some transformation of variables that leads to a concave problem. The trouble is, however, that there are no simple rules and that you have to be imaginative to find a transformation that does the job.[11]

In many applications one can safely assume that the cost function is convex. But one may feel less comfortable assuming concavity of the revenue function. So you may wonder whether one could not assume instead that the revenue function is quasiconcave and then obtain a quasiconcave profit function, which is really enough for a well-behaved decision problem. The answer is no. Just recall that the sum of a concave and a quasiconcave function need not be quasiconcave. Consult Appendix C if you are not entirely sure about this matter.

So what shall you do if the profit function is continuous but not quasiconcave in output or in any conceivable transformation of this variable? Well, you cannot avoid the tedious job of checking out all stationary points and all corners. Of course, only those stationary points can qualify where the profit function is (locally) concave. Therefore, you need only consider those stationary points at which the *second-order*

---

[11] An example of such a transformation of variables is spelled out in detail in Section C.8 of Appendix C.

or local concavity condition

$$\pi''(x) := R''(x) - C''(x) \leq 0 \qquad \text{(second-order condition)} \qquad (1.17)$$

is satisfied. But you may still be left with fairly extensive computations to compare the profits at the remaining stationary and corner points.

Example 1.3 Suppose the cost function is S-shaped (strictly concave for low and strictly convex for high outputs), and suppose demand is linear. Then the profit function has two stationary points. But the profit function is only locally concave at the one point with the higher output. Therefore, only one stationary point survives the second-order or local concavity condition. However, this point need not be a profit maximum either. Indeed, if fixed costs are sufficiently high, it is always optimal to close down the firm and choose the corner point $x = 0$.[12] Draw a diagram to illustrate this case.

1.2.2 Deadweight Loss of Monopoly

Compared to a competitive firm, the Cournot monopolist earns higher profits (if he did not, the price would have to be equal to the marginal cost at the Cournot point). This shows that monopoly power redistributes welfare from buyers to sellers. But redistribution alone does not indicate any loss of social welfare, in the sense of the Pareto criterion. However, since the Cournot monopolist can only extract more from the consumers' willingness to pay by charging a higher unit price, the monopolist reduces welfare, unless demand is completely inelastic.

If the unit price rises above the competitive level, the consumers who continue to buy at the now higher price suffer a loss in consumer surplus that is however exactly offset by the seller's gain. However, those who quit buying at the higher price suffer a loss not offset by any gain to the seller. This *deadweight loss* of Cournot monopoly is illustrated in Figure 1.3, by the shaded area D.

As always, a deviation from the welfare optimum suggests that, with a bit of imagination, one can design Pareto-improving trades. For example, starting from the Cournot point, the monopolist could propose to his customers to supply an additional $x^* - x^M$ units in exchange for an additional payment equal to the cost increment (measured by the area under the marginal cost function between x^M and x^*), plus some small bonus. Miraculously, both buyers and sellers would be better off. However, the weak Cournot monopolist cannot take advantage of these gains from trade, because he is restricted to simple linear pricing schemes, for reasons that will have to be explained from basic assumptions concerning technology and information structures.

Conceptually, the deadweight loss of monopoly is the same as the deadweight loss of taxation. In the Middle Ages, it was popular to tax real estate on the basis of the size of windows. Due to the conspicuously high price of glass, the size of

---

[12] It is useful to distinguish two cases: 1) Suppose the average cost is higher than the price at the qualifying stationary point. Then the corner point $x = 0$ is definitely optimal if fixed costs are reversible (not sunk). 2) Suppose the average variable cost is higher than the price at the qualifying stationary point. Then $x = 0$ is optimal even if fixed costs are irreversible (sunk).

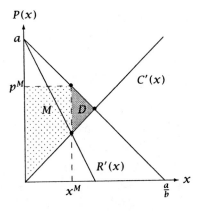

Figure 1.3. Deadweight Loss of Monopoly.

windows was correlated with wealth. Just as consumers reduce their demand when a monopolist raises the unit price, medieval citizens responded to the window tax by reducing the size of windows. In the end, they paid their taxes in any case. But on top of the direct reduction of wealth due to taxation, they sat in the dark – a visible example of the deadweight loss of taxation.

Can a government reduce or even eliminate that deadweight loss by means of corrective taxes? If the government has complete information about cost and demand functions, the task is easily accomplished. For example, a simple linear subsidy based on output – a negative excise tax – will do the job. The intuition is simple. An output subsidy smoothly reduces the effective marginal cost. By result (1.15), it follows immediately that the subsidy increases the Cournot equilibrium output. Therefore, one only needs to set the subsidy at the right level, and the monopolist is induced to produce the socially optimal level of output.

An obvious objection is that such a subsidy makes the monopolist even richer. However, this side effect of the output subsidy scheme can easily be eliminated by adding an appropriate lump-sum tax into the package.

To compute the appropriate subsidy rate and lump-sum tax, you should proceed as follows. In a first step, solve the monopolist's decision problem, given a subsidy rate s per output unit and a lump-sum tax T. Of course, the lump-sum tax does not affect the optimal output, but the subsidy does. Then, impose the requirement that the optimal output be equal to the competitive output x^M, implicitly defined by the condition $P(x^M) = C'(x^M)$. After a bit of rearranging the first-order condition you will find that the subsidy rate has to be set as follows:

$$s = \frac{-C'(x^M)}{\varepsilon(P(x^M))} > 0. \tag{1.18}$$

Finally, make the subsidy self-financing by setting the lump-sum tax equal to

$$T = sx^M. \tag{1.19}$$

It is as simple as that.[13]

---

[13] An even simpler mechanism is to impose sufficiently high penalties on any deviation from marginal cost pricing. This just shows that the regulation of monopoly is a trivial task if the regulator has complete information.

However, in most applications the regulation of Cournot monopoly is considerably more difficult. The main reason is that monopolists usually have private information about costs and sometimes even about their demand function. This raises a challenging mechanism design problem. We will address this issue in some detail in Section 2.3 of the next chapter.

Another problem has to do with the fact that monopolies are often the product of government regulation. It is hard to imagine that those agencies that restrict entry and thus permit monopolization will also tightly monitor these monopolies and direct them toward maximizing social welfare. And indeed, many economists are inclined to view regulation as industry-dominated and directed primarily to the industry's benefit. As Stigler (1971) put it: "...as a rule, regulation is acquired by the industry and is designed and operated primarily for its benefit."

1.2.3 Social Loss of Monopoly and Rent Seeking

The deadweight loss of monopoly D in Figure 1.3, however, tends to underestimate the social loss of monopoly. As Posner (1975) observed:

> The existence of an opportunity to obtain monopoly profits will attract resources into efforts to obtain monopolies, and the opportunity costs of those resources are social costs of monopoly too.

Under idealized conditions, the additional loss of monopoly is exactly equal to the monopoly profit measured by the area M in Figure 1.3. Therefore, the social cost of monopoly is the sum of the deadweight loss D and the monopoly profit M.

The additional loss may easily outweigh the traditional deadweight loss. For example, if consumers are identical and demand is perfectly inelastic, the deadweight loss vanishes, but the monopoly profit is as large as consumers' aggregate willingness to pay. This suggests that the additional cost component deserves close scrutiny.

The key assumption underlying the proposed inclusion of the monopoly profit as part of the social loss of monopoly is that obtaining a monopoly is itself a competitive activity. Even though there is perhaps no competition *in* the market, there is almost always competition *for* the market. The contestants spend resources to such an extent that, at the margin, the cost of obtaining the monopoly is exactly equal to the expected profit of being a monopolist. For if a monopoly could be acquired at a bargain, others would try to take it away until no net gain could be made. As a result, monopoly profits tend to be transformed into costs, and the social cost of monopoly is made equal to D plus M.

A simple argument illustrates this point. Suppose n identical firms spend resources, each at the level of the expected value z, to obtain a lucrative monopoly with the monopoly profit $\pi^M > 0$. Then each firm has a $1/n$ chance to win π^M. In equilibrium n and z are such that the expected value of the profit from participating the contest is equal to zero:

$$\frac{1}{n}\pi^M - z = 0. \tag{1.20}$$

Therefore, the monopoly profit is exactly equal to the overall cost of competition for the market,

$$\pi^M = nz, \qquad (1.21)$$

as asserted.[14]

Assuming competition for the market is reasonable in many applications. For example, if monopoly is based on patents, many firms can enter the patent race for this monopoly.[15] Or if monopoly is based on public licensing, many firms can enter into the political lobbying or perhaps even bribery necessary to obtain a license or raid an existing one.[16]

1.2.4 Monopoly and Innovation

Schumpeter (1975) pointed out that in perfectly competitive markets the benefits of innovation are not cashed in by the innovator, but are immediately competed away by other firms. Therefore, competitive firms have no incentive to invest in innovations. In contrast, a monopolist can easily translate cost reductions and quality improvements into higher profits. This suggests that some degree of monopoly is a prerequisite for innovation.

Although monopoly induces innovation, it does not give rise to socially optimal innovations. Consider an innovation that reduces marginal cost by \$1. The maximum social benefit of that innovation is reached if and only if the price is lowered by \$1. However, by doing this, the monopolist would give away the entire gain to his customers. Therefore, the monopolist's price reduction must be less than \$1, which in turn destroys some of the potential social benefits of innovation.

Patents

The failure of competitive markets to provide incentives to innovate gives some justification for a system of patents that grants the innovator a transferable monopoly for a certain period of time. However, Arrow (1962) observed that if one firm is awarded a patent, the incentives to innovate are not the same as in an ideal world.

In order to see this, consider a competitive industry with product price p_0 equal to marginal cost C_0'. A new technology is discovered that reduces the marginal cost to $C_1' < C_0'$. The innovation is patented, and the owner of the patent becomes a monopolist for all prices below p_0. Of course, the new price cannot be above p_0 because of potential competition from firms equipped with the old technology. Therefore, if the unconstrained Cournot monopoly price p^M is above p_0, the patent holder will set the new price just marginally below p_0, leading to a monopoly profit equal to the shaded area in Figure 1.4, whereas if p^M is below p_0, the patent holder

---

[14] Typically, the underlying "rent seeking" game has an equilibrium in mixed strategies, which is why z was interpreted as an expected value.

[15] Incidentally, Plant (1934) criticized the patent system precisely on the ground that it draws greater resources into inventions than into activities that yield only competitive returns.

[16] The case of bribery poses an intriguing problem. At first glance, one is inclined to argue that bribery is purely redistributional and therefore cannot qualify as a social loss component. However, if a political office is the recipient of substantial bribes, it is itself a lucrative monopoly, subject to its own competition for office. As a result, people will spend resources, for example in education, to be put in office and stay in office. Ultimately, it is these costs associated with competition for office that represent the social loss of monopoly.

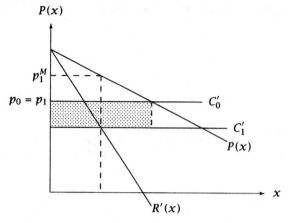

Figure 1.4. Innovation with Patent if $p_1^M > p_0$.

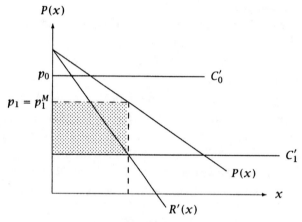

Figure 1.5. Innovation with Patent if $p_1^M < p_0$.

will lower the price to p^M and the monopoly profit is given by the shaded area in Figure 1.5. In either case, the incentive to innovate is clearly lower than in an ideal world, simply because the patent holder is unable to capture the entire increment in consumer surplus.

One can also see from the examples of Figures 1.4–1.5 that if a firm has a monopoly already at the beginning, it has less incentive to innovate than if the firm starts out in a competitive market. This is due to the fact that a competitive firm that acquires a patent not only captures the benefit of a cost reduction, but also gains market power by becoming a temporary monopolist.

To cover one of the two cases in greater detail, consider the example of Figure 1.4, which is elaborated in Figure 1.6. There, the following holds: If the initial state is already a *monopoly*, the gain from innovation G_m is measured by the area (see Figure 1.6)

$$G_m := B + C + D - (A + B) \qquad \text{(monopoly)},$$

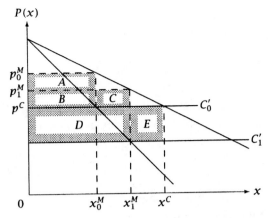

Figure 1.6. Incentives to Innovate Are Reduced Once a Firm Is a Monopoly.

whereas, starting from *competition*, the gain is

$$G_c := D + E \qquad \text{(competition)}.$$

Of course,

$$B + C \le A + B \quad \text{and hence} \quad C \le A,$$

because $A + B$ is the maximum profit at the marginal cost function C_0' (see Figure 1.6). Therefore,

$$G_c - G_m = E - (C - A) \ge E > 0,$$

as asserted.

This result suggests that the patent system poses a dilemma: On the one hand, the patent system sets strong incentives to innovate by granting a temporary monopoly, but once a monopoly has been established patents become less effective.

Duration of Patents

The duration of patents varies, ranging from 16 to 20 years. In France certain types of patents are given shorter terms if the inventions have an overall general usefulness. Incidentally, the U.S. grants patents to the party that is *first to invent*, whereas most European countries award to the party that is *first to file*. Also, in many countries, including France, Germany, and the U.K., the patent holder must pay an annual renewal fee to maintain the patent.

Sleeping Patents

Gilbert and Newbery (1982) pointed out that an incumbent monopolist has a stronger incentive to innovate than potential entrants. This is due to the fact that the profits from maintaining a monopoly are usually greater than the profits an entrant could make by sharing the market with the incumbent monopolist.

An extreme case of defending a monopoly through the patent system is the accumulation of patents not to use them, but to prevent potential competitors from obtaining them ("sleeping patents"). One way to avoid such abuses of the patent system is to force the patentee to let others use the invention (see Carlton and Perloff (1990, p. 662 ff.)).

Prizes and Innovations

Prizes are well-known incentives in academic research. However, governments can also employ prizes to spur applied inventions as an alternative to the patent system. There are several prominent examples where prizes have been successfully employed.

For example, in 1713 substantial prizes were offered in England to reward the discovery of the measurement of longitude at sea. The first substantial prize of £3,000 was won by Mayer for his method of accurately predicting the position of the moon, which allowed the computation of a ship's longitude. Later, John Harrison developed the first chronometer, for which he was able to claim the prize of £20,000. By 1815, the remarkable sum of £101,000 had been awarded.

As another example, in 1795 Napoleon Bonaparte offered a prize of 12,000 francs for a method of food preservation to be employed by the military. Fifteen years later Nicolas Appert received the prize for his method of food canning (see Wright (1983)).

Speculation as an Alternative to Patents

The patent system often fails to provide effective protection of property rights. Imitation, reverse engineering, and inventing around patents are just some examples of the erosion of property rights in innovations.

There is, however, another way in which firms can profit from innovations, without monopoly or patent protection. This is the opportunity to speculate on the relative price changes that are caused by successful innovations.

As an example, Hirshleifer (1971) cites Eli Whitney's invention of the cotton gin. Although the cotton gin was patented, Whitney was not very successful in enforcing the patent. But he could have benefited from his invention in a different way. Since the cost saving due to the gin increased the value of the land on which cotton is grown, Whitney could have captured some of the rent generated by his invention by speculating on the price of cotton-growing land.

There are, of course, some problems with this approach. Wealth constraints and the risks involved may pose some limitations. But you should not overlook its advantages. In any case, there are many innovations that are intrinsically excluded from patent protection. Think of the large area of financial, organizational, economic, legal, and political innovations – from the invention of zero coupons or poison-pill securities to corporate and political governance structures.

Internal Financing of Innovations

It is often claimed that, due to moral hazard, the innovating firm must bear a substantial share of the development cost. A firm that earns monopoly profits is, presumably, better able to undertake internal financing than a competitive firm. Moreover, borrowing requires disclosure of information about the innovation, which in turn may leak out to rival firms and destroy the advantage the firm attempted to gain. This adds yet another reason for internal financing and hence monopoly.

1.2.5 Monopoly and Product Quality

A Cournot monopolist supplies insufficient output relative to the welfare optimum. Can one extrapolate and claim that a Cournot monopolist supplies also insufficient quality?

In order to answer this question, suppose quality can be described by a single index, measured by the real-valued variable q. Let cost and inverse demand be functions of output x *and* quality q, denoted by $C(x, q)$ and $P(x, q)$, and let C be monotone increasing in x and q, and P decreasing in x and increasing in q. Also, choose C and P in such a way that the profit

$$\pi(x, q) := P(x, q)x - C(x, q)$$

and total surplus

$$T(x, q) := \int_0^x P(\tilde{x}, q) \, d\tilde{x} - P(x, q)x + \pi(x, q) = \int_0^x P(\tilde{x}, q) \, d\tilde{x} - C(x, q)$$

are strictly concave.[17] Then the choice of output and quality can be described by first-order conditions.

We compare the welfare-optimal output and quality (x^{PO}, q^{PO}) with the generalized Cournot point (x^M, q^M). The welfare optimum maximizes total surplus, whereas the Cournot point maximizes profit. Assuming interior solutions, the Cournot point solves the first-order conditions

$$\pi'_x := P + P'_x x - C'_x = 0, \tag{1.22}$$

$$\pi'_q := P'_q x - C'_q = 0 \tag{1.23}$$

whereas the welfare optimum solves

$$T'_x := P - C'_x = 0, \tag{1.24}$$

$$T'_q := \int_0^x P'_q(\tilde{x}, q) \, d\tilde{x} - C'_q = 0. \tag{1.25}$$

From (1.25) it is immediately obvious that the monopolist's choice of quality is *locally* inefficient if and only if the effect of a quality increment on the marginal willingness to pay differs across average and marginal customers:

$$\frac{1}{x} \int_0^x P'_q(\tilde{x}, q) \, d\tilde{x} \neq P'_q(x, q) \qquad \text{(local inefficiency condition)}.$$

Therefore, strict monotonicity of P'_q in x is always sufficient for a locally inefficient choice of quality, as summarized by the following proposition.

Proposition 1.1 (Local Inefficiency) *The Cournot monopolist endows his output x^M with insufficient quality if $P''_{qx} < 0$ and with excessive quality if $P''_{qx} > 0$.*[18]

---

[17] A sufficient condition is that C is strictly convex and P concave.
[18] This result was observed for the first time by Spence (1975). See also the follow-up article by Sheshinski (1976).

Proof Suppose $P''_{qx} < 0$. Evaluated at the Cournot point (x^M, q^M), one has $\pi'_q = 0$ and therefore, by (1.25),

$$
\begin{aligned}
T'_q &= x \left(\frac{1}{x} \int_0^x P'_q(\tilde{x}, q)\, d\tilde{x} - P'_q \right) \\
&> x(P'_q - P'_q) \quad \text{(by } P''_{qx} < 0) \\
&= 0.
\end{aligned}
$$

This proves that, at the Cournot point, welfare could be increased if quality were raised. Therefore, quality is locally too low. The proof of the other case is similar.   □

These results indicate that the Cournot monopolist chooses inefficient quality. But they do not tell you anything about the global comparison of q^M and q^{PO}. The latter is also influenced by the gap between the two outputs, x^M and x^{PO}, in addition to the gap between the effects of quality on the marginal willingness to pay of the average and the marginal customer.

Altogether, the global inefficiency gap of quality $(q^M - q^{PO})$ has the same sign as the local gap summarized in the above proposition if the output gap $(x^M - x^{PO})$ is relatively small. However, if the output gap $(x^M - x^{PO})$ is substantial, the monopolist may actually provide more than the socially optimal level of quality $(q^M > q^{PO})$, even if the monopolist's quality level is locally insufficient because P'_q is strictly monotone decreasing in x.

We close with a simple example in which the local and the global inefficiency gap have the same sign.

Example 1.4 Suppose $P(x, q) := (1 - x)q$ and $C(x, q) = \frac{1}{2}q^2$. Then both profit and total surplus are strictly concave in x and q. Therefore, (x^M, q^M) and (x^{PO}, q^{PO}) can be found by solving the above first-order conditions:

$$
x^M = \frac{1}{2}, \qquad q^M = \frac{1}{4},
$$
$$
x^{PO} = 1, \qquad q^{PO} = \frac{1}{2}.
$$

1.3 Price-Discriminating or Strong Monopoly

A *strong* monopoly is not required to charge all customers the same linear price function, but may price-discriminate and set nonlinear prices or discriminate between individuals or groups of customers.

Price discrimination is often defined to be present if the same good is sold at different prices to different customers. In this vein Joan Robinson defined it as "the act of selling the same article, produced under single control, at different prices to different buyers" (Robinson (1933)).

However, this definition tends to fail if one interprets the "same good" too loosely. When delivery costs differ, as for example in the delivery of clay bricks, different prices may have nothing to do with price discrimination, whereas equal prices are discriminatory. On the other hand, the definition tends to become void of meaningful applications if one views two goods as the "same" only if they share the same physical characteristics and are available at the same time, place, and state of nature, as is common in general equilibrium theory.

In view of these difficulties it is preferable to adopt a pragmatic notion of price discrimination. The emphasis should be on the monopolist's motive to base the price on customers' willingness to pay rather than simply on cost. The typical price difference between hardcover and paperback books and between first- and second-class flights is a case in point. In both instances the price difference cannot be explained by the difference in cost alone. Instead, it reflects predominantly an attempt to charge buyers according to their willingness to pay. It is this pattern that qualifies observed price differences as discriminatory.

1.3.1 First-Degree Price Discrimination

First-degree price discrimination occurs if the monopolist charges different prices both across units and across individual customers. Ever since Pigou (1920),[19] it has been common to equate first-degree price discrimination with perfect discrimination where the monopolist generates the maximal gain from trade and captures all of it. But this identification leaves out the possibility of imperfect first-degree price discrimination.

A perfectly discriminating monopoly must know the marginal willingness to pay of each potential customer, prevent customers from engaging in arbitrage transactions, and unambiguously convey to customers that it is pointless to haggle. Within this general framework the monopolist can succeed with one of two simple pricing schemes.

One way to go is a customized *take-it-or-leave-it-sales plan*

$$S_i := \{(T_i, x_i), (0, 0)\}. \tag{1.26}$$

There, each customer i is offered to either buy the stipulated x_i units for the total price T_i, or leave it $(0, 0)$. To capture the maximum gain, the monopolist only needs to offer the efficient quantities, implicitly defined by the "price = marginal cost" requirement (where $X := \sum_j x_j$)

$$P_i(x_i) = C'(X) \qquad \text{for all } i, \tag{1.27}$$

and set T_i equal to i's maximum willingness to pay for x_i.

Another way is to offer customized *two-part tariffs*

$$S_i' := \{(t_i, f_i), (0, 0)\} \tag{1.28}$$

that prescribe a certain unit price t_i plus a lump-sum price f_i. In order to capture

---

[19] Pigou (1920) introduced the standard distinction between first-, second-, and third-degree price discrimination.

the maximum gain, t_i needs to be set equal to the marginal cost $C'(\sum_j x_j)$, and f_i at the level where the total price equals i's maximum willingness to pay. Then allow each customer to buy as many units as he likes, unless he chooses the no-buy option $(0, 0)$.

The two methods of sale are equivalent as long as complete information and exclusion of arbitrage prevail.

An immediate implication of optimal first-degree price discrimination is that it maximizes social surplus. Hence, one arrives at the somewhat paradoxical conclusion that the strong monopolist gives rise to efficiency of output, whereas the monopolist that exercises restraint and adopts a uniform linear price function contributes to a welfare loss.

However, keep in mind that higher monopoly profits give rise to more wasteful expenditures in the course of the competition for the market. In Section 1.2.3 we showed that monopoly profit is a good statistic of this underlying waste. This suggests that first-degree price discrimination is the least efficient among all conceivable market forms. True, once a monopoly position has been acquired, perfect price discrimination maximizes the social surplus. But the entire social gain is completely eaten up by wasteful expenditures in the course of the preceding competition for the market.

1.3.2 Second-Degree Price Discrimination

Second-degree price discrimination occurs if unit prices vary with the number of units bought, but all customers are subject to the same nonlinear price function. It is by far the most frequently observed form of price discrimination.

For example, many products are sold in different-sized packages at a quantity discount, airlines offer frequent-flyer bonuses, and public utilities and amusement parks alike charge two-part tariffs. The opposite of a quantity discount – a quantity premium – also occurs. For example, supermarkets often impose a three–per-customer rule on discount priced items, where customers are charged the regular price except for the first three units.

The main reason for the popularity of second-degree price discrimination is the lack of precise information about individual customers' willingness to pay. Since it is so important, we cover it in detail in Section 1.4 and again, at a more advanced level, in Section 9.5.1. The particularly nice feature of models based on incomplete information is that they give an endogenous explanation of second-degree price discrimination.

1.3.3 Third-Degree Price Discrimination

Third-degree price discrimination occurs if different submarkets are charged different linear price functions. Each customer pays a constant unit price, but unit prices differ across submarkets.

Table 1.2. *Relative markups of selected cars, year 1990*

Model	Markup (%)				
	Belgium	France	Germany	Italy	U.K.
Nissan Micra	8.1	23.1	8.9	36.1	12.5
Fiat Tipo	8.4	9.2	9.0	20.8	9.1
Toyota Corolla	9.7	19.6	13.0	24.2	13.6
VW Golf	9.3	10.3	12.2	11.0	10.0
Mercedes 190	14.3	14.4	17.2	15.6	12.3
BMW 7 series	15.7	15.7	14.7	19.0	21.5

Source: Verboven (1996).

Common examples of third-degree price discrimination are senior-citizen and student discounts, lower prices at certain shopping hours (such as the "happy hour" in bars and restaurants), the infamous coupons in U.S. supermarkets, and intertemporal price discrimination.

Another example is price discrimination across national markets, as in the European car market. Table 1.2 compares the markup on costs for a sample of cars across some European countries. The spread of markups is remarkably high. The table also suggests that loyalty is a true "luxury"; the Italians are fond of their Fiats and the Germans of their VW Golf (in the U.S. known as Rabbit) – and they pay extra for this national brand loyalty.

Of course, the optimal third-degree price discrimination is a straightforward extension of the standard Cournot monopoly solution. It simply extends the Cournot markup rule to each and every submarket i:

$$P_i(x_i) \left(\frac{1 + \varepsilon_i}{\varepsilon_i} \right) = C' \left(\sum_j x_j \right), \qquad (1.29)$$

(ε_i : price elasticity of demand in submarket i).

Of course, a full account of price discrimination cannot be given in terms of price alone. Pricing is interconnected with product design, quality, and product bundling. Often product design is a prerequisite of price discrimination. As a particularly extreme example, Scherer (1980) reports that a manufacturer considered adding arsenic to his industrial plastic molding powder methyl methacrylate in order to prevent its use in denture manufacture.[20]

Third-degree price discrimination comes up again in our discussion of the time inconsistency of optimal intertemporal price discrimination, also known as the durable-goods monopoly problem, and later in the book when we deal with optimal auctions.

---

[20] This method of separating markets is also common in taxation. For example, diesel fuel can be used to heat your home or to run a diesel-engine-powered automobile. In Europe both uses are widespread. Governments wanted to tax engine fuel at a higher rate than heating fuel. This was made feasible by adding a substance to heating fuel that generates an obnoxious fume if burnt in an engine.

1.3.4 Limits of Price Discrimination

The possibilities of price discrimination are limited for at least three reasons:

1. arbitrage,
2. hidden information,
3. limited commitment power.

If different prices are charged across units or across customers, arbitrage transactions tend to be profitable. For example, if all customers are charged the same two-part tariff, customers can gain if they buy through an intermediary. This saves participating customers all except one lump-sum fee.

As a rule, the possibility of arbitrage erodes price discrimination. But, due to transaction costs, it does not usually rule it out altogether. The European car market is a case in point. In German newspapers one sees ads for low-priced "reimports" of new German cars. Car manufacturers run their own campaigns to warn potential buyers of reimports against alleged fraud. The combination of fear and bother seems to scare away most customers.

Moreover, there are many products where arbitrage is intrinsically difficult to achieve. Did you never wish you could send someone else to the dentist to have your teeth drilled? There are many examples of products and services where a transfer of ownership is seriously inhibited. Therefore, price discrimination has many applications, and indeed it flourishes in real-world markets.

The second limitation, hidden information, has to do with the fact that the monopolist typically does not know the marginal willingness to pay of each and every customer. The statistical distribution of customers' characteristics may be fairly well known. But when customers walk in, it is difficult to identify their type.

The third limitation has to do with limited commitment power and the credibility of threats. If a monopolist makes a take-it-or-leave-it offer, the leave-it threat may pose a problem. Suppose a customer has refused the initial offer and starts haggling. Then the monopolist is tempted to enter negotiations in order to avoid the loss of a profitable customer. When both sides of a transaction gain, both tend to have some bargaining power. The seller can capture the entire gain from trade only if he can make a reliable commitment to always break off negotiations after an offer has been refused. But such commitment is difficult to achieve. In some cases delegation is effective (just try to negotiate the price of a bar of soap in a department store), but if the gains are substantial, one can always ask to see the manager.

1.4 Hidden Information and Price Discrimination

Second-degree price discrimination is the most widely observed kind of price discrimination. We now take a closer look at it and elaborate on a model that explains why this kind of discrimination emerges, and how it should be done.[21]

---

[21] Here we present a two-type version of the continuous-type model by Maskin and Riley (1984a).

Consider a profit-maximizing monopolist who faces two types of customers with known payoff functions in equal proportions.[22] Arbitrage transactions between customers are not feasible. Therefore, the monopolist may price-discriminate.

However, the pricing problem is complicated by the fact that customers' type is their private or hidden information. The monopolist knows all payoff functions; but he cannot tell customers apart (he does not know who is type 1 and who is type 2). Therefore, price discrimination requires a somewhat sophisticated sorting device.

The market game is structured as follows:

1. The monopolist sets a uniform nonlinear price function in the form of a menu of price–quantity combinations, (T, x), called the *sales plan*, from which each customer is free to select one:

$$S := \{(T_1, x_1), (T_2, x_2), (0, 0)\}. \tag{1.30}$$

The $(0, 0)$ combination is included because market transactions are voluntary; customers are free to abstain from buying. Of course, $x_1, x_2 \geq 0$.

2. Customers observe the sales plan and pick that price–quantity combination that maximizes their payoff. Payments are made, and the market game ends.

Without loss of generality, the component (T_1, x_1) is designated for customer 1, and (T_2, x_2) for customer 2 (*incentive compatibility*).

Of course, the monopolist could also live with a sales plan where, for example, customer 2 picks (x_1, T_1) and 1 picks (x_2, T_2), as long as he makes no error in predicting customers' rational choice. But then incentive compatibility can be restored simply by relabeling the components of the sales plan. Moreover, one can show that any other format of sales plans is equivalent to a sales plan of the kind considered here. Therefore, the restriction to incentive-compatible sales plans is without loss of generality. This is the essence of the well-known *revelation principle*.[23]

Assumptions Five assumptions are made:

A1 (*Cost function*). Unit costs are constant and normalized to 0.
A2 (*Payoff functions*). The monopolist maximizes profit[24]

$$\pi := T_1 + T_2; \tag{1.31}$$

and customers maximize consumer surplus:

$$U_i(x, T) := \int_0^x P_i(y)\, dy - T \qquad \text{for } i = 1, 2, \tag{1.32}$$

where $P_i(x)$ denotes i's marginal willingness to pay for x.
A3 (*Declining marginal willingness to pay*). $P_i(x)$ is continuously differentiable with $P_i'(x) < 0$; also $P_i(0) > 0$, and $P_i(x) = 0$, for some $x, i \in \{1, 2\}$.
A4 (*Single crossing*). For all x

$$P_2(x) > P_1(x). \tag{1.33}$$

---

[22] Equal proportions are invoked only in order to avoid a glut of notation and obvious case distinctions.
[23] A detailed exposition and proof of this principle is given in Section 8.5.2.
[24] Alternative interpretation: there is only one customer; this customer is either type 1 or type 2 with equal chance; the monopolist maximizes expected profit.

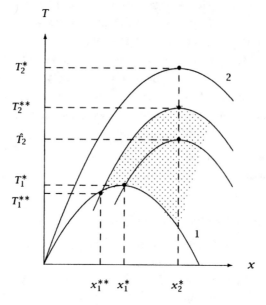

Figure 1.7. Customers' Indifference Curves.

A5 (*Concavity*). For all x

$$2P_1'(x) < P_2'(x). \tag{1.34}$$

A4 is called the single-crossing assumption for the following reason: Pick an arbitrary point in (x, T) space, say x_1^*, T_1^*, and draw the two types' indifference curves that pass through this point. Since the slope of the indifference curves is equal to $P_i(x)$, A4 assures that these curves cross only once at this given point, as illustrated in Figure 1.7.

And A5 is called "concavity" because it assures the strict concavity of the objective function, as we show later on.

Optimal Sales Plan

The optimal sales plan maximizes π subject to the *participation constraints*

$$U_1(x_1, T_1) \geq U_1(0, 0) = 0, \tag{1.35}$$

$$U_2(x_2, T_2) \geq U_2(0, 0) = 0 \tag{1.36}$$

and the *incentive constraints*

$$U_1(x_1, T_1) \geq U_1(x_2, T_2), \tag{1.37}$$

$$U_2(x_2, T_2) \geq U_2(x_1, T_1). \tag{1.38}$$

Conditions (1.35) and (1.37) assure that the component of the sales plan designated for customer 1, (x_1, T_1), is dominated neither by the $(0, 0)$ nor by the (x_2, T_2) option. Similarly, conditions (1.36) and (1.38) assure that (x_2, T_2) is dominated neither by $(0, 0)$ nor by the (x_1, T_1).

Some Preliminaries

Luckily, the program can be simplified by eliminating two constraints. Indeed, among the participation constraints only the lower type's participation constraint (1.35) binds, and among the incentive constraints only the upper type's incentive constraint (1.38) binds. (A constraint does not *bind* if eliminating it from the optimization program does not affect the solution.) Therefore it is claimed that one can eliminate constraints (1.36) and (1.37) without loss of generality.

What makes us come to this conclusion? At this point, just take it as a working hypothesis. Of course, it is only justified if it turns out that the solution of the thus restricted optimization program also satisfies the eliminated constraints – which will be confirmed later on.

1.4.1 Solution of the Restricted Program

The restricted program – restricted by eliminating constraints (1.36) and (1.37) – can be further simplified due to the following results.

Lemma 1.1 *The optimal sales plan exhibits*

$$T_1 = \int_0^{x_1} P_1(y)\, dy, \tag{1.39}$$

$$T_2 = T_1 + \int_{x_1}^{x_2} P_2(y)\, dy. \tag{1.40}$$

Proof We have noted (but not yet proved) that the upper type's incentive constraint and the lower type's participation constraints are binding. If a constraint binds, then it is satisfied with equality at the optimal sales plan. Therefore, (1.35) entails (1.39). Using this result concerning T_1 if (1.38) and (1.35) bind, one has

$$0 = U_2(x_2, T_2) - U_2(x_1, T_1)$$
$$= \int_0^{x_1} P_1(y)\, dy + \int_{x_1}^{x_2} P_2(y)\, dy - T_2, \tag{1.41}$$

which entails (1.40), as asserted. □

These price functions have a nice interpretation:

1. The low type is charged his maximum willingness to pay for x_1.
2. The high type pays the same for the first x_1 units plus his own maximum willingness to pay for the additional $x_2 - x_1$ units. Therefore, the high type makes a net gain if $x_1 > 0$, simply because he obtains the first x_1 units at a bargain price.

In view of Lemma 1.1 we can now eliminate the T-variables in the monopolist's objective function and state the restricted program in the form of the unconstrained optimization problem (except for nonnegativity)

$$\max_{x_1, x_2 \geq 0} \left(2 \int_0^{x_1} P_1(y)\, dy + \int_{x_1}^{x_2} P_2(y)\, dy \right). \tag{1.42}$$

The Kuhn–Tucker conditions of the restricted program are

$$\phi(x_1) := 2P_1(x_1) - P_2(x_1) \leq 0 \quad \text{and} \quad \phi(x_1)x_1 = 0, \qquad (1.43)$$

$$P_2(x_2) \leq 0 \quad \text{and} \quad P_2(x_2)x_2 = 0. \qquad (1.44)$$

The T's are obtained by inserting the optimal x's into (1.39), (1.40).

As you can confirm easily, A5 assures the strict concavity of the objective function. It also entails that $\phi(x_1)$ is strict monotone decreasing with $\phi(x) < 0$ for some x. This assures that (1.43) has a unique solution; however, since $\phi(x)$ may be negative everywhere, one may get the corner solution $x_1 = 0$. Also, P_2 is declining, with $P_2(0) > 0$. Therefore, (1.44) has the unique solution $x_2 > 0$, implicitly defined by $P_2(x_2) = 0$.

1.4.2 The Optimal Sales Plan

Proposition 1.2 *The optimal sales plan exhibits*

$$P_2(x_2) = 0, \quad x_2 > 0 \qquad \textit{(no distortion at top)}, \qquad \text{(i)}$$

$$x_2 > x_1, \quad T_2 > T_1 \qquad \textit{(monotonicity)}, \qquad \text{(ii)}$$

$$P_1(x_1) > 0 \qquad \textit{(distortion at bottom)}, \qquad \text{(iii)}$$

$$U_1(x_1, T_1) = 0 \qquad \textit{(no surplus at bottom)}, \qquad \text{(iv)}$$

$$U_2(x_2, T_2) \geq 0 \quad \textit{with} > \Longleftrightarrow x_1 > 0 \,\textit{(surplus at top unless } x_1 = 0). \quad \text{(v)}$$

The optimal prices are computed in (1.39) and (1.40).

Proof First we characterize the solution of the restricted program (1.42) and then show that it also solves the unrestricted program.

We have already shown that the Kuhn–Tucker conditions have a unique solution that exhibits $x_2 > 0$ and $x_1 \geq 0$.

(i): Follows immediately from the fact that $P_2(x_2) = 0$, $x_2 > 0$ and the fact that marginal cost is constant and has been normalized to zero.

(ii): By Lemma 1.1 the T's have the asserted monotonicity property if and only if it holds for the x's. We first prove weak monotonicity: Suppose $x_1 > x_2$, contrary to what is asserted. Since $x_2 > 0$, one has also $x_1 > 0$. Therefore, (1.43) is satisfied with equality, and one has, using the single-crossing assumption A4,

$$0 = 2P_1(x_1) - P_2(x_1)$$

$$\leq 2P_2(x_1) - P_2(x_1)$$

$$= P_2(x_1)$$

$$< P_2(x_2).$$

But this contradicts (i). Therefore, $x_2 \geq x_1$. Finally, note that if it were possible to have $x = x_1 = x_2 > 0$, one would need to have $P_2(x) = P_1(x) = 0$ for some x, which contradicts A4. Therefore, the monotonicity is strict.

(iii): If $x_1 = 0$, one has $P_1(x_1) > 0$, by A3. And if $x_1 > 0$, condition (1.43) combined with monotonicity (ii) entails, due to $x_2 > x_1$,

$$P_1(x_1) = \frac{1}{2}P_2(x_1) > \frac{1}{2}P_2(x_2) = 0.$$

In either case the low customer gets less than the efficient quantity, $P_1(x_1) > 0$ (distortion at bottom).

(iv): $U_1(x_1, T_1) = 0$ is obvious from (1.39). And $U_2(x_2, T_2) \geq 0$, with strict inequality if $x_1 > 0$, follows immediately from (1.40) and monotonicity.

(v): Finally, we need to confirm that the restricted program also satisfies the two omitted constraints (1.36) and (1.37). The omitted participation constraint (1.36) is obviously satisfied by (v). And the omitted incentive constraint (1.37) holds for the following reasoning (the last step uses the monotonicity property $x_2 \geq x_1$ and the single-crossing assumption A4):

$$U_1(x_2, T_2) - U_1(x_1, T_1) = \int_{x_1}^{x_2} P_1(y)\, dy - (T_2 - T_1)$$

$$= \int_{x_1}^{x_2} (P_1(y) - P_2(y))\, dy$$

$$\leq 0.$$

This completes the proof.   □

1.4.3 Why it Pays to "Distort" Efficiency

Why is it optimal to deviate from efficiency in dealing with the low type but not the high type? The intuition is simple. The high type has to be kept indifferent between (x_2, T_2) and (x_1, T_1). This is achieved by charging the high type the price T_1 for the first x_1 units and a price equal to his maximum willingness to pay for $x_2 - x_1$ units. From this observation it follows immediately that profit is maximized by expanding x_2 to a level where the marginal willingness to pay equals the marginal cost, $P_2(x_2) = 0$ (see Figure 1.7). In turn, starting from $P_1(x_1) = 0$ (see point (x_1^*, T_1^*) in that figure), a small reduction in x_1 is costless in terms of forgone profits from the low type (the marginal profit is zero at this starting point). But, as a side effect, it extends the domain where the high type is charged a price equal to his maximum willingness to pay. Altogether, it thus pays to introduce a downward distortion at the bottom, illustrated by the two-star variables in Figure 1.7.

Both Figures 1.7 and 1.8 provide illustrations of these considerations. Note that in Figure 1.8 the shaded area is the high type's consumer surplus, which can also be viewed as forgone profit from type 2 (the explanation was already provided in Lemma 1.1). That surplus is always lowered if one deviates from the efficient level of x_1.

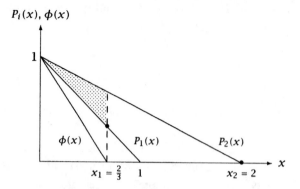

$P_i(x), \phi(x)$

$\phi(x)$ $P_1(x)$ $P_2(x)$

x

$x_1 = \frac{2}{3}$ 1 $x_2 = 2$

Figure 1.8. Optimal Sorting with Two Customers if $P_i(x) := 1 - x/i$.

1.4.4 Sorting, Bunching, and Exclusion

Finally, note that it is not always optimal to serve both customers and, if we slightly change the assumptions, it may not even be optimal to discriminate.

Altogether, the optimal price discrimination falls into one of three categories:

1. *Sorting*, with $0 < x_1 < x_2$, $T_1 < T_2$.
2. *Bunching*, or no discrimination, with $x_1 = x_2 > 0$, $T_1 = T_2$.
3. *Exclusion*, or extreme discrimination, where only the high type is served at a price equal to its maximum willingness to pay, with $0 = x_1 < x_2$, $T_2 > T_1 = 0$.

Note carefully that Proposition 1.2 excludes only case 2.

Example 1.5 Here we illustrate these three cases.

1. Suppose $P_i(x) := 1 - x/i$, $i = 1, 2$. Then the optimal price discrimination exhibits sorting with $x_1 = \frac{2}{3}$, $T_1 = \frac{4}{9}$, $x_2 = 2$, $T_2 = \frac{8}{9}$, and, incidentally, exhibits a declining unit price (quantity discount) $T_2/x_2 = \frac{4}{9} < \frac{6}{9} = \frac{2}{3} = T_1/x_1$.
2. Suppose $P_i(x) := \theta_i(1 - x)$, $i = 1, 2$, and $1 = \theta_1 < \theta_2 < 2$. Then it is optimal to abstain from discrimination (bunching). Specifically, $x_1 = x_2 = 1$, $T_1 = T_2 = \frac{1}{2}$.
3. Suppose $P_i(x) := i - x$, $i = 1, 2$. Then it is optimal to serve only the high type (exclusivity) and take away the entire surplus $x_1 = T_1 = 0$, $x_2 = 2$, $T_2 = 2$.

However, bunching is a pure borderline case and cannot occur generically. Why? A necessary condition for bunching is that there exists a quantity $\xi > 0$ for which $P_2(\xi) = P_1(\xi) = 0$ (which is, incidentally, ruled out by A4). This property cannot survive parameter perturbations; hence, it is irrelevant.

Example 1.6 Modify Example 1.5(2) by setting $\theta_2 > 2$. Then

$$\phi(x_1) = (2 - \theta_2)(1 - x)$$

is evidently not decreasing; hence, the monopolist's payoff is not concave. In that case, the Kuhn–Tucker conditions have two solutions: 1) $x_1 = x_2 = 1$ and 2) $x_1 = 0$, $x_2 = 1$ (see Figure 1.9). Comparing payoffs shows that the unique maximizer is the corner solution $x_1 = 0$, $x_2 = 1$ (exclusion).

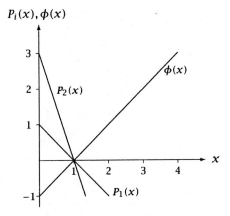

Figure 1.9. Nonconcavity: $P_i(x) := \theta_i(1-x)$, $\theta_1 = 1$, $\theta_2 = 3$.

Digression: Two-Part Tariffs

A somewhat less effective price-discrimination scheme is to offer a menu of two-part tariffs. A two-part tariff is an affine price function

$$T_i(x) := t_i x + f_i \qquad (1.45)$$

with the constant unit-price component t_i and the lump-sum component f_i. This pricing scheme is observed in many regulated industries, for example in public utilities and in the taxi business.

The two-part tariff discriminating monopolist offers a sales plan,

$$S' := \{(t_1, f_1), (t_2, f_2), (0, 0)\}, \qquad (1.46)$$

asks each customer to pick one component, and then lets each customer buy as many units as he wishes, unless he chose the no-buy option $(0, 0)$.

Using the revelation principle, one can again restrict attention to prices that satisfy the corresponding participation and incentive constraints, and then compute the optimal two-part tariffs. Again, only the low type's participation and the high type's incentive constraint bind. Therefore, the solution procedure is quite similar.

Two-part tariffs are evidently less effective. The profit earned with a menu of two-part tariffs can always be replicated by appropriately chosen price-quantity combinations, but not vice versa. You may wish to confirm this by computing the optimal two-part tariffs for the $P_i(x)$ functions assumed in the complete sorting case of Example 1.5 and show that two-part tariffs are less profitable.

Generalization*

The above generalizes in a straightforward manner to $n \geq 2$ types with the single-crossing marginal willingness-to-pay functions

$$P_1(y) < P_2(y) < \cdots < P_n(y), \qquad \forall y. \qquad (1.47)$$

In particular, if complete sorting is optimal, one can show that the optimal price discrimination exhibits

1. zero consumer surplus for the lowest type only;
2. no distortion at the top only;
3. only local downward incentive constraints bind (customer $i \geq 2$ is indifferent between (T_i, x_i) and (T_{i-1}, x_{i-1}); all other price–quantity combinations in the optimal sales plan are inferior).

Moreover, the optimal sales plan is then completely characterized by the following rules:

$$(n + 1 - i)P_i(x_i) = (n - i)P_{i+1}(x_i), \qquad i \in \{1, \ldots, n - 1\}, \qquad (1.48)$$

$$P_n(x_n) = 0, \qquad (1.49)$$

$$T_1 = \int_0^{x_1} P_1(y)\, dy, \qquad (1.50)$$

$$T_i = T_{i-1} + \int_{x_{i-1}}^{x_i} P_i(y)dy, \qquad i \in \{2, \ldots, n\}. \qquad (1.51)$$

The proof of these assertions is a fairly straightforward extension of the above analysis of the two-types case.

Follow-up Reading

If you want to know more about second-degree price discrimination under incomplete information, take a look at our follow-up analysis in Chapter 9, Section 9.6, where a continuum of types is assumed and more advanced techniques are employed.

1.5 Price Discrimination and Public Goods*

Monopolies tend to price-discriminate, but not all price discrimination is due to monopoly. Public goods are a case in point. There, price discrimination is a prerequisite for an efficient allocation, even if the supplier does not exercise monopoly power.

Many public goods happen to be supplied by monopolies. Therefore, an introduction to monopoly should include a few remarks on the relationship between price discrimination and public goods.

Usually we consider *private goods*, which are defined by two properties:

1. *rivalry in consumption:* a good consumed by one agent is no longer available to others;
2. *excludability.*

However, some goods are *nonrival* in the sense that one person's consumption does not reduce the amount available to others. And some goods are *nonexcludable* because it is impossible or too costly to exclude customers. Goods that are both nonrival and nonexcludable are often called *common goods.* However, it is useful to distinguish more narrowly between *public goods* and *club goods,* as in the classification in Table 1.3.

A good example of a nonrival good is the reception of a radio or TV broadcast. In the absence of exclusion devices one has a public good. But if the broadcast is

Table 1.3. *Private, public and club goods*

		Rivalry	
		Yes	No
Excludability	Yes	Private good	Club good
	No	No name	Public good

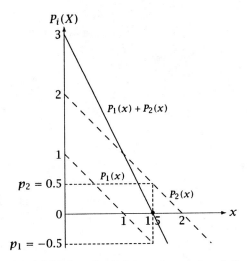

Figure 1.10. Lindahl Prices for $P_i(x) := i - x$, $i = 1, 2$ and $c = 0$.

coded and only those who have a decoder can listen to or watch the broadcast, one has a club good.

Lindahl Prices: Price Discrimination without Monopoly

Suppose there are two types of customers, as in Section 1.4, except that the good is public rather than private, and suppose marginal cost is constant at the rate $0 < c < \min\{P_1(0), P_2(0)\}$. What allocation is welfare-optimal? And can it be implemented by a set of linear prices? These questions are standard exercises in (undergraduate) microeconomics. The answers are:

1. Choose that output x^* at which the *sum* of customers' marginal willingnesses to pay is equal to marginal cost:[25]

$$P_1(x^*) + P_2(x^*) = c.$$

2. Charge each customer a unit price p_i equal to this customer's marginal willingness to pay (*Lindahl prices*):[26]

$$p_i = P_i(x^*).$$

An illustration is provided in Figure 1.10.

[25] The efficiency conditions for public goods were introduced by Samuelson (1954).
[26] Lindahl prices were introduced by Lindahl (1919).

First-Degree Price Discrimination

Suppose the public good is provided by a monopoly. If the monopolist has complete information concerning customers' marginal willingness to pay and if arbitrage transaction among customers are excluded, first-degree price discrimination is feasible. As you can easily confirm, the profit-maximizing monopolist implements the welfare optimum by setting two-part tariffs with a unit price equal to the Lindahl price and a lump-sum fee equal to customer's maximum consumer surplus. Therefore, Lindahl prices are also part of first-degree price discrimination.

Second-Degree Price Discrimination

If the monopolist operates under incomplete information, as in the Section 1.4 on hidden information and price discrimination, he cannot price discriminate, because he cannot induce sorting by supplying different price–quantity packages. Therefore, the monopolist either supplies both customers or exclusively customer 2, whichever is more profitable, and earns the maximum profit:

$$\Pi := \max\left\{\max_x 2\int_0^x P_1(y)\,dy - cx,\ \max_x \int_0^x P_2(y)\,dy - cx\right\}.$$

However, if the good is a club good because exclusion is feasible, second-degree price discrimination comes back. And the optimal price discrimination scheme is characterized by the sales plan $S := \{(T_1, x_1), (T_2, x_2)\}$ that solves

$$\max_{x_1,x_2}\left(2\int_0^{x_1} P_1(y)\,dy + \int_{x_1}^{x_2} P_2(y)\,dy - c\max\{x_1, x_2\}\right),$$

$$T_1 := \int_0^{x_1} P_1(y)\,dy,$$

$$T_2 := T_1 + \int_{x_1}^{x_2} P_2(y)\,dy.$$

1.6 Intertemporal Price Discrimination

Third-degree price discrimination is frequently observed in markets for consumer durables in the form of intertemporal price discrimination. For example, when new computer hardware, digital video-telephone receivers, or even new books are introduced, the seller typically starts out with a high unit price in order to skim the impatient high-demand customers, and then gradually lowers the price.

The rules of optimal third-degree price discrimination are a straightforward extension of the Cournot monopoly rule, which was already summarized in Section 1.3.3. However, the application to intertemporal price discrimination for durable goods poses an intriguing new problem: that of the time inconsistency of optimal plans. In the face of this problem the standard formula for optimal third-degree price discrimination needs to be modified along the following lines.

Time Inconsistency of Optimal Plans An optimal plan that calls for a sequence of actions is called *time-inconsistent* if, in the course of time, one can gain by deviating from it. Essentially such gains may occur if others rely in an important way on the execution of that plan and the decision maker takes advantage of breaching that "trust."

If an optimal sequence of actions is time-inconsistent, inflexibility and the power to make a commitment to stick to these actions become valuable. However, such commitment is difficult to achieve.

The problem of the time inconsistency of optimal plans and the search for commitment mechanisms is a matter of concern in many decision problems (think of smoking and the notorious difficulties of quitting). It already engaged the attention of Greek mythology. In his famous story of Odysseus and the sirens, Homer tells of two sirens – creatures half bird and half woman – on the rocks of Scylla who lured sailors to destruction by the sweetness of their song. The Greek hero Odysseus escaped the danger of their song by stopping the ears of his crew with wax so that they were deaf to the sirens. Yet he wanted to hear the music himself, and had himself tied to the mast so that he could not steer the ship out of course.

1.6.1 Durable-Goods Monopoly

We now consider the simplest possible durable-goods monopoly problem with a time horizon of only two periods. Although the exposition is kept at an elementary level, the issues raised show up in general settings and have a bearing on many other topics in economics, from oligopoly to monetary policy.

Suppose a monopolist produces a durable good that can be used for two periods. The average cost is constant in output and time and thus normalized to zero. There is no wear and tear. The durable good can be sold but not rented; leasing is not feasible. The monopolist is free to deviate from an earlier plan and cannot commit to a sequence of outputs or prices.

The demand side of the market is characterized by the time-invariant inverse *user demand* (or *marginal willingness to pay for use*) per period $t \in \{1, 2, \ldots\}$, defined on the consumption flow of the durable good in period t, $X_t \in [0, 1]$:

$$P(X_t) := \begin{cases} 1 - X_t & \text{for } t = 1, 2, \\ 0 & \text{for } t > 2. \end{cases} \tag{1.52}$$

Note: $P(\xi)$ is a marginal willingness for consumption or use, not ownership, and customers are interested in this good only during the first two periods.

Denote the monopolist's outputs by x_1, x_2 and normalize the rate of consumption per unit of the durable good to be equal to one. Then, since there is no wear and tear, the consumption flow available in each period bears the following relationship to past outputs:

$$X_1 := x_1, \qquad X_2 := x_1 + x_2. \tag{1.53}$$

Customers can only buy, not rent. Buying in period 1 provides a consumption flow in two periods, whereas buying in period 2 provides valuable consumption only in period 2. From these facts one can compute the *inverse demand for ownership*, as follows.

Inverse Ownership Demand

In period 2, the marginal willingness to pay or inverse ownership demand, P_2, coincides with the marginal willingness to pay for use, since the durable good is useless thereafter. Using the stock flow conversion assumption (1.53), this entails

$$P_2 = P(X_2) = P(x_1 + x_2) = 1 - x_1 - x_2. \tag{1.54}$$

In period 1, the marginal willingness to pay for ownership, P_1, takes into account that the acquired good provides services during two periods. Using the discount factor $\delta \in (0, 1]$ and assumption (1.53), one obtains the inverse ownership demand in period 1:

$$P_1 := P(X_1) + \delta P(X_2)$$

$$= P(x_1) + \delta P(x_1 + x_2)$$

$$= (1 - x_1) + \delta(1 - x_1 - x_2). \tag{1.55}$$

Evidently, in order to make the right demand decision in period 1, customers have to correctly predict the monopolist's output in period 2.

Interpretation

Many students who have difficulties with this computation of the inverse ownership demand P_1 find the following interpretation useful.

Imagine those who buy the durable good in period 1 sell it at the end of the period and then possibly buy again the quantity they want to consume, at zero transaction costs. Since new and old durable goods are perfect substitutes, the unit price at which the used good is sold at the end of period 1 is equal to $P(x_1 + x_2)$. Therefore, the inverse demand for ownership in period 1 must be equal to the marginal willingness to pay for use in period 1 plus the present value of the price earned from selling it at the end of that period, which gives $P_1 = P(x_1) + \delta P(x_1 + x_2)$, as asserted.

Payoff Functions

After these preliminaries it follows immediately that the monopolist's present values of profits in periods 1 and 2 are

$$\pi_2 := P_2(x_1, x_2)x_2$$

$$= (1 - x_1 - x_2)x_2, \tag{1.56}$$

$$\pi_1 := P_1(x_1, x_2)x_1 + \delta\pi_2$$

$$= (1 - x_1 + \delta(1 - x_1 - x_2)) x_1$$

$$+ \delta(1 - x_1 - x_2)x_2. \tag{1.57}$$

1.6.2 Time-Inconsistency Problem

The optimal output plan maximizes the present value of profits:

$$\max_{x_1,x_2 \geq 0} \pi_1(x_1, x_2). \tag{1.58}$$

Proposition 1.3 (Optimal Price Discrimination) *The optimal output plan, prices, and present value of profits are*

$$x_1 = 0.5, \qquad x_2 = 0, \tag{1.59}$$

$$p_1 = 0.5 + \delta p_2, \qquad p_2 = 0.5, \tag{1.60}$$

$$\pi_1 = 0.25(1 + \delta). \tag{1.61}$$

Proof The objective function is strictly concave. Therefore, the solution is uniquely characterized by the Kuhn–Tucker conditions

$$((1 - 2x_1)(1 + \delta) - \delta 2x_2) \leq 0 \quad \text{and} \quad (\cdots)x_1 = 0, \tag{1.62}$$

$$(1 - 2x_1 - 2x_2) \leq 0 \quad \text{and} \quad (\cdots)x_2 = 0. \tag{1.63}$$

The output plan (1.59) satisfies these two conditions. The associated prices and maximum present value of profits follow easily. □

Alternative Solution Procedure Of course, the optimal price discrimination follows already from the standard formula for optimal third-degree price discrimination. Note that if marginal cost is equal to zero, that formula requires user prices (the unit cost of consumption) to be set at the level where the corresponding price elasticities of demand are equal to -1, or equivalently (see (1.29)),

$$\frac{1}{\varepsilon_i} := \frac{\partial P}{\partial X_i} \frac{X_i}{P} = -1, \qquad i \in \{1, 2\}.$$

Since $P(X_i) = 1 - X_i$, it follows immediately that

$$\frac{X_i}{1 - X_i} = 1, \qquad i \in \{1, 2\}.$$

Hence, $X_1 = X_2 = \frac{1}{2}$, and $x_1 = X_1 = \frac{1}{2}$, $x_2 = X_2 - x_1 = 0$, user prices $= \frac{1}{2}$, and prices for ownership $p_1 = (1 + \delta)/2$, $p_2 = \frac{1}{2}$, as asserted in Proposition 1.3.

Proposition 1.4 (Time Inconsistency) *The optimal third-degree price discrimination summarized in Proposition 1.3 is time-inconsistent. In the absence of commitment the monopolist deviates from that plan.*

Proof Suppose the monopolist starts out with $x_1 = \frac{1}{2}$ and customers believe that the monopolist will continue with the optimal output plan. Then, the market clearing price in period 1 is equal to $p_1 = \frac{1}{2}(1 + \delta)$. However, when period 2 has arrived, the monopolist faces the inverse residual demand function $P_2 = 1 - \frac{1}{2} - x_2$. The maximizer of the associated profit function $\pi_2(x_2) = \frac{1}{2}x_2 - x_2^2$ is $x_2 = \frac{1}{4} > 0$.

Since the monopolist is free to deviate from any plan, he will serve the market again at the rate $x_2 = \frac{1}{4}$ – violating the optimal plan.   □

At first glance you may wonder: How can the monopolist raise his profits by deviating from the optimal plan? Of course, this works only if customers believe incorrectly that the monopolist will stick to the optimal plan and will not erode the price of the durable good in period 2. In reality, rational customers anticipate that the optimal plan is not time-consistent, adjust their marginal willingness to pay for ownership accordingly, and shift purchases to later periods when prices are lower – to the monopolist's dismay.

1.6.3 Optimal Time-Consistent Price Discrimination

If customers anticipate correctly at what rate the monopolist will serve the market in period 2, once they have observed the output rate in period 1, the monopolist is restricted to time-consistent output plans.[27] Therefore, the monopolist's decision problem is to find the optimal-time-consistent third-degree price discrimination.

Can one find a time-consistent plan? A simple way to achieve time consistency is to serve the market only during the last relevant period: $(x_1 = 0, x_2 = \frac{1}{2})$. However, such *end loading* is surely not the optimal time-consistent plan, since it completely destroys the benefits of durability.

In order to find the optimal time-consistent plan, one has to solve a dynamic programming problem. The solution procedure is that of *backward induction*. In a first step, one has to find the reaction function $x_2^*(x_1)$ that maps the first-period output into the optimal second-period output. That reaction function is employed by customers in their prediction of x_2 and in computing the optimal first-period output, given customers' predictions.

Suppose the monopolist has supplied x_1 in period 1 and customers have observed this. Then, in period 2 the monopolist will supply that quantity that solves

$$\max_{x_2} \pi_2(x_1, x_2). \tag{1.64}$$

The solution is described by the reaction function

$$x_2^*(x_1) := \max \left\{ \frac{1 - x_1}{2}, 0 \right\}. \tag{1.65}$$

Customers anticipate the monopolist's reaction and, after observing x_1, adjust their marginal willingness to pay for ownership in period 1 to

$$P_1(x_1, x_2^*(x_1)). \tag{1.66}$$

In turn, the monopolist anticipates that customers make these predictions. Therefore, the monopolist sets that output rate x_1 that maximizes the reduced form profit function:

$$\pi_1^*(x_1) := \pi_1(x_1, x_2^*(x_1)). \tag{1.67}$$

---

[27] The "revelation principle" assures that the restriction to time-consistent plans involves no loss of generality.

Proposition 1.5 (Optimal Time-Consistent Price Discrimination) *The optimal time consistent output plan, associated third-degree price discrimination, and maximum present value of profits are*

$$x_1 = \frac{2}{4+\delta}, \qquad p_1 = \frac{\delta}{2} + \frac{2}{4+\delta}, \qquad (1.68)$$

$$x_2 = \frac{2+\delta}{2(4+\delta)}, \qquad p_2 = \frac{2+\delta}{2(4+\delta)}, \qquad (1.69)$$

$$\pi_1 = \frac{(2+\delta)^2}{4(4+\delta)}. \qquad (1.70)$$

Altogether, both prices and the present value of profits are lower than in the optimal plan.

Proof Inserting (1.65) into (1.57) gives the reduced-form profit function (for $x_1 \le 1$):

$$\pi_1^*(x_1) = x_1 \left(1 - x_1 + \delta\left(1 - x_1 - \frac{1-x_1}{2}\right)\right) + \delta\frac{(1-x_1)^2}{4}.$$

$\pi_1^*(x_1)$ is strictly concave, and the first derivative of $\pi_1^*(x_1)$ vanishes at $x_1 = 2/(4+\delta)$. The asserted x_2 is the monopolist's best response to this x_1, by (1.65). And the associated prices and maximum present value of profits follow immediately. □

Example 1.7 As an exercise, suppose the durable good is subject to physical decay at the rate $\rho \in (0, 1)$ (after one period, for each unit only ρ units are left), and set the discount factor equal to 1. Then one has

$$\pi_1 = (1 - x_1)x_1 + (1 - \rho x_1 - x_2)\rho x_1 + (1 - \rho x_1 - x_2)x_2. \qquad (1.71)$$

Therefore, the following output plan is optimal:

$$x_1 = \frac{1}{2}, \qquad x_2 = \frac{1-\rho}{2}, \qquad (1.72)$$

and the optimal time consistent output plan is

$$x_1 = \frac{2}{4+\rho^2}, \qquad x_2 = \frac{1-\rho x_1}{2}. \qquad (1.73)$$

Leasing as Commitment Mechanism?

As Bulow (1982) observed, *short-term leasing* may serve as a commitment mechanism that supports optimal price discrimination. This follows immediately by the fact that the solution of (recall that the X's denote the consumption flow and the x's acquisition of ownership)

$$\max_{X_1,X_2} P(X_1)X_1 + \delta P(X_2)X_2$$

is $X_1 = X_2 = \frac{1}{2}$, and that this plan is also time-consistent because

$$\arg\max_{X_2} P(X_2)X_2 = \frac{1}{2}.$$

However, notice that observed leasing arrangements are typically long-term and thus cannot solve the durable-goods monopoly problem. Leasing can only set the right incentives to maintain the optimal price of the durable good if leasing rates are flexible and are always adjusted to the current market rate. Observed leasing arrangements are apparently geared to save taxes, not to solve a commitment problem.

Comparative Statics

1. Switching to an inefficient technology with higher marginal costs and lower fixed costs can be profitable.
2. The monopolist has an incentive to reduce durability (*obsolescence planning*).
3. If there is a constant inflow of a new generation of customers, the equilibrium price sequence can be cyclical (see Conlisk, Gerstner, and Sobel (1984)).
4. Incomplete information concerning the seller's marginal cost tends to benefit the monopolist.

1.6.4 Coase Conjecture

The durable-goods monopoly problem was discovered by Coase (1972) in one of his seminal contributions to economics. Coase did not only discover the inconsistency of the optimal plan. He also conjectured that the monopolist tends to lose all monopoly power if he can adjust prices faster and faster. The latter assertion has become known as the *Coase conjecture*. It was later proved by Stokey (1979, 1981) for particular demand functions, and generalized by Gul, Sonnenschein, and Wilson (1986) and by Kahn (1986).

The Coase conjecture is to some extent intuitively appealing. If the time span between trading periods within a given time period is reduced, the durable-goods monopolist works himself down the demand function at a faster pace. Since consumers anticipate that prices will fall, fewer and fewer transactions take place at high prices, and more and more transactions are concentrated around the competitive price. In the limit, all transactions take place in the twinkling of an eye, and the equilibrium present value of profits converges to zero.

1.6.5 An Example Where the Coase Conjecture Fails*

In the literature there are several counterexamples to the main durable-goods monopoly results. Of course, these counterexamples are based on slightly different models of the durable-goods monopoly problem.

For example, Bagnoli, Salant, and Swierzbinski (1989) assumed discrete demand instead of the continuous demand functions assumed in the bulk of the literature. Surprisingly, they showed that the standard assertions concerning the durable-goods monopoly may then fail. These claims are now explained using their main example.

Suppose there are only two customers. Each wants to buy either one unit or abstain. Their valuations are $v_A > v_B$ if the good is obtained in period 1, and δv_i

if it is obtained in period 2.[28] Specifically, v_A is taken to be so much bigger than v_B that $v_A > 2v_B$. Marginal costs are constant, and normalized to zero. The time horizon is two periods.

Suppose the monopolist plays the following *myopic* pricing strategy:

$$p_1 = v_A, \qquad (1.74)$$

$$p_2 = \begin{cases} v_A & \text{if customer A did not buy in period 1,} \\ v_B & \text{otherwise.} \end{cases} \qquad (1.75)$$

This strategy is myopic, because the monopolist simply calls the best price on *current* demand, as if there were no future to consider.

In response to this myopic strategy, consumer *A* would lose by delaying his purchase; therefore *A* buys in period 1, and *B* in period 2. In other words, consumers' best reply is the *get-it-while-you-can* strategy

$$\text{buy at } t \iff p_t \le v_i \delta^{t-1}, \, i \in \{A, B\}, \qquad t \in \{1, 2\}. \qquad (1.76)$$

In turn, the monopolist myopic strategy is a best reply to consumers' get-it-while-you-can strategy, in each of the two subgames. Therefore, in the subgame-perfect equilibrium, the durable-goods monopolist achieves almost the same payoff as the idealized, perfectly price-discriminating monopolist (the two coincide if there is no discounting, $\delta = 1$):

$$\pi^* = v_A + \delta v_B. \qquad (1.77)$$

Compare this with the profit at the Cournot point, which is $\pi^C = v_A$, in this case. It follows immediately that the durable-goods monopolist achieves a profit that is higher than at the Cournot point:

$$\pi^* = v_A + \delta v_B > v_A, \qquad (1.78)$$

contrary to what was claimed by Coase, Bulow, and others.

However, as Dudey (1995) made clear, the significance of this result is somewhat questionable.

1.7 Bilateral Monopoly and Bargaining*

So far monopoly has been equated with the power to unilaterally dictate either the unit price or some more sophisticated price discrimination scheme. In the language of game theory, monopoly pricing was modeled as an *ultimatum game* where the monopolist sets the price function and customers make their purchases accordingly.

An *ultimatum* is a final proposition or demand whose rejection will end negotiations. It requires the ultimatum player to have a reliable commitment to end negotiations if the ultimatum is rejected. Such commitment is, however, difficult to achieve. This suggests that the theory of monopoly pricing should be put into the

---

[28] There is a bit of a break here. In our first example we assumed a stationary rental demand; in this example we assume that the valuation is independent of the time when the good is available, except for the effect of discounting.

framework of more general bargaining games between buyer and seller where both
have some market power.

One way to generalize the simple ultimatum game is to permit several rounds
of haggling, while maintaining that one party has ultimately the power to make an
ultimatum, and assume that delay in reaching an agreement is costly. This is the
perspective of *finite-horizon* bargaining games.

In most bargaining settings one can always add another round of haggling. Therefore, the finite-horizon framework is not entirely satisfactory. Moreover, the two
parties may be in a *bilateral monopoly* position, where both sides have equal market
power, and no one is in the position to make an ultimatum at any point in the relationship. In either case, *infinite-horizon* bargaining games are appropriate where
no one ever has the power to set an ultimatum.

In the following, we give a brief introduction to finite- and infinite-horizon bargaining games. The emphasis is on explaining basic concepts and presenting simple
proofs of existence and uniqueness of the bargaining solution. The main limitation
is that we stick to the complete-information framework. Incomplete information
is, however, particularly important for understanding why rational bargainers may
end up with a breakdown of negotiations despite gains from trade.

1.7.1 A Finite-Horizon Bargaining Game

Consider the following three stage bargaining game: Two players, 1 and 2, bargain
over the division of a fixed sum of money, say \$1. Their utilities are linear in money,
but there is discounting with discount factors $\delta_1, \delta_2 < 1$.

The bargaining has three stages; exactly one period passes between two consec-
utive stages.

Stage 1. Player 1 asks for $x_1 \in [0, 1]$. Player 2 accepts or rejects; if he accepts, the game is
   over, if he rejects, it continues.
Stage 2. Player 2 asks for $x_2 \in [0, 1]$; if player 1 accepts, the game is over; if he rejects, it
   continues.
Stage 3. Player 1 obtains the default payment $d > 0$, and player 2 goes empty-handed.

This game has many Nash equilibria (find at least two). But since it has a subgame structure, we invoke subgame perfection. This selection principle is effective.
Indeed, the game has a unique subgame-perfect Nash equilibrium, explained as follows.

1. If stage 3 is reached, player 1 gets his default payment d; player 2 gets nothing.
2. If stage 2 is reached, player 2 asks for $x_2^*(2) = 1 - \delta_1 d$, and player 1 accepts. Acceptance
   gives player 1 the payoff $1 - x_2^*(2) = \delta_1 d$; rejection gives d one stage later, which has
   the present value $\delta_1 d$. Therefore, $x_2^*(2)$ makes player 1 indifferent between acceptance
   and rejection.
3. In stage 1, player 1 asks for $x_1^*(1) = 1 - \delta_2(1 - \delta_1 d)$ and player 2 accepts. The share
   $x_1^*(1)$ is chosen in such a way that player 2 is made indifferent between acceptance and
   rejection (the left-hand side is player 2's payoff from acceptance, the right-hand side that

from rejection):

$$1 - x_1^* = \delta_2 x_2^* = \delta_2(1 - \delta_1 d). \tag{1.79}$$

This gives $x_1^*(1) = 1 - \delta_2(1 - \delta_1 d)$, as asserted.

The associated equilibrium payoffs are

$$\pi_1^*(d, \delta_1, \delta_2) = 1 - \delta_2(1 - \delta_1 d), \tag{1.80}$$

$$\pi_2^*(d, \delta_1, \delta_2) = \delta_2(1 - \delta_1 d). \tag{1.81}$$

Evidently, each player would prefer to face an impatient rival with a high discount rate; impatience is costly.

An important special case occurs when there are no payoffs in case of disagreement ($d = 0$). Then

$$\pi_1^*(0, \delta_1, \delta_2) = 1 - \delta_2, \qquad \pi_2^*(0, \delta_1, \delta_2) = \delta_2. \tag{1.82}$$

And if agent 2 is infinitely impatient ($\delta_2 \to 0$), the solution approaches that of the ultimatum game.

The general finite bargaining game, with possibly many rounds, was solved by Ståhl (1972). The extension to an infinite game – to which we turn next – is due to Rubinstein (1982).

1.7.2 Infinite-Horizon Bargaining

Finite-horizon bargaining games are not convincing. No matter how long the parties have already bargained, they can always add another round of haggling. This suggests that, at the outset, one should not restrict the number of stages. This leads us to the bargaining game solved by Rubinstein, the solution of which is known as the *Rubinstein solution*.

The analysis of this bargaining game utilizes an important property of subgame perfectness known as the *one-stage-deviation principle*.

Proposition 1.6 (One-Stage-Deviation Principle) *Consider a multistage game with observed actions. A strategy profile is subgame perfect if and only if it satisfies the one-stage-deviation condition that no player can gain by deviating from it in a single stage while conforming to it thereafter.*

This principle applies to finite as well as to infinite-horizon games, provided events in the distant future are made sufficiently insignificant through discounting. Essentially, the one-stage-deviation principle is an application of the fundamental dynamic programming principle of *pointwise optimization*, which says that a profile of actions is optimal if and only if it is optimal in each time period.[29]

---

[29] For a proof of the one-stage-deviation-principle see Fudenberg and Tirole (1991), p. 109.

Multiplicity of Nash Equilibria

Like the finite-horizon bargaining game, the infinite-horizon game has many Nash equilibria; but only one is subgame-perfect.

An example of a Nash equilibrium that is not also subgame-perfect is the following profile of "tough" strategies:

Each player always asks for share $x = 1$ and never accepts less.

Evidently, these strategies are a Nash equilibrium (given the rival's strategy, the own strategy is a best response). However, subgame perfection is violated because these strategies are improvable by one-stage deviations.

To see why this happens, one has to identify a particular history of the game at which it pays to engage in a one-stage deviation from the candidate strategy if the rival sticks to it. A case in point is the history described by the event that the rival has just asked for $0 < x < 1$. Then, by sticking to the candidate solution strategy, one's payoff is equal to zero, whereas, if one deviates just once and then accepts, one earns $1 - x > 0$. Therefore, the candidate strategy is improvable by a one-stage deviation.

Note that a subgame-perfect equilibrium strategy must be unimprovable at *all* possible histories – not just the ones that occur in equilibrium. This is why the one-stage-deviation principle must be applied on as well as off the equilibrium path. This is precisely what we did when we showed that "always ask for $x = 1$ and never accept less" is not a subgame-perfect equilibrium.

Proposer and Responder

In the following, we call the player whose turn it is to propose the *proposer* and the player whose turn it is to either accept or reject the *responder.*

Subgame-Perfect Equilibrium

The game has a unique subgame-perfect Nash equilibrium. It exhibits stationary strategies, as follows. We first state and prove existence, and then turn to the proof of uniqueness. Since the proof of uniqueness includes a proof of existence, you may go immediately to Proposition 1.8. However, the proof of the following proposition is quite useful in exercising the one-stage deviation principle.

Proposition 1.7 (Existence) *The following strategy profile is a subgame perfect Nash equilibrium; it tells player i what to do, depending upon whether it is i's turn to propose or to accept/reject:*

1. Proposer: always ask for

$$x_i^* = \frac{1 - \delta_j}{1 - \delta_i \delta_j}. \tag{1.83}$$

2. Responder: always accept any share equal to or greater than

$$\delta_i \frac{1 - \delta_j}{1 - \delta_i \delta_j}. \tag{1.84}$$

(Note that if i asks for x_i^* then j is offered $\delta_j(1 - \delta_i)/(1 - \delta_i \delta_j)$, which j accepts.)

Proof Consider the above strategy profile. We want to show that these strategies are a subgame perfect Nash equilibrium. In view of the one-stage-deviation principle, one needs to show is that no one-stage deviation pays at any possible history of the game.

1. Suppose i is responder and i is offered at least $\delta_i(1 - \delta_j)/(1 - \delta_i\delta_j)$. The candidate strategy tells him to accept. But what if he engages in a one-stage deviation, rejects the offer, and then returns to the candidate strategy? Then the game enters into the next bargaining round where i is proposer, and since he returns to the candidate strategy, he asks for the share $(1 - \delta_j)/(1 - \delta_i\delta_j)$, which is accepted by the rival. Discounting this payoff shows that it would have been at least as good to accept the original offer. An immediate implication is that it does not pay to engage in a one-stage deviation either if the rival has offered less than $\delta_i(1 - \delta_j)/(1 - \delta_i\delta_j)$.
2. Next, suppose i is proposer. Suppose he deviates once, asks for a higher share than $(1 - \delta_j)/(1 - \delta_i\delta_j)$ (lower shares would be accepted at a loss), and thereafter returns to the candidate equilibrium strategy. Then j rejects and offers i

$$1 - \frac{1 - \delta_i}{1 - \delta_i\delta_j} = \delta_i\frac{1 - \delta_j}{1 - \delta_i\delta_j},$$

which player i accepts. Properly discounting shows that this one-time deviation would lead to a lower payoff, since

$$\delta_i^2\frac{1 - \delta_j}{1 - \delta_i\delta_j} < \frac{1 - \delta_j}{1 - \delta_i\delta_j}. \tag{1.85}$$

$\square$

Proposition 1.8 (Uniqueness) *The stationary strategies described in Proposition 1.7 are the unique subgame perfect equilibrium.*[30]

Proof Suppose the game has not yet ended at time t. Denote the subgame-perfect *continuation* payoff of the proposer at t by v and the corresponding continuation payoff of the responder by w. Define

$$\bar{v} := \sup(v), \qquad \underline{v} := \inf(v), \tag{1.86}$$

$$\bar{w} := \sup(w), \qquad \underline{w} := \inf(w). \tag{1.87}$$

We will show that the continuation payoffs are uniquely determined as follows:

$$v_i = \bar{v}_i = \underline{v}_i = \frac{1 - \delta_j}{1 - \delta_i\delta_j}, \tag{1.88}$$

$$w_i = \bar{w}_i = \underline{w}_i = \frac{\delta_i(1 - \delta_j)}{1 - \delta_i\delta_j}. \tag{1.89}$$

Then it follows immediately that (1.83) and (1.84) are the unique subgame-perfect equilibrium strategies. The associated equilibrium outcome is that player 1 opens the game asking for $x_1 = (1 - \delta_2)/(1 - \delta_1\delta_2)$, which player 2 accepts.

---

[30] The original proof by Rubinstein is rather involved. The following ingeniously simple proof was introduced by Sutton (1986).

1. *Assessing $\underline{v}$:* Suppose 1 is proposer. If he offers 2 at least as much as the present value of 2's "maximum" continuation payoff after rejection, $1 - x_1 \geq \delta_2 \bar{v}_2$, his proposal will definitely be accepted. Therefore, 1's continuation payoff cannot be below $1 - \delta_2 \bar{v}_2$. The same reasoning applies if 2 is proposer. Hence,

$$\underline{v}_i \geq 1 - \delta_j \bar{v}_j. \tag{1.90}$$

2. *Assessing $\bar{w}$:* Suppose 1 is proposer. He will never offer the responder 2 more than $\delta_2 \bar{v}_2$. Therefore, the responder's continuation payoff cannot exceed $\delta_2 \bar{v}_2$. The same reasoning applies if 2 is proposer. Hence,

$$\bar{w}_i \leq \delta_i \bar{v}_i. \tag{1.91}$$

3. *Assessing $\bar{v}$:* Suppose 1 is proposer. Since the responder will definitely reject any offer $1 - x_1 \leq \delta_2 \underline{v}_2$, player 1 cannot get more than $1 - \delta_2 \underline{v}_2$ through acceptance of his current proposal. In turn, 1 cannot get more than $\delta_1 \bar{w}_1$ through rejection of his current proposal. Therefore, 1's continuation payoff is bounded from above: $\bar{v}_1 \leq \max\{1 - \delta_2 \underline{v}_2, \delta_1 \bar{w}_1\}$. The same reasoning applies if 2 is proposer. Hence,

$$\bar{v}_i \leq \max\{1 - \delta_j \underline{v}_j, \delta_i \bar{w}_i\} \tag{1.92}$$

$$\leq \max\{1 - \delta_j \underline{v}_j, \delta_i^2 \bar{v}_i\} \quad \text{by (1.91).} \tag{1.93}$$

Next we show that $1 - \delta_j \underline{v}_j \geq \delta_i^2 \bar{v}_i$. Suppose *per absurdum* that $1 - \delta_j \underline{v}_j < \delta_i^2 \bar{v}_i$. Then $\bar{v}_i \leq \delta_i^2 \bar{v}_i$, and hence $\bar{v}_i \leq 0$ (note: $\delta, \bar{v} \leq 1$). But then (1.92)–(1.93) imply $1 - \delta_j \underline{v}_j \geq 0 \geq \delta_i^2 \bar{v}_i$, which is a contradiction. Again, similar reasoning applies if 2 is proposer. Hence,

$$\bar{v}_i \leq 1 - \delta_j \underline{v}_j. \tag{1.94}$$

4. Finally, combine all of the above, as follows:

$$\underline{v}_i \geq 1 - \delta_j \bar{v}_j \quad \text{by (1.90)}$$

$$\geq 1 - \delta_j + \delta_i \delta_j \underline{v}_i \quad \text{by (1.94)}$$

$$\implies \quad \underline{v}_i \geq \frac{1 - \delta_j}{1 - \delta_i \delta_j}, \tag{1.95}$$

and

$$\bar{v}_i \leq 1 - \delta_j \underline{v}_j \quad \text{by (1.94)}$$

$$\leq 1 - \delta_j + \delta_i \delta_j \bar{v}_i$$

$$\implies \quad \bar{v}_i \leq \frac{1 - \delta_j}{1 - \delta_i \delta_j}. \tag{1.96}$$

Hence, $v_i = \bar{v}_i = \underline{v}_i = (1 - \delta_j)/(1 - \delta_i \delta_j)$, which confirms (1.88). Similar reasoning also confirms $w_i = \bar{w}_i = \underline{w}_i = \delta_i (1 - \delta_j)/(1 - \delta_i \delta_j)$.

This proves that the continuation payoffs of the subgame-perfect equilibrium are unique. The associated equilibrium strategies stipulate that, in every subgame, the proposer offers exactly $x = \bar{v} = \underline{v}$ and the responder accepts all $x \leq \bar{v} = \underline{v}$.   □

Remark 1.1 (Nash Bargaining Solution) Make the time lag between bargaining rounds arbitrarily small. Then the above solution of the noncooperative bargaining game converges toward the well-known cooperative Nash bargaining solution (see Nash (1950a)). If both players have the same discount factor, that solution gives rise to equal sharing, $x^* = \frac{1}{2}$.

Remark 1.2 (Three or More Bargainers) Unfortunately, the uniqueness result holds only in bilateral bargaining. With three or more parties, one ends up with a multiplicity of subgame-perfect equilibrium solutions. Therefore, the celebrated uniqueness result holds only in a borderline case.

1.8 Digression: The Case Against Microsoft

Microsoft Corporation is perhaps the best-known, most successful, and most controversial monopoly in history. The Department of Justice claims that Microsoft has a monopoly in the field of personal-computer operating systems (OSs), and that it has cemented this monopoly through unlawful practices. For many years, these anticompetitive practices went virtually unchecked, which allowed Microsoft to establish and defend its dominant position in the market for personal-computer operating systems.

At the heart of the case against Microsoft are the following alleged monopolistic practices:[31]

Predatory Contracts. Microsoft offered its operating system to hardware manufacturers at a 60% discount if they agreed to pay them for every PC sold, as opposed to paying them for every PC sold with Microsoft's operating preinstalled. Therefore, if a hardware manufacturer wished to install a different operating system on some of its PCs, it would in fact have to pay for both operating systems.

Vaporware. Microsoft has a record of announcing new products long before they are ready (and of repeated delays in the release of new software) with the intent to deter customers from buying competing products. (In Silicon Valley, Microsoft became known as the "viscount of vapor.")

Deliberate incompatibility. For example, Microsoft told customers that DR-DOS would not work with Windows 3.1 (those who tried it anyway got an error message on the screen), even though there was apparently no reason why the two programs should not work together.

Bundling. Microsoft bundled its operating system with its own Internet browser with the intent to crowd out the browser software Netscape, which had the potential to develop into an alternative operating system.

The foundation of Microsoft's power is its ability to exploit *network externalities:* In the PC industry, the firm that controls the standard operating systems has an enormous advantage because software developers have an incentive to design software for the most widely used operating system. A successful operating system has more applications written for it. This, in turn, draws more developers to write programs, which further attracts customers, and so on, until, eventually, the operating system

---

[31] Cassidy (1998) gives a nice summary from which we borrow here.

that started out with a small advantage *locks in.* Competing operating systems then
stand little chance to succeed, even if they are superior.[32]

The case against Microsoft poses new challenges to antitrust authorities. The
antitrust laws, as their name suggests, were introduced at the turn of the last century
in response to the commercial trusts, like Rockefeller's Standard Oil, and J. P.
Morgan's United States Steel Corporation, that dominated the markets for oil, gas,
and steel. New principles and laws are needed to deal with the new network-
externality-based monopolies.

1.9 Concluding Remarks

The theory of monopoly has made important advances. However, we are still far
from having a unified theory that explains under which circumstances either price
discrimination or Cournot monopoly tends to emerge. We close this introduction
to monopoly with some tentative remarks on the intricate relationships between
monopoly and bargaining, and the need for further research on this topic.

A peculiar feature of price discrimination is that the monopolist draws a positive
profit not only from the collective body of customers but from each and every
individual customer. If each customer is valuable, the monopolist is tempted to
enter negotiations when a customer has refused his ultimatum. This, in turn, induces
customers to question the credibility of the ultimatum and make counteroffers.
Therefore, price discrimination can only work in the particular way in which it was
analyzed if the monopolist has found a mechanism that reliably commits him to
end negotiations when an ultimatum was rejected. And without such commitment,
price discrimination is intricately linked with bargaining problems.

Not so under Cournot monopoly. Recall that at the Cournot point the marginal
profit is equal to zero. If each customer contributes only a relatively small quantity to
market demand, it follows that the marginal profit of serving individual customers
is equal to zero. In that case, the monopolist need not worry about individual
bargaining and problems of credibility. When an individual customer has refused
the monopolist's ultimatum and starts haggling, the monopolist has no reason to
enter negotiations because losing that customer is of no concern. Therefore, the
Cournot point is *renegotiation-proof*, and hence can be maintained even if individual
customers are in doubt about the monopolist's commitment power. This is one of
the strong points of Cournot monopoly.

1.10 Bibliographic Notes

There are many good surveys on price discrimination that stress other aspects
ignored here. An extensive general survey is the book by Phlips (1983). Tirole's
(1989) chapter on price discrimination elaborates more on two-part tariffs, and
Varian (1989) analyzes whether and how a legal prohibition of price discrimination

---

[32] Some corporate giants tried it, like Digital Research with DR-DOS and IBM with OS/2, but failed.

would affect welfare. Finally, the most comprehensive survey is by Wilson (1993). There you can look up many practical applications and open problems, in particular in the area of multiproduct monopoly.

There is an extensive literature on the durable-goods monopoly problem and the Coase conjecture. In addition to the literature that attempts to formalize and prove the Coase conjecture, there is also a critical literature that focuses on its limitations. Assuming a finite set of buyers, von der Fehr and Kühn (1995) show that the durable-goods monopoly problem may have equilibrium solutions that differ radically from the Coase conjecture, including the perfectly-discriminating-monopoly outcome (see also Dudey (1995)). Levine and Pesendorfer (1995) explain why equilibria can be so radically different in a model with a finite number of agents than in a model with a continuum of agents, and apply their general results to the durable-goods monopoly problem.

Another interesting counterexample to the Coase conjecture is given by Kühn (1998), who assumes that durability and quality are positively correlated. In his model small differences in quality and cost between durables and nondurables allow a durable-goods monopolist to maintain intertemporal price discrimination, despite continuous trading.

A comprehensive survey of the literature on noncooperative *bargaining theory* is the book by Osborne and Rubinstein (1990); see also Myerson (1991).

The role of *bundling* in monopoly (mentioned in Section 1.8) is analyzed in Adams and Yellen (1976) and McAfee, McMillan, and Whinston (1989). The role of *network externalities* is worked out in Arthur (1989), Katz and Shapiro (1985, 1992), and Choi (1994). *Product preannouncement* ("vaporware") as an anticompetitive strategy is analyzed in Farrell and Saloner (1986).

2

Regulation of Monopoly

How come there's only one Monopolies Commission?

Anonymous

2.1 Introduction

It is sometimes desirable, on the ground of minimizing costs, to grant a single firm the exclusive right to serve a certain market. But how does one prevent an unleashed monopolist from exploiting consumers, and how does one assure that the monopolist operates on an efficient scale?

In the older literature on industrial organization, economists were primarily concerned with analyzing observed regulations. The most thoroughly researched examples are rate-of-return and price-cap regulation. The normative problem of how to design a satisfactory regulatory mechanism was only addressed in a meaningful framework in recent years, inspired by advances in the theory of incentive contracts under incomplete information.

Regulation is widespread in the U.S. and in western Europe, ranging from air and rail transportation to insurance, banking, and telecommunications. During the 1980s, many of these regulations came under heavy fire, which is why that decade is sometimes called the "age of deregulation." Prime examples of large-scale deregulation are the breaking up of the Bell Telephone system and the removal of entry and price regulations in the U.S. airline industry. In western Europe, the EC's program of economic and legal integration is a major force in the deregulation of industries like insurance, electric power, trucking, and banking.[1] However, the growing dissatisfaction with the long-term effects of deregulation in the U.S.[2] will probably slow down and change the process of deregulation in western Europe.

---

[1] In western Europe, public utilities are often publicly owned rather than regulated private monopolies. Therefore, the issue of deregulation is often linked with that of privatization. Public ownership was originally justified by the proponents of *Gemeinwirtschaft*. For an interesting anecdotal account of the original ideas and practices that lead to the establishment of publicly owned statewide monopoly suppliers of electric power in Germany see Staudinger (1982).

[2] In the *Wall Street Journal* of July 20, 1987, Kilman summarized this disappointment with the deregulation of the U.S. airline industry with the following headline: "An unexpected result of airline decontrol is return to monopolies."

There is an enormous literature on the various aspects of regulation that we cannot do justice to here.[3] In-depth coverage is usually given in a course on "industrial organization." Here, we can only touch some basic issues and elaborate selected examples. We start with a discussion of the Averch–Johnson effect, one of the best-known examples of a *positive* theory of regulation. Then we discuss two regulatory mechanisms as examples of the *normative* theory of regulation. Roughly, a positive theory of regulation is concerned with explaining how certain regulations work and what impact they tend to have, whereas a normative theory deals with the actual design of satisfactory regulations.

2.2 Positive Theory: The Averch–Johnson Effect

Suppose you own a power company that serves a certain community as a regulated monopoly. Your pricing and supply decisions are monitored by a government regulatory agency. Only linear prices are permitted. By experience you know that you are pretty much free to choose the most profitable price, output, and factor proportions, as long as your rate of return on capital stays within a certain limit, judged as a "fair rate of return." But as soon as you exceed this limit, the regulator may impose unfavorable prices and quantities. Wise and accommodating as you are, you decide to respect this implicit rate-of-return constraint. We ask: how does this constraint affect your optimal factor demand and product supply?

We will show that the rate-of-return constraint leads the regulated monopoly to inflate its rate base by substituting capital for labor. More surprising yet, it leads to the choice of factor proportions off the cost curve. Therefore, *profit maximization requires a deviation from cost minimization*. These results are known as the *Averch–Johnson effect* (see Averch and Johnson (1962)).

2.2.1 Assumptions

Consider a Cournot monopoly with two factors of production, capital K and labor L, and fixed user costs of labor w (wage rate) and capital r. Due to regulation, the rate of return on capital has to stay below the "fair" rate of return ρ. To rule out trivial cases, the rate-of-return constraint is assumed to be binding, and the fair return per unit of capital is taken to be greater than the user cost r. Also, the price of capital goods p_K is normalized to $p_K = 1$.[4]

Let P be the inverse demand function, defined on total sales, and f the production function, defined on capital and labor. We introduce the composite revenue function $R(K, L) := P(f(K, L))f(K, L)$, and assume that R is twice continuously differentiable and strictly concave, and that $f(0, 0) = 0$.

---

[3] An excellent, though somewhat dated introduction to the institutional issues is in Kahn (1971). When you look at this text, keep in mind that it was written before the wave of deregulation by one of its most ardent supporters. For a modern treatment of the normative theory of regulation see, for example, Guesnerie and Laffont (1986).

[4] Recall that the user cost of capital is $p_K(i + \delta - \hat{p}_k)$, where i is the rate of interest, δ the rate of depreciation, and $\hat{p}_K$ the expected rate of change of p_K.

The regulated monopolist maximizes profit $\pi := R - wL - rK$ subject to the rate-of-return constraint:

$$\frac{R(K, L) - wL}{K} \leq \rho. \tag{2.1}$$

To solve this program, we define the Lagrange function $\mathcal{L}(K, L, \lambda) := R - wL - rK + \lambda(\rho K + wL - R)$, with the Lagrange coefficient $\lambda \geq 0$, and compute the Kuhn–Tucker conditions for an interior solution (subscripts denote partial derivatives):[5]

$$K: \quad R_K(1 - \lambda) = r - \lambda\rho, \tag{2.2}$$

$$L: \quad R_L(1 - \lambda) = w(1 - \lambda), \tag{2.3}$$

$$\lambda: \quad \rho K + wL - R \geq 0 \quad \text{and} \quad \lambda(\rho K + wL - R) = 0, \tag{2.4}$$

$$\lambda \geq 0, \quad K > 0, \quad L > 0. \tag{2.5}$$

2.2.2 Effects of Regulation

In order to assess the effects of regulation, we compare the optimal solution (K^*, L^*, λ^*) with the hypothetical situation where the regulatory constraint is absent (denoted by (K^0, L^0, λ^0)). Our main goal is to show that rate-of-return regulation leads to overcapitalization in the sense that $K^* > K^0$.

The proof is built up by combining several auxiliary results. In a first step, notice that

$$\lambda^* \neq 1 \quad \text{and} \quad \pi^* := R^* - wL^* - rK^* > 0. \tag{2.6}$$

For if λ^* were equal to 1, we would have $r = \rho$ by (2.2), contrary to what was assumed. Also, since the rate-of-return constraint binds, one has $\pi^* + rk = \rho k$, and therefore $\pi^* = (\rho - r)K^* > 0$.

An immediate implication of $\lambda^* \neq 1$, combined with (2.3) is that

$$R_L^* = w. \tag{2.7}$$

Next, observe that, by the strict concavity of R and the fact that $(K^*, L^*) \neq (K^0, L^0)$ and $\lambda^0 = 0$, one has[6]

$$R^0 - R^* < R_K^*(K^0 - K^*) + R_L^*(L^0 - L^*)$$
$$= R_K^*(K^0 - K^*) + w(L^0 - L^*) \quad \text{by (2.7)}, \tag{2.8}$$

$$R^* - R^0 < R_K^0(K^* - K^0) + R_L^0(L^* - L^0)$$
$$= r(K^* - K^0) + w(L^* - L^0) \quad \text{by (2.7), (2.2)}. \tag{2.9}$$

---

[5] We mention that the program is not quite well behaved because the constraint set may not be convex (the quasiconcavity of the constraint function $\phi(K, L) := \rho K - R + wL$ is ambiguous). In view of Lemma C.4 and Theorem C.5, in Appendix C, it follows that the Kuhn–Tucker conditions are necessary but not sufficient for a global maximum. Therefore it is conceivable that these conditions have a solution, but the program itself does not have one. Do you see the trap?

[6] We use the second-partial-derivative characterization of concavity, explained in Appendix D in Part IV (see Theorem D.11). Notice that strict concavity implies strict inequality because optimal inputs are in a range where marginal revenue products are positive.

Adding (2.8) and (2.9) gives

$$0 < (r - R_K^*)(K^* - K^0). \tag{2.10}$$

Therefore,

$$K^* > K^0 \iff r > R_K^*. \tag{2.11}$$

Proposition 2.1 (Averch–Johnson) *The rate-of-return-constrained monopolist uses an excessive amount of capital, in the sense that $K^* > K^0$.*

Proof By (2.11) all we need to show is that $r > R_K^*$. Since $R(0, 0) = 0$, we conclude from the strict concavity of R, together with (2.7) and the fact that the rate of return constraint is binding,

$$
\begin{aligned}
0 = R(0, 0) \\
< R^* - R_L^* L^* - R_K^* K^* \\
= R^* - wL^* - R_K^* K^* \qquad \text{by (2.2)} \\
= (\rho - R_K^*) K^* \qquad \text{by (2.4)}.
\end{aligned}
$$

Finally, multiply this inequality with $\lambda^* > 0$, and one has

$$
\begin{aligned}
0 < \lambda^*(\rho - R_K^*) \\
= r - R_K^* \qquad \text{by (2.2).} \tag{2.12}
\end{aligned}
$$

Hence, $r > R_K^*$, as asserted. □

2.2.3 Relation to Cost Minimization

Overcapitalization also holds relative to the usual cost-minimizing factor proportions. To prepare for the proof, we first show that the Lagrangian coefficient is strictly between 0 and 1, $\lambda^* \in (0, 1)$.

You know already that $\lambda^* > 0$ (the constraint is binding), and that $\lambda^* \neq 1$, by (2.6). Therefore, all you need to show is that λ^* cannot exceed 1. For the sake of the proof, suppose that $\lambda^* > 1$. Then, by (2.2) and the assumption $\rho > r$, one has

$$R_K^*(1 - \lambda^*) = r - \lambda^* \rho < r(1 - \lambda^*).$$

Divide this inequality by $1 - \lambda^*$, which is then a negative number, and one gets $R_K^* > r$, in contradiction to Lemma 2.12. Therefore, $\lambda^* \in (0, 1)$.

Proposition 2.2 *The rate-of-return-regulated monopolist chooses a factor combination off the cost function that exhibits overemployment of capital, in the sense that the marginal rate of substitution of capital to labor exceeds the ratio of their factor prices:*

$$\frac{r}{w} > \frac{f_K^*}{f_L^*}.$$

Proof Divide (2.2) by (2.3). Since $r < \rho$ and $\lambda^* \in (0, 1)$, one obtains:

$$\frac{f_K^*}{f_L^*} = \frac{r - \lambda^*\rho}{w(1 - \lambda^*)} \tag{2.13}$$

$$\equiv \frac{r - \lambda^*r + \lambda^*r - \lambda^*\rho}{w(1 - \lambda^*)} \tag{2.14}$$

$$\equiv \frac{r}{w} + \frac{\lambda^*(r - \rho)}{w(1 - \lambda^*)} \tag{2.15}$$

$$< \frac{r}{w}. \tag{2.16}$$

□

The beautiful feature of the Averch–Johnson effect is that it presents an example for a rational, profit-maximizing deviation from cost minimization. But don't let yourself be fooled by words. For the most part, the surprise effect is only one of those tricks that language can play with us.

To show this, we propose to define the regulated monopolist's cost function on given output x *and* given capital K, as follows:

$$C(x, K) := \min_L\{wL \mid f(L, K) \geq x, \rho K - P(x)x + wL \geqq 0\}. \tag{2.17}$$

Then, the monopolist's decision problem can be put as follows:

$$\max_{K,x}[P(x)x - C(x, K)], \tag{2.18}$$

and one obtains the marginal conditions:

$$x: \quad [P(x)x]' = C_x, \tag{2.19}$$

$$K: \quad C_K = -r. \tag{2.20}$$

This puts the analysis of the regulated monopolist on a par with the usual analysis of factor demand.

2.2.4 Welfare Implication

Is overcapitalization bad? The Averch–Johnson effect is sometimes interpreted to imply that a fair rate-of-return constraint leads to an inefficient factor combination. This is, however, not quite right. Recall that the Cournot monopoly gives rise to inefficiency in the first place. Therefore, the excessive use of capital may have the desirable side effect of raising output.

Consider, for example, a production function with $f_{LK} > 0$ everywhere. Then rate-of-return regulation induces the monopolist to deliver more output to the market.[7] Therefore, the desirable welfare effect of higher output has to be weighed against the adverse effect of a distorted factor proportion.

[7] Proof: We have already shown that $K^* > K^0$. If the employment of labor L^* were not also greater than L^0, the right-hand side of (2.3) would exceed w, which is a contradiction.

2.3 Normative Theory: Two Almost Perfect Regulations

Having studied the effect of the often used rate-of-return regulation, we now turn to the more interesting task of designing good or perhaps even optimal regulations. We consider, again, a Cournot monopoly that does not face the threat of competition – say, because of licensing, patenting, or any other legal protection of the incumbent firm. We ask: how can one prevent the social loss of monopoly as well as the exploitation of consumers?

These tasks are easily accomplished if there is complete information about demand and cost functions. The regulator then only needs to set a subsidy per output unit plus a lump-sum tax in such a way that the unit price is equal to marginal cost at the subsidy-induced Cournot point, and both the social loss of monopoly and monopoly profits vanish.[8] However, this scheme requires more information than one can reasonably assume the regulator to have. Therefore, one would like to find mechanisms that require less information.

We discuss two alternative mechanisms: the *total surplus subsidy* by Loeb and Magat (1979) and the *incremental surplus subsidy* mechanism by Sappington and Sibley (1988). Neither mechanism requires that the regulator have any knowledge of the cost function or that costs are observable. However, both require knowledge of the demand function and observability of the unit price.

Important applications of these mechanisms include the regulation of natural monopolies such as public utilities or local garbage collectors.

Throughout, the following assumptions are made:

A1. Inverse demand $P(x)$ is strict monotone decreasing and continuously differentiable.
A2. The cost function $C(x)$ is strict monotone increasing, convex, and twice continuously differentiable.
A3. $\lim_{x \to 0} P(x) > \lim_{x \to 0} C'(x)$.

2.3.1 The Total Surplus Subsidy Mechanism

The *total surplus mechanism* was invented by Loeb and Magat (1979); it is ingeniously simple, but it has one disadvantage that makes it not entirely satisfactory. It is described by three rules:

- Permit the monopolist to set any unit price that it desires.
- Let the monopolist collect the entire market revenue.
- Pay the monopolist a subsidy equal to the net consumer surplus that it generates.

Proposition 2.3 *The total surplus subsidy mechanism induces the monopolist to choose the Pareto-optimal supply.*

Proof By assumption, the subsidy $S(x)$ is equal to the consumer surplus:

$$S(x) := \int_0^x P(y)\,dy - P(x)x. \tag{2.21}$$

---

[8] Of course, this requires that the cost function be *subadditive*. If cost functions are superadditive, the optimal allocation can only be reached by breaking up the monopoly – not by regulating it.

Therefore, the monopolist's earnings coincide with the total surplus (consumer plus producer surplus) $P(x)x - C(x) + S(x) = \int_0^x P(y)\,dy - C(x)$, and the profit maximum is at the socially optimal output where $P(x^*) = C'(x^*)$. This stationary point exists, and it is a global maximum, since $P'(x) - C''(x) < 0$. $\qquad\square$

Isn't this beautifully simple and yet effective? So, what's wrong with the total surplus subsidy mechanism?

The total surplus mechanism removes the social loss of monopoly, but it does not prevent exploitation of consumers and taxpayers. In fact, it assures the monopolist the entire gain from trade, leaving no gain to consumers and taxpayers. This in itself makes it unacceptable because the resulting high monopoly profits give rise to wasteful expenditures in the competition for the monopoly, as we explained in our discussion on the deadweight loss of monopoly (see Section 1.2.2).

Before completely dropping the total surplus subsidy mechanism, one may wonder whether its deficiency cannot be remedied by means of additional taxes. For example, lump-sum taxes achieve a transfer of monopoly rent that can be used to compensate consumers without affecting the monopolist's output decision. However, without knowing the cost function – or at least without observing costs – the regulator does not know how to set the right lump-sum tax. If the wrong rate is chosen, either monopoly profits persist or, worst of all, the market may collapse altogether because the monopolist is driven out of it by excessive taxes.

If several firms stand in line to do the monopolist's job, the regulator could gain the missing information by auctioning off the right to be the monopolist to the highest bidder. Even if there is no *competition on the market*, one may still have *competition for the market*. The regulator then only needs to set up the right auction to appropriate the entire rent and then plough it back to consumers.[9]

In many cases there are either no competing bidders (think of a monopoly granted by patent law), or they have widely differing cost functions,[10] or they are themselves subject to incomplete information about their prospective cost functions.[11] In either case, the total surplus subsidy mechanism fails to get rid of consumer exploitation and thus of the deadweight loss due to wasteful expenditures in the course of the competition for the monopoly market.

2.3.2 The Incremental Surplus Subsidy (ISS) Mechanism

In the literature, there are many suggested improvements of the total surplus mechanism. For example, Vogelsang and Finsinger (1979) propose an adaptive mechanism

[9] If there are at least two potential monopolists and it is common knowledge that they are subject to the same cost function, then standard auctions will sell the monopoly license at the price of the full monopoly profit, including the subsidy. A complete analysis of auction games is in Chapter 8.
[10] If costs differ, the lowest-cost monopolist will succeed in an auction and then pocket a profit equal to the difference between the second lowest and his own cost.
[11] If bidders themselves are subject to imperfect information about their prospective cost, it is no longer optimal to auction off the monopoly license by a standard auction. Instead, the optimal regulation includes price-regulation and even involves setting unit prices above marginal cost, to induce more aggressive bidding. See Riordan and Sappington (1987).

that gives rise to the Pareto-optimal output and vanishing monopoly profits after just a few rounds. However, as was pointed out by Sappington (1980), this mechanism invites strategic manipulation by the monopolist, who may benefit from inflating his costs. Therefore, it fails to assure cost minimization. But without cost minimization, it does not assure output efficiency either.

The *incremental surplus subsidy mechanism* proposed by Sappington and Sibley (1988) is free from these defects. It achieves *output efficiency*, *zero monopoly profits* after just one period, and *cost minimization*. Like the total surplus subsidy and the Vogelsang–Finsinger mechanism, it does not require that the regulator know the cost function or that costs be publicly observable. However, unlike the Finsinger–Vogelsang mechanism, it assumes that the regulator knows the demand function.

To see how the incremental surplus subsidy mechanism works, consider a Cournot monopoly that plans to serve the market for several (say $T > 1$) periods, subject to stationary market demand and costs. At each t the regulator observes the current and the previous unit price or quantity sold, the previous resource expenditures E_{t-1}, and therefore the previous accounting profit π_{t-1}. Based on this information, the regulator

- pays a subsidy equal to the *incremental* (not total) consumer surplus, and
- taxes away the previous accounting profit.

The increment in consumer surplus between period $t - 1$ and t is[12]

$$\int_{x_t}^{x_{t-1}} y P'(y)\, dy. \tag{2.22}$$

Therefore, the incremental surplus mechanism subsidizes the monopoly by the following rule:

$$S_t := \int_{x_t}^{x_{t-1}} y P'(y)\, dy - \pi_{t-1}, \tag{2.23}$$

where π denotes gross profits before subsidies,

$$\pi_t := p_t x_t - C_t - W_t, \tag{2.24}$$

x_0 and π_0 reflects initial conditions, which for convenience are set to

$$x_0 = \pi_0 = 0, \tag{2.25}$$

and p_t, C_t are shorthand expressions:

$$p_t := P(x_t), \qquad C_t := C(x_t). \tag{2.26}$$

All along, the regulator knows the inverse demand function P, but neither the cost function C nor the past cost level $C(x_{t-1})$. Although the regulator can observe resource expenditures (with a lag of one period), the waste W cannot be detected.

[12] Notice: by the product rule of differentiation one has $(yP(y))' = P(y) + yP'(y)$. Therefore, the consumer surplus is

$$\int_0^x P(y)\, dy - P(x)x = xP(x) - \int_0^x yP'(y)\, dy - xP(x) = \int_x^0 yP'(y)\, dy.$$

Therefore the monopolist may waste resources and thus inflate resource expenditures $E_t := C_t + W_t$. Waste may be a profitable way to manipulate the mechanism, as we have learned from the discussion of the Finsinger–Vogelsang mechanism.

Analysis

We will now analyze the mechanism in two steps. First we invoke the preliminary assumption that the monopolist has the power to commit once and for all to a sequence of output and waste levels. In the second step we remove this power of precommitment and analyze the *time-consistent* or *dynamically optimal* sequence of outputs and waste levels. Altogether, the analysis will be fairly simple – certainly far simpler than the proof proposed by Sappington and Sibley (1988).

Solution Under Precommitment

If the monopolist can commit once and for all to an optimal policy, the monopolist's decision problem is to choose an output vector $x := (x_1, \ldots, x_T) \geq 0$ and a vector of waste levels, $W := (W_1, \ldots, W_T) \geq 0$, in such a way that the present value of profits is maximized, given the discount rate $\delta < 1$:[13]

$$\max_{x, W \geq 0} \sum_{t=1}^{T} \delta^t (\pi_t + S_t), \tag{2.27}$$

subject to (2.23)–(2.26).

Since π is assumed to be strictly concave, this is a straightforward nonlinear programming problem. Its solution (x^*, W^*) is uniquely characterized by the Kuhn–Tucker conditions[14]

$$\left(\delta^t - \delta^{t+1}\right)(p_t - C_t') \leq 0 \quad \text{and} \quad x_t^*[\cdots] = 0, \qquad t = 1, \ldots, T-1, \tag{2.28}$$

$$\delta^T (p_T - C_T') \leq 0 \quad \text{and} \quad x_T^*[\cdots] = 0, \tag{2.29}$$

$$\delta^{t+1} - \delta^t \leq 0 \quad \text{and} \quad W_t^*[\cdots] = 0, \qquad t = 1, \ldots, T-1, \tag{2.30}$$

$$-\delta^T \leq 0 \quad \text{and} \quad -\delta^T W_T = 0. \tag{2.31}$$

Proposition 2.4 (ISS with Commitment) *Suppose the monopolist can commit once and for all to optimal output and waste levels. Then the incremental surplus subsidy mechanism leads to*

1. *cost minimization ($W_t = 0$) in all periods,*
2. *output efficiency (marginal cost pricing $p_t = C_t'$) in all periods,*
3. *zero net profits ($\pi_t + S_t = 0$), except in the first period.*

Proof Since $0 < \delta < 1$, it follows immediately that $\delta^{t+1} - \delta^t < 0$ and that $-\delta^T < 0$, and therefore $W_t^* = 0$, for all t, by (2.30) and (2.31). This assures cost minimization.

---

[13] The initial price p_0 and quantity x_0 either are inherited from the time before regulation was introduced or are themselves part of the regulatory mechanism.

[14] P_t' denotes the derivative of $P(x_t)$, and C_t' that of $C(x_t)$.

Next, (2.28) implies $x_t^* > 0$, and therefore $p_t^* = C'(x_t^*), \forall t = 1, \ldots, T$.[15] This assures output efficiency. Finally, realize that x_t^* is constant over time, for if it were not, the condition

$$p_{t+1}^* - p_t^* = C_{t+1}' - C_t'$$

would contradict the assumed convexity of the cost function. Therefore gross profits are constant, so that taxing away the previous period's gross profit assures zero net profits for all $t = 2, \ldots, T$. □

Remark 2.1 The first-period net profit is equal to the maximum social surplus (consumer plus producer surplus) $\pi^* - \int_0^{x^*} y P'(y) \, dy$, and all subsequent net profits vanish. This shows how the ISS coincides with the total surplus subsidy mechanism during the first period.

The fact that net profits do not vanish altogether gives rise to wasteful expenditures in the competition for the monopoly. This indicates that the ISS is a good mechanism but perhaps not optimal.

Of course, it is unlikely that the monopolist has the assumed power of precommitment. If she wants to deviate from a specified course of action, she is usually free to do so. This raises the question: How will the incremental surplus subsidy mechanism perform in the absence of precommitment?

Time-Consistent Solution

Suppose the monopolist is free to reconsider her course of action in each period. Then predicting the monopolist's behavior requires us to find that particular output and waste-level strategy that maximizes the present value of profits in each period, anticipating that an optimal strategy will be used thereafter. This leads us right to a dynamic programming problem.

In a dynamic program a strategy is a prescription for output and waste levels in each period t, contingent on the history of past output and waste levels. (In the language of optimal control theory one also talks about *closed-loop* or *feedback* strategies, as opposed to the *open-loop* strategies from the commitment case that were functions of calendar time only.)

Due to the mere size of the strategy space it is generally difficult to solve dynamic programs. Just think of the many ways in which one can link prescribed actions to past output and waste levels. However, there is a nice and simple characterization of optimal strategies that can be used to test any candidate strategy, even though it does not give guidance as to how to come up with a candidate solution. This characterization is known as the *one-stage-* or *one-step-deviation principle*.

Lemma 2.1 (One-Stage Deviation Principle (Bellman)) *Consider a finite dynamic program with perfectly observed (and remembered) past actions. A strategy*

---

[15] Recall that at $x = 0$ one has $p > C'$; otherwise it would be never be attractive to serve the market.

profile is a solution if and only if it is unimprovable in a single step, that is, if it never pays to deviate from it in a single period while conforming to it thereafter (see Kreps (1990) or Fudenberg and Tirole (1991)).

We now use this principle to show that the solution derived under precommitment also solves the monopolist's decision problem in the absence of precommitment.

Proposition 2.5 (ISS Without Commitment) *The results stated in Proposition 2.4 apply also if the monopolist cannot commit to a sequence of outputs and waste levels. Therefore, the ISS is almost perfect with and without the power of commitment.*

Proof Take the (stationary) solution of the program with commitment, $x_t = x^*$, $W_t = W^* = 0$, with $P(x^*) = C'(x^*)$, as summarized in Proposition 2.4, as a candidate solution of the dynamic programming problem in the absence of commitment. Suppose the monopolist deviates just once in period t and then returns to the candidate solution strategy (x^*, W^*) thereafter. Then the present value of profits, evaluated at t, is

$$G(x_t, W_t) := \pi(x_t, W_t) + S_t(x_t, x^*, W^*)$$

$$+ \delta \left(\pi(x^*, W^*) \frac{1 - \delta^{T-t+1}}{1 - \delta} + S_{t+1}(x^*, x_t, W_t) \right). \quad (2.32)$$

In order to find the optimal one-step deviation, partially differentiate with respect to x_t and W_t, and one finds immediately that it is optimal to stick to the candidate solution strategy, $x_t = x^*$, $W_t = W^*$. Therefore, by the one-stage-deviation principle, (x^*, W^*) is also a solution of the dynamic program, and all properties summarized in Proposition 2.4 confirm.   □

Remark 2.2 Suppose an unregulated monopolist learns in period 0 that the ISS will be introduced after one period. How does this affect current output if the discount factor is either close to one or close to zero?

The optimal output in the period that precedes the introduction of the ISS solves the condition

$$(1 - \delta)(P_0 - C_0') + x_0 P_0' = 0. \quad (2.33)$$

Therefore, if $\delta \to 0$ (only the present matters), x_0 approaches the one-shot Cournot monopoly solution, and if $\delta \to 1$ (no discounting), $x_0 \to 0$.

Finally, notice that the incremental surplus mechanism is pretty good, but it may not be optimal, not even in an infinite-time-horizon framework. Given the assumed information structure and technology, the properties of the optimal mechanism are still unknown. All we can say at this point is that the incremental surplus mechanism is *almost* perfect; but someone – perhaps you – may find a better one.

Discussion

Apart from the fact that it does not assure zero profits in all periods, the incremental surplus mechanism has at least three other disturbing deficiencies. One problem is that it does not perform well under cost inflation, as pointed out by Stefos (1990). But while this problem can be fixed by a slight modification of the mechanism (see the cure proposed in Sappington and Sibley (1990)), a serious and still unresolved problem has to do with managers' fringe benefits. The regulatory mechanism does not eliminate the kind of waste that benefits managers. Instead, it allows the monopoly to keep the revenue necessary to cover managers' fringe benefits. As a result, neither does the mechanism eliminate waste, nor does it give owners any reason to weed out waste, so that the buildup of wasteful expenditures goes virtually uncontrolled. In a sense, the ISS is "too effective": by eliminating profits except in the first period, it also eliminates the incentives to monitor managers and weed out wasteful fringe benefits. These observations indicate that some of the fundamental issues of how to regulate monopolies best are still unresolved.

Finally we mention that the mechanism has the desirable stationarity property only when the cost function is convex. However, many monopolies exist only because of nonconvexities due to significant economies of scale.

Conclusions

This brief review has covered some major contributions to the positive and normative theory of regulation. Of course, many other strands of thought have been left out. For example, we did not cover the important problem of regulating price-discriminating monopolies. Since public utilities tend to use two-part tariffs, this is a serious omission. Another omitted issue of great practical importance is the breaking up of the activities of alleged natural monopolies into those parts that can be decentralized, such as the running of trains or the generation of electric power, and that minimum component that cannot be decentralized, such as the supply of a network of rails or power lines. In this regard, recent regulatory practice has experimented with a number of interesting schemes, some of which were inspired by auction theory,[16] that require a separate review.

2.4 Bibliographic Notes

The assertions of the Averch–Johnson effect were posed for the first time by Averch and Johnson (1962). However, their proofs were not quite right. Corrections were later proposed by several authors, notably by El–Hodiri and Takayama (1973).

We mentioned that the decision problem is not well behaved in that the constraint set may not be convex. This issue is notoriously ignored in the literature. For example, Klevorick (1966) writes: " . . . Averch and Johnson make use of the Kuhn–Tucker conditions for a constrained maximum. These conditions are necessary as well as sufficient under our assumption of concavity of profit function."

[16] See Section 8.8.2.

A critical assumption is the concavity of the composite revenue function, defined on capital and labor. One of the reasons why the firm is regulated in the first place may be the presence of increasing returns to scale. Under increasing returns, the composite revenue function may not be concave, and rate-of-return regulation may lead to under rather than overcapitalization (see Dechert (1984)).

The Averch–Johnson effect has inspired a large theoretical and empirical literature. For a favorable empirical test, using data on the electric power industry, see Courville (1974). However, Courville's favorable analysis was countered by Boyes (1976).

While the normative literature reviewed here focuses on simple regulatory *mechanisms* that have certain desirable properties, there is also a large literature on optimal regulatory *contracts*. The common denominator is the assumption that firms have private information on costs. Therefore, in both branches of the literature, the regulator faces a tough information and incentive problem. However, while the mechanism literature allows the regulator to interfere with the monopolist's affairs only indirectly through tax and subsidy incentives, the contract approach assumes that they write comprehensive, enforceable contracts that commit the monopolist to certain pricing and supply functions.

The seminal paper on the contract model of regulation is Baron and Myerson (1982). This approach was further refined by Guesnerie and Laffont (1986) and by Laffont and Tirole (1988, 1990). This literature is reviewed and elaborated in great detail in the advanced textbook by Laffont and Tirole (1993).

One limitation of our review is that we restricted the analysis of regulatory mechanisms to linear prices (Cournot monopolies). If you look at your utilities or telephone bill, you see that many monopolists are actually able to set two-part tariffs and sometimes even a whole menu of different two-part tariffs. This suggests that one should analyze regulation also in a framework of price discrimination. Some results in this direction are in Vogelsang (1989).

3

Oligopoly and Industrial Organization

He is a fool that thinks not that another thinks.

Herbert

"Where are you going?" "To Minsk." "Shame on you! You say this to make me think you are going to Pinsk. But I happen to know you are going to Minsk."

A Jewish Anecdote

3.1 Introduction

Having looked at perfect competition and its antipode, monopoly, it is about time to turn to more relevant markets. Most of the products that we buy are manufactured by firms that have only few competitors. For example, there are only a handful of different brands of automobiles, household detergents, breakfast cereals, and even canned tomato soup, to name just a few. Typically, in most markets a small number of suppliers compete for a large number of potential buyers.

A market environment that has few suppliers but many buyers is called an *oligopoly*. In such an environment, each buyer takes market conditions as given, but each seller is aware that his actions have a significant impact upon his rivals' payoffs, and vice versa.

Apart from large firms whose products are traded all over the entire economy, even small firms are often part of oligopolies. Many markets are geographically localized, composed of more or less insulated market areas. Local banks, super-markets, bars, and restaurants in small communities or on a university campus are a case in point. Most people live in small towns, suburbs, or villages. Therefore, the importance of small-size oligopolies should not be underrated.

3.1.1 Game-Theoretic Foundations

Compared to a competitive firm or an uncontested monopoly, the typical oligopolist faces a considerably complicated decision problem. Strategic interdependency is the issue. When a price taker or a monopolist determines his optimal supply or factor demand, he may face a task that is complicated enough, but at least he need not be concerned with how *others* solve similar decision problems. Not so the oligopolist. He cannot make a good decision unless he does a good job anticipating the decisions of all rival firms. Hence, each oligopolist faces the doubly complicated task of solving his own decision problem, and at the same time forming rational expectations about how rivals do it.

At first glance, these problems seem to lead into a hopeless cycle of circular reasoning of the kind: "if you do this, then I do that, but then you do the other, etc." Luckily, game theory has taught us how to avoid this trap.

Key methodological concepts are *noncooperative games* under *imperfect* and *complete information* and the solution concepts known as

- noncooperative Nash equilibrium,
- self-enforcing agreement.

A game is called *noncooperative* if its players cannot write binding agreements because they have no access to an enforcement mechanism. Usually, oligopoly games are viewed as noncooperative because oligopolists cannot use the machinery of law enforcement to enforce cartel agreements, simply because these are prohibited by antitrust law.[1]

A noncooperative oligopoly game is said to be under *imperfect* information if each oligopolist chooses his strategy without knowing his rivals' choices. Also, we say that it is subject to *complete information* if each firm knows the market demand and the cost functions of all firms, if each firm knows that all the others know all of this, if each knows that all the others know that it knows, etc.[2]

The fundamental solution concept of noncooperative games is that of a *self-enforcing agreement*. Suppose, for the moment, that oligopolists make an agreement, constrained by antitrust law. Since no external enforcement mechanism is available, such an agreement is useless unless everyone has a built-in incentive to stick to it, provided everyone else upholds the agreement. Agreements that have this kind of bootstrap property are called *self-enforcing*.

A closely related – and in simple one-stage games identical – concept is that of a noncooperative *Nash equilibrium*. For the time being, we will not distinguish between the two concepts until we deal with more complicated multistage games.

An alternative interpretation of the solution concept that does not assume communication and agreements is in terms of *self-fulfilling expectations*. In this interpretation, a complete strategy vector is a solution of a noncooperative game if no player can do better than choose the strategy that the solution assigns to him provided he expects that all rivals play their part in it.

Essentially, the proposed solution concept excludes all those agreements or expectations that are *self-destroying* in the sense that some player has an incentive to deviate from his part of the assignment. Surely, it makes no sense to consider

---

[1] This rule has, however, more exceptions than you may think. In the U.S. many formerly regulated industries were deregulated during the Reagan years but in other countries, such as Germany, industries like insurance, public utilities, and air transportation are exempt from antitrust legislation, but subject to public regulation.

[2] The two pairs of concepts are 1) *complete–incomplete* and 2) *perfect–imperfect* information. The distinction may seem to be overly pedantic, but it is actually quite important.

strategies as a solution if it is obvious from the outset that some player will breach the agreement or that the expectations based on these strategies will be refuted. All you are asked to accept is this exclusion of self-destroying agreements or expectations. If you accept this principle, you have already accepted the game-theoretic solution concept of noncooperative games.

3.1.2 Historical Note

Oligopoly theory originated with the French mathematician and engineer Antoine Augustin Cournot (1801–77), whose work has no equal in the history of economic theory in terms of sheer originality and boldness of conception (Cournot (1838)). Cournot not only gave the first clear mathematical formulation of the oligopoly problem. He even anticipated the solution concept for noncooperative games long before the development of game theory by John von Neumann and Oscar Morgenstern (1944). It took forty-five years until Cournot's book became the subject of a book review. The reviewer was another French mathematician, Joseph Bertrand (1883). He was actually quite critical of Cournot's achievements, in particular the assumed rules of the market game.

The bone of contention was the pricing mechanism. While Cournot assumed that oligopolists set outputs as strategies and let a neutral auctioneer set the market-clearing product price, Bertrand contended that it is more plausible to let oligopolists themselves set prices, without the help of an auctioneer. More than merely raising the issue, he suggested that his proposed modification leads to radically different conclusions.

Thereafter, the theory of oligopoly largely lay dormant until the recent game-theory revolution in economics. There are, however, some notable exceptions. One is the work of Heinrich von Stackelberg (1934), who pioneered the role of commitment in oligopoly theory; the other is that of Francis Y. Edgeworth (1925), who pointed out some subtle and intriguing problems of price competition as proposed by Bertrand.

In recent years, the literature on oligopoly has mushroomed and many major new results have been obtained. But even today most of the literature can be classified as part of one of the three great traditions linked with the names of Cournot, Bertrand, and Stackelberg which marked the birth of oligopoly theory. Even the recent attempts to provide a unified treatment of oligopoly games include Bertrand, Cournot, and Stackelberg competition as summary descriptions or as constituent parts of a more complicated multistage game.

3.2 Three Perspectives

We start with an elementary treatment of Cournot, Bertrand, and Stackelberg competition. If the following pages are too simple for your taste, just skim the material until it gets more involved. The main point that we want to get across in this first section is how and why the three basic models differ in their *rules* of the market game but not in the equilibrium concept.

Assumptions Consider two oligopolists (*duopoly*). Each produces a homogeneous good at constant average cost. Market demand is given by the simple affine function, defined on the unit price p

$$X(p) := \max\{1 - p, 0\}. \tag{3.1}$$

Therefore, the inverse demand function is $P(X) := \max\{1 - X, 0\}$.

Firms' unit costs are constant, $c_1, c_2 \in (0, 1)$. Moreover, to assure interior solutions, the c's are assumed to satisfy the conditions

$$1 > 2c_i - c_j. \tag{3.2}$$

All demand and cost parameters are common knowledge.

3.2.1 The Three Market Games

Using these assumptions, the three basic models differ in their rules of the market game, as follows.

Cournot Competition

The Cournot duopoly game has three players: the two duopolists and one arbiter, the neutral auctioneer. Firms simultaneously choose their outputs x_i, which they deliver to the auctioneer. The auctioneer computes the aggregate output

$$X := x_1 + x_2$$

and the market-clearing price $P(X) := \max\{1 - X, 0\}$. Buyers pay this price, firms collect their payoffs

$$\pi_i(x_i, x_j) := (P(x_i + x_j) - c_i)x_i, \tag{3.3}$$

and the game is over. Duopolists' strategies are outputs $x_i \in [0, 1]$; the price is set by the auctioneer.

The assumed simultaneity of decisions is not to be taken literally. All that matters is that each duopolist decides without knowing the rival's choice (imperfect information).

In game theory one often describes incomplete-information games in sequential form, as follows:

Round 1. Firm 1 chooses x_1.
Round 2. Firm 2 chooses x_2 (without knowing 1's choice of x_1).
Round 3. The auctioneer sets the market-clearing price, and revenues are paid out.

Clearly, it is arbitrary who starts in round 1. As long as one maintains the imperfect-information assumption, it does not really make any difference whether one plays at round 1 or 2.

Bertrand Competition

Under Bertrand competition firms simultaneously choose their unit price p_i, subject to the commitment to serve the market at that price. Buyers shop at the cheapest seller. If a tie occurs, demand is shared equally by both sellers. Therefore, depending upon the prices p_1, p_2, the payoffs π_i are

$$\pi_i(p_i, p_j) = \begin{cases} (1 - p_i)(p_i - c_i) & \text{if} \quad p_i < p_j, \ p_i < 1, \\ \frac{1}{2}(1 - p_i)(p_i - c_i) & \text{if} \quad p_i = p_j < 1, \\ 0 & \text{otherwise.} \end{cases} \tag{3.4}$$

An equivalent sequential formulation of the Bertrand game is as follows:

Round 1. Firm 1 sets p_1.
Round 2. Firm 2 sets p_2 (without knowing p_1).
Round 3. Buyers place orders at the cheapest seller, and sellers produce and deliver as ordered.

    Unlike the Cournot model, firms themselves set prices without the help of an auctioneer, and production and delivery take place after buyers have placed their orders.

Stackelberg Competition

Under Stackelberg competition one oligopolist, say firm 1, has the power to precommit to a strategy choice and to perfectly publicize that choice before it is the rival's turn. The first mover is called the *Stackelberg leader*, the responder the *Stackelberg follower*. In principle, Stackelberg competition could be combined with either price or quantity competition. Since the combination with price competition is a trivial exercise without new results, we confine ourselves to quantity competition.
    Stated in sequential form, the rules of the Stackelberg game are as follows:

Round 1. Firm 1, the *leader*, chooses x_1, delivers to the auctioneer, and makes his choice known to firm 2.
Round 2. Firm 2, the *follower*, chooses x_2 under full knowledge of x_1, and delivers to the auctioneer.
Round 3. The neutral auctioneer computes aggregate output $X := x_1 + x_2$, and announces the market-clearing unit price $p = \max\{1 - X, 0\}$; buyers place orders, revenues are paid out, and the game is over.

Solutions

Denote the solutions of the Cournot competition game by the superscript C, of the Bertrand game by B, and of the Stackelberg game by S, and, as benchmarks, the competitive and Pareto-optimal outcome by PO and the Cournot monopoly outcome by M. We now characterize these solutions, explain how they can be determined, and give a complete welfare ranking.

3.2.2 Cournot Competition

The solution of the Cournot competition game is a pair of outputs (x_1^C, x_2^C) that satisfies the two mutual best-reply conditions

$$x_i^C \in \arg\max_{x_i}\{\pi_i(x_i, x_j^C) \mid x_i \geq 0\}, \qquad i \neq j, \quad i, j = 1, 2, \qquad (3.5)$$

where $\pi_i(x_i, x_j)$ is defined in (3.3). These conditions require, in words, that no firm can do better than stick to x_i^C if the rival sticks to his part of the Nash equilibrium.

Since π_i is strictly concave in the own strategy x_i, the maximizer is unique. Therefore, the solution is characterized by the Kuhn–Tucker conditions of the maximization problems in (3.5) for $i \neq j$, $i, j \in \{1, 2\}$:

$$1 - 2x_i - x_j - c_i \leq 0 \qquad (3.6)$$

and

$$x_i[1 - 2x_i - x_j - c_i] = 0. \qquad (3.7)$$

These are solved easily, and one obtains the equilibrium strategies x_1^C, x_2^C and equilibrium outcomes

$$x_i^C = \frac{1 - 2c_i + c_j}{3}, \qquad \pi_i^C = \frac{(1 - 2c_i + c_j)^2}{9}, \qquad (3.8)$$

$$p^C = \frac{1 + c_1 + c_2}{3}, \qquad \mathcal{S}^C = \frac{(2 - c_1 - c_2)^2}{9}. \qquad (3.9)$$

Here, $\mathcal{S}$ denotes the *consumer surplus*

$$\mathcal{S}(X) := \int_0^X P(y)\, dy - P(X)X. \qquad (3.10)$$

Reaction Functions

A useful illustration of the Cournot solution is in terms of each firm's *best-reply* or *reaction function*. Let $x_i^* : [0, 1] \to [0, 1]$ be the solution function of (3.5) with image $x_i^*(x_j)$. It is a best-reply or reaction function of firm i in the sense that if i assumes his rival j to produce x_j, the profit-maximizing response is to produce $x_i^*(x_j)$. By (3.6) one finds the reaction function

$$x_i^*(x_j) := \max\left\{\frac{1 - x_j - c_i}{2}, 0\right\}. \qquad (3.11)$$

It is graphed in Figure 3.1.

The two corner points x_i^M and x_j^{det} have a particular meaning. x_i^M is the *Cournot monopoly point*, which is of course a best response to $x_j = 0$. x_j^{det} is the *deterrence point*, which indicates the minimum output that rival j would have to supply in order to drive i out of the market. Also, since $x_i^*(x_j)$ is a maximizer of π_i given x_j, π_i reaches the highest level at $(x_i^*(x_j), x_j)$. This is indicated by the dashed *isoprofit curves*. All these illustrations, the reaction function, the two corner points, and the isoprofit curves are convenient and frequently used tools.

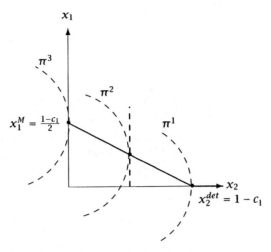

Figure 3.1. Firm 1's Reaction Function.

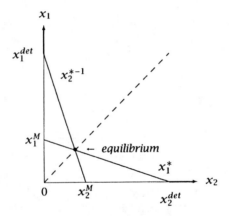

Figure 3.2. Cournot Solution.

Reaction functions are sometimes criticized for taking the rivals' choice of strategies as given, which supposedly ignores the strategic interdependency of oligopolistic decision problems. But this objection misses the point. Reaction functions are simply a tool to illustrate and find the solution of the Cournot game.

Finally, import the inverse of the rival player's reaction function $x_j^*(x_i)$ into the diagram that graphs $x_i^*(x_j)$, as in Figure 3.2. Then look at the unique intersection of the two graphs, and you see that this point gives the unique solution of the Cournot game because this and only this point satisfies the required mutual best-reply property. This shows how reaction functions are employed to find the solution.

Residual Demand

Another useful illustration is the *residual-demand representation*. Take the rival's output as given, say at the level x_j^0. Then firm i has only the *left-over* or *residual* inverse demand

$$\tilde{P}\left(x_i; x_j^0\right) := P\left(x_j^0 + x_i\right),$$

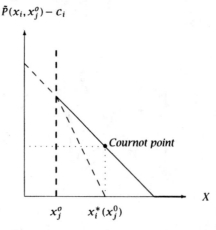

Figure 3.3. Cournot Monopoly Point in Residual-Demand Space.

and the best reply to x_j^0 is simply the Cournot monopoly solution in the residual-demand space, as illustrated in Figure 3.3. This shows neatly how Cournot monopoly ties in with Cournot duopoly.

Solution by Iterated Elimination of Dominated Strategies

We mention that the Cournot duopoly can be solved by *iterated elimination of dominated strategies*. We explain this by spelling out a few steps under the simplifying assumption $c_1 = c_2 = 0$:

1. $x_i \le x^M = \frac{1}{2}$ because no one ever supplies more than the Cournot monopoly output.
2. The rival's output is also bounded from above, by the same consideration. Therefore, firm i's best reply is bounded from below, due to $x_i = \frac{1}{2}(1 - x_j) \ge \frac{1}{2} \times \frac{1}{2} = \frac{1}{4}$.
3. Again, the rival's output is also bounded from below, by the same consideration. Therefore, firm i's best reply is bounded from above, due to $x_i = \frac{1}{2}(1 - x_j) \le \frac{1}{2} \times \frac{3}{4} = \frac{3}{8}$.
4. Again, the same consideration applies to the rival. Therefore, $x_i = \frac{1}{2}(1 - x_j) \ge \frac{5}{16}$.

Therefore, $x_i \in [\frac{5}{16}, \frac{3}{8}]$, which is already pretty close to $\frac{1}{3}$. Further application of this consideration brings us closer and closer to $x = \frac{1}{3}$, as asserted.

Remark 3.1 (Supply Matching) What if the Cournot market game is modified in such a way that producers can revise their supply decision and match their rival's supply if it exceeds their own? Show that this modified Cournot game has many Nash equilibria, among them one in which both suppliers choose $\frac{1}{2}$ of the monopoly output, giving rise to the monopoly price.

3.2.3 Bertrand Competition

The Bertrand solution is a pair of prices (p_1, p_2) – not quantities – that satisfy the corresponding mutual best-reply properties

$$p_i^B \in \arg\max_{p_i} \left\{ \pi_i \left(p_i, p_j^B \right) \right\}, \qquad i \ne j, \quad i, j = 1, 2, \qquad (3.12)$$

where π_i is defined in (3.4).

Since π_i is discontinuous you cannot characterize the solution by the Kuhn–Tucker conditions of the underlying maximization problems. But a few elementary observations explain why the Bertrand game has a unique solution, characterized by the equilibrium strategies and equilibrium outcomes:

1. If $c_2 = c_1 = c$,

$$p_i^B = c, \qquad x_i^B = \frac{1-c}{2}, \qquad \pi_i^B = 0, \qquad S^B = \frac{(1-c)^2}{2}. \qquad (3.13)$$

2. If $c_2 > c_1$ (beware: these results concern the limit of pure-strategy equilibria, as explained below),

$$p_i^B = \max\{c_1, c_2\} = c_2, \qquad x_1^B = 1 - c_2, \qquad x_2^B = 0, \qquad (3.14)$$

$$\pi_1^B = (1 - c_2)(c_2 - c_1), \qquad \pi_2^B = 0, \qquad S^B = \frac{(1-c_2)^2}{2}. \qquad (3.15)$$

In order to prove that this is indeed the solution, first suppose $c_1 = c_2 = c$. Then, $p_i = c$ is an equilibrium: if your rival quotes $p = c$, you cannot do better by quoting another price. Moreover, quoting a price above $p = c$ cannot be part of an equilibrium because it always invites underbidding. Of course, $p < c$ would be nonsense. Therefore, $p_i = c$ is indeed the unique equilibrium.

Now permit $c_2 > c_1$. Then, strictly speaking, the game has no equilibrium in pure strategies (neither $p_i > c_2$ nor $p_i < c_2$ can be part of an equilibrium, and $p_i = c_2$ invites underbidding). However, if one considers the assumed continuum of prices as an approximation of an arbitrarily fine grid of discrete prices, it is easy to see that the pure-strategy equilibria of the game converge to the asserted solution.

Reaction Mappings

It is one of the peculiar features of the simple Bertrand model that the reaction mapping is not defined for all prices above the equilibrium price. Take a look at the payoff functions $\pi_i(p_i, p_j)$ depicted in Figure 3.4 for $c_1 = c_2 = 0$. In the diagram on the left it is assumed that the rival's price p_j is above the equilibrium price and below the monopoly price p^M. In this case, the payoff function $\pi_i(p_i, p_j)$ has a discontinuity at $p_i = p_j$. Indeed, coming from $p_i > p_j$, π_i jumps up at $p_i = p_j$

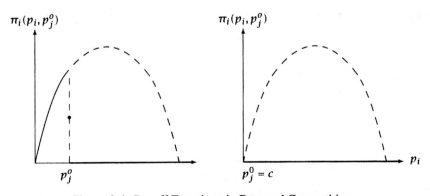

Figure 3.4. Payoff Functions in Bertrand Competition.

from 0 to $\frac{1}{2}(1 - p_i)p_i$ and again from $\frac{1}{2}(1 - p_i)p_i$ to $(1 - p_i)p_i$ as p_i is reduced below p_j. This illustrates that if the rival sets $p_j \in (0, p^M]$, it is always profitable to underbid him. But since there is no real number that is smaller and yet closest to p_j, there is no *best* response.[3]

Things change in the price range $(p^M, 1]$ and at the equilibrium price. For each $p_j \in (p^M, 1]$ the best response is of course the monopoly price p^M. However, at the equilibrium price there is not just one best response, there are infinitely many. Indeed, any price from the support $[0, 1]$ is an equally good response, as illustrated in the diagram on the right.

This latter property makes it a bit difficult to accept the equilibrium solution. Why, you may ask, should firm i respond to $p_j = 0$ with $p_i = 0$ if any other price from the support is just as good a response? The only answer that one can give in defense of this procedure is to point out that all prices other than (p_1^B, p_2^B) give rise to self-destroying expectations or agreements and hence cannot qualify as solutions.

Remark 3.2 (Price Matching) What if we modify the Bertrand market game and admit matching-offer strategies where firms independently quote a price with the provision that they match any lower price? Show that this modified Bertrand game has many Nash equilibria. In one of them, each firm quotes the monopoly price, which gives rise to the monopoly outcome.

3.2.4 Stackelberg Competition

Turning to Stackelberg competition, we come back to quantity strategies (the Stackelberg model with price strategies is trivial in the present context). Let firm 1 be the first mover, called the *Stackelberg leader*, and firm 2 the follower. Unlike in the Cournot model, firm 2 can respond to firm 1's output decision x_1. When 2 makes its choice, it has already observed some relevant history of the game. Therefore, 2's strategies are reactions to x_1, described by functions $x_2 = \xi(x_1)$ that map the observed history of the game, captured by x_1, into 2's choice.

Evidently, the Stackelberg leader has the same strategy set as under Cournot competition; but the follower's strategy set is considerably larger, for it includes all real-valued functions $\xi : [0, 1] \to [0, 1]$. This may suggest the somewhat paradoxical conclusion that the Stackelberg follower is in a stronger position and should therefore be able to earn a higher profit.

At first glance, this conjecture seems to be confirmed if you consider the strategies

$$\xi(x_1) = \begin{cases} x_2^M & \text{if} \quad x_1 = 0, \\ 1 - x_1 & \text{otherwise,} \end{cases} \tag{3.16}$$

$$x_1 = 0, \tag{3.17}$$

---

[3] The problem vanishes if one allows only discrete prices from a certain price grid. This assumption is plausible. As the mathematician Kronecker used to say, "God gave us the integers, all else is the work of man."

that award monopoly power to the Stackelberg follower. Obviously, $x_1 = 0$ is the leader's best response to the follower's strategy $\xi(x_1)$ and vice versa. Therefore, we arrive at the paradoxical conclusion that the Stackelberg follower may be a Cournot monopolist in the equilibrium of the Stackelberg game.

However, the strategy (3.16) is not credible, for the following reason: Suppose firm 2 plays (3.16), but firm 1 deviates and supplies some positive output $x_1 > 0$. Then firm 2 would do better to revise its plan and produce the quantity that is a best response to x_1. Having understood this, the Stackelberg leader calls the strategy (3.16) a bluff and anticipates that the follower will always respond to x_1 with $x_2 = x_2^*(x_1)$.

The conclusion from all of this is that one can restrict player 2's strategies to the best-reply function

$$\xi(x_1) = x_2^*(x_1) := \max\left\{ \frac{1 - c_2 - x_1}{2}, 0 \right\} \tag{3.18}$$

because no other strategy is credible. In the language of game theory, (3.18) is the unique solution of the subgame that starts at the node of the games tree where the Stackelberg follower makes his move.

Of course, the Stackelberg leader anticipates how the follower responds to his choice and utilizes this knowledge to maximize his own payoff. Therefore, the leader chooses the output that maximizes his reduced-form payoff function

$$\max_{x_1} \pi_1(x_1, x_2^*(x_1)), \tag{3.19}$$

$$\pi_1(x_1, x_2^*(x_1)) := \left(\frac{1 - x_1}{2} + \frac{c_2}{2} - c_1 \right) x_1, \tag{3.20}$$

which has the unique solution

$$x_1^S = \frac{1 - 2c_1 + c_2}{2}. \tag{3.21}$$

We conclude: the Stackelberg model has a unique subgame perfect equilibrium solution. The equilibrium strategies are (3.18), (3.21). They give rise to the equilibrium outcome

$$x_1^S = \frac{1 - 2c_1 + c_2}{2}, \qquad x_2^S = \frac{1 - 3c_2 + 2c_1}{4}, \tag{3.22}$$

$$p^S = \frac{1 + 2c_1 + c_2}{4}, \qquad \pi_1^S = \frac{(1 - 2c_1 + c_2)^2}{8}, \tag{3.23}$$

$$\pi_2^S = \frac{(1 - 3c_2 + 2c_1)^2}{16}, \qquad S^S = \frac{(3 - 2c_1 - c_2)^2}{32}. \tag{3.24}$$

Compared to the Cournot game, the Stackelberg leader is better off, and the Stackelberg follower is worse off.

Remark 3.3 (Can More Information Hurt?) A puzzling consequence of this result is that the oligopolist who knows his rival's strategy is worse off than the one who does not have this information. Does this prove that more information can be detrimental? The answer is no. What hurts the Stackelberg follower is not that he knows more, but that the rival knows that he knows more.

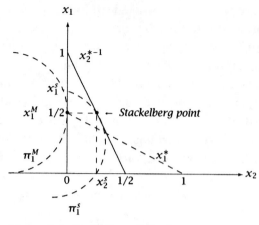

Figure 3.5. Stackelberg Point for $c_1 = c_2 = 0$.

Reaction Function

As we have shown, all points on the Stackelberg follower's reaction function are Nash equilibrium outcomes. Invoking credibility of strategies (subgame perfection), the set of equilibria shrinks to the one strategy that maximizes the Stackelberg leader's payoff over the follower's reaction function. This is illustrated in Figure 3.5. There, the solid line is the follower's reaction function, the dashed curves are the leader's isoprofit curves, and (as a reference) the dashed sloping line is the leader's reaction function. The Stackelberg point x_1^S, x_2^S is the point of tangency of the leader's isoprofit curve and the follower's reaction function. Essentially, the follower's reaction function is the leader's menu of choices; the leader picks from this menu the point that suits him the most.

Stackelberg Competition without Commitment Mechanism

How does the outcome of the game change if the leader can communicate but cannot irreversibly precommit his strategy choice? In this case, the follower has no way of knowing the leader's decision. Whatever the leader threatens to do, he can always deviate and do otherwise. Therefore, the game again turns into a game under imperfect information (neither player knows his rival's decision). Therefore, Stackelberg competition stripped of a commitment mechanism is Cournot competition.

While this argument is already conclusive, it may be useful to look at it from yet another angle. Suppose firm 1 threatens to supply x_1^S even though it cannot precommit. In that case firm 2 will ask: is this threat serious or is it just a bluff? In order to qualify it as a serious threat, the self-declared leader should have an incentive to stick to the threat if the other player takes it seriously and plays the assigned role as Stackelberg follower. However, the leader is better off by deviating because

$$x_1^* \left(x_2^* \left(x_1^S \right) \right) = \frac{3}{8}(1 - 2c_1 + c_2) < \frac{1}{2}(1 - 2c_1 + c_2) = x_1^S. \tag{3.25}$$

Therefore, the supposed follower calls the bluff a bluff and plays the Cournot equilibrium strategy, and the self-declared leader follows suit.

3.2.5 Welfare Ranking

The three market games have radically different properties that are summarized in the following welfare ranking. As a benchmark, we include the Cournot monopoly and the Pareto optimum in our comparison:

$$x^M = \frac{1-c_1}{2}, \qquad \pi^M = \frac{(1-c_1)^2}{4}, \qquad \mathcal{S}^M = \frac{(1-c_1)^2}{8} \qquad (3.26)$$

$$X^{PO} = 1-c_1, \qquad \pi_i^{PO} = 0, \qquad \mathcal{S}^{PO} = \frac{(1-c_1)^2}{2}. \qquad (3.27)$$

Ranking by *consumer surplus*, Bertrand competition is the best and Cournot competition the worst of all kinds of oligopolistic competition; Stackelberg competition ranks somewhere in between. Bertrand competition is actually Pareto-optimal if $c_1 = c_2$, just like perfect competition, but Cournot competition is not quite as bad as Cournot monopoly:

$$\mathcal{S}^{PO} \geq \mathcal{S}^B > \mathcal{S}^S > \mathcal{S}^C > \mathcal{S}^M. \qquad (3.28)$$

Judging by equilibrium profits, every firm would like best to be Stackelberg leader and least to play in a Bertrand competition game.[4] But the Stackelberg leader does not quite fare as well as the Cournot monopolist:

$$\pi^M > \pi_1^S > \pi_i^C > \pi_2^S > \pi_i^B = \pi^{PO}. \qquad (3.29)$$

Finally, judging by *total surplus*, defined as the sum total of consumer and producer surplus,

$$\mathcal{T} := \mathcal{S} + \pi_1 + \pi_2,$$

one gets the same ranking as judging by consumer surplus:

$$\mathcal{T}^{PO} = \mathcal{T}^B > \mathcal{T}^S > \mathcal{T}^C > \mathcal{T}^M. \qquad (3.30)$$

3.2.6 The Dual of Cournot Duopoly

There are many links between oligopoly and monopoly. In some cases they differ only in the interpretation placed on symbols. A case in point is the *complementary monopoly*, which turns out to be the dual of Cournot monopoly. The nice implication is that one has a well-developed body of results on complementary monopoly merely be reinterpreting known results on oligopolies.

Complementary monopolies were already studied by Cournot (1838).[5] He considered the case of two monopolists who sell complementary products – copper and one unit of zinc – to the competitive brass industry. Brass is made out of one unit each of copper and zinc, in those fixed proportions. Therefore, the demand for brass is a function of the *sum* of the two prices for copper (p_c) and zinc (p_z).

---

[4] We mention that the preference for being the Stackelberg leader is reversed if reaction functions are *upward sloping*, which may occur under product differentiation (see Dowrick (1986)).

[5] See Chapter 9 on "Mutual Relations of Producers" in his main book. The duality relationship was later pointed out by Sonnenschein (1968).

Now replace quantity by price in the description of the Cournot duopoly and you have a complete description of complementary monopoly. Indeed, each monopolist chooses his price under imperfect information, demand is a monotone decreasing function of the sum of prices, and the solution of the market game is a pair of prices that has the mutual best-response property. The formal equivalence of the two theories is thus established.

An immediate consequence is that a theorem on Cournot duopoly is a theorem on complementary monopoly. For example, the result that the output supplied under Cournot duopoly is greater than that supplied under pure monopoly translates into the result that the sum of prices charged under complementary monopoly is greater than that charged under monopoly. Of course, all other results can be translated just as well, as summarized by the following welfare ranking, where *CM* denotes complementary monopoly without a leader–follower structure, *CS* complementary Stackelberg monopoly, and *M* the merger of the two complementary monopolists:

$$S^{PO} > S^M > S^{CM} > S^{CS}, \tag{3.31}$$

$$\pi^M > \pi_1^{CS} > \pi_i^{CM} > \pi_2^{CS}. \tag{3.32}$$

3.2.7 Discussion

Having acquired a basic knowledge of the different kinds of oligopoly theory, you probably have more questions than before we started. For example, you probably wonder:

- What is the intuition for the welfare properties of Cournot, Bertrand, and Stackelberg competition?
- Do these results apply to more general demand and cost structures?
- Does anything change if oligopolies interact during many periods?
- Are there any meaningful commitment mechanisms to support Stackelberg competition?
- How could policy makers reduce the welfare loss of Cournot and Stackelberg competition?
- Which of the competing market games is the "correct" one?

Among all these issues, the plethora of oligopoly models is probably the most disturbing. In the past, many people have claimed that oligopoly theory is caught in a premature state of development because, after more than 150 years, one has not even reached an agreement on what is the right equilibrium concept.

As you have just learned, this criticism is not quite right. Oligopoly theorists have no quarrel about equilibrium concepts. Indeed, they all employ the same solution concepts of a noncooperative game.

However, the fact remains that there are several plausible oligopoly models that have widely different properties. So which is the correct one? Should we not ask oligopoly theorists to clean up their act and agree on a set of market rules before they deserve to be taken seriously?

There is probably no single right answer. Several contributors have started to endogenize the choice of market rules to determine whether price or quantity competition tends to emerge (see for example Singh and Vives (1984)). Others have argued that, given the variety of real-world market environments, the variety of models is a virtue, not a defect. Most important of all, some success has been achieved in actually providing a unified oligopoly model. Interestingly, as you will learn later in this chapter, all these attempts include Bertrand, Stackelberg, and Cournot competition as summary descriptions or as constituent parts of more complicated multistage games.

3.3 More on Stackelberg Competition

The problem with Stackelberg competition concerns the assumed credibility of precommitment. How can the leader irreversibly precommit himself to a certain strategy? How can he credibly "tie his hands" so that he can never take advantage of second-round gains? Without answering these questions, Stackelberg competition is simply not meaningful.[6]

3.3.1 Criticism and Extensions

If you see a model with Stackelberg competition, make it a habit to raise three questions:

- How does the leader actually "tie his hands" – in the language of game theory, what *commitment mechanism* is available to him?
- Why is this commitment mechanism *not* equally available to other players?
- Is the commitment level perfectly observable to rival players?

In many economic applications one can actually find meaningful commitment mechanisms. However, these are usually available to *all* players, not just to an identifiable leader. Therefore, one is led to analyze a modified model of Stackelberg competition – with strategic precommitment, but without a leader–follower structure.

There is a large and growing literature on market games in which each player has the power to precommit. For example, Dixit (1980) showed how *investment* may serve as a commitment mechanism, available to all oligopolists. Similarly, Brander and Spencer (1983) stressed the role of R&D, Brander and Lewis (1986) the role of *financial leverage* under limited liability, and Gal-Or (1990) the role of *delegation to retailers*. These and other contributions have proven that commitment plays an important role in industrial organization. And indeed, the analysis of market games with specific powers of commitment has become one of the main strands of thought in current oligopoly theory.

In view of the importance of this tradition, we will now present one simple application in some detail. This particular application concerns the role of delegation – in particular of *delegation to managers* – as commitment mechanism. It contributes to resolve a long debate in the theory of the firm, and it has some nice paradoxical results.

---

[6] Go back to our analysis of Stackelberg competition stripped of a commitment mechanism. There we showed that the only credible precommitment is the Cournot equilibrium strategy.

Later on in your reading of this book you should also compare the view of delegation expounded here with that of the classical principal–agent problem, which we discuss in Chapter 11 on "Hidden Action and Moral Hazard."

Towards the end of this section, we will also point out some fundamental flaws of the entire Stackelberg tradition in economics. This has to do with the implausible requirement of perfect observability in commitment games.

3.3.2 Managerial Incentives as Commitment Mechanism

In economics, there is a long-standing debate about the proper description of firms' objective function. Economic theorists tend to assume that profit maximization is a fairly good working hypothesis. However, critics of economic theory and practical economists alike have always contended that profit maximization is useless as a descriptive device of what goes on in firms. As J. K. Galbraith (1988) put it in one of his polemics:

> . . . it has long been accepted in fact – though not, alas, in economic theory – that the ordinary shareholder, either individually or collectively, is normally without power. . . . What did not follow was the acceptance of the fact in the established microeconomic theory. The latter depends, and absolutely, on the aforesaid commitment to maximizing profits.

The following model builds a bridge between the two seemingly irreconcilable camps. Like Galbraith, we recognize that the modern corporation is characterized by delegation of control to professional managers. Managers pursue their own goals; therefore, delegation gives rise to a principal–agent problem. However, *pace* Galbraith, profit maximization is not thrown out all the way. Instead, owners will be assumed to maximize profits *indirectly*, by selecting profit-maximizing managerial incentives. Paradoxically, you will learn that profit-maximizing owners may have an incentive to direct their managers away from profit maximization toward a more aggressive sales orientation.[7]

The Model

The choice of incentives is modeled as a two-stage oligopoly game. At *stage 1*, the owners of identical firms simultaneously select a managerial incentive plan and hire a manager. At *stage 2*, the incentive plans become public information, and managers play a Cournot competition game. Based on managers' supply decisions, the auctioneer sets the market-clearing unit price, trade takes place, and revenues and costs are paid out.

Three simplifications are assumed: 1) inverse demand takes the simplest possible form,

$$P(X) := \max\{1 - X, 0\}, \qquad X := x_1 + x_2; \tag{3.33}$$

---

[7] The following model is based on Fershtman and Judd (1987). For another contribution along similar lines see Vickers (1985).

2) average costs are uniform and constant at the rate $c \in (0, 1)$; 3) incentive plans are linear in sales and profit, the managers' profit share is α_i, and their revenue share is $1 - \alpha_i$; in addition, managers may earn a lump sum f_i.

Denoting managers' salary by M_i and gross profit by π_i, incentive plans have the following form:

$$M_i(x_i, x_j, \alpha_i, f_i) := \alpha_i \pi_i + (1 - \alpha_i) P(X) x_i + f_i \qquad (3.34)$$

$$= P(x_i + x_j) x_i - \alpha_i c x_i + f_i. \qquad (3.35)$$

Obviously, $\alpha_i = 1$ leads managers to maximize profits, and $\alpha_i = 0$ leads them to maximize sales.

Managers have a reservation price m. Therefore, in order to hire a manager, the incentive plan has to satisfy the *participation constraint*

$$M_i \geq m. \qquad (3.36)$$

Of course, m must be sufficiently small and not eat up the entire profit, and we may then normalize it to $m = 0$.

Solution Concept The analysis is in two steps. First we analyze the stage-2 Cournot competition subgame played by managers, for all possible incentive plans. The rationale for isolating and beginning with the last stage of the game is that, once incentive plans have been chosen and become public information, duopolists play a self-contained Cournot competition subgame. The results of this subgame are then used to compute owners' reduced-form payoffs as functions of incentive plans, and then solve equilibrium incentive plans. In the language of game theory, the solution concept is that of a *subgame-perfect* Nash equilibrium. A Nash equilibrium is called subgame-perfect if it is a Nash equilibrium for each subgame. Subgame perfectness is one of the most important refinements of the Nash equilibrium concept.

A Labor-Saving Device One can minimize dull and boring computations by intelligently recycling the results of Section 3.2.2. For this purpose define

$$c_i := \alpha_i c. \qquad (3.37)$$

Managers' objective function can thus be rewritten in a form that resembles the payoff function of owner-operated firms, except for the lump-sum payment f_i:

$$M_i = P(x_i + x_j) x_i - c_i x_i + f_i. \qquad (3.38)$$

Lump-sum payments do not affect optimal actions. Therefore, we can immediately use the results of Section 3.2.2 to describe the solution of the Cournot subgame between managers.

In a second step we compute owners' reduced-form payoff functions and let them simultaneously choose the c_i's and f_i's. From that point on it is a snap to compute the equilibrium incentive plan.

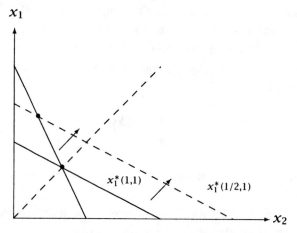

Figure 3.6. Manager 1's Reaction Function.

Equilibrium of the Cournot Subgame

Given incentive plans (c_1, f_1), (c_2, f_2), managers play a Cournot game. Each manager maximizes his own income M_i by choice of x_i. As we already noted, this game is equivalent to a Cournot game played between profit-maximizing firms with unit costs $c_i = \alpha_i c$.

By (3.8), the solution of that game is

$$x_i(c_i, c_j) = \frac{1 - 2c_i + c_j}{3}. \qquad (3.39)$$

Note that introducing a deviation from profit maximization in the direction of giving more emphasis on sales is equivalent to reducing the own unit cost c_i in an associated game between profit maximizing firms. The latter makes the own firm more aggressive, which in turn has a deterrence effect upon the rival firm. Thus, introducing a sales orientation in the incentive plan drives managers to be more aggressive. This is illustrated in Figure 3.6, where the solid line with the smaller slope is the reaction function for $c_i = c$ and the parallel dashed one is the reaction function for $c_i = \frac{1}{2}c$.

Equilibrium Incentive Plans

In the first stage, owners simultaneously chose their incentive plans. This can be viewed as a choice of c_i, f_i. The Nash equilibrium incentive plans simultaneously maximize owners' reduced-form payoff functions over c_1, f_1 and c_2, f_2, respectively.

To compute owners' reduced-form payoff functions, two steps are required. First, notice that owners can capture the entire gain by setting the lump sum f_i at the level that drives managers' income down to the minimum ($M_i = m$). This entails

$$- f_i = (P(x_i + x_j) - \alpha_i c)x_i - m. \qquad (3.40)$$

Therefore, owners' income coincides with standard profits minus the constant m:

$$(P(x_i + x_j) - c)x_i - M_i = (P(x_i + x_j) - c)x_i - m \qquad \text{by (3.40)}$$

$$=: \pi_i(x_i, x_j) - m.$$

Second, insert the solution of the Cournot subgame (3.39), and one has the *owners' reduced-form payoff function*

$$\pi_i^*(c_i, c_j, c) = \pi_i(x_i(c_i, c_j), x_j(c_i, c_j), c)$$
$$= (1 - 2c_i + c_j)(1 - 3c + c_i + c_j)/9. \quad (3.41)$$

The equilibrium c's satisfy the best-reply requirements

$$c_i^* \in \arg \max_{c_i} \pi_i^*(c_i, c_j, c), \qquad i \neq j, \quad i, j \in \{1, 2\}. \quad (3.42)$$

The associated first-order conditions are (note: nonnegativity is not required)[8]

$$6c - 4c_i - c_j - 1 = 0, \qquad i \neq j, \quad i, j \in \{1, 2\}. \quad (3.43)$$

One obtains the unique solution

$$c_1^* = c_2^* = \frac{6c - 1}{5}. \quad (3.44)$$

Putting the pieces together, the unique subgame-perfect Nash equilibrium incentive plan and payoffs are

$$\alpha_1^* = \alpha_2^* = \frac{6c - 1}{5c}, \quad (3.45)$$

$$f_1^* = f_2^* = m - \frac{4(1 - c)^2}{25}, \quad (3.46)$$

$$\pi_1^* = \pi_2^* = \frac{2(1 - c)^2}{25} - m, \quad (3.47)$$

$$M_1^* = M_2^* = m. \quad (3.48)$$

Proposition 3.1 (Equilibrium Incentive Plan) *The equilibrium managerial incentive plan has the following properties:*

1. *Profit-maximizing owners direct their managers away from profit maximization toward a more aggressive sales orientation, $\alpha_i^* < 1$, with $\alpha_i^* > 0$ for $c > \frac{1}{6}$, and $\alpha_i^* \leq 0$ for $c \leq \frac{1}{6}$.*
2. *If all managers were induced to maximize profits by setting $\alpha_i = 1$, all owners would earn higher net profits. However, this incentive plan is not part of a subgame-perfect equilibrium.*

Proof Part 1 Follows immediately by the fact that $c < 1$. Part 2: If α_i were set equal to 1, managers would maximize gross profits, as in the standard symmetric Cournot model where equilibrium profits are equal to $(1 - c)^2/9$. Obviously,

$$\frac{(1 - c)^2}{9} = \frac{2(1 - c)^2}{18} > \frac{2(1 - c)^2}{25} = \pi_i^*.$$

Therefore, the equilibrium incentive plan gives rise to lower profits than profit maximization. $\qquad \square$

---

[8] Show that the second-order condition is satisfied.

Remark 3.4 If only one firm, say firm 1, has hired a manager, it is easy to see that it can get the Stackelberg-leader profit by setting

$$c_1 = \frac{5c - 1}{4} \quad \text{and} \quad \alpha_1 = \frac{5c - 1}{4c}. \tag{3.49}$$

This brings out sharply the incentive to deviate from profit maximization.

Remark 3.5 As a variation, suppose managers play a Stackelberg game in lieu of a Cournot game. Then the owners of the Stackelberg leader firm L will choose profit maximization, $\alpha_L = 1$ – which is hardly surprising – whereas the managers of the Stackelberg follower firm F are given a stronger sales orientation,

$$\alpha_F = \frac{4c - 1}{3c} < \frac{6c - 1}{5c}.$$

Altogether, the equilibrium profit of the follower firm is higher than that of the leader,

$$\pi_F = \frac{(c - 1)^2}{12} > \frac{(c - 1)^2}{18} = \pi_L.$$

Therefore, we here have a case where it is preferable to be a follower.

Moreover, the leader is even worse off and the follower better off than in the original game with Cournot competition. This leads us to the surprising observation that the commitment device of delegation can be very powerful if it is used against a Stackelberg player who is already endowed with a direct commitment mechanism.

Discussion

At this point you may object: why should profit-maximizing owners deviate from profit maximization if this leads them only to lower net profits? Why do they not simply make an agreement to stick to profit maximization, so that are all better off?

The reason why this does not work is that an agreement to this effect is not self-enforcing. If the owners of the rival firm stick to profit maximization, it is always the best response to deviate from profit maximization and introduce a strong sales orientation. Similarly, if the rival firm's owners set $\alpha = \alpha^*$, the best reply is also to set $\alpha = \alpha^*$, not $\alpha = 1$.

The conclusion from all of this is that delegation has its price – not because managers cannot be induced to maximize profits, as in the classical principal–agent story, but because owners cannot resist using managerial incentive plans to make even higher profits, which is, alas, self-defeating.[9]

---

[9] We mention that the restriction to linear incentive plans poses a serious problem. Suppose owners can also write so-called *forcing contracts* of the form $M_i = m$ if $x_i = \bar{x}_i$ and $M_i = 0$ otherwise. Such forcing contracts are a much more powerful commitment mechanism than the linear incentive plan assumed in this section, but they have radically different consequences. Indeed, if only one owner can delegate, you get the classical Stackelberg outcome. However, if both owners can delegate and use forcing contracts, the game collapses to the usual Cournot game. Another serious problem is that effective commitment requires that the owner and the manager be able to convince others that they have not written a *new* contract superseding the one to which they claim

Finally, we mention that the philosophy of the present approach can be applied to explain other incentive schemes, such as labor contracts with a profit-sharing component. Several years ago Weitzman (1984) came out with the idea that the widespread use of profit sharing in labor contracts would cure the notorious unemployment problem, essentially because profit sharing gives rise to a permanent excess demand for labor. An obvious objection to Weitzman's claims was that individual firms and their employees have no incentive to introduce profit sharing, so that, in the absence of tax incentives, individual firms would never voluntarily undertake the proposed switch (see for example Wadhwani (1988)). However, this objection holds true only in a competitive or a monopolistic framework. If the product market is organized as a Cournot oligopoly, labor contracts with a profit-sharing component can be equilibrium labor contracts pretty much for the same reason the introduction of a sales orientation is an equilibrium incentive scheme in managerial labor contracts (see Stewart (1989)).

3.3.3 Commitment and Observability

The kind of stage games exemplified in the previous section on managerial incentives has been very popular in recent years. A large part of the field of theoretical industrial organization has been built on this foundation.[10] And even the self-proclaimed "new international trade theory," which stresses the role of subsidies, tariffs, and regulations as commitment devices, is nothing but an application of the mechanics of stage games and subgame perfectness (see for example Helpman and Krugman (1989)).

However, this entire tradition has at least three serious flaws:

- Results tend to be highly sensitive to the assumed sequence of moves.
- Finding subgame-perfect equilibria can be difficult except if one works with simple examples that permit explicit solutions and assure well-behaved reduced-form payoff functions.
- Worst of all, the strategic benefit of commitment tends to vanish if the observation of commitment levels is distorted, even if that distortion is arbitrarily small.

The first flaw – the sensitivity of results to the assumed sequence of moves – has led to the criticism that multistage games can be used to explain everything and thus nothing (Hellwig (1987)).

The second flaw explains why multistage games tend to come in the form of simple examples such as linear demand and cost functions.

The third flaw poses the most serious challenge to the entire Stackelberg tradition. For this reason, we will now elaborate on it, following an important contribution by Bagwell (1995). The argument will be based on a simple example, but it illustrates a general property.

---

to have committed. This problem is serious because, given others' belief about the managerial incentive plan chosen by one firm, it is always in the joint interest of the owner and the manager of this firm to sign a new contract instructing the manager to maximize profit.

[10] See for example the textbooks by Tirole (1989) and by Martin (1993).

Table 3.1. *Noisy Stackelberg*
game

		2	
		S	C
1	S	(5,2)	(3,1)
	C	(6,3)	(4,4)

Bagwell's Criticism

Consider a 2×2 Stackelberg game where player 1 is the Stackelberg leader, and player 2 the Stackelberg follower. Both players' action set is $A := \{S, C\}$, where S is mnemonic for Stackelberg and C for Cournot. Payoffs are described by the payoff matrix in Table 3.1.

If players have to choose their actions simultaneously, the game has the unique equilibrium strategy vector (C, C) (Cournot solution). In contrast, the two-stage Stackelberg game, where player 1 moves first, precommits to an action, and perfectly communicates it to player 2 before that player chooses his own action, has the unique subgame-perfect equilibrium (Stackelberg solution)

$$a_1 = S \qquad \text{(leader's equilibrium strategy)},$$

$$\sigma(S) = S, \qquad \sigma(C) = C \qquad \text{(follower's equilibrium strategy)}.$$

The associated equilibrium outcomes are (C, C) (Cournot) and (S, S) (Stackelberg).

Now introduce noise into the Stackelberg game. When player 1 chooses an action $a_1 \in \{S, C\}$, player 2 receives a signal $\phi \in \{S, C\}$. That signal is imperfect or distorted because both signal values occur with positive probability, as follows:

$$\Pr\{\phi = S \mid S\} = 1 - \epsilon, \tag{3.50}$$

$$\Pr\{\phi = C \mid C\} = 1 - \epsilon, \qquad \epsilon \in (0, 1). \tag{3.51}$$

Therefore, if 1 chooses a particular action, 2 observes a signal indicating the same action with probability $1 - \epsilon$. Obviously, the signals are almost perfect if ϵ is close to 0.

The pure strategies of the noisy Stackelberg game are $a_1 \in \{S, C\}$ (player 1) and $\sigma(\phi) \in \{S, C\}$ for all $\phi \in \{S, C\}$. In other words: player 2's strategies are reactions to the observed signal, whereas player 1's strategies coincide with his actions.

Pure-Strategy Equilibrium Amazingly, the value of commitment vanishes altogether if we look only at pure-strategy equilibria, even if the imperfection of observability is arbitrarily small.

Proposition 3.2 (Noisy Stackelberg game I) *The noisy Stackelberg game has exactly one pure-strategy equilibrium*

$$a_1 = C, \qquad \sigma(S) = \sigma(C) = C. \tag{3.52}$$

Player 2 does not react to the signal, and (C, C) (Cournot) is the unique equilibrium outcome.

Proof Suppose, *ad absurdum*, that in equilibrium player 2 reacts to the signal as in the strategy

$$\sigma(S) = S, \qquad \sigma(C) = C.$$

Then player 1's best reply is $a_1 = S$, provided ϵ is smaller than $\frac{1}{2}$.[11] Yet, player 2's best reply to $a_1 = S$ is $\sigma(S) = \sigma(C) = S$, which is a contradiction. By a similar argument it follows that $\sigma(S) = C, \sigma(C) = S$ cannot be part of an equilibrium either. □

Mixed-Strategy Equilibria Perhaps one can recover the value of commitment if one is willing to consider mixed-strategy equilibria.

Note that neither the simultaneous-move game nor the Stackelberg game under perfect observability has mixed-strategy equilibria. However, the noisy Stackelberg game has exactly two such equilibria. One of them does indeed recover the value of commitment and gives support to the traditional Stackelberg equilibrium. However, the other mixed-strategy equilibrium has exactly the opposite property: it destroys the value of commitment and supports the Cournot equilibrium outcome when the signal distortion becomes small.

In order to prepare for the proof of these claims, it is useful to understand which strategy profiles cannot be part of a mixed-strategy equilibrium. Mixed strategies will be denoted by

$$\lambda := \Pr\{a_1 = S\}, \qquad \eta(\phi) := \Pr\{a_2 = S \mid \phi\}. \tag{3.53}$$

Lemma 3.1 (Impossibilities) *Suppose the signal distortion is sufficiently small, $\epsilon < \frac{1}{4}$. The following strategy profiles cannot be part of an equilibrium in mixed strategies:*

1. *Only player 2 randomizes.*
2. *Only player 1 randomizes.*
3. *Player 2 randomizes at each signal.*

Proof 1: If player 1 plays a pure strategy, then player 2's best reply is unique; therefore, in equilibrium player 1 cannot randomize either. It follows that in a mixed-strategy equilibrium

$$\lambda \in (0, 1) \qquad \text{(player 1 randomizes)}. \tag{3.54}$$

2: Similarly, if player 2 plays a pure strategy, then player 1's best reply is unique. Therefore, in a mixed-strategy equilibrium,

$$\eta(S) \in (0, 1) \quad \text{or} \quad \eta(C) \in (0, 1). \tag{3.55}$$

3: Suppose player 2 randomizes at all signal realizations, i.e., $\eta(S), \eta(C) \in (0, 1)$ and $\lambda \in (0, 1)$. Then player 2 must be indifferent between the two actions S and C

---

[11] If $\epsilon > \frac{1}{2}$, the relevant strategy of 2 is $\sigma(S) = C, \sigma(C) = S$, and player 1's best reply remains the same.

regardless of which signal has been observed. Therefore, at each signal realization, the following condition of indifference between action S (LHS) and action C (RHS) must be satisfied for player 2:

$$2\gamma + 3(1 - \gamma) = \gamma + 4(1 - \gamma), \qquad \gamma \in \{\alpha, \beta\}. \tag{3.56}$$

Here α and β denote the conditional probabilities of $a_1 = S$, conditional on observing signal S and C, respectively.

Of course, these two conditions of indifference can be both satisfied only if the associated conditional probabilities are the same. Therefore, $\alpha = \beta$.

Now compute α and β. Using Bayes' rule, one obtains

$$\begin{aligned}
\alpha &:= \Pr\{a_1 = S \mid \phi = S\} \\
&= \frac{\Pr\{\phi = S \mid a_1 = S\} \Pr\{a_1 = S\}}{\Pr\{\phi = S\}} \\
&= \frac{(1 - \epsilon)\lambda}{(1 - \epsilon)\lambda + \epsilon(1 - \lambda)}.
\end{aligned} \tag{3.57}$$

By the same consideration you can solve $\beta := \Pr\{a_1 = S \mid \phi = C\}$ and confirm that it has the same solution as α if you replace the $1 - \epsilon$ in (3.57) by ϵ. Since α and β must be the same, it follows that $\epsilon = 1 - \epsilon$ and therefore $\epsilon = \frac{1}{2}$, which contradicts the assumed $\epsilon < \frac{1}{4}$. $\square$

Proposition 3.3 (Noisy Stackelberg Game II) *Suppose the signal distortion is sufficiently small, $\epsilon < \frac{1}{4}$. The noisy Stackelberg game has exactly two mixed strategy equilibria. Whereas one equilibrium supports the Stackelberg outcome,*

$$\lambda = 1 - \epsilon \quad and \quad \eta(C) = \frac{1 - 4\epsilon}{2 - 4\epsilon}, \quad \eta(S) = 1, \tag{3.58}$$

the other supports the Cournot outcome

$$\lambda = \epsilon \quad and \quad \eta(S) = \frac{1}{2 - 4\epsilon}, \quad \eta(C) = 0. \tag{3.59}$$

Proof The above Lemma 3.1 implies that a mixed-strategy equilibrium must have the following form:

$$\lambda \in (0, 1) \quad \text{and} \quad \text{either } \eta(S) \in (0, 1) \text{ or } \eta(C) \in (0, 1).$$

Using the standard property of indifference between the actions that should be played in equilibrium with positive probability, the asserted equilibria follow immediately. Note that if ϵ is made small, the first equilibrium leads almost always to the Stackelberg outcome and the second to the Cournot outcome.

To exemplify the procedure of the proof, we now show that $\lambda = 1 - \epsilon$ is a best reply to $\eta(S) = 1$, $\eta(C) = (1 - 4\epsilon)/(2 - 4\epsilon)$.

Recall that a mixed strategy can only be player 1's best reply if he or she is indifferent between the two actions $a_1 = S$ and $a_1 = C$. Player 1's payoff, if playing $a_1 = S$ is (using $\eta(S) = 1$)

$$U_1(S, \eta) = 5 \Pr\{\phi = S \mid a_1 = S\}$$
$$+ \Pr\{\phi = C \mid a_1 = S\} \left(5\eta(C) + 3(1 - \eta(C)\right)$$
$$= 5 - 2\epsilon + 2\epsilon\eta(C). \tag{3.60}$$

Similarly, player 1's payoff from playing $a_1 = C$ is

$$U_1(C, \eta) = 6 \Pr\{\phi = S \mid a_1 = C\}$$
$$+ \Pr\{\phi = C \mid a_1 = C\} \left(6\eta(C) + 4(1 - \eta(C)\right)$$
$$= 4 + 2\epsilon + 2\eta(C)(1 - \epsilon). \tag{3.61}$$

After a bit of rearranging it follows immediately that the condition of indifference, $U_1(S, \eta) = U_1(C, \eta)$, holds only if $\eta(C) = (1 - 4\epsilon)/(2 - 4\epsilon)$, as asserted. □

Altogether, these results indicate that the entire tradition of games that rely on the strategic benefits of commitment is seriously flawed.[12] This is bad news for those who hope to write important theory with the simple tools and tricks of multistage games and subgame perfection.

3.4 More on Cournot Competition

Of all oligopoly models, Cournot's is the oldest and most popular. Many economists believe that it gives the best mileage for understanding the basic principles of oligopolistic behavior. And some have even argued that it is indicative of the outcome of more realistic multistage games in which firms set prices without the help of a fictitious auctioneer.

Given the eminent importance of the Cournot market game, we now prepare for a fuller understanding of it. The emphasis in this section is on generalizing assumptions on demand and cost functions. Among other things, we will explore what happens if firms may exit and new firms may enter, and point out some surprising effects of cartel laws on equilibrium profits.

3.4.1 Existence and Uniqueness

By a well-known result due to John Nash (1950b), every noncooperative game with finite pure-strategy sets has at least one Nash equilibrium solution. Therefore, existence of a solution of the Cournot market game is always assured if each oligopolist is restricted to choose from a discrete grid of output levels. But what happens if we admit any real-valued output, and, more important, what can be said about existence and possibly uniqueness of pure-strategy equilibria?

---

[12] We mention that there are some commitment games where actions are payoff-irrelevant and signals are payoff-relevant. For example, central banks choose the stock of high-powered money, which in turn is reflected in the inflation rate. Of course, the public cares more about the signal of the authorities' actions – the inflation rate – than the underlying action. Not surprisingly, equilibrium strategies may be signal-dependent in such a case. See for example Fudenberg and Levine (1992).

Actually, as Glicksberg (1952) has shown, the restriction to a discrete grid of strategies can be replaced by the requirements that strategy sets be *compact* (closed and bounded) and payoffs be *continuous* functions of strategies. However, both these general results assure existence only in an unrestricted strategy space that permit pure as well as mixed strategies.[13] Many people feel uncomfortable with the idea that managers determine their output by the flip of a coin. Therefore, one would like to know which assumptions assure existence of a pure-strategy equilibrium.

Furthermore, multiple equilibria of a noncooperative game pose serious problems of interpretation and make comparative statics meaningless. Therefore, one would like to know even more specifically which assumptions assure a *unique* pure-strategy equilibrium.

In the oligopoly literature there is a large set of sufficient conditions for existence and uniqueness, some of which are more and some less technically demanding.[14] In the following we present one particular proof. The underlying assumptions are not the weakest requirements. However, the proof has the advantage that it is accessible without advanced mathematical prerequisites. In addition, it provides a simple solution procedure that is often useful for computing the equilibrium strategies of Cournot and other *strategically aggregable* (Selten) games.

Assumptions

Consider an industry composed of $n \geq 2$ suppliers of a homogeneous good. Firm i produces the good in quantity $x_i \geq 0$. Its cost function is $C_i(x_i)$. The inverse demand function is $P(X)$, where $X := \sum_{i=1}^{n} x_i$ is the total market supply.

(A1) Cost functions are continuous on $\mathbb{R}_+$ and twice continuously differentiable on $\mathbb{R}_{++}$ with $C_i'(x_i) > 0$.

(A2) Demand has a finite *satiation point*, $P(X) = 0, \forall X \geq \bar{X}$. P is continuous on $\mathbb{R}_+$ and twice continuously differentiable with $P(X) > 0$, and $P'(X) < 0$ on $(0, \bar{X})$.

(A3) All firms are viable if they alone serve the market: $\lim_{x_i \to 0} C_i'(x_i) < \lim_{X \to 0} P(X)$.

(A4) Cost functions are convex ($C_i''(x_i) \geq 0$) and inverse demand concave ($P''(X) \leq 0$), at least one strict.[15]

In order to prepare the proof of existence and uniqueness, we recall the rules of the Cournot oligopoly game and adopt some new notation and concepts. As before, *strategies* are outputs $x_i \in [0, \bar{X}]$, and a complete strategy choice is denoted by the *strategy vector* $x := (x_1, \dots, x_n)$. The complete *strategy set* $\mathcal{X}$ is the Cartesian product of the individual strategy set $[0, \bar{X}]$; therefore, $x \in \mathcal{X}$. In addition, define the *truncated strategy vector* as $x_{-i} := (x_1, \dots, x_{i-1}, x_{i+1}, \dots, x_n)$; viewed from the perspective of firm i, it lists the strategies of all rival players. Finally, let $\pi_i : \mathcal{X} \to \mathbb{R}$

[13] *Pure* strategies are feasible output levels; *mixed* strategies are probability distributions over the set of feasible output levels.
[14] For a review consult Friedman (1986).
[15] These assumptions can be replaced by the following weaker requirements concerning the marginal profit function: $P''(X)x_i + P'(X) < 0 \ \forall x_i > 0, X < \bar{X}, P'(X) - C_i''(x_i) < 0 \ \forall x_i > 0, X < \bar{X}$.

be firm i's profit as a function of all players' strategies:

$$\pi_i(x_i, x_{-i}) := P\left(x_i + \sum_{j \neq i} x_j\right) x_i - C_i(x_i). \qquad (3.62)$$

Definition 3.1 The output vector $x^C \in \mathcal{X}$ is a pure-strategy equilibrium of the Cournot oligopoly game if it is a mutual best response:

$$x_i^C \in \arg \max_{x_i \in [0, \bar{X}]} \pi_i\left(x_i, x_{-i}^C\right), \qquad i = 1, \ldots, n.$$

Since the profit function is strictly concave, a pure-strategy Nash equilibrium is equivalently described as the solution of the following Kuhn–Tucker conditions, for $i = 1, \ldots, n$:[16]

$$[P'(X)x_i + P(X) - C_i'(x_i)] \leq 0 \quad \text{and} \quad [\cdots]x_i = 0, \qquad (3.63)$$

$$X = \sum_{i=1}^{n} x_i. \qquad (3.64)$$

Inclusive Reaction Function – a Convenient Tool

Select the Kuhn–Tucker conditions for one particular firm i. Make a "bold" move: view $X \geq 0$ as a parameter, and summarize the solutions of the ith firm's Kuhn–Tucker conditions for all $X \in [0, \bar{X}]$ by a function $\phi_i(X)$ defined on $X \geq 0$. Adapting a terminology proposed by Selten, we call ϕ_i an *inclusive* reaction function.[17] Finally define the *aggregate* inclusive reaction function

$$\phi(X) := \sum_{i=1}^{n} \phi_i(X). \qquad (3.65)$$

You will see, in just a moment, that the Nash equilibrium has a lot to do with the *fixed point* of ϕ, which is that particular $\hat{X} \in [0, \bar{X}]$ that ϕ maps into itself:

$$\phi(\hat{X}) = \hat{X}. \qquad (3.66)$$

Example 3.1 Suppose $P(X) := \max\{1 - X, 0\}$ and $C_i(x_i) := c_i x_i$, with $c_i < 1$. Then the inclusive reaction functions ϕ_i and ϕ are as follows:

$$\phi_i(X) = \max\{1 - X - c_i, 0\}, \qquad \phi(X) = n \max\{1 - X - \bar{c}, 0\},$$

where $\bar{c}$ denotes the industry's average of marginal costs,

$$\bar{c} := \frac{1}{n} \sum_{i=1}^{n} c_i.$$

---

[16] The second partial derivative of π_i with respect to x_i is equal to $(P''x_i + P') + (P' - C_i'')$. By (A4) both terms in parenthesis are negative. Therefore, the profit function is strictly concave, and the maximum is unique (if one exists). Existence of a maximum is assured by the Weierstrass theorem, since the objective function is continuous in x_i and the associated domain $[0, \bar{X}]$ is compact.

[17] This function appears in the literature under different names. Selten (1970) calls it *"Einpassungsfunktion,"* Novshek (1984) "backward reaction mapping," and Phlips (1995) "fitting-in function."

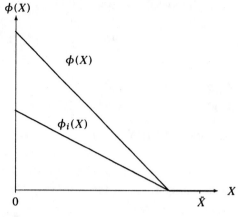

Figure 3.7. Inclusive Reaction Functions.

Properties of Inclusive Reaction Functions The functions ϕ_i and ϕ have several notable properties that follow immediately from the underlying Kuhn–Tucker conditions:

1. Since every solution of (3.63), (3.64) is a Nash equilibrium, every fixed point $\hat{X}$ of ϕ generates a Nash equilibrium

$$(\phi_1(\hat{X}), \ldots, \phi_n(\hat{X})) = (x_1^C, \ldots, x_n^C),$$

   and vice versa;
2. $\phi_i(\bar{X}) = 0$ and $\phi_i(0) > 0$, and therefore $\phi(\bar{X}) = 0$ and $\phi(0) > 0$;
3. ϕ is continuously differentiable, with $\phi'(X) < 0$, if $\phi(X) > 0$, since

$$\phi_i'(X) = -\frac{P''(X)\phi_i(X) + P'(X)}{P'(X) - C_i''(\phi_i(X))}. \tag{3.67}$$

ϕ_i, ϕ, and the fixed point $\hat{X}$ of ϕ are illustrated in Figure 3.7 and 3.8.

Basic Existence and Uniqueness Theorem

With these preliminaries, the proof of existence and uniqueness is a snap.[18]

Proposition 3.4 *Assume (A1)–(A4). The Cournot oligopoly game has a unique pure-strategy equilibrium* x^C.

Proof You have already learned that every fixed point $\hat{X}$ gives us a Nash equilibrium $(\phi_1(\hat{X}), \ldots, \phi_n(\hat{X}))$, and vice versa. Therefore, existence of equilibrium is equivalent to existence of a fixed point of ϕ. Since ϕ is continuous and strictly decreasing, ranging from $\phi(0) > 0$ to $\phi(\bar{X}) = 0$, ϕ does have a fixed point (ϕ must cross the 45° line somewhere, as illustrated in Figure 3.8). Also, since ϕ is strict monotone decreasing if $\phi(x) > 0$, it cannot have more than one fixed point. Therefore, the fixed point is unique.   □

---

[18] The following proof is usually attributed to Szidarovszky and Yakowitz (1977). However, it appeared seven years earlier in Chapter 9 of Selten (1970). Selten even generalized the procedure of this proof to cover Cournot oligopoly models with joint production and interdependent demand.

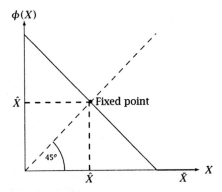

Figure 3.8. Fixed Point of ϕ.

Example 3.2 In order to see how the inclusive reaction function provides a simple solution procedure, go back to the assumptions and notation of Example 3.1. It is a snap to compute the fixed point $\hat{X}$, which is exclusively determined by the industry's average of marginal costs $\bar{c}$:

$$\hat{X} = \frac{n}{n+1}(1 - \bar{c}).$$

Finally, insert $\hat{X}$ into the functions ϕ_i, and one has the equilibrium strategies

$$x_i^C = (1 - c_i) - \frac{n}{1+n}(1 - \bar{c})$$

$$= \frac{1}{n+1}[(1 - c_i) - n(c_i - \bar{c})].$$

(If some of the thus determined outputs are not positive, eliminate the firm with the highest c_i, and repeat the entire procedure until all outputs are positive.)

Notice how the distribution of equilibrium outputs x_i^C is governed by the deviation of individual marginal costs from the industry's average. Also notice that the Cournot equilibrium price is exclusively determined by that industry average and unaffected by any reshuffling of individual marginal costs.

Moreover, note that if the c's are changed in such a way that the average, $\bar{c}$, remains unchanged, the equilibrium outputs change as follows:

$$\left. \frac{dx_i}{dc_i} \right|_{\bar{c} = \text{const}} = -1.$$

This suggests that the Treasury can raise tax revenue without affecting the market price by taxing output of low-cost firms (where the tax base is high) and subsidizing output of high-cost firms (where the tax base is low). This issue is picked up in Example 3.5.

Example 3.3 As another example consider the simple linear Cournot oligopoly from Section 3.2 with three firms. Suppose firms have a collusive agreement that binds them to not exceed the output quotas

$$\bar{x}_1 = 0.6, \qquad \bar{x}_2 = 0.4, \qquad \bar{x}_3 = 0.$$

Determine the equilibrium outputs in the Cournot game.

In a first step show that the inclusive reaction functions are

$$\phi_i(X) = \max\{0, \min\{1 - X, \bar{x}_i\}\},$$

$$\phi = \begin{cases} 1.1 & \text{if } X \in [0, 0.4], \\ 1.5 - X & \text{if } X \in [0.4, 0.6], \\ 2.1 - 2X & \text{if } X \in [0.6, 0.9], \\ \max\{3 - 3X, 0\} & \text{if } X \geq 0.9. \end{cases}$$

It follows immediately that the unique fixed point $\phi(X^*) = X^*$ is $X^* = 0.7$. Insert X^* into $\phi_i(X)$), and one has the unique equilibrium outputs

$$x_1^* = x_2^* = 0.3, \qquad x_3^* = 0.1.$$

Multiplicity and Nonexistence

The above conditions for existence and uniqueness may seem fairly innocuous. But it does not take all that much to violate them and end up with multiple equilibria and even nonexistence.

Take a look at the following example, which is also an instructive application of the inclusive reaction function. The only deviation from the assumptions (A1)–(A4) is that the demand function has a discontinuity.

Example 3.4 Let the inverse demand be given by the discontinuous function P : $[0, 1] \rightarrow \mathbb{R}_+$ with

$$P(x) := \begin{cases} 2 - X & \text{for } X \in [0, \tilde{X}], \\ 1 - X & \text{for } X \in (\tilde{X}, 1] \end{cases}$$

with $\tilde{X} = 0.75$, and let there be two identical firms with zero marginal costs.

Using these data, determine the inclusive reaction functions ϕ_i: one obtains

$$\phi_i(X) = \begin{cases} 2 - X & \text{for } X \in [0, \tilde{X}], \\ 1 - X & \text{for } X \in (\tilde{X}, 1]. \end{cases}$$

Therefore, the aggregate inclusive reaction function ϕ is

$$\phi(X) := \begin{cases} 4 - 2X & \text{for } X \in [0, \tilde{X}], \\ 2 - 2X & \text{for } X \in (\tilde{X}, 1]. \end{cases}$$

Plot the graph of ϕ, and you see immediately that ϕ does not have a fixed point (see Figure 3.9). Therefore, no pure-strategy equilibrium exists. (Of course, if you have nonexistence in pure strategies, you may go to randomized or mixed strategies.)

Generalizations

Before we conclude this glimpse of the existence and uniqueness problem, we mention that there is an enormous literature on these issues and a host of alternative necessary or sufficient conditions.

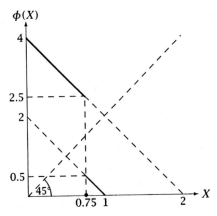

Figure 3.9. Nonexistence of Cournot Equilibrium.

A fundamental result that can be applied here is a well-known existence theorem by Debreu (1952), which says that one has always a pure-strategy equilibrium if 1) strategy sets are convex and compact, 2) all payoff functions are continuous in the entire strategy vector, and 3) all payoff functions are quasiconcave in the players' own strategies. Application of this result allows us to loosen the requirements for concavity of market revenue and convexity of cost function and still have existence, though not necessarily uniqueness.

But there are many further conditions that cannot be subsumed under Debreu's existence theorem. For example, Roberts and Sonnenschein (1976) allow general (downward-sloping) inverse demand and prove existence and uniqueness if there are n identical firms with nondecreasing marginal cost. One limitation of this result is that it assumes identical firms. Allowing different cost functions, Novshek (1985) extends our existence result to arbitrary continuous cost functions, so that one can do without our convexity assumption and assure existence, though not necessarily uniqueness.

Finally, Kolstad and Mathiesen (1987) provide a tight necessary *and* sufficient condition for uniqueness. Essentially, this condition requires that the effect of a small change in a firm's output on its own marginal profit must be greater than the effect on its marginal profit from a similar output change on the part of all rival firms.

3.4.2 Digression: A Prescription for Leviathan*

As a brief application, consider the tax-revenue-maximizing Leviathan in the framework of Cournot oligopoly. Let $t_i^0 \in (0, 1)$ be the current tax rate per output unit levied upon firm i. You are hired as an advisor. Your job is to figure out whether and how these rates should be changed. The preset goal is to maximize tax revenue. However, there is one constraint. Whatever you recommend, you should not change the product price or the overall supply, so that consumers are not upset by your proposed tax reform.

In order to simplify matters, assume constant marginal costs. Now everything is fairly simple, and you can start with your job.

A useful property of the Cournot equilibrium price is that it is invariant with regard to changes in marginal costs as long as their sum remains unchanged.[19] This result follows immediately if you sum over the Kuhn–Tucker conditions (3.63) of all active firms, and hence obtain

$$P'(X^C)X^C + nP(X^C) = \sum_{i=1}^{n} C_i'(x_i^C). \qquad (3.68)$$

Denote the constant marginal cost by $c_i > 0$. Since the inclusion of the tax rate t_i^0 has the same effect as an increase in marginal cost, $c_i + t_i^0$ can be viewed as the *effective marginal cost* of firm i. It follows immediately that any reshuffling of tax rates that leaves their sum unchanged has no effect on equilibrium price and quantity.

Using this result, a second useful property is that the Cournot equilibrium strategies x_i^C are affected only by firm i's own tax rate t_i and independent of the t's of other firms, as long as the sum of tax rates is unchanged. Indeed, by (3.68), one has in this case

$$x_i^C(t_i) = -\frac{P(X^C) - c_i - t_i}{P'(X^C)}. \qquad (3.69)$$

Combining both results, your job is now reduced to finding those tax rates that solve the following simple maximization problem:

$$\max_{t_i \in (0,1)} \sum_{i=1}^{n} t_i x_i^C(t_i) \qquad \text{s.t.} \quad \sum_{i=1}^{n} (t_i - t_i^0) = 0. \qquad (3.70)$$

Obviously, this decision problem is well behaved, and it follows from the first-order conditions that tax rates should satisfy the following requirement:

$$t_i - t_j = \frac{1}{2}(c_j - c_i) \qquad \forall i \neq j. \qquad (3.71)$$

Therefore, all firms that have the same marginal cost should also be taxed the same, and the higher the marginal cost, the lower should be the tax rate.

This result is quite surprising at first glance because any zero-sum reshuffling of tax rates leads to a zero-sum reshuffling of outputs but not of tax receipts.[20] However, given the fact that aggregate output remains unchanged, it is clear that one can generate tax revenue by imposing a tax on those who have a high tax base (high output due to low marginal costs), and neutralize its effect on price by paying an equal subsidy per unit output to those who have a low output and hence subsidy base.

Example 3.5 Consider the Cournot duopoly with linear inverse demand and constant marginal costs:

$$P(X) := 1 - X, \qquad c_1 = 0, \qquad c_2 = 0.2.$$

---

[19] This observation is due to Bergstrom and Varian (1985b).
[20] Oligopoly theory offers a rich mine for public finance. For another taste of it, take a look at Levin (1985), where it is shown that an output tax, designed to reduce the emission of an undesirable by-product, such as air or water pollution, may actually *increase* pollution. This could never happen in a competitive framework.

Suppose firm 1's output is taxed and firm 2's output is subsidized, both at the same rate t. Then the equilibrium outputs are a function of the tax rate t, as follows:

$$x_1^C(t) = 0.4 - t, \qquad x_2^C(t) = 0.2 + t. \tag{3.72}$$

Therefore, the tax receipt maximizing tax rate is

$$t = \frac{1}{20}. \tag{3.73}$$

The associated tax receipt amounts to 0.0005 units.

3.4.3 What Does a Cournot Equilibrium Maximize?*

Isn't this a silly question? Oligopolists maximize their own profit. They do not care about how the outcome affects their rivals' payoffs. Therefore, it is not likely that the Cournot equilibrium maximizes the objective function of any single player or that it maximizes social welfare. So, what sense does this question make?

Even though all of these observations are correct, it would still be useful to know that the Cournot equilibrium can also be derived as the maximizer of a certain fictitious objective function.

Indeed, it can, if cost functions are uniform.[21] Among other applications, this happens to be useful in assessing the welfare properties of Cournot equilibria.

Proposition 3.5 *Assume (A1)–(A4) and uniform cost functions. The Cournot equilibrium output per firm, $z := X^C/n$, is the unique maximizer of the weighted sum of total surplus and aggregate profits, represented by the function $F : [0, \bar{X}] \to \mathbb{R}_+$, with image $F(z)$:*

$$F(z) := (n - 1)T(z) + n\pi(z), \tag{3.74}$$

$$T(z) := \int_0^{nz} P(t)\, dt - nC(z), \tag{3.75}$$

$$\pi(z) := P(nz)z - C(z). \tag{3.76}$$

Proof F is strictly concave; therefore, the maximizer of F must be the unique solution of the Kuhn–Tucker condition ((A3) assures existence of an interior solution)

$$P(nz) + P'(nz)z - C'(z) = 0.$$

But this condition is precisely the same as condition (3.63). □

The fictitious objective function F has a suggestive welfare interpretation. In the first term $T(nz)$ is the total surplus (net consumer plus producer surplus), which is a measure of social welfare, and in the second term $\pi(z)$ is the profit per firm. If there is only one firm, total surplus is assigned zero weight, and z is determined exclusively by profit maximization. However, as the number of firms is increased,

---

[21] This result is due to Bergstrom and Varian (1985a). Unfortunately, it cannot be extended to the case of different cost functions.

total surplus gets a higher and higher weight relative to profits, and industry output gradually approaches its social optimum.

3.4.4 What If Suppliers Form a Cartel?

Which outputs would firms choose if they could write an enforceable cartel agreement? The following strictly concave program gives the answer. Here it is assumed that the cartel maximizes the sum of its members' profits, which may then be redistributed appropriately:[22]

$$\max_{x,X} P(X)X - \sum_{i=1}^{n} C_i(x_i) \tag{3.77}$$

$$\text{s.t.} \quad \sum_{i=1}^{n} x_i - X \geq 0 \quad \text{and} \quad x \geq 0. \tag{3.78}$$

Since the decision problem is strictly concave, its solution is unique and characterized by the Kuhn–Tucker conditions (existence of an interior solution is assured by (A3))

$$P'(X)X + P(X) - C_i'(x_i) = 0 \qquad \forall i. \tag{3.79}$$

Denote the *cartel solution* by the superscript K. It differs from the Cournot solution as follows:

Proposition 3.6 *The cartel produces less output and earns higher profits than the Cournot equilibrium.*

Proof Suppose, *per absurdum*, that $X^K \geq X^C$. Then there must exist at least one firm, say firm r, that produces at least as much as under the C-regime: $x_r^C \leq x_r^K$. Since all firms produce positive quantities (recall that interior solutions are assured), it follows by (3.63) and the fact that $P'(X^C) < 0$ that

$$P'(X^C)X^C + P(X^C) < P'(X^C)x_r^C + P(X^C) = C_r'(x_r^C).$$

By the convexity of the cost functions, combined with (3.79), one has

$$C_r'(x_r^C) \leq C_r'(x_r^K) = P'(X^K)X^K + P(X^K).$$

Therefore, putting the two pieces together, marginal revenue is strictly increasing in X:

$$P'(X^K)X^K + P(X^K) > P'(X^C)X^C + P(X^C).$$

But this contradicts the assumed concavity of the market revenue function.[23] Finally, in order to prove that the cartel earns higher aggregate profits, just think of the fact that the cartel could always stick to the Cournot equilibrium output vector. But, as we have just seen, it can do better.   □

---

[22] This requirement is incidentally a property of the standard solution concepts of cooperative bargaining solutions. However, it may be more appropriate to view the bargaining over the distribution of profits as a noncooperative game, with sequential moves and countermoves, which was reviewed in Chapter 1.

[23] Recall the second-derivative characterization of concave functions explained in *Appendix C*.

The Cartel Instability Problem

If you were part of a cartel, would you rely on your fellow cartel members' promise to stick to the terms of the agreement even if no external enforcement is available because cartel agreements are illegal?

A fundamental yet simple observation suggests that the answer is negative.

Proposition 3.7 *The cartel solution x^K is not self-enforcing. Each firm's best response to x^K_{-i} is to exceed his output quota x^K_i.*

Proof We have already shown that the cartel solution differs from the Cournot solution. By definition, each Cournot solution is self-enforcing and vice versa. Therefore, the cartel solution cannot be self-enforcing. To show that each firm has an incentive to exceed his output quota, compute firm i's marginal profit at the point x^K; using the fact that P is strict monotone decreasing, that each $x^K_i > 0$, and (3.79), one obtains

$$P(X^K) + P'(X^K)x^K_i - C'_i(x^K_i) > P(X^K) + P'(X^K)X^K - C'_i(x^K_i) = 0.$$

Therefore, if rivals stick to the cartel agreement, it is more profitable to violate the agreement and produce more than the output quota. □

If no external enforcement is available, why doesn't the cartel invent its own *internal* enforcement mechanism? Surely, the cartel could threaten to punish all those "bad guys" who breach the agreement? If the penalties are sufficiently high, cheating is deterred and the cartel agreement holds. However, the threat of sanctioning those who breach the cartel agreement poses a serious credibility problem. Once a breach has occurred, the execution of the sanctions cannot possibly undo it. Hence, once a violation has occurred, the execution of sanctions has costs but no benefits. In this situation, no rational cartel would stick to its threat, unless it had found a way to "tie its hands." But, of course, it is difficult to imagine any such commitment mechanism.

The Role of the Antitrust Office

This suggests that the prohibition of cartels is sufficient to actually prevent cartels. Interestingly, this works without an antitrust office that collects evidence to detect hidden cartels and then triggers legal sanctions. All that is needed is that the services of law enforcement, which are part of contract law, are not extended to cartel agreements.

Of course, this does not imply that one does not need an antitrust office at all. After all, someone has to figure out whether a contract that coordinates the actions of some firms – be it a full-scale merger or just a joint advertising campaign – falls under the domain of antitrust law.[24]

---

[24] In many applications, the distinction between enforceable and illegal agreements is rather loose. This suggests an intriguing research problem: to analyze self-enforcing cartel agreements under uncertainty about the enforcement of antitrust laws.

Disguised Cartel Agreements

The task of the antitrust office is in many ways considerably more complicated than it may seem at first glance. Many cartel agreements come in disguise and then often pass as legal agreements, served by the machinery of law enforcement.

For example, referring to environmental concerns, the firms of an industry could write an agreement to restrict the emission of certain pollutants. If pollution is a function of outputs, this joint restriction of pollution is really a deceptively packaged system of monopolistic output quotas. Similarly, the firms and workers of an industry may take advantage of the right to collective bargaining – one of the major exemptions from antitrust law – and write an industry-wide labor contract that restricts employment and thus outputs. These are just two of many widely used practices that make the job of the lawmaker and antitrust officer despairingly difficult.

An Externality Interpretation

The choice of quantity strategy by each oligopolist has a measurable effect on the market price and hence on the payoffs of all rival suppliers. This side effect is the source of an *externality* problem. As each individual supplier is concerned only with his own costs and returns, he ignores the negative externality that he exerts upon his rivals whenever he increases his own supply. Hence, each oligopolist tends to produce too much, relative to what is optimal for *all* suppliers. This tendency toward "overproduction" corresponds to the fact that each supplier has an incentive to exceed his output quota whenever rival suppliers stick to the joint profit-maximizing cartel agreement.

3.4.5 Selten's "Four Are Few and Six Are Many"

In the previous section we assumed that firms would join an all-inclusive cartel if they could write enforceable cartel agreements. However, as Selten (1973) has shown, this is only true if the market is sufficiently small. In large markets, with many competitors, only some firms will join a cartel, while others stay independent. The surprising part is that four or fewer firms tends to be a "small" market, while six or more is "large." We now illustrate this important "four are few and six are many" property, using the simple linear model from Section 3.2.

Suppose there are $n \geq 2$ firms, each with constant marginal cost, normalized to zero, and the inverse market demand function $P(X) := 1 - X$, $X := \sum x_i$. The market game has three stages: In *stage 1*, firms either join a cartel or stay out; in *stage 2*, cartel members propose output quotas, and, provided they propose the same quotas, write an enforceable cartel agreement that binds each member to his quota. Finally, in *stage 3*, firms play a Cournot market game, knowing who is a cartel member.

Denote cartel members by $K := \{1, \ldots, k\}$, nonmembers by $N := \{k + 1, \ldots, n\}$, and the respective aggregate and individual supplies by X_K, x_{iK}, X_N, x_{iN}. Then the equilibrium supplies and profits are functions of the number of cartel members, k, and the size of the market, n, as follows.

Proposition 3.8 *Suppose $0 \leq k \leq n$ firms join the cartel. Then the subgame perfect-equilibrium outputs and profits of stages 2 and 3 are*

$$X_K(k, n) = \frac{1}{2}, \qquad x_{iK}(k, n) = \frac{1}{2k},$$

$$X_N(k, n) = \frac{n-k}{2(n-k+1)}, \qquad x_{iN}(k, n) = \frac{1}{(2(n-k+1))},$$

$$\pi_K(k, n) = \frac{1}{4k(n-k+1)}, \qquad \pi_N(k, n) = \frac{1}{4(n-k+1)^2},$$

where x_{iK} is also the output quota of cartel member i.

Proof Stages 2 and 3 are a Stackelberg leader–follower game in which the cartel has the role of leader and the $n - k$ nonmembers the role of independent followers. It is straightforward to see that the followers' best reply to X_K is

$$x_{iN} = \frac{1 - X_K}{n - k + 1};$$

hence,

$$X_N = \frac{(n-k)(1 - X_K)}{n - k + 1}.$$

From this it follows easily that the cartel's overall profit is maximized by $X_K = \frac{1}{2}$, regardless of k, and the asserted equilibrium supplies and profits follow easily. $\square$

Corollary 3.1 *In equilibrium all firms join the cartel if and only if the market size is four or less firms. If there are six or more firms, equilibrium cartels include only some firms.*

Proof The all-inclusive cartel is stable if and only if

$$\pi_K(n, n) \geq \pi_N(n - 1, n).$$

As one can easily confirm, this occurs if and only if $k \leq 4$, as asserted. If $k > 4$, one can find the equilibrium size of cartels by imposing the conditions that it should not be profitable for a cartel member to quit membership, $\pi_K(k, n) \geq \pi_N(k - 1, n)$, or for a nonmember to join, $\pi_N(k, n) \geq \pi_K(k + 1, n)$. $\square$

Example 3.6 Suppose $n = 5$ or $n = 6$ ($n = 9$ or $n = 10$). Then the equilibrium size of the cartel is $k = 4$ ($k = 6$). Also note that nonmembers consistently earn higher equilibrium payoffs.

Selten's "four are few and six are many" theory is often viewed as a noncooperative theory of cartels (see for example Martin (1993, p. 98)). However, this is quite misleading. True, Selten explicitly models the participation decision of potential cartel members. However, he assumes that once a cartel has formed, members can neither quit nor deviate from the agreed-upon output quota. In other words, membership is voluntary, but those who became members write an enforceable quota agreement. The assumed enforceability of output quota agreements is, of course, inconsistent with cartel laws in most countries.

3.4.6 Are Mergers Profitable?

Firms are better off if they collude. But does this property extend to mergers of *some* firms? You may be very much surprised, but it does not, without qualification.[25]

In order to explain this point, go back to our simple example of an n-firm Cournot oligopoly with a linear inverse demand function $P(X) = 1 - X$ and constant average cost, normalized to be equal to zero.

If none of these n firms merge, each oligopolist produces an output equal to $1/(n + 1)$ and hence earns a profit

$$\pi(n) = \frac{1}{n+1}\left(1 - \frac{n}{n+1}\right) = \frac{1}{(n+1)^2}.$$

Evidently, $\pi(n)$ is strictly diminishing in n, and so are aggregate profits $\Pi(n) := n\pi(n)$, and the equilibrium price $p(n) = 1/(n+1)$. So far, nothing is new.

But now suppose a subgroup of $m + 1$ firms merge, so that m firms leave the market. What is their gain from a merger?

The merger reduces the number of firms from n to $n - m$. Therefore, the merged firms' profit is equal to $\pi(n - m)$, whereas before the merger the coalition of $m + 1$ firms earned a sum total of $(m + 1)\pi(n)$. Hence, the *gain from merger* is equal to

$$g(n, m) := \pi(n - m) - (m + 1)\pi(n)$$

$$= \frac{1}{(n - m + 1)^2} - \frac{m + 1}{(n + 1)^2}.$$

We show that a merger is profitable if and only if almost all firms are part of it.

Proposition 3.9 *Consider the linear-demand, constant-average-cost Cournot oligopoly, with a given number n of firms. Suppose $m + 1$ firms merge, where $m + 1 < n$ (no grand merger). The merger is profitable if and only if at least 80% of the firms merge.*

Proof Obviously, $g(n, 0) = 0$ (the *singleton coalition* is just the status quo) and $g(n, n - 1) > 0$ (the *grand coalition* reaps the monopoly profit). Next, observe that g is decreasing at $m = 0$ and convex over its entire domain:

$$\left.\frac{\partial g}{\partial m}\right|_{m=0} = \frac{1 - n}{(n + 1)^3} \qquad < 0,$$

$$\frac{\partial^2 g}{(\partial m)^2} = \frac{6}{(n - m + 1)^4} > 0 \qquad \forall m < n - 1.$$

Therefore, the graph of $g(n, m)$ is as in Figure 3.10.

This graph shows clearly that a merger is not profitable unless it includes many firms. But how many is many? In order to answer this question, we determine the breakeven point m^*.

Let $m^* + 1$ be the number of firms in the coalition that makes a merger neither profitable nor beneficial. Define the *breakeven fraction* of firms in the coalition as

$$\alpha(n) = \frac{m^*(n) + 1}{n}.$$

[25] This observation is due to Salant, Switzer, and Reynolds (1983).

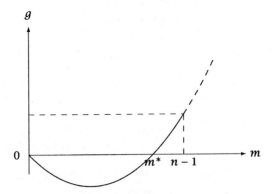

Figure 3.10. Profitability of Merger.

Then $\alpha(n)$ is implicitly determined as the solution of

$$0 = \frac{1}{[n - \alpha(n)n + 2]^2} - \frac{\alpha(n)n}{(n + 1)^2}.$$

It has three roots,

$$\alpha_1 = \frac{1}{n}, \qquad \alpha_2 = \frac{2n + 3 - \sqrt{4n + 5}}{2n}, \qquad \alpha_3 = \frac{2n + 3 + \sqrt{4n + 5}}{2n}.$$

The third root is greater than 1 and hence inadmissible, and the first gives the singleton coalition for all n. Therefore, only the second root is of interest. Finally, compute the first and the second derivative of α_2 with respect to n; one finds that α_2 has a minimum at $n = 5$, with $\alpha_2(5) = 0.8$, for

$$\frac{d}{dn}\alpha_2(n) = 0 \quad \Leftrightarrow \quad 3\sqrt{4n + 5} - (2n + 5) = 0,$$

$$\frac{d^2}{dn^2}\alpha_2(5) > 0.$$

This completes the proof. □

What is the intuition for this surprising result? In a Cournot oligopoly the industry as a whole gains from a merger, since the aggregate equilibrium profit $\Pi(N) := n\pi(n) = n/(n + 1)^2$ is strictly increasing in n. However, since this gain comes in the form of a price reduction, it is shared also by those who are not part of the merging coalition and who thus take a *free ride*. This free-rider problem is aggravated because the merging coalition's reduction in output induces free riders to expand their output. Consequently, a merger is profitable for those who merge if and only if a sufficiently large number of firms take part in it.[26]

In the applied industrial-organization literature, it has always been claimed that real-world mergers are rarely profitable. As Scherer (1980) put it:

---

[26] We mention that this paradoxical property is a feature of Cournot competition. Under Bertrand competition with differentiated products, mergers tend to be profitable even if they include only two firms (see Deneckere and Davidson (1985)).

...the weight of the postmerger profitability evidence for an assortment of nations suggests that on average the private gains from mergers were either negative or insignificantly different from zero.

This suggests that the observations made in this section are often learned the hard way, after incurring heavy losses.[27]

3.4.7 The Welfare Loss of Cournot Oligopoly

We have shown that the Cournot oligopoly produces *too much*, relative to the cartel solution. Now we show that it also produces *too little*, relative to the Pareto optimum. As welfare criterion we use again the total surplus function $T : [0, \bar{X}] \to \mathbb{R}$ given by

$$T(X) := \int_0^X P(\tilde{X}) \, d\tilde{X} - \sum_{i=1}^n C_i(x_i), \quad X := \sum_{i=1}^n x_i. \tag{3.80}$$

The Pareto optimum is defined as the maximizer of T and denoted by the superscript *PO*.

Proposition 3.10 *The Cournot oligopoly produces too little, relative to the Pareto optimum* $(X^C < X^{PO})$.

Proof In two steps: First, we prove the assertion assuming well-behavedness of the welfare optimization problem; second, we prove well-behavedness.

By the well-behavedness assumption, the unique maximizer x^{PO} of T is characterized by the Kuhn–Tucker conditions (existence of interior solutions is guaranteed by (A3))

$$P(X^{PO}) = C_i'(x_i^{PO}) \quad \forall i, \quad \text{where} \quad \sum_{i=1}^n x_i^{PO} = X^{PO}.$$

Assume, *per absurdum*, that $X^C \geq X^{PO}$. Then there exists at least one firm, say firm r, that produces at least as much under the Cournot equilibrium, $x_r^C \geq x_r^{PO}$. Therefore, by the convexity of cost functions,

$$P(X^{PO}) = C_r'(x_r^{PO}) \leq C_r'(x_r^C).$$

By (3.63) and the fact that P is strictly monotone decreasing, one has

$$P(X^C) > P'(X^C)x_r^C + P(X^C) = C_r'(x_r^C).$$

Therefore, by combining the two results, one concludes that $P(X^C) > P(X^{PO})$, which contradicts the assumption that P is monotone decreasing in X.

The welfare maximization problem is well behaved if T is strictly concave in the vector x. We now show that this property holds. Recall, from the Appendix C, that

---

[27] More evidence to support this claim was published by Ravenscraft and Scherer (1989).

$\mathcal{T}$ is strictly concave if its Hessian matrix, $H(\mathcal{T})$, is negative definite. Obviously,

$$H(\mathcal{T}) := \begin{bmatrix} P' - C_1'' & P' & P' & \cdots & P' \\ P' & P' - C_2'' & P' & \cdots & P' \\ \vdots & \vdots & \vdots & \ddots & \vdots \\ P' & P' & P' & \cdots & P' - C_n'' \end{bmatrix}$$

$$= P' \begin{bmatrix} 1 & \cdots & 1 \\ 1 & \cdots & 1 \\ \vdots & \ddots & \vdots \\ 1 & \cdots & 1 \end{bmatrix} - \begin{bmatrix} C_1'' & 0 & \cdots & 0 \\ 0 & C_2'' & \cdots & 0 \\ \vdots & \vdots & \ddots & \vdots \\ 0 & 0 & \cdots & C_n'' \end{bmatrix}.$$

Pre- and postmultiply with x^T and x respectively, and one has, for all $x \in \mathbb{R}^n$, $x \neq 0$,

$$x^T H(\mathcal{T}) x = P' \left(\sum_{i=1}^n x_i \right)^2 - \sum_{i=1}^n C_i'' x_i^2 < 0,$$

which proves negative definiteness. ☐

Combining this with previous results, we summarize with the following rankings:

$$X^{PO} > X^C > X^K \quad \text{and} \quad \mathcal{T}^{PO} > \mathcal{T}^C > \mathcal{T}^K. \tag{3.81}$$

You probably guessed this result. Haven't we shown already that the Cournot equilibrium does not maximize total surplus, but instead maximizes a weighted sum of total surplus and total profits, giving "too much" weight to profits? However, do not overlook that this representation of the Cournot equilibrium is feasible only if firms have uniform cost functions.

3.4.8 A Corrective Tax

If the Cournot equilibrium gives rise to a welfare loss, perhaps an intelligent government can do something about it. If the government has complete information about demand and cost functions, this task is indeed fairly easy. Just adapt the lessons from corrective taxation of Cournot monopoly. The basic idea is to induce firms to produce more by paying an appropriate subsidy per output unit, and at the same time skim profits by a simple lump-sum tax. The only difficulty is to determine the right subsidy and tax rates.

A corrective tax should have various properties that characterize an ideal mechanism.

Definition 3.2 An ideal mechanism 1) implements the maximum total surplus as a corrected Cournot equilibrium, 2) does not contribute to an unbalanced budget, and 3) makes no one worse off. In addition, one may require that it eliminate profits.

Consider the *tax scheme* (s_i, t_i, T), where s_i denotes a fixed subsidy per output unit, t_i a lump-sum tax on firm i, and T a lump-sum tax on the group of consumers.

Set (s_i, t_i, T) as follows:

$$s_i := -P'(X^{PO})x_i^{PO} > 0, \quad t_i := s_i x_i^{PO} - \left(\pi_i^C - \pi_i^{PO}\right), \quad T := \sum_{i=1}^{n}\left(\pi_i^C - \pi_i^{PO}\right),$$

where π_i is the profit before tax and subsidy.

Proposition 3.11 *The tax scheme* (s_i, t_i, T) *is an ideal mechanism.*

Proof It is immediately obvious that the mechanism leaves net profits and the government's budget unchanged if and only if x^{PO} is the unique tax-*cum*-subsidy-induced Cournot equilibrium. Consequently, if the mechanism succeeds, the entire welfare gain goes to consumers, and nobody is made worse off. Therefore, all that remains to be shown is that x^{PO} is indeed the unique equilibrium. Compute marginal profits, evaluated at x^{PO}, and one finds, using the specification of s_i,

$$\frac{\partial \pi_i(x^{PO})}{\partial x_i} = P(X^{PO}) - C_i'(x_i^{PO}) = 0 \qquad \forall i.$$

Therefore, x^{PO} is indeed a tax-*cum*-subsidy-induced Cournot equilibrium, and by our basic existence theorem it is the only one.[28]   □

Remark 3.6 If the mechanism should also eliminate profits, just remove the lump-sum tax on consumers, which simplifies it considerably, and change the lump-sum tax on firms to $t_i := s_i x_i^{PO} - \pi_i^{PO}$.

Of course, it is hardly reasonable to assume that a government agency has reliable information about firms' cost functions. But without this information, the mechanism cannot work. This suggests a search for ideal or at least acceptable mechanisms that have lower information requirements, just as in Section 2.3.

3.4.9 The Generalized ISS Regulatory Mechanism*

Recall the *incremental surplus subsidy* (ISS) mechanism from Section 2.3.2. It is easy to adapt it to the Cournot oligopoly environment.

For simplicity, suppose n identical firms operate repeatedly in a market characterized by stationary demand and cost functions. Consider symmetric equilibria $(X_t = nx_t)$. In the spirit of the ISS mechanism the regulator subsidizes the increment of consumer surplus between periods $t-1$ and t, and taxes away the profit earned in $t-1$, as stated in the following subsidy rule:[29]

$$S_t := \int_{x_t}^{x_{t-1}} y P'(ny)\, dy - (P(X_{t-1})x_{t-1} - C(x_{t-1})). \tag{3.82}$$

---

[28] Include the tax and subsidy as part of the cost function, and it follows immediately that the tax scheme does not change assumptions (A1)–(A4). Therefore, existence and uniqueness follow from our basic existence theorem.

[29] The following slightly more complicated subsidy rule was proposed by Schwermer (1995):

$$S_t := \int_{x_t}^{0} y P(X_t^- + y)\, dy - \int_{x_{t-1}}^{0} y P(X_{t-1}^- + y)\, dy - (P(X_{t-1})x_{t-1} - C(x_{t-1})),$$

where X^- denotes the aggregate output of all rival firms. The proof is again straightforward.

Proposition 3.12 *The incremental surplus subsidy rule (3.82) induces output efficiency $(P(X_t) = C'(x_t))$ in all periods and zero profits in all periods except the first.*

Proof The proof is the same as in the case of monopoly regulation. □

The ISS is appealing in that it does not require the regulator to know firms' cost functions. However, it lacks incentives to control managers' appetite for fringe benefits, as we emphasized in Chapter 2, and it needs to be adjusted if the demand or cost environment is not stationary. Also keep in mind that it may be just as important to change the number of active firms as to correct the output distortion. If unit costs are decreasing, the best regulatory policy is to transform oligopoly into monopoly, and then apply monopoly regulation.

3.4.10 Entry*

Up to this point, the number of oligopolists in the market has been given. Similarly, we have assumed that the actions of suppliers in other markets either are given or can be ignored. This procedure is not entirely satisfactory for at least two reasons:

- markets are open and admit free entry and exit, unless the law restricts entry by direct regulation or through patents and licensing;
- the demand for different products is interdependent, so that firms are subject to strategic interdependency both within and across markets.

The second criticism points at a limitation of *partial analysis* – to which we will nevertheless confine ourselves in this chapter. Therefore, we concentrate on the first issue and ask: How does the Cournot equilibrium change as the number of firms is increased, and what are the consequences of free entry?

Limiting Properties

As the number of firms is increased, one may conjecture that the market becomes more competitive and continuously approaches the familiar model of competitive price-takership. Plausible as this may sound, it is, however, not quite correct. True, as more firms enter and each firm produces a diminishing share of market supply, the elasticity of demand facing the firm eventually tends to infinity. But the effect of additional output on price depends on the *slope* of the demand function, not the elasticity.[30] Therefore, you may increase the number of firms as much as you like and still not always end up with price-takership.

In order to describe some limiting properties of the Cournot equilibrium in the long run without much technical apparatus, suppose all cost functions are uniform, so that the solution is symmetric. Also suppose all fixed costs are reversible (which is surely plausible in the assumed long run). Denote output per firm by $z := X/N$. Since X is bounded (see (A2) in Section 3.4.1), z tends to zero as N tends to infinity.

[30] This point was raised by Ruffin (1971).

The average cost is defined as the ratio of two functions $A(z) := C(z)/z$ that both tend to zero as z tends to zero.[31] Therefore, by L'Hospital's rule,

$$\lim_{N\to\infty} A(z(N)) = \lim_{z\to 0} A(z) = \lim_{z\to 0} C'(z) = \lim_{N\to\infty} C'(z(N)),$$

and by (3.63),

$$\lim_{N\to\infty} P(Nz(N)) = \lim_{N\to\infty} [C'(z(N)) - z(N)P'(z(N))] = \lim_{z\to 0} C'(z).$$

Hence, in the limit, the Cournot equilibrium price approaches marginal *and* average costs.

As is well known, in a (long-run) competitive equilibrium, the product price is equal to the minimal average cost, $\min_z A(z)$, and therefore the Cournot equilibrium price and quantity converge to the competitive solution if and only if $\lim_{z\to 0} C'(z) = \min_z A(z)$.

This condition is indeed satisfied as long as we stick to convex cost functions.

Proposition 3.13 *If the average cost function is convex, the Cournot equilibrium price and quantity converge to the competitive solution.*

However, once we remove the convexity of the cost function, we still have existence of a unique (symmetric) Cournot equilibrium,[32] but it does not converge to the competitive solution.

Proposition 3.14 *If the average cost function A is U-shaped, the Cournot equilibrium price always exceeds the competitive price.*

Proof This follows immediately from the well-known fact that average and marginal cost coincide at the point where the average cost reaches its minimum, and that average costs exceed marginal costs at all higher outputs.   □

Equilibrium Size

In the presence of indivisibilities and hence fixed costs, only a limited number of firms can be squeezed into a given market. So how many firms will enter, if entry is not restricted by patents or any other legal monopoly licensing?

The standard explanation of equilibrium size in symmetric oligopoly models is to treat the equilibrium number of firms as the largest integer $\bar{n}$ such that equilibrium profit per firm is nonnegative:

$$\bar{n} = \max\{n \in \mathbb{N} \mid P(nx^C)x^C - C(x^C) \geq 0\}. \tag{3.83}$$

But while this yields *one* equilibrium number of firms, the equilibrium size is usually not unique[33] unless all fixed costs are sunk.

In order to explain this point and show how large the range of equilibrium sizes may be, go back to our simple example of an n-firm Cournot oligopoly with a linear

[31] This would of course change if some fixed costs were irreversible, for then C would converge to the level of these reversible fixed costs and hence not to zero.
[32] Recall the result due to Roberts and Sonnenschein (1976) that was reported in Section 3.4.1.
[33] This was noticed, among others, by Mankiw and Whinston (1986).

inverse demand $P(X) := \max\{1 - X, 0\}$ and zero marginal cost, to which we now add fixed costs $F > 0$ of which the fraction $s \in [0, 1]$ is sunk. Denote the gross profit (before deducting F) in the n-firm Cournot equilibrium by

$$\Pi(n) := P(nx^C)x^C = \frac{1}{(1+n)^2}. \tag{3.84}$$

Also, let $\pi(n)$ denote the maximum gross profit that an $(n + 1)$th firm can earn by optimally responding to the n-firm industry equilibrium output level

$$\pi(n) := P(nx^C + x^*(nx^C))x^*(nx^C) = \frac{\Pi(n)}{4}. \tag{3.85}$$

Obviously, there cannot be more than $\bar{n}$ firms that enter in equilibrium, because otherwise at least one would make a loss. But there can also be strictly fewer. The reason is that, even if $n < \bar{n}$ firms are in the market, an $(n + 1)$th firm may be deterred from entering, if there is an equilibrium of the postentry Cournot subgame at which the $(n + 1)$th firm would not actually produce. This is possible if the $(n + 1)$th firm cannot cover its *nonsunk* fixed costs $(1 - s)F$, provided that the n firms threaten to stick to the n-firm equilibrium outputs x^C:

$$\pi(n) < (1 - s)F. \tag{3.86}$$

If (3.86) holds, this threat is credible, because it is an equilibrium of the Cournot subgame for the n firms to stick to the threat and for the $(n + 1)$th entrant not to produce.

In order to determine the range of equilibrium size, compute the real number n_1 that solves $\Pi(n_1) - F = 0$:

$$n_1 = \frac{1}{\sqrt{F}} - 1, \tag{3.87}$$

and the real n_0 that solves $\pi(n_0) - (1 - s)F = 0$:

$$n_0 = \frac{1}{2\sqrt{(1 - s)F}} - 1. \tag{3.88}$$

Obviously,

$$n_1 > n_0 \iff s < 0.75.$$

Therefore, we summarize:

Proposition 3.15 *Consider the linear-demand, zero-marginal-cost Cournot oligopoly with fixed cost $F \in (0, 1)$ of which the proportion $s \in (0, 1)$ is sunk. If $s < 0.75$, any integer $N \in [n_0, n_1]$ is an equilibrium number of firms. The equilibrium size is unique and then equal to $\bar{n}$ if and only if $s \geq 0.75$.*

Obviously, the range of equilibrium size increases as the degree of sunkness is diminished; and as s tends to zero, n_0 approaches $\frac{1}{2}n_1$.

As an illustration, suppose $F = 0.000001$ and $s = 0.001$.[34] Then, $n_1 = 1000$, so that 1000 is an equilibrium number of firms (even if all fixed costs were sunk).

---

[34] Notice: F may be a larger number, in natural units. Recall that we have normalized the physical units in such a way that the unit price is in the interval [0, 1].

However, given the relatively small degree of sunkness, any integer between 501 (almost $\frac{1}{2}\bar{n}$) and 1000 is an equilibrium number of active firms.

In the face of this potential multiplicity of equilibria, what prediction of equilibrium size is the most plausible? One disturbing aspect of the equilibria that involve $n < \bar{n}$ firms is that they assume an asymmetry in the strategies that the n firms play relative to what the $(n + 1)$th entrant does. Asymmetric equilibria pose a difficult coordination problem, in particular since the active entrants earn positive profits and hence are strictly better off than the passive one. It is difficult to imagine how potential firms could resolve this coordination problem. This is why one is inclined to favor symmetric equilibria. But once we impose the requirement that the equilibria of each subgame should be *symmetric*, an additional entrant could always anticipate that the n incumbent firms accommodate its entry, so that $\bar{n}$ would be the unique equilibrium size. Therefore, the symmetry requirement supports the usual explanation of equilibrium size.

However, even the standard explanation of equilibrium size poses an unresolved coordination problem, as it fails to explain who enters and who stays out. This suggests that one should perhaps break more radically with the standard approach, and analyze entry decisions in the framework of symmetric mixed-strategy equilibria.[35]

Mixed Entry Strategies*

If all N potential competitors are identical, the equilibrium in mixed entry strategies is easy to develop. Let F be the sunk entry cost, and assume that equilibrium gross profits are decreasing in the number of active firms, for example as in the $\Pi(n)$ function stated in (3.84).

Suppose, in equilibrium each firm enters with probability μ. Consider any one firm. Randomizing can only be its best response, if it is indifferent between entry and nonentry. As usual in the analysis of mixed-strategy equilibria, this requirement helps us to actually determine μ.

There are $N - 1$ others. If n of them enter together with the one firm, the industry has altogether $n + 1$ active firms, and each earns the profit $\Pi(n + 1) - F$. The probability that n other firms enter is

$$\phi(n) := \binom{N-1}{n} \mu^n (1 - \mu)^{N-1-n}.$$

Therefore, the firm's payoff from *entry* is $\sum_{n=0}^{N-1} \phi(n)\Pi(n + 1) - F$. The payoff from *nonentry* is zero.

Putting pieces together, it follows that the equilibrium probability of entry must solve the following condition of indifference between entry and nonentry:[36]

$$\sum_{n=0}^{N-1} \binom{N-1}{n} \mu^n (1 - \mu)^{N-1-n} \Pi(n + 1) - F = 0. \qquad (3.89)$$

---

[35] For a strong defense of mixed entry strategies see Dixit and Shapiro (1986). Their model is summarized in the following subsection.

[36] Using the tools of first-order stochastic dominance, it is relatively easy to show that (3.89) has indeed a unique solution $\mu \in (0, 1)$. The proof is spelled out in detail in Section 5.5.

The mixed-strategy equilibrium is particularly interesting in a dynamic framework if entry is possible in each of many successive rounds of the market game. The model then gives rise to an appealing explanation of the evolution of the market structure. Typically, the industry starts out with a small number of active firms, leading to transient profits. These profits are then eliminated by successive entry, until an absorbing state is reached where no further entry is profitable, often ending with overcrowding and irrecoverable losses. Paradoxically, high transient profits speed up the subsequent entry process to such an extent that the early incumbents would actually prefer to start out with more competitors. Therefore, the worst that can happen to a firm is to find itself in the transient position of a monopolist.[37]

Are Cartel Laws Good for Business?

In a closed market, cartel laws are definitely not in the interest of firms, as we showed in Section 3.4.6. Interestingly, this assessment does not extend to open markets with free entry and exit. As Selten (1984) has shown, under free entry quite the opposite may be true. Paradoxically, equilibrium profits may be higher if cartels are effectively prevented by cartel laws, so that firms themselves should be the most ardent supporters of antitrust legislation.

What is so radically different about the effect of cartel laws if we admit free entry and exit? The key observation is that collusive joint profit maximization permits a greater number of firms in the market than noncollusive behavior, essentially because, at each given number of firms, collusion restricts output. Therefore, if cartels are legal, markets tend to be overcrowded. This entry effect counteracts the obvious advantages of collusion. And as Selten (1984) has shown, under reasonable assumptions on the distribution of market parameters it even outweighs it, so that, ironically, the expected sum of all profits is indeed increased by cartel laws.

*3.4.11 Exit**

We have discussed entry in markets with stationary demand. But what about the exit decision in shrinking markets?

Markets with shrinking demand are part of a changing economy. New goods tend to crowd out other, less desirable ones. This change may be sudden and violent, forcing firms to exit immediately. But often it is gradual and progresses at a fairly predictable pace.

Sooner or later, the oligopolists facing a shrinking market have to leave it. If they all hang on, everyone makes losses, and if they all leave, profit opportunities are forgone. Therefore, the order in which they exit does matter. But who leaves first and who last? Clearly, no individual oligopolist can decide for himself without making conjectures about his rivals' exit decisions. Therefore, the exit decision is a strategic decision problem.

Strategic exit decisions have been analyzed by several authors, notably by Fudenberg and Tirole (1986), Ghemawat and Nalebuff (1985, 1990), Lieberman

---

[37] See the simulations reported in Dixit and Shapiro (1986) where the value of incumbency is increasing in n until the static equilibrium number of firms is reached.

(1990), and Whinston (1988). Here we will briefly review the model by Ghemawat and Nalebuff in a simple duopoly framework. The main result will be that it is always the larger firm that exits first. After analyzing the exit game we will also briefly discuss an integrated entry plus exit game. As it turns out, adding the exit stage to a commonly used entry game leads to considerably changed predictions.

Assumptions

We stay in the framework of the Cournot duopoly, but modify two assumptions:

(A1) The inverse demand function $P(X, t)$ is strictly monotone decreasing in time t and in demand X; as t becomes arbitrarily large, $P(X, t)$ comes arbitrarily close to zero; however, marginal revenue is always positive.[38]

(A2) Each firm has a given capacity K_i; therefore, $x_i(t) \leq K_i$ $\forall t$.

(A3) Firm 1 is larger than firm 2: $K_1 > K_2$.

(A4) The cost functions C_i, defined on $[0, K_i]$, exhibit constant operating costs (normalized to zero) and *reversible* (or quasi-) fixed costs (with $c > 0$):

$$C_i(x_i) = \begin{cases} cK_i & \text{if } x_i > 0, \\ 0 & \text{otherwise.} \end{cases} \qquad (3.90)$$

(A5) Exit is irreversible.

(A6) Each duopolist maximizes the present value of profits; the discount rate r is constant.

At the beginning of the planning horizon, $t = 0$, both firms just break even under full capacity utilization:

$$P(K_1 + K_2, 0) = c. \qquad (3.91)$$

Since demand shrinks, there exists a finite date t_i^* at which firm i exits even if it is an uncontested monopoly at full capacity utilization:

$$P(K_i, t_i^*) = c. \qquad (3.92)$$

Obviously,

$$t_1^* < t_2^*. \qquad (3.93)$$

Solution of the Exit Game

Each duopolist has to choose two actions: the date of exit, τ_i, and the supply $x_i(t)$ for all t prior to τ_i. We begin with some elementary properties of pure-strategy equilibria $(\tau_i^*, x_i^*(t))$.

Proposition 3.16 *A pure-strategy Nash equilibrium has the following properties:*

1. $x_i^*(t) = K_i$ for all $t \in [0, \tau_i^*]$ *(full capacity utilization)*;
2. $\tau_i^* \leq t_i^*$ *(τ_i is bounded)*;
3. *either* $\tau_1^* = 0$ *or* $\tau_2^* = 0$ *(exactly one firm exits immediately)*.

---

[38] As an illustration, consider the constant-elasticity inverse demand function $P(X, t) := X^\beta e^{-t}$ with $\beta \in (-1, 0)$.

Proof 1: By assumption, marginal revenue is always positive. Therefore, each firm will choose full capacity utilization unless it exits. 2: By definition of t_i^*, it never pays to stay in the market beyond time t_i^*. Part 3 follows immediately from the fact that the two firms cannot coexist without suffering losses. □

In a pure-strategy Nash equilibrium one duopolist leaves right away, at $t = 0$. But who leaves and who stays? The answer depends on the monopoly payoff that the smaller firm 2 can earn during the $(t_1^*, t_2^*]$ period, relative to the loss that it would have to endure during the period $[0, t_1^*]$ if the rival firm 1 also stayed until time t_1^*.

Evidently, the smaller firm 2 has $\tau_2 = t_2^*$ as its dominant strategy if the present value of the monopoly profit during the interval $[t_1^*, t_2^*]$ exceeds the present value of the loss that it suffers in the worst case during the interval $[0, t_1^*]$ (if firm 1 ever stays in the market that long):

$$\int_{t_1^*}^{t_2^*} [P(K_2, t) - c]K_2 e^{-rt}\, dt \geq - \int_0^{t_1^*} [P(K_1 + K_2, t) - c]K_2 e^{-rt}\, dt \quad (3.94)$$

In that case the larger firm 1 exits right away, and the smaller firm 2 stays until t_2^*. However, except for this extreme case, there are always two equilibria: one where firm 1 yields and exits right away, and one where firm 2 yields. Therefore:

Proposition 3.17 *The exit game has the following Nash equilibria:*

1. *if the present-value condition (3.94) applies, then $\tau_1^* = 0$, $\tau_2^* = t_2^*$ is the unique equilibrium;*
2. *if condition (3.94) does not hold, $\tau_1 = t_1^*$, $\tau_2 = 0$ is also an equilibrium.*

In either case, $x_i^*(t) = K_i \ \forall t \in [0, \tau_i^*]$.

Proof Using the results of Proposition 3.16, it is obvious that the strategies have the mutual best-response property. If the present-value condition (3.94) holds, it is a dominant strategy for the smaller firm 2 to stay until t_2^*. The asserted equilibria are in pure strategies. The impossibility of a mixed-strategy equilibrium is shown in the proof of Proposition 3.18. □

This leaves us with a multiplicity problem. But, as you will see in just a moment, only one equilibrium is meaningful because only one passes the subgame-perfectness test.

The Unique Subgame-Perfect Equilibrium

By assumption, no duopolist can precommit to a certain date of exit, which means that firms may always reconsider their exit strategy until they have actually left the market. Also, the exit decision is one under complete information. Therefore, at each point in time, the duopolists play a well-defined exit subgame. Consequently, subgame perfectness is the appropriate equilibrium concept.[39] Subgame perfectness

---

[39] As we explained before, a Nash equilibrium is subgame-perfect if it is a Nash equilibrium of each subgame.

eliminates all those Nash equilibria that are not plausible because they involve an exit strategy that is not credible.

Proposition 3.18 *The exit game has a unique subgame-perfect Nash equilibrium: the larger firm exits right away, and the smaller firm stays until t_2^*.*[40]

Proof Define the time t_A as the first date such that the smaller firm 2 is willing to sustain losses during the period $[t_A, t_1^*]$ to reap monopoly profits during the period (t_1^*, t_2^*). Since the larger firm 1 exits no later than at t_1^*, the smaller firm 2 will definitely stay until t_2^* if it is still in the market at date t_A. But then firm 1 will exit right away, and firm 2 enjoys monopoly profits during the entire period $(t_A, t_2^*]$. Given this solution of the t_A-subgame, define t_B as the first date such that firm 2 is willing to sustain losses during the period $(t_B, t_A]$ to reap monopoly profits during the interval $(t_A, t_2^*]$. Again, it follows that the equilibrium exit strategy of the t_B-subgame requires firm 1 to exit right away and firm 2 to stay until t_2^*. Next, compute t_C, applying the same consideration, and note that t_C is a larger step back from t_B than t_B was from t_A, since inverse demand is increasing as one moves backwards in time. Therefore, the steps are moving toward the origin at an increasing rate. Hence, this process of backward induction continues until $t = 0$. A similar argument excludes mixed strategy equilibria. Just note that firm 1 will not randomize its exit decision at the t_A-subgame. Thus firm 1 will exit with probability 1 at t_A. Using a procedure such as the above, one can work backwards to time t_B etc. until time $t = 0$. □

Discussion

The analysis of strategic exit decisions took firms' capacities as given. But capacities are chosen at some point. Rational firms anticipate the outcome of the later exit game already when they contemplate entry. Typically, firms go through a life cycle, beginning with entry and expansion and ending with shrinking outputs and ultimate exit. This suggests that one should merge the analysis of entry and exit, rather than study them in isolation. As it turns out, this merger leads to some rather surprising and unusual results, which are in stark contrast to the predictions of isolated entry models.

For example, consider the entry model in the spirit of Dixit (1980). Assume that one firm, the incumbent, enters before the rival contemplates entry. Entry requires a certain fixed entry cost that is fully sunk, plus the choice of capacity which serves as a commitment mechanism. After both firms have made their entry decision and chosen their capacities, in sequential order, they play a standard Cournot-competition game. Therefore, the model has a Stackelberg leader–follower structure.

Assuming a stationary (or a one-shot) demand, the entry model predicts that the incumbent chooses a higher capacity than in the corresponding Cournot model and

---

[40] In a subsequent paper, Ghemawat and Nalebuff (1990) analyze the case in which firms can divest incrementally rather than on an all-or-nothing basis. In this case, the larger firm divests first in equilibrium, and continues to do so until it has shrunk to the size of the smaller firm. Subsequently, both firms gradually shrink together.

than an uncontested monopolist. The reason is that it uses its first-mover position to induce the rival to choose a low capacity – under certain circumstances, even to stay out of the market altogether. An immediate implication is that *potential entry* is socially useful, because it gives rise to a higher market output than an uncontested monopoly – even if the incumbent deters entry.

As it turns out, these predictions no longer hold true if the entry model is augmented by assuming that demand will shrink after some time so that firms face an exit game, at some point. To the contrary, it turns out that after adding the exit stage, potential competition may be socially harmful, even if the exit stage is arbitrarily short. We close with a brief sketch of the main arguments that lead to this conclusion.[41]

In a first step, notice, from the solution of the above exit game, that the firm with the smaller capacity will exit at time $t_0(K)$, implicitly defined by the condition[42]

$$P(K, t_0(K)) = c, \qquad K := K_1 + K_2. \tag{3.95}$$

Therefore, it is straightforward to compute the *reduced-form profit function*, defined on capacities K_1, K_2. Denote this function by Π with image $\Pi(K_1, K_2)$. Then it is easy to solve for the equilibrium capacities, as follows.

Let firm 1 be the incumbent and firm 2 the Stackelberg follower. Since 2 chooses its capacity after K_1 has become public information, firm 2's equilibrium choice of capacity is fully described by the reaction function $k : \mathbb{R}_+ \to \mathbb{R}_+$, defined as

$$k(K_1) := \arg\max_K \Pi(K, K_1), \tag{3.96}$$

and therefore, firm 1's equilibrium strategy is

$$K_1^* := \arg\max_K \Pi(K, k(K)). \tag{3.97}$$

Which capacities actually are chosen in equilibrium depends on the parameters. Three parameters play a pivotal role. These are the capacities that would be chosen by a monopolist,

$$K^M := \arg\max_K [P(K, t) - c]K,$$

and the two capacities at which a monopolist exactly breaks even:[43]

$$\tilde{K} := \min\{K \in \mathbb{R}_+ \mid [P(K, t) - c]K = 0\},$$

$$C := \max\{K \in \mathbb{R}_+ \mid [P(K, t) - c]K = 0\}.$$

We now give two examples. In both of them we assume that the phase during which demand shrinks away is very short, so that it has a negligible effect on payoffs.

---

[41] For a more detailed analysis of the integrated entry plus exit game, see Fishman (1990).

[42] In equilibrium, firms will never choose the same capacity; therefore, we need not be concerned with this case.

[43] Why are there two such levels of capacity? Just recall that there are two cost components: the proportional capacity cost plus the sunk entry cost. Therefore, the average cost function intersects the inverse demand function either twice or not at all. If it did not intersect at all, the market would not be feasible in the first place, which is why this case is ignored.

Example 3.7 Suppose $K^M > C/2$, $k(C/2) = 0$, $\Pi(C/2, 0) > 0$. Then the equilibrium capacities are

$$K_1 = \frac{C}{2}, \qquad K_2 = 0. \tag{3.98}$$

Why? First of all, $K_1 = 0$ is a best response to firm 1's choice because $k(C/2) = 0$. Of course, firm 1 would like to increase capacity up to K^M if it could still keep 2 out of the market. But, if 1 increases capacity above $C/2$, it is 2's best response to follow suit and choose a capacity just marginally below K_1. For, in this case, the overall capacity is greater than C, so that the larger firm 1 is forced to exit right away, hence assuring a positive profit to the second mover, firm 2. This shows how adding an exit phase may give rise to *full entry deterrence*, and this at a supply which is paradoxically below that of an uncontested monopoly.

Example 3.8 Suppose $\tilde{K} > C/2$. Then there are two equilibrium capacities: one that gives rise to *full entry deterrence* at a price at which the incumbent earns zero profits,

$$K_1 = \tilde{K}, \qquad K_2 = 0, \tag{3.99}$$

and another where the entrant stays out and the second mover, firm 2, sets the monopoly capacity,

$$K_1 = 0, \qquad K_2 = K^M. \tag{3.100}$$

The capacities (3.99) are an equilibrium outcome because firm 2 has to choose at least $\tilde{K}$ if it enters (this is the minimum capacity – everything less leads to a sure loss). Therefore, if firm 2 enters, it will be the larger firm. And since overall capacity is above C, firm 2 thus induces an immediate exit game in which it will be forced to leave right away. Similarly, the capacities (3.100) are an equilibrium outcome, as $K_1 = 0$ gives zero profits just like $K_1 = \tilde{K}$, combined with $K_2 = 0$. In either case, potential competition does not contribute to drive output above that of an uncontested monopoly. True, if capacities are chosen as in (3.100), potential competition drives profits down to zero. However, paradoxically, the overall output is below that of an uncontested monopoly, so that potential competition is actually harmful.

Both examples show that adding an exit stage to a standard entry model gives rise to quite unusual and paradoxical results, even if the exit stage is arbitrarily short. The most counterintuitive result was that *potential competition may be harmful* under reasonable circumstances.

3.5 More on Bertrand Competition

Of all three basic oligopoly models, Bertrand's is the most appealing in terms of the assumed pricing mechanism, but the least plausible in terms of results. The nice feature is that firms themselves set prices without the help of a fictitious auctioneer. The unconvincing feature – sometimes referred to as the *Bertrand paradox* – is that it gives rise to the perfectly competitive outcome, regardless of the number of oligopolists if there are at least two. Of course, this result may be well liked by those who are committed to the simple competitive paradigm (which is why it is sometimes ridiculed by saying that "in Chicago two is a large number"). But most economists have more confidence in the Cournot result despite the bothersome role of the auctioneer.

On a closer look it turns out that price competition is not the villain. Rather, the Bertrand paradox is due to other specific assumptions of Bertrand's modeling of price competition, such as the assumed lack of capacity constraints and the particular cost functions. Once you deviate just slightly from this particular case, the paradox vanishes.

The importance of Bertrand competition is that it can provide economists with a convincing price formation story. Therefore, it is well worthwhile to invest some more effort to get a fuller understanding of it.

The emphasis in this section is on the effect of capacity constraints. Among other results, you will learn that the Bertrand model may lead to some very noncompetitive results. In particular, even the monopoly outcome is a Bertrand equilibrium if capacities are sufficiently scarce. Furthermore, we will show that, for an intermediate range of capacities, no pure-strategy equilibrium exists, and Bertrand competition gives rise to random sales. As capacity is further increased, the equilibrium reaches the perfectly competitive outcome, as in the simple Bertrand story.

3.5.1 Capacity-Constrained Price Competition: An Example

Go back to our basic Bertrand competition duopoly, and add the assumption that each firm has the same fixed production capacity, denoted by $k \in \mathbb{R}_+$. All other assumptions of the basic model are maintained. In particular, marginal cost is zero, and market demand has the simplest possible form,

$$X(p) := \max\{1 - p, 0\}. \tag{3.101}$$

In addition to the assumptions of the standard Bertrand model we assume that there are n identical consumers. Therefore, consumers' demand functions X_ν are equal to

$$X_\nu(p) := \frac{1}{n} X(p), \qquad \nu = 1, \ldots, n. \tag{3.102}$$

With limited capacity it can now happen that one firm is unable to serve the demand for its product, so that some demand spills over to the rival seller. But how much spills over depends on the particular rationing rule employed by the capacity constrained seller. In this section we consider a particular case known as *random rationing*.

Random Rationing

Suppose the two firms have set distinct prices. Let p_l be the low and p_h the high price, and assume that p_l is such that firm l is capacity-constrained, $1 - p_l > k$.

Then firm l cannot serve the entire demand, and some demand spills over to the high-price seller.

Under *random rationing* each buyer has the same chance of buying at the low price. The number of buyers who are served by the low-price seller is $k/X_v(p_l)$, and the number of buyers who are not served at the discount price is (ignoring integer constraints)

$$n_h := n - \frac{k}{X_v(p_l)} = n\left[1 - \frac{k}{X(p_l)}\right].$$

Therefore, the high-price seller h faces the *residual demand* $\tilde{X}$, which is determined as follows:

$$\tilde{X}(p_h, p_l, k) := n_h X_v(p_h)$$
$$= \frac{X(p_l) - k}{X(p_l)} X(p_h)$$
$$= \max\left\{\frac{1 - p_l - k}{1 - p_l}(1 - p_h), 0\right\}.$$
(3.103)

Some Preliminaries

To prepare the analysis of the modified Bertrand model, we introduce some useful concepts and basic relationships. First, we ask: what price would be set by a monopolist seller? Obviously, a monopolist calls the *monopoly price*

$$p^M(k) := \max\left\{\tfrac{1}{2}, 1 - k\right\}$$
(3.104)

where $\tfrac{1}{2}$ is the unconstrained monopoly price if capacity does not bind.

Next, ask: what price would a monopolist call who controls only *residual demand* $\tilde{X}$? The answer is similar. The residual-demand monopolist calls the *residual-demand monopoly price*

$$\tilde{p}^M(k, p_l) := \max\left\{\tfrac{1}{2}, \hat{p}\right\},$$
(3.105)

where $\hat{p}(k, p_l)$ is the price at which residual demand matches the given capacity supply:

$$\hat{p}(k, p_l) := 1 - k\frac{1 - p_l}{1 - p_l - k}.$$
(3.106)

The price $\tfrac{1}{2}$ enters simply because the maximizer of

$$p_h \tilde{X}(p_h, p_l) = \frac{1 - p_l - k}{1 - p_l}(1 - p_h)p_h$$

over p_h is the same as that of $p_h X(p_h) = p_h(1 - p_h)$, which is the unconstrained monopoly price $\tfrac{1}{2}$.

Another useful concept is the *accommodating price*, $p^A(k)$, defined as the price that clears the market if both sellers dump their entire capacity. The accommodating price is equal to

$$p^A(k) := P(2k) = \max\{1 - 2k, 0\}, \tag{3.107}$$

And if both firms call $p^A(k)$, the firms' profit is equal to

$$\pi^A(k) := p^A(k)k. \tag{3.108}$$

Using these concepts, we collect three useful results:

Lemma 3.2 $\pi^A(k)$ *has a unique global maximum at the capacity that supports the monopoly outcome, which is* $k = \frac{1}{4}$. *Therefore*

$$\pi^A(k) < \pi^A(\tfrac{1}{4}) = \tfrac{1}{8} \qquad \forall k \neq \tfrac{1}{4}. \tag{3.109}$$

Lemma 3.3 (Best-Response Properties) *1) If firm i calls $p_i > p^M(k)$, it is firm j's best response to underbid i and call the monopoly price $p^M(k)$; 2) if a firm is committed to call a higher price than its rival, it should call the residual demand monopoly price $\tilde{p}^M(k, p_l)$.*

Proof Obvious. □

Lemma 3.4 *A pure-strategy equilibrium must be symmetric.*

Proof Suppose, *per absurdum*, that there is an asymmetric pure-strategy equilibrium where firms set distinct prices, $p_h > p_l$. By Lemma 3.3 it follows that one must have $p_l \leq p^M(k)$. If $p_l < p^M(k)$, the low price-seller would gain by raising his price, moving towards $p^M(k)$ while staying below p_h. In turn, if $p_l = p^M(k) < p_h$, the high-price seller would gain by lowering his price just marginally below $p^M(k)$. □

Low Capacities – Some Very Noncompetitive Results

In stark contrast to the simple Bertrand model, which predicts the competitive outcome, low capacities give rise to some very noncompetitive results. Even the monopoly outcome can be a Bertrand equilibrium. Indeed, under random rationing, any price at or above the monopoly price is a Bertrand equilibrium, if capacities are sufficiently scarce.

Proposition 3.19 *Suppose $k \in [0, \frac{1}{4}]$ or $k \geq 1$. The Bertrand-competition game has a unique pure-strategy equilibrium that has both firms call the accommodating price $p^A(k)$.*

Proof If $k \geq 1$, firms are never capacity-constrained, which takes us right back to the standard Bertrand model. As we know already, the unique equilibrium is then $p^A(k) = 0$. Therefore, we need only consider the case $k \in [0, \frac{1}{4}]$.

First, we prove that $p^A(k)$ is indeed a pure-strategy equilibrium. For this purpose, suppose the rival sets $p^A(k)$. Then *underbidding* does not pay, since the firm has already full capacity utilization at $p^A(k)$ and cannot take advantage from extra demand anyway. But could it gain from *overbidding*? The answer is no, for the following reason. By Lemma 3.3 we know that if one chooses to overbid, one should always call the residual demand monopoly price. But

$$\tilde{p}^M(k, p^A(k)) = \max\left\{\frac{1}{2}, 1 - k\frac{1 - p^A(k)}{1 - p^A(k) - k}\right\}$$

$$= \max\left\{\frac{1}{2}, 1 - 2k\right\} \qquad \text{by (3.107)}$$

$$= p^A(k), \qquad \text{since} \quad k \leq \frac{1}{4}.$$

Therefore, overbidding does not pay either.

Second, we prove uniqueness by contradiction. Suppose, *per absurdum*, that the game has another pure strategy equilibrium. By Lemma 3.4 this equilibrium must be symmetric. Therefore, the uniform equilibrium price is either higher or lower than $p^A(k)$. If it is lower, at least one firm cannot serve all demand and therefore benefits from raising its price, and if it is higher, at least one firm cannot sell its entire capacity and therefore has an incentive to underbid. Therefore, the equilibrium is also unique.   □

Corollary 3.2 *The equilibrium price is equal to the unconstrained Cournot monopoly price for $k = \frac{1}{4}$ and even higher for $k < \frac{1}{4}$.*

High Capacities – Nonexistence of a Pure-Strategy Equilibrium

But what happens if capacity is in the range $(\frac{1}{4}, 1)$? If the above existence result also applied in this case, even the Cournot outcome would be a Bertrand equilibrium for $k = \frac{1}{3}$. However, under random rationing this cannot hold true.[44] In fact, for all capacities in this range the Bertrand-competition game has no pure-strategy equilibrium at all.

Proposition 3.20 *Suppose $k \in (\frac{1}{4}, 1)$. The Bertrand-competition game has no pure-strategy equilibrium.*

Proof Recall that a pure-strategy equilibrium must be symmetric by Lemma 3.4. We proceed by trying all possible candidates for an equilibrium solution – but they all fail.

1. Obviously, no price above the accommodating price can be an equilibrium because underbidding is then better than matching.
2. This incentive to underbid vanishes once you reach $p^A(k)$, where both suppliers exhaust their capacity. However, if the rival has set $p^A(k)$, it is always better to overbid. For

---

[44] This result is, however, due to the particular rationing mechanism. Later, when we turn to parallel rationing, the Cournot price is not only a pure-strategy equilibrium, it is even the only equilibrium if capacities are choice variables in a two-stage game.

example, if $k \geq \frac{1}{2}$, matching yields the price $p^A(k) = 0$, whereas a price slightly higher than $p^A(k)$ yields a positive profit. And if $k \in (\frac{1}{4}, \frac{1}{2})$, matching $p^A(k)$ yields

$$\pi_i(p^A(k), p^A(k)) = \pi^A(k) < \frac{1}{8} \quad \forall k \in (\tfrac{1}{4}, 1), \quad \text{by (3.109)},$$

whereas overbidding up to $p = \frac{1}{2} > p^A(k)$ gives definitely more, since

$$\pi_i\left(\frac{1}{2}, p^A(k)\right) = \frac{1}{2} \min\left\{k, \max\left\{0, \frac{1 - p^A(k) - k}{1 - p^A(k)}\left(1 - \frac{1}{2}\right)\right\}\right\}$$

$$= \frac{1}{2} \min\left\{k, \frac{1}{4}\right\} \quad \text{by (3.107)}$$

$$= \frac{1}{8}, \quad \text{since} \quad k > \frac{1}{4}.$$

3. Of course, no price $p < p^A(k)$ can be a symmetric equilibrium because in that case at least one firm could not serve the entire demand, and therefore would benefit from raising its price. □

Incidentally, the nonexistence of a pure-strategy equilibrium for certain high levels of capacity was already observed by Edgeworth (1925) in his path-breaking contribution. He concluded that prices would be *cyclical* in this situation with successive underbidding, starting from the monopoly price down to a certain positive price, at which point one supplier raises the price back to the monopoly price and the whole sequence starts all over again. But, of course, such price dynamics could only occur if it were assumed from the outset that firms set prices repeatedly in some fixed sequential order.[45]

Random Sales

If a game has no pure-strategy equilibrium, you may always go to mixed strategies. In the present context, a mixed strategy is a probability distribution over the set of feasible prices. Therefore, if firms play mixed strategies, they pick their price at random. The outcome may be a cautious, high price at or near the monopoly price, or an aggressive price equal to the accommodating price, or anything in between. Such price-setting behavior can be interpreted as random sales.

Is existence, and possibly uniqueness, of a mixed-strategy equilibrium assured for all $k \in (\frac{1}{4}, 1)$? As simple as the present model may be, the answer is far from obvious. Indeed, standard existence theorems do not apply here. Recall that the existence theorem by Glicksberg (1952) that was quoted in Section 3.4.1 requires continuity of payoff functions in strategies. But as prices are changed, profits can make a discontinuous jump, violating continuity. However, since Glicksberg's condition is only sufficient and not also necessary, you cannot conclude that no equilibrium exists.

For the present example, the existence of mixed-strategy equilibria was proven by Beckmann and Hochstädter (1965),[46] who solved the equilibrium strategies

---

[45] In the literature on *dynamic* oligopoly games this sort of cyclical pricing has been derived from a dynamic game with staggered price setting, employing the concept of a "Markov perfect Nash equilibrium." See the section on "Edgeworth Cycles" in Maskin and Tirole (1988).

[46] If you read this article, watch out for one flaw in the proof of uniqueness.

explicitly. A similar result was obtained by Levitan and Shubik (1972) for the alternative, *parallel* rationing rule (see the next subsection for this rule). Finally, Dasgupta and Maskin (1986) have generalized Glicksberg's theorem in such a way that the continuity requirement is softened. As they showed, this generalization assures existence for a large class of capacity-constrained Bertrand models, including the present example. Their results were further generalized by Dixon (1984) for general convex cost functions, and by Simon (1987) to admit fixed costs.

Summary

If capacity is sufficiently scarce – the critical value is $k = \frac{1}{4}$ – the Bertrand game has a unique pure-strategy equilibrium. In this case, both firms set the accommodating price, which is at or above the monopoly price. Due to the shortage of capacity, underbidding does not pay, and since the price is at or above the monopoly price, overbidding does not pay either. Hence, shortage of capacity leads to quite noncompetitive results. If capacity is increased beyond this critical value, accommodation is no longer an equilibrium, and the game becomes more competitive. In an intermediate range of capacity, the game has an equilibrium only in mixed strategies, where firms pick a price at or below the monopoly price at random. If capacity is further increased to or beyond $k = 1$, the capacity constraint never binds and the market becomes perfectly competitive, as in the simple Bertrand story.

3.5.2 An Alternative Rationing Rule

The above example assumed random rationing. Of course, one can easily design alternative rationing rules. Their adoption may lead to a different price competition game. Therefore it is important to decide which rationing rule is the most plausible.

At first glance random rationing looks like a fairly reasonable assumption. Sellers have usually little if no information about the preferences of individual customers. But without such information it would seem that firms sell on a first-come, first-served basis, which supports random rationing.

However, it turns out that sellers have a strong incentive to use more sophisticated rationing rules. And these are feasible even if firms are subject to incomplete information about individual preferences. More important yet, random rationing induces buyers to trade at an aftermarket, and the prospect of being able to trade there affects buyers' willingness to pay in the primary market in such a way that random rationing tends to lead to the same market outcome as more sophisticated rationing rules.

Parallel vs. Random Rationing

You may have noticed it already: random rationing is not efficient. Efficiency requires that the marginal willingness to pay be at least as high as marginal cost. From the perspective of buyers, the marginal cost of output is equal to the high price, say p_h. Yet those who were so lucky as to be served by the low-price seller buy as long

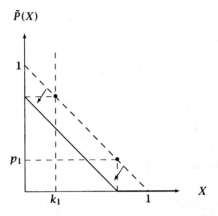

Figure 3.11. Residual Demand under Parallel Rationing.

as their marginal willingness to pay is not lower than the discount price p_l. Hence, with random rationing not all gains from trade are exploited.

In order to ration efficiently, customers have to be served in the order of their willingness to pay. By a well-known result from demand theory, the inverse market demand function can be interpreted as the aggregate marginal-willingness-to-pay function. Therefore, if the capacity of the low-price seller is rationed efficiently and P is strictly monotone decreasing, the marginal willingness to pay of the group of customers served by him must be greater or equal to $P(k)$. Consequently, the willingness-to-pay function facing the high-price seller is just

$$\tilde{P}(x_j, k) = P(x_j + k). \tag{3.110}$$

Therefore, under *efficient rationing*, the residual demand function $\tilde{X}$ is independent of the rival's discount price p_l and determined as

$$\tilde{X}(p_h, k) := \max\{X(p_h) - k, 0\}. \tag{3.111}$$

It is illustrated in Figure 3.11. Evidently, its graph is obtained by a parallel shift of the market inverse demand function. This is why efficient rationing is often called *parallel* rationing.

Parallel Rationing: Why and How

If a firm can choose between random and efficient rationing, which should it apply? At least two reasons suggest that efficient rationing is the better choice.

As a first observation, notice that parallel rationing leaves less residual demand to the rival firm because the highest willingness to pay is skimmed off first. This may suggest that parallel rationing is the more likely choice on the ground that it fits better to the noncooperative, rivalrous relationship between oligopolists. However, this argument is not compelling. Firms maximize their own profit. Why should they care to inflict harm on others if this does not raise their own profit?

A more convincing argument is that parallel rationing is more profitable, if it is done right. All that is needed is to sell *coupons* that give the bearer a transferable right to obtain output at the announced discount price. These coupons may be sold or distributed at a nominal fee on a first-come, first-served basis. No matter how their sale is organized, the aftermarket for coupons takes care of their efficient allocation.[47] For all those whose willingness to pay is below the high price p_h sell the coupons they have, whereas those whose willingness to pay is at or above p_h buy and exercise coupons. Therefore, the use of coupons implements efficient rationing. At the same time, coupons can be issued at a positive price, up to the difference between $\max\{\tilde{P}(k), p_h\}$ and the discount price p_l. Hence, parallel rationing is efficient as well as profitable.

Coupons are widely used in the U.S. in the retailing of groceries. In these applications coupons are used primarily to compete for the highly price-sensitive consumers. However, coupons have also been introduced into other markets. For example, airline coupons were introduced by United Airlines in 1979, after a long strike. United Airlines issued transferable coupons that entitled the bearer to a 50% discount on flights. Within a short time, an aftermarket developed, with active trading of coupons, and other airlines followed suit and issued similar coupons.[48]

3.5.3 Generalizations

Based on our discussion, there are several urgent generalizations:

1. One should analyze capacity-constrained price competition under parallel rather than random rationing.
2. One should consider the case when firms hold different capacities.
3. The choice of capacities should be endogenized.
4. Finally, one should allow general demand functions and introduce the costs of building and maintaining capacity.

All these generalizations will be pursued in the following section.

Having shown that the introduction of capacity constraints may lead to some very noncompetitive results, so that two is no longer a large number, one should also reexamine the effect of large numbers on the equilibrium outcome. This important topic was pursued by Allen and Hellwig (1986). Assuming exogenously given capacities and random rationing, they showed that the equilibrium probability distribution of prices converges towards the competitive outcome in the sense that, as the number of firms is increased, the probability mass is more and more concentrated in a small neighborhood of the competitive price, even though the support of prices always includes the monopoly price, regardless of the number of sellers. In a sequel article Vives (1986) explored the same issues under parallel rationing and showed that this leads to even nicer limit results, as even the support of prices tends to shrink to the competitive price in this case.[49]

---

[47] If all customers have similar individual demand functions, those who got a sufficient number of coupons exercise only some and sell the rest.
[48] Incidentally, Gelman and Salop (1983) showed how coupons can be used by a small-sized entrant to build a profitable yet uncontested niche in a market dominated by a large incumbent.
[49] For a simpler variation of the Bertrand–Edgeworth model see Dudey (1992).

3.6 A Defense of Cournot Competition*

After these preliminaries on capacity-constrained Bertrand competition it is time to generalize and come to an assessment of Cournot vs. Bertrand competition. Following Kreps and Scheinkman (1983), we consider a two-stage duopoly game. In the first stage firms choose capacity without knowing their rival's choice. Thereafter, capacities become common knowledge, and firms play a capacity-constrained Bertrand competition game with parallel rationing and unit prices as strategies.

The surprising result will be that the equilibrium outcome of the game is as if duopolists played a Cournot-market game. Hence, Cournot competition may be a good predictor of oligopolistic behavior even if firms set prices without the help of a fictitious auctioneer.

Assumptions

We work with a general downward-sloping demand function, assume parallel rather than random rationing, and introduce irreversible or sunk costs of building up capacity. The assumptions on demand and cost functions are borrowed from the general Cournot model in Section 3.4.1, except that assumptions on the cost function now refer to the cost of building up capacity. In addition there may be operating costs, but these are taken to be constant and hence are normalized to zero.

Procedure and Solution Concept

We proceed in two steps. First we analyze the stage-two-price competition subgame for all possible combinations of capacities. The rationale for isolating and beginning with the last stage of the game is that, once capacities have been chosen, the duopolists play a self-contained price-competition subgame, simply because they have complete information at this stage and because they cannot precommit to price strategies. The results of this subgame are used to compute the reduced-form payoffs as functions of capacities. These reduced-form payoffs serve as payoff functions of the stage-1 subgame, with capacities as strategies. In the language of game theory, the solution concept is that of a *subgame-perfect* Nash equilibrium.[50]

3.6.1 Benchmark Cournot Equilibrium

Our goal is to show that the equilibrium outcome of the two-stage game is the same as that of the corresponding, hypothetical Cournot game. For this purpose, we need to know the benchmark Cournot equilibrium, defined as the pair of outputs that are a Nash equilibrium of the corresponding Cournot game.

Two benchmark Cournot equilibria are considered: one if there are costs of output represented by the capacity cost functions C, and one if there are no such costs. The Cournot equilibrium with costs is denoted by k_1^C, k_2^C, and the one without by k_1^0, k_2^0.

---

[50] Recall that a Nash equilibrium is called subgame-perfect if it is a Nash equilibrium of each subgame. This solution concept was already used in Section 3.3 on Stackelberg competition.

Definition 3.3 (Cournot Reaction Functions) Write $r(k_j)$ for firm i's reaction function of the benchmark Cournot game with capacity costs, and $r_0(k_j)$ for the reaction function in the absence of capacity costs:

$$r(k_j) := \arg\max_x [P(x + k_j)x - C(x)],$$
$$r_0(k_j) := \arg\max_x P(x + k_j)x.$$

As one can easily confirm, these reaction functions exist, are continuous, and are monotone decreasing. Furthermore, one has

Lemma 3.5 *The best response output with capacity costs $r(k_j)$ is smaller than that without $r_0(k_j)$,*

$$r_0(k_j) > r(k_j) \qquad \text{for all } k_j,$$

unless $r_0(k_j) = 0$.

Proof This follows immediately from an analysis of the reaction functions in the Cournot oligopoly model.   □

Also, the benchmark Cournot equilibria (k_1^C, k_2^C), (k_1^0, k_2^0) are unique.

3.6.2 The Price-Competition Subgame

This subgame is played after firms' capacities are common knowledge. The game rule is that firms simultaneously call a unit price, subject to the commitment to service demand, up to capacity. Consumers shop at the discount seller unless demand is rationed, in which case some demand spills over to the high-price seller. Parallel rationing is used. If a tie occurs, demand is split evenly between the two firms.

As in the previous section, the equilibrium strategies depend upon what capacities are given. A unique pure-strategy equilibrium exists if and only if capacities are either "small" or "very large", each in a sense to be made precise below. In the intermediate range, the price competition game has only mixed-strategy equilibria.

Again, it is useful to define the *accommodating price* p^A, the *monopoly price* p_i^M, and the *residual demand monopoly price* $\tilde{p}_i^M$, as follows:[51]

$$p^A := P(k_1 + k_2), \tag{3.112}$$

$$p_i^M := \max\{P(k_i), P(r_0(0))\}, \tag{3.113}$$

$$\tilde{p}_i^M := \max\{p^A, P(k_j + r_0(k_j))\}. \tag{3.114}$$

Pure-Strategy Equilibria

Lemma 3.6 *In a pure-strategy equilibrium both firms name the accommodating price p^A.*

---

[51] If you wonder why r_0 rather than r enters, just recall that capacity costs are already sunk when the price-competition subgame is played.

Proof Suppose, *per absurdum*, that the equilibrium pure strategies differ, say $p_2 > p_1$. Then firm 1 is a monopolist for all prices $p \in [0, p_2)$, so that $p_1 = p_1^M$ must hold.[52] But then, the discount seller 1 leaves no residual demand to the high-price seller 2, regardless of the question whether capacity binds or not. Therefore, seller 2 has an incentive to undersell 1 just slightly in order to catch some demand at a positive price. This proves symmetry. Next, suppose the equilibrium price is $p > p^A$. Then at least one firm has excess capacity and gains by underselling p just slightly. Finally, if $p < p^A$, both firms ration their customers. By naming the higher price p^A, firm 1 nets a higher profit, since

$$\pi_1(p^A, p) = p^A \tilde{X}(p^A, p)$$
$$= p^A(X(p^A) - k_2)$$
$$= p^A(k_1 + k_2 - k_2)$$
$$= p^A k_1$$
$$> p k_1$$
$$= \pi_1(p, p). \qquad \square$$

While this lemma tells us what prices are named in a pure-strategy equilibrium, it does not tell us whether a pure-strategy equilibrium does exist. This question is answered as follows.

Lemma 3.7 *A pure-strategy equilibrium exists if and only if* $\forall i$: *either* $k_i \leq r_0(k_j)$ *or* $k_i \geq \bar{X}$.

Proof Sufficiency: Suppose $k_i \leq r_0(k_j)$, for both i. By Lemma 3.6, in a pure-strategy equilibrium both firms set the accommodating price. At this price no firm has an incentive to undersell. But can a firm gain by overbidding p^A? Suppose, *per absurdum*, that firm i benefits from overbidding. Then one must have $P(k_j + r_0(k_j)) > p^A$. Since P is strictly monotone decreasing, it follows that $r_0(k_j) < k_i$, contrary to what was assumed. Finally, if firms' capacities exceed the satiation point, capacities never bind, and we are back to the simple Bertrand model which predicts a price equal to zero, which is the accommodating price at these high capacities.

Necessity: Suppose a pure-strategy equilibrium exists. Then, by Lemma 3.6, p^A is the equilibrium price. Now suppose that one firm, say firm i, has $k_i > r_0(k_j)$. Then $k_j + k_i > r_0(k_j) + k_j$ and hence $P(k_j + r_0(k_j)) > p^A$ – which contradicts the assumption that $(p^A(k), p^A(k))$ is an equilibrium. $\qquad \square$

The pure-strategy range of capacities is represented by the shaded area in Figure 3.12.

An immediate implication of these results is

---

[52] This assumes $p^M < p_2$. If $p^M \geq p_2$, firm 1 would try to match p_2 as closely as possible; therefore, different prices could not be part of an equilibrium in this case.

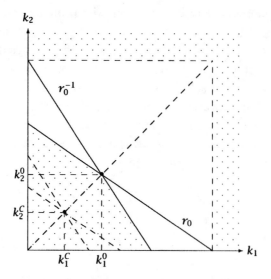

Figure 3.12. Pure-Strategy Range of Capacities.

Corollary 3.3 *The reduced-form gross and net profit functions* π_i^* *and* Π_i^* *have the exact Cournot form*

$$\Pi_i^*(k_i, k_j) = \pi_i^*(k_i, k_j) - C(k_i)$$

$$\pi_i^*(k_i, k_j) = P(k_i + k_j)k_i$$

if and only if $\forall i$: $k_i \leq r_0(k_j)$ *or* $k_i \geq \bar{X}$.

Proof The reduced-form payoff functions map the capacity vector (k_1, k_2) into firm i's gross or net profit respectively, assuming that both firms call the equilibrium prices of the resulting price competition subgame. Using this definition, the assertion follows immediately by Lemma 3.6 and Lemma 3.7.   □

Mixed-Strategy Equilibria

If firms' capacities are in the intermediate range, represented by the area that is *not* shaded in the diagram, the game has no pure-strategy equilibrium. Does it have one in mixed strategies? If existence of an equilibrium is assured, the answer is yes, by exclusion. But existence does not follow readily from the standard existence theorems reviewed in Section 3.4.1.

Since we deal with a continuous-strategy game, it would seem that Glicksberg's theorem is the appropriate one. However, this assumes that payoffs are continuous functions of strategies – which is violated in Bertrand models, including the present one. In recent contributions, Dasgupta and Maskin (1986) and Simon (1987) weakened this continuity requirement and showed that existence is assured in the present capacity-constrained Bertrand game.[53]

---

[53] See Theorem 1 in Dasgupta and Maskin, Part II. Incidentally, Kreps and Scheinkman (1983) explicitly solve for the equilibrium mixed strategies, which also proves existence, without recourse to the general results of Dasgupta and Maskin.

Referring to these general existence results, we can assume existence of equilibrium and turn right away to the properties of mixed-strategy equilibria if capacities are in the intermediate range where the equilibrium cannot be in pure strategies. The main result will be that the larger firm's reduced (gross) profit function has the exact Stackelberg-follower form. This result makes it easy to assess the effect of a unilateral increase in capacity.

The support of equilibrium mixed strategies is the interval $[\underline{p}_i, \bar{p}_i]$. Loosely speaking, you may refer to $\underline{p}_i$ as the lowest and to $\bar{p}_i$ as the highest price.

A first result concerns the location of the two "highest" prices and the probability weights assigned to them.

Lemma 3.8 *In a mixed-strategy equilibrium one cannot have* $\bar{p}_i = \bar{p}, i = 1, 2,$ *and* $\Pr\{p_i = \bar{p}\} > 0,$ *for both i; in other words, if the two "highest" prices are the same, they cannot both be called with positive probability.*

Proof We have already shown that p^A dominates all prices below p^A, so that the "lowest" prices must be at or above p^A and the "highest" prices must exceed p^A (if they were equal to p^A, we would have a pure-strategy equilibrium, by Lemma 3.6). Now assume, *per absurdum*, that the two "highest" prices coincide and are both called with positive probability. Then each player is strictly better off by shifting probability mass away from $\bar{p}$ to a price just marginally below $\bar{p}$. Therefore, the assumed strategies cannot be equilibrium strategies. $\qquad\square$

An immediate implication is that we have either one of two cases:

$$\bar{p}_1 > \bar{p}_2 \quad \text{or} \quad [\bar{p}_1 = \bar{p}_2 \text{ and } \Pr\{p_2 = \bar{p}_2\} = 0] \qquad \text{(case I)},$$
$$\bar{p}_2 > \bar{p}_1 \quad \text{or} \quad [\bar{p}_2 = \bar{p}_1 \text{ and } \Pr\{p_1 = \bar{p}_1\} = 0] \qquad \text{(case II)}.$$

Lemma 3.9 *Suppose case I holds. Then*

1. $\bar{p}_1 = P(k_2 + r_0(k_2))$ *(Stackelberg-follower price),*
2. $k_1 > r_0(k_2)$ *(excess capacity at Stackelberg-follower price),*
3. $\pi_1^*(k_1, k_2) = P(k_2 + r_0(k_2))r_0(k_2)$ *(reduced-form gross profit function has exact Stackelberg-follower form),*
4. $k_1 \geq k_2.$

The extension to case II is obtained by interchanging subscripts 1 and 2.

Proof In order to prove parts 1 and 2, notice that firm 1 is undersold with certainty whenever it calls $\bar{p}_1$. Therefore, $\bar{p}_1$ must be the residual-demand monopoly price (otherwise $\bar{p}_1$ would not be part of the equilibrium support of prices), which is equal to

$$\bar{p}_1 = \tilde{p}_1^M = P(k_2 + r_0(k_2)), \qquad \text{since} \quad p^A < \bar{p}_1.$$

By the monotonicity of P it follows that $k_1 > r_0(k_2)$, as asserted.

3: If firm 1 calls $\bar{p}_1$, its payoff is equal to $P(k_2 + r_0(k_2))r_0(k_2)$. By a known property of mixed-strategy equilibria, the equilibrium payoff $\pi_1^*(k_1, k_2)$ is the same as the payoff that occurs when firm 1 replies to the rival's equilibrium strategy with one of the pure strategies (including $\bar{p}_1$) over which the player randomizes. Therefore, $\pi_i^*(k_1, k_2) = P(k_2 + r_0(k_2))r_0(k_2)$, as asserted.

The proof of part 4 is rather long and unenlightening, and hence omitted.

The extension to case II is obvious.   □

Two immediate implications of these results are

Corollary 3.4 *Suppose capacities are in the intermediate, mixed-strategy equilibrium range. Then case I applies if $k_1 \geq k_2$, and case II if $k_2 \geq k_1$.*

Corollary 3.5 *In the mixed strategy range of capacities the larger firm's reduced form payoff function has the exact Stackelberg-follower form*

$$k_i > k_j \iff \pi_i^*(k_1, k_2) = P(k_j + r_0(k_j))r_0(k_j).$$

3.6.3 Equilibrium of the Overall Game

We are now ready to characterize the solution of the overall game.

Proposition 3.21 *The overall game has a unique subgame-perfect Nash equilibrium. It gives rise to the Cournot outcome: $k_i = k^C$ and $p_i = p^A$, $i = 1, 2$.*

Proof The proposition claims that the Cournot solution is an equilibrium outcome and that the equilibrium is unique. We prove the first part but omit the proof of uniqueness (which would require a few more steps).

Since the equilibria of the price competition subgame are already represented in the reduced-form payoff functions, we only need to show that the Cournot capacities have the mutual best-response property. Since the Cournot capacities are within the pure-strategy range (see Lemma 3.7), the resulting equilibrium prices follow from Lemma 3.6. Now consider firm 1, and suppose the rival firm 2 has chosen $k_2 = k^C$. We show that it does not pay to switch from $k_1 = k^C$ to any other capacity level. Evidently, it never pays to switch to another capacity level from within the pure-strategy set $\{k \in \mathbb{R} \mid k_1 \leq r_0(k^C) \text{ or } k_1 \geq \bar{X}\}$ because the reduced-form payoff function has the exact Cournot form in this range (see Lemma 3.3), and because the Cournot equilibrium is unique.

But what about moving into the mixed-strategy range of capacities? As firm 1 moves into this range, one has $k_1 > k_2$. Therefore, by Corollary 3.5, firm 1's reduced profit function has the exact Stackelberg-follower form, and one obtains

$$
\begin{aligned}
\Pi_1^*(k_1, k^C) &= \pi_1^*(k_1, k^C) - C(k_1) \\
&= P(k^C + r_0(k^C))r_0(k^C) - C(k_1) \\
&< P(k^C + r_0(k^C))r_0(k^C) - C(r_0(k^C)) \quad \text{(by Lemma 3.9)} \\
&< P(k^C + r(k^C))r(k^C) - C(r(k^C)) \quad \text{(since $r(k)$ maximizes Π_1^*)} \\
&= P(k^C + k^C)k^C - C(k^C) \quad \text{(by definition of Cournot equilibrium)} \\
&= \Pi_1^*(k^C, k^C).
\end{aligned}
$$

Therefore, $k_1 = k^C$ is the best response to $k_2 = k^C$, and vice versa. This completes the proof. $\qquad\qquad\qquad\qquad\qquad\qquad\qquad\qquad\qquad\qquad\qquad\qquad\quad$ □

3.6.4 Excess Capacity and Collusion

The present model has been used by Osborne and Pitchik (1987) and Davidson and Deneckere (1990) to analyze the relationship between excess capacity and collusion. They assumed that firms choose their capacities before they enter into collusive agreements. If collusion fails, firms return to the Bertrand game with limited capacity.

In this framework, a higher capacity gives firms a stronger bargaining position in the negotiation concerning cartel quotas. And excess capacity turns out to be a prerequisite of stable collusion.

To a certain extent, these models illustrate the capacity race that was observed during the 1920s, which was a period of widespread cartelization. As Scherer (1980, p. 370) reports:

In Germany, during the 1920's and 1930's, shares were allocated on the basis of production capacity. Cartel members therefore raced to increase their sales quotas by building more capacity ... Even when market shares are not linked formally to capacity, a cartel member's bargaining power depends upon its fighting reserves ... Recognizing this, companies participating in market sharing cartels will be tempted to invest more in capacity than they need to serve foreseeable demands at anticipated collusive price levels.

3.6.5 Discussion

We close this ingenious defense of the Cournot model with some remarks.

The main limitation of this defense is that it does not hold under alternative rationing schemes such as random rationing. You can see immediately why it does not hold for random rationing, by going back Section 3.5.1 where random rationing was used. There we showed that the Cournot outcome cannot be an equilibrium outcome of the overall game, simply because the price-competition subgame has no pure-strategy equilibrium for the Cournot capacities. This point was made with greater generality by Davidson and Deneckere (1986), who pointed out that the Cournot outcome cannot emerge as an equilibrium for virtually any rationing rule other than parallel rationing.

Another limitation is that this defense assumes complete information concerning the choice of capacities, as firms enter into the price-competition subgame. During World War II, the British army drew up dummy tanks in order to mislead German air reconnaissance about the strength of its tank corps. Similarly, firms may have many ways to mislead rivals about their true capacity.

This and other examples suggest that we have reached the limitations of the complete-information analysis of oligopoly. Many of the stylized features of oligopolistic markets – such as entry deterrence through limit pricing – are difficult to explain within a complete-information framework. Recent contributions have increasingly turned to models of incomplete information. A full review of these developments is the subject of specialized courses on theoretical industrial organization.

3.7 Bibliographic Notes

If you want to know more about oligopoly theory and industrial organization, we recommend five books: the classic text by Scherer (1980), Tirole's (1989) textbook, the textbooks by Shy (1995) and Martin (1993), and the survey by Phlips (1995). While Scherer's book is a rich mine of IO themes and cases, Tirole's book has extensive coverage of the incomplete-information theory of oligopoly that we have excluded from the present chapter. The books by Shy and Martin supplement Tirole and are generally at a more introductory level. The book by Phlips surveys important contributions on collusion and oligopoly.

One important area in oligopoly theory that we have not covered is the analysis of product differentiation. To underline its importance, recall that the analysis of oligopolies with heterogeneous products is often a better model of monopolistic markets than the given-demand-function approach in standard monopoly theory, as we pointed out in the introduction to the monopoly chapter.

Product differentiation is well covered in other texts. A good introduction can be found in Friedman (1983) or in Singh and Vives (1984). One prominent application is that of spatial competition, originating with a famous contribution by Hotelling (1929). Concise introductions to the Hotelling model and the complications that come with it are Gabszewicz and Thisse (1986) and Anderson, de Palma, and Thisse (1992).

Two other important fields not covered here are price discrimination in oligopoly (see Stole (1995)), and the repeated-game theory of oligopoly and the theory of price wars due to Green and Porter (1984). On the latter issue see also Slade (1989) and Klemperer (1989).

Part II

Risk, Stochastic Dominance, and Risk Aversion

4

Stochastic Dominance: Theory

Only risk is sure.
Erica Jong

4.1 Introduction

Decision problems under uncertainty concern the choice between random payoffs. For a rational agent with a known utility function, one random variable is preferred if it maximizes expected utility. This is easy enough in theory. However, in practice it is often difficult to find an agent's utility function. Therefore it would be most useful to know whether a random variable is the dominant choice because it is preferred by *all* agents whose utility functions share certain general characteristics.

In this chapter, we introduce two such rankings, known as first- and second-order stochastic dominance. These notions apply to pairs of random variables. They indicate when one random variable ranks higher than the other by specifying a condition which the difference between their distribution functions must satisfy.

Essentially, first-order stochastic dominance is a *stochastically larger* and second-order stochastic dominance a *stochastically less volatile* or *less risky* relationship. While the larger random variable is preferred by all agents who prefer higher realizations, the less volatile random variable is preferred by all agents who also dislike risk. In this sense, stochastic dominance theory gives *unanimity rules*, provided utility functions share certain properties.

Stochastic dominance theory has a bearing on the old issue whether one can judge a random variable as more risky than another regardless of who is the judge, provided that utility functions belong to a class with certain common properties. For many years, economists thought that mean and variance are a satisfactory measure of comparative risk. But this was not quite right. Indeed, mean and variance can only serve this purpose if agents' utility functions are quadratic or if all probability distributions are normal distributions. Surely, normal distributions are far too restrictive.[1] And quadratic utility functions are unsatisfactory. Not only do they imply that utility reaches a maximum, they also entail that the absolute degree of

---

[1] For example, studies have shown that stock price changes are inconsistent with the assumption of normal probability distributions (see Mandelbrot (1963) and Breen and Savage (1968)).

risk aversion is increasing in wealth, approaching infinity as utility approaches its maximum. Consequently, one is led to the absurd result that the willingness to gamble for a bet of fixed size should decrease as wealth is increased.

Stochastic dominance is interesting in itself. But we are mostly interested in what it contributes to the solution of complex decision problems and their comparative statics of risk. Keeping this in mind, we will not only give a detailed exposition of the theory, but also elaborate on a number of applications from various fields in economics. Among other examples, we address the following issues:

- Will the competitive firm increase its supply if the random product price becomes "larger"? What if it is subject to less risk?
- Consider the labor-supply and saving decision if the return from saving is risky. Will labor supply increase if the return from saving becomes more volatile?
- Consider the entry decision in an oligopoly market. Is there a symmetric equilibrium in mixed entry strategies, and how does the equilibrium entry probability change if more firms contemplate entry?
- Can one unanimously rank distributions of wealth in a society if all agents agree on some general ethical principles represented by a social welfare function with certain properties?
- Does it pay to diversify a financial portfolio, and should one always invest more in an asset if its return becomes "larger" or if it is subject to less risk?

4.2 Assumptions and Definitions

We use capital letters such as X and Y to denote random variables, and the corresponding lowercase letters to denote realizations. Capital letters such as F and G denote distributions, and f and g the associated density functions. For convenience, all random variables have the same (extended) support $I := [\underline{x}, \bar{x}]$, $-\infty < \underline{x} < \bar{x} < +\infty$. All expected values are assumed to be finite.

The decision maker has a preference ordering over all possible outcomes, which is represented by a von Neumann–Morgenstern utility function. Two properties of the utility function are emphasized: *monotonicity* (more is better than less) and *concavity* (risk aversion). The set of utility functions that are monotone increasing is denoted by $\mathcal{U}_1$, and the set of functions that are monotone increasing *and* concave by $\mathcal{U}_2$. Differentiability requirements will be invoked as needed. All utility functions are bounded.

Obviously, $U \in \mathcal{U}_1$ if and only if the argument of U is regarded as a good, and $U \in \mathcal{U}_2$ if and only if the decision maker is also risk-averse.

4.3 First-Order Stochastic Dominance (FSD)

We say that the random variable X *first-order stochastically dominates* (FSD) the random variable Y, written $X \succsim_{\mathrm{FSD}} Y$, if

$$\Pr\{X > z\} \geq \Pr\{Y > z\} \qquad \text{for all } z, \qquad (4.1)$$

or equivalently, if

$$\bar{F}(z) \geq \bar{G}(z) \qquad \text{for all } z \qquad (4.2)$$

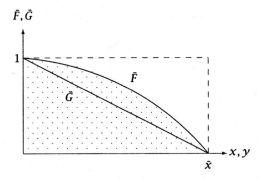

Figure 4.1. First-Order Stochastic Dominance, FSD (dotted area = $E[X]$).

(where $\bar{F}(z) := 1 - F(z)$ and $\bar{G}(z) := 1 - G(z)$). If the inequality is strict for some z, the dominance relationship is *strict*.

In the literature, (4.2) is often written in the form

$$F(z) \leq G(z) \qquad \text{for all } z. \tag{4.3}$$

However, since it is slightly easier to remember that the dominant random variable is stochastically *larger*, we find formulation (4.2) slightly more appealing.

An illustration of first-order stochastic dominance is in Figure 4.1.

4.3.1 Main Results

The following result is useful in several proofs. It also indicates that Y cannot FSD-dominate X if its expected value is lower. This offers a quick test for FSD.

Lemma 4.1 $X \succsim_{\text{FSD}} Y \implies E[X] \geq E[Y]$.

Proof Suppose X and Y are nonnegative random variables. Then, by a known property of expected values,[2] the assumed FSD implies

$$E[X] = \int_0^{\bar{x}} \bar{F}(t)\, dt \geq \int_0^{\bar{x}} \bar{G}(t)\, dt = E[Y]. \tag{4.4}$$

If $\underline{x} < 0$ one has[3]

$$E[X] = \int_0^{\bar{x}} dx - \int_{\underline{x}}^{\bar{x}} F(x)\, dx$$

$$\geq \int_0^{\bar{x}} dx - \int_{\underline{x}}^{\bar{x}} G(x)\, dx$$

$$= E[Y]. \qquad \square$$

Proposition 4.1 (FSD Theorem) *X is unanimously preferred to Y by all agents with monotone increasing utility functions if and only if $X \succsim_{\text{FSD}} Y$:*

$$X \succsim_{\text{FSD}} Y \iff E[U(X)] \geq E[U(Y)] \quad \text{for all } U \in \mathcal{U}_1.$$

The preference ranking is reversed if utility functions are decreasing.

---

[2] Consult rule R6 in Appendix D (Section D.4.1).
[3] Consult rule R5 in Appendix D (Section D.4.1).

Proof Suppose $X \succsim_{FSD} Y$. Then[4]

$$\Pr\{U(X) > z\} = \Pr\{X > U^{-1}(z)\}$$
$$\geq \Pr\{Y > U^{-1}(z)\}$$
$$= \Pr\{U(Y) > z\}.$$

Therefore, $U(X) \succsim_{FSD} U(Y)$, and Lemma 4.1 implies $E[U(X)] \geq E[U(Y)]$.

Suppose $E[U(X)] \geq E[U(Y)]$ for all $U \in \mathcal{U}_1$. For each z consider the particular monotone increasing function[5]

$$U_z(x) := \begin{cases} 1 & \text{if} \quad x > z, \\ 0 & \text{otherwise.} \end{cases}$$

Evidently, $E[U_z(X)] = \Pr\{X > z\}$, $E[U_z(Y)] = \Pr\{Y > z\}$, and therefore $X \succsim_{FSD} Y$.

□

4.3.2 FSD and the "Stochastically Larger" Relationship*

Proposition 4.1 links the FSD stochastic order relationship and a preference order shared by all agents who prefer more to less. This already indicates that FSD can be viewed as a "stochastically larger" relationship. The following result makes this interpretation even more compelling. It shows that if $X \succsim_{FSD} Y$, then it is possible to represent X and Y by probabilistically equivalent gambles, X^* and Y^*, in such a way that X^* is unambiguously larger than Y^* for all events.

Proposition 4.2 *If $X \succsim_{FSD} Y$, one can find random variables X^* and Y^* that have the same probability distributions as X and Y and that satisfy the "stochastically larger" relationship*

$$\Pr\{X^* \geq Y^*\} = 1. \tag{4.5}$$

Proof Notice that the random variable $Y^* := G^{-1}(F(X))$ has distribution G just like random variable Y because

$$\Pr\{Y^* \leq x\} = \Pr\{G^{-1}(F(X)) \leq x\}$$
$$= \Pr\{F(X) \leq G(x)\}$$
$$= \Pr\{X \leq F^{-1}(G(x))\}$$
$$= F(F^{-1}(G(x)))$$
$$= G(x)$$
$$=: \Pr\{Y \leq x\}.$$

Now set $X^* = X$, and observe that $\Pr\{X^* \geq Y^*\} = \Pr\{X \geq G^{-1}(F(X))\} = \Pr\{G(X) \geq F(X)\} = 1$, as asserted.

□

---

[4] Define $U^{-1}(z) := \sup\{x | U(x) = z\}$. This may seem a bit pedantic. But it allows you to cover the case when U is monotone but not *strictly* monotone increasing. Notice, however, that continuity is required to make this work.

[5] Generally, we assume continuous utility functions (see the remark in the preceding footnote). So how can we dare to use a discontinuous function in the proof of one of the key results? Don't worry about this. One can always approximate this function by a continuous function as closely as one desires.

Examples There are many examples of first-order stochastic dominance. Two of the more frequently used examples are listed below:

1. The binomial distribution with the density function

$$f(x; N, p) := \binom{N}{x} p^x (1-p)^{N-x}$$

increases stochastically both as N and as p are increased.

2. The normal distribution increases stochastically with its mean.

4.3.3 Relationship to Other Stochastic Orderings

In the economics of information one frequently encounters some other stochastic orderings, such as the likelihood ratio and hazard-rate orderings (see Chapters 8, 9, 11, and the survey by Jewitt (1991)). Both these orderings are even stronger requirements than FSD.

Definition 4.1 (MHRC) Let X and Y be continuous nonnegative random variables with respective distributions functions F, G and densities f, g. Then X is said to be larger in the sense of the monotone hazard-rate condition, written as $X \succsim_{MHRC} Y$, if

$$h_X(x) := \frac{f(x)}{1 - F(x)} \le \frac{g(x)}{1 - G(x)} =: h_Y(x) \qquad \forall x.$$

Definition 4.2 (MLRC) Similarly, X is said to be larger in the sense of the monotone likelihood-ratio condition, written as $X \succsim_{MLRC} Y$, if

$$r_X(x) := \frac{f(x)}{g(x)} \le \frac{f(y)}{g(y)} =: r_Y(y) \qquad \forall x \le y.$$

Proposition 4.3

$$X \succsim_{MLRC} Y \quad \Rightarrow \quad X \succsim_{MHRC} Y \quad \Rightarrow \quad X \succsim_{FSD} Y.$$

Proof Since $X \succsim_{MLRC} Y$, it follows that for all $y \ge x$,

$$f(y) \ge g(y) \frac{f(x)}{g(x)},$$

and hence

$$h_X(x) = \frac{f(x)}{1 - F(x)}$$

$$= \frac{f(x)}{\int_x^{+\infty} f(\tau)\, d\tau}$$

$$\le \frac{f(x)}{\int_x^{+\infty} g(\tau) \frac{f(x)}{g(x)}\, d\tau}$$

$$= \frac{g(x)}{\int_x^{+\infty} g(\tau)\, d\tau}$$

$$= h_Y(x).$$

This proves that MLRC $\Rightarrow$ MHRC.

Table 4.1. *Two probability distributions that violate FSD*

	x_1	x_2	x_3
$\Pr\{X = x_i\}$	0.2	0.2	0.6
$\Pr\{Y = x_i\}$	0.1	0.4	0.5

Now assume $X \succsim_{\text{MHRC}} Y$; then one has for all x that $h_X(x) \le h_Y(x)$. Therefore, one has also

$$\int_0^x \frac{f(\tau)}{1 - F(\tau)}\, d\tau \le \int_0^x \frac{g(\tau)}{1 - G(\tau)}\, d\tau,$$

which is obviously equivalent to $\ln(1 - F(x)) \ge \ln(1 - G(x))$, and hence to $F(x) \le G(x)$, for all x. Therefore, MHRC $\Rightarrow$ FSD. $\square$

A Reminder If you only skimmed through the main result, you may mistakenly equate FSD with the monotonicity of utility functions. Therefore, we remind you that the FSD theorem is an *unanimity result*. It gives a necessary and sufficient condition under which *all* agents with monotone increasing utility functions agree on a preference ranking of two random variables. At the risk of unnecessary repetition, we stress that for random variables that do not satisfy FSD, one can always find monotone increasing utility functions that give higher rank to either the one or the other, as in the following discrete example. But this cannot occur if random variables can be ranked according to FSD.

Example 4.1 Consider the probability distribution functions over the three outcomes x_1, x_2, x_3 stated in Table 4.1 and two monotone increasing utility functions: a) $U(x_1) = 0.5, U(x_2) = 1, U(x_3) = 2$ and b) $U(x_1) = 0.5, U(x_2) = 1.5, U(x_3) = 2$. Obviously, b) $\Longrightarrow E[U(Y)] > E[U(X)]$, and a) $\Longrightarrow E[U(Y)] < E[U(X)]$.

4.4 Second-Order Stochastic Dominance

We say that random variable X *second-order stochastically dominates* (SSD) random variable Y, written $X \succsim_{\text{SSD}} Y$, if

$$\int_{\underline{x}}^k \Pr\{X > x\}\, dx \ge \int_{\underline{x}}^k \Pr\{Y > y\}\, dy \qquad \text{for all } k, \tag{4.6}$$

which is equivalent to

$$\int_{\underline{x}}^k \bar{F}(x)\, dx \ge \int_{\underline{x}}^k \bar{G}(y)\, dy \qquad \text{for all } k. \tag{4.7}$$

If the inequality in (4.6) is strict for some k, the dominance relationship is *strict*.

In the literature, condition (4.7) is often written in the form

$$\int_{\underline{x}}^k F(x)\, dx \le \int_{\underline{x}}^k G(y)\, dy \qquad \text{for all } k. \tag{4.8}$$

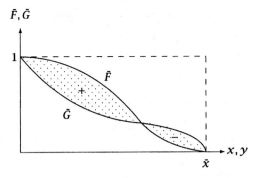

Figure 4.2. Second-Order Stochastic Dominance (SSD).

An illustration of SSD dominance is in Figure 4.2.

4.4.1 Main Results

Of course, FSD $\Longrightarrow$ SSD – but not vice versa. Also, computing expected values offers a simple test for SSD:

Lemma 4.2 $X \succsim_{\mathrm{SSD}} Y \implies E[X] \geq E[Y]$.

Proof The assertion follows immediately by the fact that $E[X] = \int_0^{\bar{x}} \bar{F}(t)\, dt$ if $\underline{x} \geq 0$, and $E[X] = \int_0^{\bar{x}} dx - \int_{\underline{x}}^{\bar{x}} F(x)\, dx$ if $\underline{x} < 0$. $\qquad\square$

Proposition 4.4 (SSD Theorem) *X is unanimously preferred to Y by all agents with monotone increasing and concave utility functions if and only if* $X \succsim_{\mathrm{SSD}} Y$:

$$X \succsim_{\mathrm{SSD}} Y \iff E[U(X)] \geq E[U(Y)] \quad \text{for all } U \in \mathcal{U}_2.$$

The preference ranking is reversed if utility functions are decreasing and convex.

Proof Suppose $E[U(X)] \geq E[U(Y)]$ for all $U \in \mathcal{U}_2$. Consider the following function:

$$U_k(x) := \begin{cases} x & \text{if } x \leq k, \\ k & \text{if } x > k. \end{cases}$$

Obviously, $U_k \in \mathcal{U}_2$. Suppose $\underline{x} \geq 0$. Then

$$E[U_k(X)] = \int_0^k \bar{F}(x)\, dx \qquad \text{for each } k.$$

Therefore the assumption implies $\int_0^k \bar{F}(x)\, dx \geq \int_0^k \bar{G}(x)\, dx$ for all k, and hence $X \succsim_{\mathrm{SSD}} Y$. Similar reasoning applies if $\underline{x} < 0$.

We show that $X \succsim_{\mathrm{SSD}} Y \implies U(X) \succsim_{\mathrm{SSD}} U(Y)$ for all utility functions $U \in \mathcal{U}_2$. Since monotonicity implies differentiability almost everywhere, and since risk aversion entails that U' is monotone decreasing, we can invoke differentiability with

$U' > 0$, $U'' \leq 0$ almost everywhere. Using a transformation of random variables from X to $U^{-1}(X)$ and integration by parts, one obtains

$$\int_{\underline{x}}^{k} \Pr\{U(X) > x\}\, dx = \int_{\underline{x}}^{k} \Pr\{X > U^{-1}(x)\}\, dx$$

$$= \int_{\underline{x}}^{k} \bar{F}(U^{-1}(x))\, dx$$

$$= \int_{\underline{z}}^{z} \bar{F}(\tilde{z}) U'(\tilde{z})\, d\tilde{z}$$

$$= \int_{\underline{z}}^{z} U'(\tilde{z}) \frac{d}{dv} \int_{\underline{z}}^{v} \bar{F}(\tilde{v})\, d\tilde{v}\, d\tilde{z}$$

$$= U'(z) \int_{\underline{z}}^{z} \bar{F}(\tilde{v})\, d\tilde{v} - \int_{\underline{z}}^{z} U''(\tilde{z}) \int_{\underline{z}}^{v} \bar{F}(\tilde{v})\, d\tilde{v}\, dz.$$

Since $U' > 0$, $U'' \leq 0$, the assumed $X \succsim_{\mathrm{SSD}} Y$ implies immediately that $U(X) \succsim_{\mathrm{SSD}} U(Y)$. Combining this with Lemma 4.2, we conclude $E[U(X)] \geq E[U(Y)]$ for all $U \in \mathcal{U}_2$.[6]   □

4.4.2 SSD and the "Stochastically More Risky" Relationship*

Proposition 4.4 links the SSD stochastic order relationship and a preference order shared by all agents who prefer more to less and are risk-averse. This already indicates that SSD can be viewed as a "stochastically more risky" relationship. The following result makes this interpretation even more compelling. It shows that if $X \succsim_{\mathrm{SSD}} Y$, then it is possible to represent X and Y by probabilistically equivalent gambles, X^* and Y^*, in such a way that Y^* is more risky than X^* for all events.

Proposition 4.5 *If $X \succsim_{\mathrm{SSD}} Y$, one can find random variables X^* and Y^* that have the same probability distributions as X and Y and satisfy the "more risky" relationship*

$$\Pr\{E[Y^*|X^*] \leq X^*\} = 1. \tag{4.9}$$

Examples The most frequently used example of SSD consists of two *single-crossing* distributions; the *mean-preserving spread* is a special case. Two distribution functions are called single-crossing if they intersect exactly once, as in Figure 4.2. An important implication of single crossing is that one random variable has more probability mass on *both* tails of the distribution.

Another implication of the single crossing is that the relationship between expected values and SSD can be strengthened as follows:

---

[6] Sketch of alternative proof (using integration by parts twice): Let $Z(x) := \bar{F}(x) - \bar{G}(x) = G(x) - F(x)$. Then $E[U(X)] - E[U(Y)] = -\int_{\underline{x}}^{\bar{x}} U(x)\, dZ(x) = \int_{\underline{x}}^{\bar{x}} U'(x) Z(x)\, dx = U'(\bar{x}) \int_{\underline{x}}^{\bar{x}} Z(y)\, dy - \int_{\underline{x}}^{\bar{x}} U''(x) \int_{\underline{x}}^{x} Z(y)\, dy\, dx \geq 0.$

Proposition 4.6 (Single Crossing and SSD) *Suppose X and Y are nonnegative random variables that are single-crossing with $\bar{F}(x) \geq \bar{G}(x)$ for low and $\bar{F}(x) \leq \bar{G}(x)$ for high x. Then $X \succsim_{SSD} Y \iff E[X] \geq E[Y]$.*

Proof Lemma 4.2 already shows that $X \succsim_{SSD} Y \implies E[X] \geq E[Y]$. Therefore, we need only prove that $E[X] \geq E[Y] \implies X \succsim_{SSD} Y$. By the assumed single crossing property, it follows immediately that $\int_{\underline{x}}^{z}[\bar{F}(t) - \bar{G}(t)]\,dt \geq 0$ for all $z \in [\underline{x}, c)$, where c denotes the crossing point. We now show that this relationship extends also to all $z \in [c, \bar{x}]$. For this purpose, assume $z \in (c, \bar{x}]$; then one has

$$0 \leq E[X] - E[Y]$$
$$= \int_{0}^{\bar{x}}[\bar{F}(t) - \bar{G}(t)]\,dt$$
$$= \int_{0}^{z}[\bar{F}(t) - \bar{G}(t)]\,dt + \int_{z}^{\bar{x}}[\bar{F}(t) - \bar{G}(t)]\,dt$$
$$\leq \int_{0}^{z}[\bar{F}(t) - \bar{G}(t)]\,dt.$$

Hence, $\int_{0}^{z}[\bar{F}(t) - \bar{G}(t)]\,dt \geq 0$ holds for all z.   □

Another example concerns normal distributions.

Proposition 4.7 (Normal Distributions) *Suppose X and Y are normally distributed and Y has a higher variance or a lower expected value than X. Then $X \succsim_{SSD} Y$.*

Proof If the variance is the same, but the expected value of X is greater than that of Y, then we know already that $X \succsim_{FSD} Y$, which, of course, implies SSD. If the variance of X is lower while expected values are the same, the two distributions are single-crossing.[7] Therefore, $X \succsim_{SSD} Y$, by Proposition 4.6. If X has both a higher expected value and a lower variance than Y, the assertion follows by the transitivity of stochastic dominance relationships (see Proposition 4.8 below).   □

This last fact proves that the mean–variance analysis in finance is justified if the returns of financial securities are normally distributed.

4.5 An Invariance Property*

Stochastic dominance is preserved when the original random variables are multiplied by a constant or when another independent random variable is added.[8]

Proposition 4.8 (Transitivity) *Consider three independent nonnegative random variables X, Y, and W, and the linear combination $aX + bW$ and $aY + bW$ with $a > 0$, $b \geq 0$. Then:*

---

[7] The crossing point is $z = E[X] = E[Y]$, which is where the density function has its peak.
[8] This result is needed in the starred application on optimal portfolio selection (Section 5.7). You may skip it if you do not cover this application.

1. $X \succsim_{\text{FSD}} Y \implies (aX + bW) \succsim_{\text{FSD}} (aY + bW)$.
2. $X \succsim_{\text{SSD}} Y \implies (aX + bW) \succsim_{\text{SSD}} (aY + bW)$.

Proof See Hadar and Russell (1971).   □

4.6 Ranking Transformations of Random Variables*

Suppose the random variable X is transformed using the deterministic function $t(x)$. This transformation maps each possible outcome of the original random variable into a new value. Let t be monotone increasing (to assure that the transformation does not reverse the preference ranking) and differentiable.

We begin with two results that provide necessary and sufficient conditions for FSD and SSD dominance of $t(X)$ over X. In the light of what you have already learned, these results are plausible. Therefore the proofs are omitted.

Proposition 4.9 *Consider the transformation $t(X)$, and define $k(X) := t(X) - X$. Then*

$$t(X) \succsim_{\text{FSD}} X \iff k(x) \geq 0 \quad \forall x, \tag{4.10}$$

$$t(X) \succsim_{\text{SSD}} X \iff \int_0^x k(t)\, dF(t) \geq 0 \quad \forall x. \tag{4.11}$$

Strict dominance requires strict inequalities for some x.

Proof To prove the FSD relationship note that

$$\Pr\{t(X) > x\} = \Pr\{X > t^{-1}(x)\}$$

$$> \Pr\{X > x\}$$

$$\iff \quad t^{-1}(X) < x \iff X < t(X).$$

The proof of the SSD relationship is left as an exercise.   □

Frequently used transformations are affine transformations, $t(x) := \alpha + \beta x$. But these are often more specialized than necessary to derive unambiguous comparative statics of risk.

Example 4.2 (Stretching) Consider the affine transformation of X

$$t(X) := \alpha + \beta X \tag{4.12}$$

with $\alpha \geq 0$, $\beta \geq 1$, at least one strict. Then $t(X) \succ_{\text{FSD}} X$. Obviously, $t(X)$ can be viewed as a stretching of X.

The direct proof follows from a simple assessment as follows:

$$\Pr\{t(X) > z\} = \Pr\left\{X > \frac{z - \alpha}{\beta}\right\} \geq \Pr\{X > z\}.$$

But it is also a consequence of Proposition 4.9.

Example 4.3 (Single Crossing) Consider a single-crossing transformation $t(x)$, with $t(x) \geq x$ for $x \leq x^*$ and $t(x) \leq x$ otherwise. Also assume the mean-preserving property $E[t(X)] \geq E[X]$. Then the integral condition in (4.11) is satisfied; therefore, $t(X) \succsim_{SSD} X$.

4.7 Comparative Statics of Risk

Economic models of uncertainty usually examine optimal decisions in the face of random outcomes. In comparative statics, we explore how the optimal action responds to parameter changes. Comparative statics of risk concerns changes in the nature of the underlying uncertainty. In this section we lay the foundations for the comparative statics of risk, for a class of decision problems. The results will then be used in the analysis of various typical applications.

4.7.1 Framework

Suppose the decision maker has the objective function

$$V(a, X) := U(\pi(a, X)),$$

where a is his action variable and $\pi(a, X)$ the random outcome, codetermined by his action a and the nonnegative[9] random variable X. The function π (which could be the profit function of a firm) is strictly concave in a, and $\pi_a = 0$ is satisfied for some finite a, for each x.

The decision maker maximizes expected utility:

$$\max_{a \geq 0} E[V(a, X)].$$

Existence of an interior solution a^* that solves

$$E[V_a(a^*, X)] = 0 \quad \text{and} \quad E[V_{aa}(a^*, X)] < 0 \qquad (4.13)$$

is assumed.

4.7.2 *Key Issue

We want to find out how a^* changes when the random variable X is altered by a FSD or SSD transformation. For this purpose consider the convex linear combination of X and $t(X)$ given by

$$Z(\theta) := \theta t(X) + (1 - \theta)X, \qquad \theta \in [0, 1]$$

$$= X + \theta k(X)$$

where

$$k(X) := t(X) - X.$$

---

[9] In the following, nonnegativity is invoked only in order to avoid cumbersome case distinctions.

We will analyze the solution function

$$a^*(\theta) := \arg\max_a E[V(a, Z(\theta))],$$

in particular its derivative at the point $\theta = 0$. The sign of $a^{*\prime}(0)$ determines the effect of the transformation $t(X)$ on the optimal action.

Since $a^*(\theta)$ solves the first-order condition $E[V_a] = 0$, one has by the implicit-function theorem

$$a^{*\prime}(0) = -\frac{E[V_{ax}k]}{E[V_{aa}]},\tag{4.14}$$

where all functions are evaluated at the point (a^*, X). By the second-order condition, $E[V_{aa}] < 0$. Thus,

$$\operatorname{sign} a^{*\prime}(0) = \operatorname{sign} E[V_{ax}k],\tag{4.15}$$

and the comparative statics problem is reduced to determining the sign of $E[V_{ax}k]$.

Proposition 4.10 (FSD Transformations I) *The optimal action increases (decreases) $[a^{*\prime}(0) \geq 0 \ (\leq 0)]$ for all FSD transformations if $V_{ax}(a^*, X) \geq 0 \ (\leq 0)$ everywhere.*

Proof Follows immediately by (4.15) and the fact that $k(X) \geq 0$ (FSD).   □

Proposition 4.11 (SSD Transformations I) *The optimal action increases (decreases) $[a^{*\prime}(0) \geq 0 \ (\leq 0)]$ for all SSD transformations if $V_{axx}(a^*, x) \leq 0 \ (\geq 0)$ everywhere, in addition to the condition stated in Proposition 4.10.*

Proof Using integration by parts one obtains

$$\begin{aligned}
E[V_{ax}k] &= \int_0^{\bar{x}} V_{ax}(a^*, x)\frac{d}{dx}\left(\int_0^x k(t)\,dF(t)\right)dx \\
&= V_{ax}(a^*, \bar{x})\int_0^{\bar{x}} k(x)\,dF(x) \\
&\quad - \int_0^{\bar{x}} V_{axx}(a^*, x)\int_0^x k(t)\,dF(t)\,dx.
\end{aligned}$$

Since $\int_0^x k\,dF \geq 0 \ \forall x$, by SSD, the sign of $E[V_{ax}k]$ is unambiguous when $V_{ax}(a^*, \bar{x}) < 0$ and $V_{axx} \geq 0$ for all x, and the assertion follows immediately.   □

As an interpretation of these results, we introduce what has been called the *generalized* risk aversion[10]

$$R := \frac{-U''\pi_a\pi_x}{U'}.$$

[10] Notice: If $\pi_a\pi_x = 1$, the measure reduces to the *absolute* risk aversion, and if $\pi_a\pi_x = ax$, to the *partial relative* risk aversion proposed by Menezes and Hanson (1970).

Then V_{ax} and V_{axx} can be rewritten as follows:

$$V_{ax} = U'(\pi_{ax} - R), \tag{4.16}$$

$$V_{axx} = U'(\pi_{axx} - R_x) + U''\pi_x(\pi_{ax} - R). \tag{4.17}$$

Therefore, the conditions in Propositions 4.10 and 4.11 can be replaced by requirements concerning the function π and the generalized risk aversion R.

For example, if $\pi(a, X) := aX$, one has $\pi_{ax} = 1$ and therefore $a^{*\prime}(0) > 0$ for all SSD transformations if $R(a^*, x) < 1$, $R_x(a^*, x) > 0$.

The conditions summarized in Propositions 4.10 and 4.11 are sufficient for determining the sign of $a^{*\prime}(0)$, but not necessary. This suggests that there is room for other sufficient conditions. We close with two further results that are useful in several applications. Key requirements are that $k'(X) \leq 0$ and that the *absolute* risk aversion, $A := -U''/U'$, must be monotone decreasing. Whereas the emphasis of the previous conditions is on the degree of risk aversion, the emphasis of the following conditions is on the functional form of the transformation rule.

Proposition 4.12 (FSD Transformations II) *The optimal action increases for all FSD transformations if all of the following conditions hold everywhere:*

1. $U' > 0$, $U'' \leq 0$, $A' \leq 0$,
2. $\pi_x > 0$, $\pi_{xx} \leq 0$, $\pi_{ax} \geq 0$,
3. $k'(x) \leq 0$.

Proof Using the absolute risk aversion A, V_{ax} can be written in the form

$$V_{ax} = U'(\pi_{ax} - A\pi_x\pi_a). \tag{4.18}$$

Therefore,

$$E[V_{ax}k] = \int_0^{\bar{x}} U'\pi_{ax}k\,dF - \int_0^{\bar{x}} U'A\pi_x\pi_ak\,dF. \tag{4.19}$$

The first integral is obviously nonnegative for all FSD transformations. In order to determine the sign of the second integral, notice two facts: 1) $A\pi_x k$ is positive and decreasing in x; and 2) $U'\pi_a$ is negative for low x, say for all $x < x_1$, and positive for all $x > x_1$ in such a way that the first-order condition $\int U'\pi_a\,dF = 0$ holds. Combining these facts, one has

$$\int_0^{x_1} (Ak\pi_x)U'\pi_a\,dF \leq (Ak\pi_x)|_{x=x_1} \int_0^{x_1} U'\pi_a\,dF, \tag{4.20}$$

$$\int_{x_1}^{\bar{x}} (Ak\pi_x)U'\pi_a\,dF \leq (Ak\pi_x)|_{x=x_1} \int_{x_1}^{\bar{x}} U'\pi_a\,dF. \tag{4.21}$$

Therefore, by the first-order condition concerning a,

$$\int_0^{\bar{x}} Ak\pi_x U'\pi_a\,dF \leq (Ak\pi_x)|_{x=x_1} \int_0^{\bar{x}} U'\pi_a\,dF = 0, \tag{4.22}$$

and hence $E[V_{ax}k] \geq 0$. $\qquad\qquad\qquad\qquad\square$

Table 4.2. *Sufficient conditions for $a^{*\prime}(0) \geq 0$*

Propositions	FSD transformations	SSD transformations
4.10 and 4.11	$V_{ax} \geq 0$	$\ldots$ and $V_{axx} \leq 0$
4.12 and 4.13	$A', k', \pi_{xx} \leq 0, \quad \pi_x, \pi_{ax} \geq 0$	$\ldots$ and $\pi_{axx} \leq 0$

Note: $A := -U''/U'$; $\quad R := A\pi_a\pi_x$, $\quad V_{ax} = U'(\pi_{ax} - R)$,
$V_{axx} = U'(\pi_{axx} - R_x) + U''\pi_x(\pi_{ax} - R)$

Finally, a similar result applies to all SSD transformations, if one makes the stronger requirement that the *marginal product* π_a must not only increase but must also be concave in x.

Proposition 4.13 (SSD Transformations II) *The optimal action increases for all SSD transformations if $\pi_{axx} \leq 0$ in addition to the conditions stated in Proposition 4.12.*

Proof Look at the first integral term on the RHS of (4.19). Using integration by parts, this can be written as

$$\int_{\underline{x}}^{\bar{x}} U'\pi_{ax}k\, dF = \int_{\underline{x}}^{\bar{x}} U'\pi_{ax} \frac{d}{dx}\left(\int_{\underline{x}}^{x} k(y)\, dy\right) dF(x)$$

$$= U'\pi_{ax} \int_{\underline{x}}^{x} k(y)\, dy\Big|_{x=\bar{x}}$$

$$- \int_{\underline{x}}^{\bar{x}} (U''\pi_{ax} + U'\pi_{axx}) \int_{\underline{x}}^{x} k(y)\, dy\, dF(x).$$

Using an argument similar to the one developed in the previous proof, the assertion follows easily. □

4.7.3 Summary Table

Since we make extensive use of these results in the following applications, we summarize these sufficient conditions for $a^{*\prime}(0) \geq 0$ in Table 4.2.

4.8 Bibliographic Notes

The exposition of the theory of stochastic dominance is based on Hadar and Russell (1969, 1971), Meyer (1989), Meyer and Ormiston (1983), Ross (1983), and Ormiston (1992). For further details the reader is referred to the collection of essays edited by Whitmore and Findlay (1982), especially the contributions by Fishburn and Vickson (1978) and Hadar and Russell (1982).

The extension to third- and higher-order stochastic dominance is straightforward. The interested reader is referred to Whitmore (1970).

5

Stochastic Dominance: Applications

Chance favors only the prepared mind.
`Louis Pasteur`

5.1 Introduction

In the introduction to this part of the book (Section 4.1) it was claimed that stochastic dominance theory is useful in many areas of economics. We now put this claim to a proof with a sample of applications – ranging from a simple portfolio selection problem to the measurement of income inequality in society.

5.2 Portfolio Selection I

A risk-averse investor considers dividing given wealth w between two assets: one riskless asset with the sure return r, and one risky asset with the random return $r + X$. Short sales are not feasible. The decision problem is to choose that investment in the risky asset $a \in [0, w]$, which maximizes expected utility:

$$\max_a E[U(\pi(a, X))] \quad \text{where} \quad \pi(a, X) := wr + aX. \tag{5.1}$$

To assure an interior solution, $a^* \in (0, w)$, $E[X] > 0$ is assumed.[1]
Evidently, one has

$$\pi_a = X, \quad \pi_{ax} = 1, \quad \pi_{axx} = 0, \quad \pi_x = a, \quad \pi_{xx} = 0, \quad R = -\frac{U''}{U'}aX. \tag{5.2}$$

Therefore,

$$V_{ax} = U'(1 - R), \quad V_{axx} = -U'R_x + U''a(1 - R). \tag{5.3}$$

Proposition 5.1 *Investment in the risky asset will increase if*

1. *its return is subject to a FSD transformation and $R < 1$ everywhere;*
2. *its return is subject to a SSD transformation and $R < 1$, $R_x > 0$ everywhere.*

---

[1] The first-order condition for an interior solution is $E[U'X] = 0$. Since $E[U'X] = E[U']E[X] + \text{Cov}(U', X)$, it follows that an interior solution exists if and only if $E[X] > 0$. Notice: $\text{Cov}(U', X) < 0 \iff a > 0$, because U' is strict monotone decreasing.

Proof See Table 4.2 and (5.2), (5.3).   □

The two requirements in Proposition 5.1 are fairly restrictive. Indeed, $R < 1$ excludes some commonly used utility functions, and the alternative requirement $R_x > 0$ contradicts the usual assumption of diminishing risk aversion.

However, by restricting the permitted transformations of the return of the risky asset, one can show that the demand for the risky asset tends to increase also under more reasonable assumptions concerning the degree of risk aversion.

Proposition 5.2 *Investment in the risky asset will increase if its return is subject to a SSD transformation, with $t'(x) \leq 1$ (equivalently $k'(x) \leq 0$), and the absolute risk aversion is diminishing ($A' \leq 0$).*

Proof See Table 4.2 and (5.2).   □

As an illustration, suppose the premium on the risky asset is increased by a fixed amount θ at all realizations of X. This leads to the transformation $t(X) = X + \theta$. Hence, $k(X) = \theta$, $k'(X) = 0$, and the demand for the risky asset will increase by the first part of Proposition 5.2. As another illustration, suppose that the earnings on the risky asset are subject to an income tax. Suppose the tax is reduced in such a way that the tax reduction is high at low and low at high realizations x. Then $k(X) = t(X) - X > 0$ and $k'(X) = t'(X) - 1 < 0$. Again, the demand for the risky asset will increase, by the second part of Proposition 5.2.

Interestingly, if $t'(x) > 1$ (equivalently, if $k' > 0$), the higher return of the risky asset may lead the investor to hold less of it. An interpretation of this paradoxical *Giffen-good effect* makes use of the distinction between an income effect and a substitution effect, adapted from traditional demand theory. The fact that $t(x) \geq x$ ($k(x) \geq 0$) implies that the *substitution effect* is positive, which indicates that a^* should increase. However, if $t' > 1$ ($k' > 0$), the transformed random variable is riskier, and the *income effect* may be negative and larger than the substitution effect.[2]

5.3 The Competitive Firm under Price Uncertainty

Consider a risk-averse competitive firm with the convex cost function $C(a)$, defined on output a with fixed costs $\lim_{a \to 0} C(a) > 0$. Production is subject to a time lag; therefore, production decisions have to be made before the market price is known. The firm is a price taker in the sense that the product price is a nonnegative random variable X. To assure an interior solution, $E[X] > \min_a C(a)/a$ is assumed.

The firm maximizes the expected utility of profits π by choosing nonnegative output a:

$$\max_{a \geq 0} E[U(\pi(a, X))], \quad \text{where} \quad \pi(a, X) := Xa - C(a). \quad (5.4)$$

---

[2] If the demand for the risky asset may diminish when its return increases, you may rightly suspect that the demand for the riskless asset may also increase if its (safe) return diminishes. This possibility was noticed by Fishburn and Porter (1976). Necessary and sufficient conditions for this to occur are described in Fishburn and Porter (1976) and in Pratt (1989).

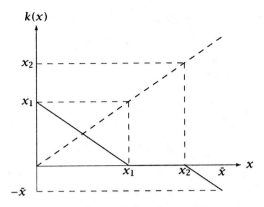

Figure 5.1. Effect of Price Support Program.

Evidently,[3]

$$\pi_a = X - C'(a), \qquad \pi_{ax} = 1, \qquad \pi_{xx} = \pi_{axx} = 0, \qquad \pi_x = a. \qquad (5.5)$$

Proposition 5.3 *The competitive firm will increase output if the product price is subject to a SSD transformation ($\int_0^x k\,dF \geq 0$), with $k'(x) = t'(x) - 1 \leq 0$, and the absolute risk aversion is decreasing in x.*

Proof See Table 4.2 and (5.5).   □

As an illustration, suppose output is subsidized at a fixed rate $\theta > 0$. Then $t(x) = x + \theta$ and $k(x) = t(x) - x = \theta > 0$, $k'(x) = 0$. Alternatively, let this subsidy be regressive in the sense that the subsidy rate is positive but monotone decreasing in the price x. Then $k(x) > 0$ and $k'(x) < 0$. In both cases output will increase, provided absolute risk aversion is not increasing.[4]

Finally, suppose the government introduces a price support program where it buys or sells from its inventory in such a way that the price is confined to a narrower range, say $[x_1, x_2] \subset [\underline{x}, \bar{x}]$. Such price support or buffer stock programs are observed in many markets for natural resources and agricultural products. Stated formally, they lead to the transformation (see Figure 5.1)

$$t(X) = \begin{cases} X + (x_1 - X) & \text{if } X \leq x_1, \\ X & \text{if } X \in (x_1, x_2), \\ X - (X - x_2) & \text{if } X \geq x_2. \end{cases}$$

Therefore,

$$k(X) = \begin{cases} x_1 - X & \text{if } X \leq x_1, \\ 0 & \text{if } X \in (x_1, x_2), \\ x_2 - X & \text{if } X \geq x_2. \end{cases}$$

If x_1 is chosen sufficiently high or x_2 sufficiently low, one can assure that $t(X) \succsim_{\text{SSD}} X$. The exact condition is $x_1^2 > (\bar{x} - x_2)^2$ (see Proposition 4.9 and the

---

[3] Note that $R = -(U''/U')(X - C')a$, which is why R is positive for high x, and negative for low x.
[4] Notice, however, that the effect of an *ad valorem* subsidy is ambiguous because in this case $t(x) = \theta x, \theta > 0$, and therefore $k'(x) = \theta > 0$.

illustration), which is of course always satisfied if the price support intervenes only to assure a minimum price. In this case, Proposition 5.3 indicates that the price support program leads to higher output (provided the absolute risk aversion is not increasing), which in turn may lead to a buildup of public inventories, epitomized by the infamous butter mountain of the European Community.

5.4 Labor Supply

A risk-averse household chooses a labor supply a facing a fixed real wage rate $w > 0$ and random earnings on nonhuman capital, $X \geq 0$. The endowment with time is one unit; time spent without working is leisure. All income is spent on a fixed basket of consumption goods; therefore, the number of units consumed is

$$\pi(a, X) := wa + X. \qquad (5.6)$$

The household maximizes expected utility:

$$\max_{a \in [0,1]} E[V(a, X)].$$

The objective function is based on the twice continuously differentiable and concave utility function U, with the two arguments a and $\pi(a, X)$:

$$V(a, X) := U(a, \pi(a, X)).$$

Of course, $U_a < 0$, $U_\pi > 0$, $U_{\pi\pi} \leq 0$. To assure an interior solution, $a^* \in (0, 1)$, the usual Inada conditions are assumed.

The important difference between this and all previous applications is that the utility function U now has two arguments, $\pi(a, x)$ and a. This must be kept in mind when one applies the general theory of the comparative statics of risk.

We want to find out under which conditions labor supply tends to either increase or diminish if random property income is subject to FSD or SSD transformations. In contrast with previous applications, we now also need assumptions concerning the behavior of the cross derivative of the utility function.

To obtain clear-cut results, we admit only utility functions that display either $U_{a\pi} + wU_{\pi\pi} < 0$ or > 0 everywhere. In the well-known deterministic labor-supply model, these inequalities correspond to leisure being either a *normal* or an *inferior* good, respectively. We will stick to this interpretation of the sign of $U_{a\pi} + wU_{\pi\pi}$.

As you know from Section 4.7, the signs of V_{ax} and V_{axx} play an essential role in explaining the labor-supply response. The nice feature of the present model is that there is a one-to-one correspondence between the sign of these functions and the nature of the leisure good. Therefore, the supply response is unambiguously determined by the income elasticity of the demand for leisure.

Proposition 5.4 *Labor supply diminishes (increases) for all FSD transformations of property income, if leisure is a normal (inferior) good everywhere.*

Proof This follows immediately by Proposition 4.10 and the fact that

$$V_{ax} = U_{a\pi} + wU_{\pi\pi} \lesseqqgtr 0 \quad \text{if leisure is} \begin{cases} \text{normal,} \\ \text{neutral,} \\ \text{inferior.} \end{cases} \qquad \square$$

This result can be pushed a bit further if one adds assumptions concerning the behavior of the cross derivative of the utility function. For example, suppose the consumption of leisure does not affect the household's willingness to take gambles. Specifically, suppose the *absolute* risk aversion A is independent of the consumption of leisure:

$$\frac{d}{da} A(a, \pi(a, x)) = 0 \qquad \text{everywhere.} \qquad (5.7)$$

Then whether leisure is a normal or an inferior good determines not only the sign of V_{ax}, but also that of V_{axx}:

Lemma 5.1 *Suppose (5.7) holds. Then* sign $V_{axx} = -$sign V_{ax}.

Proof Since $\pi_x = 1$, one has $(d/dx) \ln U_\pi = U_{\pi\pi}/U_\pi = -A$. Therefore, by the assumed invariance of A with respect to a and the fact that the order of differentiation does not matter, one has

$$0 = \frac{d}{da}\frac{d}{dx} \ln U_\pi$$

$$= \frac{d}{dx}\frac{d}{da} \ln U_\pi$$

$$= \frac{d}{dx}\left(\frac{U_{\pi a} + wU_{\pi\pi}}{U_\pi}\right)$$

$$= \frac{d}{dx}\left(\frac{V_{ax}}{U_\pi}\right)$$

$$= \frac{V_{axx} + V_{ax}A}{U_\pi}.$$

Therefore, $V_{axx} = -V_{ax}A$, and the assertion follows immediately. $\square$

Using this result one can extend the labor-supply response described in Proposition 5.4 to all SSD transformations of property income.

Proposition 5.5 *The labor supply diminishes (increases) for all SSD transformations of property income if leisure is a normal (inferior) good.*

Proof This follows immediately by Proposition 4.11 and Lemma 5.1. $\square$

5.5 Entry in Cournot Oligopoly

Consider the mixed-strategy equilibrium of the entry game in a Cournot oligopoly, explained in Chapter 3 on Oligopoly and Industrial Organization (see Section 3.4.10).

There we showed that the equilibrium probability of entry, μ, must satisfy the condition of indifference between entry (leading to the payoff stated on the left-hand side) and nonentry (leading to zero payoff):

$$\sum_{n=0}^{N-1} \phi_N(n, \mu)\Pi(n+1) - F = 0, \tag{5.8}$$

where $\phi_N(n, \mu)$ is the probability of the event that n rivals enter,

$$\phi_N(n, \mu) := \binom{N-1}{n}\mu^n(1-\mu)^{N-1-n}, \tag{5.9}$$

$\Pi(n)$ the gross profit as a function of the number of active firms, N the number of potential competitors, and F the sunk entry cost. N is taken to be so large that $\pi(N) < F$; in other words: If all firms entered with certainty, they would suffer losses.

The prize question is: Does this indifference condition have a solution $\mu \in (0, 1)$, and if so, is it unique? Having mastered stochastic dominance, the answer is easy to prove.

Proposition 5.6 (Mixed Entry Strategies in Oligopoly) *The simultaneous-entry model has a unique mixed-strategy equilibrium where each potential competitor enters with positive probability less than one.*

Proof The proof proceeds in several steps:

1. Confirm that the left-hand side of (5.8) is positive if $\mu = 0$, and negative if $\mu = 1$. This is the easiest part.
2. Consider the probability distribution of the random number of rival entrants, $\tilde{n}$, as a function of μ:

$$\bar{\Phi}_N(n, \mu) := \Pr\{\tilde{n} > n\} = \sum_{m=n+1}^{N-1} \binom{N-1}{m}\mu^m(1-\mu)^{N-1-m}. \tag{5.10}$$

By a known result one can write (5.10) in the equivalent form[5]

$$\bar{\Phi}_N(n, \mu) = \frac{(N-1)!}{n!(N-n-2)!} \int_0^\mu \tau^n(1-\tau)^{N-n-2}\, d\tau, \tag{5.11}$$

from which you see immediately that $\bar{\Phi}_N$ is strictly monotone increasing in μ. In other words, increasing μ leads to FSD dominance. Since Π is *decreasing* in n, it follows that the expected profit from entry (the left-hand side of (5.8)) must be strict monotone decreasing in μ, by Proposition 4.1.
3. Putting pieces together, it follows that (5.8) has a unique solution $\mu \in (0, 1)$. □

Another question concerns the effect of potential competition on the equilibrium entry strategy. Again, stochastic dominance gives the clue.

Proposition 5.7 (Comparative Statics) *The equilibrium probability of entry μ is a strict monotone decreasing function of the number of potential competitors N.*

---

[5] See rule (R18) in the brief introduction to order statistics in Appendix D, Section D.4.5.

Proof Follows immediately from the fact that the binomial distribution $\phi_N(n, \mu)$ is stochastically increasing (in the sense of FSD) in N as well as in μ.   □

5.6 Auctions

Consider the English (E) and Dutch (D) auction in the symmetric framework of independent private values with $N \geq 2$ bidders. Assume uniformly distributed valuations on the support $[0, 1]$ and risk-neutral bidders.

In Chapter 8, we show in detail that the equilibrium bid functions are $b_D(v) = (1 - 1/N)v$ and $b_E(v) \equiv v$. The associated equilibrium prices are the random variables P_D and P_E. Their probability distribution functions (cdf's) are (see (8.21) and (8.22))

$$F_D(x) = \left(\frac{N}{N-1}\right)^N x^N, \tag{5.12}$$

$$F_E(x) = x^N + N\left(x^{N-1} - x^N\right). \tag{5.13}$$

The equilibrium price in both auctions is equal to the highest bid. In the Dutch auction it is

$$P_D = b_1^*\left(V_{(N)}\right) \tag{5.14}$$

and in the English auction

$$P_E = b_2^*\left(V_{(N-1)}\right). \tag{5.15}$$

Here $V_{(N)}$, $V_{(N-1)}$ denote the highest and second highest order statistic of a sample of N identically and independently distributed iid random valuations, respectively.

An important result in auction theory is that the expected values of equilibrium prices in the Dutch and English auction are the same, $E[P_D] = E[P_E]$. However, the random variables differ in their risk attributes. Indeed:

Proposition 5.8 (Dutch vs. English Auction) *The random equilibrium price of the Dutch auction, P_D, second-order stochastically dominates that of the English auction, P_E. In other words, every risk-averse seller should strictly prefer the Dutch auction.*

Proof In order to prove the asserted stochastic dominance relationship, we show that the two cdf's are single-crossing. Since the expected values of the two equilibrium prices are the same, one can employ the single-crossing Theorem 4.6. The dominated random equilibrium price is the one that has more probability mass on both tails of the distribution. This happens to be P_E. The details are spelled out in Chapter 8 on Auctions, in Section 8.2.5 (see also Figure 8.2).   □

5.7 Portfolio Selection II*

Using the mean–variance approach, it is relatively straightforward to find out whether it pays to mix two risky assets in a portfolio even if one asset would be strictly preferable if one had to choose just one of them.[6] The mean–variance approach is however not sufficiently general.[7] Therefore, it is high time to return to this issue, using stochastic dominance instead of mean–variance rankings.

Consider portfolios consisting of a mixture of two random prospects. We are interested in conditions under which diversification is optimal for all risk-averse agents. Let the two prospects be described by two independent and positive random variables X_1 and X_2. Then a portfolio is characterized by a new random variable $P(\lambda)$:

$$P(\lambda) := \lambda X_1 + (1 - \lambda) X_2. \tag{5.16}$$

The portfolio selection problem is to choose a $\lambda \in \mathbb{R}$ that maximizes the investor's expected utility, $E[U(P(\lambda)]$. We will say that diversification is optimal if for all $U \in \mathcal{U}_2$ there exists some $\lambda \in (0, 1)$ for which $E[U(P(\lambda))] > \max\{E[U(P(0))],$ $E[U(P(1))]\}$.

A first result that also helps in other proofs is

Proposition 5.9 *Let X_1 and X_2 be two independent, identically distributed random variables. Then diversification pays in the strong sense that*

$$E[U(P(\lambda))] > \max\{E[U(P(1))], E[U(P(0))]\} \qquad \forall \lambda \in (0, 1).$$

Proof See Hadar and Russell (1971). □

But does diversification pay even if one of the two random prospects, say X_1, SSD-dominates X_2? Surprisingly, the answer is yes – provided the dominance is not excessive in a sense to be made precise.

Before proceeding, it has to be stressed that this question makes sense only if the two prospects have the same mean: $E[X_1] = E[X_2]$. Why this? First of all, the assumption that X_1 SSD-dominates X_2 implies $E[X_1] \geq E[X_2]$, by Lemma 4.2. Therefore, if $E[X_1]$ differed from $E[X_2]$, one would have $E[X_1] > E[X_2]$. But then $\forall \lambda \in (0, 1)$, $EP(1) = E[X_1] > \lambda E[X_1] + (1 - \lambda)E[X_2] =: EP(\lambda)$, so that – again by Lemma 4.2 – $P(\lambda)$ cannot SSD dominate X_1, $\lambda \in (0, 1)$, so that the assertion could not possibly hold true. Anyway, the assumption $E[X_1] = E[X_2]$ is not restrictive. If assets are divisible, it is only a matter of the choice of units.

As a second preliminary question we now ask: What precisely do we mean by saying that X_1 dominates X_2 – but not *excessively* so? For the purpose of formalizing this notion, we introduce yet another random variable. Let Y be independent of X_2, yet identically distributed. Then, by combining X_2 and Y, one gets a new random variable that SSD-dominates X_2 (see Proposition 4.8). Utilizing this property, we now make the following assumption:

Assumption 5.1 There exists a set $S \subset (0, 1)$, $S \neq \varnothing$, such that $\forall \lambda \in S$, $\tilde{P}(\lambda) :=$ $\lambda X_2 + (1 - \lambda)Y$ SSD-dominates X_1.

This gives precise meaning to the statement that X_1 SSD-dominates X_2, but not excessively so.

---

[6] See the supplementary section on variance-minimizing portfolios (Section 5.9).

[7] Recall that variance is an unambiguous measure of risk only if the utility function is quadratic or if probability distributions are normal.

With these preliminaries we come to our main optimality-of-diversification result.

Proposition 5.10 *Let X_1 and X_2 be two independent nonnegative random variables with identical means. Suppose X_1 SSD-dominates X_2, and suppose the above assumption holds. Then, for all $\lambda \in S$, $P(\lambda) := \lambda X_1 + (1 - \lambda)X_2$ SSD-dominates X_2 as well as X_1.*

Proof In the proof we make use of certain properties of the *artificial portfolio* described in Assumption 5.1 that involves a convex combination of the two random variables X_2 and Y, $\tilde{P}(\lambda) := \lambda X_2 + (1 - \lambda)Y$, $\lambda \in S$. Since X_2 and Y are identically and independently distributed, the probability distributions of $P(\lambda)$ and $\hat{P}(\lambda) := \lambda X_1 + (1 - \lambda)Y$ must be the same. Next, notice that, by Proposition 4.8, $\hat{P}(\lambda)$ SSD-dominates $\tilde{P}(\lambda)$.[8] Combining this with the other assumptions, one thus arrives at the following combination of SSD relationships:

$$P(\lambda) := \lambda X_1 + (1 - \lambda)X_2$$
$$\succsim_{\mathrm{SSD}} \lambda X_1 + (1 - \lambda)Y =: \hat{P}(\lambda)$$
$$\succ_{\mathrm{SSD}} \lambda X_2 + (1 - \lambda)Y =: \tilde{P}(\lambda)$$
$$\succ_{\mathrm{SSD}} X_1$$
$$\succ_{\mathrm{SSD}} X_2.$$

The assertion follows immediately by the transitivity of stochastic dominance. □

5.8 Income Inequality*

As an economist you are well trained to rank social states by their efficiency on the basis of the Pareto criterion. But how do you rank income distributions? For example, you may be asked to answer questions such as these:

- Has the distribution of income become less or more equal during the past decade?
- Is the distribution of income in France less or more equal than in Germany?
- Does the introduction of the value added tax in the U.S. give rise to greater or less income inequality?

How would you go about to answer these questions?

As a first shot you might use the *Gini coefficient*, a well-known summary statistic of inequality. However, we all have some rough notion of what income inequality should mean, and given any such notion one can always find examples of income distributions for which the ranking by the Gini coefficient blatantly contradicts that notion of inequality. Indeed, you may try as hard as you wish, but you cannot find any acceptable social welfare function that consistently ranks income distributions in the same way as the Gini coefficient, as was shown rigorously by Newbery (1970).

Already in the earlier 1920s Dalton (1920) suggested that the study of income inequality should start with a statement of the underlying welfare norm in the form of a social welfare function. The modern economic theory of ethics has laid

---

[8] In applying Proposition 4.8 set $a = \lambda$ and $b = 1 - \lambda$.

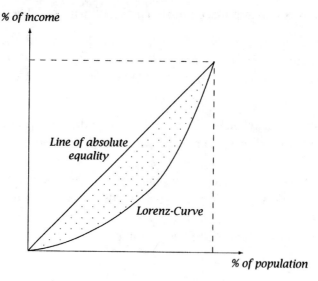

Figure 5.2. Lorenz Curve.

out various properties that reasonable social welfare functions should share, such as symmetry and additive separability. The rationale of imposing these and other properties is the notion that ethical rankings of social states must be impartial vis à vis all individuals in society.[9]

In the following, we adopt Dalton's advice and use a social welfare function to rank income distributions. Specifically, we consider income distributions with equal means μ characterized by their distribution functions such as $F : [0, \bar{y}] \rightarrow [0, 1]$ and $F^* : [0, \bar{y}] \rightarrow [0, 1]$ with images $F(y)$, $F^*(y)$. These are ranked according to the social welfare function $W : \mathcal{F} \rightarrow \mathbb{R}$, defined on the set of all distribution functions $\mathcal{F}$ with domain $[0, \bar{y}]$,

$$W(F) := \int_0^{\bar{y}} U(y)\, dF(y). \tag{5.17}$$

The only additional requirement will be that the utility function $U : \mathbb{R} \rightarrow \mathbb{R}$ be an element of the class $\mathcal{U}_2$.

We ask: *Under which conditions does F rank higher than F* regardless of the particular form of the utility function* $U \in \mathcal{U}_2$? This leads us to the notion of Lorenz dominance and – even though no random variables are involved here – back to the SSD.

You surely are familiar with the ingenious statistical representation of income distributions by Lorenz curves. The *Lorenz curve* plots percentages of the population, ordered by their income level from bottom to top, and their respective percentage shares of total income, as depicted in Figure 5.2. The diagonal represents

---

[9] Social welfare functions that have these properties are usually referred to as *utilitarian*. One of the most ardent and sophisticated defenders of modern utilitarianism is Harsanyi, and you may wish to consult one of his beautifully clear contributions on this important subject, in the collection of his essays on this topic (Harsanyi (1976)).

the line of absolute equality. Therefore, Lorenz curves are always on or below the diagonal.[10]

Stated formally, the Lorenz curve (due to Lorenz (1905)) is the graph of a function $\varphi : [0, 1] \to [0, 1]$ that maps the images of the distribution functions $F(y)$ and $F^*(y)$ into income shares as follows:

$$\varphi(z; F) := \frac{1}{\mu} \int_0^{F^{-1}(z)} y\, f(y)\, dy \qquad (5.18)$$

$$\varphi(z; F^*) := \frac{1}{\mu} \int_0^{F^{*-1}(z)} y\, f^*(y)\, dy, \qquad (5.19)$$

where $\mu := \int y f(y)\, dy = \int y f^*(y)\, dy$.

Based on this familiar concept, we now define *Lorenz dominance*:

Definition 5.1 Consider two income distributions with equal mean, described by the distribution functions F and F^*. F Lorenz-dominates F^* ($F \succ_L F^*$) if F is above F^* everywhere, i.e., if $\forall z \in [0, 1]$, $\varphi(z; F) \geq \varphi(z; F^*)$.

Of course, any welfare function W ranks distributions the same way as Lorenz dominance. But Lorenz dominance induces only a partial ordering of income distributions. However, as shown in the following main result, the welfare function W cannot consistently rank distributions in the same manner for all utility functions $U \in \mathcal{U}_2$, unless these distributions can be ranked by Lorenz dominance. Interestingly, the proof employs SSD, which is why the present material is an application of stochastic dominance theorems.

Proposition 5.11 *The income distribution function F ranks higher than F^* ($W(F) \geq W(F^*)$) for all utility functions $U \in \mathcal{U}_2$ if and only if F Lorenz dominates F^* ($F \succ_L F^*$).*

Proof By Proposition 4.4, the statement $W(F) \geq W(F^*) \,\forall U \in \mathcal{U}_2$ is equivalent to the statement that F dominates F^* in the sense of SSD. Therefore, one only needs to show that Lorenz dominance is equivalent to SSD. The details of the proof are spelled out in Atkinson (1972). □

5.9 Supplement: Variance-Minimizing Portfolios*

We close this chapter with a supplementary section, dealing with the basics of the mean–variance analysis of portfolio selection. This material may be used independently, for example to motivate the analysis of portfolio selection scattered over different sections of this part of the book.

Suppose you want to invest \$1 million. You are offered two financial assets, say two different bonds or stocks. Stripped of all unimportant detail, these assets are fully characterized by their random returns X and Y. Both assets promise the same

---

[10] Incidentally, the Gini coefficient is defined as the ratio of the area between the Lorenz curve and the line of absolute inequality to the area under the line of full equality.

average return $E[X] = E[Y]$ and have the same unit price.[11] But X is at least as risky and perhaps riskier than Y. You are risk-averse. *Would you be well advised to invest in a mixed portfolio, with a positive fraction of your wealth invested in X and Y, or should you rather put it all into the low-risk asset Y?*

5.9.1 Portfolios

Given these assumptions, a feasible (budget-balancing) portfolio is characterized by a new random variable Z, defined as a linear combination of the random returns of its constituent assets:

$$Z := \alpha X + (1 - \alpha)Y, \qquad \alpha \in \mathbb{R}. \tag{5.20}$$

Since the two assets' average returns are the same, the average return of the portfolio Z is unaffected by the asset mix. Therefore, you can be single-minded and focus on the effect of mixing assets on risk. Your decision problem is thus reduced to choosing that particular α that minimizes the risk of the resulting portfolio.

While we are particularly interested in finding out whether the optimal α is a real number between 0 and 1, which represents diversification, notice that we have not excluded that α is negative or greater than 1. A negative α indicates that the investor actually sells or issues the asset X, and $\alpha > 1$ that he issues Y.

5.9.2 Conjectures

Before you continue with the formal analysis, sit back for a moment and let your intuition guide you. As X is at least as risky as Y (and perhaps even riskier), you may think that by combining them one can only increase risk relative to that from holding only the low-risk asset. Therefore, it would seem that you should stay away from the high-risk asset X. On the other hand, you may recall the old adage that one should never put all one's eggs in one basket, which suggests that it is always better to diversify.

5.9.3 Outlook

As it turns out, neither conjecture holds true without qualification. If the covariance (or the correlation) of X and Y is sufficiently low, risk is subadditivity (the total is less than the sum of its parts), and diversification is beneficial. But diversification actually increases risk if the covariance is sufficiently high. Therefore, it all depends on the degree of association between the two assets' returns, measured by their covariance or correlation.

Essentially, risk is like toxic chemicals. To determine the toxic properties of a blend of chemicals, it is less important how poisonous the ingredients are than how they work together. Some perfectly harmless substances combine to a deadly mixture, while other highly toxic ingredients completely neutralize each other.

---

[11] Assuming both identical expected values and identical unit prices makes this analysis a special case. Nevertheless, some of the following results, such as the convexity of the variance of a portfolio, are central to the general mean–variance analysis of portfolio choice. A nice introductory text is Sharpe (1970).

5.9.4 Assumptions

In the following exercise, we develop a tight, necessary, and sufficient condition for the optimality of diversification. In line with the mean–variance approach to the theory of finance, we assume that the variance of Z is a suitable measure of risk.[12] As a convention, we let

$$\sigma_x^2 := \mathrm{Var}(X) \geq \mathrm{Var}(Y) =: \sigma_y^2. \tag{5.21}$$

By a known result (see rule (R3), Appendix D), one has

$$\sigma_z^2 := \mathrm{Var}(Z) = \alpha^2 \sigma_x^2 + (1-\alpha)^2 \sigma_y^2 + 2\alpha(1-\alpha)\,\mathrm{Cov}(X,Y). \tag{5.22}$$

The question is: Does σ_z^2 have a minimum for some $\alpha \in (0,1)$?

5.9.5 A Lemma That Clears the Road

Lemma 5.2 *Suppose $\sigma_x^2 > \sigma_y^2$ or X and Y are not perfectly correlated. Then σ_z^2 reaches a minimum at*

$$\alpha^* = \frac{\sigma_y^2 - \mathrm{Cov}(X,Y)}{\sigma_x^2 + \sigma_y^2 - 2\,\mathrm{Cov}(X,Y)}. \tag{5.23}$$

Proof Define the function $\phi : \mathbb{R} \to \mathbb{R}$, $\phi(\alpha) := \sigma_z^2$. Then ϕ is twice continuously differentiable, and one has

$$\phi'(\alpha) = 2\alpha\sigma_x^2 - 2(1-\alpha)\sigma_y^2 + 2\,\mathrm{Cov}(X,Y) - 4\alpha\,\mathrm{Cov}(X,Y). \tag{5.24}$$

Therefore, α^* is a stationary point of $\phi(\alpha)$.

Denote the standard deviations by σ_x, σ_y (these are the nonnegative square roots of σ_x^2, σ_y^2), and the correlation by $\rho := \mathrm{Cov}(X,Y)/(\sigma_x\sigma_y)$. Also recall that $\rho \in [-1, 1]$ (by rule (R7), Appendix D). Therefore,

$$\begin{aligned}
\phi''(\alpha) &= 2\sigma_x^2 + 2\sigma_y^2 - 4\,\mathrm{Cov}(X,Y) \\
&= 2\sigma_x^2 + 2\sigma_y^2 - 4\rho\sigma_x\sigma_y \\
&\geq 2\sigma_x^2 + 2\sigma_y^2 - 4\sigma_x\sigma_y \quad (\text{by } \rho \leq 1) \\
&= 2(\sigma_x - \sigma_y)^2 \\
&\geq 0 \quad (\text{by } 5.21),
\end{aligned} \tag{5.25}$$

with at least one inequality holding strict because $\rho < 1$ or $\sigma_x > \sigma_y$. Hence, ϕ is strictly convex, and therefore the stationary point α^*, determined in (5.23), is a unique global minimum. (Note: By (5.25) the denominator of (5.23) is equal to $\frac{1}{2}\phi''(\alpha) > 0$ and hence does not vanish.) □

---

[12] As we have explained in this chapter, variance can only serve this purpose if utility functions are quadratic or if probability distributions of X and Y are normal distributions (see Section 5.7). These conditions are, of course, extremely restrictive.

5.9.6 Main Result

It remains to be shown that $\alpha^* \in (0, 1)$ under reasonable circumstances. This question is answered by the following main result

Proposition 5.12 *Suppose* $\sigma_x \geq \sigma_y$. *Diversification is optimal,* $\alpha^* \in (0, 1)$, *if and only if the correlation is sufficiently low:* $\rho < \sigma_y/\sigma_x$.

Proof We need to show that ϕ reaches a minimum at $\alpha^* \in (0, 1)$. Since ϕ is convex (see (5.25)) and $\phi(0) = \text{Var}(Y) \leq \text{Var}(X) = \phi(1)$, the proof is complete if $\phi'(0) < 0$, as illustrated in Figure 5.3. Insert $\alpha = 0$ into (5.24) and one obtains

$$\phi'(0) = 2\big[\text{Cov}(X, Y) - \sigma_y^2\big]$$
$$= 2\big(\rho\sigma_x\sigma_y - \sigma_y^2\big)$$
$$< 0 \quad \Longleftrightarrow \quad \rho < \frac{\sigma_y}{\sigma_x}. \qquad\qquad \square$$

Example 5.1 Assume the joint probability distribution of two assets' random returns X and Y summarized in Table 5.1. Then one obtains $E(X) = E(Y) = 10$, $\text{Var}(X) = 100$, $\text{Var}(Y) = 12$, $\text{Cov}(X, Y) = 0$, and hence $\alpha^* \approx 0.107$. Therefore, almost 11% of the entire investment should be put into the high-risk asset X.

Table 5.1. *Probability distribution of returns*

	Pr(X, Y)		
	$Y = 8$	$Y = 16$	Σ
$X = 5$	3/5	1/5	4/5
$X = 30$	3/20	1/20	1/5
Σ	3/4	1/4	1

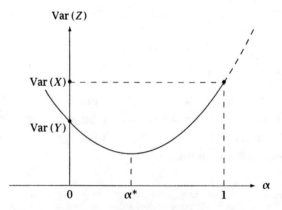

Figure 5.3. The Variance of a Mixed Portfolio.

5.9.7 Summary

We have shown that the optimality of diversification hinges upon the degree of association between the individual assets' returns. Diversification reduces risk and hence is beneficial if and only if the correlation is sufficiently low. This occurs, for example, if 1) both assets are equally risky ($\sigma_y = \sigma_x$), but $\rho < 1$, or 2) the correlation is negative or vanishes ($\rho \leq 0$). In turn, diversification actually increases risk if the two assets are highly correlated – ρ is positive and close to 1 – and one asset is more risky than the other.

Having obtained clear-cut results, summarized by the necessary and sufficient condition in Proposition 5.12, you may be ready to look at the generalized analysis, using a less restrictive measure of risk, in Section 5.7 of this chapter.

5.9.8 Discussion

As an exercise, consider the effect of price variations. Normalize the price of asset Y to 1, denote the (relative) price of X by π, and suppose the investor's budget is equal to $m > 0$. Using the investor's budget constraint, feasible portfolios are then described by the random return (where α now is the demand for asset X)

$$Z = \alpha X + (m - \alpha \pi)Y,$$

and the variance-minimizing demand is

$$\alpha^* = \frac{m(\pi \sigma_y^2 - \mathrm{Cov}(X, Y))}{\sigma_x^2 + \sigma_y^2 \pi^2 - 2\,\mathrm{Cov}(X, Y)}.$$

It follows immediately that the variance-minimizing demand for the riskier asset X can increase with its price π. In particular,

$$\pi < \rho \frac{\sigma_x}{\sigma_y} \quad \Rightarrow \quad \alpha^* < 0,$$

$$\pi > \rho \frac{\sigma_x}{\sigma_y} \quad \Rightarrow \quad \alpha^* > 0.$$

Therefore, as π is increased in this manner, the variance-minimizing investor switches from a negative to a positive demand. This takes us to the somewhat paradoxical conclusion that the riskier asset can be a Giffen good – provided the investor is preoccupied with variance and pays little attention to the expected return. Economists are usually hard pressed to find meaningful examples of Giffen goods. You may view this exercise as an addition to a very short list of Giffen goods.

5.10 Bibliographic Notes

The applications to the diversification of simple portfolios are based on Hadar and Russell (1982). If you want to know more about this topic, take a look at Fishburn and Porter (1976), Hadar and Seo (1990a, 1990b), and Landsberger and Meilijson (1990a).

The application on the competitive firm is based on Hadar and Russell (1982) and Ormiston (1992). For further aspects, see Sandmo's (1971) seminal contribution. The distinction between the income and substitution effects may have seemed misplaced to you in the context of the theory of the firm. In that case, take a look at Davis (1989).

The application to labor supply uses results derived in the analysis of social security risk by Prinz and Wolfstetter (1991).

The application to mixed entry strategies in a Cournot oligopoly uses the entry model by Dixit and Shapiro (1986).

The application to income inequality and stochastic dominance is based on a celebrated result by Atkinson (1972). In the current literature, the concept of Lorenz dominance has been generalized so that it can also be applied to income distributions with different means, and the so-called Atkinson theorem has been extended correspondingly. If you are interested in these matters, take a look at Yitzhaki (1982) and Amiel and Cowell (1997). For a general survey on income inequality, we also recommend Sen's (1972) monograph very highly.

An important topic that has been omitted here concerns the relationship between stochastic dominance and Marschak's measure of informativeness, which is quite a bit more general than the usual measures of riskiness, such as the one proposed by Rothschild and Stiglitz (1970). For an informal introduction to these concepts – and detailed references to the literature – the interested reader is referred to Part I of Nermuth (1982).

In the literature, there are many more applications of stochastic dominance. We mention the explanation of the optimal deductible in insurance contracts by Arrow (1963) and Eeckhoudt, Gollier, and Schlesinger (1991), the theory of wage indexation by Adolph and Wolfstetter (1991), and Holmstrom's (1979) analysis of the principal–agent problem, which will be discussed extensively in Chapter 11.

Finally, we refer the reader to the well-known ranking of risk proposed by Rothschild and Stiglitz (1970, 1971) and its critical evaluation by Landsberger and Meilijson (1990b).

6
Risk Aversion

Great deeds are usually wrought at great risk.
Herodotus

6.1 Introduction

Stochastic dominance concerns the assessment and comparative statics of risk. It asks: What is meant by one prospect being more risky than another? A natural complementary issue concerns the problem of characterizing agents' attitude towards risk. We close this part with a brief discussion of this issue. In particular, we ask: What is meant by one agent being more risk-averse than another, how are these differences measured, and how useful are these measures in illuminating economic issues?

The *Arrow–Pratt* measures are the best-known measures of risk aversion. They are widely used to characterize the optimal allocation of risk, ranging from the demand for insurance and portfolio selection to the analysis of tax evasion. However, despite their success, these measures are not strong enough to always yield economically plausible results. This becomes apparent when they are applied to an incomplete-markets framework where agents cannot cover all risks.

The purpose of this brief chapter is to introduce important measures of risk aversion, spell out typical applications, and point out limitations and open issues. In particular, we address the following questions:

1. How should risk aversion be measured?
2. Is more risk aversion associated with a higher willingness to pay for insurance?
3. Should a more risk-averse investor hold more high-risk assets in his portfolio?
4. Should wealthier agents exhibit lower risk premiums or hold more high-risk assets if risk aversion is decreasing in wealth?

6.2 Absolute and Relative Risk Aversion

Consider two von Neumann–Morgenstern utility functions U_A, U_B, defined on $\mathbb{R}$, that are strictly monotone increasing, strictly concave (risk aversion), and in C^3 (at least three times continuously differentiable). The *coefficients of risk aversion* are defined as follows:

Definition 6.1 (Absolute Risk Aversion) U_A exhibits (strictly) higher risk aversion, in the sense of Arrow and Pratt, if its coefficient of absolute risk aversion is higher:

$$(\forall x): \quad -\frac{U_A''(x)}{U_A'(x)} \geq -\frac{U_B''(x)}{U_B'(x)} \tag{6.1}$$

(with strict inequality almost everywhere).

An alternative ranking is based on the coefficient of relative risk aversion (which is the elasticity of the marginal utility of wealth),

$$(\forall x): \quad -\frac{U_A''(x)}{U_A'(x)}x \geq -\frac{U_B''(x)}{U_B'(x)}x. \tag{6.2}$$

In general, these coefficients are *local* measures of risk aversion, except for the following *constant-risk-aversion utility functions*, for $\beta > 0$:

$$U(x) := \alpha - \beta e^{-ax} \qquad (a = \text{absolute risk aversion}),$$

$$U(x) := \alpha - \beta x^{-r+1} \qquad (r = \text{relative risk aversion}).$$

Another representation is gained by integrating the above coefficients twice. This establishes the existence of a strictly monotone increasing transformation G such that

$$U_A(x) \equiv G(U_B(x)).$$

Therefore, U_A exhibits more risk aversion than U_B if U_A can be obtained by *concavification* of U_B (see also Appendix C, Section C.8).

6.2.1 Pratt's Theorem

Is the Arrow–Pratt measure acceptable? The answer depends on how useful it is in illuminating economic issues. Pratt (1964) himself proposed such an economic test and claimed that his measure passes it with flying colors.

The canonical economic choice problem relates to risk-averse agents' willingness to pay for insurance. If the measure of risk aversion makes economic sense, then a more risk-averse agent should be willing to pay more for insurance. Define the insurance premium as the maximum willingness to pay to avoid having a given monetary lottery X with $E[X] = 0$. Stated formally, the insurance premium π is the certainty equivalent of X that satisfies the condition (where w denotes initial wealth)

$$E[U_i(w + X)] = U_i(w - \pi_i), \qquad i \in \{A, B\}. \tag{6.3}$$

Proposition 6.1 (Pratt) *The following three conditions are equivalent (Pratt (1964)):*

$$(\forall x) \quad -\frac{U_A''}{U_A'} \geq -\frac{U_B''}{U_B'}, \tag{i}$$

$$(\exists G) \quad G' \geq 0, \;\; G'' \leq 0, \quad U_A \equiv G(U_B), \tag{ii}$$

$$(\forall w) \quad \pi_A \geq \pi_B. \tag{iii}$$

Proof (i) $\Rightarrow$ (ii): Since U_B is monotone, we can define G implicitly by $U_A = G(U_B)$. Differentiating twice gives, after a bit of rearranging,

$$0 \geq \frac{U_A''}{U_A'} - \frac{U_B''}{U_B'} = \frac{G''}{G'}U_B',$$

which confirms that G is a monotone, concave transformation.

(ii) $\Rightarrow$ (iii): Follows immediately from the following chain of inequalities (which uses Jensen's inequality)

$$U_A(w - \pi_A) = E[U_A(w + X)]$$
$$= E[G(U_B(w + X)]$$
$$< G(E[U_B(w + X)])$$
$$= G(U_B(w - \pi_B))$$
$$= U_A(w - \pi_B).$$

(iii) $\Rightarrow$ (i): Without loss of generality, consider the binary lottery $L := (w+\epsilon, w-\epsilon; \frac{1}{2})$ (L gives either the monetary payoff $w + \epsilon$ or $w - \epsilon$ with equal probability). The associated risk premia, π_A, π_B, are implicitly defined as follows:

$$E[U_A(L)] := \frac{1}{2}(U_A(w + \epsilon) + U_A(w - \epsilon)) = U_A(w - \pi_A),$$

$$E[U_B(L)] := \frac{1}{2}(U_B(w + \epsilon) + U_B(w - \epsilon)) = U_B(w - \pi_B).$$

Expanding each, using a Taylor's series around w, one obtains for small ϵ the associated risk premia

$$\pi_i \approx -\frac{1}{2}\frac{U_i''(w)}{U_i'(w)}\epsilon^2, \qquad i \in \{A, B\}.$$

Hence, $\pi_A \geq \pi_B \Rightarrow$ (i), as asserted. $\qquad\square$

Apparently, the Arrow–Pratt measure of absolute risk aversion is in line with our intuition in the simple insurance problem. But it can easily be upset, as is shown in the following subsection.

6.2.2 An Incomplete-Insurance Puzzle

Typically, agents can only partially insure; some gambles can be insured against, while others have to be retained. As Ross (1983) observed, if only incomplete insurance is accessible, the Arrow–Pratt measure of absolute risk aversion is not sufficiently strong to support the plausible association between the size of the risk premium and the measure of risk aversion.

The following example, which is due to Ross, is a case in point: Suppose wealth is distributed according to the compounded lottery

$$L := [L_1, w_2; p],$$
$$L_1 := \left[w_1 - \epsilon, w_1 + \epsilon; \frac{1}{2}\right]$$

(L gives with probability p the binary lottery L_1 and with probability $1 - p$ the monetary payoff w_2; and L_1 gives either the monetary payoff $w_1 - \epsilon$ or $w_1 + \epsilon$, with equal probability). The agent can only buy partial insurance and get rid of the risk due to lottery L_1 and thus cannot avoid bearing some risk. The associated risk premium is implicitly defined by the requirements

$$E[U(L_2)] = E[U(L)],$$

$$L_2 := [w_1 - \pi_u, w_2 - \pi_u; p]$$

(π_u is the maximum willingness to pay for trading in lottery L_1 for a sure payoff).

For small ϵ one obtains, applying a Taylor approximation,

$$E[U(L)] = \frac{p}{2}\left(U(w_1 - \epsilon) + U(w_1 + \epsilon)\right) + (1 - p)U(w_2)$$

$$\approx pU(w_1) + (1 - p)U(w_2) + \frac{p}{2}U''(w_1)\epsilon^2,$$

$$E[U(L_2)] = pU(w_1 - \pi_u) + (1 - p)U(w_2)$$

$$\approx pU(w_1) + (1 - p)U(w_2)$$

$$-(pU'(w_1) + (1 - p)U'(w_2))\pi_u.$$

Combining yields

$$\pi_u = -\frac{pU''(w_1)\epsilon^2}{2\left(pU'(w_1) + (1 - p)U'(w_2)\right)}. \tag{6.4}$$

Now consider the constant-absolute-risk-aversion utility functions U_A, U_B given by

$$U_A(x) := -e^{-ax}, \quad U_B(x) := -e^{-bx}, \qquad a > b.$$

Obviously, U_A exhibits greater absolute risk aversion than U_B:

$$-\frac{U_A''}{U_A'} = a > b = -\frac{U_B''}{U_B'}.$$

However, for $w_1 - w_2$ sufficiently large one has

$$-\frac{U_A''(w_1)}{U_A'(w_2)} = ae^{a(w_2 - w_1)} < be^{b(w_2 - w_1)} = -\frac{U_B''(w_1)}{U_B'(w_2)}. \tag{6.5}$$

Hence, from (6.4), (6.5) one arrives at the counterintuitive conclusion that if p is sufficiently small, more risk aversion is associated with a lower risk premium: $\pi_A < \pi_B$.

6.3 Strong Absolute Risk Aversion*

The failure of the plausible association between higher risk aversion and a higher risk premium was one of the motivations for Ross's proposal of a new ordering called *strong absolute risk aversion*.

Definition 6.2 (Ross) U_A exhibits more strong absolute risk aversion than U_B if

$$(\exists \lambda > 0)\,(\forall x_1, x_2) \qquad \frac{U_A''(x_1)}{U_B''(x_1)} \geq \lambda \geq \frac{U_A'(x_2)}{U_B'(x_2)}.$$

This new ordering is indeed strictly stronger than the Arrow–Pratt measure.

Proposition 6.2 *If U_A exhibits more strong absolute risk aversion than U_B, then it also exhibits more absolute risk aversion, but not vice versa.*

Proof The asserted implication follows immediately by rearranging the definition. To show that the converse fails, consider the utility functions $U_i(x) := -e^{-a_i x}$, $i \in \{A, B\}$, with $a_A > a_B$. Obviously, U_A exhibits higher absolute risk aversion than U_B, but

$$\frac{U_A'(x_2)}{U_B'(x_2)} = \frac{a_A}{a_B} e^{a_B - a_A x_2},$$

$$\frac{U_A''(x_1)}{U_B''(x_1)} = \left(\frac{a_A}{a_B}\right)^2 e^{(b-2)x_1}.$$

Hence, for $x_1 - x_2$ sufficiently large, one has

$$\frac{U_A''(x_1)}{U_B''(x_1)} > \frac{U_A'(x_2)}{U_B'(x_2)},$$

which violates strong absolute risk aversion. □

6.3.1 Ross's Theorem

Proposition 6.3 *The following conditions are equivalent:*

$$(\exists \lambda > 0)\,(\forall x_1, x_2) \qquad \frac{U_A''(x_1)}{U_B''(x_1)} \geq \lambda \geq \frac{U_A'(x_2)}{U_B'(x_2)}, \tag{i}$$

$$(\exists G, \lambda > 0) \quad G' \leq 0, G'' \leq 0, \quad U_A \equiv \lambda U_B + G. \tag{ii}$$

Proof (i) ⇒ (ii): Assume (i), and define G by

$$U_A = \lambda U_B + G.$$

Differentiating gives

$$G' = U_A' - \lambda U_B',$$

$$\frac{U_A''}{U_B''} = \lambda + \frac{G''}{U_B''} \geq \lambda,$$

which also implies $G'' \leq 0$. The proof of the converse, (ii) ⇒ (i), is omitted. □

Ross introduced this new risk-aversion relationship in order to reestablish an unambiguous relationship between risk aversion and the size of the risk premium. This goal was achieved for the particular lottery considered in the example of the above insurance puzzle. However, as we exemplify with the following portfolio selection example, Ross's new ordering does not generally perform satisfactorily.

6.3.2 A Portfolio Selection Puzzle

In simple insurance problems it seemed natural to hope that a more risk-averse individual should have a higher risk premium. Similarly, in simple portfolio selection problems one would expect that a more risk-averse individual should demand less high-risk assets. However, this intuition is again not supported by the Arrow–Pratt measure.

The failure of this intuition was one of the reasons for Ross's construction of his strong absolute risk aversion measure. Ross showed that the strongly more risk-averse investor should hold a smaller proportion of high-risk assets, provided "riskier" is defined according to a new definition introduced by Ross (1983). However, his proof critically depends upon this peculiar definition of "riskier," and indeed fails if "riskier" is properly defined in terms of a second-order stochastic dominance relationship. Therefore, strong absolute risk aversion is still too weak to support intuitively plausible results.

To see why this is the case, take a look at the following example, which is due to Hadar and Seo (1990b). Consider two risky assets, denoted by their random returns X and Y. Let Y be riskier in the sense of second-order stochastic dominance (SSD), $X \succsim_{\text{SSD}} Y$, and let $E[X] > E[Y]$.[1] Investors' utility functions are

$$U_i(x) := x - \gamma_i x^2, \qquad x < \frac{\gamma_B}{2}, \qquad i \in \{A, B\},$$

$$\gamma_A > \gamma_B > 0,$$

and investors' portfolios are denoted by the random variables

$$Z(\alpha_i) := \alpha_i Y + (1 - \alpha_i)X,$$

which is characterized by the diversification parameter $\alpha_i \in \mathbb{R}$.

U_A is strongly more risk-averse than U_B. To prove this, define

$$G(x) := U_A(x) - U_B(x) = -(\gamma_a - \gamma_b)x^2.$$

Hence, one can write

$$U_A(x) = U_B(x) + \lambda G(x), \qquad \lambda = 1,$$

and $G(x)$ is monotone decreasing and concave – as required by Proposition 6.3(ii).

Next, compute the expected utilities of portfolio Z:

$$u_i(\alpha_i) := E[U_i(Z)] = E[Z] - \gamma_i E[Z^2].$$

The optimal portfolios satisfy the first-order conditions

$$u_i'(\alpha_i) = E[Y - X] - 2\gamma_i E[Z(Y - X)] = 0.$$

Since we assumed $E[Y - X] < 0$, these conditions entail

$$E[Z(Y - X)] < 0$$

in both cases.

---

[1] Recall that $X \succsim_{\text{SSD}} Y \Rightarrow E[X] \geq E[Y]$ by Proposition 4.2; therefore our assumption is slightly stronger than SSD.

Now note that

$$Z(Y - X) = (\alpha_i Y + (1 - \alpha_i)X)(Y - X)$$
$$= \alpha_i(Y - X)^2 + X(Y - X).$$

Therefore, by the above first-order conditions,

$$1 < \frac{\gamma_a}{\gamma_b} = \frac{\alpha_B E[(Y - X)^2] + E[X(Y - X)]}{\alpha_A E[(Y - X)^2] + E[X(Y - X)]}.$$

This entails (recall that $E[Z(Y - X)] < 0$)

$$\alpha_A E[(Y - X)^2] > \alpha_B E[(Y - X)^2].$$

Hence, $\alpha_A > \alpha_B$: *the strongly more risk-averse investor invests more in the riskier asset Y.*

Of course, since strong absolute risk aversion is stronger than absolute risk aversion by Proposition 6.2, this example also applies to the Arrow–Pratt measure.

6.4 Wealth–Dependent Risk Aversion*

In economic applications one often encounters the assumption of wealth-dependent risk aversion. Particularly, most people expect wealthier individuals to be less reluctant to bear risk. This leads to the assumption of decreasing risk aversion.

Definition 6.3 (DARA) The utility function $U(x)$ displays decreasing absolute risk aversion (DARA) if

$$(\forall x, \forall y > 0): \quad \frac{U''(x + y)}{U'(x + y)} \geq \frac{U''(x)}{U'(x)},$$

and decreasing strong absolute risk aversion if

$$(\forall x \forall y > 0)\,(\exists \lambda): \quad \frac{U''(x + y)}{U''(x)} \leq \lambda \leq \frac{U'(x + y)}{U'(x)}.$$

(Similarly, one has "increasing absolute risk aversion" if these inequalities are reversed.)

Proposition 6.4 (Equivalent Conditions for DARA) *The utility function $U(x)$ displays decreasing absolute risk aversion if and only if*

$$(\forall x) \quad \frac{U'''(x)}{U''(x)} \geq \frac{U''(x)}{U'(x)}.$$

(A sufficient condition is $U''' < 0$.)

Proof The proof is obvious. ☐

Do wealthier agents exhibit lower risk premiums, or should they hold more high-risk assets if risk aversion is decreasing in wealth? Of course, the answer is positive only if the relationship between risk aversion and both the risk premium and the demand for high-risk assets is unambiguous. Unfortunately, this is not assured. Therefore, the search for a meaningful measure of risk aversion is still on the agenda.

6.5 Bibliographic Notes

The basic notions of risk, risk aversion, and optimal decisions under uncertainty are reviewed in Hirshleifer and Riley (1992), Part I. The presentation in this chapter follows closely the seminal contributions by Pratt (1964) and Ross (1983). A sample of the follow-up literature is Hadar and Seo (1990b), Menezes and Hanson (1970), and Laffont (1990).

An important topic not covered here is the extension of the notion of risk aversion to the many-goods case. On this issue consult Kihlstrom and Mirman (1974) and Kihlstrom and Laffont (1979).

Part III

Incomplete Information and Incentives

7

Matching: The Marriage Problem*

No enemy can match a friend.
Jonathan Swift

7.1 Introduction

Many economic problems concern the need to match members of one group of agents with one or more members of a second group. For example, workers need to be matched with firms, graduate students with graduate schools, authors with publishers, landlords with tenants, and men with women, to name just a few.

Matching problems pose three central issues:

- Is there a *stable* matching – one that cannot be upset by individual negotiations?
- What *procedures* or *institutions* accomplish stable matchings?
- Are these procedures *manipulable*?

This chapter gives a brief introduction to the economics of two-sided matching.[1] To keep matters as simple as possible, we focus on one particular class of matching problems: the matching of two distinct groups (two-sided matching).

7.2 Notation and Basic Assumptions

Consider the problem of matching two distinct groups, say $W := \{w_1, \ldots, w_n\}$ and $M := \{m_1, \ldots, m_n\}$, metaphorically referred to as the *marriage problem*. Keeping the particular application of marriage in mind, W may be remembered as the group of *women* and M as the group of *men*.

Each man is assumed to have a complete and transitive strict preference defined on W, and each woman has such a preference defined on M. These are conveniently described by a *preference matrix*, as in the following example.

Example 7.1 The preference matrix below gives the rankings of three men and three women. The first number of each pair in the matrix gives the ranking of women by the men, and the second the ranking of men by the women. Thus, m_1

---

[1] Most of the results and examples are taken from the beautiful paper by Gale and Shapley (1962).

ranks w_1 highest, m_2 most prefers w_2, and m_3 most prefers w_3; women have just the opposite rankings:

	w_1	w_2	w_3
m_1	1,3	2,2	3,1
m_2	3,1	1,3	2,2
m_3	2,2	3,1	1,3

How many matchings are conceivable? If M and W have each n elements, there are altogether $n!$ matchings. This is obvious once you introduce the convention that each matching is represented by an n-dimensional vector:

$$\left(w_{i_1}, w_{i_2}, \ldots, w_{i_n} \right),$$

to be read as: m_1 is matched with w_{i_1}, m_2 with w_{i_2}, etc., and m_n with w_{i_n}. For then, the number of conceivable matchings is the same as the number of permutations of a set of n elements, which you know is equal to $n!$. Therefore, Example 7.1 has altogether six matchings.

7.3 Stable Two-Sided Matchings

Loosely speaking, a matching is *unstable* if a man and a woman who are not married to each other are better off if they "divorce" their current partners and marry each other. Stated formally:

Definition 7.1 A matching is called unstable if there are two M's and two W's who are matched to each other, say (m_1, w_1) and (m_2, w_2), even though m_1 prefers w_2 to w_1 and w_2 prefers m_1 to m_2:

$$w_2 \succ_{m_1} w_1 \quad \text{and} \quad m_1 \succ_{w_2} m_2.$$

A matching that is not unstable is called stable.

In Example 7.1 there are altogether six possible matchings, of which three are stable. One stable matching is reached if each man is assigned to his first choice. It is stable simply because no woman can convince any man to divorce his first choice. Similarly, the second stable matching is reached if each women is given her first choice. And the third stable matching gives everyone his or her second choice. An example of an unstable matching is (m_1, w_1), (m_2, w_3), (m_3, w_2); for m_3 and w_1 are then better off if they divorce their partners and get together with each other.

This suggests that one might always find stable two-sided matchings simply by giving either men or women their first choice. Unfortunately, this does not always work: just imagine that two or more members of each group give the highest rank to the very same member of the other group.

Do all matching problems have at least *one* stable matching, regardless of preferences? The answer is no, as you can see from the following example. Unlike the marriage problem, it concerns the matching of the members of one group with each other.[2]

Example 7.2 (Roommate Problem) Four students, $\{s_1, \ldots, s_4\}$, are to be divided up into pairs of roommates. Their preferences are summarized by the following matrix, which includes only the essential rankings. Evidently, nobody wants to share a room with s_4, and whoever is matched with s_4 can always find someone else who would prefer to share the room with him rather than with his current roommate.[3] Therefore, no stable matching exists.

	s_1	s_2	s_3	s_4
s_1		1		3
s_2			1	3
s_3	1			3
s_4				

In view of this negative result, it is the more surprising that the marriage problem has always a stable matching. Amazingly, it makes all the difference whether one has to match one population with another or with itself.

Proposition 7.1 *The marriage problem has at least one stable matching, regardless of preferences.*

Proof The proof constructs a procedure that actually finds a stable matching. This procedure may be called "man proposes to woman." It works as follows:

Step 1: (a) Each man proposes to his most preferred woman.
(b) Each woman rejects all except the one whom she most prefers and keeps the most preferred as her suitor.

⋮

Step k: (a) Each man who was rejected in the previous step proposes to the most preferred of those women to whom he has not yet proposed.
(b) Each woman keeps as her suitor the man she most prefers among those who have proposed and rejects the rest.

⋮

The procedure terminates when all women have received at least one proposal, at which point each woman has one suitor. This occurs after at most n^2 steps, simply because each man can propose to each woman at most once.[4]

---

[2] The following example could be turned into a two-sided matching problem if the students cared about the room to which they are assigned and not about the roommate with whom they have to share it. One-sided matching problems are analyzed in Hylland and Zeckhauser (1979) and in Zhou (1990).

[3] For example, if s_1 is matched with s_4, it follows that s_2 must be matched with s_3. But s_3 most prefers to be matched with s_1. Therefore, s_3 and s_1 should move together and "divorce" their current roommates. The instability of all other possible matchings follows by similar reasoning.

[4] While this is an obvious upper bound, it is not the smallest one. The smallest upper bound of steps is $(n-1)^2 + 1$. Math whizzes, try your teeth on this.

The outcome is stable, since any woman preferred by a man to his current wife must have already rejected him in favor of her current partner.   □

7.4 Who Benefits from Which Procedure?

The procedure constructed in the proof of existence of stable matchings is only one of many possible procedures. Moreover, when there is more than one stable matching, it generates an outcome that is heavily biased in favor of men. Indeed, there is an entirely symmetric procedure with women proposing to men that also leads to a stable matching, yet is always preferred by women, unless the stable matching is unique.

Example 1 offers a nice illustration of this point. In this example, all men get their first choice of women if they are allowed to propose. But if the procedure is changed in such a way that women instead of men propose, all women end up with their first choice of men and all men are worse-off. This suggests that, if there is more than one stable matching, the selection gives rise to a kind of "class conflict" of interest between the group of men and the group of women.

Proposition 7.2 *Among all stable matchings, one is weakly preferred by every man and one by every woman. Therefore, there is a "men-optimal" and a "women-optimal" stable matching unless the stable matching is unique.*

Proof Consider the stable matching selected if men propose. We will show that in every other stable matching no man will get a more desirable partner. The symmetry of the problem implies that the corresponding property holds in the alternative procedure when women propose.

For each man m_i, call a woman w_j *possible* for him if there is a stable matching that assigns her to him. Suppose that, up to step $k - 1$ of the "man proposes to woman" procedure, no man has been rejected by a possible woman and that, at step k, m_i is rejected by w_j. Then, as we will show, w_j cannot be possible for m_i. As no man is ever rejected by a woman who is possible for him, it follows that no man is ever rejected by his most preferred possible woman, and the proof is complete.

Suppose, *per absurdum*, that w_j is possible for m_i, even though w_j rejects m_i at step k. Then, at step k, another man, say m_r, was kept as suitor by w_j. Therefore,

$$m_r \succ_{w_j} m_i$$

and, since m_r has not been rejected by a woman possible for him,

$$w_j \succ_{m_r} w_k \qquad \text{for all } w_k \text{ possible for him.}$$

But then the matching of w_j with m_i and of m_r with any woman possible for him is unstable. Therefore, w_j cannot be possible for m_i, contrary to what was assumed.   □

7.5 Strategic Issues

Up to this point, matching procedures were only used in the constructive proof of certain properties of stable matchings. New problems come up if a procedure is actually used as a mechanism to resolve matching problems. The source of trouble is *strategic voting*. It comes up if agents know only their own preference and not that of others.[5]

A mechanism consists of a certain procedure that maps preferences into a stable matching. Without loss of generality, one may look at direct mechanisms. A mechanism is *direct* if each man and each woman is only asked to report his or her preference, which is then taken at face value and processed by the given procedure.

The adoption of direct mechanisms gives rise to a noncooperative game under *imperfect* information (no one knows the preferences stated by others) as well as *incomplete* information (no one knows the true preferences of others). Each man's strategy is a ranking of all women, and each woman's strategy a ranking of all men.

A key question is whether one can design a stable matching procedure that induces truthful revelation of preferences. The literature on this topic is still evolving. We will report some of the more important recent results (mostly without spelling out the proofs), and then close with a brief note on successful applications of these findings to the analysis of entry-level labor markets.

7.5.1 Two Impossibility Results

We start out with two negative results. The first one shows that one cannot design a procedure that makes truthful revelation a dominant strategy in all matching problems.

Proposition 7.3 *No stable matching procedure exists for which the revelation of true preferences is a dominant strategy for all preferences.*

Proof In order to prove the assertion it is sufficient to present a matching problem for which no stable matching procedure has truthful revelation of preferences as a dominant strategy. For this purpose, consider the marriage problem characterized by the following preference matrix:

	w_1	w_2	w_3
m_1	2,1	1,2	3,1
m_2	1,3	2,3	3,2
m_3	1,2	2,1	3,3

It has exactly two stable matchings: the women-optimal (I) and the men-optimal matching (II):

(I) (w_1, w_3, w_2),

(II) (w_2, w_3, w_1).

---

[5] If preferences are public information, the procedure can be delegated to a neutral third party such as an appropriately programmed computer.

Now consider any stable matching procedure. It selects either (I) or (II). Suppose it selects the men-optimal matching (II). But then, by misrepresenting her preference, woman w_1 can influence the selection in her own favor. For if w_1 states the untrue preference

$$m_1 \succ_{w_1} m_2 \succ_{w_1} m_3,$$

the matching (II) is no longer stable (w_1 could induce m_2 to break up with w_3). At the same time, (I) is then the only stable matching. Therefore, by appropriately misrepresenting her preference, woman w_1 can force the stable matching procedure to select the preferred women-optimal matching (I). Similarly, if the given procedure selects the women-optimal matching (I), some man can be shown to benefit from misrepresenting his preference. Therefore, no procedure exists that makes truth revelation a dominant strategy.   □

This negative result does not imply that truthful revelation of preferences cannot be achieved. It only says that truth revelation cannot be a *dominant* strategy in *all* matching problems. However, as Roth has shown, one can strengthen this negative result and show that:[6]

Proposition 7.4 *No stable matching mechanism exists that makes truth telling by all players a Nash equilibrium for all preferences.*

After these negative results, one would like to know whether one can at least find mechanisms that are stable both in terms of stated and in terms of true preferences. One can. The deferred acceptance procedures, labeled "man proposes to woman" and "woman proposes to man," give the clue.

7.5.2 Stable Matchings?

Consider, for example, the "man proposes to woman" mechanism. If it is applied, truth telling is a dominant strategy for all men, even under incomplete information about preferences. Indeed, as Roth and Sotomayor have shown:

Proposition 7.5 *The "man proposes to woman" mechanism makes it a dominant strategy for each man to state his true preference. (Similarly, the "woman proposes to man" mechanism makes it a dominant strategy for each woman to state her true preference.)*

However, even though honesty is a best policy for men under the "men proposes to woman" rule, women can usually do better by responding with strategic voting, as we have already seen in Example 7.5. Now consider the equilibrium in which women optimally respond to mens' truthfully reported preferences. Will the resulting matching be stable with respect to true preferences?[7]

---

[6] The proof is in Roth (1989) and (in a slightly easier form) in Roth and Sotomayor (1990).

[7] The fact that it is stable with respect to reported messages follows from the properties of an equilibrium.

Roth and Sotomayor found that the answer is affirmative:

Proposition 7.6 *Suppose women choose preferences that are a best response to mens' true preferences under the "man proposes to woman" mechanism. Then the corresponding matching is stable both with regard to stated and with regard to true preferences.*

Altogether, these results indicate that one can find simple mechanisms that lead to stable matchings even under incomplete information. If these mechanisms are applied, somebody tends to manipulate by misrepresenting his or her preference. Therefore, the resulting matching is stable but generally not Pareto-optimal.

7.6 Bibliographic Notes

The matching problem has been applied to housing, college admission, and first-entry labor markets. So far, the most thoroughly researched application is the work of Al Roth on the matching of medical interns to hospitals in the U.S. and in England (see Roth (1984, 1991)). In his study, Roth shows that the American market was subject to chaotic last-minute recontracting with students who had often already accepted a position elsewhere, until in 1952 a centralized matching algorithm was introduced. This algorithm was successful precisely because it produced stable outcomes. In turn, in England, similar problems led to the introduction of centralized regional matching procedures, some of which were not stable and therefore did not resolve the chaotic recontracting problem. Interestingly, all the successful mechanisms applied in the U.S. and in England are variations of the "man proposes to woman" and "woman proposes to man" mechanisms. This emphasizes the eminent practical significance of Propositions 7.5 and 7.6.

However, new problems have come up with the increasing number of couples that look for internships at the same location. This has opened an important and still unresolved new twist of the matching problem.

Labor markets are a natural application of two-sided matching models. However, in most of these applications matching is related to wage determination. In an important contribution Shapley and Shubik (1972) showed that the properties of stable matchings generalize to models where matching and wage determination are interrelated.

Some recent contributions of the matching literature have focused on the timing of transactions. Bergstrom and Bagnoli (1993) explore reasons for delay in marriages, and Roth and Xing (1994) and Li and Rosen (1998) explain the tendency for transactions to become earlier, which is observed in some markets for highly skilled employees.

8

Auctions

Men prize the thing ungained more than it is.
William Shakespeare

8.1 Introduction

Suppose you inherit a unique and valuable good – say a painting by van Gogh or
a copy of the 1776 edition of Adam Smith's *Wealth of Nations*. For some reason
you are in desperate need for money, and decide to sell. You have a clear idea of
your valuation. Of course, you hope to earn more than that. You wonder: isn't there
some way to reach the highest possible price? How should you go about it?

If you knew the potential buyers and their valuations of the object for sale, your
pricing problem would have a simple solution. You would only need to call a
nonnegotiable price equal to the highest valuation, and wait for the right customer
to come and claim the item. It's as simple as that.[1]

8.1.1 Information Problem

The trouble is that you, the seller, usually have only incomplete information about
buyers' valuations. Therefore, you have to figure out a pricing scheme that performs
well even under incomplete information. Your problem begins to be interesting.

8.1.2 Basic Assumptions

Suppose there are $n > 1$ potential buyers, each of whom knows the object for sale
well enough to decide how much he is willing to pay. Denote buyers' valuations by
$V := (V_1, \ldots, V_n)$. Since you, the seller, do not know V, you must think of it as a
random variable, distributed by some joint probability distribution function (CDF)
$\mathcal{F} : [\underline{v}_1, \bar{v}_1] \times \cdots \times [\underline{v}_n, \bar{v}_n] \to [0, 1]$, $\mathcal{F}(v_1, \ldots, v_n) := \Pr(V_1 \leq v_1, \ldots, V_n \leq v_n)$. Similarly, potential buyers know their own valuation but not that of others.
Therefore, buyers also view valuations as a random variable, except their own.

---

[1] Of course, it is not really easy to make something nonnegotiable.

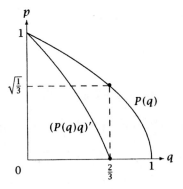

Figure 8.1. Optimal Take-It-Or-Leave-It Price When There Are Two Potential Buyers.

8.1.3 Cournot-Monopoly Approach

Of course, you could stick to the take-it-or-leave-it pricing rule, even as you are subject to incomplete information about buyers' valuations. You would then call a nonnegotiable price p at or above your *own valuation* r, and hope that some customer has the right valuation and is willing to buy. Your pricing problem would then be reduced to a variation of the standard Cournot monopoly problem. The only unusual part would be that the trade-off between price and quantity is replaced by one between price and the probability of sale.

Alluding to the usual characterization of Cournot monopoly, you can even draw a "demand curve," with the nonnegotiable price p on the "price axis" and the probability that at least one bidder's valuation exceeds the listed price p

$$\pi(p) = 1 - G(p), \quad G(p) := \mathcal{F}(p, \ldots, p), \tag{8.1}$$

on the "quantity axis" (as in Figure 8.1). You would then pick that price p that maximizes the expected value of your gain from trade, $\pi(p)(p - r)$.

Equivalently, you can state the decision problem in quantity coordinates, as is customary in the analysis of Cournot monopoly, where "quantity" is represented by the probability of sale, $q := 1 - G(p)$:

$$\max_q (P(q) - r)\, q, \quad P(q) := G^{-1}(1 - q). \tag{8.2}$$

Computing the first-order condition, the optimal price p^* can then be characterized in the familiar form as a relationship between *marginal revenue* (MR) and *marginal cost* (MC):[2]

$$\text{MR} := p - \frac{1 - G(p)}{G'(p)} = r =: \text{MC}. \tag{8.3}$$

Example 8.1 Suppose valuations V_i are independent and uniformly distributed over the interval $[0, 1]$, and the seller's own valuation is $r = 0$. Then, for all $p \in [0, 1]$,

---

[2] As always, this condition applies only if the maximization problem is well behaved. Well behavedness requires that revenue be continuous and marginal revenue strictly monotone increasing in p.

$G(p) = F(p)^n = p^n$. Hence, the optimal take-it-or-leave-it price is

$$p^*(n) = \sqrt[n]{\frac{1}{n+1}}. \tag{8.4}$$

The resulting expected price paid (price asked times probability of success) is

$$\bar{p}(n) := p^*(n)(1 - G(p^*(n))) = p^*(n)\frac{n}{n+1}. \tag{8.5}$$

Both $p^*(n)$ and $\bar{p}(n)$ are strictly monotone increasing in n, starting from $p^*(1) = 1/2$, $\bar{p}(1) = 1/4$, and approaching 1 as $n \to \infty$.[3]

Take-it-or-leave-it pricing is one way to go. But generally you can do better by setting up an auction. This brings us to the analysis of auctions, and the design of optimal auction rules. Interestingly, the particular Cournot monopoly price $p^*(1)$ that holds for $n = 1$, will continue to play a role as an optimal minimum price in the optimal auction setting, as you will learn in the section on optimal auctions.

8.1.4 Auctions – What, Where, and Why

An auction is a bidding mechanism, described by a set of auction rules that specify how the winner is determined and how much he has to pay. In addition, auction rules may restrict participation and feasible bids and impose certain rules of behavior.

Auctions are widely used in many transactions – not just in the sale of art and wine. Every week, the U.S. Treasury auctions-off billions of dollars of bills, notes, and bonds. Governments and private corporations solicit delivery-price offers on products ranging from office supplies to tires and construction jobs. The Department of the Interior auctions off the rights to drill oil and other natural resources on federally owned properties. And private firms auction off products ranging from fresh flowers, fish, and tobacco to diamonds and real estate. Altogether, auctions account for an enormous volume of transactions.

Essentially, auctions are used for three reasons:

- speed of sale,
- to reveal information about buyers' valuations,
- to prevent dishonest dealing between the seller's agent and the buyer.

The agency role of auctions is particularly important if government agencies are involved in buying or selling. As a particularly extreme example, think of the recent privatization programs in Eastern Europe. Clearly, if the agencies involved, such as the *Treuhandanstalt* that was in charge of privatizing the state-run corporations of formerly communist East Germany, had been free to negotiate the terms of sale, the lucky winner probably would have been the one who made the largest bribe or political contribution. However, if assets are put up for auction, cheating the taxpayer is more difficult and costly, and hence less likely to succeed.

---

[3] For a simple proof of monotonicity, work with $\ln \bar{p}$, which is obviously a monotone transformation of $\bar{p}$.

Table 8.1. *The most popular auctions*

Open	Closed
Ascending-price (English)	Second-price (Vickrey)
Descending-price (Dutch)	First-price

8.1.5 Popular Auctions

There are many different auction rules. Actually, the word itself is something of a misnomer. *Auctio* means increase but not all auctions involve calling out higher and higher bids.

One distinguishes between *oral* and *written* auctions. In oral auctions, bidders hear each other's bids and can make counteroffers; each bidder knows his rivals. In closed auctions, bidders submit their bids simultaneously without revealing them to others; often bidders do not even know how many rival bidders participate.

The best known and most frequently used auction (Table 8.1) is the ascending price or English auction, followed by the first-price closed-seal bid or Dutch auction, and the second-price closed-seal bid (also known as Vickrey auction).[4]

In the ascending-price or *English* auction, the auctioneer seeks increasing bids until all but the highest bidder(s) are eliminated. If the last bid is at or above the minimum price, the item is awarded or *knocked down* to the remaining bidder(s). If a tie bid occurs, the item is awarded for example by a chance rule. In one variation, used in Japan, the price is posted on a screen and raised continuously. Any bidder who wants to be active at the current price pushes a button. Once the button is released, the bidder has withdrawn and is not permitted to reenter the bidding.

Instead of letting the price rise, the descending-price or *Dutch* auction follows a descending pattern. The auctioneer begins by asking a certain price, and gradually lowers it until some bidder(s) shout "Mine" to claim the item. Frequently, the auctioneer uses a mechanical device called the *Dutch clock*. This clock is started, and the asking price ticks down until someone calls out. The clock then stops and the buyer pays the indicated price. Again, provisions are made to deal with tie bids.[5]

Finally, in a written auction bidders are invited to submit a sealed bid, with the understanding that the item is awarded to the highest bidder. Under the first-price rule the winner actually pays as much as his own bid, whereas under the second-price rule the price is equal to the second highest bid.

---

[4] Many variations of these basic auctions are reviewed in Cassady (1967).

[5] An interesting Dutch auction in disguise is *time discounting*. In many cities in the U.S. discounters use this method to sell clothes. Each item is sold at the price on the tag minus a discount that depends on how many weeks the item was on the shelf. As time passes, the price goes down by (say) 10% per week, until the listed bottom price is reached.

This terminology is not always used consistently in the academic, and in the financial literature. For example, in the financial community a multiple-unit, single-price auction is termed a Dutch auction, and a multiple-unit, sealed bid auction is termed an English auction (except by the English, who call it an American auction). In the academic literature, the labels English and Dutch would be exactly reversed. In order to avoid confusion, keep in mind that here we adhere to the academic usage of these terms, and use English as equivalent to ascending and Dutch as equivalent to descending price.

8.1.6 Early History of Auctions

Probably the earliest report on auctions is found in Herodotus in his account of the bidding for men and wives in Babylon around 500 B.C. These auctions were unique, since bidding sometimes started at a negative price.[6] In ancient Rome, auctions were used in commercial trade, to liquidate property, and to sell plundered war booty. A most notable auction was held in 193 A.D. when the Praetorian Guard put the whole empire up for auction. After killing the previous emperor, the guards announced that they would appoint the highest bidder as the next emperor. Didius Julianus outbid his competitors, but after two months was beheaded by Septimius Severus, who seized power – a terminal case of the winner's curse?

8.2 The Basics of Private-Value Auctions

We begin with the most thoroughly researched auction model, the *symmetric independent private values* (SIPV) model with risk-neutral agents. In that model

- a single indivisible object is put up for sale to one of several bidders (*single-unit auction*);
- each bidder knows his valuation – no one else does (*private values*);
- all bidders are indistinguishable (*symmetry*);
- unknown valuations are independent and identically distributed (iid) and continuous random variables (*independence, symmetry, continuity*);
- bidders are *risk-neutral*, and so is the seller (unless stated otherwise).

We will model bidders' behavior as a noncooperative game under incomplete information. One of our goals will be to rank the four common auctions. To what extent does institutional detail matter? Can the seller get a higher average price by an oral or by a written auction? Is competition between bidders fiercer if the winner pays a price equal to the second highest rather than the highest bid? And which auction, if any, is strategically easier to handle?

8.2.1 Some Basic Results on Dutch and English Auctions

The comparison between the four standard auction rules is considerably facilitated by the fact that the Dutch auction is equivalent to the first-price and the English

[6] See Shubik (1983).

to the second-price closed auction. Therefore, the comparison of the four standard auctions can be reduced to comparing the Dutch and the English auction. Later you will learn the far more surprising result that even these two auctions are payoff-equivalent.

The strategic equivalence between the Dutch auction and the first-price closed auction is immediately obvious. In either case, a bidder has to decide how much he should bid or at what price he should shout "Mine" to claim the item. Therefore, the strategy space is the same, and so are the payoff functions and hence the equilibrium outcomes.

Similarly, the English auction and the second-price closed auction are equivalent, but for different reasons and only as long as we stick to the private-values framework. Unlike in a sealed-bid auction, in an English auction bidders can respond to rivals' bids. Therefore, the two auction games are not strategically equivalent. However, in both cases bidders have the obvious (weakly) dominant strategy to bid an amount or set a limit equal to their own true valuation. Therefore, the equilibrium outcomes are the same as long as bidders' valuations are not affected by observing rivals' bidding behavior, which always holds true in the private-values framework.[7]

The essential property of the English auction and the second-price closed auction is that the price paid by the winner is exclusively determined by rivals' bids. Bidders are thus put in the position of price takers who should accept any price up to their own valuation. The *truth-revealing* strategy where one always bids one's own valuation is a (weakly) dominant strategy. The immediate implication is that both auction forms have the same equilibrium outcome, provided bidders never play a weakly dominated strategy.

8.2.2 Revenue Equivalence

We have established the payoff equivalence of Dutch and first-price and of English and second-price auctions. Remarkably, payoff equivalence is a much more general feature of auction games. Indeed, *all* auctions that award the item to the highest bidder and lead to the same bidder participation are payoff-equivalent. The four standard auctions are a case in point. We now turn to the proof of this surprising result and then explore modifications of the SIPV framework.

We mention that the older literature conjectured that Dutch auctions lead to a higher average price than English auctions because, as Cassady (1967, p. 260) put it, in the Dutch auction ". . . each potential buyer tends to bid his highest demand price, whereas a bidder in the English system need advance a rival's offer by only one increment." Both the reasoning and the conclusion are wrong.

Before we go into the general solution of SIPV auction games, in the following subsection we elaborate on an extensive example and solve several standard auction

[7] Obviously, if rivals' bids signal something about the underlying common value of the item, each bidder's estimated value of the item is updated in the course of an English auction. No such updating can occur under a sealed-bid auction, where bidders place their bids before observing rivals' behavior. Therefore, if the item has a *common* value component, the English auction and the second-price sealed bid do not have the same equilibrium outcome.

games for the case of uniformly distributed valuations. This serves as motivation for our general results and as a playground to exercise the standard solution procedure that is typically employed in the literature.

The standard procedure to solve a particular auction, as in any other game, is to first solve for equilibrium strategies and then compute equilibrium payoffs. This procedure can, of course, be applied to arbitrary probability distribution functions, not just to uniform distributions. But when we come to the general solution of SIPV auction games, we will switch – with good reason – to an alternative solution procedure. Since you can learn from both, it is advisable neither to jump immediately to the general solution in Section 8.2.5 nor to skip the latter.

8.2.3 Solution of Some Auction Games – Assuming Uniformly Distributed Valuations

Example 8.2 Suppose all bidders' valuations are uniformly distributed on the support $[0, 1]$, as in Example 8.1, and the seller's own valuation and minimum bid are equal to zero. Then the unique equilibrium bid functions $b^* : [0, 1] \to \mathbb{R}_+$ are[8]

$$b^*(v) = v \qquad \text{(English auction)}, \tag{8.6}$$

$$b^*(v) = \left(1 - \frac{1}{n}\right)v \qquad \text{(Dutch auction)}. \tag{8.7}$$

In both auctions, the expected price is

$$\bar{p} = \frac{n-1}{n+1}, \tag{8.8}$$

and the equilibrium payoffs are

$$U^*(v) = \frac{v^n}{n} \qquad \text{(bidders' expected gain)}, \tag{8.9}$$

$$\Pi = \bar{p} = \frac{n-1}{n+1} \qquad \text{(seller's expected gain)}. \tag{8.10}$$

This implies payoff equivalence. Moreover, more bidders mean fiercer competition, to the seller's advantage and to the bidders' disadvantage.

We now explain in detail how these results come about. The proof uses two preliminary assumptions that will then be confirmed to hold: the symmetry of equilibrium and the strict monotonicity of equilibrium strategies.

Dutch (First-Price) Auction

Suppose bidder i bids the amount b, and all rival bidders bid according to the strictly monotone increasing equilibrium strategy $b^*(v)$. Then bidder i wins if and only if all rivals' valuations are below $b^{*-1}(b)$. Since the V's are continuous random variables and $b^*(v)$ is strictly monotone increasing, ties have zero probability. Therefore, the

---

[8] Uniqueness of the English auction assumes elimination of weakly dominated strategies. More on this below.

probability of winning when bidding the amount b against rivals who play the strategy $b^*(v)$ is

$$
\begin{aligned}
\rho(b) &= \Pr\{b^*(V_j) < b, \ \forall j \neq i\} \\
&= \Pr\{V_j < \sigma(b), \ \forall j \neq i\}, \qquad \sigma := b^{*-1} \\
&= F(\sigma(b))^{n-1}.
\end{aligned}
\tag{8.11}
$$

Here $\sigma(b)$ is the inverse of $b^*(v)$, which indicates the valuation that leads to bidding the amount b when strategy $b^*(v)$ is played.

In equilibrium, the bid b must be a best response to rivals' bidding strategies. Therefore, b must be a maximizer of the expected utility

$$
U(b, v) := \rho(b)(v - b),
\tag{8.12}
$$

leading to the first-order condition

$$
\frac{\partial}{\partial b} U(b, v) = \rho'(b)(v - b) - \rho(b) = 0.
\tag{8.13}
$$

Moreover, b itself must be prescribed by the equilibrium strategy $b^*(v)$ or, equivalently, one must have

$$
v = \sigma(b).
\tag{8.14}
$$

And a bidder with valuation 0 should bid zero, or equivalently

$$
\sigma(0) = 0.
\tag{8.15}
$$

Using (8.14), one can rewrite (8.13) in the form

$$
(n-1) f(\sigma(b)) (\sigma(b) - b) \sigma'(b) - F(\sigma(b)) = 0.
\tag{8.16}
$$

This simplifies, due to $F(\sigma(b)) = \sigma(b)$ (uniform distribution), to

$$
(n-1)(\sigma(b) - b)\sigma'(b) - \sigma(b) = 0.
\tag{8.17}
$$

Given the initial condition $\sigma(0) = 0$, this differential equation has the obvious solution $\sigma(b) = [n/(n-1)]b$.[9] Finally, solve this for b and you have the asserted equilibrium strategy[10]

$$
b^*(v) = \left(1 - \frac{1}{n}\right)v.
\tag{8.18}
$$

Notice that the margin of profit that each player allows himself in his bid decreases as the number of bidders increases.

Based on this result, you can now determine the expected price $\bar{p}(n)$ by the following consideration: In a Dutch auction, the random equilibrium price, P_D, is equal to the highest bid, which can be written as $b^*(V_{(n)})$, where $V_{(n)}$ denotes the

[9] Why is it obvious? Suppose the solution is linear; then you will easily find the solution, which also proves that there is a linear solution.

[10] This raises the question whether the equilibrium is unique. The proof is straightforward for $n = 2$. In this case, one obtains from (8.17) $\sigma \, d\sigma = \sigma \, db + b \, d\sigma = d(\sigma b)$. Therefore, $\sigma b = \frac{1}{2}\sigma^2 + \sigma(0)$. Since $b(0) = 0$, one has $\sigma(0) = 0$ and thus $\sigma(b) = 2b$. Hence, the unique equilibrium strategy is $b^*(v) = \frac{1}{2}v$. In order to generalize the proof to $n > 2$, apply a transformation of variables from (σ, b) to (z, b), where $z := \sigma/b$. Then one can separate variables and uniquely solve the differential equation by integration.

highest order statistic of the entire sample of n valuations. Therefore, by a known result on order statistics,[11]

$$\bar{p}(n) = E\left[b^*(V_{(n)})\right]$$

$$= \frac{n-1}{n}E\left[V_{(n)}\right] \quad \left(\text{since } b^*(v) = \frac{n-1}{n}v\right)$$

$$= \frac{n-1}{n+1}, \tag{8.19}$$

as asserted.

English (Second-Price) Auction

Recall that in an English auction truthful bidding, $b(v) \equiv v$, is a weakly dominant strategy. Therefore, if one eliminates weakly dominated strategies, the bidder with the highest valuation wins and pays a price equal to the second highest valuation. The random equilibrium price P_E is equal to the order statistic $V_{(n-1)}$ of the given sample of n valuations. And the expected price is

$$\bar{p}(n) = E\left[V_{(n-1)}\right] = \frac{n-1}{n+1}. \tag{8.20}$$

Notice, however, that the English auction is plagued by a multiplicity problem. For example, the "wolf–sheep" strategy combination

$$b_1(v) = 1, \qquad b_i(v) = 0, \quad i = 2, \ldots, n,$$

where bidder 1 bids very aggressively and bidders 2 to n hold back, is also an equilibrium, even though it prescribes rather pathological behavior. These equilibria are overlooked if one eliminates weakly dominated strategies. (This is why game theorists view the elimination of *weakly* dominated strategies as problematic.)

Can one eliminate these pathological equilibria with a plausible equilibrium refinement? Yes, one can. These equilibria fail the test of *trembling-hand perfection* (see Fudenberg and Tirole (1991)).

Comparison

Since the two expected prices are the same, this example illustrates the general principle of revenue equivalence. (It is left to the reader to confirm the stronger payoff equivalence, asserted in (8.9) and (8.10).[12]) Notice, however, that random prices differ in their risk characteristics. Indeed, the random equilibrium price in the Dutch auction, P_D, second-order stochastically dominates that of the English auction, P_E. Therefore, all *risk-averse* sellers unanimously prefer the Dutch to the English auction.

---

[11] Let $V_{(r)}$ be the rth order statistic of a given sample of n independent and identically distributed random variables V_i with distribution function $F(v) =, v$ on the support $[0, 1]$. Then $E[V_{(r)}] = r/(n+1)$ and $\text{Var}(V_{(r)}) = r(n-r+1)/(n+1)^2(n+2)$. See rules (R18), (R19) in Appendix D, Section D.4.

[12] Note that in an English auction $U^*(v) = F(v)^{N-1}(v - E[V_{(n-1)} \mid V_{(n)} = v])$; use (D.42), from Appendix B, to compute the conditional expected value.

To illustrate this, recall that one random variable second-order stochastically dominates another if their expected values are the same and their probability distribution functions (cdf's) are single-crossing. This result is often referred to as the *mean-preserving spread* theorem. A mean-preserving spread of a given distribution shifts probability mass towards both tails of the distribution. It is plausible that this induces *more* risk (for a proof see Section 4.4.2). Since the seller prefers higher prices, the dominated random variable is the one that has more probability mass on the tails of the distribution.

The cdf's of $P_D := b^*(V_{(n)})$ and of $P_E := V_{(n-1)}$ are

$$F_D(x) = \Pr\left\{ b^*\left(V_{(n)}\right) < x \right\} = \min\left\{ \left(\frac{n}{n-1}\right)^n x^n, 1 \right\}, \qquad (8.21)$$

$$F_E(x) = \Pr\left\{ V_{(n-1)} < x \right\} = \min\{x^n + n(x^{n-1} - x^n), 1\}. \qquad (8.22)$$

Consider the difference

$$\phi(x) := F_D(x) - F_E(x) = \left(\left(\frac{n}{n-1}\right)^n + (n-1)\right)x^n - nx^{n-1}. \qquad (8.23)$$

Evidently, $\phi(x)$ is an nth-order polynomial with only one change in the sign of its coefficients. By Descartes's rule, $\phi(x)$ has at most one real positive root. Also, $\phi(x)$ must have at least one real root in $(0, 1)$ because the expected values of P_D and P_E are the same. Hence, $\phi(x)$ has exactly one real root in $(0, 1)$. This confirms single crossing.

Finally, observe that P_E has more probability mass on both tails of the distribution than P_D because

$$1 - F_E(x) > 1 - F_E(1) = 0 = 1 - F_D(x) \qquad \forall x \in \left[\frac{n-1}{n}, 1\right],$$

as illustrated in Figure 8.2. Therefore, P_D second-order stochastically dominates P_E.

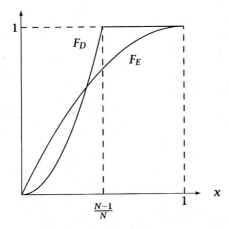

Figure 8.2. Probability distributions of P_D, P_E for $n = 2$.

Third- and Higher-Price Auctions*

Consider a generalization of the second-price auction: the *third-price* auction, where the highest bidder wins but pays only as much as the third highest bid, and, more generally the *k th-price* auction, where the winner pays the kth highest bid.[13] It has the following solution:[14]

$$b_k^*(v) = \frac{n-1}{n-k+1} v, \qquad \text{for} \quad n > 2, \quad k = 1, \dots, n. \qquad (8.24)$$

Third- and higher-price auctions have four striking properties: 1) bids are higher than the own valuation; 2) equilibrium bids increase when one moves to a higher-price auction; 3) equilibrium bids diminish as the number of bidders is increased (since $(n-1)/(n-k+1) > n/(n-k+2)$); and 4) the variance of the random price P_k,

$$\text{Var}(P_k) = \text{Var}\left(b_k^*(V_{(n-k+1)})\right) = \frac{k(n-1)}{(n-k+1)(n+1)^2(n+2)^2}, \qquad (8.25)$$

increases in k, and more generally, P_k second-order stochastically dominates P_{k+1} for all $k = 1, \dots, n-1$.

Once you have figured out why it pays to "speculate" and bid higher than the own valuation, it is easy to interpret the second property. Just keep in mind that a rational bidder may get burned and suffer a loss because the kth highest bid is above the own valuation. As the number of bidders is increased, it becomes more likely that the kth highest bid is close to the own valuation. Therefore, it makes sense to bid more conservatively when the number of bidders is increased, even though this may seem somewhat puzzling at first glance.

Finally, the fourth property suggests that a risk-averse seller should always prefer lower-order kth-price auctions and should most prefer the Dutch auction. While the English auction is always appealing because of its overwhelming strategic simplicity, third- and higher-price auctions are strategically just as complicated as the Dutch auction, and in addition expose the seller to unnecessary risk.

Nobody has ever, to our knowledge, applied a third- or higher-price auction in a single-unit framework. So is this just an intellectual curiosity, useful only to challenge your intuition and technical skills?

Experimental economists have exposed inexperienced subjects to third-price sealed-bid auctions and examined their response to a larger number of bidders. Amazingly, the majority of bidders reduced their bid, just as the theory recommends (see Kagel and Levin (1993)). The authors take great pride in this result; they take it as evidence that inexperienced subjects are not as unsophisticated as is often

---

[13] Third-price auctions were analyzed for the first time by Kagel and Levin (1993), assuming uniformly distributed valuations.

[14] Hints: Suppose the equilibrium bid function of the kth-price auction is linear in the own valuation, $b^*(v) = \alpha_k v$. Revenue equivalence applies also to the kth-price auction (the proof follows in Section 8.2.5). Therefore, the expected price must be the same as under the English auction: $E[V_{(n-1)}] = E[b^*(V_{(n-k+1)})] = \alpha_k E[V_{(n-k+1)}]$. Compute the two expected values and you have the asserted bid function (8.24). Once you have a candidate for solution, you only need to confirm that it does indeed satisfy the mutual best-response requirement. Notice, however, that this sketch raises the question whether the equilibrium strategy is linear.

suspected by critics of the experimental approach. The particular irony is that, if asked to make a guess, trained theorists tend to come up with the wrong hunch concerning the relationship between the number of bidders and equilibrium bids until they actually sit down and do the computations.

All-Pay Auctions

As a last example consider an auction that is frequently used in charities; we call it the *charity* or *all-pay* auction for lack of a better name. Its peculiar feature is that all bidders are required to actually pay their bid. Just as in a standard auction, the item is awarded to the highest bidder. But unlike in standard auctions, all bidders must pay their bid, even those who are not awarded the item.

Using a procedure similar to the above, the equilibrium bid function is[15]

$$b^*(v) = \frac{n-1}{n} v^n. \tag{8.26}$$

This is in line with the observation that bidders often bid only nominal amounts of money for relatively valuable items.

In order to determine the seller's expected revenue, notice that the seller collects the following expected payment from each bidder:

$$E[b^*(V)] = \frac{n-1}{n} \int_0^1 v^n \, dv = \frac{n-1}{n(n+1)}. \tag{8.27}$$

Take the sum over all bidders, and one obtains $E[nb^*(V)] = (n-1)/(n+1)$, which confirms revenue equivalence.

The crucial feature of charity or all-pay auctions is that they make winners and losers pay. We mention that this is also a feature of the not so charitable seller-optimal auction if bidders are risk-averse (see Matthews (1983))[16] or if bidders are financially constrained (see Laffont and Robert (1996)).

All-pay auctions have also been used to model political lobbying, political campaigns, research tournaments, and job promotion (the last two interpretations view bids as agents' effort).[17] An early example of an all-pay auction under complete information is Posner's (1975) well-known reinterpretation of the social loss of monopoly.

Finally, note that instead of requiring all bidders to pay their own bid, one may instead require them pay the second, third, or kth highest bid. In this sense, it would be more precise to describe the above auctions as "first-price all-pay" auctions.

---

[15] The probability of winning is the same as under the Dutch auction (see (8.11)). However, since all bids must actually be paid, the equilibrium bid must be a maximizer of $\rho(b)v - b$; hence it must solve the differential equation $\rho' v = 1$. Combining these two building blocks leads to the differential equation $\sigma(b)^{n-1}\sigma'(b) = 1/(n-1)$. Integration entails $(1/n)\sigma(b)^n = [1/(n-1)]b$, and therefore $b^*(v) = [(n-1)/n]v^n$, as asserted.

[16] However, Matthews also showed that the fee should be negative for sufficiently high valuation types.

[17] See, for example, Baye, Kovenock, and de Vries (1993).

Incidentally, the *war-of-attrition* game – used in oligopoly theory to model strategic exit – is essentially a second-price all-pay auction.

Participation Fees

So far we have considered auction rules where all bidders have an incentive to participate because no one can lose. All these auctions were payoff-equivalent. This suggests the following questions: Is there any common auction that gives rise to different equilibrium payoffs, and if so, is it ever desirable to adopt such a deviation from standard auctions?

Many seemingly innocuous modifications of standard auction rules affect bidder participation and drive a wedge between those who participate, typically those with high valuations, and those who exit, typically because their valuation is below a certain critical valuation v_0. Adding such a distortion is profitable to the seller, even though it involves the risk that no sale takes place.

In the following we discuss one particular example: the introduction of a uniform entry or participation fee. The purpose of this exercise is to motivate and explain the notion of a *critical valuation* v_0 below which it does not pay to participate and to show that standard auctions are not seller-optimal, which motivates the search for optimal auction rules.

Example 8.3 (Participation Fee) Suppose the seller requires a participation fee $c \in [0, 1]$ from each bidder in an English auction. Let there be two bidders with uniformly distributed valuations on the support $[0, 1]$.

Then a bidder participates if and only if his valuation is at or above the critical level $v_0 := \sqrt{c}$. The expected-revenue-maximizing entry fee is $c^* = \frac{1}{4}$, and the maximum expected revenue $\frac{5}{12}$. Therefore, for $n = 2$, the participation-fee-augmented English auction is more profitable than the standard English auction and than the optimal take-it-or-leave-it price (see Examples 8.1 and 8.2).

The proof is sketched as follows:

1. In order to compute v_0, consider the marginal bidder with valuation v_0. His cost of participation, c, must be exactly matched by the expected gain from bidding, $\Pr\{\text{winning}\}v_0 - c = 0$. Note that a bidder with valuation v_0 can win only if the rival does not participate because his valuation is below v_0, in which case the price is equal to zero. Therefore, $\Pr\{\text{winning}\} = v_0$, and hence $v_0^2 - c = 0$, or equivalently $v_0 = \sqrt{c}$, as asserted.

2. Notice that the seller collects the entry fee from both bidders if and only if $V_{(1)} \geq v_0$, in which case the price is equal to $V_{(1)}$. The seller has no earnings if and only if $V_{(2)} < v_0$. And finally, only one bidder participates if and only if $V_{(1)} < v_0 \leq V_{(2)}$. Then the price goes all the way down to zero, and the seller's only earning is the entry fee paid by the one and only active bidder. Therefore, the seller's expected profit is equal to

$$\Pi := \Pr\left\{V_{(1)} \geq v_0\right\} \left(E\left[V_{(1)} \mid V_{(1)} \geq v_0\right] + 2c\right)$$
$$+ \Pr\left\{V_{(1)} < v_0 \leq V_{(2)}\right\}c.$$

Of course,

$$\Pr\left\{V_{(1)} \geq v_0\right\} = (1 - v_0)^2,$$

$$\Pr\left\{V_{(1)} < v_0 \leq V_{(2)}\right\} = 2v_0(1 - v_0),$$

$$E\left[V_{(1)} \mid V_{(1)} \geq v_0\right] = \frac{2}{(1 - v_0)^2} \int_{v_0}^{1} v(1 - v)\,dv$$

$$= \frac{2v_0 + 1}{3}.$$

Hence, by all of the above,

$$\Pi = \frac{(1 - \sqrt{c})(4c + \sqrt{c} + 1)}{3}.$$

3. Evidently, Π is strictly concave in c, and $c^* = \frac{1}{4}$ solves the first-order condition $1 - 2\sqrt{c} = 0$, which completes the proof.

While the introduction of an entry fee raises the sellers' payoff (the optimal c is not equal to zero), we will later show that there are many ways to achieve the seller's maximum revenue. The seller-optimal auction is characterized by a particular critical valuation v_0, which can be implemented in many ways, for example by setting the right minimum bid or the right entry fee.

8.2.4 An Alternative Solution Procedure*

There are many ways to solve an auction. In the previous subsection you were introduced to the standard solution procedure, which is straightforward though a bit cumbersome. The purpose of this subsection is to raise your virtuosity and exercise a more elegant solution of a first-price or Dutch auction. This solution procedure is also useful in other auction problems, and it breaks the ground for the analysis in Section 8.2.5.

Proposition 8.1 *First-price and Dutch auctions have a unique symmetric equilibrium strategy*

$$b^*(v) = E\left[V_{(n-1)} \mid V_{(n-1)} < v\right] < v. \tag{8.28}$$

Proof We proceed as follows: Assume b^* is strict monotone increasing (which will be confirmed later on). Consider one bidder, and suppose all other bidders play the strategy b^*. Then that bidder must only consider bids from the range $[b^*(0), b^*(1)]$. Therefore, all relevant deviating bids can be generated by bidding the equilibrium strategy b^* as if the valuation were $x \in [0, 1]$ rather than v, which leads to a bid $b^*(x) \neq b^*(v)$.

Let $U(x, v)$ denote that bidder's payoff, and $\rho(x)$ his probability of winning the auction, provided: 1) his true valuation is v, 2) all others play the strategy b^*, and 3) he bids the amount $b^*(x)$. In a first-price or Dutch auction $U(x, v) := \rho(x)(v - b^*(x))$ and, due to the monotonicity of b^*, $\rho(x) := \Pr\{b^*(V_{(n-1)}) < b^*(x)\} = \Pr\{V_{(n-1)} < x\} = F(x)^{n-1}$.

The strategy b^* is a symmetric Bayesian Nash equilibrium if and only if it never pays to deviate from the equilibrium bid $b^*(v)$, i.e.,

$$v \in \arg\max_x U(x, v) \qquad \forall v. \tag{8.29}$$

A necessary condition for (8.29) is that for all v

$$0 = \frac{\partial}{\partial x} U(x, v)\big|_{x=v} = \rho'(v)(v - b^*(v)) - \rho(v)b^{*'}(v).$$

This condition can be written in the form $v \, d\rho = d(\rho b)$. Since $b^*(0) = 0$, integration yields $b\rho = \int_0^v x \, d\rho$, which implies the assertion $b^*(v) = E[V_{(n-1)} \mid V_{(n-1)} < v]$.

Partial integration of (8.28) gives

$$b^*(v) = v - \int_0^v \left(\frac{F(x)}{F(v)}\right)^{n-1} dx < v,$$

which confirms bid shading. And differentiation gives

$$b^{*'}(v) = (n - 1)\frac{F'(v)}{F(v)}(v - b^*(v)) > 0,$$

which confirms the assumed monotonicity of b^*.

The necessary conditions are also sufficient if each stationary point is a global maximum. This requirement holds because $U(x, v)$ is increasing in x iff $x < v$ and decreasing if and only if $x > v$, as shown in the appendix on the pseudoconcavity of bidders' payoff functions (Section 8.10). $\qquad\qquad\square$

8.2.5 General Solution of Symmetric Auction Games

In many noncooperative games it is difficult, if not impossible, to find a closed-form equilibrium solution unless one works with particular functional specifications. The SIPV auction game framework is an exception. In this framework all standard auctions – indeed, all auctions that select the highest bidder as winner – have a unique symmetric equilibrium.

As we show in this subsection, the general solution of SIPV auction games can be found quite easily. The trick is to begin with a more abstract account of auction games, and then solve for equilibrium payoffs, and establish general revenue-equivalence properties before solving for equilibrium strategies.

Once equilibrium payoffs have been determined, one can turn to particular auction games such as the auctions considered in the previous subsection. Knowing payoffs and the details of the considered auction, it is, in most cases a snap to compute the associated equilibrium bid functions.

The advantage of putting the usual solution procedure upside down is twofold: 1) payoffs are determined and revenue equivalence is established for a large array of auction rules (this could never be achieved by solving all conceivable auctions one by one) and 2) the technique is remarkably simple (no need to do dull manipulations of first-order conditions and solve nonlinear differential equations).

To prepare the more abstract account of auction games, we begin with some slightly technical definitions and remarks.

Probability Distribution

Since bidders' valuations are iid random variables, their joint distribution function $\mathcal{F}$ is just the product of their separate distribution functions $F : [0, \bar{v}] \to [0, 1]$, which are in turn identical due to the assumed symmetry. Therefore,

$$\mathcal{F}(v_1, v_2, \ldots, v_n) = F(v_1)F(v_2) \cdots F(v_n). \tag{8.30}$$

Strategies

Bidders' strategies are their *bid function* $b : [0, \bar{v}] \to \mathbb{R}_+$ and their *participation rule* $\xi : [0, \bar{v}] \to \{0, 1\}$. Without loss of generality we characterize symmetric equilibria where all bidders play the same strategies. And we assume that all bidders have an incentive to participate, provided their valuation is not below a certain critical value $v_0 \geq 0$, so that $\xi(v) = 1 \iff v \geq v_0$. This reduces strategies to bid functions $b(v)$ and critical valuations $v_0 \in [0, \bar{v}]$.

Representation of Auction Rules

All auction rules can be represented by an *allocation rule* $\hat{\rho}$ and a *payment rule* $\hat{x}$, where $\hat{\rho}(b_1, \ldots, b_n)$ is i's probability of winning the auction, and $\hat{x}(b_1, \ldots, b_n)$ i's payment to the auctioneer.[18] The advantage of this representation is that, given rivals' strategies, each bidder's decision problem can be viewed as one of choosing through his bid b a *probability of winning* and a *payment*.

Consider one bidder, say bidder 1, and suppose bidders 2 to n bid according to the equilibrium strategy $b^*(v)$. Then the probability of winning and the expected payment are solely functions of the own action b, as follows:

$$\rho(b) := \mathop{E}_{V_2,\ldots,V_n} [\hat{\rho}(b, b^*(V_2), \ldots, b^*(V_n))], \tag{8.31}$$

$$\mathcal{E}(b) := \mathop{E}_{V_2,\ldots,V_n} [\hat{x}(b, b^*(V_2), \ldots, b^*(V_n))]. \tag{8.32}$$

Due to the independence assumption, both ρ and $\mathcal{E}$ depend only on the bid b but not *directly* on the bidder's own valuation v.

Payoff Functions

Suppose rivals play the equilibrium strategy $b^*(v)$. Using the $\rho, \mathcal{E}$ representation, the bidders' payoff function is

$$U(b, v) := \rho(b)v - \mathcal{E}(b). \tag{8.33}$$

Equilibrium

The strategies $(b^*(v), v_0)$ are a (symmetric) Bayesian Nash equilibrium if (for $v \geq v_0$)

$$U(b^*(v), v) \geq U(b, v) \qquad \forall b, \tag{8.34}$$

$$U(b^*(v_0), v_0) = 0. \tag{8.35}$$

---

[18] In principle, payments may be determined by a lottery. Therefore, $\hat{x}_i(\cdot)$ should be viewed as an expected value.

Results

As a first result, we establish the strict monotonicity of the equilibrium bid function.

Lemma 8.1 (Monotonicity) *The equilibrium bid function $b^*(v)$ is strictly monotone increasing.*

Proof The expected utility of a bidder with valuation v who chooses the bid (action) b when all rivals play the equilibrium strategy $b^*(v)$ is (8.33). The equilibrium action $b = b^*(v)$ must be a best reply. Therefore, the *indirect utility* function is

$$U^*(v) := U(b^*(v), v) = \rho(b^*(v))v - \mathcal{E}(b^*(v)). \qquad (8.36)$$

Since $U^*(v)$ is a maximum-value function, the envelope theorem applies, and one has[19]

$$U^{*\prime}(v) = \frac{\partial}{\partial v} U(b^*(v), v) = \rho(b^*(v)). \qquad (8.37)$$

Obviously, $U^*(v)$ is convex.[20] Therefore, $U^{*\prime}(v) = \rho(b^*(v))$ is increasing in v. And since $\rho(b)$ is increasing in b, it follows that the equilibrium bid function $b^*(v)$ is increasing in v. In view of the fact that the optimal bid cannot be the same for different valuations, the monotonicity is strict.[21] □

An immediate implication of strict monotonicity, combined with symmetry, is:

Lemma 8.2 (Probability of Winning) *The bidder with the highest valuation wins the auction, provided that valuation is above v_0. Therefore, the equilibrium probability of winning is (for $v \geq v_0$)*

$$\rho^*(v) := \rho(b^*(v)) = \Pr\{\text{rivals' } V\text{'s are below } v\} = F(v)^{n-1}. \qquad (8.38)$$

This brings us to the amazing payoff equivalence of a large class of auction games.

Proposition 8.2 (Payoff Equivalence) *All auctions that select the highest bidder as winner have a symmetric equilibrium and share the same critical valuation v_0 give rise to the same expected payoffs.*

---

[19] You may wonder whether a second-order condition is satisfied. The answer is yes, as we show in the appendix (Section 8.10).

[20] The proof is a standard exercise in microeconomics. Choose $v_1 \neq v_2$, $\hat{v} := \lambda v_1 + (1 - \lambda)v_2$. By definition of a maximum, $\rho^*(\hat{v})v_i - \mathcal{E}^*(\hat{v}) \leq \rho^*(v_i)v_i - \mathcal{E}^*(v_i)$, $i \in \{1, 2\}$. Rearrange, and you get $U^*(\hat{v}) \leq \lambda U^*(v_1) + (1 - \lambda)U^*(v_2)$, which proves convexity. Make sure that you also understand the intuition of this result. Notice that the bidder could always leave the bid unchanged when v changes, as a fallback. Therefore, U^* must be at or above its gradient hyperplane, which is convexity.

[21] Suppose the bid function contains some flat portion in the interval (v_1, v_2). Then a bidder with some valuation from this interval, say v_2, can raise his expected payoff by marginally raising his bid because then he always wins when the second highest valuation is in that same interval.

Proof Suppose $v \geq v_0$. Integrating (8.37), one obtains, using (8.38) and the fact that $U^*(v_0) = 0$,

$$U^*(v) = \int_{v_0}^{v} U^{*\prime}(x)\,dx + U^*(v_0)$$

$$= \int_{v_0}^{v} \rho(b^*(x))\,dx$$

$$= \int_{v_0}^{v} F(x)^{n-1}\,dx. \qquad (8.39)$$

Next, solve (8.36) for bidders' expected payment, and one finds (for $v \geq v_0$)

$$\mathcal{E}^*(v) := \mathcal{E}(b^*(v))$$

$$= vF(v)^{n-1} - \int_{v_0}^{v} F(x)^{n-1}\,dx. \qquad (8.40)$$

These results prove that bidders' equilibrium payoff, probability of winning, and expected payments are the same for all permitted auction rules.

Finally, compute the seller's expected revenue Π. The seller earns from each bidder an expected payment $\mathcal{E}^*(v)$. Since he does not know bidders' valuations, he has to take an expected value, which gives

$$\mathop{E}_{V_{(n)} \geq v_0} [\mathcal{E}^*(V)] = \mathop{E}_{V_{(n)} \geq v_0} [V F(V)^{n-1} - U^*(V)]$$

$$= \frac{1}{n} \mathop{E}_{V_{(n)} \geq v_0} [V_{(n)}] - \mathop{E}_{V_{(n)} \geq v_0} [U^*(V)].$$

Sum over all n, and one has the seller's expected revenue

$$\Pi(n, v_0) = n \mathop{E}_{V \geq v_0} [\mathcal{E}^*(V)]$$

$$= \mathop{E}_{V_{(n)} \geq v_0} [V_{(n)}] - n \mathop{E}_{V \geq v_0} [U^*(V)] \qquad (8.41)$$

$$= \int_{v_0}^{\bar{v}} v \frac{d}{dv} F(v)^n\,dv$$

$$\quad - n \int_{v_0}^{\bar{v}} \left(\int_{v_0}^{v} F(x)^{n-1}\,dx \right) \frac{d}{dv} F(v)\,dv.$$

Using integration by parts gives

$$\int_{v_0}^{\bar{v}} \left(\int_{v_0}^{v} F(x)^{n-1}\,dx \right) \frac{d}{dv} F(v)\,dv = \int_{v_0}^{\bar{v}} F(v)^{n-1}\,dv - \int_{v_0}^{\bar{v}} F(v)^n\,dv$$

$$= \frac{1}{n} \int_{v_0}^{\bar{v}} \left(\frac{d}{dv} F(v)^n \right) \frac{1 - F(v)}{f(v)}\,dv.$$

Therefore, the seller's expected revenue is

$$\Pi(n, v_0) = \int_{v_0}^{\bar{v}} \left(v - \frac{1 - F(v)}{f(v)} \right) \left(\frac{d}{dv} F(v)^n \right)\,dv, \qquad (8.42)$$

which is also the same for all permitted auction rules. $\qquad \square$

Note that (8.41) indicates nicely how the social surplus from trade (the conditional expected value of $V_{(n)}$, conditional on $V_{(n)} \geq v_0$) is divided between bidders and the seller. It follows immediately that this surplus is maximized by setting $v_0 = 0$. Therefore, the considered auction rules are Pareto-optimal if and only if $v_0 = 0$.

As you can see from the ingredients in the proofs, revenue equivalence applies not only to the four standard auctions but to all auctions that select the highest bidder as winner, provided they share the same critical valuation v_0. However, expected payoffs are usually not the same when critical valuations differ. In particular, while standard auctions are payoff-equivalent when the critical valuation is the same, varying the critical valuation gives rise to a different class of payoff-equivalent auctions with a different payoff level. Keep this in mind if you apply revenue equivalence.

Remark 8.1 Note that the factor that appears in the integrand of (8.42),

$$\gamma(v) := v - \frac{1 - F(v)}{f(v)}, \tag{8.43}$$

can be interpreted as "marginal revenue" (see Section 8.1.3) or as a "priority level" (Myerson).[22] In this light it follows immediately from (8.42) that the seller's expected revenue is equal to the expected value of the highest priority level:

$$\Pi(n, v_0) = \mathop{E}_{V_{(n)} \geq v_0} \left[\gamma \left(V_{(n)} \right) \right]. \tag{8.44}$$

Proposition 8.3 (Equilibrium Bid Functions I) *Suppose valuations are drawn from the continuous probability distribution function $F(v)$, and the minimum bid is $v_0 \geq 0$. Then the equilibrium bid functions of standard auction games are (for $v \geq v_0$)*

$$b^*(v) = v - \int_{v_0}^{v} \left(\frac{F(x)}{F(v)} \right)^{n-1} dx \qquad \text{(Dutch auction)}, \tag{8.45}$$

$$b^*(v) = v \qquad \text{(English auction)}. \tag{8.46}$$

Of course, the English auction has also several asymmetric equilibria, but these are weakly dominated.

Proof In the Dutch auction, the winner pays his bid, and the loser goes free. Therefore, $\mathcal{E}^*(v) = \rho^*(v) b^*(v)$. Solve this for $b^*(v)$, and one has immediately (8.45).

To establish the asserted symmetric equilibrium bidding rule for the English auction, recall that truth telling is a (weakly) dominant strategy. This proves immediately the asserted solution. However, as an exercise we now also derive the symmetric equilibrium strategy using our solution procedure: By (??) one has

$$\mathcal{E}^*(v) = \int_{v_0}^{v} y \frac{d}{dy} (F(y)^{n-1}) \, dy$$

$$= E\left[V_{(n-1:n-1)} \mid V_{(n-1:n-1)} \in [v_0, v] \right] \Pr \left\{ V_{(n-1:n-1)} \in [v_0, v] \right\}.$$

---

[22] Myerson (1981) shows that, if valuations are drawn from different distributions, the optimal auction awards the item to the bidder with the highest priority level and charges him an amount equal to the lowest valuation that would still assure winning.

In an English auction the winner pays the second highest bid, and only the winner pays; therefore,

$$\mathcal{E}^*(v) = E\left[b^*\left(V_{(n-1:n-1)}\right)\middle|V_{(n-1:n-1)} \in [v_0, v]\right]\Pr\left\{V_{(n-1:n-1)} \in [v_0, v]\right\}.$$

Hence, $b^*(v) = v$, $\forall v \geq v_0$. $\qquad\qquad\qquad\qquad\qquad\qquad\qquad\qquad$ □

Proposition 8.4 (Equilibrium Bid Functions II) *Suppose valuations are drawn from the continuous probability distribution function $F(v)$. Then the equilibrium bid functions of some of the other auction games analyzed before are (for $v \geq v_0$)*

$$b^*(v) = vF(v)^{n-1} - \int_{v_0}^{v} F(x)^{n-1}\,dx \qquad \text{(all-pay auction),} \qquad (8.47)$$

$$b^*(v) = v + \frac{k-2}{n-k+1}\frac{F(v)}{f(v)} \qquad \text{(kth-price auction, } k \geq 2\text{).} \qquad (8.48)$$

Proof In the all-pay auction all bidders actually pay their bid with certainty, whether they win or lose. Therefore, $b^*(v) = \mathcal{E}(b^*(v))$, and the asserted bid function follows immediately from (**??**). The solution of the third-price auction is a bit more involved and hence omitted (see Wolfstetter (1998)). $\qquad\qquad$ □

In order to illustrate the effect of the minimum bid upon the bid function in the first-price auction, take a look at Figure 8.3, where we plot the equilibrium bid functions for the case of uniformly distributed valuations on the support $[0, 1]$, and two bidders under $v_0 = 0$ (dashed curve) and $v_0 = \frac{1}{2}$ (solid curve).

Remark 8.2 In a first-price auction the minimum bid p_0 induces the same critical valuation $v_0 = p_0$, which is why we identified v_0 and p_0 in this case. However, the two do not coincide in all auctions. For example, in an all-pay auction the critical valuation v_0 bears the following relationship to the minimum price:

$$v_0 = \frac{p_0}{\rho(v_0)} > p_0,$$

because the bidder with valuation v_0 is indifferent between participation and non-participation if and only if $\rho(v_0)v_0 - p_0 = 0$.

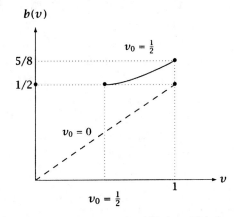

Figure 8.3. Effect of Minimum Price v_0 on Equilibrium Bids in a First-Price Auction.

Also note the following interpretation of equilibrium bidding.

Proposition 8.5 (Interpretation) *In equilibrium each bidder bids so high that his expected payment, conditional upon winning, exactly matches the item's value to rival bidders:*

$$\mathcal{E}^*(v) = \rho^*(v) E\left[V_{(n-1)} \mid V_{(n)} = v\right]. \tag{8.49}$$

Therefore, the equilibrium bid function of the first-price auction can also be written as

$$b^*(v) = E\left[V_{(n-1)} \mid V_{(n)} = v\right] \qquad \text{(first-price auction)}. \tag{8.50}$$

Finally we mention that the second-order stochastic dominance relationship between the seller's payoff under the Dutch and the English auction, $P_D \succ_{SSD} P_E$, holds generally and not just for uniformly distributed valuations.

Proposition 8.6 (Stochastic Dominance) *The equilibrium price under the Dutch auction, P_D, second-order stochastically dominates that under the English auction, P_E. Therefore, a risk-averse seller prefers the Dutch over the English auction.*

Proof (Sketch) Suppose the highest valuation is v. Then the conditional cdf's of P_D and P_E, conditional on $V_{(n)} = v$, are single-crossing. Note that the Dutch auction puts all probability mass on $b^*(v)$, whereas under the English auction P_E is determined by the random variable $V_{(n-1)}$. Moreover, $E[P_D \mid V_{(n)} = v] = E[P_E \mid V_{(n)} = v]$ since $\mathcal{E}^*(v \mid V_{(n)} = v)$ is the same under both auctions, by (??). Therefore, for each $V_{(n)} = v$, P_E is a mean-preserving spread of P_D, and P_D second-order stochastically dominates P_E. Since this applies to all possible highest valuations, it also applies to the average highest valuation. □

8.2.6 Vickrey Auction as a Clarke–Groves Mechanism*

In his analysis of the efficient provision of public goods, Clarke (1971) proposed his well-known *pivotal mechanism* that implements the efficient allocation in dominant strategies. This mechanism was later generalized by Groves (1973).[23] Interestingly, the Vickrey auction is a special case of the Clarke–Groves mechanism.

The Clarke–Groves mechanism, denoted by (t, k, k'), is defined by a transfer rule t and the allocation rules k and k' that prescribe an allocation and payments, contingent upon agents' valuations v. The allocation rule $k(v)$, $v := (v_1, \ldots, v_n)$, prescribes the allocation that is efficient for the valuations v reported by all agents. And the allocation rules $k'_{-i}(v_{-i})$ prescribe the efficient allocations that would result if agent i were not present, where $v_{-i} := (v_1, \ldots, v_{i-1}, v_{i+1}, \ldots, v_n)$. Finally, the transfer rule stipulates payments to agents if $t_i(v) > 0$ (and from agents if $t_i(v) < 0$),

---

[23] Green and Laffont (1979) showed that the Clarke–Groves mechanism is the only one that implements the efficient allocation in dominant strategies. They also showed that budget balancing (the requirement that the sum of all transfers vanish) cannot generally be achieved by dominant-strategy mechanisms. However, as shown by d' Aspremont and Gérard–Varet (1979), efficiency and budget balancing can be implemented as a Bayesian Nash equilibrium.

contingent upon agents' reported valuations, as follows:

$$t_i(v) := \sum_{j \neq i} u_j(k(v), v_j) - \sum_{j \neq i} u_j(k'_{-i}(v_{-i}), v_j), \qquad (8.51)$$

where u_i denotes i's payoff as a function of the allocation and the own valuation.

Note that $t_i(v) > 0$ represents the positive externality that i exerts upon the welfare of the $n - 1$ other agents. It is the difference in welfare of others if agent i is present and if i is absent. In turn, if $t_i(v) < 0$, agent i is required to pay a "tax" equal to the negative externality that he inflicts upon others.

Now apply the Clarke–Groves mechanism to the allocation of a single indivisible unit of a private good. In this case, the allocation rule k stipulates that the good is awarded to the agent with the highest valuation, and that $u_i(k, v_i) = v_i$ if v_i is the highest valuation, and that $u_i(k, v_i) = 0$ otherwise. Therefore, by (8.51),

$$t_i(v) = \begin{cases} -v_{(n-1)} & \text{if } v_i = v_{(n)}, \\ 0 & \text{otherwise,} \end{cases} \qquad (8.52)$$

i.e., the agent with the highest valuation is required to pay a transfer equal to the second highest valuation, while all others pay nothing. This shows that, in the present framework, the Clarke–Groves mechanism is precisely the social choice rule implemented by the Vickrey auction.

8.3 Robustness*

Assuming the SIPV framework with risk-neutral agents, we have derived the amazing result that *all* auctions that award the item to the highest bidder and give rise to the same critical valuation below which it does not pay to participate share the same equilibrium payoffs. In other words, if all participants are risk-neutral, many different auction forms – including the four standard auctions – are nothing but irrelevant institutional detail. And if the seller is *risk-averse,* he should favor the Dutch over the English auction (and the English over all higher-order kth-price auctions).

These results are in striking contrast to the apparent popularity of the second-price auction as an oral auction and the first-price auction for sealed bids. Has the SIPV model missed something of crucial importance, or have we missed something at work even in this framework?

A strong argument in favor of the English auction is its strategic simplicity. In this auction bidders need not engage in complicated strategic considerations. Even an unsophisticated bidder should be able to work out that setting a limit equal to one's true valuation is the best one can do. Not so under the Dutch auction. This auction game has no dominant strategy equilibrium. As a result, understanding the game is conceptually more demanding, not to speak of computational problems.

However, if the auction cannot be oral, say, because it would be too costly to bring bidders together at the same time and place, there is a very simple reason why one should favor a first-price sealed-bid auction, even though it is strategically more complicated than a second-price or Vickrey auction.

Second-price auctions can easily be manipulated by soliciting *phantom* bids close to the highest submitted bid. This suggests that second-price sealed bid auctions should not be observed if the seller is profit-oriented.

There are several further good reasons why the seller should favor the Dutch auction. But these come up only as we modify the SIPV model. We now turn to this task. In addition, we will give a few examples of auctions that violate the prerequisites of revenue equivalence and on that ground fail to be payoff-equivalent to the four common auctions.

8.3.1 Introducing Numbers Uncertainty

In many auctions bidders are uncertain about the number of participants (*numbers uncertainty*). This seems almost inevitable in sealed-bid auctions where bidders do not convene in one location but make bids each in their own office.

Notice, however, that the seller can easily eliminate numbers uncertainty if he wishes to do so. He only needs to solicit *contingent* bids where each bidder makes a whole list of bids, each contingent on a different number of participating bidders. Therefore, the seller has a choice. The question is: Is it in the interest of the seller to leave bidders subject to numbers uncertainty?

McAfee and McMillan (1987b) explored this issue. They showed that if bidders are risk-averse and have constant or decreasing absolute risk aversion, numbers uncertainty leads to more aggressive bidding in a first-price closed auction. Since numbers uncertainty obviously has no effect on bidding strategies under the three other auction rules, one can conclude from the revenue equivalence (Proposition 8.2) that numbers uncertainty favors the first-price closed auction. Incidentally, this result is used in experiments to test whether bidders are risk-averse (see Dyer, Kagel, and Levin (1989)).

8.3.2 Discrete Valuations

If valuations are *discrete* random variables, say $V \in \{0, v_1, v_2, \ldots, v_r\}$, the Dutch auction has only a mixed-strategy equilibrium. This equilibrium has remarkable properties that make it a truly interesting case and not just a technical side issue.

When you hear that bidders use mixed strategies, you may suspect that efficiency and hence revenue equivalence are sacrificed. By chance, high-valuation bidders may bid low and a low-valuation bidder bid high, in which case the item is not awarded to the highest-valuation bidder.

However, this cannot occur. The equilibrium mixed strategies are continuous probability distribution functions with a remarkable monotonicity property: the supports of bids associated with $v_1 < v_2 < \cdots < v_n$ are

$$[0, b_1], [b_1, b_2], \ldots, [b_{n-1}, b_n],$$

where $b_1 < b_2, \ldots, < b_n$. Due to this neighboring property of the supports, efficiency is maintained despite randomization, and revenue equivalence prevails.[24]

---

[24] For an ingeniously simple proof see Riley (1989).

As an illustration, suppose there are only two bidders, and their valuations are either 0 or 1, with equal probability. Then the unique symmetric equilibrium is as follows: if the valuation is equal to 0, do not participate; if it is equal to 1, participate and bid according to the probability distribution function[25]

$$B(x) := \Pr\{\text{bid} < x\} = \frac{x}{1-x}, \qquad x \in [0, \tfrac{1}{2}], \qquad (8.53)$$

with $B(0) = 0$, $B(\tfrac{1}{2}) = 1$.

In a mixed-strategy equilibrium, all actions from the support of the equilibrium mixed strategy, $[0, \tfrac{1}{2}]$, are an equally good response to $B(x)$. Therefore, bidders' equilibrium payoffs in the Dutch-auction game are $U^*(0) = 0$, $U^*(1) = \tfrac{1}{2}$.

Finally, consider the English auction. There, bidders stick to the truth-telling pure strategy $b^*(v) \equiv v$. A bidder with valuation $v = 1$ has an equal chance to face a rival either with valuation $v = 0$ or with $v = 1$. If the rival has $v = 1$, the item is sold at price 1 by using some tie rule, and neither bidder gains or loses. And if the rival has $v = 0$, the item is sold at price zero at a gain equal to 1. From this you see immediately that bidders' equilibrium payoffs are the same as in the Dutch-auction game. Finally, since it is always the highest valuation that wins the item, the overall gain from trade and therefore the seller's expected revenue are also the same.

8.3.3 Removing Bidders' Risk Neutrality

A more substantial modification is obtained by introducing risk-averse bidders. Obviously, this modification does not affect the equilibrium strategy under the English auction. Therefore, the expected price in this auction is unaffected as well.

However, strategies and payoffs change under the Dutch auction. Recall that in this auction form bidders take a chance and *shade* their bid below their valuation. When risk aversion is introduced, shading becomes less attractive because the marginal increment in wealth associated with winning the auction at a slightly reduced bid weighs less heavily than the possible loss of not winning due to such a reduced bid. Therefore, a risk-averse bidder shades his bid less than a risk-neutral bidder. Of course, bidders thus raise the seller's payoff and, alas, reduce their own.[26]

Proposition 8.7 *Suppose bidders are risk-averse. Then the seller prefers the Dutch to the English auction.*

8.3.4 Removing Independence: Correlated Beliefs

Finally, remove independence from the SIPV model and replace it by the assumption of a positive correlation between bidders' valuations. Positive correlation (this is

---

[25] Make sure to check that all bids (actions) $x \in [0, \tfrac{1}{2}]$ are maximizers of $\tfrac{1}{2}(1-x)(1+B(x))$, and therefore best replies to $B(x)$.

[26] For a formal proof see Riley and Samuelson (1981). On the design of optimal auctions when bidders are risk-averse see Maskin and Riley (1984b).

a special case of *affiliation*) means that a high own valuation makes it more likely that rival bidders' valuations are high as well.

The main consequence of positive correlation is that it makes bidders bid lower in a Dutch auction. Of course, correlation does not affect bidding in an English auction, where truth telling is always the dominant strategy. Therefore, the introduction of correlation reduces the expected price under the Dutch auction but has no effect on the expected price under the English auction. In other words, correlation entails that the seller should prefer the English to the Dutch auction.

Proposition 8.8 *In the symmetric private-values model with positively correlated valuations, the seller's payoff is higher under the English than under the Dutch auction, and that of potential buyers is lower.*[27]

The intuition for this result is sketched as follows: Each bidder knows that he will win the auction if and only if all other bidders' valuations are lower than his own. The introduction of correlation means that those with low valuations also think it is more likely that rival bidders have low valuations as well. Therefore, bidders with lower valuations shade their bids more. In turn this convinces high-valuation bidders that they do not have to bid so aggressively (for an instructive example see Riley (1989, p. 48 ff.)).

The introduction of correlation has a number of comparative-statics implications with interesting public policy implications. In particular, the release of information about the item's value should raise bids in a Dutch auction. Incidentally, this comparative-statics property was used by Kagel, Harstad, and Levin (1987) to test the predictions of auction theory in experimental settings.

You may return to the analysis of auctions with correlated valuations in Section 8.7, where you will find a more detailed analysis and some simple proofs.

8.3.5 Removing Symmetry

The symmetry assumption is central to the revenue-equivalence result. For if bidders are characterized by different probability distributions of valuations, under the Dutch auction it is no longer assured that the object is awarded to the bidder with the highest valuation. But precisely this property was needed in the proof of Proposition 8.2.

Example 8.4 Suppose there are two bidders, A and B, characterized by their random valuations, with supports $(\underline{a}, \bar{a})$ and $(\underline{b}, \bar{b})$, with $\bar{a} < \underline{b}$. Consider the Dutch auction. Obviously, B could always win and pocket a gain by bidding the amount $\bar{a}$. But B can do even better by shading the bid further below $\bar{a}$. But then the low-valuation bidder A wins with positive probability, violating Pareto optimality.

An important implication is that Pareto optimality is only assured by second-price bids. If a public authority uses auctions as an allocation device, efficiency should be

---

[27] The formal proof is in Milgrom and Weber (1982).

the primary objective. This suggests that public authorities should employ second-price auctions.

A detailed study of asymmetric auctions is in Maskin and Riley (1996). They state sufficient conditions under which first-price auctions are preferred by the seller. Altogether, their results suggest that the first-price auction tends to generate higher expected revenue when the seller has less information about bidders' preferences than bidders do about each others' preferences. But if the seller is equally well informed and therefore is in a position to set an appropriate minimum price, the ranking is most likely reversed.[28]

Based on these observations, Maskin and Riley suggest that

... in procurement bidding, where the procurer almost certainly knows less about the suppliers than they do about each other, the sealed first-price auction is very likely to be preferred by the procurer.

whereas

... in art auctions, where the auctioneer is likely to have at least as much information about buyers' reservation prices as each buyer has about his competitors, this presumption in favor of the sealed first-price auction no longer obtains.

8.3.6 Multiunit Auctions

Suppose the seller has more than one unit of a good and auctions them simultaneously. Then everything generalizes quite easily as long as each buyer demands at most one unit. But revenue equivalence generally fails if buyers are interested in buying several units and their demand is a function of price.

Consider the case if each buyer wants at most one unit. First of all we need to generalize the notions of first- and second-price auctions. Suppose k units are put up for sale. In a generalized second-price auction, a uniform price is set at the level of the highest rejected bid. The highest k bidders receive one unit each and pay that price. This shows how the kth-price auctions reviewed earlier are important in a multiunit setting. Of course, in a generalized first-price auction, the highest k bidders are awarded the k items and each pays his own bid. Therefore, the generalized first-price auction involves price discrimination.

Just as in the single-unit case, one can show that all auction rules are revenue-equivalent, provided they adhere to the principle of awarding each item to the highest bidder (see Harris and Raviv (1981)). However, this does not generalize when bidders may buy several units depending on the price.

A simple analysis of price-dependent demand is in Hansen (1988), who showed that first-price auctions lead to a higher expected price, so that revenue equivalence breaks down in this case. An important application concerns industrial procurement

---

[28] Another study of asymmetric auctions is Plum (1992). However, Plum considers a very special case, focuses on issues of existence and uniqueness, and does not address the ranking of different auctions by their expected revenue.

contracts in private industry and government. Hansen's results explain why procurement is usually in the form of a first-price seal-bid auction. For a fuller analysis of this matter, see Section 8.8.1 on auctions and oligopoly below.

Altogether, the theory of multiunit auctions is not very well developed. Until recently, one has often avoided modeling the auction as a game and instead analyzed bidders' optimal strategy, assuming a given probability distribution of being awarded the demanded items.[29] However, Maskin and Riley (1989) have generalized the theory of optimal auctions to include the multiunit case. And Spindt and Stolz (1989) showed that as the number of bidders or the quantity put up for auction is increased, the expected stopout price (the lowest price served) goes up, which generalizes well-known properties of single-unit auctions.

The most important applications of multiunit auctions are in financial markets. For example, the U.S. Treasury sells marketable bills, notes, and bonds in more than 150 regular auctions per year, using a sealed-bid, multiple-price auction mechanism. Some of the institutional details of the government securities market are sketched in Section 8.8.3 below.

8.3.7 Split-Award Auctions

Consider a procurement problem – say, the government wants to buy a sophisticated piece of military hardware. There are only two potential suppliers. Suppose it is cost-minimizing to break down the production into two subunits and to let each subunit be produced by a different supplier, due to sufficiently strong decreasing returns to scale. Then the government faces a dilemma: on the one hand, it would like to have each supplier produce one subunit because subdivision assures cost efficiency, and on the other hand, it would like to have competition between suppliers, as a safeguard against monopolistic pricing. How can it reconcile both goals?

One answer is to introduce a *split-award auction*. Such an auction asks each supplier to submit two bids: one for the subunit and one for the complete unit. The auctioneer selects those bids that minimize the cost of the complete unit. In equilibrium each supplier is awarded one subunit at a price that is lower than the monopoly price, due to competition between firms for the entire unit. Unfortunately, split-award auctions do not always perform so well (see Anton and Yao (1989, 1992)).

8.3.8 Repeated Auctions

If a seller has several units, he may also sell them sequentially, one unit after the other. This method of sale gives rise to a *repeated-auction* problem.

Sequential auctioning is common, for example, in the sale of wine, race horses, and used cars. In some of these markets it has been observed that prices tend to follow

---

[29] See for example the analysis of Treasury-bill auctions by Scott and Wolf (1979) and Nautz and Wolfstetter (1997). Treasury-bill auctions are explained in Section 8.8.3.

a declining pattern (Ashenfelter (1989), Ashenfelter and Genovese (1992)). Several explanations have been proposed for this declining-price anomaly.[30]

Ashenfelter suggested that risk aversion among bidders may explain declining prices in sequential auctions of identical objects, such as identical cases of wine or virtually identical condominiums. However, McAfee and Vincent (1993) could only generate declining prices by assuming that bidders' absolute degree of risk aversion is *nondecreasing* – which seems to violate most peoples' attitude towards risk. Therefore, risk aversion alone is probably not the answer.

While there is no compelling reason for declining prices when identical objects are auctioned, declining prices follow easily if each bidder's valuations for the different objects are independently drawn from an identical distribution, and each bidder wants to buy only one unit (see Bernhardt and Scoones (1994)).

To understand why prices fall in a sequential second-price auction of stochastically identical objects, it is useful to compare with the case of identical objects. In his study of a sequential second-price auction of exactly identical objects, Weber (1983) pointed out that bidders should bid less than their valuation in the first round to allow for the option value of participating in subsequent rounds. Since Weber assumed identical objects, bidders with a higher valuation have also a higher option value, and therefore they should shade their bids in the first round by a greater amount than bidders with a lower valuation. This way, all gains to waiting are arbitraged away and, as Weber showed, the expected prices in all rounds are the same.

However, if the objects for sale are only stochastically the same, all bidders have the same option value, regardless of their valuation for the first object put up for sale. For a precise statement of equilibrium suppose there are $n > 3$ bidders and two stochastically identical units sold in a sequence of second-price auctions. Each bidder wants to acquire only one unit.

Bidders' expected gain in the second auction is

$$\xi := \frac{1}{n-1} \left(E\left[V_{(n-1:n-1)}\right] - E\left[V_{(n-2:n-1)}\right]\right). \tag{8.54}$$

Since a bidder could always delay bidding until the second round, and since he is interested in just one unit, ξ is the *option value* of delay.

Another explanation of declining prices is based on the assumption of stochastic scale effects, in the form of either economies or diseconomies of scale (see Jeitschko and Wolfstetter (1998)).

8.4 Auction Rings

So far we have analyzed auctions in a noncooperative framework. But what if bidders collude and form an *auction ring*? Surely, bidders can gain a lot by collusive agreements that exclude mutual competition. But can they be expected to achieve a stable and reliable agreement? And if so, which auctions are more susceptible to collusion than others?

---

[30] On the role of information transmission and learning in repeated auctions see Jeitschko (1998).

To rank different auctions in the face of collusion, suppose all potential bidders have come to a collusive agreement. They have selected their *designated winner*, who we will assume is the one with the highest valuation, recommended him to follow a particular strategy, and committed others to abstain from bidding. However, suppose the ring faces an enforcement problem because ring members cannot be prevented from breaching the agreement. Therefore, the agreement has to be self-enforcing. Does it pass this test at least in some auctions?

Consider the Dutch auction (or first-price sealed bid). Here, the designated winner will be recommended to place a bid roughly equal to the seller's minimum price, whereas all other ring members are asked to abstain from bidding. But then each of those asked to abstain can gain by placing a slightly higher bid, in violation of the ring agreement. Therefore, the agreement is not self-enforcing.

Not so under the English auction (or second-price closed-seal auction). Here the designated bidder is recommended to bid up to his own valuation and everyone else to abstain from bidding. Now, no one can gain by breaching the agreement, because no one will ever exceed the designated bidder's limit.

Therefore:[31]

Proposition 8.9 *Collusive agreements between potential bidders are self-enforcing in an English but not in a Dutch auction.*[32]

These results give a clear indication that the English auction (or second-price closed auction) is particularly susceptible to auction rings, and that the seller should choose a Dutch instead of an English auction if he has to deal with an auction ring that is unable to enforce agreements.

Even if auction rings can write enforceable agreements, the ring faces the problem of how to select the designated winner and avoid strategic behavior of ring members. This is usually done by running a pre-auction. But can one set it up in such a way that it always selects that ring member with the highest valuation?

In a pre-auction, every ring member is asked to place a bid, and the highest bidder is chosen as the ring's sole bidder at the subsequent auction. But if the bid at the pre-auction only affects the chance of becoming designated winner at no cost, each ring member has every reason to exaggerate his valuation. Therefore, the pre-auction problem can only be solved if one makes the designated winner share his alleged gain from trade.

Graham and Marshall (1987) proposed a simple scheme that resolves the pre-auction problem by an appropriate side-payment arrangement. Essentially, this scheme uses an English auction (or second-price closed auction) to select the designated winner. If the winner of the pre-auction also wins the main auction, he is required to pay the difference between the price paid at the main auction and the second highest bid from the pre-auction bid to a third party. This way, the entire

[31] This point was made by Robinson (1985).
[32] To be more precise, under an English auction the bidding game has two equilibria: one where everybody sticks to the cartel agreement and one where it is breached. The latter can, however, be ruled out on the ground of payoff dominance.

game (pre- plus main auction) is made equivalent to a second-price auction without collusion, which solves the pre-auction problem.

In order to prevent all the gains from collusion from going to the third party, the ring has to sell the entitlement to this payment to an interested party and divide that payment equally, prior to the pre-auction. This way, all ring members capture a share of the gains from collusion.

Alternatively, the ring could arrange the pre-auction without using a third party. For example, the ring could require the winner to pay to all ring members an equal share of the difference between the price paid at the main auction and the second highest bid from the pre-auction. Such auction games have been analyzed by Engelbrecht–Wiggans (1994).

Notice, however, that these solutions work only if the ring can enforce the agreed-upon side payments. In the absence of enforcement mechanisms, auction rings are plagued by strategic manipulation, so that no stable ring agreement may get off the ground.

In their analysis of *weak cartels* McAfee and McMillan (1992) come to the conclusion that the impossibility of transfer payments precludes efficiency. Tacit collusion implies bidding strategies of the following form (for some $\hat{v} \in (0, 1)$):

$$b^*(v) = \begin{cases} 0 & \text{if } v < \hat{v}, \\ \hat{v} & \text{if } v \geq \hat{v}, \end{cases} \tag{8.55}$$

which evidently entails inefficiency.

Incidentally, this tacit collusion strategy has an empirical counterpart. As mentioned by Scherer (1980),

Each year the Federal and State governments receive thousands of sets of identical bids in the sealed bid competitions they sponsor.

Finally, we mention that the seller may fight a suspected auction ring by "pulling bids off the chandelier," that is, by introducing imaginary bids into the proceedings. In 1985, the New York City Department of Consumer Affairs proposed to outlaw imaginary bids after it had become known that Christie's had reported the sale of several paintings that had in fact not been sold. This proposed regulation was strongly opposed by most New York-based auction houses, precisely on the ground that it would deprive them of one of their most potent weapons to fight rings of bidders.

8.5 Optimal Auctions

Among all possible auctions, which one maximizes the seller's expected profit? At first glance, this question seems unmanageable. There is a myriad of possible auction rules limited only by one's imagination. Whatever your favorite auction rule, how can you ever be sure that someone will not come along and find a better one?

On the other hand, you may ask, what is the issue? Did we not show that virtually all auction rules are payoff-equivalent?

The breakthrough that made the problem of optimal auction design tractable is due to two contributions, one by Riley and Samuelson (1981) and the other by Myerson (1981).

In a superficial interpretation, the two contributions differ in the style of how they approach the optimal-auction problem. Whereas Riley and Samuelson start out with a simple characterization of revenue-equivalence relationships (much of which has entered into our analysis of standard auctions) and then reduce the optimal-auction problem to the optimal choice of minimum price, Myerson poses optimal auctions as a mechanism design problem.

However, the difference goes deeper. The approach by Riley and Samuelson is more restrictive, for two reasons:

- Whereas Riley and Samuelson assume that the item is awarded to the highest bidder, Myerson shows the limitations of this commonly used allocation rule.
- Whereas Riley and Samuelson assume that all bidders' valuations are drawn from the same distribution, Myerson allows them to be drawn from different distributions (asymmetric auctions).

In the following we first review the solution by Riley and Samuelson, which builds directly upon our previous results. Then we explain Myerson's mechanism-design approach. And finally we add some remarks on how optimal-auction results change if one takes into account the cost of participation and stochastic entry.

8.5.1 A Simplified Approach

In the symmetric case it is easy to characterize optimal auctions, without employing the apparatus of the mechanism-design approach if one is ready to restrict attention to the allocation rule awarding the item to the highest bidder. This simplified approach follows Riley and Samuelson (1981). We will later confirm that the assumed allocation rule is not restrictive in the symmetric case. Therefore, the only serious limitation is the symmetry assumption.

For this purpose, go back to our solution of the seller's equilibrium payoff (8.42). There, the only remaining choice variable for the seller is the critical valuation v_0. Therefore, the seller-optimal auction is the one that maximizes $\Pi(n, v_0)$ over v_0.

Proposition 8.10 (Optimal Auctions without Entry) *The seller optimal auction sets the cutoff valuation v_0^* (below which it does not pay to bid) that satisfies the condition*

$$v_0^* = \frac{1 - F(v_0^*)}{f(v_0^*)}, \tag{8.56}$$

independent of the number of bidders n. Therefore, a modified second-price auction – modified by imposing a minimum bid equal to v_0^* – is optimal. For example, if valuations are uniformly distributed on the support $[0, 1]$, then $v_0^* = 1/2$ (Figure 8.4).

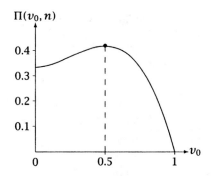

Figure 8.4. Optimal Auction: Uniform Distribution and $n = 2$.

Proof Differentiate $\Pi^*(v_0, n)$ from (8.42) with respect to v_0, and one obtains

$$\frac{\partial}{\partial v_0}\Pi^*(n, v_0) = \varphi(v_0)\frac{\partial}{\partial v_0}F(v_0)^n, \tag{8.57}$$

$$\varphi(v) := \frac{1 - F(v)}{f(v)} - v. \tag{8.58}$$

Note that (8.57) has also a stationary point at $v_0 = 0$. However, since $\Pi^*(v_0, n)$ is strictly increasing for all positive v_0 close to 0, the stationary point at $v_0 = 0$ is a minimum. Therefore, the maximizer must solve (8.56). Existence is assured because $\varphi(0) = 1/f(0) > 0$ and $\varphi(\bar{v}) = -\bar{v} < 0$. We mention that if the *hazard rate* $f(v)/(1 - F(v))$ is strictly monotone increasing, v_0^* is unique.[33]

If you are still somewhat surprised by this result, take a look at the following intuitive argument.

Suppose the minimum price is v_0, and the seller raises it to $v_0 + \delta$. In which case does this matter? The seller gains δ only if he squeezes a single bidder who bids at or above $v_0 + \delta$, which occurs with probability $nF(v_0)^{n-1}(1 - F(v_0 + \delta))$. And the seller loses v_0 if the maximum bid happens to be between v_0 and $v_0 + \delta$, which occurs with probability

$$nF(v_0)^{n-1}\left(F(v_0 + \delta) - F(v_0)\right).$$

Therefore, the net expected gain, per increment in v_0, is

$$\Delta(\delta) := nF(v_0)^{n-1}(1 - F(v_0 + \delta)) - nF(v_0)^{n-1}\frac{F(v_0 + \delta) - F(v_0)}{\delta}v_0.$$

Taking the limit gives

$$\lim_{\delta \to 0}\Delta(\delta) = nF(v_0)^{n-1}\left((1 - F(v_0)) - f(v_0)v_0\right),$$

and setting $\Delta = 0$, one obtains the asserted $v_0^* = [1 - F(v_0^*)]/f(v_0^*)$. □

Remarkably, the optimal minimum bid is independent of the number of bidders.

---

[33] Otherwise, (8.56) may have multiple roots, in which case one has to evaluate the seller's payoff at all roots, to find out which is the global maximizer.

8.5.2 The Mechanism-Design Approach

We now turn to Myerson's mechanism-design approach. Recall that this approach is more general in that it permits asymmetries and does not impose arbitrary restrictions concerning the allocation rule.

Myerson observed that in the search for optimal auctions one may restrict attention, without loss of generality, to incentive-compatible, direct auctions. This fundamental insight applies the famous *revelation principle*, which is also due to Myerson (1979), and which has been useful in many areas of modern economics, from the public-good problem to the theory of optimal labor contracts.

Direct Auctions

An auction is called *direct* if each bidder is only asked to report his valuation to the seller, and the auction rules select the winner and bidders' payments. Closed auctions are direct auctions; English and Dutch auctions are indirect.

Incentive Compatibility

A direct auction is *incentive-compatible* if honest reporting of valuations is a Nash equilibrium. A particularly strong and strategically simple case is an auction where truth telling is a dominant strategy.

Since we consider optimality from the point of view of the seller, incentive compatibility requires only that buyers reveal their true valuations; we do not require that the seller reports his own true valuation before bids are solicited. Again, the second-price closed auction is a good illustration. Obviously, it is incentive-compatible in the sense that all buyers bid truthfully. But, as we have already learned, it is not truthful with regard to the seller's own valuation because it is in the seller's interest to set a minimum bid above his own valuation.

Revelation Principle

The revelation principle says that *for any equilibrium of any auction game, there exists an equivalent incentive-compatible direct auction that leads to the same probabilities of winning and expected payments.* Therefore, the auction that is optimal among the incentive-compatible direct auctions is also optimal for all types of auctions.

To prove the revelation principle, consider an equilibrium of some arbitrarily chosen auction game. We will show that the following procedure describes an equivalent incentive-compatible direct auction, characterized by an allocation rule ρ and a payment rule x, both contingent on the vector of valuations $v := (v_1, \ldots, v_n)$:

1. Ask each bidder to report his valuation.
2. Write down bidders' equilibrium bidding strategies of the assumed auction game, and compute the associated probabilities of winning ρ_i and payments x_i as functions of bidders' valuations v.
3. Set the probabilities of winning $\rho_i(v)$ and payments $x_i(v)$ as in the given equilibrium of the assumed auction game.
4. Select the winner, and collect payments accordingly.

Evidently, if all bidders are honest, this direct auction is equivalent to the given equilibrium of the assumed auction game. Finally, this direct auction is also incentive-compatible. For if it were profitable for any bidder to lie in the direct auction, it would also be profitable for him to lie to himself in executing his equilibrium strategy in the original auction game. It is as simple as that.

Example 8.5 Consider the equilibrium in dominant strategies of the second-price auction. To construct a payoff-equivalent, direct, incentive-compatible auction (ρ, x), set

$$\rho_i(v) = \begin{cases} 1 & \text{if} \quad v_i = \max v, \\ 0 & \text{otherwise,} \end{cases} \tag{8.59}$$

$$x_i(v) = \begin{cases} \max v_{-i} & \text{if} \quad v_i = \max v, \\ 0 & \text{otherwise,} \end{cases} \tag{8.60}$$

where v_{-i} denotes the truncated vector of valuations obtained from v by omitting v_i.

Similarly, the equilibrium of the symmetric first-price auction game can be translated into a payoff-equivalent, incentive-compatible direct auction (ρ, x) by setting ρ as in (8.59) and

$$x_i = \begin{cases} \frac{n-1}{n} v_i & \text{if} \quad v_i = \max v, \\ 0 & \text{otherwise.} \end{cases} \tag{8.61}$$

Feasible Direct Auctions

A direct auction is described by the allocation rule ρ and the payment rule x, both defined on the product set of the support of valuations. Here $\rho_i(v)$ denotes the ith bidder's probability of winning and $x_i(v)$ his payment (notice: the bidder may have to make a payment even if he does not win the auction). To be *feasible*, these functions have to satisfy the following three conditions.

First, because there is only one object to allocate, the probabilities $\rho_i(v_1, \ldots, v_n)$ must sum to no more than 1 for all valuations (notice: the sale may fail with positive probability):

$$\sum_{i=1}^{n} \rho_i(v) \leq 1 \qquad \text{(budget constraint).} \tag{8.62}$$

Second, the direct auction has to be incentive-compatible. That is, if a bidder's true valuation is v_i, reporting the truth must be at least as good as reporting any other valuation $\hat{v}_i \neq v_i$. The utility of an agent whose valuation is v_i but who reports the valuation $\hat{v}_i$ is

$$U_i(\hat{v}_i \mid v_i) := \mathrm{E}\left[\rho_i(V_1, \ldots, \hat{v}_i, \ldots, V_n)v_i\right]$$
$$-\mathrm{E}\left[x_i(V_1, \ldots, \hat{v}_i, \ldots, V_n)\right]. \tag{8.63}$$

(The V's are random variables; v_i and $\hat{v}_i$ particular realizations.) Therefore, incentive compatibility requires that, for all $v_i, \hat{v}_i \in [\underline{v}_i, \bar{v}_i]$,

$$U_i(v_i \mid v_i) \geq U_i(\hat{v}_i \mid v_i) \qquad \text{(incentive compatibility).} \tag{8.64}$$

Third, participation must be voluntary, i.e., each bidder must be assured a non-negative expected utility,

$$U_i(v_i \mid v_i) \geq 0 \quad \forall v_i \in [\underline{v}_i, \bar{v}_i] \quad \text{(participation constraint)}. \tag{8.65}$$

The Programming Problem

In view of the revelation principle and the above feasibility considerations, the optimal auction design problem is reduced to the choice of (ρ, x) in such a way that the seller's expected profit is maximized (recall that r is the seller's own valuation):

$$\max_{\{\rho_i, x_i\}} \sum_{i=1}^{n} E[x_i(V_1, \ldots, V_n)] - \sum_{i=1}^{n} E[\rho_i(V_1, \ldots, V_n)]r, \tag{8.66}$$

subject to the budget (8.62), the incentive compatibility (8.64), and the participation constraints (8.65). What looked like an unmanageable mechanism design problem has been reduced to a straightforward optimization problem.

In the following we review and interpret the solution. If you want to follow the mathematical proof you have to look up Myerson's (1981) contribution.

Solution

In order to describe the solution, the so-called *priority levels* associated with a bid play the pivotal role. Essentially, these priority levels resemble and play the same role as individual customers' marginal revenue in the analysis of monopolistic price discrimination.

The priority level associated with valuation v_i is defined as

$$\gamma_i(v_i) := v_i - \frac{1 - F_i(v_i)}{f_i(v_i)}. \tag{8.67}$$

We assume that priority levels are monotone increasing in the v_i's.[34]

Going back to the Cournot monopoly problem under incomplete information, reviewed in the introduction (see (8.3)), $\gamma_i(v_i)$ can be interpreted as the marginal revenue from offering the item for sale to buyer i at a take-it-or-leave-it price equal to $p = v_i$. Therefore, the monotonicity assumption means that marginal revenue is diminishing in "quantity," that is, in probability of sale.[35] Of course, the priority level is always less than the underlying valuation v_i.

With these preliminaries, the optimal auction is summarized by the following rules. The first set of rules describes how one should pick the winner, and the second how much the winner shall pay.

---

[34] Notice $[1 - F_i(v_i)]/f_i(v_i)$ is the reciprocal of the so-called *hazard rate*. Therefore, the assumed monotonicity of priority levels is satisfied whenever the hazard rate is not decreasing. A sufficient condition is obviously the log concavity of the complementary distribution function $\bar{F}(v) := 1 - F(v)$. ($\bar{F}$ is called log concave if $\ln \bar{F}$ is concave.) This condition holds, for example, if the distribution function F is uniform, normal, logistic, chi-squared, exponential, or Laplace. See Bagnoli and Bergstrom (1989).

[35] Myerson (1981) also covers the case when priority levels are not monotone increasing.

Selection of Winner

1. Ask each bidder to report his valuation, and compute the associated priority levels.
2. Award the item to the bidder with the highest priority level, unless it is below the seller's own valuation r.
3. Keep the item if all priority levels are below the seller's own valuation r (even though the highest valuation may exceed r).

Pricing Rule To describe the optimal pricing rule we need to generalize the second-price auction rule. Suppose i has the valuation v_i, which leads to the highest priority level $\gamma_i(v_i) \geq r$. Now ask: By how much could i have reported a lower valuation and still have won the auction under the above rules?

Let z_i be the lowest reported valuation that would still lead to winning,

$$z_i := \min\{\tilde{v} \mid \gamma_i(\tilde{v}) \geq r, \ \gamma_i(\tilde{v}) \geq \gamma_j(v_j), \ \forall j \neq i\}. \tag{8.68}$$

Then the optimal auction rule says that the winner shall pay z_i. This completes the description of the auction rule.

Interpretation Essentially, the optimal auction rule combines the idea of a second-price (or Vickrey) auction with that of third-degree monopolistic price discrimination.[36] As a first step, customers are ranked by their marginal revenue $v_i - [1 - F_i(v_i)]/f(v_i)$, evaluated at the reported valuation. Since only one indivisible unit is up for sale, only one customer can win. The optimal rule selects the customer who ranks highest in the marginal-revenue hierarchy, unless it falls short of the seller's own valuation r. In this sense the optimal selection of the winner rule employs the techniques of third-degree price discrimination.

But the winner is asked to pay neither his marginal revenue nor his reported valuation. Instead, the optimal price is equal to the lowest valuation that would still make the winner's marginal revenue equal to or higher than that of all rivals. In this particular sense, the optimal auction rule employs the idea of a "second-price" auction.

Illustrations

As an illustration, take a look at the following two examples. The first one shows that the optimal auction coincides with the second-price sealed-bid auction supplemented by a minimum price above the seller's own valuation, if customers are indistinguishable. The second example then brings out the discrimination aspect, assuming that bidders are different.

In both examples, the seller deviates from the principle of selling to the highest bidder (which underlies revenue equivalence), and the equilibrium outcome fails to be Pareto-optimal with positive probability. This indicates that the four standard auctions are not optimal. However, the optimal auction itself poses a credibility problem that will be discussed toward the end of this section.

---

[36] Recall that in the theory of monopoly one distinguishes between three kinds of price discrimination: perfect or *first-degree* price discrimination, imperfect or *second-degree* price discrimination by means of self-selection devices (offering different price–quantity packages), and finally *third-degree* price discrimination based on different signals about demand (for example, different national markets).

Example 8.6 (Identical Bidders) Suppose valuations are uniformly distributed on [0, 1]. Then the priority levels are

$$\gamma_i(v_i) = v_i - \frac{1 - v_i}{1} = 2v_i - 1,$$

and a sale occurs only if the highest valuation exceeds $\frac{1}{2} + r/2$. The winner pays either $\frac{1}{2} + r/2$ or the second highest bid, whichever is higher. The optimal auction is equivalent to a modified second-price sealed-bid auction where the seller sets a minimum price equal to $\frac{1}{2} + r/2$. Since that minimum price is higher than the seller's own valuation, the optimal auction is not Pareto-efficient.

With two bidders and a zero seller's own valuation the optimal minimum price is $\frac{1}{2}$, and the expected revenue is equal to $\frac{5}{12}$.[37] Compare this with the Cournot approach, the English auction, and the participation-fee-augmented English auction (see Examples 8.1, 8.2, 8.3).

Example 8.7 (Bidder Heterogeneity) Suppose two bidders, A and B, have uniformly distributed valuations; A's support is [0, 1] and B's [0, 2]. Set $r = 0$. Then the priority levels are

$$\gamma_A(v_A) = 2v_A - 1, \qquad \gamma_B(v_B) = 2v_B - 2.$$

Obviously, B can only win if his valuation exceeds that of A by $\frac{1}{2}$. Thus, the optimal auction discriminates against B in order to encourage more aggressive bidding. Note that if B were not discriminated against, he would never report a valuation greater than 1 and never pay more than 1, whereas in the optimal auction he might have to pay up to $\frac{3}{2}$.

Remark

In the symmetric case, the optimal auction can be implemented by a modified second-price auction. This is, however, not the only way. In fact, the optimum can be implemented by any mechanism that awards the item to the highest valuation that exceeds the optimal critical valuation. The list of possible auctions includes first-price, second-price, and even all-pay auctions, supplemented by an optimal minimum price.

The Case of Two Bidders and Two Valuations*

This brief introduction to optimal auctions has stressed essential properties and left out proofs and computations. This may leave you somewhat unsatisfied. Therefore, we now add a full-scale example with two identical bidders and two valuations.[38] Its main purpose is to exemplify the computation of optimal auctions in a particularly simple case where the price-discrimination aspect of optimal auctions cannot play any role. (See, however, the closing remarks in this sub-subsection.)

---

[37] The expected revenue is $\Pr\{V_{(1)} \geq \frac{1}{2}\}E[V_{(1)} \mid V_{(1)} \geq \frac{1}{2}] + \frac{1}{2}\Pr\{V_{(1)} < \frac{1}{2} \leq V_{(2)}\}$, with $E[V_{(1)} \mid V_{(1)} \geq \frac{1}{2}] = \frac{2}{3}$, and $\Pr\{V_{(1)} \geq \frac{1}{2}\} = \frac{1}{4}$, $\Pr\{V_{(1)} < \frac{1}{2} \leq V_{(2)}\} = \frac{1}{2}$. As an alternative, just plug $n = 2$ and $F(v) = v$ into (8.42).

[38] The example is borrowed from Binmore (1992, pp. 532–536).

Suppose the two bidders are identical in the sense that they have either a low (v_l) or a high valuation (v_h). These valuations occur with the probabilities $\Pr\{V = v_l\} = \pi, \Pr\{V = v_h\} = 1 - \pi$.

In the framework of this example, a direct auction will be described by 1) the conditional probabilities $\rho_h := E[\rho(V, v_h)]$, $\rho_l := E[\rho(V, v_l)]$ of obtaining the item, and 2) the bidders' expected payments $\mathcal{E}_h := E_V[x(v_h, V)]$, $\mathcal{E}_l := E_V[x(v_l, V)]$.

Optimization Problem The optimal auction maximizes the expected gain from each bidder,

$$\max_{\rho_h,\rho_l,\mathcal{E}_h,\mathcal{E}_l} G := (1 - \pi)\mathcal{E}_h + \pi\mathcal{E}_l, \tag{8.69}$$

subject to the *incentive compatibility*

$$\rho_h v_h - \mathcal{E}_h \geq \rho_l v_h - \mathcal{E}_l, \tag{8.70}$$

$$\rho_l v_l - \mathcal{E}_l \geq \rho_h v_l - \mathcal{E}_h, \tag{8.71}$$

and *participation* constraints

$$\rho_h v_h - \mathcal{E}_h \geq 0, \tag{8.72}$$

$$\rho_l v_l - \mathcal{E}_l \geq 0. \tag{8.73}$$

An immediate implication of incentive compatibility is the monotonicity property

$$\rho_h \geq \rho_l, \quad \mathcal{E}_h \geq \mathcal{E}_l. \tag{8.74}$$

Restrictions due to Symmetry Having stated the problem, we now make it more user-friendly. The key observation is that symmetry implies three further restrictions on the probabilities ρ_h, ρ_l.

From the seller's perspective each bidder wins the item with probability $(1 - \pi)\rho_h + \pi\rho_l$; in a symmetric equilibrium this probability cannot exceed $\frac{1}{2}$. Therefore,

$$(1 - \pi)\rho_h + \pi\rho_l \leq \frac{1}{2}. \tag{8.75}$$

Also, in a symmetric equilibrium type h must lose with probability $\frac{1}{2}$ or more whenever he faces a type-h rival. Therefore, $1 - \rho_h \geq \frac{1}{2}(1 - \pi)$, or equivalently

$$\rho_h \leq 1 + \frac{1}{2}(1 - \pi) = \frac{1}{2}(\pi + 1). \tag{8.76}$$

And similarly, type l must lose with probability $\frac{1}{2}$ or more when he faces a type-l rival, so $1 - \rho_l \geq \frac{1}{2}\pi$, or equivalently

$$\rho_l \leq 1 - \frac{1}{2}\pi. \tag{8.77}$$

Combining these restrictions, the set of feasible probabilities ρ_h, ρ_l is illustrated in Figure 8.6. Similarly, the set of feasible expected payments $\mathcal{E}_h, \mathcal{E}_l$ is illustrated in Figure 8.5. In both diagrams, the dashed lines represent the seller's indifference curves.

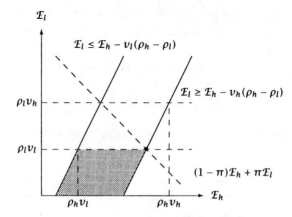

Figure 8.5. Optimal Auction: Optimal $\mathcal{E}$'s.

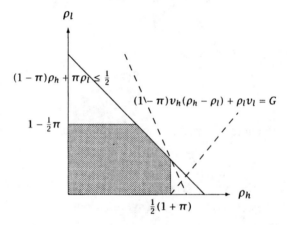

Figure 8.6. Optimal Auction: Optimal ρ's.

Why Some Constraints Do Not Bind As you can see immediately from Figure 8.5, only two constraints are binding: the truth-telling condition concerning type h and the participation constraint concerning type l. Therefore, you can ignore inequalities (8.71), (8.72) and replace inequalities (8.70), (8.73) by equalities.

User-Friendly Optimization Problem Using these results, you can now eliminate the expected payment variables and find the optimal auction as the solution of the following linear programming problem:

$$\max_{\rho_h, \rho_l} G := (1 - \pi) v_h (\rho_h - \rho_l) + \rho_l v_l, \tag{8.78}$$

subject to (8.75)–(8.77).

The only variables are ρ_h, ρ_l.

Solution The solution is easily characterized by the two diagrams. Take a look at the seller's indifference curves (the dashed lines) in Figure 8.6. Evidently, the marginal rate of substitution can be positive or negative, depending on the prior probability π. In particular, if type l is sufficiently likely ($\pi \geq (v_h - v_l)/v_h$), the marginal rate of substitution is negative (the dashed indifference curve slopes downwards), whereas

Table 8.2. *Optimal auction*

π	ρ_l	$\mathcal{E}_l$	ρ_h	$\mathcal{E}_h$
$\pi \leq \frac{v_h - v_l}{v_h}$	0	0	$\frac{1}{2}(1+\pi)$	$\frac{1}{2}(\pi+1)v_h$
$\pi > \frac{v_h - v_l}{v_h}$	$\frac{1}{2}\pi$	$\frac{1}{2}\pi v_l$	$\frac{1}{2}(1+\pi)$	$\frac{1}{2}(v_h + \pi v_l)$

if it is sufficiently unlikely ($\pi \leq (v_h - v_l)/v_h$), the marginal rate of substitution is positive (the dashed indifference curve slopes upwards). Therefore, the solution is at one of two corners of the set of feasible ρ's, depending upon the size of the prior probability π, as summarized in Table 8.2.

Remarks While this example highlights some aspects of optimal auctions, it has also some peculiar properties. In our general statement of the optimal-auction problem, we stressed that optimal auctions are standard auctions supplemented by a minimum-price requirement. However, this holds true only if valuations are continuous random variables. With discrete valuations, as in the present example, the optimal auction is typically not a standard auction.

To see why a standard auction is not optimal in the present example, take a look at the case $\pi > (v_h - v_l)/v_h$. Clearly, if one tries to implement the optimal auction by a second-price sealed-bid auction supplemented by a minimum-price requirement, the optimal $\mathcal{E}_l$, stated in the second row of Table 8.2, requires a minimum price equal to $p = v_l$. However, with this minimum price one cannot also implement the optimal value for $\mathcal{E}_h$.

8.5.3 Secret Reservation Price?

In many auctions the seller keeps his reservation price secret. Secrecy is often justified as a means to fight auction rings. But can a secret reservation price still raise the seller's revenue, or does it destroy the value of commitment?

Consider a first-price auction. If the seller commits to a reservation price and announces it to bidders, he thus induces more aggressive bidding (see Figure 8.3 in Section 8.2.5). The catch is that the seller runs the risk that no transaction takes place, even if the bidders' highest valuation is above the seller's valuation. Therefore, the seller would like bidders to believe that he is committed to a certain reservation price above his own valuation; however, once they are convinced, the seller would most like to revoke that reservation price and not forgo profitable transactions. This suggests that secrecy makes the power of commitment useless, as in the commitment-and-observability problem discussed in Section 3.3.3.

Proposition 8.11 *Consider a first-price auction, and suppose the seller keeps his reservation price secret. Then the equilibrium reservation-price strategy is to set it equal to the seller's own valuation, $\hat{v}$, for all $\hat{v}$.*

Proof In a first-price auction setting the reservation price p_0 induces the critical valuation $v_0 = p_0$. Therefore, we save notation by identifying the reservation price with v_0.

If the seller with valuation $\hat{v}$ sets the secret reservation price $v_0 \geq \hat{v}$, his expected profit is a function of v_0 and $\hat{v}$, as follows (to simplify notation, define $G(y) := \Pr\{V_{(n)} < y\} = F(y)^n, g(y) := G'(y)$):

$$\pi(v_0, \hat{v}) = \hat{v} + \Pr\left\{b^*\left(V_{(n)}\right) \geq v_0\right\}\left(E\left[b^*\left(V_{(n)}\right) \mid b^*\left(V_{(n)}\right) \geq v_0\right] - \hat{v}\right)$$

$$= \hat{v} + \int_{b^{*-1}(v_0)}^{1} \left(b^*(y) - \hat{v}\right) dG(y). \tag{8.79}$$

Due to the strict monotonicity of b^*,[39]

$$\frac{\partial \pi}{\partial v_0} = \left(\hat{v} - b^*(b^{*-1}(v_0))\right) g\left(b^{*-1}(v_0)\right) b^{*-1'}(v_0)$$

$$= (\hat{v} - v_0) g\left(b^{*-1}(v_0)\right) \frac{1}{b^{*'}(v_0)}. \tag{8.80}$$

Therefore, the optimal minimum bid is $v_0 = \hat{v}$. $\square$

However, if the seller runs a second-price or Vickrey auction, secrecy does not hurt him, because in a second-price or Vickrey auction truthful bidding is a weakly dominant strategy, no matter what reservation price is announced. Therefore, the reservation price poses neither a commitment problem nor a commitment-and-observability problem.

The bottom line is that the implementation of the optimal auction requires neither the ability to commit to the optimal reservation price nor its perfect observability, provided the seller adopts a second-price or Vickrey auction. If the seller adopts a first-price or Dutch auction, secrecy completely destroys the power of commitment.

8.5.4 Optimal Auctions with Stochastic Entry*

We close the discussion of optimal auctions with some results concerning the relationship between the minimum price and bidder participation.

The standard analysis of optimal auctions ignores the problem of entry in the face of costly participation. We now show that optimal auctions differ drastically if this entry problem is taken into account.[40] Recently, Levin and Smith (1994) explored whether one should use a minimum price or entry fees when participation is costly. Here we present a simple and straightforward proof of one of their main assertions.[41]

Suppose bidders have to spend resources to inspect the item for sale, before they know their own valuation. Once the own valuation is known, the cost of inspection, c, is sunk and does not affect further bidding behavior. In this sense, inspection constitutes entry into the bidding game.

---

[39] Note: since the reservation price is secret, bidders cannot react to it; therefore, bidders' strategy is independent of v_0.

[40] A simple complete-information model of auctions with stochastic entry is in Elberfeld and Wolfstetter (1999). There it is shown that more potential competition lowers the seller's expected revenue, which implies that the seller should restrict the number of bidders.

[41] Incidentally, Tan (1992) analyzed a similar entry problem where bidders in a procurement auction invest in R&D in order to learn their production cost. That game has reasonable pure-strategy equilibria; but, again, the seller should not impose a price ceiling.

The optimal auction problem is now posed as a three-stage game. At *stage 1*, the seller selects an auction rule from the class of auctions considered in previous sections. At *stage 2*, each of m potential bidders decides whether to enter. Entry entails the fixed cost c. Finally, at *stage 3*, the number of active bidders, $n \leq m$, who have entered becomes common knowledge, and they play the usual bidding game.

The number of potential bidders, m, is taken to be so large that all bidders suffer a loss if they all enter, $E[U^*(V; m, v_0)] < c$. If this condition fails, entry is not an issue.

At stage 3 equilibrium payoffs are as shown in Proposition 8.2. Therefore, at stage 2, when bidders do not yet know their own valuation, their reduced-form payoff as a function of n and v_0 is $E[U^*(V; n, v_0)] - c$. Note that $E[U^*(V; n, v_0)]$ is strictly monotone decreasing in n and v_0, and positive (negative) for low (high) n.

Now consider the entry subgame that begins at stage 2. Denote the (mixed) entry strategy by $q := \Pr\{\text{entry}\}$. Then the equilibrium strategy $q^* \in [0, 1]$ must solve the condition of indifference between entry and nonentry,

$$\sum_{n=0}^{m-1} p_{n:m-1}(q) E[U^*(V; n+1, v_0)] - c = 0. \tag{8.81}$$

Here $p_{n:m-1}(q)$ denotes the probability that n rival firms enter (out of a sample of $m - 1$),

$$p_{n:m-1}(q) := \binom{m-1}{n} q^n (1-q)^{m-n-1}, \qquad m > n. \tag{8.82}$$

Note that as bidders randomize their entry decision, the number of active bidders becomes a random variable, denoted by the capital letter $0 \leq N \leq m$. Its probability distribution is a binomial distribution, with the following property that will be used repeatedly.

Lemma 8.3 (Stochastic Dominance (FSD)) *When the probability of entry, q, is increased, the random number of bidders, N, increases in the sense of first-order stochastic dominance (FSD). The same applies to an increase in m.*

Proof By a known result, one can write the (complementary) binomial probability distribution function, for $k \in \mathbb{N}$, $0 < k \leq m$,[42]

$$\bar{\Phi}(k; q, m) := \Pr\{N \geq k\} = \sum_{n=k}^{m} p_{n:m}(q) \tag{8.83}$$

$$= \frac{m!}{(k-1)!(m-k)!} \int_0^q \tau^{k-1}(1-\tau)^{m-k} \, d\tau. \tag{8.84}$$

The asserted FSD relationship follows immediately: $q_2 > q_1 \implies \bar{\Phi}(k; q_2, m) > \bar{\Phi}(k; q_1, m)$. ☐

---

[42] This formula is proved by repeated integration by parts. See Fisz (1963), equations (10.3.7), (10.3.8).

Proposition 8.12 (Equilibrium Entry Strategy) *The entry subgame has a unique symmetric equilibrium strategy $q^* \in (0, 1)$ that is strictly monotone decreasing in v_0.*

Proof At $q = 0$ the left-hand side (LHS) of (8.81) is positive, and at $q = 1$ negative. Since $E[U^*(V; n, v_0)]$ is strictly monotone decreasing in n, the FSD relationship established in Lemma 8.3 implies that the LHS of (8.81) is strictly monotone decreasing in q. By continuity, there must be a q^* where the indifference condition holds with equality. The asserted comparative statics also follows from Lemma 8.3. □

Using these preliminary results we now turn to the stage 1 subgame and solve the seller optimal auction. For this purpose, use the seller's reduced-form payoff function

$$G(v_0, m) := \sum_{n=1}^{m} p_{n:m}(q^*(v_0))\Pi^*(n, v_0). \tag{8.85}$$

Note that $\Pi^*(n, v_0)$ is increasing in n, and it has a maximum in v_0, which is independent of n, by Proposition 8.10.

Proposition 8.13 (Optimal Auctions with Stochastic Entry) *In the face of stochastic entry, the seller optimal auction sets a minimum price below the static optimum. The optimal auction moves towards the unmodified standard second-price auction, with $v_0^* = 0$.*

Proof Compute the derivative of the seller's expected payoff $G(v_0, m)$ with respect to v_0:

$$\frac{\partial G}{\partial v_0} = \sum_{n=1}^{m} p'_{n:m}q^{*\prime}\Pi^* + \sum_{n=1}^{m} p_{p_{n:m}}\frac{\partial \Pi^*}{\partial v_0}. \tag{8.86}$$

Evaluated at or above the static optimum v_0^*, one has

$$\frac{\partial}{\partial v_0} G(v_0, m) < 0,$$

since $\partial \Pi^*/\partial v_0 \le 0$, $q^{*\prime} < 0$, and an increase in q "increases" the random number of bidders in the sense of FSD. This shows that the optimal minimum bid is lower than the static optimum. By similar reasoning one can see that $\frac{\partial}{\partial v_0} G(v_0, m) < 0$ also at $v_0 = 0$ (recall: $\Pi^*(v_0, n)$ always has a stationary point at $v_0 = 0$). Therefore, it may very well be optimal to set $v_0 = 0$. □

Remark on Deterministic Entry Consider (one of the many) alternative pure strategy equilibria, where bidders enter until their expected payoff has vanished.[43] Interestingly, even in this framework, no minimum price should be imposed.

---

[43] Since n is an integer, the precise equilibrium number of bidders is the largest n^* for which $E[U^*(V; n^*)] \ge c$. These equilibria are meaningful if bidders enter sequentially and learn about how many have already entered. They were studied by McAfee and McMillan (1987c) (see also Engelbrecht–Wiggans (1993)).

8.6 Common-Value Auctions and the Winner's Curse

In a famous experiment, Bazerman and Samuelson (1983) filled jars with coins, and auctioned them off to MBA students at Boston University. Each jar had a value of $8, which was not made known to bidders. The auction was conducted as a first-price sealed-bid auction. A large number of identical runs were performed. Altogether, the *average bid* was $5.13; however, the *average winning bid* was $10.01. Therefore, the average winner suffered a loss of $2.01; alas, the winners were the ones who lost wealth ("winner's curse").

What makes this auction different is just one crucial feature: the object for sale has an *unknown common* value rather than *known private* values. The result is typical for common-value auction experiments. So what drives the winner's curse; and how can bidders avoid falling prey to it?

Most auctions involve some common-value element. Even if bidders at an art auction purchase primarily for their own pleasure, they are usually also concerned about eventual resale. And even though construction companies tend to have private values, for example due to different capacity utilizations, construction costs are also affected by common events, such as unpredictable weather conditions, the unknown difficulty of specific tasks, and random input quality or factor prices. This suggests that a satisfactory theory of auctions should cover private as well as unknown common value components.

Before we consider combinations of private and common value components, we now focus on pure common-value auctions. In a pure common-value auction, the item for sale has the same value for each bidder (e.g., the jar in the above experiment contains the same number of coins for each bidder). At the time of the bidding, this common value is unknown. Bidders may have some imperfect estimate (everyone has his own rule of thumb to guess the number of coins in the jar); but the item's true value is only observed after the auction has taken place.

To sketch the cause of the winner's curse, suppose all bidders obtain an unbiased estimate of the item's value. Also assume bids are an increasing function of this estimate. Then the auction will select the one bidder as winner who received the most optimistic estimate. But this entails that the average winning estimate is higher than the item's value.

To play the auction right, this *adverse selection bias* must already be allowed for at the bidding stage by shading the bid. Failure to follow this advice will result in winning bids that earn less than average profits or even losses.

8.6.1 An Example: The Wallet Auction

An instructive example is the following *wallet auction*, which was introduced by Klemperer (1998): Ask each of two students to check the contents of his wallet without revealing it to the other; then, sell a sum of money equal to the contents of both wallets to the same two students in an English auction.

Each bidder $i = 1, 2$ knows the contents of his own wallet x_i, but neither one knows the sum $v := x_1 + x_2$. Therefore, the item sold has a common value, which is, however, unknown at the time of bidding and only becomes known after the auction, when the contents of both wallets have been revealed.

Proposition 8.14 (Wallet Auction) *The wallet auction has a symmetric equilibrium, described by the strategy* $b^*(x) = 2x$.

Proof Suppose rival j plays the candidate equilibrium strategy b^*. Then, if rival j quits bidding at price p, bidder i updates his valuation to

$$v_i := E[x_i + X_j \mid b^*(X_j) = p] = x_i + \frac{p}{2}.$$

In order to maximize his payoff, bidder i should stay active as long as $v \geq p$, i.e., as long as $p \leq 2x_i$. Hence, the optimal limit at which i should quit is $b^*(x_i) := 2x_i$. In other words, $b^*(x_i)$ is a best reply to $b^*(x_j)$, and vice versa. $\qquad\square$

How can one interpret this equilibrium, and how do bidders avoid the winner's curse? When the price is at the level p, bidder i knows that the wallet of rival j must contain at least $p/2$. Therefore, the conditional expected value v_i, conditioned on the event that $p = 2x_i$ has been reached, is equal to or greater than $2x_i$. But then, why should i quit bidding at $p = 2x_i$, and not bid higher?

Here the selection bias enters. If bidder i contemplates whether he should quit bidding at $p = 2x_i$, he must ask himself what is the conditional expected value v_i, conditional on the event that he wins at $p = 2x_i$; because bidder j just quit bidding at this price. Since j plays the strategy $b^*(x_j) = 2x_j$, his quitting at $p = 2x_i$ entails $x_j = x_i$ and hence $v_i = x_i + x_j = 2x_i$. This explains why bidder i should bid neither more nor less than $2x_i$.

We conclude that in a symmetric equilibrium bidder i bids exactly as if rival j had the same amount of money in his wallet, i.e.,

$$b^*(x) = E[X_i + X_j \mid X_i = X_j = x].$$

Incidentally, the wallet auction has also a continuum of asymmetric equilibria, which have entirely different properties. Indeed, the following strategies are an asymmetric equilibrium for all $\alpha > 1$ (of course, the symmetric equilibrium is obtained for $\alpha = 2$):

$$b_1^*(x_1) = \alpha x_1, \qquad b_2^*(x_2) = \frac{\alpha}{\alpha - 1} x_2.$$

These asymmetric equilibria strongly favor one bidder, to the seller's disadvantage.

8.6.2 Some General Results

Now consider a more general framework, under the following simplifying assumptions:[44]

(A1) The common value V is drawn randomly from a uniform distribution on the domain $(\underline{v}, \bar{v})$.

---

[44] Assumptions (A1) and (A2) were widely used by John Kagel and Dan Levin in their various experiments on common-value auctions. See for example Kagel and Levin (1986).

(A2) Before bidding, each bidder receives a private signal S_i, drawn randomly from a uniform distribution on $(V - \epsilon, V + \epsilon)$. The unknown common value determines the location of the signals' support. A lower ϵ indicates greater signal precision.

(A3) The auction is first-price, like a Dutch auction or a sealed-bid auction.[45]

As an illustration you may think of oil companies interested in the drilling rights to a particular site that is worth the same to all bidders. Each bidder obtains an estimate of the site's value from its experts and then uses this information in making a bid.

Computing the Right Expected Value

Just as in the private-values framework, each bidder has to determine the item's expected value and then strategically shade his bid, taking a bet on rival bidders' valuations. Without shading the bid, there is no chance to gain from bidding. The difference is that it is a bit more tricky to determine the right expected value, in particular since this computation should allow for the built-in adverse selection bias.

For signal values from the interval $s_i \in [v - \epsilon, v + \epsilon]$, the *expected value* of the item conditional on the signal s_i is[46]

$$E[V|S_i = s_i] = s_i. \tag{8.87}$$

This estimate is unbiased in the sense that the average estimate is equal to the site's true value.

Nevertheless, bids should not be based on this expected value. Instead, a bidder should anticipate that he would revise his estimate whenever he actually wins the auction. As in many other contexts, the clue to rational behavior is in thinking one step ahead.

In a symmetric equilibrium, a bidder wins the auction if he actually received the highest signal.[47] Therefore, when a bidder learns that he won the auction, he knows that his signal s_i was the largest received by all bidders. Using this information, he should value the item by its expected value conditional on having the highest signal, denoted by $E[V \mid S_{\max} = s_i]$, $S_{\max} := \max\{S_1, \ldots, S_n\}$.

Evidently, the *updated expected value* is lower:

$$E[V \mid S_{\max} = s_i] = s_i - \epsilon \frac{n-1}{n+1}$$
$$< E[V \mid S_i = s_i]. \tag{8.88}$$

Essentially, a bidder should realize that if he wins, it is likely that the signal he received was unusually high, relative to those received by rival bidders.

Notice that the adverse selection bias, measured by the difference between the two expected values, is increasing in n and ϵ. Therefore, raising the number of

---

[45] Second-price common-value auctions are easier to analyze, but less instructive. A nice and simple proof of their equilibrium properties, based entirely on the principle of *iterated dominance*, is in Harstad and Levin (1985). The procedure proposed in this paper requires, however, that the highest signal be a *sufficient statistic* of the entire signal vector.

[46] Here and elsewhere we ignore signals near corners, that is $v \notin (\underline{v}, \underline{v} + \epsilon)$ and $v \notin (\bar{v} - \epsilon, \bar{v})$.

[47] This standard property follows from the monotonicity of the equilibrium bid function; in the present context, it is confirmed by the equilibrium bid function stated below.

bidders or lowering the precision of signals gives rise to a higher winner's curse, if bidders are subject to judgmental failure and base their bid on $E[V \mid S_i = s_i]$ rather than on $E[V \mid S_{\max} = s_i]$.

Equilibrium Bids

The symmetric Nash equilibrium of the common-value auction game was found by R.B. Wilson (1977b) and later generalized by Milgrom and Weber (1982) to cover auctions with a combination of private- and common-value elements.

In the present framework, the symmetric equilibrium bid function is[48]

$$b(s_i) = s_i - \epsilon + \phi(s_i), \tag{8.89}$$

where

$$\phi(s_i) := \frac{2\epsilon}{n+1} e^{-(n/2\epsilon)[s_i - (\underline{v}+\epsilon)]}. \tag{8.90}$$

The function $\phi(s_i)$ diminishes rapidly as s_i increases beyond $\underline{v} + \epsilon$. Ignoring it, the bid function is approximately equal to $b(s_i) = s_i - \epsilon$, and the expected profit of the high bidder is positive and equal to $2\epsilon/(n + 1)$.

Conclusions

The main lesson to be learned from this introduction to common-value auctions is that bidders should shade their bids, for two different reasons. First, without shading bids there can be no profits in a first-price auction. Second, the auction always selects the one bidder as winner who received the most optimistic estimate of the item's value, and thus induces an adverse selection bias. Without shading the bid to allow for this bias, the winning bidder regrets his bid and falls prey to the winner's curse.

The discount associated with the first reason for shading bids will decrease with increasing number of bidders, because signal values are more congested if there are more bidders. In contrast, the discount associated with the adverse selection bias increases with the number of bidders, because the adverse selection bias becomes more severe as the number of bidders is increased.

Thus, increasing the number of bidders has two conflicting effects on equilibrium bids. On the one hand, competitive considerations require more aggressive bidding. On the other hand, allowing for the adverse selection bias requires greater discounts. In the above example with bid function (8.89), the adverse selection bias predominates, and bids are always decreasing in n. But for a number of common distribution functions such as the normal and lognormal case, the competitive effect prevails for small numbers of bidders, where the bid function is increasing in n; but eventually the adverse selection effect takes over and the equilibrium bid function decreases in n (see Wilson (1992)).

Altogether, it is clear that common-value auctions are more difficult to play and that unsophisticated bidders may be susceptible to the winner's curse. Of course,

---

[48] Again, we restrict the analysis to signal values from the interval $s_i \in [\underline{v} + \epsilon, \bar{v} - \epsilon]$.

the winner's curse cannot occur if bidders are rational and take proper account of the adverse selection bias. The winner's curse is strictly a matter of judgmental failure; rational bidders do not fall prey to it.

The experimental evidence demonstrates that it is often difficult to avoid the winner's curse. Even experienced subjects who are given plenty of time and opportunity to learn often fail to bid below the updated expected value. And most subjects fail to bid more conservatively when the number of bidders is increased.[49]

Similarly, many real-life decision problems are plagued by persistent winner's-curse effects. For example, in the field of book publishing, Dessauer (1981) reports that "... most of the auctioned books are not earning their advances." Capen, Clapp, and Campbell (1971) claim that the winner's curse is responsible for the low profits of oil and gas corporations on drilling rights in the Gulf of Mexico during the 1960s. And Bhagat, Shleifer, and Vishny (1990) observe that most of the major corporate takeovers that made the financial news during the 1980s have actually reduced the bidding shareholders' wealth (see also Roll (1986)).

8.7 Affiliated Values*

The assumption of independent private values is appropriate for nondurable consumption goods and services, but it is far too restrictive when it comes to the auctioning of durable goods.

As an example, consider the auctioning of a well-known painting. In order to apply the independent-private-values model, two prerequisites must be met:

1. each bidder must have his own private valuation, and
2. private valuations must be stochastically independent.

The first assumption rules out any consideration concerning a possible resale in the future, and the second assumption rules out the influence of fashion.

In this regard, the common-value model may seem more appealing, because it assumes that valuations are (perfectly) correlated. However, it completely ignores differences in bidders' preferences.

Clearly, one would like to have a more general model that combines both common- and private-value aspects and covers both basic auction models as special cases. This leads us to the *affiliated-values model* by Milgrom and Weber (1982), which is one of the most influential contributions to auction theory.

8.7.1 *Private and Common Value Generalized*

We now assume that bidders' valuations are influenced by their own preferences but are also dependent upon other bidders' quality assessment. Since each bidder knows only his own assessment, bidders do not exactly know their valuation of the object for sale.

---

[49] A comprehensive review of the experimental evidence is in Kagel (1995).

Specifically, we assume that the valuation of bidder i, V_i, is a function of all bidders' quality signals $X_1, X_2, \ldots, X_n$ and of the seller's quality signal X_0:

$$V_i := u(X_0, X). \tag{8.91}$$

The function u is nonnegative, continuous, monotone increasing, and symmetric in $\{X_j\}_{j \neq i}$; moreover, $E[V_i]$ is finite.

This formulation is sufficiently general to include both basic auction models as special cases. In particular, the private-values model is obtained by setting $V_i = X_i$, and the common-value model by setting $V_i = X_0$.

In the following we consider only symmetric equilibria. This allows us to view bidders' behavior from the perspective of one particular bidder, say bidder 1, who has observed the quality signal X_1.

We denote the order statistics of bidders' quality signals by $Y_1 \geq Y_2, \ldots, Y_{n-2} \geq Y_{n-1}$. Due to the symmetry assumption, we can thus write the valuation of bidder 1 as follows:

$$V_1 = u(X_1, Y_1, \ldots, Y_{n-1}, X_0). \tag{8.92}$$

8.7.2 Stochastic Similarity: Affiliation

As a second modification we now replace stochastic independence by affiliation. Affiliation is a statistical concept. Roughly speaking, the affiliation of random variables means that similarity of realizations is the most likely outcome. For example, if quality signals are affiliated, and bidder i has observed a high quality signal X_i, then he should believe that rival bidders have most likely also observed a high signal.

Let $f(x)$ denote the joint probability density function (pdf) of $X := (X_0, X_1, \ldots, X_n)$. Consider two realizations $x \neq x'$, and denote the componentwise maximum of (x, x') by $x \vee x'$ and the componentwise minimum by $x \wedge x'$. Quality signals are called *affiliated* if the following inequality holds for all x, x':

$$f(x \vee x')f(x \wedge x') \geq f(x)f(x'). \tag{8.93}$$

As an illustration, consider the two realizations $x := (10, 2)$ and $x' := (5, 7)$. The associated *similar* realizations are $x \vee x' = (10, 7)$ and $x \wedge x' = (5, 2)$.

Affiliation of signals (X, X_0) implies that the conditional expected values of V_1,

$$w(x, y, z) := E[V_1 \mid X_1 = x, \ Y_1 = y, \ X_0 = z], \tag{8.94}$$

$$v(x, y) := E[V_1 \mid X_1 = x, \ Y_1 = y], \tag{8.95}$$

are strictly monotone increasing in all variables. Note that $v(x, y)$ and $w(x, y, z)$ are the conditional expected valuations of bidder 1 after he has observed the signal realizations $X_1 = x, Y_1 = y$ and $X_1 = x, Y_1 = y, X_0 = z$, respectively.

8.7.3 Generalized Solution of the Vickrey Auction

Consider the Vickrey auction. Is truthful bidding a dominant strategy also in the present affiliated-values framework?

When the auction takes place, bidders do not exactly know their valuations. Therefore, it is unclear what "truthful bid" possibly means in this case. Does it mean that bidder 1 should bid an amount equal to his expected valuation, conditional on his own quality signal $X_1 = x$, $E[V_1 \mid X_1 = x]$? This may seem reasonable, because at the time of bidding the signal $X_1 = x$ is the best information available to bidder 1. However, beware of the selection bias. If bid functions are strictly monotone increasing, the auction is always won by the bidder who observed the most favorable quality signal. Bidders should take this additional information into account.

The wallet game from the previous section gives the clue. It suggest that bidders should bid truthfully in the particular sense of bidding *as if* the relevant rival had observed the same quality signal.

Proposition 8.15 *The Vickrey auction has a symmetric equilibrium, described by a strategy $b^*(x)$, which is a function of the own quality signal. Depending upon whether the seller keeps his own signal X_0 secret or makes it common knowledge, one has*

$$b^*(x) = v(x, x) \qquad \text{(if X_0 is kept secret),} \tag{8.96}$$

$$b^*(x; x_0) = w(x, x, x_0) \qquad \text{(if X_0 is common knowledge).} \tag{8.97}$$

Proof We sketch an intuitively accessible proof, assuming that the seller hides information concerning his own quality signal. The proof of the other case is similar and hence omitted.

In Figure 8.7 we plot the equilibrium bid function $b^*(y)$ and the conditional expected value $v(x, y) := E[V \mid X = x, \; Y_1 = y]$ for a given quality signal of the bidder $X = x$. As a working hypothesis it is assumed that b^* is strictly monotone increasing. The graphs of these functions intersect at the point $y = \hat{y}$. (Hint: for small values of y one has $v(x, y) > b^*(y)$, and for large ones $v(x, y) < b^*(y)$.)

The bidder knows his own quality signal x, but not that of his relevant rival, Y_1. Which bid is the best reply to $b^*(Y_1)$?

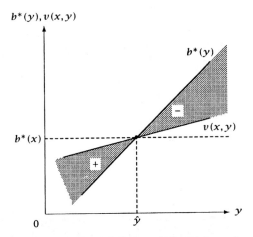

Figure 8.7. Generalized Solution of the Vickrey Auction.

The answer is simple: bidder 1 should bid the amount $b = b^*(\hat{y})$ because this way he will win if and only if his payoff $v(x, y) - b^*(y)$ is nonnegative (see Figure 8.7). Therefore, in a symmetric equilibrium one must have

$$b^*(x) = b^*(\hat{y}) = v(x, \hat{y}).$$

From the assumed strict monotonicity of b^* it follows immediately that $\hat{y} = x$, which implies the assertion $b^*(x) = v(x, x)$. And the assumed monotonicity of b^* follows from the monotonicity of $v(x, x)$.   □

If a bidder succeeds with the bid $b^*(x)$, he knows for sure that the relevant rival has a lower quality signal, i.e., $Y_1 < x$. If the bidder loses, he knows for sure that $Y_1 > x$. Therefore, the implicit estimate of Y_1, implicit in the bid (8.96), is biased as follows, by the monotonicity of $v(x, y)$.

Corollary 8.1 (Biased Estimator) *Consider the equilibrium strategy of the Vickrey auction. The successful bid overestimates the quality signal of the relevant rival, Y_1, whereas the unsuccessful bid underestimates it.*

This result plays a pivotal role in the interpretation of the linkage principle, to which we turn below.

To avoid misunderstanding, note that the biased-estimator property does not reflect any deviation from optimal behavior. Just keep in mind that the winner of the Vickrey auction pays less than his own bid because the price is equal to the second highest bid.

8.7.4 Linkage Principle

The linkage principle says the following: Suppose the private quality signal of the seller is affiliated with bidders' (affiliated) private quality signals. Then a policy of always revealing the seller's private information increases the seller's expected payoff.

The seller's private information could be due to an expert assessment of a painting's authenticity or of the state of a building. The linkage principle advises the seller to make a commitment to reveal favorable as well as unfavorable information.

Proposition 8.16 *Consider the Vickrey auction with revelation (r) and without revelation (n) of the seller's quality signal X_0. Denote the associated expected values of equilibrium prices by p_r, and p_n. Then*

$$p_r = E\left[w(Y_1, Y_1, X_0) \mid \{X_1 > Y_1\}\right] \tag{8.98}$$

$$\geq E\left[v(Y_1, Y_1) \mid \{X_1 > Y_1\}\right] \tag{8.99}$$

$$= p_n. \tag{8.100}$$

Proof The proof is sketched in three steps:

1. If bidder 1 wins the auction, the equilibrium price P is equal to the highest unsuccessful bid: with revelation, $P_r = w(Y_1, Y_1, X_0)$, and without revelation, $P_n = v(Y_1, Y_1)$. Due to the assumed symmetry, these prices apply regardless of the bidder's identity.

2. Consider the price-making bid (which is the highest unsuccessful bid). If the seller keeps his information secret, it is $b^*(Y_1) = v(Y_1, Y_1)$. Due to the biased-estimator property stated in Corollary 8.1, this bid underestimates the signal of the winning bidder, which is X_1. The signals X_0 and X_1 are affiliated. Therefore, the price-making bid $v(Y_1, Y_1)$ also underestimates the distribution of X_0.

3. Now, suppose the seller is committed to reveal X_0. Then the price-making bid $w(Y_1, Y_1, X_0)$ is based on the true signal X_0. Therefore, the expected value of the equilibrium price P_r, conditioned on the true signal X_0, is higher than the expected equilibrium price P_n which is computed on the basis of a downward-biased estimated distribution of X_0. Hence, $p_r > p_n$, as asserted. □

8.7.5 Why the English Auction Benefits the Seller

There are many variants of the English auction. They differ with respect to pricing rules and the revelation of information. We exclusively consider the following variant, which is particularly favorable concerning the revelation of information: The auctioneer calls a sufficiently low initial price, which is depicted on a so-called English clock and which goes up at a preset speed. At that initial price all bidders are active, and they remain active until they irreversibly quit the auction. As the clock goes up, some bidders quit, until finally only one bidder remains active. The item is then awarded the last active bidder, who pays an amount of money equal to the price at which the last rival quit the auction.

In this auction game the strategy of a bidder is a stopping rule, which says at which price the bidder should quit, depending upon who else has quit and at which price. Let k be the number of bidders who have already quit at the prices $p_1 \leq p_2 \leq \cdots \leq p_k$. Then the strategy of a bidder with quality signal x is described by the function $b_k(x \mid p_1, \ldots, p_k)$, which indicates at which price that bidder should also quit, provided k bidders have already quit at prices $p_1, \ldots, p_k$.

As a working hypothesis, suppose the equilibrium is symmetric and the equilibrium strategy is strictly monotone increasing in x. This assures that an active bidder can deduce the underlying quality signal of those who quit, just by observing the price at which they quit.

At the beginning of the auction, when all bidders are still active, no one knows the others' quality signals. As soon as one bidder quits, the others infer that bidder's signal. The more bidders quit, the more information is revealed until, in the last round, when only two bidders remain active, all but the highest two signals are common knowledge. This built-in transmission of information allows bidders to continuously upgrade their quality assessment which, on average, leads to higher bidding, to the benefit of the seller.

Proposition 8.17 *The English auction has a symmetric equilibrium; the equilibrium strategy is a vector $b^*(x) = (b_0^*(x), \ldots, b_{n-1}^*(x))$, in which $b_k^*(x)$ is the bidders' price limit, contingent upon the prices $p_1, \ldots, p_k$ at which k bidders have* *quit the auction:*

$$b_0^*(x) = E[V_1 \mid X_1 = Y_1 = \ldots = Y_{n-1} = x], \qquad (8.101)$$

$$b_k^*(x \mid p_1, \ldots, p_k) = E\left[V_1 \mid X_1 = Y_1 = \ldots = Y_{n-k-1} = x,\right.$$

$$b_{k-1}^*(Y_{n-k} \mid p_1, \ldots, p_{k-1}) = p_k, \ldots,$$

$$\left. b_0^*(Y_{n-1}) = p_1\right], \qquad k = 1, \ldots, n-2. \quad (8.102)$$

Proof (Sketch) Suppose bidder 1 observes the signal $X_1 = x$, and all rival bidders quit exactly when the price reaches the level $p = b_0^*(y)$. Then bidder 1 knows for sure that $Y_1 = Y_2 = \cdots = Y_{n-1} = y$ wins the auction, and earns the payoff

$$E[V_1 \mid X_1 = x, \ Y_1 = Y_2 = \cdots, \ Y_{n-1} = y] - b_0^*(y).$$

Using a diagram similar to Figure 8.7, it becomes clear that (8.101) is the best reply of bidder 1 if everyone else plays the strategy (8.101).

In a similar fashion one can show that $b_1^*(x)$ is the best reply to $b_0^*(y)$, $b_1^*(y)$, etc. Finally, the strategies are strictly monotone increasing in the own quality signal, which confirms the assumed monotonicity of all components of $b_k(x)$. $\qquad \square$

Proposition 8.18 *The seller's expected profit is higher in the English than in the Vickrey auction.*

Proof (Sketch) In the English auction there are two phases: In the first phase the bidders with the lowest $n - 2$ quality signals reveal their signal realizations by quitting the auction at prices $p_1 \leq p_2 \leq p_{n-2}$. In the second phase the remaining two bidders play a Vickrey auction. By Proposition 8.16 it is known that revealing the seller's signal increases the seller's expected profit. Similar reasoning explains why revealing some bidders' signals raises the seller's expected profit as well. $\quad \square$

Milgrom and Weber (1982) generalized this result, as follows:

Proposition 8.19 *The equilibrium expected profits of the four most common auctions rank as follows:*

$$Dutch = first\text{-}price \leq Vickrey \leq English. \qquad (8.103)$$

The relatively low profitability of the Dutch and first-price auctions is due to the fact that in the course of these auctions no useful information is revealed.

This result is often used to justify the use of an open, increasing auction, like the English auction. However, one can design sealed-bid auction rules that are at least as profitable as the English auction and yet less susceptible to collusion (see Perry, Wolfstetter, and Zamir (1998)).

8.7.6 Limits of the Linkage Principle

In many auctions one sells many units of identical or similar goods. And often the bidders are also interested in acquiring more than one good. Unfortunately, the theory of multiunit auctions is still fairly undeveloped. The theory of single-unit auctions can be easily generalized to multiunit auctions if each bidder demands only one unit. However, if bidders demand more than one unit, many questions are still unanswered. In particular, it is not clear whether the revenue ranking known from single-unit auctions also applies to the auctioning of many units.

Some negative results are already known. For example, we know that the linkage principle does not always apply to multiunit auctions. True, the revelation of private quality signals also raises the average unsuccessful bid and lowers the average successful bid. However, unlike in the single-unit case, it can occur that the revelation of a private quality signal turns a successful bid into an unsuccessful one, and vice versa. This upsets the linkage principle, which suggests that the English auction may be less profitable to the seller than a first-price or Dutch auction.

When practical advice is sought concerning the design of new auctions, one naturally relies on the intuition developed for the well-researched single-unit case. For example, when auction theorists were called upon to design an auction for the sale of spectrum rights for the operation of wireless telephones, they relied on the validity of the linkage principle and recommended the use of an open, increasing auction.[50] The Federal Communications Commission decided that the advantageous effect of the information revelation, which is built into an open auction, outweighs the danger of collusion, which is intrinsic to open auctions.[51]

Another problematic prerequisite of the linkage principle is the symmetry assumption. If it is common knowledge that some bidders have higher valuations than others, the linkage principle may again be upset, and the first-price or Dutch auction can be more profitable than the English auction (see Landsberger, Rubinstein, Wolfstetter, and Zamir (1998)).

Moreover, Klemperer (1998) developed several examples of auctions with *almost* common values where the seller is better off if bidders receive no information concerning other bidders' valuations. This again suggests that there are close limits to the validity of the linkage principle, and that open, increasing auctions may not always be the most profitable for the seller. To close with a positive perspective: This just shows you that auction theory is still a rich mine for further research.

8.8 Further Applications*

We close with a few remarks on the use of the auction selling mechanism in financial markets, in dealing with the natural-monopoly problem, and in oligopoly theory. Each application poses some unique problem.

8.8.1 Auctions and Oligopoly

Recall the analysis of price competition and the Bertrand paradox ("two is enough for competition") in Chapter 3 on Oligopoly and Industrial Organization. There

---

[50] See McMillan (1994), Milgrom (1998), and Milgrom (1997).
[51] Evidence concerning widespread collusion was reported in the *Economist,* May 17, 1997.

we elaborated on one proposed resolution of the Bertrand paradox that had to do with capacity-constrained price competition and that culminated in a defense of the Cournot model. This resolution was successful, though a bit complicated – but unfortunately not quite robust with regard to the assumed rationing rule.

A much simpler resolution of the Bertrand paradox can be found by introducing incomplete information. This explanation requires a marriage of oligopoly and auction theory, which is why we sketch it here in two examples.

Example 8.8 (Another Resolution of the Bertrand Paradox) Consider a simple Bertrand oligopoly game with inelastic demand and $n \geq 2$ identical firms. Each firm has constant unit costs c and unlimited capacity. Unlike in the standard Bertrand model, each firm knows its own cost, but not those of others. Rivals' unit costs are viewed as identical and independent random variables, described by a uniform distribution with the support $[0, 1]$.

Since the lowest price wins the market, the Bertrand game is a Dutch auction with the understanding that we are dealing here with a "buyers' auction" rather than the "seller's auction" considered before. Since costs are independent and identically distributed, we can employ the apparatus and results of the *SIPV* auction model. Strategies are price functions that map each firm's unit cost c into a unit price $p(c)$.

The unique equilibrium price strategy is characterized by the markup rule

$$p^*(c) = \frac{1}{n} + \frac{n-1}{n}c. \tag{8.104}$$

The equilibrium price is $p^*(C_{(1)})$, the equilibrium expected price[52]

$$\bar{p}(n) := E\left[p^*(C_{(1)})\right] = E\left[C_{(2)}\right] = \frac{2}{n+1}, \tag{8.105}$$

and each firm's equilibrium expected profit

$$\bar{\pi}(c, n) = \frac{(1-c)^n}{n}. \tag{8.106}$$

Evidently, more competition leads to more aggressive pricing, beginning with the monopoly price $p^*(1) = 1$ and approaching the competitive pricing rule $p = c$ as the number of oligopolists becomes very large. Similarly, the expected-price rule and profit are diminishing in n, beginning with $\bar{p}(1) = 1$, $\bar{\pi}(1) = 1 - c$, and with $\lim_{n \to \infty} \bar{p}(n) = 0$ and $\lim_{n \to \infty} \bar{\pi}(n) = 0$. Hence, numbers matter. Two is not enough for competition.

In order to prove these results, all we need to do is to use a transformation of random variables and then apply previous results on Dutch auctions.

For this purpose, define

$$b := 1 - p \quad \text{and} \quad v := 1 - c. \tag{8.107}$$

[52] Notice that $E[p^*(C_{(1)})] = E[C_{(2)}]$ is the familiar *revenue equivalence* that holds for all distribution functions. (If the market were second-price, each firm would set $p^*(c) \equiv c$, the lowest price would win, and trade would occur at the second lowest price; therefore, the expected price at which trade occurs would be equal to $E[C_{(2)}]$.)

This transformation maps the price competition game into a Dutch auction, where the highest bid b (the lowest p) wins. Also, $b, v \in [0, 1]$, and v is uniformly distributed. Therefore, we can apply the equilibrium bid function from Example 8.2, which was $b(v) := [(n-1)/n]v$. We conclude

$$
\begin{aligned}
p^* &= 1 - b \\
&= 1 - \frac{n-1}{n}v \\
&= 1 - \frac{n-1}{n}(1-c) \\
&= \frac{1}{n} + \frac{n-1}{n}c,
\end{aligned} \tag{8.108}
$$

as asserted.

Remark 8.3 (Why Numbers Matter) By revenue equivalence one has

$$
\bar{p}(n) := E[p^*(C_{(1)}] = E[C_{(2)}]. \tag{8.109}
$$

Therefore, the "two is enough for competition" property of the Bertrand paradox survives in terms of expected values. Still, numbers matter, essentially because $E[C_{(1)}]$ and $E[C_{(2)}]$ move closer together as the size n of the sample is increased. The gap between these statistics determines the aggressiveness of pricing because the price function has the form $p^*(c) = (1 - \beta) + \beta c$ with

$$
\beta := \frac{n-1}{n} = \frac{1 - E[C_{(2)}]}{1 - E[C_{(1)}]}. \tag{8.110}
$$

Example 8.9 (Extension to Price-Elastic Demand*) Suppose demand is a decreasing function of price, as is usually assumed in oligopoly theory.[53] Specifically, assume the simplest possible inverse demand function $P(X) := 1 - X$. Otherwise, maintain the assumptions of the previous example. Then the equilibrium is characterized by the following markup rule $p^* : [0, 1] \to [0, 1]$:

$$
p^*(c) = \frac{1 + nc}{n + 1}. \tag{8.111}
$$

Obviously, $p^*(1) = 1$ and $p^*(0) = 1/(n+1)$.

Compare this with the equilibrium markup rule in the inelastic-demand framework analyzed in the previous example, which was $p^*(c) = [1 + (n-1)c]/n$. Evidently, pricing is more aggressive if demand responds to price. Of course, if the auction were second-price, bidding would not be affected, since $p^*(c) = c$ is a dominant strategy in this case.

We conclude: If demand is a decreasing function of price, a first-price auction leads to higher expected consumer surplus. This may explain why first-price sealed bids are the common auction form in industrial and government procurement.

[53] This case was considered by Hansen, as already noted in Section 8.3.6.

This is just the beginning of a promising marriage of oligopoly and auction theory. Among the many interesting extensions, an exciting issue concerns the analysis of the repeated Bertrand game. The latter is particularly interesting because it leads to a dynamic price theory where agents successively learn about rivals' costs, which makes the information structure itself endogenous.

8.8.2 Natural-Gas and Electric Power Auctions

As a next example, recall the natural-monopoly problem discussed in Chapter 2. There we discussed regulatory mechanisms designed to minimize the cost of monopoly, when monopolization is desirable due to indivisibilities in production and associated economies of scale.

In many practical applications, it has often turned out that the properties of a natural monopoly apply only to a small part of an industry's activity. And vertical disintegration often contributed to reduce the natural-monopoly problem.

The public utility industry (gas and electric power) has traditionally been viewed as the prime example of natural monopoly. However, the presence of economies of scale in the production of energy has always been contested. An unambiguous natural monopoly exists only in the transportation and local distribution of energy. This suggests that the natural-monopoly problem in public utilities can best be handled when one disintegrates production, transportation, and local distribution of energy.

In the U.K. the electric power industry has been reshaped in recent years by the privatization of production combined with the introduction of electric power auctions. These auctions are run on a daily basis by the National Grid Company. At 10 a.m. every day, the suppliers of electric power make a bid for each of their generators to be operated on the following day. By 3 p.m., the National Grid Company has finalized a plan of action for the following day in the form of a merit order, ranked by bids from low to high. Depending upon the random demand on the following day, the spot price of electric power is then determined in such a way that demand is matched by supply, according to the merit order determined on the previous day.

Similar institutional innovations have been explored, dealing with the transportation of natural gas in long-distance pipelines and in the allocation of airport landing rights in the U.S. Interestingly, these innovations are often evaluated in laboratory experiments before they are put to a real-life test.[54]

A similarity between auctions in a regulatory setting and oligopoly with price-elastic demand is that bidders typically decide on a two-dimensional object: a price bid and a nonprice variable. For example, the nonprice bid could be quantity, as in the oligopoly application, or quality of service in a regulatory problem. Formally, the oligopoly problem with elastic demand is equivalent to a procurement problem where the social planner faces a declining social benefit function.

[54] See for example Rassenti, Smith, and Bulfin (1982) and McCabe, Rassenti, and Smith (1989).

The literature that discusses optimal mechanisms in this kind of environment includes Laffont and Tirole (1987). Che (1993) showed that the optimal mechanism can be implemented by a two-dimensional version of a first- or second-price auction that uses a *scoring rule* of the kind often seen in auctions by the U.S. Department of Defense. Typically, the optimal scoring rule gives exaggerated weight to quality.

8.8.3 Treasury-Bill Auctions

Each week the U.S. Treasury uses a discriminatory auction to sell Treasury bills (T–bills).[55] On Tuesday the Treasury announces the amount of 91-day and 182-day bills it wishes to sell on the following Monday and invites bids for specified quantities. On Thursday, the bills are issued to the successful bidders. Altogether, in fiscal year 1991 the Treasury sold over $1.7 trillion of marketable Treasury securities (bills, notes, and bonds).

Prior to the early 1970s, the most common method of selling T-bills was that of a *subscription offering*. The Treasury fixed an interest rate on the securities to be sold and then sold them at a fixed price. A major deficiency of this method of sale was that market yields could change between the announcement and the deadline for subscriptions.

The increased market volatility in the 1970s made fixed-price offerings too risky. Subsequently, the Treasury switched to an auction technique in which the coupon rate was still preset by the Treasury, and bids were made on the basis of price. The remaining problem with this method was that presetting the coupon rate still required forecasting interest rates, with the risk that the auction price could deviate substantially from the par value of the securities.

In 1974 the Treasury switched to auctioning coupon issues on a yield basis. Thereby, bids were accepted on the basis of an annual percentage yield with the coupon rate based the weighted-average yield of accepted competitive tenders received in the auction. This freed the Treasury from having to preset the coupon rate.

Another sale method was used in several auctions of long-term bonds in the early 1970s. This was the closed, uniform-price auction method.[56] Here, the coupon rate was preset by the Treasury, and bids were accepted in terms of price. All successful bidders were awarded securities at the lowest price of accepted bids.

In the currently used auction technique, two kinds of bids can be submitted: *competitive* and *noncompetitive*. Competitive bidders are typically financial intermediaries who buy large quantities. A competitive bidder indicates the number of bills he wishes to buy and the price he is willing to pay. Multiple bids are permitted. Noncompetitive bidders are typically small or inexperienced bidders. Their bids indicate the number of bills they wish to purchase (up to $1,000,000), with the

---

[55] For more details see Tucker (1985).

[56] In the financial community, a single-price, multiple-unit auction is often called "Dutch" (except by the English, who call it "American"). Be aware of the fact that in the academic literature one would never call it Dutch. Because of its second-price quality one would perhaps call it "English."

understanding that the price will be equal to the quantity-weighted average of all accepted competitive bids.

When all bids have been made, the Treasury sets aside the bills requested by noncompetitive bidders. The remainder is allocated among the competitive bidders beginning with the highest bidder, until the total quantity is placed. The price to be paid by noncompetitive bidders can then be calculated.

T-bill auctions are unique discriminatory auctions because of the distinct treatment of competitive and noncompetitive bids. Compared to the standard discriminatory auction, there is an additional element of uncertainty because competitive bidders do not know the exact amount of bills auctioned to them.

Another distinct feature is the presence of a secondary after-auction market and of pre-auction trading on a when-issued basis, which serves a price-discovering purpose where dealers typically engage in short sales.

In many countries, central banks use similar discriminatory auctions to sell short-term repurchase agreements to provide banks with short-term liquidity.[57] Several years ago, the German Bundesbank switched from a uniform-price auction to a multiple-price, discriminatory auction. The uniform-price auction had induced small banks to place very high bids because this gave them sure access to liquidity without the risk of having a significant effect on the price to be paid. Subsequently, large banks complained that this procedure put them at a competitive disadvantage, and the Bundesbank responded by switching to a discriminatory auction. However, this problem could also have been solved without changing auction procedures simply by introducing a finer grid of feasible bids (see Nautz (1997)).

In recent years, the currently used discriminatory auction procedures have become the subject of considerable public debate. Many observers have claimed that discriminatory auctions invite strategic manipulations and, perhaps paradoxically, lead to unnecessarily low revenues. Based on these observations, several prominent economists have proposed to replace the discriminatory by uniform-price auction procedures.

The recent policy debate was triggered by an inquiry into illegal bidding practices by one of the major security dealers, Salomon Brothers. Apparently, during the early 1990s, Salomon Brothers repeatedly succeeded in cornering the market by buying up to 95% of a security issue. This was in violation of U.S. regulations that do not allow a bidder to acquire more than 35% of an issue.[58] Such cornering of the market tends to be profitable because many security dealers engage in short sales between the time when an issue is announced and the time it is actually issued. This makes them vulnerable to a short squeeze.

Typically, a short squeeze develops during the when-issued period before a security is auctioned and settled. During this time, dealers already sell the soon-to-

---

[57] The procedures used by the Federal Reserve are described in *The Federal Reserve System: Purposes and Functions*, Board of Governors of the Federal Reserve System, Washington, D.C.

[58] Salomon Brothers circumvented the law by placing unauthorized bids in the names of customers and employees at several Treasury auctions. When these practices leaked, the Treasury security market suffered a substantial loss of confidence. For a detailed assessment of this crisis and some recommended policy changes consult the *Joint Report on the Government Securities Market* (Brady, Breeden, and Greenspan (1992)).

be-available securities and thus incur an obligation to deliver on the issue date. Of course, dealers must later cover this position, either by buying back the security at some point in the when-issued market, or in the auction, or in the post-auction secondary market, or in any combination of these. If those dealers who are short do not bid aggressively enough in the auction, they may have difficulty in covering their positions in the secondary market.

Are discriminatory auctions the best choice? Or should central banks and the Treasury go back to single-price auction procedures? This is still an exciting and important research issue. Already during the early 1960s, Friedman (1964) made a strong case in favor of a uniform-price sealed-bid auction. He asserted that this would end cornering attempts by eliminating gains from market manipulation. And, perhaps paradoxically, he also claimed that total revenue would be raised by surrendering the possibility to price-discriminate. Essentially, both claims are based on the expectation that the switch in auction rules would completely unify the primary and secondary markets and induce bidders to reveal their true willingness to pay.[59]

8.9 Bibliographic Notes

There are several good surveys of auction theory, in particular Phlips (1988), McAfee and McMillan (1987), Milgrom (1987), Milgrom (1989), Wilson (1992), and Matthews (1995b). Laffont (1997) reviews some of the empirical work on auctions. Cramton (1998) debates the pros and cons of open vs. closed (sealed-bid) auctions. And Krishna and Perry (1998) provide a unified treatment of optimal multiunit auctions and public-good problems based on a generalized Vickrey–Clarke–Groves mechanism.

Friedman and Rust (1993) review the literature on *double auctions*, which we have completely ignored here. Milgrom (1997, 1998), McMillan (1994), and Cramton (1995) review the experience with the auctioning of spectrum licenses in the U.S. And Schmidt and Schnitzer (1997) discuss the role of auctions in the privatization of public enterprises.

8.10 Appendix: Second-Order Conditions (Pseudoconcavity)

When we derived the symmetric equilibrium of SIPV auctions, we (implicitly) employed the first-order condition

$$U_b'(b, v) = \rho'(b)v - \mathcal{E}'(b) = 0, \qquad (8.112)$$

which underlies the envelope theorem. But we did not verify that a sufficient second-order condition holds. Here, in this appendix, we make up for that omission.

The second-order condition that we employ is not your usual concavity or quasiconcavity condition. Instead, we show that $U(b, v)$ is increasing in b for $b < b^*(v)$,

---

[59] For a discussion of Friedman's ideas, see Goldstein (1962) and Bikchandani and Huang (1989, 1998).

and decreasing for $b > b^*(v)$. Naturally, this implies that bidders' payoff is maximized at $b = b^*(v)$. In the optimization literature this second-order condition is known under the name of *pseudoconcavity*.[60]

Differentiate $U_b'(b, v)$ with respect to v, and one has

$$U_{bv}''(b, v) = \rho'(b) > 0. \tag{8.113}$$

Now, suppose $b < b^*(v)$. Let $\hat{v}$ be the valuation that would lead to the bid b if strategy b^* were played, that is, $b^*(\hat{v}) = b$. By the strict monotonicity of b^* it follows that one must have $v > \hat{v}$. Therefore, by (8.113), for all $b < b^*(v)$,

$$U_b'(b, v) \geq U_b'(b, \hat{v}) \equiv U_b'(b^*(\hat{v}), \hat{v}) \equiv 0. \tag{8.114}$$

In words, $U(b, v)$ is increasing in b for all $b < b^*(v)$.

Similarly one can show that $U(b, v)$ is decreasing in b for all $b > b^*(v)$. Therefore, $b^*(v)$ is a global maximizer, and hence $b^*(v)$ is an equilibrium.

---

[60] A differentiable function $f : \mathbb{R}^n \to \mathbb{R}$ is called *pseudoconcave* if for all $x, y \in \mathbb{R}^n$, $(y - x)\nabla f(x) \leq 0 \implies f(y) \leq f(x)$. Pseudoconcavity is a sufficient second-order condition, because if f is pseudoconcave and the gradient vector is $\nabla f(x^*) = 0$, then x^* maximizes f. Note that if $n = 1$, as in the present context, the graph of a pseudoconcave function is single-peaked.

9

Hidden Information and Adverse Selection

More will mean worse.
Kingsley Amis

9.1 Introduction

This chapter studies the interaction in markets when there is one-sided private or hidden information. The emphasis is on markets rather than simple bilateral relationships.

The key assumption is that the party that sets the terms of the contract lacks information about some relevant characteristics of its customers. This is often paraphrased as the *uninformed-party-moves-first* assumption.

The main conclusions are:

1. Hidden information gives rise to an efficiency problem. But the nature of the distortion differs radically according as one has adverse or positive selection.
2. There is an incentive to introduce self-selection or screening of customers in the form of rationing or nonlinear pricing.
3. In a screening equilibrium, the least preferred customers exert a negative externality upon the more preferred types. This externality is completely dissipative.
4. A screening equilibrium is generally improvable.
5. However, a screening equilibrium does not always exist.

The chapter closes with an in-depth analysis of bilateral trading between a monopolist and his customer, which generalizes the theory of second-degree price discrimination from Chapter 1 to a continuum of types. Bilateral trading relationships do not pose the existence problem that plagues the analysis of markets under hidden information.

9.2 Adverse Selection

Consider a market for goods of different quality. Sellers can observe the quality of what they sell, but buyers can only assess average quality. In the absence of some device to allow buyers to identify quality, bad products will always be sold together with good products, and, provided buyers' and sellers' quality ranking is the same, the best products are withheld from the market. This introduces an *adverse selection* bias that generally leads to inefficient trade and sometimes even a complete breakdown of trade.

Economists have long recognized that adverse selection may interfere with the efficient operation of markets. Sir Thomas Gresham observed already in the year 1558 that if two coins have the same nominal value but are made from metals of unequal value, the cheaper coin tends to drive out the other of circulation. This "bad money drives out good" principle – ever since known as *Gresham's law* – is the prototypical example of adverse selection in economics.

Problems of hidden information and adverse selection are important in many markets. For example:

- A bank grants a loan to fund an investment; typically, the investor knows more about the probability of failure than the lender.
- An insurance company offers automobile liability insurance; typically, drivers know more about their driving skills and habits than the insurer.
- A firm hires workers or a manager; typically, the firm knows less about their skills and work attitude.

Recently, the oldest living woman in France was interviewed on the occasion of her 120th birthday. When she told the highlights of her life she mentioned that, at the age of 80, she had sold her house as a "life estate", keeping the right to use the house until the event of her death. Forty years later, she still enjoyed the benefits of that house, while the buyer had died years before. *Caveat emptor* – let the buyer beware.

9.2.1 The Market for Lemons

The modern treatment of adverse selection was triggered by George Akerlof's (1970) paper on the "market for lemons." As the title suggests, Akerlof considered a stylized market for used cars in which bad cars drive out good.

Following Akerlof, suppose the quality index X of used cars is drawn from a uniform distribution with support $[0, \bar{x}]$, $\bar{x} > 0$. Sellers' valuation of a car is equal to its quality x; but buyers value the same car more highly, at αx, with $\alpha > 1$. This asymmetry assures gains from trade. In particular, assuming a sufficiently large number of buyers, all cars should be sold. However, only sellers know the quality of their cars, whereas buyers only know the distribution from which quality is drawn.

If buyers could observe quality, the market price for used cars would be a function of quality: $p(x) = \alpha x$, and all cars would be traded. However, under the assumed incomplete information buyers can only assess average quality, and therefore all cars traded must go for the same price.

At a given price p a potential seller will only supply if the quality of his car is sufficiently low: $X \leq p$. Therefore, in view of the uniform distribution assumption, it follows that the expected value of quality is $\rho(p) := E[X \mid X \leq p] = p/2$.

In turn, buyers will buy only if $\alpha(\rho(p)) = \alpha p/2 \geq p$. Hence, trade occurs only if buyers value the good much more highly ($\alpha \geq 2$), and the market breaks down if $\alpha < 2$. This danger of market breakdown lurks in the back of all adverse-selection problems.

9.2.2 Adverse Selection in Labor Markets

We now adapt and extend Akerlof's lemons model to labor markets. This application will recur later in this chapter when we discuss two important market responses to adverse selection: *screening* and *signaling*. Rather than follow Akerlof's traditional competitive equilibrium modeling, we will now model adverse selection in a simple game.

Suppose a worker can work either in one of two firms or in self-employment. If employed in a firm, the worker's productivity is x, and in self-employment it is y. The worker knows his or her own productivities (x, y), whereas the employer only knows the distribution from which they are drawn.

For simplicity, y is either constant or a deterministic and monotone increasing function of x.[1] With slight abuse of notation, this function is denoted by $y(x)$.

Market Game

1. "Nature" draws productivity from the distribution $F : [\underline{x}, \bar{x}] \rightarrow [0, 1]$; only the worker observes the realization x.
2. The two firms, a and b, simultaneously make wage offers $w_i(y)$, $i \in \{a, b\}$.
3. The worker observes wage offers and either chooses self-employment or accepts the high-wage firm as employer (if both wages are the same, the employer is chosen by the flip of a fair coin).

Payoffs

All players are risk-neutral and maximize the expected value of their payoff. If employed, the worker's payoff is w, and if self-employed, $y(X)$. Firms' payoff is $X - w$ if an offer is accepted, and 0 otherwise.

Subgame

Just as in the lemons model, self-selection is at work in this model of the labor market. Suppose the highest wage offer is w. Then the worker accepts if that offer is more attractive than self-employment. Therefore, the worker's equilibrium strategy is

$$\text{accept employment} \iff y(X) \leq w. \tag{9.1}$$

Firms have rational expectations, and they anticipate the worker's equilibrium strategy when they assess the expected value of productivity. The expected value of productivity is thus a function of the maximum wage, as follows:

$$\rho(w) := E[X \mid y(X) \leq w]. \tag{9.2}$$

---

[1] The case of a decreasing function is covered in the section on positive selection.

(Of course, if w is so low that the worker goes into self-employment with certainty, $\rho(w)$ is not defined; in this case we set $\rho(w) = w$.) Evidently, ρ is increasing in w, since y is either constant or increasing in x. Therefore, adverse selection is at work here.

Solution

The subgame-perfect equilibrium of the market game is characterized as follows. Both firms set the same wage w^*, and that wage assures zero profits and the self-confirming productivity estimate $\rho(w^*) = w^*$, as in similar Bertrand competition games. (If the fixed point w^* is not unique, the only wage that rules out overbidding is the highest w^*.) Therefore:

Proposition 9.1 *The subgame-perfect Nash equilibrium strategies of the labor market game are*

$$w_a = w_b = w^* := \max\{w \mid \rho(w) = w\}, \tag{9.3}$$

$$accept\ employment \iff y(X) \leq w^*. \tag{9.4}$$

Inefficiency: Under- and Overemployment

We now turn to some examples to highlight the efficiency problems of this hidden-information game. First we assume that productivities are uncorrelated; this gives rise to strong inefficiency, in the form of either high underemployment or high overemployment. Then we move on to positively correlated productivities; typically, this gives rise to underemployment. Negatively correlated productivities are analyzed in Section 9.3.

Proposition 9.2 (Uncorrelated Productivities) *Suppose the productivity in self-employment, y, is constant, and let $\underline{x} < y < \bar{x}$ and $F(y) \in (0, 1)$. Then the subgame perfect equilibrium exhibits*

1. *overemployment if $E[X] \geq y$,*
2. *underemployment if $E[X] < y$.*

Proof The efficient allocation is to send the worker either to employment if $X \geq y$ or to self-employment if $X < y$. However, the subgame-perfect equilibrium prescribes an inefficient allocation for all x because it entails either employment of all x or self-employment of all x. Thus, the pivotal role is played by $E[X]$.

1. If $E[X] \geq y$, then $w^* = E[X]$, and in equilibrium all x accept employment. The associated beliefs $\rho(w^*) = E[X]$ are self-confirming because $y(X) \leq w^*$ is satisfied for all x, and therefore $E[X \mid y(X) \leq w^*] = E[X]$.
2. If $E[X] < y$, then $w^* = E[X]$ and no x accepts employment. The associated beliefs $\rho(w^*) = E[X]$ are also satisfied because we agreed to set $E[X \mid y(X) \leq w^*] = E[X]$ if the set of x for which $y(X) \leq w^*$ is satisfied is the empty set. $\qquad\square$

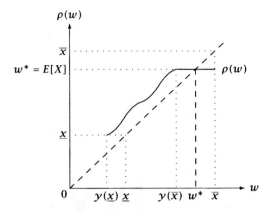

Figure 9.1. Equilibrium with Efficient Employment.

Now suppose the two productivities are positively correlated, i.e., y is monotone increasing in x. As a particularly extreme case, let $y(x) \leq x$ everywhere, and

$$y(\underline{x}) \leq \underline{x} < y(\bar{x}) < \bar{x}.$$

Then the efficient allocation is again very simple because the worker should be employed regardless of x. However, this can only be an equilibrium outcome if the unconditional expected value of X is sufficiently high. Otherwise it exhibits underemployment or even complete market breakdown.

Figure 9.1 illustrates the extreme case $E[X] \geq y(\bar{x})$ and $y(\underline{x}) < \underline{x}$. The function $\rho(w)$ starts at $(y(\underline{x}), \underline{x})$, above the 45° line. For all $w \geq y(\underline{x})$ the worker accepts employment with certainty. Therefore $\rho(w) = E[X]$, and $\rho(w)$ has its maximum fixed point at wage $w^* > y(\bar{x})$. The equilibrium implements the efficient allocation in this case.

However, efficiency is easily upset by lowering $E[X]$ below $y(\bar{x})$. Figures 9.2 and 9.3 illustrate this case. There, the subgame-perfect equilibrium exhibits under-employment in the sense that the worker moves into self-employment with positive probability whereas the efficient allocation stipulates employment regardless of x.

Proposition 9.3 (Positively Correlated Productivities) *Suppose the productivity in self-employment y is a strictly monotone increasing function of x and $E[X] < y(\bar{x})$. Then the subgame-perfect equilibrium exhibits underemployment and, if $y(\underline{x}) = \underline{x}$, even market breakdown.*

Proof Figure 9.2 illustrates the equilibrium if $y(\underline{x}) < \underline{x}$. There, the function $\rho(w)$ starts at $(y(\underline{x}), \underline{x}))$, above the 45° line, and the maximum fixed point is $w^* < y(\bar{x})$. Therefore, the equilibrium exhibits underemployment in the sense that the worker moves into self-employment with positive probability, whereas efficiency requires employment regardless of x.

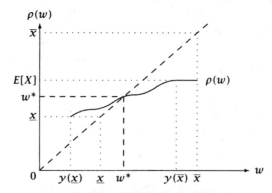

Figure 9.2. Equilibrium with Underemployment.

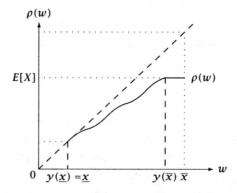

Figure 9.3. Equilibrium with Market Breakdown.

The extent of underemployment can go all the way to market breakdown where no employment takes place. This is illustrated in Figure 9.3, where $E[X] < y(\bar{x})$ and $y(\underline{x}) = \underline{x}$ are assumed. Here, $\rho(w)$ has its only fixed point at $w = \underline{x}$; therefore, in equilibrium no employment takes place.   □

9.3 Positive Selection: Too Many Professors?

You have just learned how adverse selection may explain underemployment. Here is an entertaining and yet equally important variation in which adverse selection is replaced by positive selection and underemployment by overemployment.

The story is nice for several reasons. First of all, it explains why there may be too many professors – which you may have suspected all along. Second, and even less pleasing, this selection bias calls for corrective taxes.

9.3.1 Assumptions

Consider the choice between accepting employment as a professor and self-employment, say as a plumber. Casual experience suggests that good professors are bad plumbers and vice versa. On this basis we assume that productivity as a plumber,

y, is a strictly decreasing function of productivity as a professor, x, described by the function $y(x)$ with $\underline{x} < y(\underline{x})$ and $y(\bar{x}) < \bar{x}$.

The worker knows his own productivities, but universities cannot observe productivity. Hence, x is hidden information. In the face of this incomplete information, universities view the worker's productivity as a random variable X, drawn from the probability distribution F with support $[\underline{x}, \bar{x}]$ and density function $f(x) > 0$.

A professor's salary is w, and a plumber's income y. At least two universities compete for the worker's service as a professor, and all players are risk-neutral. In other words, all assumptions of Section 9.2.2 are maintained except that y is now a strictly monotone *decreasing* function of x.

9.3.2 Occupational Choice

Who chooses to be a professor, and who takes up plumbing? An income maximizer becomes a professor if and only if he or she would earn less in plumbing:

$$\text{choose professorship} \quad \Leftrightarrow \quad y(X) \leq w. \tag{9.5}$$

And what choice of occupation is socially desirable? The efficient assignment is determined by the principle of *comparative advantage*. Accordingly, one should become a professor if and only if $X \geq Y$.

9.3.3 Positive vs. Adverse Selection

An *adverse* selection bias occurs if a reduction in price tends to reduce quality. Similarly, one can speak of a *positive* selection bias if a reduction in price tends to increase quality. The present model is an example of positive selection. For, if w is lowered, the least productive professors will move into plumbing, which raises the average productivity of professors.

Stated formally, the expected value of a professor's productivity is a function of w, as follows:

$$\begin{aligned} \rho(w) &:= E[X \mid y(X) \leq w] \\ &= E[X \mid X \geq \phi(w)], \qquad \phi := y^{-1} \\ &= \frac{1}{1 - F(\phi(w))} \int_{\phi(w)}^{\bar{x}} z \, dF(z). \end{aligned} \tag{9.6}$$

Therefore, (note that $\phi' < 0$ and $\rho > \phi$)

$$\rho'(w) = \frac{f(\phi(w)) \, \phi'(w)}{1 - F(\phi(w))} (\rho(w) - \phi(w)) < 0. \tag{9.7}$$

This confirms that the assumed negative correlation between productivities gives rise to a *positive* selection bias.

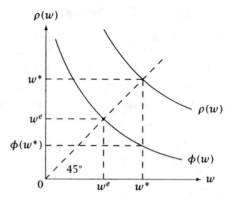

Figure 9.4. Equilibrium with Overemployment.

9.3.4 Subgame-Perfect Equilibrium

What wage do professors earn, and what is the profile of productivities in equilibrium? As before, the equilibrium wage is the maximal fixed point

$$w^* = \max\{w \mid \rho(w) = w\}. \tag{9.8}$$

Since $\rho'(w) < 0$, and $\underline{x} < y(\underline{x})$, and $y(\bar{x}) < \bar{x}$, existence and uniqueness are assured (see Figure 9.4).

Proposition 9.4 (Negatively Correlated Productivities) *Suppose the productivity as a plumber, y, is a strict monotone decreasing function of the productivity as a professor, x. Then the subgame-perfect equilibrium exhibits overemployment of professors.*

Proof Since $w^e = \phi(w^e) < \rho(w^e)$, the efficient allocation cannot be an equilibrium. As you can see from Figure 9.4, the equilibrium wage w^* must be higher than w^e. Hence, in equilibrium every $X \geq \phi(w^*)$ becomes a professor, which includes the efficient assignments, $X \geq \phi(w^e)$, plus others. Therefore, overemployment of professors occurs. Society would benefit if all $X \in (\phi(w^*), w^*)$ could be moved into plumbing.   □

Example 9.1 Suppose that X is uniformly distributed on the support $[0, 1]$, and that $y(x) := 1 - x$ and $\phi(w) := 1 - w$. Then the efficient occupational choice is reached at $w^e = 1/2$. However, this cannot be a subgame-perfect equilibrium because $\rho(w^e) = 3/4 > 1/2 = w^e$.

The unique equilibrium wage is $w^* = 2/3$. It gives rise to overemployment of professors because every $X \geq 1/3$ becomes a professor, not just those with $X \geq 1/2$.

9.3.5 A Corrective Tax

Can one implement the efficient choice of occupations by a corrective tax, and if so how? The answer is simple. By imposing a proportional tax t on professors' income one can move the equilibrium to the socially desired outcome. This is achieved if

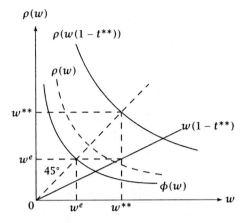

Figure 9.5. Corrective Tax.

one finds a tax rate t^{**} and resulting equilibrium wage w^{**} that make the after-tax equilibrium wage equal to w^e and yet satisfy the zero-profit condition

$$w^{**}(1 - t^{**}) = w^e,$$

$$w^{**} = \rho(w^{**}).$$

Why does the tax shift the equilibrium in the right direction? Given w, levying a tax $t > 0$ drives the least productive professors into plumbing and hence raises the average productivity of professors. In Figure 9.5 this effect is illustrated by the rightward shift of the average productivity curve. The only question is whether one can always find a tax that exactly implements the efficient allocation.

Rather than dwell into a general proof of existence of corrective taxes, we close with an example.

Example 9.2 Using the assumptions of Example 9.1, the unique corrective tax is $t^{**} = 1/3$.

In order to induce efficiency, the after-tax wage must be equal to w^e, i.e., $w^{**}(1 - t^{**}) = w^e = \frac{1}{2}$. Therefore, the corrective tax must solve the condition

$$w^{**} = \frac{1}{2(1 - t^{**})} = \rho(w^e) = \frac{3}{4}.$$

The unique solution is $w^{**} = \frac{3}{4}, t^{**} = \frac{1}{3}$.

Note that this corrective tax reduces professors' after-tax wage from $\frac{2}{3}$ to $\frac{1}{2}$; so, please, do not tell anybody about it.

Perhaps you do not like some aspects of this model. Make a better one. This may very well contribute to your first job as a professor.

9.4 Adverse Selection and Rationing

Adverse-selection problems are also prominent in insurance and credit markets. For example, when a bank raises its interest rate on loans, it tends to crowd out

Table 9.1. *Probability of investment returns $\underline{R}$*

$\underline{R}$	$\Pr(R \mid \ell)$	$\Pr(R \mid h)$
0	1/2	3/4
2.2	1/2	0
3.8	0	1/4

low-risk investors, which, in turn, contributes to reducing the bank's profit. In the face of this adverse selection effect, credit markets break down altogether unless banks invent some device that prevents this market failure.

As a simple example, suppose two investors want to borrow $1. One investor is a high (h) and the other a low risk (ℓ). The bank knows the probability distributions of investment returns (Table 9.1) but not the identity of the investor. Liability is limited to the collateral, which is set at $\$\frac{3}{4}$.

With these assumptions, the demand for loans is a function of the rate of interest r, as follows:

$$D(r) = \begin{cases} 2, & r \leq 0.45, \\ 1, & r \in (0.45, 0.55], \\ 0, & r > 0.55. \end{cases}$$

Note: as the interest rate is raised above 45%, adverse selection comes into effect because the low-risk investor is crowded out, while the high-risk investor remains in the market for all $r \leq 0.55$.

Suppose the bank can attract $1 deposits at a low interest rate, say $r = 0$. Then there is no interest rate at which the market is cleared, for in order to match the demand, the interest rate would have to be $r \in (0.45, 0.55)$, at which the bank would suffer a loss. Therefore, the competitive credit market breaks down.

However, this market failure can be avoided by some *credit rationing scheme*. Let the bank set the interest sufficiently low, at $r = 0.45$. Then both low- and high-risk investors apply for the loan. And if the bank picks one of the two loan applications by the flip of a fair coin, the low-risk investor has an equal chance to be served. Altogether, this is profitable because it raises the bank's expected profit to a positive level equal to 0.0125. Hence, in this example, the introduction of credit rationing improves the market outcome even though rationing obviously cannot establish maximum efficiency. This observation is at the heart of the theory of credit rationing proposed by Stiglitz and Weiss (1981) and Wilson (1980).

9.5 Adverse Selection and Screening

Both adverse and positive selection call for more complex market arrangements. In the previous section you have already learned that rationing may improve the equilibrium outcome. Here, we discuss another more common market response: *screening* or *self-selection* of types.

Screening can only be achieved if the party that sets the terms of the contract is able to:

- play with at least one additional variable, in addition to price, that affects customers' marginal willingness to pay;
- restrict customers to choose among particular combinations of variables from a menu of choices.

Such additional variables are, for example, quantity in monopolistic price discrimination, coverage in insurance, collateral in lending, and output in labor contracts.

If these conditions are met and the marginal willingness to pay functions are single-crossing, one can generally design a menu of contracts in such a way that it is in each type's best interest to pick the contract designated for this particular type. Moreover, in the face of competition, *pooling* of types cannot be part of an equilibrium. This suggests a strong case for screening. However, existence of equilibrium is generally not assured.

9.5.1 Screening in Insurance Markets

Consider an insurance market with (at least) two insurance companies and a large population of customers. Customers come in two types, either high (h) or low (ℓ) risk, in the proportions λ and $1 - \lambda$. The customers' type is their private information. Insurance companies offer complete insurance contracts that stipulate different combinations of insurance premium p and insurance coverage c, from which customers are free to select one. After insurance contracts have been signed, nature draws either one of two states, called good (g) or bad (b).[2]

Customers' initial endowment is described by the binary lottery

$$L_i^0 := [w_g^0, w_b^0; \rho_i], \qquad w_g^0 > w_b^0, \quad i \in \{h, \ell\}, \tag{9.9}$$

where w_g^0 denotes wealth in state g, w_b^0 wealth in state b, and ρ_i the probability of state b for customer type i. The difference $w_g^0 - w_b^0 > 0$ is the loss, in case state b has occurred. The only distinction between types is that high-risk customers suffer that loss with greater probability:

$$1 > \rho_h > \rho_\ell > 0. \tag{9.10}$$

Buying insurance with coverage c and premium p means trading the lottery L_i^0 for the lottery $L_i, i \in \{h, \ell\}$, where

$$L_i := [w_b^i, w_g^i; \rho_i], \tag{9.11}$$

$$w_b^i := w_b^0 + c_i, \tag{9.12}$$

$$w_g^i := w_g^0 - p_i. \tag{9.13}$$

Insurance companies are risk-neutral, and customers risk-averse. All customers have the same utility function $u(w)$ with $u'(w) > 0, u''(w) < 0$.

---

[2] The following model is due to Rothschild and Stiglitz (1976). This seminal contribution is often referred to as the *Rothschild–Stiglitz model*.

The Market Game

1. Insurance companies simultaneously offer a menu of complete contracts (for convenience we state contracts in terms of w_g and w_b),

$$C := \{(w_b^\ell, w_g^\ell), (w_b^h, w_g^h), (w_b^0, w_g^0)\}. \tag{9.14}$$

The contract (w_b^0, w_g^0) represents no trade; it is included because market transactions are voluntary.

2. Customers pick the best contract from the menus offered by insurers and sign it; if both insurers offer the same contracts, the demand is divided equally.

3. Nature draws either state g or state b, that drawing becomes common knowledge, payments are made, and the market game is over.

Payoffs and Marginal Rates of Substitution

Customers' expected utility $E[U(L)]$ and insurance companies' expected profit $E[\pi(L)]$ are (type index omitted)

$$E[u(L)] := \rho u(w_b) + (1 - \rho)u(w_g), \tag{9.15}$$

$$E[\pi(L)] := \rho(w_b^0 - w_b) + (1 - \rho)(w_g^0 - w_g). \tag{9.16}$$

Therefore, one obtains the following marginal willingness-to-pay or marginal rate-of-substitution (MRS) functions (type index omitted)

$$-\frac{dw_b}{dw_g}\bigg|_{E[u(L)] = \text{const}} = \frac{1 - \rho}{\rho} \frac{u'(w_g)}{u'(w_b)}, \tag{9.17}$$

$$-\frac{dw_b}{dw_g}\bigg|_{E[\pi(L)] = \text{const}} = \frac{1 - \rho}{\rho}. \tag{9.18}$$

Note: Since $\rho_h > \rho_\ell$, the MRS of h is always lower than that of ℓ. In words, h is willing to forgo less wealth in state b in exchange for one extra dollar in state g, because the event in which this extra dollar is obtained occurs with lower probability. Similarly, insurance companies' MRS is lower if they deal with customer h. These are the *single-crossing* properties that you have already met in our introduction to monopolistic second-degree price discrimination in Chapter 1.

Efficiency and Equilibrium under Complete Information

An efficient allocation of risk requires that customers' and insurers' MRSs be made equal. An immediate implication is that marginal utilities must be the same across states ($u'_g = u'_b$), which in turn implies the optimality of *full insurance*: ($w_g = w_b$).

If insurance companies knew their customers' type, the efficient risk allocation would also be the equilibrium outcome of the market game. Indeed, in the market equilibrium under complete information both insurers allow each group of customers to trade in their initial endowment L_i^0 for that riskless lottery L_i:

$$L_i = (\bar{w}^i, \bar{w}^i; \rho_i), \tag{9.19}$$

$$\bar{w}^i := E[L_i^0] := \rho_i w_b^0 + (1 - \rho_i)w_g^0, \tag{9.20}$$

which pays out the expected value of L_i^0 in each state realization.

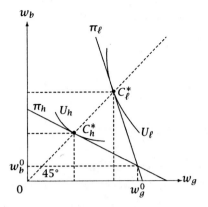

Figure 9.6. Efficient Risk Allocation.

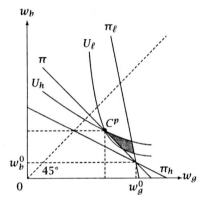

Figure 9.7. Pooling Cannot Occur in Equilibrium.

Figure 9.6 illustrates the efficient risk allocation. There (w_g^0, w_b^0) is the *initial endowment*, the lines π_ℓ, π_h are the *zero-profit* lines (assuming exclusive service of either h or ℓ, respectively), and the convex curves are customers' indifference curves. The equilibrium contracts exhibit full insurance and zero expected profits.

Subgame-Perfect Equilibrium under Incomplete Information

Suppose insurance companies pool risks and offer the same contract to both h and ℓ. Can this be part of a subgame-perfect equilibrium of the market game?

If pooling occurs in equilibrium, the pooling contract has to yield zero expected profits, as at point C^P on the zero-expected-profit line associated with pooling π in Figure 9.7, because otherwise insurers have an incentive to underbid. Now recall that the MRS of type ℓ exceeds that of type h at all (w_g, w_b). Therefore, at the equilibrium pooling contract C^P the indifference curve of type ℓ must cross that of h from above, as illustrated in Figure 9.7.

Now consider the shaded area in Figure 9.7. Each contract C in this set satisfies the following properties: 1) $C \succ_\ell C^P$ (ℓ prefers C to C^P); 2) $C^P \succ_h C$ (h prefers C^P to C); 3) insurers prefer C to C^P, provided C is only demanded by low-risk customers. Due to the single-crossing relationship between the MRSs, the set of contracts that share these properties is not empty.

Proposition 9.5 (No Pooling) *A pooling contract cannot be part of a subgame-perfect equilibrium.*

Proof Suppose, *per absurdum,* that one insurer offers a pooling contract that gives a zero expected profit if a representative sample of customers is served. Then the other insurer can exclusively attract all low-risk customers by offering a contract from the shaded area in Figure 9.7 (which has already been shown to be not empty) at a positive expected profit. This upsets the pooling property of the rival's contract. Therefore, pooling cannot be part of a subgame-perfect equilibrium. ☐

If the market game has an equilibrium, it has the following properties: High-risk customers are offered efficient insurance (no distortion), and low-risk customers are offered that contract (w_g^ℓ, w_b^ℓ), which keeps high-risk customers indifferent between this contract and the contract designated for them. The latter exhibits underinsurance, $w_g^\ell > w_b^\ell$.

Proposition 9.6 (Screening Equilibrium) *Suppose the market game has a sub-game-perfect equilibrium (in pure strategies). Then both insurers offer the same menu of contracts, which satisfies the conditions*

$$w_g^h = w_b^h = \bar{w}^h, \tag{9.21}$$

$$\rho_h u\left(w_b^\ell\right) + (1 - \rho_h)u\left(w_g^\ell\right) = u(\bar{w}^h), \tag{9.22}$$

$$\rho_\ell\left(w_b^0 - w_b^\ell\right) + (1 - \rho_\ell)\left(w_g^0 - w_g^\ell\right) = 0. \tag{9.23}$$

And each customer type picks the contract designated for that type. These contracts are independent of the proportion of high-risk customers in the population.

Proof Assuming existence, the equilibrium contracts must induce self-selection (by Proposition 9.5), yield zero expected profits, and not be improvable. As you can see from Figure 9.8, these properties are only satisfied for the asserted contracts. [3]

☐

Existence of Equilibrium?

Unfortunately, an equilibrium does not always exist. The reason is quite simple. We have already noted that equilibrium contracts are independent of the proportion of high-risk customers. In order to induce self-selection and zero expected profits, low-risk customers have to suffer a severe deviation from the efficient risk allocation, just

---

[3] Exercise: Suppose we give low-risk customers the efficient insurance. Why can this not be part of an equilibrium? Which requirement is violated? (Hint: Show that one cannot induce self-selection and zero expected profits in this case.)

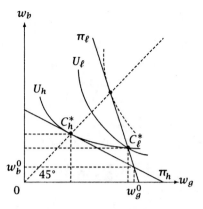

Figure 9.8. Screening Equilibrium.

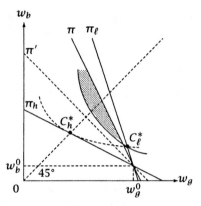

Figure 9.9. Nonexistence If High-Risk Customers Are Rare.

in order to keep high-risk customers away. This arrangement becomes ridiculous if the proportion of high-risk customers is small. For in that case, the cost of sorting by far outweighs the gain, and low-risk customers are better off if risks are pooled. This induces insurers to offer pooling contracts, which, however, cannot be an equilibrium.

Proposition 9.7 (Nonexistence of Equilibrium) *Suppose the proportion of high-risk customers is small. Then the market game has no equilibrium (in pure strategies).*

Proof If the proportion of high-risk customers is small, the zero-expected-profit line associated with pooling risks is close to the one associated with serving low-risk customers only. Now suppose one insurer offers the candidate solution of a screening equilibrium (as described in Proposition 9.6). Then the rival insurer's best reply is to offer a pooling contract from the shaded area in Figure 9.9, which attracts all customers and thus destroys screening. That shaded area is not empty if λ is sufficiently small. Since a pooling contract cannot be part of an equilibrium by Proposition 9.5, no equilibrium exists in this case. □

Welfare Properties

The presence of high-risk customers exerts a negative externality on low-risk customers. That externality is completely dissipative – there are losses to low risk customers, but the high-risk customers are not better off than they would be in isolation. As Rothschild and Stiglitz put it:

If only the high-risk individuals would admit to their having high accident probabilities, all individuals would be made better-off without anyone being worse-off.

However, make sure you understood why high-risk customers would never volunteer that information.

9.5.2 Screening in Labor and Credit Markets

The above analysis of insurance markets can be applied to many other markets simply by changing words.

Consider a labor market where (at least) two firms compete for workers that are either able (ℓ) or not so able (h). Ability is workers' private information. Both workers produce a random *output* or *revenue* that has one of two realizations. Ability only affects the probability distribution of outputs, and ℓ obtains the greater output with higher probability than h. Firms set menus of screening contracts; each contract stipulates wages contingent upon output, workers can be restricted to these choices, and workers either accept or reject.

This labor-market model is nothing but a reinterpretation of the insurance-market model. Simply interpret w_g^0, w_b^0 as high and low output, and w_g, w_b as the wages contingent upon the output realization, either g or b. If workers remain self-employed, they have the initial endowment lottery $L_i^0, i \in \{h, \ell\}$. Once they enter employment, they exchange their initial endowment L_i^0 for a wage lottery L_i.

In an employment relationship the employer is *residual claimant* (he "owns" the output or revenue) and the worker has a contractual claim on wage payments. In the present framework, each wage contract is essentially a piece-rate contract.

With this reinterpretation of variables, the entire analysis of the insurance market applies to this model of the labor market.

Similarly, one can apply the Rothschild–Stiglitz model to credit markets. Bester (1985) explored this application using the assumption that collateral is used as screening variable, whereas Milde and Riley (1988) linked repayment and loan size.

9.5.3 Alternative Equilibrium Concepts

The Rothschild–Stiglitz model was examined independently by C. Wilson (1977a). His work has two additional features that received some attention in the literature.

First, Wilson considers an alternative definition of equilibrium and shows that with this definition existence of equilibrium is always assured. His notion of equilibrium drops the assumption that firms will introduce any new menu of contracts that makes money, provided all other menus of contracts remain in the market. Instead,

Wilson assumes that firms only introduce new menus if these make money even if some other menus are withdrawn by other firms, so that all menus of contracts that exist break-even.

Second, Wilson analyzes the role of government intervention to bring about Pareto improvements in these markets. He shows that in many instances cross subsidization schemes and compulsory insurance requirements can bring about Pareto improvements.

Miyazaki (1977) utilized the benefits of cross subsidization in the framework of labor contracts.

9.5.4 Limits of Screening

Many people seem to believe that screening models make the earlier vintage of adverse-selection models obsolete. This overlooks the fact that screening is often not feasible.

First of all, recall that screening requires an unambiguous ranking of marginal-willingness-to-pay functions, which was called the single-crossing assumption. Such an unambiguous ranking is, however, quite restrictive. Second and perhaps more important, screening is often not feasible because customers cannot be restricted to the set menu of choices, for they can undermine it by engaging in arbitrage. Using the insurance example, insurers cannot even pick an arbitrary pooling contract in this case, because by engaging in side dealings with each other, customers can buy any volume of coverage at a fixed unit price per dollar of coverage. Therefore, the only feasible contract is an incomplete contract in the form of a linear price, where each customer is free to buy as much coverage as he or she wants.

9.6 Screening without Competition*

Before closing the book on adverse selection, one should at least address two more issues: 1) to add an example of screening without competition, and 2) to show how to generalize the simple two-type models.

As we have already mentioned in the introduction, screening without competition is much easier because it leads to a straightforward maximization problem and avoids problems of existence of equilibrium. This is why it is advisable to take up the task of generalization in the simpler framework of screening without competition.

As a particular application we now return to the topic of second-degree price discriminiation, which was already spelled out in full detail in a simple model with only two types of customers in the chapter on monopoly, Section 1.4. We will extend this analysis to a continuum of customer types and thereby exercise some more advanced techniques.

9.6.1 Price Discrimination with a Continuum of Types

In Chapter 1 on monopoly we showed already how hidden information may give rise to second-degree price discrimination. There we covered the simplest case of two types of customers. We are now ready to exercise more advanced techniques and extend that analysis to a continuum of customers.[4]

The basic notation and assumptions of Section 1.4 are maintained. However, the monopolist now faces a continuum of customer types from the type space $\Theta := [0, \bar{\theta}]$, $\bar{\theta} > 0$. Customers' type is their private or hidden information. The monopolist only knows that types are drawn from the probability distribution $F : \Theta \rightarrow [0, 1]$, which is common knowledge.

From the revelation principle we know that every sales plan is equivalent to a *direct incentive-compatible sales plan.* [5] Accordingly, the monopolist announces a sales plan composed of the functions $x(\theta)$ (quantity) and $T(\theta)$ (total payment):

$$S := (x(\theta), T(\theta)), \tag{9.24}$$

and invites customers to choose a combination of quantity and total payment, $(x(\tilde{\theta}), T(\tilde{\theta}))$, by self-declaring their type $\tilde{\theta} \in \Theta$. Since the monopolist does not know customers' type, they may cheat and declare some $\tilde{\theta} \neq \theta$. However, an incentive-compatible sales plan induces all customers not to cheat and to declare their true type, $\tilde{\theta} = \theta$.

As in Section 1.4, customers' payoff function is

$$U(x, T; \theta) := W(x; \theta) - T. \tag{9.25}$$

Here $W(x; \theta)$ denotes θ's *willingness to pay* for the quantity x,

$$W(x; \theta) := \int_0^x P(y; \theta)\, dy, \tag{9.26}$$

and $P(x; \theta) = \partial W/\partial x$ the associated *marginal willingness to pay.* Customers maximize their payoff by self-declaring their type.

Assuming constant unit costs that are normalized to zero (as in Section 1.4), the monopolist's profit from a certain customer type is that type's total payment $T(\theta)$. Therefore, the optimal sales plan maximizes the monopolist's expected profit ($F(\theta)$ is the cdf of customers' types):

$$\max_{\{x(\theta), T(\theta)\}} \int_0^{\bar{\theta}} T(\theta)\, dF(\theta), \tag{9.27}$$

subject to the following *participation* (9.28) and *incentive constraints* (9.29):

$$U(x(\theta), T(\theta); \theta) \geq U(0, 0; \theta) = 0 \qquad \forall \theta \in \Theta, \tag{9.28}$$

$$\theta \in \arg\max_{\tilde{\theta}} U(x(\tilde{\theta}), T(\tilde{\theta}); \theta) \qquad \forall \tilde{\theta}, \theta \in \Theta. \tag{9.29}$$

Further Assumptions

In Section 1.4 we assumed that marginal willingness-to-pay functions are decreasing and single-crossing and that unit costs are constant. We now adapt and strengthen these assumptions and add assumptions concerning the probability distribution:

---

[4] We follow the seminal contribution by Maskin and Riley (1984a), simplifying some proofs and leaving out some extensions.

[5] The revelation principle was stated and proved in Section 8.5.2.

(A1) $P(x; \theta)$ is twice continuously differentiable with the partial derivatives $P_1 < 0$, $P_2 > 0$, $P_{22} < 0$, and unit costs are constant and normalized to zero.

(A2) The price elasticity of demand is increasing in θ; stated in terms of inverse demand P,

$$x, P > 0 \quad \Rightarrow \quad \frac{\partial}{\partial \theta} \left(\frac{-x}{P} \frac{\partial P}{\partial x} \right) < 0.$$

(A3) The cdf of θ, $F(\theta)$, is continuously differentiable with $F'(\theta) > 0$ everywhere on Θ and $F(0) = 1 - F(\bar{\theta}) = 0$.

Auxiliary Results

Fortunately, the optimization problem can be simplified, due to the following auxiliary results.

Let $U^*(\theta)$ denote the indirect utility function of customer θ:

$$U^*(\theta) := \max_{\tilde{\theta} \in \Theta} U(x(\tilde{\theta}), T(\tilde{\theta}); \theta). \tag{9.30}$$

Lemma 9.1 (Monotonicity) *The sales plan S is incentive-compatible if and only if*

$$U^{*\prime}(\theta) = \frac{\partial W}{\partial \theta}(x(\theta); \theta) \geq 0 \tag{9.31}$$

and

$$x'(\theta) \geq 0. \tag{9.32}$$

Proof Necessity: Applying the envelope theorem to the customers' maximization problem (9.30) gives

$$U^{*\prime}(\theta) = \frac{\partial W}{\partial \theta}(x(\theta); \theta),$$

which is positive because $P_2 > 0$. Note that (9.31) incorporates the first-order condition of the customers' maximization problem.

Moreover $U^*(\theta)$ is convex;[6] therefore,

$$0 \leq U^{*\prime\prime}(\theta)$$
$$= \frac{\partial^2 W}{\partial x \, \partial \theta}(x(\theta); \theta) x'(\theta) + \frac{\partial^2 W}{\partial \theta^2}(x(\theta); \theta)$$
$$= P_2(x(\theta); \theta) x'(\theta) + P_{22}(x(\theta); \theta).$$

And since $P_{22} < 0$ and $P_2 > 0$, we conclude that $x'(\theta) \geq 0$.

The proof of sufficiency is by contradiction.[7] Consider a sales plan that satisfies the two conditions, yet suppose type θ_1 prefers to "cheat" and declare $\theta_2 \neq \theta_1$. Define the customers' payoff as a function of their true and declared type $(\theta, \tilde{\theta})$, for a given sales plan, as $\bar{U}(\theta, \tilde{\theta}) := U(x(\tilde{\theta}), T(\tilde{\theta}); \theta)$. Then $\bar{U}(\theta_1, \theta_2) > \bar{U}(\theta_1, \theta_1)$,

---

[6] The proof of convexity is a standard exercise in microeconomics; it was sketched in Section 8.2.5.
[7] The proof is adapted from Laffont and Tirole (1993).

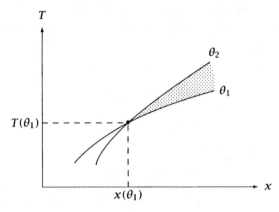

Figure 9.10. Incentive Compatibility and Monotonicity of $x(\theta)$.

and after a few tautological rearrangements, also using the first-order condition $\bar{U}_2(\theta, \theta) \equiv 0$ (third line), one obtains

$$0 < \bar{U}(\theta_1, \theta_2) - \bar{U}(\theta_1, \theta_1)$$

$$= \int_{\theta_1}^{\theta_2} \bar{U}_2(\theta_1, z)\, dz$$

$$= \int_{\theta_1}^{\theta_2} (\bar{U}_2(\theta_1, z) - \bar{U}_2(z, z))\, dz$$

$$= \int_{\theta_1}^{\theta_2} \int_{z}^{\theta_1} \bar{U}_{12}(r, z)\, dr\, dz$$

$$= \int_{\theta_1}^{\theta_2} \int_{z}^{\theta_1} P_2(x(z); r) x'(z)\, dr\, dz.$$

Let $\theta_2 > \theta_1$; then $z \geq \theta_1$ for all $x \in [\theta_1, \theta_2]$, and the inequality cannot hold. Similarly, let $\theta_1 > \theta_2$; then $z \leq \theta_1$ for all $z \in [\theta_2, \theta_1]$, which is again a contradiction. □

The monotonicity of $x(\theta)$ is illustrated by the indifference curves of two distinct types, $\theta_2 > \theta_1$, in Figure 9.10. There, if type θ_1 gets $(x(\theta_1), T(\theta_1))$, the price–quantity combination offered to type θ_2 must be in the shaded area, above θ_1's and below θ_2's indifference curves that pass through the point $(x(\theta_1), T(\theta_1))$. Hence, $x(\theta_2)$ must be either the same as $x(\theta_1)$ or exceed it.

Lemma 9.2 *An incentive-compatible sales plan satisfies all participation constraints if and only if $U^*(0) \geq 0$.*

Proof Follows immediately by the monotonicity of $U^*(\theta)$. □

The monotonicity of $x(\theta)$ implies that $x(\theta)$ is differentiable almost everywhere. In the following we consider the smaller class of piecewise differentiable functions. This is a prerequisite of using the calculus of variations or optimal control.[8]

---

[8] A piecewise differentiable function has continuous derivatives almost everywhere, and when it has no derivative it always has left and right derivatives.

Lemma 9.3 (Total Payment) *Consider a nondecreasing function $x(\theta)$. Incentive compatibility is assured if and only if*

$$T(\theta) = W(x(\theta); \theta) - \int_0^\theta \frac{\partial W}{\partial z}(x(z); z)\,dz - U^*(0). \qquad (9.33)$$

Proof Since $x(\theta)$ is nondecreasing, incentive compatibility is assured if and only if $U^{*\prime}(\theta)$ is set as in (9.31). Integrate $U^{*\prime}(\theta)$, and one obtains

$$U^*(\theta) \equiv \int_0^\theta U^{*\prime}(z)\,dz + U^*(0) = \int_0^\theta \frac{\partial W}{\partial z}(x(z); z)\,dz + U^*(0).$$

Solving $U^*(\theta) = W(x(\theta); \theta) - T(\theta)$ for $T(\theta)$ gives (9.33). $\qquad\square$

Proposition 9.8 *The monopolist's decision problem is equivalent to the variational problem*

$$\max_{\{x(\theta)\}} \left\{ \int_0^{\bar\theta} \Pi(x(\theta); \theta)\,dF(\theta) \mid x'(\theta) \geq 0 \right\} \qquad (9.34)$$

where

$$\Pi(x(\theta); \theta) := W(x(\theta); \theta) - \frac{1}{h(\theta)} \frac{\partial W}{\partial \theta}(x(\theta); \theta) \qquad (9.35)$$

and

$$h(\theta) := \frac{F'(\theta)}{1 - F(\theta)} \qquad \text{(hazard rate)} \qquad (9.36)$$

(provided $T(\theta)$ is set as in (9.33) and also $U^*(0) = 0$).

Proof The monopolist maximizes the expected value of $T(\theta)$. By the above lemmas, the incentive and participation constraints are equivalent to choosing $T(\theta)$ as in (9.33) combined with $U^*(0) \geq 0$, $x'(\theta) \geq 0$.

Leaving a surplus to the lowest type, $U^*(0) > 0$, is costly. Therefore, the monopolist sets $U^*(0) = 0$. In view of (9.33) the expected profit is hence equal to

$$\int_0^{\bar\theta} W(x(\theta); \theta)\,dF(\theta) - \int_0^{\bar\theta} \int_0^\theta \frac{\partial W}{\partial z}(x(z); z)\,dz\,dF(\theta). \qquad (9.37)$$

Apply integration by parts to the second term and substitute the hazard rate $h(\theta)$, defined in (9.36). After a few rearrangements this gives

$$\int_0^{\bar\theta} \int_0^\theta \frac{\partial W}{\partial z}(x(z); z)\,dz\,dF(\theta) = \int_0^{\bar\theta} \frac{\partial W}{\partial \theta}(x(\theta); \theta)\frac{1}{h(\theta)}\,dF(\theta). \qquad (9.38)$$

Finally, insert (9.38) into (9.37), and one has the program stated in the proposition. $\qquad\square$

Complete Sorting Solution

Consider the program obtained from (9.34) by omitting the monotonicity constraint $x'(\theta) \geq 0$. Call it the *restricted program*, and denote its solution by $\bar{x}(\theta)$, $\bar{T}(\theta)$.

Lemma 9.4 (Restricted Program) *The solution $\bar{x}(\theta)$ of the restricted program is characterized by the conditions*

$$\bar{x}(\theta) > 0 \quad \Rightarrow \quad P(\bar{x}(\theta); \theta) = \frac{1}{h(\theta)} P_2(\bar{x}(\theta); \theta). \tag{9.39}$$

It exhibits distortions, $P(\bar{x}(\theta); \theta) > 0$, everywhere on Θ except at the top, where $P(x(\bar{\theta}); \bar{\theta}) = 0$ ("no distortion at the top").

Proof In a variational problem the principle of optimality is that of *pointwise optimality* (Euler's equation).[9] In other words, $\bar{x}(\theta)$ maximizes Π for every θ. Hence, either $\bar{x}(\theta) = 0$ or $\bar{x}(\theta)$ satisfies the first-order condition $\partial\Pi/\partial x = 0$. Therefore,

$$\bar{x}(\theta) > 0 \quad \Rightarrow \quad P(\bar{x}(\theta); \theta) - \frac{1}{h(\theta)} P_2(\bar{x}(\theta); \theta) = 0. \tag{9.40}$$

Note that $P_2 > 0$, $h \geq 0$, and $1/h = 0 \iff \theta = \bar{\theta}$. Therefore, $P(\bar{x}(\theta); \theta) > 0$ everywhere except at $\theta = \bar{\theta}$, where $P(\bar{x}(\bar{\theta}); \bar{\theta}) = 0$.   □

We now show that the solution of the restricted program also solves the full program, provided the probability distribution function satisfies a certain concavity condition. That condition is weaker than the assumption of a monotone increasing hazard rate that plays a prominent role in the incomplete-information literature.

Proposition 9.9 (Complete Sorting) *Suppose the probability distribution function $F(\theta)$ is log-concave.[10] Then the solution of the restricted program, $\bar{x}(\theta)$, also solves the full program (9.34).*

Proof F is log-concave if and only if

$$\rho(\theta) := \theta - \frac{1}{h(\theta)} \tag{9.41}$$

is monotone increasing. Since $\bar{x}(\theta)$ maximizes $\Pi(x(\theta); \theta)$, either

$$\bar{x}(\theta) = 0 \quad \text{or} \quad \frac{\partial\Pi}{\partial x}(\bar{x}(\theta); \theta) = 0.$$

Totally differentiating the latter gives

$$\bar{x}'(\theta) = -\frac{\partial^2\Pi/\partial x\,\partial\theta}{\partial^2\Pi/\partial x^2}. \tag{9.42}$$

Therefore, if at $\bar{x}(\theta)$ one has $\partial^2\Pi/\partial x^2 < 0$ and $\partial^2\Pi/\partial x\,\partial\theta \geq 0$, the solution of the restricted program $\bar{x}(\theta)$ also solves the full program.

[9] For an introductory exposition of the calculus of variations and optimal control consult Kamien and Schwartz (1991).

[10] F is *log-concave* if $\ln F$ is concave. A monotone increasing hazard rate $h(\theta)$ is sufficient for log-concavity, but not necessary. Many standard distributions are log-concave; examples are normal, uniform, and exponential distributions. See Bagnoli and Bergstrom (1989).

From now on all terms are evaluated at $\bar{x}(\theta) > 0$. By (9.39) one has $1/h = P/P_2$. Compute $\partial^2 \Pi / \partial x^2 = P_1 - P_{21}/h$, substitute $1/h$, and use the monotonicity of the elasticity of demand (A2), and one confirms

$$\frac{\partial^2 \Pi}{\partial x^2} = P_1 - \frac{P_{21} P}{P_2} = \frac{P^2}{x P_2} \frac{\partial}{\partial \theta} \left(-\frac{x P_1}{P} \right) < 0.$$

Similarly, compute $\partial^2 \Pi / \partial x \, \partial \theta = P_2 - (P_{22}h - P_2 h')/h^2$, substitute ρ, and utilize the monotonicity of ρ. After a few rearrangements (also using $P_2 > 0$, $P_{22} \le 0$) one confirms

$$\frac{\partial^2 \Pi}{\partial x \, \partial \theta} = P_2 \left(\rho' - \frac{P_{22}}{P_2} \frac{1}{h} \right) \ge 0. \qquad \square$$

In Section 1.4 we showed that the optimal second-degree price discrimination may also exhibit bunching. Evidently, the fairly strong assumptions imposed in this section exclude bunching over a measurable set of types. However, if these assumptions are weakened, bunching occurs in some subsets of Θ. In that case, one must reintroduce the monotonicity constraint into the optimization program and preferably state it as an optimal-control problem. Optimal control is better suited to deal with such inequality constraints.[11]

9.6.2 Implementation by Nonlinear Pricing

At first glance the direct incentive-compatible sales plan discussed here seems hopelessly unrealistic. Have you ever seen a monopolist playing a direct revelation game with customers? Therefore, it is important to realize that the frequently observed second-degree price discrimination, where all customers are charged the same nonlinear price function – that makes payments exclusively a function of quantity – and are free to buy as much as they want, is nothing but a direct incentive-compatible sales plan in disguise.

Proposition 9.10 (Second-Degree Price Discrimination) *The optimal incentive-compatible sales plan is equivalent to second-degree price discrimination with the following nonlinear price function:*

$$\tilde{T}(x) := T(\phi(x)) = \int_0^x P(z; \phi(z)) \, dz, \qquad (9.43)$$

where $\phi(z)$ is the (generalized) inverse of $x(\theta)$:

$$\phi(z) := \min\{\theta \mid x(\theta) = z\}. \qquad (9.44)$$

Proof We apply a change of variables using the inverse function $\phi := x^{-1}$. That inverse exists, since $x(\theta)$ is monotone.

---

[11] In principle, one can also adapt the calculus of variations to deal with inequality constraints; but the procedure, due to Valentine, is cumbersome and hopelessly old-fashioned. See Pierre (1969), p. 95 ff.

Start from the optimal $T(\theta)$ function (9.33) using $U^*(0) = 0$, and employ the *change-of-variables theorem* [12]; after a few more manipulations one obtains

$$T(\phi(x)) = W(x; \phi(x)) - \int_0^x \frac{\partial W}{\partial \phi(z)}(z; \phi(z))\phi'(z)\, dz$$

$$= W(x; \phi(x)) - \int_0^x \left(\frac{\partial W}{\partial z}(z; \phi(z)) - \frac{\partial W}{\partial z}(z; \phi(z)) \right) dz$$

$$= \int_0^x \frac{\partial W}{\partial z}(z; \phi(z))\, dz$$

$$= \int_0^x P(z; \phi(z))\, dz,$$

as asserted.   □

An interesting follow-up problem is to look for necessary and sufficient conditions for the frequently observed quantity discounts in nonlinear pricing. Quantity discounts are equivalent to strict concavity of the price function $\tilde{T}(x)$.

9.7 Bibliographic Notes

One disturbing aspect of the screening model is the possible nonexistence of equilibrium. The literature has responded in two ways: One approach is to establish existence in a larger strategy space that admits mixed strategies (see Dasgupta and Maskin (1986) and Baye, Tian, and Zhou (1993)). The other is to consider modifications of the equilibrium concept (see C. Wilson (1977a) and Riley (1987)).

Another disturbing aspect of the screening model (and of all models presented in this Part of the book) is the restrictiveness of the stochastic order assumptions invoked here. One would like to know what remains if these strong assumptions do not hold. An important recent contribution to this issue, in the context of insurance, is Landsberger and Meilijson (1999).

The screening model assumes that the uninformed party makes the first move and offers the contract. An obvious alternative is to let the informed party offer the contract. This leads us to the signaling models presented in the next chapter.

We mention at this point that signaling models have radically different properties. This is another disturbing property. All these models are necessarily grand simplications of reality. However, if market outcomes are so sensitive to seemingly arbitrary modeling choices, one may be led to conclude that these contributions have little predictive ability (see Hellwig (1987)).

There are many applications of the adverse-selection and screening model. We just mention two contributions from the area of finance: the explanation of the bid-ask spread by Glosten and Milgrom (1985) and the analysis of security design by Rahi (1996).

---

[12] See Bartle (1976), p. 234, or in any other good calculus text.

10

Hidden Information and Signaling

He's a sheep in sheep's clothing.
Winston Churchill on Attlee

Oh, what a tangled web we weave,
When first we practice to deceive!
Sir Walter Scott

10.1 Introduction

Another market response to the problems of adverse selection is *signaling*. Here, the informed party makes a first move and attempts to reveal his or her private information by signaling his or her type. Regarding the labor-market application, we allow workers to signal their productivity with their educational achievements.

Signaling is also widespread outside the realm of education. For example, a joint stock company may issue debt instruments in lieu of equity in order to indicate to potential shareholders that the market underestimates its future earnings. Similarly, a firm may engage in costly advertising just in order to tell its customers or rivals that it is not a fly-by-night outfit. Or a monopolist may choose a high-cost product supply – despite forgone monopoly profits – just in order to warn potential entrants that they face a low-cost supplier (see Milgrom and Roberts (1982a, 1982b)). In animal populations, high-quality males may advertise their quality by displaying handicaps, such as a longer tail or brighter plumage, that make it more difficult to survive.[1]

In the following, we consider one particular signaling model, Spence's (1973) justly famous *job-market signaling*, and we state it explicitly as a noncooperative game. As it turns out, the analysis requires the employment of several advances in game theory. In particular, the presence of asymmetric information between workers and employers leads to a game with *incomplete information*, the timing of decisions and absence of commitment mechanisms to the application of the idea of *subgame perfectness*, the combination of both to the concept of a *sequential*

---

[1] In biology, the idea that cost might be associated with signals in order to ensure their honesty was proposed in the so-called *handicap principle*. See for example Grafen (1990).

Table 10.1. *Correlation between productivity and*
signaling cost

Type	Marginal revenue product	Cost of education	Prior probability
1	0	y	$1 - q_0$
2	1	$y/2$	q_0

equilibrium (introduced by Kreps and Wilson (1982)), and the plethora of sequential equilibria to the adoption of equilibrium *refinements*.

10.2 The Education Game

Suppose a worker may be either of *low* ability (*type 1*) or of *high* ability (*type 2*). The worker knows her talent; the employer does not. However, the worker can attempt to signal her ability by her educational achievement. This relationship becomes interesting because the employer has an incentive to deduce the worker's type from such a signal while the worker may have an incentive to mislead the employer.

Suppose type 2 occurs with probability $q_0 \in (0, 1)$, which is common knowledge. The worker chooses an education represented by an index $y \geq 0$ of educational achievement. Education does not affect a worker's productivity; however, ability is positively correlated with productivity and negatively with the cost of education, as summarized in Table 10.1.

After the worker has completed the education, two firms, compete over her services in Bertrand-competition fashion. Firms can observe the educational choice, but not the underlying type. Therefore, hiring involves a gamble. Each firm quotes a wage, and the worker picks the more attractive offer.

Altogether, there are four players: worker type 1, worker type 2, and the two identical firms a and b. The market game that they play is specified by the following sequence of rules, payoff functions, and equilibrium concept.

10.2.1 Rules of the Game

1. "Nature" draws the type (either 1 or 2), the worker learns her type, and nobody else does.
2. The worker chooses an education $y \geq 0$, which becomes common knowledge.[2]
3. Firms simultaneously make wage offers $w_i(y)$, $i \in \{a, b\}$, contingent upon the observation of y.
4. The worker observes wage offers and chooses the high-wage firm as employer; if $w_a(y) = w_b(y)$, the choice is determined by the flip of a fair coin.

---

[2] Implicitly this requires that workers can reliably commit themselves to a certain education. If educational achievement is interpreted as enrollment in a certain program, this kind of commitment is difficult to justify, simply because a student can always quit school. But in the absence of a commitment mechanism, the pooling equilibria described below break down: firms would hire students immediately after they have enrolled and thus sorted themselves – at a discount. But then, of course, all types would enroll, and hence the sorting would break down. This criticism was made by Weiss (1983).

10.2.2 Payoff Functions

All players maximize expected payoffs. The payoff to a type-n worker who chooses the education y is $w(y) - y/n$. In turn, a firm's payoff is equal to $(n-1) - w(y)$ if a type-n worker who chose education y is hired, and equal to zero if the firm fails to hire.

10.2.3 Subgame

By the rules of the game, firms cannot reliably precommit to a wage schedule prior to the worker's choice of education. Therefore, for given beliefs about workers' type there is a well-defined subgame: the price competition game between the two firms that compete over the services of a worker with given and known education.[3]

The solution of this subgame depends upon firms' beliefs concerning the relationship between observable education and unobservable types. Such beliefs are described by the probability function

$$q(y) := \Pr\{\text{worker is type } 2 \mid y\}, \qquad (10.1)$$

which gives the probability that the firm assigns to the worker's having type 2, conditional on observing the educational choice y.

Given beliefs, the subgame has a unique solution with the following properties:[4]

$$w_a(y) = w_b(y) = w(y) \qquad \text{(symmetric equilibrium)}, \qquad (10.2)$$

$$w(y) = q(y) \qquad \text{(zero expected profit)}. \qquad (10.3)$$

10.2.4 Sequential Equilibrium

The solution of the market game is the collection of strategies and beliefs that have the following properties:

- given equilibrium beliefs, the strategies have to be a subgame-perfect Nash equilibrium,
- given equilibrium strategies, beliefs have to be self-fulfilling.

We describe the solution by the functions (a_1, a_2, q, w_a, w_b), where $a_i(y)$ denotes the probability that type $i \in \{1, 2\}$ chooses action y, $q(y)$ denotes the probability that firms assign to the worker having type 2, conditional on observing y, and $w_j(y)$ denotes the wage firm $j \in \{a, b\}$ offers in this case. The first three functions have to be probabilities. In addition, (a_1, a_2, q, w_a, w_b) has to satisfy the equilibrium conditions (10.2), (10.3), and beliefs have to be consistent with equilibrium strategies. Using Bayes' rule, the consistency requirement can be written

---

[3] If firms can commit to a wage schedule prior to workers' choice of education, one obtains a screening game, as shown in Section 10.5.

[4] If a firm hires, its expected payoff is $q(y)1 + (1 - q(y))0 - w(y)$. Since we have Bertrand competition in the input market, the equilibrium expected payoff is equal to zero.

in the form

$$q(y) := \Pr\{\text{worker is type 2} \mid y\} \qquad (10.4)$$

$$= \frac{\Pr\{y \mid \text{worker is type 2}\} \Pr\{\text{worker is type 2}\}}{\Pr\{y\}} \qquad (10.5)$$

$$= \frac{a_2(y)q_0}{a_2(y)q_0 + a_1(y)(1 - q_0)} \qquad \text{(whenever possible)}. \qquad (10.6)$$

And, for given beliefs and wage schedules, the worker's best-reply requirements are

$$a_i(y) := \Pr\{\text{worker type } i \text{ chooses } y\} > 0$$

$$\Rightarrow \quad y \in \arg\max_{\tilde{y}} \left[w(\tilde{y}) - \frac{\tilde{y}}{i} \right]. \qquad (10.7)$$

Condition (10.4) requires that beliefs be consistent with Bayes' rule whenever the right-hand side is defined (that is, whenever y is chosen with positive probability). Condition (10.7) says that a worker of type i puts positive probability mass on action y only if that action is a maximizer of her payoff, given the wage schedule $w(y)$ and the belief system $q(y)$.

10.3 Equilibrium – Embarrassment of Riches

The signaling game has pure- as well as mixed-strategy equilibrium solutions. The disturbing part is that it admits an infinite number of such equilibria. We will now describe the different classes of equilibria and inquire into the reasons for this multiplicity.

There are two kinds of pure-strategy equilibria: *separating* (or *revealing*) and *pooling* (or *nonrevealing*) solutions. In a pooling equilibrium, both types of workers choose the same signal. Therefore, that signal does not reveal the underlying type of worker. In a separating equilibrium, different types choose different education, so that education is a perfect signal of the underlying type. Both kinds of equilibria occur.

Proposition 10.1 (Separating Equilibria) *The following strategies and beliefs are separating (or sorting) sequential equilibria:*

$$q(y) = \begin{cases} 1 & \text{if } y \geq y^*, \\ 0 & \text{if } y < y^* \end{cases} \quad \textit{(equilibrium beliefs)}, \qquad (10.8)$$

$$w_a(y) = w_b(y) = q(y) \quad \textit{(equilibrium wages)}, \qquad (10.9)$$

$$a_1(0) = 1 \quad \textit{(type 1 chooses } y = 0 \textit{ with certainty)}, \qquad (10.10)$$

$$a_2(y^*) = 1 \quad \textit{(type 1 chooses } y = y^* \textit{ with certainty)}, \qquad (10.11)$$

$$y^* \in [1, 2] \quad \textit{(equilibrium threshold)}. \qquad (10.12)$$

Proof The proof is straightforward.

Take the beliefs (10.8) as given. Then the action $y = 0$ is type 1's best reply to the wage schedule (10.9), since type 1 cannot raise her payoff by choosing any other y. Similar reasoning applies to type 2. In turn, the firms' wage schedule is the best reply to workers' choice of education (10.10), (10.11), and they are a solution of the price competition subgame because they satisfy conditions (10.2) and (10.3).

Take the equilibrium strategies as given. Since type 1 chooses $y = 0$ and type 2 chooses $y = y^*$, the beliefs (10.8) are self-fulfilling. Hence, (10.8)–(10.12) are a separating sequential equilibrium. □

Since the threshold level y^* can assume any value between 1 and 2, there are an infinite number of such separating equilibria. However, since firms have no benefit from raising type 2's cost of education above level 1, these equilibria can be ranked by the Pareto criterion. The unique Pareto-dominant (or efficient) separating sequential equilibrium is obtained by setting $y^* = 1$.

Proposition 10.2 (Pooling Equilibria) *The following strategies and beliefs are sequential equilibria with the pooling property:*

$$q(y) = \begin{cases} q_0 & \text{if } y = y^*, \\ 0 & \text{if } y \neq y^*, \end{cases} \tag{10.13}$$

$$w_a(y) = w_b(y) = q(y), \tag{10.14}$$

$$a_1(y^*) = a_2(y^*) = 1, \tag{10.15}$$

$$y^* \in [0, q_0]. \tag{10.16}$$

Proof The proof is left as an exercise. □

Again, there are an infinite number of such pooling equilibria, and the unique Pareto-dominant (or efficient) pooling equilibrium is obtained for $y^* = 0$.

In addition to the plethora of pure-strategy equilibria, the game has also equilibria in mixed strategies where type 1 mimics type 2 with positive probability less than one. It is appropriate to refer to them as *hybrid* equilibria. Hybrid equilibria are supported by the following strategies and beliefs: firms set a threshold level $y^* \in (q_0, 1)$; type 1 randomizes over the educational choices $y \in \{0, y^*\}$; and type 2 chooses y^* with certainty.

Proposition 10.3 (Hybrid Equilibria) *The following strategies and beliefs are sequential equilibria where type 1 mimics type 2 with positive probability less than one:*

$$q(y) = \begin{cases} y^* & \text{if } y = y^*, \\ 0 & \text{if } y \neq y^*, \end{cases} \tag{10.17}$$

$$w_a(y) = w_b(y) = q(y), \tag{10.18}$$

Table 10.2. *Equilibrium payoffs for different threshold levels y^**

Player	Pooling $y^* \in [0, q_0]$	Hybrid $y^* \in (q_0, 1)$	Separating $y^* \in [1, 2]$
1	$q_0 - y^*$	0	0
2	$q_0 - y^*/2$	$y^*/2$	$1 - y^*/2$
Firms	0	0	0

$$a_1(y^*) = \frac{q^0}{1 - q_0} \frac{1 - y^*}{y^*}, \qquad a_1(0) = 1 - a_1(y^*), \tag{10.19}$$

$$a_2(y^*) = 1, \tag{10.20}$$

$$y^* \in (q_0, 1). \tag{10.21}$$

Proof The proof is in three steps:

1. First, type 1's asserted equilibrium strategy is obviously optimal, given $w(y)$ and $q(y)$, since the two actions over which type 1 is supposed to randomize, $y = 0$ and $y = y^*$, yield the same payoff and no other actions are superior. Thus, $a_1(y^*) \in (0, 1) \iff y^* \in (q_0, 1)$.
2. Similarly, type 2's asserted equilibrium action y^* is obviously optimal, given $w(y)$ and $q(y)$.
3. Finally, beliefs are consistent with equilibrium strategies, since by (10.4),

$$q(y^*) = \frac{a_2(y^*)q_0}{a_2(y^*)q_0 + a_1(y^*)(1 - q_0)} = y^* \tag{10.22}$$

and $q(0) = 0$. □

Again, there are an infinite number of such hybrid equilibria, and the unique Pareto-dominant hybrid equilibrium is obtained by setting $y^* = 1$.

Summary The complete set of equilibria is summarized in Table 10.2. Also note that the efficient pooling equilibrium with the threshold level $y^* = 0$ is the unique Pareto-dominant equilibrium, provided type 2 is sufficiently predominant (the exact condition is $q_0 > \frac{1}{2}$). However, if type 2 is rare ($q_0 \leq \frac{1}{2}$), equilibrium selection poses a conflict of interest: Type 2 then prefers the efficient separating equilibrium ($y^* = 1$), whereas type 1 prefers pooling, as always.

10.4 Equilibrium Selection: Intuitive Criterion*

Why does the signaling game admit so many solutions? The cause of this multi-plicity is that the concept of sequential equilibrium does not restrict firms' beliefs concerning all those educational choices that do not occur if workers stick to their corresponding equilibrium strategies. This comes out most clearly in the above pooling equilibria. Here firms can entertain fairly arbitrary beliefs as long as the threshold level y^* is so low that the inference to be drawn from observing any reasonable educational choice $y \neq y^*$ is never put to a test, because no one ever chooses any education $y \neq y^*$ when firms are assumed to stick to the beliefs underlying that pooling equilibrium. The question then is: Can one somehow restrict admissible beliefs and thereby arrive at a unique equilibrium? This leads us to consider refinements of the sequential equilibrium, in particular Pareto dominance and the so-called intuitive criterion.

The *intuitive criterion* was proposed by Cho and Kreps (1987) (see also van Damme (1987, pp. 289–293)). It weeds out all equilibria except the best separating equilibrium with $y^* = 1$. However, its application is only convincing if $q_0 \leq \frac{1}{2}$. For $q_0 > \frac{1}{2}$ the criterion is not "intuitive," to say the least. In turn, Pareto dominance applies only when the intuitive criterion is not meaningful (that is when $q_0 > \frac{1}{2}$), in which case it selects the best pooling equilibrium with $y^* = 0$.

10.4.1 The Criterion When Type 2 Is Rare

The intuitive criterion is best explained by the following hypothetical events and dialog, assuming $q_0 \leq \frac{1}{2}$: Suppose players consider to play a particular pooling equilibrium with some threshold level $y^* \in [0, q_0]$. Now, let something unexpected happen: One worker chooses education $y \in [1, 2]$ in the expectation that she can convince firms to revise their pessimistic assessment, recognize her as type 2, and pay $w(y) = 1$.

As an illustrative device, suppose the worker who chose $y \in [1, 2]$ addresses firms with the following speech in order to convince them to change their pessimistic assessment:

Speech 1 (Worker): Look, I have worked hard in school, and acquired the education $y \in [1, 2]$, because I was sure this would identify me as the type 2 who I really am. Surely, I would not have done this if I were type 1.

Firms are not so easily convinced and respond:

Speech 2 (Firm): Your point is well taken. We can see that your choice of action raises your payoff if we follow your advice and recognize you as the type 2 who you claim to be. While this indicates that you make this speech if you are type 2, how can we be assured that you are not type 1 in disguise?

Finally, the worker puts all remaining doubts to rest with the following reply:

Speech 3 (Worker): If I were type 1, I would earn the payoff $q_0 - y^* > 0$ if I did not attempt to revise your beliefs; this is more than what I earn if my attempt is successful $(1 - y \leq 0)$. Therefore, you can safely exclude that I am type 1 and recognize me as the type 2 who I am.

Stated more formally, the intuitive criterion requires:

Definition 10.1 (Intuitive Criterion) Consider an equilibrium and associated belief system. The belief system satisfies the intuitive criterion if, for all out-of-equilibrium actions y, it puts zero probability on that type who is sure to lose by taking this action y, relative to that type's payoff in the assumed equilibrium.

All pooling equilibria evidently violate the intuitive criterion because they fail to rule that $q(y) = 1$ for all $y \in [1, 2]$.

At this point you probably wonder where and how it matters whether the probability q_0 is smaller or greater than $\frac{1}{2}$. Recall: So far we have assumed that $q_0 < \frac{1}{2}$. This played a role in showing that type 2 does indeed gain if she makes that speech and is able to convince firms to revise their beliefs accordingly.

10.4.2 The Criterion When Type 1 Is Rare

Now suppose $q_0 \geq \frac{1}{2}$ and consider the efficient pooling equilibrium, with threshold level $y^* = 0$. Then it is still true that the speech would never make sense if the worker were type 1; but (and this is the catch) it would not make sense for type 2 either.

Clearly, it would not make sense to choose $y \geq 1$ and make the speech, not even for type 2. Check this. However, type 2 might choose either $y \in (q_0, 1)$ (the education that is supported by a mixed-strategy equilibrium) or $y \in (0, q_0)$, $y \neq y^*$ (the education supported by other pooling equilibria). Does that make sense?

At first glance, it seems that one can find an out-of-equilibrium y at which the above dialog applies. Consider $\hat{y} := 1 - q_0 + \epsilon$, with $\epsilon > 0$ and small. Then type 2 is better off choosing that $\hat{y}$ than in the best pooling equilibrium, if firms recognize her as type 2 with certainty:[5]

$$1 - \frac{1}{2}\hat{y} = 1 - \frac{1}{2}(1 - q_0 + \epsilon) > q_0. \tag{10.23}$$

At the same time, type 1 would definitely be worse off if she chose $\hat{y}$, even if she were identified as type 2 with certainty, because

$$1 - \hat{y} = 1 - (1 - q_0 + \epsilon) = q_0 - \epsilon < q_0. \tag{10.24}$$

Therefore, we can summarize:

Proposition 10.4 (Equilibrium Selection) *The intuitive criterion rules out all pooling equilibria, regardless of q_0.*

However, the intuitive criterion is not compelling if $q_0 \geq \frac{1}{2}$. For firms could never believe that they face type 2 *with certainty* if $y \in (1 - q_0, 1)$ is observed. Indeed, if $q_0 \geq \frac{1}{2}$, all educational choices $y \in (1 - q_0, 1)$ are only consistent with either a pooling or a mixed-strategy equilibrium.

In other words, if the worker chose the action $y = 1 - q_0 + \epsilon$ and made a speech similar to the above, firms should counter along the following lines:

Speech 4 (Firm): Your argument sounds all right. However, as you must also know, in equilibrium I will never believe that anybody who chooses $y \in (1 - q_0, q_0)$ is type 2 with

[5] Proof: 1) Type 2 is already better off if she chooses $y' := 1 - q_0$, provided she is recognized as type 2 with certainty, because $1 - \frac{1}{2}y' > 1 - y' = 1 - (1 - q_0) = q_0$. 2) Of course, this inequality is preserved if y is slightly increased from $y' = 1 - q_0$ to $\hat{y} = 1 - q_0 + \epsilon$.

certainty. And if instead I use the equilibrium belief that corresponds to your choice of y, then I cannot see how you could benefit from choosing this action. Therefore, your action leaves me confused – not convinced.

We conclude that the intuitive criterion is successful in weeding out pooling equilibria, but it should only be applied if $q_0 < \frac{1}{2}$.

Also notice that one can meaningfully employ either the intuitive criterion or the criterion of Pareto dominance to weed out all separating equilibria except the efficient one with the threshold level $y^* = 1$. This is left as an exercise.

10.5 Screening vs. Signaling

In the introduction to this chapter, we indicated that in a signaling game the informed party makes the first move, whereas in a screening game the uninformed party is the first mover. This suggests that by reversing the sequence of moves one should always be able to transform a signaling problem into a screening problem, and vice versa.

In this vein, let us modify the signaling game from Section 10.4. Suppose firms make the first move and offer the worker a menu of contracts

$$C = \{(w_1, y_1), (w_2, y_2)\}. \tag{10.25}$$

Then each type of worker chooses the best contract, if any. Both contracts are declined only if the worker's payoff is negative. Firms compete by means of contracts, and in equilibrium they earn zero expected profits.

The equilibrium contract is either *pooling* (only one contract is offered) or *separating* (each type is induced to choose a different contract). The question is: Which case occurs in equilibrium, and when does an equilibrium exist at all?

Since we have already treated screening games, the analysis can be performed quickly with the help of two simple diagrams.

In a first step, we establish that pooling contracts cannot be part of an equilibrium. For this purpose, look at Figure 10.1. Suppose, *per absurdum,* that firms offer a pooling contract. Such a contract would have to yield zero profits, as at point C of this diagram. But if one firm offers C, it follows immediately that the other firm could gain by offering a contract from the shaded area in Figure 10.1. For such a contract would only attract type 2 workers and give rise to a positive profit.

If the equilibrium contract cannot be pooling, either it must be separating, or no equilibrium exists at all. Suppose it is separating. Then the equilibrium contracts must be represented by the points (w_1, y_1), (w_2, y_2) in Figure 10.2. For these are the only contracts that induce self-selection and give rise to zero expected profits. If q_0 is sufficiently small (the precise condition is $q_0 \leq \frac{1}{2}$), such an equilibrium does exist. However, if type 1 is sufficiently rare (the precise condition is $q_0 > \frac{1}{2}$), the separating contract cannot be an equilibrium either. For if one firm offers it, the other can gain by offering a pooling contract from the shaded area in Figure 10.2, which attracts both types, and yet earns a positive expected profit.

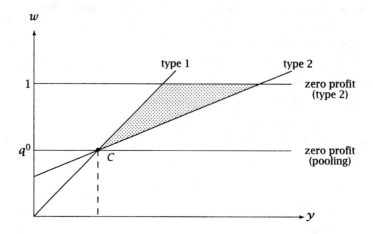

Figure 10.1. Pooling Contracts Cannot Occur in Equilibrium.

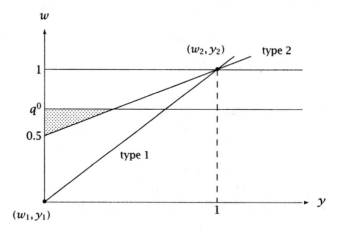

Figure 10.2. Nonexistence of Equilibrium When $q_0 > \frac{1}{2}$.

We have thus shown that the signaling game can be transformed into a screening game. That screening game has a unique (separating-contract) solution whenever it is plausible to apply the intuitive criterion in order to select a unique (separating) equilibrium in the associated signaling game. Yet, for all values of the parameter q_0 where it is not plausible to let the intuitive criterion select an equilibrium in the signaling game, the associated screening game does not even have an equilibrium.

10.6 Bibliographic Notes

We mention that the equilibrium refinements discussed in this chapter fail to accomplish a unique prediction if there are more than two types of workers. For an account of the stronger requirements that need to be invoked in this case see Fudenberg and Tirole (1991).

There are many other applications of signaling besides education, insurance, and labor. Some other examples from the literature are *warranties* (Grossman (1981), Emons (1988, 1989)), *delay in bargaining* (Admati and Perry (1987)), *limit pricing* (Milgrom and Roberts (1982a, 1982b)), and *jump bidding* in auctions (Fishman (1988)).

Finally, we mention that costless signals, called *cheap talk*, may also affect equilibrium selection if a coordination-game aspect is present (see Farrell (1987) and Crawford and Sobel (1982)).

11

Hidden Action and Moral Hazard

If you want something done right, do it yourself.
Benjamin Franklin

"Sorry to hear about the fire, Joe."
"Ssh – it's tomorrow."
Anonymous

11.1 Introduction

In the previous two chapters we analyzed market relationships when, at the time of contracting, one party has private information concerning the quality of the traded good. Now we turn to bilateral contracting problems when relevant private information is expected to emerge *after* contracts have been signed. This problem has been named the problem of *postcontractual opportunism*, or simply the *principal–agent problem*.

Postcontractual opportunism is endemic to relationships that involve the delegation of activities to another party. The prototypical example is the employment relationship, where a person called the *principal* hires another person to act as his or her *agent*. But there is an abundance of other applications. For example, a principal–agent relationship exists between a landowner and a farmer, a car owner and her no-fault insurer, a doctor and her patient, a lawyer and her client, a borrower and a lender, and a regulator and a public utility, to name just a few.

It is useful to distinguish between two kinds of informational asymmetries that may emerge in a principal–agent relationship: *hidden information* and *hidden action*. If a manager is put in charge of sales, in the process of doing his job he typically acquires a better understanding of the firm's market; thus, he acquires private or hidden information.[1] Similarly, if a saleswoman is assigned to sell the firm's products in a certain region, her employer cannot observe precisely how much diligence she put into her job; hence, the principal–agent relationship involves a hidden-action aspect.

---

[1] Other examples are: the relationship between the branches of large firms, between public utilities and the regulator, or between citizens and the tax authorities.

Hidden action is also known as the *moral-hazard* problem. This characterization has its origin in the insurance literature, where it describes the hazards, additional to the risk covered by the insurance, that are due to the lack of precaution induced by insurance.

In the present chapter we focus on the hidden-action version of the principal–agent model. The hidden-information model is ignored, since it is closely related to the adverse-selection problems, which were already covered in Chapter 9.

Two variations of the hidden-action model are distinguished:

1. The contracting between a risk-neutral principal and a risk-averse agent under unlimited liability (covered in Section 11.2);
2. The contracting between a risk-neutral principal and risk-neutral agent who is subject to limited liability (covered in Section 11.3).

In addition we discuss the *renegotiation problem* and possible solutions (Section 11.4).

The particular issues of contracting between *one* principal and *several* agents are addressed in Chapter 12.

11.2 Risk Aversion and Incentives

The most frequently used hidden-action model analyzes the contracting relationship between a risk-neutral principal and a risk-averse agent under unlimited liability. This model offers a framework to analyze the trade-off between the efficient risk allocation and effort incentives and to show why implementing high effort makes it necessary to expose the agent to some income risk (coinsurance).

Consider, for a moment, the contracting problem when both parties are risk-neutral and subject to unlimited liability. Then, the contracting problem has a simple solution: The principal offers a *franchise contract* that "leases" the job to the agent in exchange for a fixed rental fee. This contract exposes the agent to high income risk, while it fully insures the principal's income. But since the agent is risk-neutral, he does not mind taking that risk. The advantage of this contract is that it sets full-powered effort incentives. The private and social marginal benefits of effort coincide when the agent is made into a residual claimant who collects the entire surplus (net after deducting of a fixed rental fee). Therefore, if the agent is risk-neutral, the contracting problem has a trivial solution, and there is no trade-off between efficient risk allocation and effort incentives. Such a trade-off occurs only if the agent cares about risk or if limited-liability considerations preclude efficient incentive schemes.

11.2.1 A Simple Model

We start with a simple 2×2 model, with two states and two effort levels, that gives some basic insight without a great deal of technicalities. In terms of tools and procedures, this model is quite similar to the analysis of insurance and screening in Section 9.5.1. If you have read that section carefully, you may just skim through these pages until you reach the general analysis in Section 11.2.2.

Consider a risk-neutral principal who may hire a risk-averse agent (from a pool of potential agents).[2] If a contract is signed, the agent performs a certain task and chooses an action from the action set $\{a_\ell, a_h\}$, $a_h > a_\ell$, where h and ℓ are mnemonic for *high* and *low*. The agent's action is his private or hidden information. The principal earns a random output or revenue $Y \in \{y_g, y_b\}$, $y_g > y_b$, where g and b represent the *good* and the *bad* state of nature, respectively. The agent's choice of effort affects the probability distribution of Y, but the support is the same for all actions. In particular, high effort gives rise to a higher probability of the good state output y_g. Denoting the conditional probability of $Y = y_g$, conditional on the choice of effort a_i, by p_i, $i \in h, \ell$, it is assumed that $1 > p_h > p_\ell > 0$.

Rules of the Game

1. The principal offers a complete contract, $C = \{w_g, w_b, a_i\}$, that stipulates the agent's effort and remuneration, contingent upon the state realization $i \in \{h, \ell\}$.
2. The agent either accepts or rejects the contract; rejection earns him the reservation utility $\bar{u}$.
3. If the agent accepts, he exerts effort, either high (h) or low (ℓ).
4. Nature draws either the *good* (g) or the *bad* (b) state, with probability p_i or $1 - p_i$, respectively, that drawing becomes common knowledge, payments are made, and the market game is over.

Payoffs and Marginal Rates of Substitution

The expected utility of the agent who accepts the contract C and exerts effort a_i is

$$U(a_i) := p_i u(w_g) + (1 - p_i)u(w_b) - c(a_i), \qquad i \in \{h, \ell\}$$

where u is a strictly concave function (risk aversion). And the associated expected utility of the principal is

$$\Pi_i := p_i(y_g - w_g) + (1 - p_i)(y_b - w_b), \qquad i \in \{h, \ell\}.$$

Therefore, the marginal rates of substitution (MRS) are, for $i \in \{h, \ell\}$,

$$-\frac{dw_b}{dw_g}\bigg|_{U(a_i)=\text{const}} = \frac{p_i}{1 - p_i}\frac{u'(w_g)}{u'(w_b)},$$

$$-\frac{dw_b}{dw_g}\bigg|_{\Pi_i=\text{const}} = \frac{p_i}{1 - p_i}.$$

Since $p_h > p_\ell$, the MRS of the high-effort agent is always higher than that of the low-effort agent. In words, the agent who exerts effort a_h is willing to forgo more wealth in the bad state b in exchange for obtaining one extra dollar in the good state g because the event in which this extra dollar is forthcoming occurs

---

[2] The risk neutrality of the principal reflects the possibilities of diversification of financial assets; the risk aversion of the agent reflects the fact it is difficult to diversify human capital.

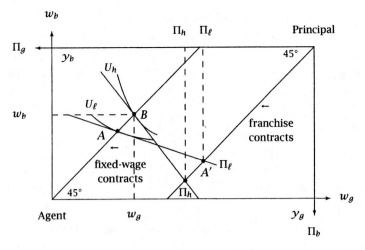

Figure 11.1. Efficient Allocation.

with higher probability. Similarly, the principal's MRS is higher if he deals with a high-effort agent. These are the *single-crossing* properties that you came across already in several places in this book.

Efficiency and the Optimal Contract under Complete Information

An efficient allocation is fully characterized by three requirements:

1. The MRSs of principal and agent are equal.
2. The agent earns his reservation expected utility: $U(a_i) = \bar{u}$.
3. The agent's effort a_i maximizes the principal's expected utility.

An immediate implication of the MRS condition is that marginal utilities must be the same across states: $u'_g = u'_b$. Hence, efficient wages are state-independent ($w_g = w_b$), i.e., the principal offers full income insurance to the agent.[3]

The Edgeworth box diagram in Figure 11.1 offers a useful illustration of the efficient allocation. There, the U_h and U_ℓ curves represent the agent's indifference curves that assure the reservation expected utility $\bar{u}$. Similarly, the Π_h and Π_ℓ curves represent the principal's indifference curves if the agent exerts high and low effort, respectively. The marginal rates of substitution of principal and agent are the same on the *fixed-wage contracts* line, whereas the principal's expected profits Π_h, Π_ℓ can be read from the intersection of the principal's indifference curves with the *franchise contracts* line. Evidently, in this illustration one has $\Pi_h > \Pi_\ell$. Therefore, in this case a_h is the principal's best choice and the optimal allocation is as follows:

$$a = a_h, \qquad w_g = w_b, \qquad U_h = \bar{u}, \qquad \Pi = \Pi_h.$$

---

[3] It is often overlooked that the full-insurance property is an artifact of the assumed additive separability of the utility. With more general utility functions, equality of the MRSs entails either over- or underinsurance, depending upon the income elasticity of the supply of effort; for a full characterization of the optimal risk allocation see Brown and Wolfstetter (1985).

If the principal could observe the agent's effort, the efficient risk allocation would also be prescribed by the optimal contract. However, since the principal cannot observe effort, the provision of complete insurance to the agent destroys effort incentives. Indeed, if the agent is offered the (first best) efficient contract, he will shirk and exert only the low effort. Therefore, the principal has to deviate from the (first best) efficient contract, and either settle with low effort and maintain full income insurance or give up full income insurance and implement high effort.

The Optimal Contract under Hidden Action

It is useful to decompose the search for the optimal contract under hidden action into two steps:

1. find the optimal wage schedule $\{w_h, w_\ell\}$; that implements a given action a_i at the lowest expected wage cost;
2. find the action that maximizes the expected profit, given the cost of implementation determined in step 1.

Obviously, if he wants to implement the lowest action a_ℓ, the principal minimizes the cost of implementing that action by offering the expected utility $\bar{u}$ combined with full income insurance, as in the efficient allocation (see point A in Figure 11.1). The intuition is straightforward: start with another wage scheme on the same indifference curve of the low-effort agent. Then the principal can lower the average wage and still keep the agent indifferent by offering a smoother income profile. The lowest expected wage is reached at the point of full income insurance.

However, if one wants to implement the high-effort action a_h, full income insurance (as in point B of Figure 11.1) is not feasible, because if full income insurance is offered, the agent shirks and exerts only low effort a_ℓ. It follows that implementation of the high effort is only possible by exposing the agent to some income risk in the form of paying him more in the good than in the bad state of nature.

The intuition for this necessity of income risk is straightforward. If one increases pay in the good state by a certain amount, the high-effort agent is willing to give up more income in the bad state than the low-effort agent, simply because high effort reduces the probability with which the bad state occurs.[4] Therefore, if one moves sufficiently far along the indifference curve U_h towards the right, one can induce the agent to work hard, and thus implement a_h.

In Figure 11.2 the shaded area represents all wage schedules $\{w_h, w_\ell\}$ that implement a_h, because there the agent earns his reservation expected utility or more and prefers high effort. The least-cost implementation of a_h is reached at point B, where the two indifference curves U_h, U_ℓ and the principal's indifference curve Π'_h all intersect.[5]

Finally, which effort should be implemented? Evidently, in Figure 11.2 the high effort is optimal for the principal, since $\Pi'_h > \Pi_\ell$, even though the presence of hidden action lowers the expected profit from Π_h to Π'_h.

---

[4] Of course, this is really the meaning of the assumed single crossing of the MRSs.

[5] Make sure that you see why all other points in the shaded area give rise to a lower expected profit, given $a = a_h$.

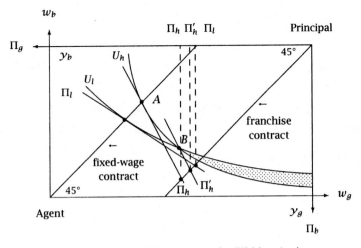

Figure 11.2. Optimal Contract under Hidden Action.

However, the optimality of a_h can easily be turned around. As an exercise, just play with Figure 11.2 and make high effort less attractive by lowering the parameter y_g. Then, the ranking of expected profits can be turned around and from some point onwards the low-effort fixed-wage contract is optimal.

Example 11.1 Suppose $U(w, a) := \sqrt{w} - a^2$, $a_h = 2$, $a_\ell = 1$, $p_h = 0.5$, $p_\ell = 0.25$, $\bar{u} = 2$. Then, the optimal contracts implementing a_h and a_ℓ are respectively

$$w_g = w_b = 9 \quad \text{(optimal contract implementing } a_\ell), \quad (11.1)$$

$$w_g = 144, \quad w_b = 0 \quad \text{(optimal contract implementing } a_h). \quad (11.2)$$

The associated maximum expected profits of the principal are .

$$\Pi(a_h) = 0.5(y_g + y_b - 144), \quad (11.3)$$

$$\Pi(a_\ell) = 0.25y_g + 0.75y_b - 9. \quad (11.4)$$

Therefore, it is optimal to implement a_h using contract (11.2) if and only if $y_g \geq y_b + 252$.

Digression: The Linear Principal–Agent Model*

Here we digress briefly and describe a simple version of the hidden-action principal–agent model, which we refer to as the *linear model*. This model is sometimes used in the literature, and it plays an important role in the extension to *multitask problems* by Holmstrom and Milgrom (1987, 1990, 1991).

The key assumptions of the linear model are[6]:

1. Linearity of agent's wage in output: $W = w_0 + sX$.
2. Linear production function with additive noise Y: $X = a + Y$.
3. Normal distribution: Y is normally distributed with mean zero and finite variance σ^2.

---

[6] What makes these assumption special and somewhat unappealing?

4. Constant risk aversion: the agent has a constant-absolute-risk-aversion utility function $U(W, a) := u(W) - \frac{1}{2}a^2$ with $u(W) := -e^{-rW}$, where $r > 0$ is the absolute degree of risk aversion. The agent's reservation utility is normalized to zero.

5. The action variable is continuous: the agent chooses from a real-valued interval of possible action levels.

Note that the wage is made conditional on output rather than on the signal. Of course, since output is monotone in Y, the choice of format does not matter.

Proposition 11.1 (Linear PA Model) *The linear principal–agent model has the following solution:*

$$a^*(s) = s, \tag{11.5}$$

$$s^* = \frac{1}{1 + r\sigma^2}, \qquad w_0^* = \frac{r\sigma^2 - 1}{2(r\sigma^2 + 1)^2}, \tag{11.6}$$

$$U^* = 0, \qquad \Pi^* = \frac{1}{2(1 + r\sigma^2)}. \tag{11.7}$$

Proof If a random variable is normally distributed, its linear transformation is also normally distributed. $W = (a+Y)s + w_0$ is a linear transformation of Y. Therefore, W is normally distributed.[7]

By a well-known formula, the assumption of constant absolute risk aversion, combined with a normal distribution, implies the following *certainty equivalent* of W, denoted by $\hat{w}$:[8]

$$u(\hat{w}) = E[u(W)] \iff \hat{w} = \mu_w - \frac{r}{2}\sigma_w^2,$$

where μ_w is the mean and σ_w^2 the variance of W.

Due to the assumed linearity of the sharing rule,

$$\mu_w = w_0 + sa, \qquad \sigma_w^2 = s^2\sigma^2.$$

Therefore, the agent's expected utility, $U(a) := E[u(W)] - \frac{1}{2}a^2$, is

$$U(a) = \hat{w} - \frac{1}{2}a^2$$

$$= w_0 + sa - \frac{r}{2}s^2\sigma^2 - \frac{1}{2}a^2.$$

Given the contract (s, w_0), the agent solves $\max_a U(a)$, which gives

$$a^*(s) = s.$$

The principal anticipates the agent's choice of action, computes the reduced-form expected profit function, and solves the optimal contract (s^*, w_0^*). The principal's profit is $\pi(a, s, w_0, Y) := (a + Y)(1 - s) - w_0$. Therefore, the reduced-form expected profit function is

$$\pi^*(s, w_0) := E[\pi(a^*(s), s, w_0, Y)] = s(1 - s) - w_0.$$

---

[7] Of course, if $s = 0$ the wage is no longer random.
[8] Consult (R14) in Appendix D (Section D.4.3), where this rule is stated and proved.

Given s, the principal sets the smallest w_0 that assures participation by the principal; therefore,

$$w_0(s) = \frac{1}{2}s^2(r\sigma^2 - 1).$$

Finally, the principal solves $\max_s \pi^*(s, w_0^*(s))$, which gives

$$s^* = \frac{1}{1 + r\sigma^2}$$

$$w_0^* = \frac{r\sigma^2 - 1}{2(r\sigma^2 + 1)^2}.$$

and the principal's equilibrium payoff $\Pi^* := \pi^*(s^*, w_0(s^*))$ follows immediately.

□

Note that the principal prefers more noise in the production technology (a higher σ^2), and he prefers to deal with a more risk-averse agent (a higher r). This is due to the fact that the principal's source of income is insurance.

Essentially, the principal trades a risky lottery for a less risky one. In exchange he collects an insurance premium. Of course, that premium is increasing in the agent's measure of risk aversion, r, and in the measure of risk, σ^2.

If there were competition among principals for the services of the agent, the entire gain from trade would go to the agent, and the entire gain relative to autarky would be the agent's benefit from obtaining insurance. Of course, insurance is limited due to moral hazard.

This concludes the digression on the linear model with a continuum of actions.

11.2.2 Generalization

We now return to the main theme, and generalize the simple 2×2 model from Section 11.2.1. In particular, we allow for more than two actions and more than two states. The main objective is to give a general account of the optimal implementation of a given action, and to find sufficient conditions for the monotonicity of the associated wage schedule.[9]

Assumptions

We maintain the assumptions of Section 11.2.1 except that we permit $n \geq 2$ states of nature and $m \geq 2$ action levels. However, we also add some assumptions concerning the probability distribution of events. As we show, these assumptions are sufficient for the monotonicity of the wage schedule.

After the agent has exerted effort, both principal and agent observe a real-valued signal $Y \in \{y_1, \ldots, y_n\}$, $n \geq 2$, which may be interpreted as output or revenue, drawn from a family of probability distributions $\{p_s(a_i), \ i = 1, \ldots, m, \ s = 1, \ldots, n\}$ with the following properties:

[9] The presentation follows the seminal paper by Grossman and Hart (1983) and adopts some simplifications due to Kreps (1990, Chapter 16).

Assumption 11.1 (Full Support) The (conditional) probability distribution $p_s(a_i)$:= $\Pr\{Y = y_s \mid a_i\}$ is positive for all s and i, and twice continuously differentiable in a_i.

Assumption 11.2 (MLRC) Higher effort gives rise to a stochastically larger signal in the sense of the monotone likelihood-ratio condition:[10]

$$a_i > a_j, \quad s > r \quad \Rightarrow \quad \frac{p_s(a_i)}{p_s(a_j)} \geq \frac{p_r(a_i)}{p_r(a_j)}. \tag{11.8}$$

Assumption 11.3 (CDFC) The cumulative probability distribution of Y,

$$P_r(a_i) := \sum_{s=1}^{r} p_s(a_i), \tag{11.9}$$

is convex in a_i for all $s = 1, \ldots, n$ and $i = 1, \ldots, m$ ("convexity-of-the-distribution-function condition").

Interpretation

If the family of probability distributions p_{si} satisfies the MLRC, it also satisfies the first-order stochastic dominance FSD relationships:[11]

$$a_i > a_r \quad \Rightarrow \quad P_r(a_i) \leq P_r(a_j) \quad \forall r = 1, \ldots, n.$$

In words, higher effort gives rise to a stochastically larger random signal. Note, however, that FSD does not also imply the MLRC; therefore, the MLRC is stronger than the already restrictive FSD relationship.

In contrast, the CDFC says that an increase in effort has a negative but increasing marginal impact on the probability of low outcomes. Equivalently, it says that higher effort has a positive but decreasing marginal impact on the probability of high outcomes. Essentially, this is a "law of return" (diminishing marginal product) assumption.

Optimal Contract

Denote the agent's expected utility for a given contract $C = \{w_1, \ldots, w_n, a_i\}$ by

$$U(a_i) := \sum_{s=1}^{n} p_s(a_i)u(w_s) - c(a_i). \tag{11.10}$$

Then the optimal contract offered by the principal maximizes his expected payoff subject to the following *participation* and *incentive constraints*:

$$\max_{\{w_s, a_i\}} \sum_{s=1}^{n} p_s(a_i)\,(y_s - w_s) \tag{P}$$

s.t. $U(a_i) \geq \bar{u}$ (participation constraint),

$\quad\quad U(a_i) \geq U(a_j) \quad \forall j = 1, \ldots, n$ (incentive constraints).

---

[10] For some useful relationships between the MLRC and FSD, you may wish to go back to Section 4.3.3 in the chapter on stochastic-dominance theory.

[11] Consult the chapter on stochastic dominance, in particular Proposition 4.3 in Section 4.3.3.

The participation constraint is imposed because the agent must be induced to sign the contract voluntarily (market transactions are voluntary). And the incentive constraints are due to the revelation principle. That principle says that one can restrict attention to incentive-compatible contracts (i.e., contracts that satisfy the incentive constraints), because the equilibrium payoffs of a game induced by a contract that is not incentive-compatible can be replicated by an incentive-compatible contract.[12]

Following Grossman and Hart (1983), it is convenient to decompose the solution of program (P) into 1) the solution of the expected-wage-cost-minimizing implementation of a given effort and 2) the choice of the effort level that maximizes the reduced-form expected-profit function.[13] In the following we concentrate on optimal implementation and provide sufficient conditions for the monotonicity of the associated optimal wage schedule.

Optimal Implementation of a Given Action

The contract that implements a given effort level a_i at the lowest possible expected wage cost solves the following concave maximization problem (note how minimization of expected wage costs has been transformed into a maximization problem):

$$\max_{\{w_s\}} - \sum_{s=1}^{n} p_s(a_i) w_s \qquad \text{(P1)}$$

s.t. $U(a_i) \geq \bar{u}$ (participation constraint),

$\quad U(a_i) \geq U(a_j) \quad \forall j = 1, \ldots, m$ (incentive constraints).

The associated first-order conditions are

$$\frac{1}{u'(w_s)} = \lambda + \sum_{j=1}^{m} \mu_j \left(1 - \frac{p_s(a_j)}{p_s(a_i)}\right), \qquad s = 1, \ldots, n. \qquad (11.11)$$

We now come to the main result:

Proposition 11.2 (Montonicity) *The optimal wage schedule implementing the action a_i, is monotone nondecreasing:* $w_n \geq w_{n-1} \geq \cdots \geq w_1$.

Proof Suppose, for the moment, that incentive constraints are binding only "downwards," i.e., $\mu_j > 0$ for some $j < i$ and $\mu_j = 0$ for all $j > i$. Then one obtains from the first-order conditions (11.11), combined with the assumed MLRC and the fact that $\mu_j \geq 0$ (Lagrangians are nonnegative),

$$s > r, \quad i > j \implies \frac{1}{u'(w_s)} - \frac{1}{u'(w_r)} = \sum_{j=1}^{m} \mu_j \left(\frac{p_{rj}}{p_{ri}} - \frac{p_{sj}}{p_{si}}\right)$$

$$\geq 0.$$

[12] A precise statement and proof of the revelation principle are in Section 8.5.2.
[13] Reduced form in the sense that for each effort level one applies the wage schedule that yields optimal implementation of that effort.

Therefore, $u'(w_r) \geq u'(w_s)$, and hence (due to the strict concavity of u), $w_s \geq w_r$, which proves the asserted monotonicity.

It remains to be shown that incentive constraints are indeed only binding "downwards" as assumed above. This is where the CDFC assumption comes in. The proof is a bit long and hence relegated to an appendix (Section 11.6).   □

Can Contracts Fail to be Monotone?

We close with an example that shows that monotonicity of the wage schedule can easily be destroyed. This should not be terribly surprising, given that strong assumptions had to be invoked to assure monotonicity.

Example 11.2 Suppose $u(w) := \ln(w)$, $n = 3$ (three states) and $m = 2$ (two effort levels), and assume the conditional probability distributions summarized in the following table ($y_3 > y_2 > y_1$, $a_2 > a_1$):

i	p_{1i}	p_{2i}	p_{3i}
ℓ	1/3	1/3	1/3
h	1/9	5/9	3/9

Then the optimal wage schedule implementing a_h is not monotone. In fact, employing (11.11), one obtains (note that λ, $\mu_1 > 0$)

$$w_1 = \lambda + \mu_1 \left(1 - \frac{p_{1\ell}}{p_{1h}}\right) < \lambda,$$

$$w_2 = \lambda + \mu_1 \left(1 - \frac{p_{2\ell}}{p_{2h}}\right) > \lambda,$$

$$w_3 = \lambda + \mu_1 \left(1 - \frac{p_{3\ell}}{p_{3h}}\right) = \lambda.$$

Hence, w_s is not monotone.

11.3 Limited Liability and Incentives

Now suppose the agent is risk-neutral but faces a liability constraint. This also gives rise to an incentive problem that is, however, easier to solve and generalize.

At the outset it should be clear that if risk neutrality is combined with *unlimited* liability, the incentive problem has a simple solution. Just make the agent a residual claimant who pays a fixed sum to the principal, collects the entire revenue, and thus bears all risk. Such a *franchise* contract, as it is often called, is efficient because it makes private and social benefits of agents' effort coincide, while risk does not matter under risk neutrality.

In some circumstances franchising is quite meaningful. For example, in London taxi drivers typically pay a fixed rental for their cab and then keep their entire revenue. In the taxi business, revenue fluctuations are probably not terribly significant. Therefore the benefits of effort efficiency may outweigh the unfavorable risk allocation.[14]

---

[14] However, this raises a puzzle: why are cab operators almost everywhere *except* in London remunerated like sharecroppers, earning a 50% share of their daily revenue?

However, in many cases franchising is not feasible. Often agents have insufficient wealth for bonding, or the law severely restricts penalties.

In the following we consider a framework where franchise contracts are not feasible because their adoption would violate the liability limit in some states. We will characterize the optimal contract that implements a given action. Again we start with a simple two-state model, which will then be generalized. Unlike in the previous section, we admit a continuum of actions right from the beginning.[15]

11.3.1 A Simple Model

Consider the two-state principal–agent model from Section 11.2. Only two assumptions are changed:

1. The agent's action space is the interval $A := [0, \bar{a}]$, $\bar{a} > 0$.
2. The agent is risk-neutral and has the utility function $u(w, a) := w - c(a)$, where $c(a)$ is the twice continuously differentiable cost-of-effort function with $c(0) = 0$, $c'(a) > 0$, $c''(a) \geq 0$.

After the agent has chosen his action, both principal and agent observe a binary signal $y \in Y := \{y_g, y_b\}$, $y_g > y_b$, which may be interpreted as output or revenue. Here g is mnemonic for "good" and b for "bad" signal realization. The signal is drawn from the family of twice continuously differentiable probability distributions

$$p(a) := \Pr\{Y = y_g \mid a\}, \qquad a \in A, \tag{11.12}$$

with the following properties for all $a \in A$:

$$p(a) \in (0, 1), \qquad p'(a) > 0, \qquad p''(a) \leq 0. \tag{11.13}$$

The first of these requirements excludes the trivial case of a moving support, the condition $p'(a) > 0$ means that $Y = y_g$ is favorable information with respect to the agent's action, and the concavity requirement $p''(a) \leq 0$ assures that the agent's decision problem is well behaved.

Optimal Contract to Implement a Given Action

Suppose the principal wants to induce the agent to choose the given action $a > 0$ at the minimum expected wage cost. The optimal contract $\{w_g, w_b\}$ solves the following optimization problem (note that $\max -E[w(Y)]$ is equivalent to $\min E[w(Y)]$):

$$\max_{w_g, w_b} \quad -(w_b + p(a)(w_g - w_b)) \tag{11.14}$$

$$\text{s.t.} \quad U(a) := w_b + p(a)(w_g - w_b) - c(a) \geq 0, \tag{11.15}$$

$$a \in \arg\max_{\tilde{a} \in A} U(\tilde{a}), \tag{11.16}$$

$$w_b + L \geq 0, \tag{11.17}$$

$$w_g + L \geq 0. \tag{11.18}$$

---

[15] The presentation in this section borrows heavily from Demougin and Fluet (1998, 1999). Some results were also derived by Sappington (1983, 1991), Innes (1990), and Park (1995).

Here (11.15) is the *participation constraint* (the agent's reservation utility is normalized to zero), (11.16) *the incentive compatibility constraint*, and (11.17)–(11.18) are the *liability constraints*.

Proposition 11.3 (Optimal Contract) *The optimal contract, implementing the given action $a > 0$, is the following increasing wage schedule:*

$$w_g = w_b + \frac{c'(a)}{p'(a)} > w_b, \tag{11.19}$$

$$w_b = \max\left\{-L, c(a) - \frac{p(a)}{p'(a)}c'(a)\right\}. \tag{11.20}$$

The associated expected wage cost $C^w(a, L)$ is

$$C^w(a, L) = \max\left\{-L + \frac{p(a)}{p'(a)}c'(a), c(a)\right\}. \tag{11.21}$$

Proof The first-order condition of the agent's decision problem (11.16) implies

$$w_g - w_b = \frac{c'(a)}{p'(a)} > 0.$$

The concavity assumption concerning $p(a)$ assures that this condition holds at a global maximum and not elsewhere.

Having shown that $w_g > w_b$, it follows that (11.18) is implied by (11.17). Therefore (11.18) can be eliminated. And assertion (11.20) follows immediately from the remaining constraints (11.15), (11.17), after substituting (11.19). Assertion (11.21) follows easily.   □

Is the optimal contract implementing a given action efficient? Efficient implementation means that the expected wage cost equals the cost of effort: $C^w(a, L) = c(a)$.

Proposition 11.4 (Inefficiency?) *The optimal contract, implementing a given action $a > 0$, is*

1. efficient if and only if liability constraint (11.17) is not binding;
2. inefficient if the liability limit L is sufficiently small.

Proof 1: By (11.21), $C^w(a, L) = c(a)$ if and only if $c(a) \geq -L + [p(a)/p'(a)]c'(a)$, which is equivalent to $w_b = c(a) - [p(a)/p'(a)]c'(a)$. This is the solution that one would also obtain if the liability constraint were omitted from the program.

2: The optimal contract is inefficient if $C^w(a, L) > c(a)$. By (11.21)

$$C^w(a, L) - c(a) = -L + \frac{p(a)}{p'(a)}c'(a) - c(a).$$

We will show that $[p(a)/p'(a)]c'(a) > c(a)$. Therefore $C^w(a, L) > c(a)$ if L is sufficiently small.

The assumptions $c(0) = 0$, $c'(a) > 0$, $c''(a) \leq 0$ for all $a > 0$ imply $c(0) \geq c(a) - ac'(a)$; hence for all $a > 0$

$$a \geq \frac{c(a)}{c'(a)}.$$

Similarly, the assumptions $p(0) > 0$, $p(a) > 0$, $p'(a) > 0$, $p''(a) \leq 0$ imply for all $a > 0$

$$a \leq \frac{p(a) - p(0)}{p'(a)} < \frac{p(a)}{p'(a)}.$$

Combine the two and one has $[p(a)/p'(a)]c'(a) > c(a)$, as asserted. $\qquad\square$

We summarize: The optimal contract pays a fixed wage plus a bonus equal to $c'(a)/p'(a)$ if y_g has been observed. The value of the fixed wage depends upon whether the liability or the participation constraint is binding. If the liability constraint binds, the fixed wage is equal to $-L$, the expected wage cost to the principal is $C^w(a, L) > c(a)$, and the agent earns rent. If the participation constraint binds, one has efficiency $C^w(a, L) = c(a)$, and the agent earns no rent. Inefficient implementation and rent occur in tandem.

Discussion

Why does efficient implementation not follow already from the properties of the optimal franchise contract spelled out in the introduction to this section? And how could one get efficient implementation of a certain action if the franchise contract violates the liability limit in some state?

True, the optimal franchise contract implements the optimal action a^* at which marginal revenue equals marginal cost of effort: $p'(a^*)(y_g - y_b) = c'(a^*)$, but it does not implement every arbitrary action $a \in A$. It may very well occur that a certain action $a \neq a^*$ admits efficient implementation: $C^w(a, L) = c(a)$, even though a^* cannot be implemented efficiently because $C^w(a^*, L) > c(a^*)$. *Efficient implementation of a given action* and *implementation of the efficient action* must be distinguished.

11.3.2 Generalization

We now generalize the model to $n \geq 2$ signal realizations. Amazingly, the results of the binary signal model generalize in a strong sense. Indeed, the optimal contract to implement a given action is a *bonus contract* that pays a flat wage in all states, unless the most favorable signal is observed, in which case it adds a bonus payment to the flat wage. An immediate implication is that the principal can, without loss of generality, aggregate information and distinguish only between a *good* state (the most favorable) and a *bad* state (all other states). Therefore the n-signal model can be reduced to the simple binary signal model.

Assumptions

After the agent has exerted effort, both principal and agent observe a real-valued signal $y \in Y := \{y_1, \ldots, y_n\}$, $n \geq 2$ (which may be interpreted as output or revenue), drawn from a family of probability distributions $\{p(y, a), \ a \in A, \ y \in Y\}$ with the following properties:

Assumption 11.4 The probability distribution

$$p(y, a) := \Pr\{Y = y \mid a\}$$

is positive and twice continuously differentiable everywhere.

Assumption 11.5 (MLRC) Y satisfies the strict monotone likelihood-ratio condition

$$\frac{\partial}{\partial y} \left(\frac{p_a(y, a)}{p(y, a)} \right) > 0 \qquad \forall a \in A.$$

Assumption 11.6 (CDFC) Y satisfies the convexity-of-the-distribution-function condition, i.e.,

$$P(y', a) := \sum_{y \leq y'} p(y, a)$$

is convex in a for every $y' \in Y$.

Optimal Implementation

The optimal contract implementing a given action $a > 0$ minimizes the expected wage $E[w(Y)]$ (equivalently, maximizes $-E[w(Y)]$), subject to the constraints of participation $(U(a) \geq 0)$, incentive compatibility $(a \in \arg\max_{\tilde{a} \in A} U(\tilde{a}))$, and liability $(w(Y) + L \geq 0)$.

Assumptions 11.4–11.6 assure that the first-order approach to the principal–agent problem is valid. This allows us to replace the incentive-compatibility requirement by the first order condition of the agent's maximization problem (see Rogerson (1985b)). Therefore the Lagrange function of the maximization problem can be written in the form

$$\mathcal{L} := -\sum_{y \in Y} p(y, a)w(y) + \alpha \left(\sum_{y \in Y} p_a(y, a)w(y) - c'(a) \right)$$

$$+ \beta \left(\sum_{y \in Y} p(y, a)w(y) - c(a) \right) + \sum_{y \in Y} \gamma(y) \left(w(y) + L \right),$$

where α, β, and $\gamma(y)$ are the multipliers associated with the agent's incentive compatibility, participation, and liability constraints.

Proposition 11.5 (Bonus Contract) *The optimal contract implementing the given action a is a bonus contract. It offers a base wage w_b in all states, plus a bonus $b := w_g - w_b > 0$ if and only if signal y_n is observed, exactly as in the binary signal model summarized in Proposition 11.3.*

Proof Suppose $\beta = 0$ (the participation constraint does not bind). Compute the first-order condition concerning $w(y)$. Since the multipliers $\gamma(y)$ associated with the liability constraints are nonnegative, one obtains

$$0 = -p(y, a) + \alpha p_a(y, a) + \gamma(y) \geq -p(y, a) + \alpha p_a(y, a).$$

Therefore

$$\alpha \leq \frac{p(a, y)}{p_a(y, a)}, \tag{11.22}$$

where the equality holds if and only if the liability constraint does not bind ($\gamma = 0$). Now recall that p/p_a is strictly decreasing in y, by the MLRC. Therefore, (11.22) is satisfied either with inequality for all y (which is equivalent to $\gamma > 0$ everywhere) or with equality at and only at $y = y_n$ (which is equivalent to $\gamma(y_n) = 0$ and $\gamma(y) > 0$ elsewhere).

The case $\gamma(y) > 0$ everywhere can be ruled out. For if it were true, one would have $w(y) = -L$ everywhere, and hence

$$\sum_{y \in Y} p_a(y, a) w(y) - c'(a) = -L \sum_{y \in Y} p_a(y, a) - c'(y)$$

$$= -c'(a) < 0.$$

But this contradicts the first-order condition concerning the agent's effort decision. We are thus left with

$$\gamma(y_n) = 0 \quad \text{and} \quad \gamma(y) > 0 \quad \forall y \neq y_n.$$

Hence the optimal contract is a bonus contract

$$w(y) = -L \qquad \forall y \neq y_n, \tag{11.23}$$

$$w(y_n) = -L + \frac{c'(a)}{p_a(y_n, a)}. \tag{11.24}$$

Now suppose $\beta > 0$ (the participation constraint binds). Then the optimal implementation of a is efficient: $C^w(a, L) = c(a)$. Therefore the limited liability constraint cannot bind, and the optimal contract is

$$w(y) = w_0 := c(a) - \frac{p(y_n, a)}{p_a(y_n, a)} c'(a) \qquad \forall y \neq y_n,$$

$$w(y_n) = w_0 + \frac{c'(a)}{p_a(y_n, a)}.$$

Define the binary statistic (where y_g and y_b are reals with $y_g > y_b$, for example $y_g := y_n, y_b := y_1$)

$$X := \begin{cases} y_g & \text{if} \quad Y = y_n, \\ y_b & \text{if} \quad Y \neq y_n. \end{cases}$$

Then the optimal contract implementing a is exactly the solution of the simple binary static model summarized in Proposition 11.3. $\qquad\qquad\square$

Remark 11.1 (Further Generalization) This result can be further generalized. Remove Assumption 11.5 (MLRC), and assume instead that the likelihood ratio has a maximum for some $y \in Y$. Then Proposition 11.5 also holds with the proviso that the maximizer of the likelihood ratio takes the place of y_n (see Demougin and Fluet (1998)).

11.3.3 Monitoring and Incentives*

Having shown that signals can be summarized by a binary statistic, we are now able to extend the principal–agent model to include monitoring and the associated choice of information system. This puts the principal–agent problem into a broader perspective.

We now assume that the principal can choose between different information systems characterized by a family of binary random variables: $Y_i \in \{y_g, y_b\}$. Naturally, we assume that more precise information requires more monitoring, which in turn involves higher cost of monitoring. Therefore, "more precise" means that a given action can be implemented at lower expected wage cost.

Signal Precision

Proposition 11.3 indicates that the likelihood ratio plays a pivotal role in the ranking of binary information systems. In the following we employ the dimension-free elasticity of the probability of the favorable signal as a ranking criterion.

Definition 11.1 Consider two binary signals, Y_i, Y_j, with the associated probability distributions $p_i(a)$, $p_j(a)$. The signal Y_i is called more precise than Y_j for implementing a if the elasticity of $p_i(a)$ is greater than that of $p_j(a)$:

$$\theta_i(a) > \theta_j(a), \tag{11.25}$$

$$\theta(a) := \frac{a p'(a)}{p(a)} \quad \text{(elasticity of } p(a)\text{)}. \tag{11.26}$$

Lemma 11.1 *The elasticity of the probability of the favorable signal is bounded as follows:*

$$\theta(a) \in [0, 1]. \tag{11.27}$$

Proof $\theta(a) \geq 0$ follows from the fact that $p(a)$, $p'(a) > 0$. In order to prove that $\theta(a) \leq 1$, note that, due to $p''(a) \leq 0$,

$$p(0) \leq p(a) - a p'(a).$$

Rearrange, and one obtains

$$\theta(a) := \frac{a p'(a)}{p(a)} \leq 1 - \frac{p(0)}{p(a)} \leq 1. \qquad \square$$

Proposition 11.6 *Consider two binary signals, Y_i and Y_j. The expected wage cost of implementing a given action is monotone decreasing in signal precision:*

$$C_i^w(a, L) \leq C_j^w(a, L) \quad \Longleftrightarrow \quad \theta_i(a) \geq \theta_j(a). \tag{11.28}$$

Proof Using (11.25), the expected wage cost of implementing a, which was given in (11.21), can be written in the form

$$C_i^w(a, L) = \max\left\{-L + \frac{ac'(a)}{\theta_i(a)}, c(a)\right\}. \tag{11.29}$$

Also recall that $C_i^w(a, L) > c(a)$ if and only if liability constraint (11.17) binds, which necessarily occurs if the liability limit L is sufficiently small (see Proposition 11.4). Therefore $C_i^w(a, L)$ is either increasing in $\theta_i(a)$ (which occurs if and only if (11.17) binds) or independent of $\theta_i(a)$. $\square$

Optimal Monitoring and Incentive Package

Now suppose there is a continuum of binary information systems, characterized by the precision measure θ, and let the cost of monitoring be a continuously differentiable function of θ with $C_\theta^m(a, \theta) > 0$ everywhere.

Then the total cost of implementing a given action, $C^t(a, L)$, is the sum total of the expected wage cost and the cost of monitoring. And the principal's problem of implementing a given action at minimum cost is to solve

$$C^t(a, L) := \min_{\theta \in (0,1)} C^m(a, \theta) + C^w(a, L, \theta)$$

$$= c(a) + \min_{\theta \in (0,1)} \{R(a, \theta) + C^m(a, \theta)\}, \tag{11.30}$$

where

$$R(a, \theta) := C^w(a, L, \theta) - c(a) \tag{11.31}$$

denotes the agent's rent.

If the liability constraint (11.17) binds, the agent earns rent. In that case the optimal monitoring intensity θ^* must equalize the marginal cost of monitoring and the marginal benefit due to a reduction in the agent's rent,

$$C_{\theta*}^m(a, \theta^*) = R_\theta(a, \theta^*). \tag{11.32}$$

If the liability constraint (11.17) does not bind, and thus the agent earns no rent, the optimal monitoring intensity is the smallest θ compatible with zero rent, which, by definition of R and θ, is

$$\bar{\theta} := \min\left\{\frac{ac'(a)}{L + c(a)}, 1\right\}. \tag{11.33}$$

By construction, if $\theta = \bar{\theta}$, the agent's rent is equal to zero, and if $\theta < \bar{\theta}$, his rent is positive and strictly decreasing in θ. Therefore, using the definition of rent R, one can rewrite the principal's problem (11.30) as follows:

$$C^t(a, L) = \min_{\theta \leq \bar{\theta}} -L + \frac{ac'(a)}{\theta} + C^m(a, \theta). \tag{11.34}$$

And the marginal condition for an interior solution $\theta \in (0, \bar{\theta})$ can be written as

$$\theta C_\theta^m(a, \theta) = \frac{ac'(a)}{\theta} := B(a, \theta), \tag{11.35}$$

where $B(a, \theta)$ is the expected wage bonus.

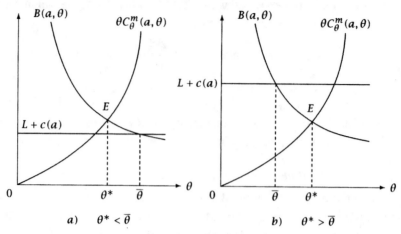

Figure 11.3. Optimal Monitoring Intensity.

Comparing (11.34) with (11.30), we conclude: *the optimal monitoring is equal to θ^* unless $\theta^* > \bar{\theta}$, in which case the solution is to set $\theta = \bar{\theta}$.*

Figure 11.3 illustrates the solution of the optimal-monitoring problem. There $\bar{\theta}$ is the monitoring intensity at which the bonus curve $B(a, \theta)$ intersects the no-rent line $L + c(a)$, and θ^* is the monitoring intensity where the bonus curve intersects the θC_θ^m curve. The optimal monitoring intensity is defined by the point E. In part a) of Figure 11.3 the solution is $\theta = \theta^*$, and the agent's rent is the vertical distance between E and $L + c(a)$, whereas in part b) the solution is $\theta = \bar{\theta}$ and the agent earns no rent. The latter occurs if the liability limit is high or the marginal cost of monitoring is small.

Comparative Statics

Suppose the liability limit L is increased. This pushes up the no-rent line $L + c(a)$ in Figure 11.3. In case a) both θ and B are unaffected and the agent's rent is diminished, whereas in case b) monitoring is lowered and the expected bonus is increased. Therefore, stronger incentives are substituted for monitoring expenditures.

Next, suppose the marginal cost of monitoring C_θ^m is increased. In case b) this has no effect on monitoring and incentives, whereas in case a) monitoring is reduced and the expected bonus is increased. Again, stronger incentives are substituted for monitoring expenditures.

Example of Monitoring Technology

We close with a nice example of a monitoring technology introduced by Demougin and Fluet (1999).

Suppose the agent makes mistakes in carrying out his job. The agent's action determines the probability distribution of mistakes, and the principal's monitoring intensity determines the probability distribution of mistakes detected by the principal.

Denote the number of mistakes by the random variable Y, and the number of mistakes detected by the principal by Z. Both random variables are Poisson-distributed:

$$\Pr\{Y = k\} = e^{-\lambda}\frac{\lambda^k}{k!}, \qquad k = 0, 1, \ldots, \tag{11.36}$$

$$\Pr\{Z = k\} = e^{-\theta\lambda}\frac{(\theta\lambda)^k}{k!}, \qquad k = 0, 1, \ldots \tag{11.37}$$

By a well-known property of Poisson distributions, the parameter λ is the expected number of mistakes, and $\theta\lambda$ is the expected number of detected mistakes, given the monitoring intensity θ. As an interpretation, you could look at Y as the number of defective output units and the monitoring intensity θ as the proportion of outputs that are quality-inspected.

Next, measure the agent's action a by the *probability of no mistake*,

$$a := \Pr\{Y = 0\} = e^{-\lambda}. \tag{11.38}$$

Putting pieces together, one obtains the following probability distribution of detected mistakes:

$$\Pr\{Z = k \mid a\} = a^{\theta}\frac{(-\theta \ln a)^k}{k!}, \qquad k = 0, 1, \ldots, \tag{11.39}$$

which is decreasing in a and increasing in θ.

A contract implementing a given probability of no mistake conditions the wage on the number of detected mistakes, $w(Z)$. Given a cost-of-monitoring function $C^m(\theta, a)$, the principal can compute the contract and monitoring package that optimally implements a given action a.

11.4 Renegotiation Problem

A fundamental yet frequently overlooked problem in information economics is the fact that optimal contracts are not renegotiation-proof. At some point in the contract relationship both parties have an incentive to renegotiate the original contract. Both parties can gain from it. However, the anticipation of future renegotiation typically destroys incentives. This suggests that the contractual solution of information problems requires a reliable commitment never to renegotiate, which is, however, difficult to achieve.

In order to explain the renegotiation problem in the present context, suppose the two parties have signed the contract that implements some effort level greater than a_1 at minimum expected wage cost. Then, once the agent has exerted effort, but just before the signal realization is observed, both parties have an incentive to tear up that contract and replace it by a fixed-wage contract. For, once the agent has executed his action, effort incentives are superfluous, and all that matters is the allocation of income risk. At this point, the agent is willing to trade the initial contract for a fixed-wage contract and pay an insurance premium in the form of a lower expected wage cost. This way, both principal and agent are better off.

However, once this is understood, the agent anticipates that the original contract will later be replaced by a fixed-wage contract. And therefore, the agent will chisel and exert only the lowest possible effort level. Effort incentives are thus completely destroyed. This suggests that optimal implementation cannot work unless the principal commits himself never to renegotiate, no matter how much he could gain from renegotiation.

Of course, such a commitment may be difficult to achieve. Therefore, one would like to know how bilateral trade is affected if one adds a renegotiation stage to the principal–agent game.

If one assumes that one party makes a take-it-or-leave-it renegotiation offer, there are still two quite different specifications of the renegotiation game. Essentially, it matters a great deal who makes the offer. If it is the principal who makes the offer, he does so without knowing the agent's effort choice, whereas if it is the agent, he can use the offer to signal his effort choice, which turns the renegotiation game into a signal game.

Both approaches are pursued in the literature. In Fudenberg and Tirole (1990), Ma (1991), and Maskin and Tirole (1992) it is the principal who makes the renegotiation offer. In Ma (1994) and Matthews (1995a) the informed party, the agent, makes the offer.

If the principal makes the renegotiation offer, the equilibrium is fairly complicated. The principal offers a menu of renegotiation-proof contracts, the agent uses a mixed effort strategy, and altogether payoffs are lower than if renegotiations are ruled out.

If the agent makes the renegotiation offer, the equilibrium is a very simple arrangement. The principal simply offers a franchise contract as initial contract and waits for the agent to renegotiate it to the contract that yields the optimal implementation of the desired effort; the agent chooses the desired action, and equilibrium payoffs are unaffected by renegotiations.

Specifically, in the 2×2 framework, the principal proposes the franchise contract described by point A' in Figure 11.2. If this initial contract is not renegotiated, the principal earns as much as he would earn if he had optimally implemented the lowest effort a_ℓ. However, the franchise contract A' sets high-powered incentives, and the agent chooses effort a_h and makes the renegotiation offer to replace A' by contract B. Evidently, this renegotiation offer makes sense only if the agent has indeed exerted high effort a_h. Thus, the renegotiation offer signals the agent's choice of high effort. The principal accepts the offer, and altogether both, parties earn the same payoffs as in the world without renegotiations.[16]

---

[16] The details are spelled out in Matthews (1995a).

11.5 Bibliographic Notes

The most influential contribution to the principal–agent model with risk–incentive trade-off is probably Holmstrom (1979), even though a number of similar contributions was published at around the same time (see for example Harris and Raviv (1979)). The further literature focused on variations and extensions of the basic model and on other applications surveyed in Hart and Holmstrom (1987).

One important extension concerns repeated agency relationships, with the aim to understand whether a long-term relationship may ease the trade-off between insurance and incentives (see Rogerson (1985b) and Holmstrom and Milgrom (1990)).

Another important contribution by Holmstrom and Milgrom (1987) shows that long-term contracts may be simple linear contracts. This indicates that complicating the model may actually give rise to simpler and more realistic contract formats. (Recall: a similar conclusion was reached in our analysis of the renegotiation problem.)

While most contributions assume one-dimensional effort, Holmstrom and Milgrom (1991) focus on multitask principal–agent problems.

Another branch of the literature contributes to the ranking of information systems, the characterization of optimal monitoring policies, and problems of collusion associated with the employment of third parties engaged with monitoring. Some of these issues were already sketched in Section 11.3, in the framework of the alternative limited-liability principal–agent model. There, however, the role of third parties in monitoring and the related problems of collusion were left out.

Work on collusion and the role of third parties is still in progress. Early contributions on collusion and collusion proofness are Tirole (1986) and Brown and Wolfstetter (1989). Important recent contributions are Kofman and Lawarrée (1993, 1996), Laffont and Martimort (1997), and Dittmann (1997).

An alternative perspective on monitoring that combines the renegotiation problem with the problem of optimal monitoring is sketched in Crémer (1995). He makes the interesting observation that lowering the cost of monitoring may actually be counterproductive because it tends to make a commitment not to renegotiate less credible.

Among the many applications of the principal–agent problem we mention finance and health economics. An excellent survey of the corporate finance literature on security design that focuses on agency costs and corporate control is Harris and Raviv (1989). A useful collection of papers on health economics is McGuire and Riordan (1994).

For a more applied outlook take a look at Lazear (1995a, 1995b). The latter includes an account of some real-life experiments on reward structures for production workers, carried out at Safelite Glass Corporation.

We close with a note on a technical issue. If one assumes a continuum of effort levels (as in Section 11.3), one has a continuum of incentive constraints. This raises technical difficulties. Researchers at first attempted to circumvent these difficulties by replacing the continuum of incentive constraints by one first-order condition:

$a \in \arg\max_a U(a)$, which lead to a tractable problem known as the *first-order approach to the principal–agent problem* (see for example Harris and Raviv (1979), Holmstrom (1979), and Shavell (1979)). However, as Mirrlees (1975) pointed out, the first-order approach may lead one astray. Subsequently, researchers have searched for conditions under which the convenient first-order approach is justified. As long as one sticks to an additively separable utility function of the agent, the equivalent of the assumptions (11.1)–(11.3) is sufficient for the validity of the first-order approach (see Rogerson (1985a) and Jewitt (1988)). However, more stringent requirements are needed if one allows for more general utility functions (see Brown, Chiang, Ghosh, and Wolfstetter (1986) and Alvi (1997)).

11.6 Appendix

Here we spell out the last part of the proof of Proposition 11.2. The proof is split up into two lemmas.

Lemma 11.2 *Consider a monotone nondecreasing wage schedule:* $w_1 \leq w_2 \leq \cdots \leq w_n$. *Then* $U(a_i) = \sum_{s=1}^n p_{si} u(w_s) - c(a_i)$ *is concave in* a_i.

Proof Let $\delta_s := u(w_s) - u(w_{s-1})$ for $s = 2, \ldots, n$, and $\delta_1 := u(w_1)$. Then[17]

$$U(a_i) = \sum_{s=1}^n \left(p_s(a_i) \sum_{j=1}^s \delta_j \right) - c(a_i)$$

$$= \sum_{s=1}^n \left(\delta_s \sum_{j=1}^s p_j(a_i) \right) - c(a_i)$$

$$= \delta_1 + \sum_{r=2}^n \delta_r \bar{P}_r(a_i) - c(a_i),$$

where $\bar{P}_r(a_i) := 1 - P_r(a_i)$. By the assumed CDFC of $P_r(a_i)$, the function $\bar{P}_r(a_i)$ is concave in a_i for all r. Hence, $U(a_i)$ is the sum of a linear combination of the concave functions $\bar{P}_r(a_i)$ (with nonnegative weights), the constant δ_1, and the concave function $-c(a_i)$. The sum of concave functions is also concave (see Section C.3 in Appendix C). Therefore $U(a_i)$ is a concave function of a_i, as asserted. □

Lemma 11.3 *Consider the optimal implementation of* a_i, $i > 1$, *ignoring the upward incentive constraints, i.e.,*[18]

$$\max_{\{w_s\}} - \sum_{s=1}^n w_s p_s(a_i) \qquad \text{(P2)}$$

$$\text{s.t.} \quad U(a_i) \geq \bar{u},$$

$$U(a_i) \geq U(a_j) \qquad \forall j = 1, \ldots, i.$$

Every solution of program (P2) is also a solution of program (P1).

---

[17] Use pencil and paper to check the step from the second to the third equality.
[18] Note: compared to (P1), in program (P2) the incentive constraints for $a_{i+1}, \ldots, a_m$ are missing.

Proof From the first part of the proof of Proposition 11.2 we know that in the absence of upward incentive constraints the optimal contract implementing a_i is monotone nondecreasing. Suppose the incentive constraint $r < i$ is binding.[19] Then one has $U(a_i) = U(a_r)$. Now consider an action a_j, for $j > i$. Obviously, the action a_i can be represented as a convex combination of a_r and a_j, i.e., $a_i = \alpha a_r + (1-\alpha)a_j$ for some $\alpha \in (0, 1)$. Therefore, using the concavity of $U(a)$ established in Lemma 11.2, one obtains

$$U(a_i) = U(\alpha a_r + (1 - \alpha)a_j)$$
$$\geq \alpha U(a_r) + (1 - \alpha)U(a_j) \qquad \text{(since } U(a) \text{ is concave)}$$
$$= \alpha U(a_i) + (1 - \alpha)U(a_j) \qquad \text{(since } U(a_i) = U(a_r)\text{).}$$

Hence, $U(a_i) \geq U(a_j)$. In other words: the solution of the program that omits upward incentive constraints also satisfies these constraints. And therefore every solution of (P2) is also a solution of (P1). □

Finally, notice that the solutions of both (P1) and (P2) are unique, because both are concave maximization problems. Therefore, the optimal contract implementing a_i, $i > 1$, has the monotonicity property established for the solution of (P2). This completes the proof.

---

[19] Some incentive constraint must be binding, because otherwise the optimal contract entails a state-independent wage, which can only implement the lowest action a_1.

12

Rank-Order Tournaments

Well in our country, said Alice, still panting a little, you'd generally get
to somewhere else – if you ran very fast for a long time, as we've been
doing. A slow sort of country, said the Queen. Now here you see, it takes
all the running you can do to keep in the same place.

Lewis Carroll

12.1 Introduction

In our analysis of the principal-agent problem we explained why labor contracts may
have a piece-rate component. While piece rates reward workers according to their
absolute output, we now turn to incentive schemes based on relative performance,
known as rank-order tournaments.[1]

A rank-order tournament is a competition between several workers who perform
similar tasks. The employer announces a set of prizes to be awarded in the order of
observed output. Workers then compete with their effort to gain rewards for high
and avoid punishment for low performance.

In many applications an important advantage of tournaments is that they require only a ranking or ordinal measurement of outputs. The latter may already
explain why tournaments are popular in academics, for example in the awarding of
assistantships and scholarships to graduate students and tenure to professors.[2]

12.2 A Simple Model

Suppose a risk-neutral firm engages two workers $i = 1, 2$ to perform similar tasks.
Their production functions x and utility functions U are

$$x(a_i, \tilde{\theta}_i) := a_i + \tilde{\theta}_i, \tag{12.1}$$

$$U(w_i, a_i) := u(w_i) - c(a_i), \tag{12.2}$$

---

[1] The seminal paper on tournaments is by Lazear and Rosen (1981). For further developments and empirical
evidence on tournaments see Lazear (1995a).

[2] In industry, the most commonly used tournaments take the form of promotion schemes. For an empirical study
of the use of tournaments in managerial compensation see Antle and Smith (1986).

where a_i denotes the action or effort, w_i the wage, and $\tilde{\theta}_i$ a random output distortion. Output distortions are independently and identically distributed (iid), with zero mean, $E[\tilde{\theta}] = 0$, and variance σ^2. Both u and c are twice continuously differentiable, with

$$u', c' > 0, \qquad u'' \leq 0, \qquad c'' > 0, \qquad \lim_{a_i \to 0} c'(a_i) < \lim_{w_i \to 0} u'(w_i). \quad (12.3)$$

Workers do not know the output distortion $\tilde{\theta}_i$ before effort is chosen, and the employer only observes output and neither θ nor a (*hidden action*).

The firm's problem is to design a reward structure that maximizes their expected value of profits.

12.2.1 First Best Effort and Wage

As a point of reference suppose, for the moment, that workers' effort is public information. Then firms can write complete contingent contracts $\{w(\theta), a\}$ with each individual worker. These contracts stipulate effort a and a wage $w(\theta)$ as a function of the output distortion θ. In principle, the contract can condition on both output distortions, but that is of no use as long as output distortions are stochastically independent.

The first best optimal labor contract maximizes the firm's expected profit subject to workers' participation condition. Normalizing workers' reservation utility to be equal to zero, this gives

$$\max_{\{w(\theta),a\}} E[x(a, \tilde{\theta})] \qquad \text{s.t.} \quad E[u(w(\tilde{\theta})) - c(a)] \geq 0. \quad (12.4)$$

The optimization problem is well behaved. Therefore, the optimal contract solves the Euler–Lagrange conditions[3] (λ is the Lagrangian)

$$w(\theta): \ u'(w(\theta)) - \lambda = 0 \quad \forall \theta, \quad (12.5)$$

$$a: \ c'(a) - \lambda = 0, \quad (12.6)$$

$$\lambda: \ E[u(w(\tilde{\theta}))] - c(a) = 0. \quad (12.7)$$

If workers are *risk-averse*, the solution is unique. In this case, the optimal contract exhibits a state-independent wage w^* and a choice of w^* and a^* that satisfies the following requirement concerning the marginal rate of substitution between income and effort:

$$\frac{dw}{da}\bigg|_{U=\text{const}} = \frac{u'(w^*)}{c'(a^*)} = 1 \quad (12.8)$$

and the participation condition

$$u(w^*) - c(a^*) = 0. \quad (12.9)$$

In contrast, if workers are *risk-neutral*, the optimal contract has many solutions. One particular optimal contract is the already familiar *franchise contract* that

---

[3] See Kamien and Schwartz (1991).

makes workers into residual claimants who effectively "lease" their job from the employer:

$$w^*(\theta) = w_0^* + \theta, \qquad w_0^* = c(a^*), \qquad c'(a^*) = 1. \qquad (12.10)$$

This contract has the distinct advantage that it works even under hidden action.

12.2.2 Tournament Game

Tournaments are an alternative to individual contracting. A tournament game is played between workers who compete for given prizes with their effort.

In the present context, the players are two identical neutral workers who perform a similar but independent task, and the firm that sets the prizes. The game has the following stages:

Stage 0. Nature independently draws output distortions from the same distribution. That drawing is not revealed, either to workers or to the firm. However, the distribution of output distortions is common knowledge.

Stage 1. The firm sets two prizes $w_g > w_b$, and commits to pay w_g to the high- and w_b to the low-output worker (g is mnemonic for "good" and b for "bad").

Stage 2. Each worker chooses his or her effort without knowing the rival's choice; outputs are observed, the firm collects revenue, prizes are paid out, and the game is over.

The game is solved by backward induction, using the prior beliefs concerning nature's drawing, as follows: First solve the tournament subgame for given prizes. Then compute the firm's reduced-form expected-profit function and find optimal prizes.

12.3 Tournaments under Risk Neutrality

Assume workers are risk-neutral. This simplifies the analysis, even though tournaments are an unnecessarily complicated incentive system scheme in this case.

12.3.1 Tournament Subgame

Two workers, who have signed on with the firm, simultaneously choose their effort. Denote the probability of winning the high prize w_g by p. Then worker i's expected utility is[4]

$$U_i = w_b + p_i(w_g - w_b) - c(a_i).$$

It is obvious that p_i must be increasing in the own effort and decreasing in that of the rival worker. However, we need to know the exact relationship. For this purpose, follow each step of the following consideration. It will establish that p_i equals the cumulative probability distribution (cdf) of the difference of two random variables,

---

[4] The possibility of a tie is payoff-irrelevant because the probability distribution is continuous, as we show below.

$\tilde{\xi} := \tilde{\theta}_j - \tilde{\theta}_i$, evaluated at $\xi = a_i - a_j$ (the cdf of ξ is denoted by $G(\xi)$):

$$
\begin{aligned}
p_i(a_i, a_j) &= \Pr(X_i > X_j) \\
&= \Pr(a_i + \tilde{\theta}_i > a_j + \tilde{\theta}_j) \\
&= \Pr(\tilde{\xi} < a_i - a_j), \qquad \tilde{\xi} := \tilde{\theta}_j - \tilde{\theta}_i \\
&=: G(a_i - a_j).
\end{aligned}
\tag{12.11}
$$

The equilibrium effort levels (a_i^*, a_j^*) satisfy the best-reply requirements (for $i, j = 1, 2, i \neq j$)

$$
a_i^* = \arg\max_{a_i}(w_b + G(a_i - a_j^*)(w_g - w_b) - c(a_i)).
\tag{12.12}
$$

Provided the objective function is quasiconcave,[5] best replies are unique and the tournament subgame has a unique symmetric equilibrium in pure strategies, a^*, which satisfies the first-order conditions together with the requirement that equal efforts entail an equal chance to win the high prize:

$$
g(0)(w_g - w_b) = c'(a^*),
\tag{12.13}
$$

$$
p_i = G(0) = \frac{1}{2}, \qquad i = 1, 2.
\tag{12.14}
$$

Note that, since $c(a)$ is strictly increasing and strictly convex, the equilibrium effort a^* is strict monotone increasing in the wage spread $w_g - w_b$. By choosing an appropriate wage spread the firm can induce any feasible effort level as the equilibrium of the tournament subgame.

12.3.2 Equilibrium Prizes

Now we turn to determine equilibrium prizes. Using the solution of the tournament subgame, firms choose those prizes that maximize the expected value of profits, subject to the workers' participation condition (market exchange is voluntary):

$$
\max_{w_g, w_b} 2\left(a^*(w_b, w_g) - \frac{1}{2}(w_g + w_b)\right)
\tag{12.15}
$$

$$
\text{s.t.} \quad w_b + \frac{1}{2}(w_g - w_b) - c(a^*(w_b, w_g)) \geq 0.
\tag{12.16}
$$

Recall that the firm can induce any feasible effort level by choosing an appropriate wage spread. Therefore, one can also view the firm as directly choosing the effort level. After substituting (12.16) in the form of an equality into (12.15), the firm's decision problem can thus be reduced to

$$
\max_{a} 2(a - c(a)).
\tag{12.17}
$$

---

[5] The quasiconcavity requirement is not met for arbitrary distribution functions G, but we will assume it here. Recall that the sum of two quasiconcave functions is not necessarily quasiconcave. Therefore, the quasiconcavity of G does not assure the quasiconcavity of the objective function. Of course, if G is concave, the objective function is concave. And concavity implies quasiconcavity. Therefore, the concavity of G assures well-behavedness.

Therefore, the equilibrium effort level solves

$$c'(a^*) = 1, \tag{12.18}$$

and the firm sets wages in such a way that they make this effort level an equilibrium of the subsequent tournament subgame and assure participation.

We have thus all the pieces together to characterize the equilibrium outcome (a^*, w_g, w_b) of the overall game,

$$c'(a^*) = 1, \tag{12.19}$$

$$(w_g - w_b)g(0) = c'(a^*), \tag{12.20}$$

$$\frac{1}{2}(w_g + w_b) = c(a^*), \tag{12.21}$$

and conclude:

Proposition 12.1 *If workers are risk-neutral, the equilibrium tournament implements the first best effort and expected utilities.*

12.3.3 Two Illustrations

We close with two examples that explicitly solve the tournament game for different probability distributions of the productivity shock. Both examples assume the quadratic cost function

$$c(a) := \frac{1}{2}a^2.$$

Example 12.1 (Normal Distribution) Suppose the $\tilde{\theta}$'s are normally distributed with zero mean and variance σ^2. Then $\tilde{\xi} := \tilde{\theta}_j - \tilde{\theta}_i$ is also normally distributed with zero mean and variance $\sigma_{\xi}^2 = 2\sigma^2$.[6] The probability density function (pdf) of $\tilde{\xi}$ is[7]

$$g(\xi) = \frac{1}{2\sigma\sqrt{\pi}}e^{-\xi^2/4\sigma^2}.$$

Therefore, $g(0) = 1/(2\sigma\sqrt{\pi})$ and

$$a^* = 1, \qquad w_b^* = \frac{1}{2} - \sigma\sqrt{\pi}, \qquad w_g^* = \frac{1}{2} + \sigma\sqrt{\pi}.$$

Example 12.2 (Uniform Distribution) Suppose the $\tilde{\theta}$'s are uniformly distributed on the support $(-\frac{1}{2}, +\frac{1}{2})$. Then $\tilde{\xi} := \tilde{\theta}_j - \tilde{\theta}_i$ has the following triangular pdf:[8]

$$g(\xi) := \begin{cases} 1+\xi & \text{for } \xi \in (-1,0), \\ 1-\xi & \text{for } \xi \in (0,1), \\ 0 & \text{otherwise.} \end{cases}$$

---

[6] The sum of independent and normally distributed random variables is again normally distributed.
[7] Recall that the variance of the weighted sum of two independent random variables $Z := aX + bY$ is $\sigma_z^2 = a^2\sigma_x^2 + b^2\sigma_y^2$.
[8] See Appendix D, Rule (R16) in Section D.4.4.

Therefore, $g(0) = 1$, and

$$a^* = 1, \quad w_b^* = 0, \quad w_g^* = 1.$$

12.3.4 Discussion

If workers are risk-neutral, tournaments are not the only incentive scheme that achieves optimality. Just recall that the franchise contract is both incentive-compatible and efficient in this case. Therefore, unless you like the idea of using a steam hammer to crack a nut, tournaments must be judged as useless, unless they prove themselves in a framework of risk aversion where no individual-performance-based contract is able to implement the first best expected utilities.

However, as Green and Stokey (1983) showed, individual-performance-based contracts Pareto-dominate tournaments if output disturbances are stochastically independent and workers are risk-averse. Therefore, the introduction of risk aversion leads us to reject tournaments in favor of individual-performance-based contracts, unless further modifications are introduced.

At this point you may wonder whether tournaments are ever superior to individual-performance-based contracts? Luckily, the picture changes if you allow risk aversion *and* replace idiosyncratic output disturbances by a common shock. Then, at last, tournaments are optimal incentive schemes that implement the first best optimum, despite risk aversion – unmatched by individual-performance-based contracts. We close the section with an illustration of this claim.

12.4 Tournaments under Common Shocks

Suppose the output distortion is a common shock. Consider a tournament with a continuum of prizes where worker i is awarded a prize w_i that depends upon the first best effort a^* and the difference between his and his rival's output, according to the following rule (where $f > 0$):[9]

$$w_i = \begin{cases} u^{-1}(c(a^*) - (x_i - x_j)^2) & \text{if} \quad x_i \geq x_j, \\ u^{-1}(-f) & \text{if} \quad x_i < x_j. \end{cases} \tag{12.22}$$

Then, at last, the tournament game implements the first best expected utilities, even if workers are risk-averse. This result should be compared with the well-known finding that individual-performance-based contracts, such as the familiar piece-rate system, cannot implement the first best if workers are risk-averse. Therefore, tournaments are superior labor contracts under some circumstances.

Proposition 12.2 (Common Shock) *Suppose the output disturbance is a common shock. Then, given the reward scheme (12.22), the first best effort a^* is an equilibrium of the tournament subgame – even if workers are risk-averse.*

---

[9] Notice: this tournament requires that outputs can be ranked on a cardinal scale.

Proof Due to risk aversion, the first best optimal labor contract prescribes the fixed wage w^* and the effort level a^* that satisfy conditions (12.8), (12.9). We show that $a_1 = a_2 = a^*$ is a Nash equilibrium of the tournament subgame if prizes are given by (12.22).

1. Suppose $a_j = a^*$. Then $a_i < a^*$ cannot be a best response, since for all $a < a^*$ worker i's expected utility $U_i(a_i, a_j)$ drops, as

$$U_i(a_i, a^*) = -f - c(a) < 0 = U_i(a^*, a^*).$$

2. Suppose $a_j = a^*$. Then for all $a_i \geq a^*$ the right derivative is

$$\frac{\partial U_i}{\partial a_i}(a_i, a^*) = -2(a_i - a^*) - c'(a_i) < 0.$$

Hence, deviating from a^* to higher effort does not pay either.   □

Notice, however, that there is a continuum of alternative equilibria. Indeed, every feasible $a \leq a^*$ is an equilibrium of the tournament subgame.

12.5 Bibliographic Notes

The basic model of tournaments under risk neutrality follows Lazear and Rosen (1981), Hirshleifer and Riley (1992, Chapter 10), and Lazear (1995a). For a variation of this model that uses multiplicative rather than additive shocks see Nalebuff and Stiglitz (1983). Multiplicative shocks affect the marginal product of effort and therefore lead to somewhat different results.

For a deeper understanding of tournaments consult Holmstrom (1982) or Green and Stokey (1983). Green and Stokey assume additive shocks but introduce a common shock component. Their main result is that tournaments dominate individual-performance-based contracts only if the common shock component is sufficiently strong. While Green and Stokey assume additive shocks and compare tournaments only with linear piece-rate contracts, Holmstrom admits both kinds of shocks and examines arbitrary contracts. His main result is that the mean output is a sufficient statistic for all of the information concerning the common shock. Therefore, an optimal contract makes the wage dependent only upon workers' own output and upon the mean output of the entire pool of workers.

Tournaments are only part of the literature on the relationship between one principal and many agents. The more recent literature has focused on conditions under which efficiency can be achieved. For example, Legros and Matthews (1993) use the framework of Holmstrom's deterministic team model and show that, with limited liability, efficiency can be achieved almost completely.

Part IV

Technical Supplements

Appendix A

Nonlinear Optimization: The Classical Approach

Nothing gives such weight and dignity to a book as an appendix.

Herodotus

A.1 Introduction

We begin with the simplest case of unconstrained problems and then proceed to nonlinear optimization under constraints that are in the form of equalities. The mathematics involved dates back a few centuries – hence the name classical.

The more modern approach deals with constraints in the form of inequalities. All the classical results can be obtained as special cases of the modern theory. Also, many economic problems do involve inequality constraints. You may thus ask: why bother with the classical approach at all?

There are at least two good reasons. First of all, the classical approach serves as a bridge between standard calculus and the more advanced subject of mathematical optimization. As it is more accessible, it gives a much easier introduction to the subject. More important yet, the tools and methods of the classical approach are utilized anyway in solving inequality-constrained optimization problems. So you can rest assured that your time and effort are not wasted.

A.2 Unconstrained Optimization

Consider a real-valued function $f : D \to \mathbb{R}$, $D \subset \mathbb{R}^n$ an open set. f is said to have a *local maximum* at $x^* \in D$ if there exists a δ-neighborhood, $N_\delta(x^*) := \{x \in D \mid \| x - x^* \| \leq \delta\}$, such that

$$\forall x \in N_\delta(x^*), \qquad f(x^*) \geq f(x). \tag{A.1}$$

If the inequality is reversed, we say that f has a *local minimum*, and if the inequalities are strict (except for $x = x^*$), we say that the maximum (minimum) is *strict*. Also, if the inequality holds for all $x \in D$ and not just for a small neighborhood of x^*, we say that we have a *global maximum (minimum)*.

An *extreme value* is either a maximum or a minimum. Not every real-valued function has an extreme value.[1] Of course, a global extreme value is also a local one, but the converse is generally false.

Suppose $x \in D \subset \mathbb{R}^n$ is a point where the partial derivatives of f, $\partial f(x)/\partial x_i$, $i = 1, \ldots, n$, exist and are continuous functions. We then say that f is in the class of functions that are continuously differentiable (C^1), at x. Define the *gradient* of f at x as the vector $\nabla f(x)$ given by

$$\nabla f(x)^T := \left[\frac{\partial f(x)}{\partial x_1}, \ldots, \frac{\partial f(x)}{\partial x_n} \right]. \tag{A.2}$$

Then for all direction vectors $y \in \mathbb{R}^n$, the *directional derivatives* of f at x in the direction y,

$$Df(x; y) := \lim_{t \to 0} \frac{f(x + ty) - f(x)}{t},$$

exist. In fact, $Df(x; y)$ is then equal to a linear combination of the partial derivatives, with the components of the direction vector serving as weights:[2]

$$Df(x; y) = y^T \cdot \nabla f(x).$$

If f is twice continuously differentiable at x, we say that f is in class C^2, $f \in C^2$, and define the *Hessian matrix* of f at x as the $n \times n$ matrix $\nabla^2 f(x)$ given by

$$\nabla^2 f(x) := \left[\frac{\partial^2 f(x)}{\partial x_i \, \partial x_j} \right], \qquad i, j = 1, \ldots, n. \tag{A.3}$$

As f is in C^2, $\nabla^2 f(x)$ is *symmetric*, and the second directional derivative of f at x in the direction y is equal to

$$D^2 f(x; y) = y^T \cdot \nabla^2 f(x) \cdot y.$$

For convenience, from now on we will use the abbreviation

$$f_i(x) := \frac{\partial f(x)}{\partial x_i}, \qquad f_{ij}(x) := \frac{\partial^2 f(x)}{\partial x_i \, \partial x_j} \tag{A.4}$$

whenever there is no risk of confusion.

There follows a collection of major results without proofs.

Proposition A.1 (Necessary Condition) *Let x^* be an interior point of D at which f has a local extreme value. Also, suppose $f \in C^1$ at x^*. Then*

$$\nabla f(x^*) = 0. \tag{A.5}$$

---

[1] If $f : D \to \mathbb{R}$ is continuous over D and D is *compact*, it is known by the Weierstrass theorem that f must have at least one extreme value. But so far we have not assumed compactness of the domain. Incidentally, a set $D \subset \mathbb{R}^n$ is compact if and only if it is bounded and closed. (This equivalence does, however, not necessarily apply to spaces other than $\mathbb{R}^n$.)

[2] To be more precise: if the directional derivatives exist for all directions and are equal to a linear combination of its partial derivatives, one says that f is *Gateaux-differentiable*. We will not be concerned here with other notions of differentiability.

Proposition A.2 (Sufficient Condition) *Let x^* be an interior point of D at which $f \in C^2$. If*

$$\nabla f(x^*) = 0, \tag{A.6}$$

$$\forall z \in \mathbb{R}^n, \quad z \neq (0), \qquad z^T \cdot \nabla^2 f(x^*) \cdot z < 0, \tag{A.7}$$

then f has a strict local maximum at x^*. If the inequality in (A.7) is reversed, then f has a strict local minimum at x^*.

The conditions in Proposition A.2 are only sufficient but not necessary. In other words, for many purposes Proposition A.2 is far too stringent. It is easy to generate functions that have a local extreme value, yet violate condition (A.7). An obvious example is a function that is constant in a small neighborhood of x^*. But, should not Proposition A.2 be sufficient for a *strict* local extreme value? Plausible as it may seem, this conjecture is wrong. There follows a proof by example.

Example A.1 Let $f(x) = x^{2\alpha}$, $\alpha \in \mathbb{N}_+$, with domain $D = \mathbb{R}$. As you can easily confirm, f has a strict global minimum at $x^* = 0$. Of course, at this point one has $\nabla f(0) = 0$. For $\alpha = 1$, $\nabla^2 f(0) = 2$, and the conditions of Proposition A.2 are satisfied. However, if $\alpha > 1$, $\nabla f^2(0) = 0$, and the sufficient condition stated in Proposition A.2 is violated at $x = 0$ even though f has a strict global minimum at this point.

Propositions A.1 and A.2 refer to the behavior of f at x^*, its local extreme value. The following results investigate the behavior of f in a δ-neighborhood of x^*, denoted by $N_\delta(x^*) := \{x \in D \mid \|x - x^*\| < \delta\}$.

Proposition A.3 (Necessary and Sufficient N_δ-Condition) *Let x^* be an interior point of $D \subset \mathbb{R}^n$, and $f \in C^2$ on D. Necessary for a local maximum of f at x^* are the conditions*

$$\nabla f(x^*) = 0, \tag{A.8}$$

$$\forall z \in \mathbb{R}^n, \qquad z^T \cdot \nabla^2 f(x^*) \cdot z \leq 0. \tag{A.9}$$

Sufficient for a local maximum are that condition (A.8) holds and that

$$\exists \delta > 0, \quad \forall x \in N_\delta(x^*), \quad \forall z \in \mathbb{R}^n, \qquad z^T \cdot \nabla^2 f(x) \cdot z \leq 0. \tag{A.10}$$

If the inequalities in (A.8) and (A.9) are reversed, the proposition applies to a local minimum.

Again, you may ask: are the conditions (A.8) and (A.9) not also sufficient? The answer is: no. The proof is by counterexample.

Example A.2 Let $D = \mathbb{R}$, and assume

$$f(x) = \begin{cases} x^4 & \text{if } x \geq 0, \\ -x^4 & \text{if } x < 0. \end{cases}$$

Obviously, at $x^* = 0$ the function f satisfies (A.8) as well as (A.9); yet f does not have an extreme value.

Finally, we present a sufficient condition for a strict local extreme value that is also based on a neighborhood of x^*.

Proposition A.4 (Sufficient N_δ-Condition for Strict Extreme Value) *Let x be an interior point of $D \subset \mathbb{R}^n$ and $f \in C^2$ on D. If*

$$\nabla f(x^*) = 0, \tag{A.11}$$

$$\exists \delta > 0, \quad \forall x \in N_\delta(x^*), \quad \forall z \in \mathbb{R}^n,$$

$$z \neq (0) \implies z^T \cdot \nabla^2 f(x) \cdot z < 0, \tag{A.12}$$

then f has a strict local maximum at x^*. If the inequality in (A.12) is reversed, the proposition applies to a strict local minimum.

To compare Proposition A.4 with Proposition A.2, go back to the case $\alpha > 1$ in Example A.1. Obviously, Proposition A.2 does not recognize that f has a minimum at $x = 0$, but Proposition A.4 does.

A.3 Equality-Constrained Optimization

We now study extreme-value problems where the solution has to lie in a specified region, called the *feasible set*, described by a finite set of *equality constraints* with constraint functions $g^i : D \to \mathbb{R}$,

$$g^i(x) = 0, \qquad i = 1, \ldots, m < n. \tag{A.13}$$

The problem is then to find an extreme value of f in the feasible set described by equations (A.13).

A first and intuitively most plausible method involves the elimination of m variables. The conditions for elimination will be stated in the *implicit-function theorem*. This theorem assumes that all g_i are C^1, and that the $m \times n$ Jacobian matrix $[\partial g_i(x)/\partial x_j]$ has rank m.

However, the actual elimination of variables is often a cumbersome, if not impossible, task. For this reason, one tends to apply an alternative method proposed by Lagrange. Like the elimination method, the method of Lagrange transforms the constrained optimization problem into an unconstrained one.

The following proposition is the basis of the elimination method, which is also used in the proof of the method of Lagrange.

Proposition A.5 (Implicit-Function Theorem) *Suppose the $m < n$ functions $g^i :$ $D \to \mathbb{R}, D \subseteq \mathbb{R}^n$, are C^1 on D, and $\forall i \in \{1, \ldots, m\}$ $g^i(x^0, y^0) = 0$, where $x^0 \in \mathbb{R}^m$, $y^0 \in \mathbb{R}^{n-m}$. Assume the Jacobian matrix $[\partial g^i(x^0, y^0)/\partial x_j]$ has rank m. Then there exists a $\delta > 0$, an open set $E \subset \mathbb{R}^{n-m}$ containing y^0, and functions $\psi_k : E \to \mathbb{R}, k = 1, \ldots, m$, which are C^1 on E, such that the following conditions* *are satisfied:*

$$x_k^0 = \psi_k(y^0), \qquad k = 1, \ldots, m, \tag{A.14}$$

$$\forall\, y \in E, \qquad g_i(\psi_1(y), \ldots, \psi_m(y), y) = 0, \quad i = 1, \ldots, m, \tag{A.15}$$

$$\forall\, y \in E, \quad \forall\, x \in N_\delta(x^0), \quad \left[\frac{\partial g^i(x)}{\partial x_j}\right] \text{ has rank } m. \tag{A.16}$$

The following result gives the clue for the method of Lagrange.

Proposition A.6 *Let $f : D \to \mathbb{R}$ and $g_i : D \to \mathbb{R}$, $i = 1, \ldots, m$, $D \subset \mathbb{R}^n$, be C^1 in a neighborhood of $N_\delta(x^*)x^*$. Suppose x^* is a local maximum of f for all points $x \in N_\delta(x^*)$ that also satisfy*

$$g^i(x) = 0, \qquad i = 1, \ldots, m. \tag{A.17}$$

Also assume the $m \times n$ Jacobian matrix $[\partial g^i(x^*)/\partial x_j]$ has rank m. Then the gradient $\nabla f(x^*)$ is a linear combination of the gradients $\nabla g^i(x^*)$, $i = 1, \ldots, m$; i.e., there exist real numbers $\lambda_1^*, \ldots, \lambda_m^*$ such that

$$\nabla f(x^*) = \sum_{i=1}^{m} \lambda_i^* \nabla g^i(x^*). \tag{A.18}$$

This leads to the formulation of the Lagrangian $L(x, \lambda)$:

$$L(x, \lambda) := f(x) - \sum_{i=1}^{m} \lambda_i g^i(x), \tag{A.19}$$

where the coefficients $\lambda_i \in \mathbb{R}$ are called *Lagrange multipliers* and $\lambda := [\lambda_1, \ldots, \lambda_m]$.

The method of Lagrange transforms an equality-constrained optimization problem into the problem of finding a stationary point of L, as shown in the following result.

Proposition A.7 (Necessary Condition) *Suppose x^* is a local maximum of f for all points $x \in N_\delta(x^*)$ that also satisfy $g^i(x) = 0$, $i = 1, \ldots, m$. Then under the assumptions of Proposition A.7 there exists a vector $\lambda^* \in \mathbb{R}^m$, such that* [3]

$$\nabla_x L(x^*, \lambda^*) = 0. \tag{A.20}$$

Proposition A.8 (Sufficient Conditions) *Suppose $f : D \to \mathbb{R}$ and $g^i : D \to \mathbb{R}$, $i = 1, \ldots, m$, are C^2 on D. If there exist vectors $x^* \in D$, $\lambda^* \in \mathbb{R}^m$ such that*

$$\nabla_x L(x^*, \lambda^*) = 0, \tag{A.21}$$

and if

$$\forall z \in \mathbb{R}^n, \quad z \neq 0, \qquad z^T \cdot \nabla g^i(x^*) = 0 \implies z^T \cdot \nabla_x^2 L(x^*, \lambda^*) \cdot z < 0, \tag{A.22}$$

---

[3] Generally, ∇ denotes a gradient vector; ∇_x means that partial derivatives are taken with respect to the vector x.

then f has a strict local maximum at x*, subject to $g_i(x) = 0$, $i = 1, \ldots, m$. If the inequality in (A.22) is reversed, the proposition applies to a strict local minimum.

This sufficient condition involves the checking of the definiteness of the matrix $\nabla_x^2 L(x^*, \lambda^*)$, subject to the linear constraints: $z^T \cdot \nabla g^i(x^*) = 0$, $i = 1, \ldots, m$. How does one perform this check? Here, a result due to Mann, which can be found in Section A.4, is handy.

Suppose now that the $n \times m$ Jacobian matrix $[g_j^i]$, $g_j^i := \partial g^i(x^*)/\partial x_j$, has rank m. Also, let the variables be indexed in such a way that

$$\det \begin{bmatrix} g_1^1(x^*) & \cdots & g_1^m(x^*) \\ \vdots & \ddots & \vdots \\ g_m^1(x^*) & \cdots & g_m^m(x^*) \end{bmatrix} \neq 0. \tag{A.23}$$

Then we can restate Proposition A.9 as follows:

Corollary A.1 (Sufficient Condition) *Suppose $f : D \to \mathbb{R}$ and $g^i : D \to \mathbb{R}$, $i = 1, \ldots, m < n$, are C^2 on D and condition (A.23) is satisfied. If there exist vectors $x^* \in D$, $\lambda \in \mathbb{R}^m$ such that*

$$\nabla_x L(x^*, \lambda^*) = 0, \tag{A.24}$$

and if $\forall p \in \{m + 1, \ldots, n\}$

$$(-1)^p \det \begin{bmatrix} L_{11}(x^*, \lambda^*) & \cdots & L_{1p}(x^*, \lambda^*) & g_1^1(x^*) & \cdots & g_1^m(x^*) \\ \vdots & & \vdots & \vdots & & \vdots \\ L_{p1}(x^*, \lambda^*) & \cdots & L_{pp}(x^*, \lambda^*) & g_p^1(x^*) & \cdots & g_p^m(x^*) \\ g_1^1(x^*) & \cdots & g_p^1(x^*) & 0 & \cdots & 0 \\ \vdots & & \vdots & \vdots & & \vdots \\ g_p^1(x^*) & \cdots & g_p^m(x^*) & 0 & \cdots & 0 \end{bmatrix} > 0, \tag{A.25}$$

then f has a strict local maximum at x*, subject to the constraints

$$g^i(x^*) = 0, \qquad i = 1, \ldots, m. \tag{A.26}$$

The corresponding result for strict local minima is obtained by replacing $(-1)^p$ by $(-1)^m$ in (A.25).

Propositions A.7 and A.8 and Corollary A.1 assumed that the Jacobian matrix $[\partial g^i(x^*)/\partial x_j]$ has rank m ($< n$), which is equal to the number of constraints. The following result does not require this qualification.

Proposition A.9 *Assume $f : D \to \mathbb{R}$ and $g^i : D \to \mathbb{R}$, $i = 1, \ldots, m < n$, $D \subset \mathbb{R}^n$, are C^1 over D. If x^* is a local extreme value of f for all points x in a neighborhood of x^* satisfying*

$$g^i(x) = 0, \qquad i = 1, \ldots, m, \tag{A.27}$$

then there exist $m + 1$ real numbers, $\lambda_0^*, \lambda_1^*, \ldots, \lambda_m^*$, not all equal to zero, such that

$$\lambda_0^* \nabla f(x^*) - \sum_{i=1}^{m} \lambda_i^* \nabla g^i(x^*) = 0. \qquad (A.28)$$

Remark A.1 If the rank of the Jacobian matrix $[\partial g^i(x^*)/\partial x_j]$ is not equal to the number of constraints, it can occur that λ_0^* must vanish. This may happen for example in degenerate optimization problems where the feasible set has only one point.

Example A.3 Let $f : \mathbb{R} \to \mathbb{R}$, $g : \mathbb{R} \to \mathbb{R}$, and consider $\min f(x) = x$, subject to $g(x) := x^2 = 0$. Obviously, the feasible set has only one element: $x = 0$. At this point, the Jacobian is $[\partial g(0)/\partial x] = [0]$, and hence $\det[\partial g(0)/\partial x] = [0] = 0$. Therefore, at $x = 0$, the Jacobian matrix has rank 0. From (A.28) we get

$$\lambda_0^* - \lambda_1^* 0 = 0;$$

and hence,

$$\lambda_0^* = 0.$$

This is indicative of what can happen. The derivative characterization addresses the question: What happens if things are changed a little near x^*? In the above example the feasible set is $\{0\}$, so that there is no room for change whatsoever. As a result we get a characterization of an optimum that is completely independent of the objective function f. To save us from this embarrassment, we would like to be assured that $\lambda_0 \neq 0$. The conditions for this come under the name *constraint qualification* or rank condition. In the present framework, this condition requires that the Jacobian matrix $[\nabla g_j^i]$ have rank m at x^*. When it is satisfied, then $\lambda_0 > 0$. In fact, we can then normalize $\lambda_0 \equiv 1$, a result that was implicitly used in Corollary A.1.

From here on, there are two urgent issues:

1. to allow for inequality constraints;
2. to find necessary and sufficient conditions for global extreme values.

We address these issues in this order in the next appendix.

A.4 Digression: Quadratic Forms

The propositions in Section A.2 contain conditions that involve *quadratic forms*:

$$z^T \cdot \nabla^2 f(x) \cdot z := \sum_i \sum_j f_{ij}(x) z_i z_j, \qquad (A.29)$$

where $\nabla^2 f(x)$ is symmetric, $f_{ij}(x) = f_{ji}(x)$, and $f_{ij}(x) := \partial^2 f(x)/\partial x_i \, \partial x_j$.

In order to determine the sign of quadratic forms for all $z \in \mathbb{R}^n$, $z \neq 0$ (as required in the above propositions) one compares the determinants

$$d_k(x) := \det \begin{bmatrix} f_{11}(x) & \cdots & f_{1k}(x) \\ \vdots & \ddots & \vdots \\ f_{k1}(x) & \cdots & f_{kk}(x) \end{bmatrix}. \qquad (A.30)$$

One says the matrix $\nabla^2 f(x)$ is *negative definite (semidefinite)* if

$$\forall z \in \mathbb{R}^n, \quad z \neq (0), \qquad z^T \cdot \nabla^2 f(x) \cdot z < 0 \quad (\leq 0), \qquad (A.31)$$

and *positive definite (semidefinite)* if the inequality in (A.31) is reversed.

Lemma A.1 *The $n \times n$ symmetric matrix $\nabla^2 f(x)$ is negative definite if*

$$\forall k \in \{1, \ldots, n\}, \qquad \text{sign } d_k = (-1)^k, \qquad (A.32)$$

and positive definite if

$$\forall k \in \{1, \ldots, n\}, \qquad d_k > 0. \qquad (A.33)$$

For semidefiniteness, replace the strict by weak inequalities.

Remark A.2 If the matrix $\nabla^2 f(x)$ has full rank, the conditions in Lemma A.1 are both necessary and sufficient for definiteness; however, if its rank is less than n, the conditions are sufficient but not necessary.

These checks are useful when one is interested in the behavior of f at a certain point, as in Proposition A.2. But they are quite impractical if n is large, and hopeless if one has to determine the definiteness of the quadratic form in an entire neighborhood of x, as in Proposition A.3.

Example A.4 Of course, a symmetric matrix may not be definite. As an example, consider

$$C := \begin{bmatrix} -2 & \sqrt{6} & 0 \\ \sqrt{6} & -3 & 0 \\ 0 & 0 & 3 \end{bmatrix}.$$

Choose $z^T = (0, 0, 1)$, and one obtains: $z^T \cdot C \cdot z = 3 > 0$. Next, choose $y^T = (1, 0, 0)$, and one has $y^T \cdot C \cdot y = -2 < 0$. Therefore C is not definite.

This example is also instructive for another reason. It makes forcefully clear that Lemma A.1 must be applied to all permutations of coordinate labels. For if this lemma were applied only to the given labeling of the coordinates, one would obtain

$$d_1 = \det(-2) = -2 < 0, \qquad d_2 = \det \begin{bmatrix} -2 & \sqrt{6} \\ \sqrt{6} & -3 \end{bmatrix},$$

$$d_3 = \det(C) = 3 d_2 = 0.$$

Therefore, one would be inclined to infer from Lemma A.1 that C is negative semidefinite, which it is not. However, it is really quite arbitrary which of the two coordinates is called coordinate 1 and which is called 2. But, if you perform all permutations of coordinates, there are really three d_1's:

$$d_1 = \det(-2) = -2 < 0, \qquad d_1 = \det(-3) = -3 < 0,$$

$$d_1 = \det(3) = 3 > 0.$$

This already proves that C is not definite.

Let $A = [a_{ij}]$ be a real $n \times n$ matrix and $B = [b_{ij}]$ a real $n \times m$ matrix. Denote by M_{pq} the matrix obtained from a matrix M by keeping only the elements in the first p rows and q columns.

Lemma A.2 (Mann's Proposition) *Suppose* $\det[B_{mm}] \neq 0_i$. *Then the quadratic form*

$$\xi^T \cdot A \cdot \xi \tag{A.34}$$

is negative definite for all $\xi \in \mathbb{R}^n$, $\xi \neq (0)$, *that also satisfy the linear constraints*

$$B \cdot \xi = 0 \tag{A.35}$$

if and only if

$$\forall p \in \{m+1, \ldots, n\}, \qquad (-1)^p \det \begin{bmatrix} A_{pp} & B_{pm} \\ B_{pm}^T & 0 \end{bmatrix} > 0. \tag{A.36}$$

Similarly, (A.34) is positive definite for all $\xi \in \mathbb{R}^n$, $\xi \neq (0)$, *satisfying (A.35) if and only if*

$$\forall p \in \{m+1, \ldots, n\}, \qquad (-1)^m \det \begin{bmatrix} A_{pp} & B_{pm} \\ B_{pm}^T & 0 \end{bmatrix} > 0. \tag{A.37}$$

For semidefiniteness the strict inequalities are replaced by weak inequalities.

Appendix B

Inequality-Constrained Optimization

Economic maxim: everything is twice more continuously differentiable than it needs to be.

Anonymous

B.1 Introduction

In most economic applications one deals with inequality constraints. For example, a consumer has a limited budget, but who says that he must spend it all? Similarly, a firm may face a borrowing constraint, but it is free to borrow less than this limit. As noted before, the introduction of inequality constraints marks the end of the classical area and the beginning of the modern theory of optimization.

B.2 The Problem

Consider the optimization problem

$$\min_{x \in D} f(x), \tag{B.1}$$

subject to the constraints (in brief: s.t.)

$$g^i(x) \geq 0, \quad i = 1, \ldots, m, \tag{B.2}$$

$$h^j(x) = 0, \quad j = 1, \ldots, p, \tag{B.3}$$

where the functions $f : D \to \mathbb{R}$, $g^i : D \to \mathbb{R}$, $h^j : D \to \mathbb{R}$ are all C^1 over $D \subset \mathbb{R}^n$. From now on we will refer to this formulation as the general optimization problem.

In case you have some doubts about its generality, some remarks are in order.

Remark B.1 If you are given an inequality in the form $\phi(x) \leq 0$, it can always be transformed into an equivalent inequality $\psi(x) \geq 0$ by defining the function $\psi(x) := -\phi(x)$. Hence, (B.2) involves no loss of generality.

Also, since a function $g(x)$ reaches a maximum whenever $f(x) := -g(x)$ has a minimum, there is no need to distinguish maximization and minimization problems.

An equivalent formulation of the general optimization problem is to define the *feasible set*

$$X := \{x \in D \mid h^j(x) = 0, \ j = 1, \ldots, p\} \tag{B.4}$$

$$\cap \{x \in D \mid g^i(x) \geq 0, \ i = 1, \ldots, m\} \tag{B.5}$$

and then write

$$\min_{x \in X} \ f(x). \tag{B.6}$$

B.3 First-Order Necessary Conditions

We now say that $x^* \in X$ is a *local minimum* if

$$\exists \delta > 0, \quad \forall x \in X \cap N_\delta(x^*), \qquad f(x^*) \leq f(x). \tag{B.7}$$

If this inequality holds for all $x \in X$ and not only in a small neighborhood of x^*, the minimum is a *global* one, and if the inequality is strict, we say the minimum is *strict*.

Every point in a neighborhood of x^* can be written as the sum of two vectors: the point x^* and the direction vector $z \in \mathbb{R}^n$. The vector z is called a *feasible direction vector* from x^* if

$$\exists \delta > 0, \quad \forall \theta \in [0, \delta], \qquad x + \theta z \in X \cap N_\delta(x^*). \tag{B.8}$$

Obviously, if x^* is a local minimum and z is a feasible direction vector from x^*, then one must have $f(x^*) \leq f(x^* + \theta z)$ for sufficiently small θ.

At x^*, the inequality constraints (B.2) may be satisfied with equality or not. To distinguish these cases, define

$$I(x^*) := \{i \in N \mid g^i(x^*) = 0\}. \tag{B.9}$$

$I(x^*)$ is the index set of constraints that are satisfied with equality at x^*. The following result should be plausible. Its proof follows easily by taking the limit of a Taylor expansion of $g^i(x^*)$.

Lemma B.1 *Suppose z is a feasible direction vector from x^*. Then*

$$\forall k \in I(x^*), \qquad z^T \cdot \nabla g^k(x^*) \geq 0, \tag{B.10}$$

$$\forall j \in \{1, \ldots, p\}, \qquad z^T \cdot \nabla h^j(x^*) = 0. \tag{B.11}$$

It is possible to derive a weak necessary first-order condition, based on the *weak Lagrangian* $\tilde{L}$, defined as

$$\tilde{L} := \lambda_0 f(x) - \sum_{i=1}^{m} \lambda_i g^i(x) - \sum_{j=1}^{p} \mu_j h^j(x). \tag{B.12}$$

Proposition B.1 (Fritz John Necessary Condition) *Let $x^* \in X$ be a local minimum. Then, there exist vectors $\lambda^0 = (\lambda_0^*, \lambda_1^*, \ldots, \lambda_m^*)$ and $\mu \in \mathbb{R}^p$ such that*

$$\nabla_x \tilde{L}(x^0, \lambda^0, \mu^0) \equiv \lambda_0^* \nabla f(x^*) - \sum_{i=1}^{m} \lambda_1 \nabla g^i(x^*) - \sum_{j=1}^{p} \mu_j^* \nabla h^j(x^*) = 0,$$

$$\lambda_i^* g^i(x^*) = 0, \qquad i = 1, \ldots, m,$$

$$(\lambda^*, \mu^*) \neq (0), \qquad \lambda^* \geq 0.$$

The main problem with this result is that it is possible for λ_0^* to be equal to zero, in which case we get again a characterization of a minimum that is independent of the objective function. To avoid this embarrassment, one would like to assure that $\lambda_0^* > 0$. As in the previous section, the conditions for this travel under the name constraint qualification.

Imposing a certain constraint qualification, Kuhn and Tucker were able to strengthen the Fritz John theorem. Subsequently, various weakened constraint qualifications were proposed in the literature. Here, we ignore this more difficult discussion. Rather than explaining constraint qualification in its weakest form, we state the following frequently invoked conditions:

Proposition B.2 (Arrow–Hurwicz–Uzawa) *Constraint qualification can be dispensed with if the $p \times n$ Jacobian matrix $[\nabla h^j(x)]$ has rank p and if any of the following conditions hold:*

1. *The functions $g^i(x)$, $i = 1, \ldots, m$, are convex.*
2. *The functions $g^i(x)$, $i = 1, \ldots, m$, are affine (this is really a special case of 1).*
3. *The set $\{x \in \mathbb{R}^n \mid g^i(x) \geq 0, \ i = 1, \ldots, m\}$ is convex, it possesses an interior point, and at x^* one has $\forall i \in I(x^*)$, $\nabla g^i(x^*) \neq (0)$.*
4. *The rank of the Jacobian matrix $[\nabla g^i(x^*) \mid i \in I(x^*)]$ is equal to the number of elements of $I(x^*)$.*

With these preliminaries, we now state stronger necessary conditions for an optimum, known as the Kuhn–Tucker necessary conditions.

Proposition B.3 (Kuhn–Tucker Necessary Conditions) *Let x^* be a local minimum, and suppose constraint qualification holds true at x^*. Then there exist vectors $\lambda^* \in \mathbb{R}^m$, $\mu^* \in \mathbb{R}^p$ such that*

$$\nabla_x L(x^*, \lambda^*, \mu^*) := \nabla f(x^*) - \sum_{i=1}^{m} \lambda_i^* \nabla g^i(x^*) - \sum_{j=1}^{p} \mu_j^* \nabla h^j(x^*) = 0, \quad \text{(B.13)}$$

$$\lambda_i^* g^i(x^*) = 0, \qquad i = 1, \ldots, m, \qquad\qquad \text{(B.14)}$$

$$\lambda^* \geq 0. \qquad\qquad\qquad\qquad\qquad \text{(B.15)}$$

In many economic applications, the variables are required to be nonnegative, so that one has the additional constraints

$$x_i \geq 0, \qquad i = 1, \ldots, n. \qquad\qquad\qquad \text{(B.16)}$$

For this more specialized optimization problem, the Kuhn–Tucker necessary conditions are as follows.

Proposition B.4 (Specialized Kuhn–Tucker Conditions) *Let x^* be a local minimum of the optimization problem with the additional nonnegativity constraints (B.16). Then Proposition B.3 holds with the modification that conditions (B.13) are replaced by*

$$\nabla_x L(x^*, \lambda^*, \mu^*) \leq 0, \tag{B.17}$$

$$x^{*T} \cdot \nabla_x L(x^*, \lambda^*, \mu^*) = 0. \tag{B.18}$$

Remark B.2 The verification of constraint qualification is often an impossible task. In economic applications, constraint qualification is usually not a problem. Therefore, it is justifiable to assume the existence of $(\lambda_1^*, \ldots, \lambda_m^*)$, as is often done in the economics literature.

B.4 Second-Order Conditions

The following complements the Kuhn–Tucker first-order necessary conditions. Define

$$\hat{Z}^1(x^*) := \{z \in \mathbb{R}^n \mid \forall i \in I(x^*), \; z^T \cdot \nabla g^i(x^*) = 0$$
$$\forall j = 1, \ldots, p, z^T \cdot \nabla h^j(x^*) = 0\}. \tag{B.19}$$

Proposition B.5 (Necessary Condition) *Let x^* be a local minimum, and suppose there exist vectors $\lambda^* \in \mathbb{R}^m$, $\mu^* \in \mathbb{R}^p$ satisfying (B.13)–(B.15). Then*

$$\forall z \in \hat{Z}^1(x^*), \qquad z^T \cdot \nabla_x^2 L(x^*, \lambda^*, \mu^*) \cdot z \geq 0. \tag{B.20}$$

This condition can be useful to reduce the number of points satisfying the first-order Kuhn–Tucker conditions.

Finally, we turn to *sufficient* conditions for optimality. Denote by $\hat{I}(x^*)$ the index set for which $g^i(x^*) = 0$ *and* at the same time (B.13)–(B.15) are satisfied with $\lambda_i^* > 0$. Obviously, $\hat{I}(x^*)$ is a subset of $I(x^*)$. Define

$$\tilde{Z}^1(x^*) := \{z \in \mathbb{R}^n \mid \forall i \in \hat{I}(x^*), z^T \cdot \nabla g^i(x^*) = 0$$
$$\forall j = 1, \ldots, p, z^T \cdot \nabla h^j(x^*) = 0\}. \tag{B.21}$$

Proposition B.6 (Sufficient Condition) *Let x^* be a feasible solution. If there exist vectors $\lambda^* \in \mathbb{R}^m$, $\mu^* \in \mathbb{R}^p$ satisfying*

$$\nabla_x L(x^*, \lambda^*, \mu^*) = 0, \tag{B.22}$$

$$\lambda_i^* g_i(x^*) = 0, \qquad i = 1, \ldots, m, \tag{B.23}$$

$$\lambda^* \geq 0, \tag{B.24}$$

$$\forall z \in \tilde{Z}(x^*), \quad z \neq (0), \qquad z^T \cdot \nabla_x L(x^*, \lambda^*, \mu^*) \cdot z > 0, \tag{B.25}$$

then x^* is a strict local minimum.

Appendix C

Convexity and Generalizations

"Contrariwise," continued Tweedledee, "if it was so, it might be; and if it were so, it would be: but as it isn't, it ain't. That's logic."

Lewis Carroll

C.1 Introduction

Without more specific assumptions there is not much else one can say about the optimization problem (A.1)–(A.3). However, if the objective function and the feasible set satisfy certain convexity properties, we can characterize global rather than local extreme values and state conditions for their uniqueness. These issues are of vital importance. After all, a local extreme value can be almost as bad as the worst possible choice. So what good does it do to know a local extreme value unless one can be assured that it is also a global one?

Smoking is a good example for a local maximum that is not also a global one. Giving it up temporarily makes most smokers worse off; but there are tremendous gains if you kick the habit altogether.

In this section we explain some basic facts about convex sets and functions and apply these to characterize convex optimization problems. In addition we cover various generalized notions of convexity – such as strong convexity, and variations of quasi- and *pseudoconvexity* – that play an important role in economic applications.

C.2 Convex Sets

A set $S \subset \mathbb{R}^n$ is called convex if every linear combination of two of its points is also an element of it; or visually, if the line joining these points lies entirely in S.

Consider $[x_1, x_2] := \{y \in \mathbb{R}^n \mid y := \alpha x_1 + (1 - \alpha)x_2, \ \alpha \in [0, 1]\}$. We define formally: $S \subset \mathbb{R}^n$ is *convex* if

$$\forall x_1, x_2 \in S, \qquad [x_1, x_2] \in S. \tag{C.1}$$

Important families of convex sets are the *hyperplanes*

$$H(a, \beta) := \{x \in \mathbb{R}^n \mid a^T x = \beta\}, \qquad \text{where} \ \ a \in \mathbb{R}^n, \ \ a \neq 0, \ \ \beta \in \mathbb{R}, \tag{C.2}$$

and the associated *half spaces*

$$H^+(a, \beta) := \{x \in \mathbb{R}^n \mid a^T x \geq \beta\}, \tag{C.3}$$

$$H^-(a, \beta) := \{x \in \mathbb{R}^n \mid a^T x \leq \beta\}. \tag{C.4}$$

Obviously, $H^+ \cup H^- = \mathbb{R}^n$ and $H^+ \cap H^- = H$.

The major importance of these sets stems from the following result, which plays a key role in several proofs of results listed below.

Proposition C.1 (Separating-Hyperplane Proposition) *Let A and B be two non-empty, convex, and disjoint sets in $\mathbb{R}^n$. Then there exists a hyperplane $H(a, \beta)$ and associated half spaces H^+ and H^- such that $A \subset H^+$ and $B \subset H^-$.*

You may wish to visualize this result in $\mathbb{R}^2$ and ask yourself why it requires $A \cap B = \emptyset$.

Also recall that the intersection of any number of convex sets is convex as well, whereas the union of convex sets need not be convex.

C.3 Convex Functions

If you draw the graph of a function $f : \mathbb{R} \to \mathbb{R}$, you may find that the chord connecting any two points of the curve $f(x)$ lies on or above the curve. Functions that have this property are called *convex*. They are closely related to convex sets. Indeed, in the following illustrations the shaded areas above convex curves (called hypographs) are convex sets. As this property is generally true, the convexity of the hypograph of f can also be used to define convex functions.

Now consider a function $f : D \to \mathbb{R}$, with a convex domain $D \subset \mathbb{R}^n$. We define formally that f is *convex* if $\forall x_1, x_2 \in D$, $\forall \lambda \in [0, 1]$

$$f(\lambda x_1 + (1 - \lambda)x_2) \leqq \lambda f(x_1) + (1 - \lambda)f(x_2). \tag{C.5}$$

If the inequality is strict for $x_1 \neq x_2$, $\lambda \in (0, 1)$, then f is called *strictly convex*.

Also, we say that f is (strictly) *concave* if $-f$ is (strictly) convex, which occurs if and only if the inequality in (C.5) is reversed. Obviously, the sum of two convex functions is convex, and the difference between a convex function and a concave function is convex as well. Convexity is also preserved by multiplication with a positive scalar.

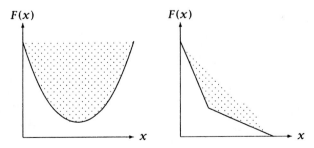

Figure C.1. Examples of Convex Functions and Hypographs.

An alternative characterization of convex functions – already suggested by the above illustrations – is in terms of the *hypograph* of f, HG(f), defined as

$$\text{HG}(f) := \{(x, y) \in D \times \mathbb{R} \mid f(x) \le y\}. \tag{C.6}$$

In fact, the convexity of HG(f) is equivalent to the convexity of f, so that the former can also be used as an alternative definition of the convexity of f.

Proposition C.2 *Let $D \subset \mathbb{R}^n$ be a convex set. The function $f : D \to \mathbb{R}$ is convex if and only if HG(f) is a convex set.*

Analogously the concavity of f is equivalent to the convexity of the epigraph of f, EG(f), defined as

$$\text{EG}(f) := \{(x, y) \in D \times \mathbb{R} \mid f(x) \ge y\}. \tag{C.7}$$

One of the nice properties of convex functions is that they are continuous everywhere except possibly at the boundaries of D (if D is not open). Differentiability is of course not implied by the convexity of f.[1] But if one assumes that f is not only concave but also in C^1 or C^2, one arrives at a characterization of convex functions that is usually far easier to check than the definition (C.5) or the convexity of the hypograph of f.

Proposition C.3 (First-Derivative Characterization) *Let $f : D \to \mathbb{R}$ be C^1 on the open and convex set $D \subset \mathbb{R}^n$. Then f is convex if and only if $\forall\, x, x^* \in D$*

$$f(x) \ge f(x^*) + (x - x^*)^T \cdot \nabla f(x^*); \tag{C.8}$$

it is strictly convex if the inequality (C.8) is strict for $x \ne x^*$.

Inequality (C.8) has an appealing geometric interpretation. It says that at any point of the graph of a convex function the tangent plane to the graph at that point lies entirely on or below the graph, as illustrated in Figure C.2.

This characterization of a differentiable and convex function involves a condition on two points. If f is C^2, there is a characterization by second derivatives at just one point:

Proposition C.4 (Second-Derivative Characterization) *Let $f : D \to \mathbb{R}$, be C^2 on the open and convex set $D \subset \mathbb{R}^n$. Then f is convex if and only if the Hessian matrix $\nabla^2 f(x)$ is positive semidefinite, i.e.,*

$$\forall\, x \in D, \qquad \nabla^2 f(x) \text{ is positive semidefinite.} \tag{C.9}$$

Proposition C.4 cannot be sharpened to cover *strictly* convex functions by replacing the word semidefinite with the word definite. True, if the inequality in (C.9) is strict, one can be assured that f is strictly convex; but the converse is not true. For a simple proof by counterexamples just go back once again to Example A.1, which gives a strictly convex function, $f : \mathbb{R} \to \mathbb{R}$, with a vanishing Hessian matrix at

---

[1] But notice that a convex function is almost everywhere differentiable. It need *not* be continuously differentiable, but it will be continuously differentiable on an open set if it is differentiable on that set.

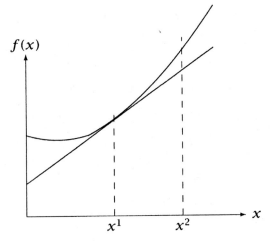

Figure C.2. A Convex Function and Its Linear Approximation.

$x = 0$. We make a point of this because it is frequently confused in the economics literature.

Example C.1 The function $f(x) := -x_1^{\alpha_1} x_2^{\alpha_2}$, with domain $\mathbb{R}_+$ and $\alpha_1, \alpha_2 \in \mathbb{R}_+$, is convex if $\alpha_1 + \alpha_2 \leq 1$, and neither *convex* nor concave if $\alpha_1 + \alpha_2 > 1$.

C.4 Strongly Convex Functions

Strong convexity is a slightly stronger requirement than strict convexity. Strong convexity plays an important role in economics.

A function $f : D \to \mathbb{R}$ defined on the convex set $D \subset \mathbb{R}^n$ is called *strongly convex* if there exists a convex function $\psi : D \to \mathbb{R}$ and a scalar $\alpha > 0$ such that $\forall x \in D$

$$f(x) = \psi(x) + \frac{1}{2}\alpha x^T \cdot x; \qquad (\text{C.10})$$

similarly, f is called strongly concave if $-f$ is strongly convex.

Since $\frac{1}{2}\alpha x^T \cdot x$ is a strictly convex function and since the sum of a strictly convex and a convex function is strictly convex, it follows that every strongly convex function is strictly convex. But not every strictly convex function is also strongly convex; therefore,

strong convexity $\Rightarrow$ strict convexity $\Rightarrow$ convexity,

but not vice versa.

Example C.2 Go back once again to the function $f(x) := x^4$. As you already know, this function is strictly convex. Yet, f is not strongly convex. To show this, suppose *per absurdum* that there exists a convex function $\psi(x)$ and a scalar $\alpha > 0$

so that $\forall x \in D$, $f(x) = \psi(x) + \frac{1}{2}\alpha x^T x$. But then, at the origin $x = 0$, one must have

$$0 = f''(0) = \psi''(0) + \alpha,$$

and therefore $\psi''(0) = -\alpha < 0$ – in contradiction to the assumed convexity of ψ.

Strongly convex functions can be characterized as follows:

Proposition C.5 (Strong-Convexity Properties) *Let* $f : D \to \mathbb{R}$ *be defined on the convex and open set* $D \subset \mathbb{R}^n$. *Then* f *is strongly convex if and only if there exists a scalar* $\alpha > 0$ *such that*

1. for all $x^1, x^2 \in D$ *and for all* $\lambda \in [0, 1]$

$$f(\lambda x^1 + (1 - \lambda)x^2) \leq \lambda f(x^1) + (1 - \lambda)f(x^2)$$
$$-\frac{\alpha}{2}\lambda(1 - \lambda)\|x^2 - x^1\|^2; \qquad (C.11)$$

2. if f *is also* C^1, *(C.11) can be replaced by:* $\forall x^1, x^2 \in D$

$$f(x^2) \geq f(x^1) + (x^2 - x^1)^T \cdot \nabla f(x^1)$$
$$+\frac{1}{2}\alpha\|x^2 - x^1\|^2; \qquad (C.12)$$

3. if f *is* C^2, *(C.11) can be replaced by:* $\forall x \in D$

$$[\nabla^2 f(x) - \alpha I] \quad \text{is positive semidefinite}, \qquad (C.13)$$

where I *denotes the identity matrix.*

Strong concavity is used in economics, for example, in the theory of the firm. If the production function is C^2 and strongly concave, one can be assured that the supply and factor demand functions are C^1 – if they exist. The differentiability of these solution functions is a prerequisite for using calculus techniques in comparative statics. Contrary to what one often reads, the strict concavity of the production function is not quite enough for this. An example of a production function that is strongly concave is the Cobb–Douglas function $f(x) := \prod x_i^{\alpha_i}$, with $\alpha_i > 0$ and $\sum \alpha_i < 1$.

C.5 Convexity and Global Extreme Values

Convexity properties greatly simplify and strengthen the necessary and sufficient conditions for extreme values. If we deal with an unconstrained minimization problem, one has

Proposition C.6 (Global Minimum) *Suppose* $f : D \to \mathbb{R}$ *is* C^1 *and convex on the convex and open set* $D \subset \mathbb{R}^n$. *Then* $x^* \in D$ *is a global minimum if and only if* $\nabla f(x^*) = 0$.

This gives us a simple procedure for finding a global minimum: simply check whether f is a convex function, and whether D is a convex and open set, and then find a stationary point of f over D.

Proposition C.7 (Maximum Number of Extreme Values) *A strictly convex function on an open and convex domain cannot have more than one minimum.*

These results extend to the general minimization problem (A.1)–(A.3) with inequality or equality constraints, provided the feasible set X is convex. A key question is then: under what conditions is the constraint set

$$X := \{x \in \mathbb{R}^n \mid g^i(x) \le 0, \quad i = 1, \ldots, m\}$$
$$\cap \{x \in \mathbb{R}^n \mid h^j(x) = 0, \quad j = 1, \ldots, p\} \tag{C.14}$$

indeed convex? We close this discussion with some results on a specialized version of program (A.1)–(A.3), known as a convex program.

Program (A.1)–(A.3) is called a *convex program* if three requirements are met:

1. $f(x)$ is convex and C^1;
2. all equality constraint functions $h^j(x)$ are affine functions:

$$h^j(x) := (a^j)^T \cdot x - b_j, \quad j = 1, \ldots, m,$$

where $a^j \in \mathbb{R}^n$, $b \in \mathbb{R}$, and $\det[a_{ij}] \neq 0$;
3. all inequality constraint functions $g^i(x)$ are C^1 and concave.

The constraint set X of such a convex program is convex. Indeed, the solution set of an affine function is convex, the solution set of concave inequality constraints $g^i(x) \le 0$ is convex, and finally the intersection of convex sets is convex.

Proposition C.8 (Kuhn–Tucker Sufficient Condition) *Consider a convex program. If there exist vectors x^*, λ^*, μ^* satisfying the constraints (A.2) and (A.3), and*

$$\nabla f(x^*) - \sum \lambda_i^* \nabla g^i(x^*) - \sum \mu_j^* \nabla h^j(x^*) = 0, \tag{C.15}$$
$$\lambda_i^* g^i(x^*) = 0, \quad i = 1, \ldots, m, \tag{C.16}$$
$$\lambda^* \ge 0, \tag{C.17}$$

then x^* is a global minimum.

C.6 Generalized Convexity: Quasiconvexity

If a convex function over a convex domain has an extreme value, you can rest assured that it is the unique global extreme value. In this sense, convexity is sufficient for a unique global extreme value. But convexity is not also necessary; indeed, convexity is far too strong a requirement. As an economist you should be happy about this fact. There are several important economic optimization problems where convexity (or concavity for that matter) cannot possibly be assumed. As an example, consider the standard consumer demand problem in a deterministic framework. While the feasible set can be taken to be convex (indeed, for positive linear prices the budget set is convex), concavity of the utility function cannot be assumed. This stems from two facts: utility functions are unique only up to positive monotone transformations (this follows from the definition of an ordinal utility function), yet concavity is obviously not preserved by all monotone transformations. Luckily, it turns out that some weaker notions of concavity have the required invariance property and yet suffice to guarantee a unique global optimum.

The first and best-known generalization of convexity is quasiconvexity. A function $f : D \to \mathbb{R}$ defined on a convex set $D \subset \mathbb{R}^n$ is called *quasiconvex* if $\forall x_1, x_2 \in D$

$$\forall \lambda \in [0, 1], \qquad f(\lambda x_1 + (1 - \lambda)x_2) \leq \max\{f(x_1), f(x_2)\}, \qquad \text{(C.18)}$$

and *quasiconcave* if $-f$ is quasiconvex.[2]

Similarly, f is called *strictly quasiconvex* (quasiconcave) if the inequality is strict for $x_1 \neq x_2$, $\lambda \in (0, 1)$.

Just as the convexity of a function is equivalent to the convexity of its hypograph, quasiconvexity is equivalent to the convexity of its lower contour set. The *lower contour* set of f for the value y, $\text{LC}(f, y)$, is defined as

$$\text{LC}(f, y) := \{x \in D \mid f(x) \leq y\}. \qquad \text{(C.19)}$$

Proposition C.9 *Let $f : D \to \mathbb{R}$ be defined on a convex set $D \subset \mathbb{R}^n$. Then f is (strictly) quasiconvex if and only if the lower contour sets $\text{LC}(f, y)$ are (strictly) convex for all $y \in \mathbb{R}$.[3]*

Analogously, f is (strictly) quasiconcave if and only if the *upper contour sets*

$$\text{UC}(f, y) := \{x \in D \mid f(x) \geq y\} \qquad \text{(C.20)}$$

are (strictly) convex for all $y \in \mathbb{R}$.

Every convex function is also quasiconvex. But the converse is not generally true. Hence,

$$\text{convexity} \Rightarrow \text{quasiconvexity},$$

but not vice versa.

Example C.3 Consider the function $f(x) := x^{\frac{1}{2}}$ defined on $\mathbb{R}$. Obviously, f is quasiconvex, yet strictly concave, and hence not convex.

Unlike convex functions, quasiconvex functions can be discontinuous in the interior of their domain, and they can have local minima that are not global. Illustrations are in Figures C.3 and C.4.

The significance of quasiconvexity for optimization theory comes out in the following result.

Proposition C.10 *If x^* is a strict local minimum of a quasiconvex function f, then x^* is also a global minimum.*

However, this should not be mistaken to mean that a stationary point of a quasiconvex function is a global extreme value. As an example, consider the function

---

[2] Prove that f is quasiconcave if and only if $f(\lambda x_1 + (1 - \lambda)x_2) \geq \min\{f(x_1), f(x_2)\}$.
[3] A convex set is strictly convex if for two boundary points x_1, x_2 all points on the joining line are in the interior of the set.

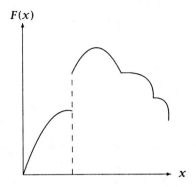

Figure C.3. Discontinuous Quasiconvex Function with Local Minimum That Is Not Global.

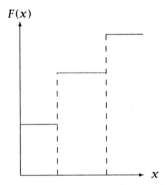

Figure C.4. Another Discontinuous Quasiconvex Function with Local Minimum That Is Not Also Global.

$f(x) = -x^3$ with domain $\mathbb{R}$. Obviously, $f'(x) = 0 \Leftrightarrow x = 0$. However, the point $x = 0$ is not even an extreme value. Therefore, be careful when you apply quasiconvexity. If you have found a stationary point, you should first check whether this point is indeed a strict local minimum. If it is, then it is safe to infer that you have found the global minimum. But without this check you cannot be sure that you have found an extreme value at all.

If f is C^1, one has:

Proposition C.11 (First-Derivative Characterization) *Let $f : D \to \mathbb{R}$ be C^1 on an open and convex set $D \subset \mathbb{R}^n$. Then f is quasiconvex if and only if $\forall x^1, x^2 \in D$*

$$f(x^1) \le f(x^2) \implies (x^1 - x^2)^T \cdot \nabla f(x^2) \le 0, \qquad \text{(C.21)}$$

and quasiconcave if and only if $\forall x^1, x^2 \in D$

$$f(x^1) \ge f(x^2) \implies (x^1 - x^2)^T \cdot \nabla f(x^2) \ge 0. \qquad \text{(C.22)}$$

Unfortunately, there seems to be no useful first-derivative characterization for the entire class of strictly quasiconvex functions. But if f is nonstationary, one has:

Proposition C.12 *Let* $f : D \to \mathbb{R}$ *be* C^1 *and nonstationary on an open and convex set* $D \subset \mathbb{R}^n$. *Then* f *is strictly quasiconvex if and only if* $\forall x^1, x^2 \in D$, $x_1 \neq x_2$,

$$f(x^1) \leq f(x^2) \quad \Longrightarrow \quad (x^1 - x^2)^T \cdot \nabla f(x^2) < 0, \tag{C.23}$$

and strictly quasiconcave if and only if $\forall x^1, x^2 \in D$, $x_1 \neq x_2$

$$f(x^1) \leq f(x^2) \quad \Longrightarrow \quad (x^1 - x^2)^T \cdot \nabla f(x^2) > 0. \tag{C.24}$$

Second-derivative characterizations of quasiconvex functions are quite complicated. The matter is considerably simplified if we restrict ourselves to the class of nonstationary, strictly quasiconvex functions. Luckily, this is not a restriction in most economic applications. But you should notice a further limitation of the following results. Like the second-derivative characterization of strictly concave functions, the following characterization provides necessary conditions and sufficient conditions that are not quite the same.

Define the *bordered Hessian* submatrices $\tilde{H}_k(x)$, $k = 1, \ldots, n$, of f:

$$\tilde{H}_k(x) := \begin{bmatrix} f_{11} & f_{12} & \cdots & f_{1k} & f_1 \\ f_{21} & f_{22} & \cdots & f_{2k} & f_2 \\ \vdots & \vdots & \ddots & \vdots & \vdots \\ f_{k1} & f_{k2} & \cdots & f_{kk} & f_k \\ f_1 & f_2 & \cdots & f_k & 0 \end{bmatrix}. \tag{C.25}$$

Proposition C.13 (Second-Derivative Characterization) *Let* $f : D \to \mathbb{R}$ *be* C^2 *and nonstationary on an open and convex set* $D \subset \mathbb{R}^n$. *Necessary for the strict quasiconvexity of* f *is the condition*

$$\forall x \in D, \qquad \tilde{H}_n(x) \text{ is positive semidefinite.} \tag{C.26}$$

In contrast, sufficient for the strict quasiconvexity of f *is the condition*

$$\forall x \in D, \qquad \tilde{H}_n(x) \text{ is positive definite.} \tag{C.27}$$

To characterize strict quasiconcavity of a nonstationary function, replace positive definiteness by negative definiteness.

Applying Mann's proposition (see A.4), one arrives at the following necessary and sufficient conditions for quasiconvexity in terms of the bordered Hessian submatrices $\tilde{H}_k(x)$, $k = 1, \ldots, n$:

Corollary C.1 *Given the assumptions of Proposition C.12, the condition*

$$\forall x \in D, \qquad \det \tilde{H}_k(x) \leq 0, \quad k = 1, \ldots, n \tag{C.28}$$

is necessary for the strict quasiconvexity of f, *and the condition*

$$\forall x \in D, \qquad \det \tilde{H}_k(x) < 0, \quad k = 1, \ldots, n \tag{C.29}$$

is sufficient for its strict quasiconvexity. To obtain conditions for strict quasiconcavity, replace (C.28) by

$$\forall x \in D, \qquad (-1)^k \det \tilde{H}_k(x) \geq 0, \quad k = 1, \ldots, n, \tag{C.30}$$

and (C.29) by

$$\forall x \in D, \qquad (-1)^k \det \tilde{H}_k(x) > 0, \quad k = 1, ..., n. \qquad (C.31)$$

We have emphasized before that even though a convex function is also quasi-convex, the reverse inference is generally not true. There is, however, an important class of functions for which quasiconvexity implies convexity, and therefore quasiconvexity is equivalent to convexity. The class of functions for which this holds true, comprises all functions $f : \mathbb{R}^n_{++} \to \mathbb{R}$ that are positive-valued, C^1, and homogeneous of degree 1. Since this result is quite useful, we state it formally as follows.

Proposition C.14 *Assume* $f : \mathbb{R}^n_{++} \to \mathbb{R}$ *is* C^1, *homogeneous of degree 1, and positive-valued. Then* f *is convex if and only if* f *is quasiconvex.*

C.7 Convexity Properties of Composite Functions

Referring to utility functions, we have already indicated that a monotone increasing transformation of a concave function need not be concave. Here we will see that quasiconcavity and quasiconvexity are invariant with regard to such transformations and add some more general results on composite functions. There is yet another important reason to study the convexity properties of composite functions: it provides eminently practical results for identification of convexity and quasiconvexity that you should try to apply when the conditions on the subdeterminants of the (bordered) Hessian matrix are impracticable.

We begin with two fairly obvious results.

Proposition C.15 *Suppose* $f : D \to \mathbb{R}$ *and* $g : D \to \mathbb{R}$ *are convex functions defined on the convex domain* $D \subset \mathbb{R}^n$. *Then* $f + g$ *is also convex, and so is* λf *for all* $\lambda > 0$.

Now consider composite functions in general. Suppose $f : D \to \mathbb{R}$ is defined on the convex set $D \subset \mathbb{R}^n$, and let $g : E \to \mathbb{R}$ be defined on the range of values of f, denoted by E. Assume both f and g are convex functions. Does it follow that the composite function of a function $h : D \to \mathbb{R}$, $h(x) := g[f(x)]$, is convex as well? The following example shows that the answer is no.

Example C.4 Let $f(x) := -\ln x$ and $g(f) := -f$. Obviously, f is convex, and g is linear and hence also convex. Yet, h defined by $h(x) := g[f(x)] = \ln x$ is strictly concave and hence not convex.

Suppose, however, that g is C^1, has the property $g' > 0$ (is a monotone increasing function), and is convex. We then call the composition $g[f(x)]$ a convex monotone increasing transformation of f. This particular transformation preserves convexity.

Proposition C.16 *Suppose* $f : D \to \mathbb{R}$ *is defined on the convex set* $D \subset \mathbb{R}^n$ *and* $g : E \to \mathbb{R}$ *on the range of values of* f. *Let* g *be monotonically increasing, and let both* f *and* g *be convex. Then the convex monotone increasing transformation of* f, $h : D \to \mathbb{R}$, $h(x) := g[f(x)]$, *is also convex.*

While convex monotone increasing transformations of convex functions are convex, it is not generally true that convex transformations of convex functions are convex nor that increasing transformations of convex functions are convex. Find counterexamples.

Now turn to *quasiconvexity*. Again, one has:

Proposition C.17 *Suppose $f : D \to \mathbb{R}$ is quasiconvex on the convex set $D \subset \mathbb{R}^n$. Then λf is also quasiconvex for all $\lambda > 0$.*

However, *the sum of two quasiconvex functions is generally not quasiconvex.* As this may surprise you, take a look at the following example.

Example C.5 Let $f : \mathbb{R} \to \mathbb{R}$, $f(x) := -x^2$ and $g : \mathbb{R} \to \mathbb{R}$, $g(x) := x$. Obviously, both f and g are quasiconvex. Consider the function $h : \mathbb{R} \to \mathbb{R}$, $h(x) := f(x) + g(x) = -x^2 + x$. Compute the lower contour set of h for the value 0, $LC(h; 0)$, and one obtains $LC(h; 0) = (-\infty, -1] \cup [1, +\infty]$, which is obviously *not* convex. Hence, the sum of the two quasiconvex functions f and g is not quasiconvex.

Turning to monotone increasing transformations of quasiconvex functions, we confirm that quasiconvexity has stronger invariance properties than convexity.

Proposition C.18 *Suppose $f : D \to \mathbb{R}$ is defined on the convex set $D \subset \mathbb{R}^n$, and $g : E \to \mathbb{R}$ on the range of values of f. Let g be monotone increasing and f quasiconvex. Then the monotone increasing transformation of f given by $h : D \to \mathbb{R}$, $h(x) := g[f(x)]$, is also quasiconvex.*

More generally than this, the operation of taking monotone increasing transformations of a function (not just of quasiconvex or quasiconcave functions) leaves the upper and lower contour sets unchanged in a sense described in the following proposition.

Proposition C.19 *Given the assumptions of Proposition C.18, one has, for all y in the range of f, the following properties of lower and upper contour sets:*

$$LC(h; h(y)) \equiv LC(f; y), \tag{C.32}$$

$$UC(h; h(y)) \equiv UC(f; y). \tag{C.33}$$

Of course, since any convex function is also quasiconvex, any monotone increasing transformation of a convex function must be quasiconvex.

Finally, we mention that all of the above results can be strengthened to strict convexity (quasiconvexity) if the underlying functions are themselves strictly convex (quasiconvex) and strictly monotone.

Example C.6 This example shows how the above results can be utilized to check convexity. Let $f : \mathbb{R}^n \to \mathbb{R}$, $f(x) := (\sum x_i^2)^{1/2}$. Define $g : \mathbb{R}^n \to \mathbb{R}$, $g(x) := \sum x_j^2$ and $h : \mathbb{R} \to \mathbb{R}$, $h(g) := g^{1/2}$. The function g is obviously strictly convex (its Hessian matrix is a diagonal matrix with positive entries on the main diagonal), and therefore g is also quasiconvex. The function h is a monotone increasing transformation of the quasiconvex function g. Hence, $f = h(g)$ is quasiconvex, by Proposition C.18. This result can even be strengthened as follows. Notice that f is homogeneous of degree 1, since $f(\lambda x) = [\sum (\lambda x_i)^2]^{1/2} = \lambda (\sum x_i^2)^{1/2} = \lambda f(x)$. Therefore, by Proposition C.14, the already confirmed quasiconvexity of f implies convexity of f.

We close this section with an application to a frequently used functional form in economics.

Is the Cobb–Douglas Function Concave? The Cobb–Douglas function

$$f(x) := \prod_{i=1}^{n} x_i^{\alpha_i}, \qquad \alpha_i > 0, \tag{C.34}$$

is frequently used in maximization problems in economics. Therefore it is eminently important to know whether this function is concave or at least quasiconcave.

Using some of the above results, we now summarize some of its properties.

Proposition C.20 *Consider the Cobb–Douglas function (C.34). It has the following concavity properties:*

1. *f is quasiconcave.*
2. *f is concave if $\sum \alpha_i \le 1$.*
3. *f is neither concave nor convex if $\sum \alpha_i > 1$.*

Proof The assertions are easy to prove if $n = 2$. In this case you can utilize the sign conditions concerning the principal minors of the Hessian matrix of f, stated above. However, these conditions are hopeless if n is large. Therefore, one has to find some other procedure. The following is a sketch of a somewhat ingenious proof that uses several of the above results in three steps.

1. Consider the transformation of f given by

$$g := \ln f = \sum \alpha_i \ln x_i$$

   instead of f. Compute the Hessian matrix of g, and show that it is a diagonal matrix. It is easy to see that g must be concave. Since $g(x) \equiv \ln f(x)$, it follows that $f(x) \equiv e^{g(x)}$. Hence, f is also a monotone increasing transformation of the concave function g. Every monotone increasing transformation of a concave function is quasiconcave (see Proposition C.18). Hence, f is quasiconcave.
2. Show that f is concave if $\sum \alpha_i = 1$. Note that, in this particular case, f is a homogeneous function of degree 1, is positive everywhere, is C^1, and is quasiconcave. Therefore, by a known property of homogeneous functions, f must be concave.
3. Using a tautological transformation, one has

$$f(x) \equiv \left(\prod x_i^{\alpha_i/\gamma} \right)^\gamma =: h(x)^\gamma, \qquad \gamma := \sum \alpha_i.$$

   The function h is obviously itself a Cobb–Douglas function with a sum of exponents $\gamma/\gamma \equiv 1$. Using step 2, it then follows that h must be concave. Let $\gamma := \sum \alpha_i \le 1$. Then the function h^γ is a monotone increasing concave transformation of the concave function h. Therefore, f is also concave, which completes the proof. $\qquad \square$

C.8 Convexifiable Quasiconvex Programs

The properties of a convex program described in Section C.5 can be extended to convexifiable programs. The prerequisite for weakening convexity requirements is that quasiconvex objective functions be convexifiable by means of monotone increasing transformations and that quasiconcave constraint function be concavifiable. In the following we state a sufficient condition and explain why the possibility of convexification and concavification is so important.

The key insight comes from the following observation: suppose the objective function is quasiconvex rather than convex, or some constraint functions are only quasiconcave rather than concave. Also suppose there exists a set of strict monotone increasing transformations such that the objective function becomes convex and all constraint functions become concave. Then it is not so difficult to see that the thus convexified program has the same solution as the original program, after applying the inverses of these transformations. Therefore, the convexity and concavity requirements of Proposition C.8 can be weakened to quasiconvexity and quasiconcavity – provided the objective function is convexifiable and the constraint functions are concavifiable.

Formally, we say that a quasiconvex function $f : D \to E$, $D \subset \mathbb{R}^n$, $E \subset \mathbb{R}$, is *convexifiable* if there exists a strictly monotone increasing and C^1 transformation $h : E \to \mathbb{R}$, such that the composite function $h(f)$ is *convex*. The definition of concavifiability is phrased correspondingly. The following proposition gives a sufficient condition for convexifiability of a quasiconvex function.

Proposition C.21 *Assume* $f : D \to E$, $E \subset \mathbb{R}$, *is* C^2 *and quasiconvex (quasiconcave),* $D \subset \mathbb{R}^n$ *is open and convex, and* $f_i'(x) > 0$, $\forall x \in D$. *Then* f *is convexifiable (concavifiable).*

Example C.7 In economic applications, most quasiconcave functions (such as utility or production functions) are concavifiable. A simple example of a quasiconcave function that is not concavifiable is the function $f : \mathbb{R} \to \mathbb{R}$, $f(x) := x^3$. Confirm that f is quasiconcave. Why does Proposition C.21 not apply?

It is surely nice to know which quasiconvex functions are convexifiable. But how does one actually convexify? The answer is particularly simple if $f : D \to \mathbb{R}$, $D \subset \mathbb{R}$, is C^2 and monotone increasing and D is convex and open. In this case f^{-1} exists and is itself monotone increasing, and

$$f^{-1}[f(x)] = x =: g(x)$$

is convex. Therefore, the inverse of f can be used to convexify f.

Unfortunately, this trick does not help as you go from one to several variables. But even then, convexification is fairly straightforward. For this purpose consider the monotone increasing transformation $g : D \to \mathbb{R}$, $D \subset \mathbb{R}^n$, with image

$$g(x) = \exp(rf(x)),$$

where r is some positive constant. Differentiation gives

$$g''(x) = [rf'(x)]^2 \exp(rf(x)) + rf''(x) \exp(rf(x)),$$

and since $f'(x) > 0$,

$$g''(x) = rf'(x)^2 \exp(rf(x)) \left[r + \frac{f''(x)}{f'(x)^2} \right].$$

For all $x \in D$, the factor outside the square brackets is positive. Consider a compact set $C \subseteq D$. Since f is C^2 and $f'(x) > 0$, the function f''/f'^2 is continuous. Therefore, by the Weierstrass theorem, f''/f'^2, must have a minimum over C. Call this minimum $m \in \mathbb{R}$. Now choose $r \geq -m$, and it is assured that the factor in brackets is nonnegative over C. But then g is convex over C; thus, convexification is assured over $C \subseteq D$.

We may now say that we are dealing with a *convexifiable quasiconvex program* if the following conditions are met:

1. $f : D \to \mathbb{R}$ is C^2, is strictly quasiconvex on the open and convex domain $D \subset \mathbb{R}^n$, and has $f'_i(x) > 0 \, \forall x \in D$.
2. All equality constraints $h^j : D \to \mathbb{R}$ are affine functions:

$$h^j(x) := (a^j)^T x - b_j, \qquad j = 1, \dots, m,$$

   where $a^j \in \mathbb{R}^n$, $b \in \mathbb{R}$ and $\det[a_{ij}] \neq 0$.
3. All inequality constraints $g^i : D \to \mathbb{R}$ are C^2 and strictly quasiconcave, with $\nabla g^i(x) > 0 \, \forall x \in D$.

We may then summarize:

Proposition C.22 (Convexifiable Quasiconvex Program) *Consider a convexifiable program. If there exist vectors x^*, λ^*, μ^* satisfying the constraints (B.2) and (B.3) and the Kuhn–Tucker conditions (C.15)–(C.17), then x^* is a global minimum.*

Application: A Concavifiable Theory of the Firm Problem Consider the factor demand and product supply decision of an egalitarian *labor-managed firm* (LMF) that operates in competitive markets. An egalitarian labor managed firm is defined as follows: It is owned by its employees (called members), and it is committed to share its net return equally among all members; new members are never charged an entry fee, and members who quit are never compensated.

Denote the product price by p, factor prices (for factors other than labor) by the row vector $w \in \mathbb{R}^n_+$, factor demand by the column vector $X \in \mathbb{R}^n_+$, product supply by Y, fixed costs by $F > 0$, and number of members by M. The production function $f(M, X)$ is strictly monotone increasing and strictly concave.

The competitive LMF maximizes the payoff per member, subject to sales and nonnegativity constraints

$$\max_{M,X,Y} \frac{pY - wX - F}{M} \tag{P}$$

$$\text{s.t.} \quad f(M, X) - Y \geq 0, \quad Y, X \geq 0, \quad M > 0.$$

Is program (P) well behaved? Obviously, the constraint function $f(M, X) - Y$ is strictly concave; but the objective function is strictly convex in M, and hence not concave.

However, we can transform program (P) into an equivalent concave program. For this purpose, define the new variables

$$y := Y/M, \qquad x := X/M, \qquad m := 1/M.$$

Apply a change of variables, and one obtains the equivalent program

$$\max_{m,x,y} py - wx - mF \qquad (P')$$

$$\text{s.t.} \quad mf\left(\frac{1}{m}, \frac{x}{m}\right) - y \geq 0, \quad m > 0, \quad x \geq 0, \quad y \geq 0.$$

Evidently, the new objective function is linear and hence concave. However, it remains to be shown that the new constraint set is strictly convex.

Denote the constraint function by $g(m, x, y) := mf(1/m, x/m) - y$. Consider two elements of the constraint set, say $(m_1, x_1, y_1) \neq (m_2, x_2, y_2)$, the real $\lambda \in (0, 1)$, and the convex linear combination

$$(m_3, x_3, y_3) := \lambda(m_1, x_1, y_1) + (1 - \lambda)(m_2, x_2, y_2).$$

Then, by the strict concavity of f,

$$g(m_3, x_3, y_3) = m_3 f\left(\frac{1}{m_3}, \frac{x_3}{m_3}\right) - y_3$$

$$= m_3 f\left(\frac{\lambda + (1 - \lambda)}{m_3}, \frac{\lambda x_1 + (1 - \lambda)x_2}{m_3}\right) - y_3$$

$$= m_3 f\left(\lambda \frac{m_1}{m_3}\frac{1}{m_1} + (1 - \lambda)\frac{m_2}{m_3}\frac{1}{m_2},\right.$$
$$\left.\lambda \frac{m_1}{m_3}\frac{x_1}{m_1} + (1 - \lambda)\frac{m_2}{m_3}\frac{x_2}{m_2}\right) - y_3$$

$$> m_3\lambda \frac{m_1}{m_3} f\left(\frac{1}{m_1}, \frac{x_1}{m_1}\right) + m_3(1 - \lambda)\frac{m_2}{m_3} f\left(\frac{1}{m_2}, \frac{x_2}{m_2}\right)$$
$$- \lambda y_1 - (1 - \lambda)y_2$$

$$= \lambda g(m_1, x_1, y_1) + (1 - \lambda)g(m_2, x_2, y_2)$$

$$\geq 0.$$

Therefore, the constraint set is convex and program (P') is concave.

Appendix D

From Expected Values to Order Statistics

All's well that ends well.
William Shakespeare

D.1 Introduction

This last appendix lists some important rules concerning random variables, from expected values to order statistics. It should be a useful source and is geared to the prerequisites of several chapters in this book.

D.2 Expected Value

Let $X, Y \in \mathbb{R}$ be random variables, $\Phi : \mathbb{R}^2 \to \mathbb{R}_+$ their joint distribution function (cdf), and $Z : \mathbb{R}^2 \to \mathbb{R}$ an integrable function with respect to Φ.

The expected-value operator E maps a random variable into a real number. The expected value can be regarded as the center of gravity of that probability distribution. It is defined as

$$E[X] := \int_{-\infty}^{+\infty} x \, dF(x), \tag{D.1}$$

$$E[Y] := \int_{-\infty}^{+\infty} y \, dG(y), \tag{D.2}$$

where F and G denote the respective cdf's of X and Y:

$$F(x) := \Pr\{X \le x\} = \int_{-\infty}^{x} \int_{-\infty}^{+\infty} \Phi(x, y) \, dy, \tag{D.3}$$

$$G(y) := \Pr\{Y \le y\} = \int_{-\infty}^{y} \int_{-\infty}^{+\infty} \Phi(x, y) \, dx. \tag{D.4}$$

The expected-value operator can also be applied to deterministic transformations of random variables such as the function Z. In principle, one then needs to determine the cdf of the new random variable $Z(X, Y)$. However, it can be shown that $E[Z(X, Y)]$ can always be calculated directly from the relation

$$E[Z(X, Y)] = \int_{-\infty}^{+\infty} \int_{-\infty}^{+\infty} Z(x, y) \, d\Phi(x, y). \tag{D.5}$$

This result has been called the "law of the unconscious statistician" because many people have been accused of using it without realizing that it is not a definition.

D.3 Variance, Covariance, and Correlation

All three operators, the variance Var, the covariance Cov, and the correlation ρ, map random variables into real numbers.

The variance

$$\mathrm{Var}(Z) := \mathrm{E}\left[(Z - \mathrm{E}[Z])^2\right] \qquad (\mathrm{D.6})$$

is a measure of the *spread* or *dispersion* of the distribution around its expected value. A small variance indicates that the distribution is concentrated around its expected value.[1]

The covariance

$$\mathrm{Cov}(X, Y) := \mathrm{E}\left[(X - \mathrm{E}[X])(Y - \mathrm{E}[Y])\right] \qquad (\mathrm{D.7})$$

is a measure of the degree of association between two random variables. Loosely speaking, a positive covariance indicates that the two random variables tend to move in the same direction.

Finally, the correlation

$$\rho := \frac{\mathrm{Cov}(X, Y)}{\sqrt{\mathrm{Var}(X)}\,\sqrt{\mathrm{Var}(Y)}} \qquad (\mathrm{D.8})$$

is a measure of the extent to which two random variables are *linearly* related. If the joint distribution of two random variables is concentrated around a straight line that has a positive slope, the correlation will be close to one.

In the following it is assumed that all these quantities exist and are finite.

D.4 Rules to Remember

D.4.1 Expected Value

Rule (R1)

$$\forall \alpha, \beta \in \mathbb{R}, \qquad \mathrm{E}\left[\alpha X + \beta Y\right] = \alpha \mathrm{E}[X] + \beta \mathrm{E}[Y]. \qquad (\mathrm{D.9})$$

Rule (R2)

$$\mathrm{Cov}(X, Y) = \mathrm{E}[XY] - \mathrm{E}[X]\mathrm{E}[Y]. \qquad (\mathrm{D.10})$$

Rule (R3)

$$\mathrm{E}[XY]^2 \le \mathrm{E}[X^2]\mathrm{E}[Y^2] \qquad \text{(Schwarz's inequality).} \qquad (\mathrm{D.11})$$

---

[1] However, both the variance and the expected value can be made arbitrarily large by placing even a very small but positive amount of probability far enough from the origin of the real line.

Rule (R4)

$$E[X] = \arg\min_{\lambda} E[(X - \lambda)^2].$$ (D.12)

Rule (R5)

$$E[X] = \int_0^{+\infty} [\bar{F}(x) - F(-x)]\,dx,$$ (D.13)

where $\bar{F}(x) := 1 - F(x)$.

Rule (R6) If X is nonnegative, then

$$E[X] = \int_0^{+\infty} \bar{F}(x)\,dx = \int_0^{\infty} \Pr\{X > x\}\,dx.$$ (D.14)

In general, one can write any random variable X as the difference between two nonnegative random variables $X := X_+ - X_-$, where

$$X_+ := \begin{cases} X & \text{if } X \geq 0, \\ 0 & \text{otherwise,} \end{cases}$$

$$X_- := \begin{cases} -X & \text{if } X \leq 0, \\ 0 & \text{otherwise,} \end{cases}$$

Therefore, by the above rule,

$$E[X] = E[X_+] - E[X_-]$$

$$= \int_0^{\infty} [\Pr\{X_+ > x\} - \Pr\{X_- > x\}]\,dx.$$ (D.15)

D.4.2 Variance, Covariance, Correlation

Rule (R7) $\forall \alpha, \beta \in \mathbb{R}$:

$$\text{Var}(\alpha X + \beta Y) = \alpha^2 \,\text{Var}(X) + 2\alpha\beta \,\text{Cov}(X, Y) + \beta^2 \,\text{Var}(Y).$$ (D.16)

Generalization: let $Z := (Z_1, Z_1, \ldots, Z_n)$ be a vector of random variables, $\alpha \in \mathbb{R}_+^n$, and M the covariance matrix of Z. Then

$$\text{Var}\left(\sum \alpha_i Z_i\right) = \alpha^T M \alpha.$$ (D.17)

Rule (R8)

$$\text{Cov}(X, Y) = E[X(Y - E[Y])]$$

$$= E[(X - E[X])Y].$$ (D.18)

An immediate implication is obtained by setting $Y = X$:

$$\text{Var}(X) = E[X^2] - E[X]^2.$$ (D.19)

Rule (R9)

$$\text{Cov}(X, Y)^2 \leq \text{Var}(X)\text{Var}(Y). \tag{D.20}$$

Rule (R10) The correlation ρ is bounded with

$$\rho \in [-1, +1]. \tag{D.21}$$

Rule (R11) The covariance matrix

$$M := \begin{bmatrix} \text{Cov}(X_1, X_1) & \text{Cov}(X_1, X_2) & \cdots & \text{Cov}(X_1, X_n) \\ \text{Cov}(X_2, X_1) & \text{Cov}(X_2, X_2) & \cdots & \text{Cov}(X_2, X_n) \\ \vdots & \vdots & & \vdots \\ \text{Cov}(X_n, X_1) & \text{Cov}(X_n, X_2) & \cdots & \text{Cov}(X_n, X_n) \end{bmatrix}$$

is positive semidefinite.

Rule (R12)

$$\text{Var}(X) = \min_{\lambda} \text{E}\left[(X - \lambda)^2\right]. \tag{D.22}$$

D.4.3 Expected Utility

Rule (R13) Suppose $U : D \to \mathbb{R}$ is C^1, strict monotone, and concave on the convex set $D \subset \mathbb{R}$. Then

$$\text{E}[U(X)] \leq U(\text{E}[X]) \qquad \text{(Jensen's inequality).} \tag{D.23}$$

The inequality is strict if U is strictly concave, and reversed if U is convex.

Rule (R14) Suppose $U(X) := -e^{-rX}$ (where r is the constant degree of absolute risk aversion), and assume the random variable X has a normal distribution with mean μ and variance σ^2. Then[2]

$$\text{E}[U(X)] = -e^{-r(\mu - r\sigma^2/2)}. \tag{D.24}$$

Moreover, the *certainty equivalent* of X, denoted by $\hat{x}$, which is implicitly defined as

$$U(\hat{x}) = U\left(E[U(X)]\right), \tag{D.25}$$

is equal to

$$\hat{x} = \mu - \frac{r}{2}\sigma^2. \tag{D.26}$$

---

[2] This relationship is often used in mean–variance analysis in finance.

D.4.4 Transformations of Random Variables

Rule (R15) Suppose X has a continuous pdf $f(x)$ with support $D \subset \mathbb{R}$. Let Y be a transformation of X with support $T \subset \mathbb{R}$, defined by the one-to-one differentiable function

$$y = r(x), \quad \text{or equivalently} \quad x = s(y), \quad s := r^{-1}. \tag{D.27}$$

Then the pdf of Y is

$$g(y) := \begin{cases} f(s(y))|s'(y)| & \text{for } y \in T, \\ 0 & \text{otherwise.} \end{cases} \tag{D.28}$$

This rule generalizes as follows.

Let X and Y be n-dimensional vectors of random variables, f the joint pdf of X, and $r : D \to T$ and $s := r^{-1} : T \to D$, with $D, T \subset \mathbb{R}^n$. Then the joint pdf of Y is

$$g(y) = \begin{cases} f(s(y))|J| & \text{for } y \in T, \\ 0 & \text{otherwise,} \end{cases} \tag{D.29}$$

where J denotes the *Jacobian* of $s(y)$,

$$J := \det \begin{bmatrix} \dfrac{\partial s_1}{\partial y_1} & \cdots & \dfrac{\partial s_1}{\partial y_n} \\ \vdots & & \vdots \\ \dfrac{\partial s_n}{\partial y_1} & \cdots & \dfrac{\partial s_n}{\partial y_n} \end{bmatrix}. \tag{D.30}$$

Rule R16 Suppose Y is a linear transformation of X:

$$y = r(x) := Ax, \quad \text{or equivalently} \quad x = s(y) := A^{-1}y, \tag{D.31}$$

where A is a real-valued, invertible $n \times n$ matrix. Then the joint pdf of Y is

$$g(y) = f(A^{-1}y)\frac{1}{|\det(A)|}. \tag{D.32}$$

As an example consider the difference between two random variables, $Y := X_1 - X_2$. The pdf of Y is

$$g(y) = \int_{-\infty}^{+\infty} f(y+z, z)\, dz. \tag{D.33}$$

If in addition X_1 and X_2 are iid and uniformly distributed on the support $(-\frac{1}{2}, +\frac{1}{2})$, then the support of Y is $(-1, +1)$ and one obtains the triangular distribution

$$g(y) = \begin{cases} 1 + y & \text{for } y \in (-1, 0], \\ 1 - y & \text{for } y \in [0, 1), \\ 0 & \text{otherwise.} \end{cases} \tag{D.34}$$

On the other hand, if X_1 and X_2 are iid and normally distributed, with mean zero and variance σ^2, one obtains

$$g(y) := \frac{1}{2\sigma\sqrt{\pi}} \exp\left(-\frac{1}{2}\frac{y^2}{2\sigma^2}\right). \tag{D.35}$$

The nice feature of normal distributions is that every linear combination of normally distributed and iid random variables is again normally distributed. This is one of the reasons why finance people love the normal-distribution assumption.

D.4.5 Order Statistics

Let $X_1, X_2, \ldots, X_n$ be a sample of n independent random variables, each having the same probability distribution function $F(x)$ with density $f(x) = F'(x)$. Suppose we always rank the realizations of the series in increasing order:

$$x_{v_1} \le x_{v_2} \le \cdots \le x_{v_k} \le \cdots \le x_{v_n}.$$

Then we define the kth *order statistic* as the function $X_{(k)}$ that assigns to each realization of the series $(X_1, \ldots, X_n)$ the kth smallest value x_{v_k}.[3] Altogether, there are n order statistics

$$X_{(1)}, X_{(2)}, \ldots, X_{(n)}.$$

Of course, each order statistic is a random variable.

Rule (R17) The kth order statistic $X_{(k)}$ of the series of random variables $X_1, \ldots, X_n$ has the following cdf:

$$F_{(k)}(x) = \sum_{j=k}^{n} \binom{n}{j} F(x)^j [1 - F(x)]^{n-j}. \tag{D.36}$$

Rule (R18) $F_{(k)}(x)$ is also equal to

$$F_{(k)}(x) = \frac{n!}{(k-1)!(n-k)!} \int_0^{F(x)} \tau^{k-1}(1-\tau)^{n-k}\, dt. \tag{D.37}$$

Therefore, the density function $f_{(k)}(x)$ is

$$f_{(k)}(x) = \frac{n!}{(k-1)!(n-k)!} F(x)^{k-1}[1 - F(x)]^{n-k} f(x). \tag{D.38}$$

Moreover, the *conditional pdf* of $X_{(r)}$, given $X_{(s)} = v$ $(s > r)$, is just the pdf of $X_{(r)}$ in the smaller sample size $(s-1)$ drawn from the parent distribution truncated

[3] Suppose $n = 2$ and $x_i \in \{0, 1\}$. Then the random vector (x_1, x_2) can assume the following realizations: $(0,0), (0,1), (1,0), (1,1)$. In this case, there are two functions $X_{(k)}$, namely $X_{(1)}$ and $X_{(2)}$. The associated realizations of $X_{(1)}$ are $(0,0,0,1)$, and those of $X_{(2)}$ are $(0,1,1,1)$.

on the right at v.[4] Therefore, for $x < v$,

$$f_{X_{(r)}|X_{(s)}=v}(x) = \frac{(s-1)!}{(r-1)!(s-r-1)!} \frac{f(x)F(x)^{r-1}(F(v)-F(x))^{s-r-1}}{F(v)^{s-1}}. \tag{D.39}$$

Rule (R19) The *expected value* of the kth order statistic $X_{(k)}$ is

$$E[X_{(k)}] := \int_{\underline{x}}^{\bar{x}} x f_{(k)}(x)\, dx \tag{D.40}$$

$$= \frac{n!}{(k-1)!(n-k)!} \int_{\underline{x}}^{\bar{x}} x F(x)^{k-1}[1-F(x)]^{n-k} f(x)\, dx.$$

If X is uniformly distributed on the domain $[0, 1]$, one obtains

$$E[X_{(k)}] = \frac{k}{n+1}, \tag{D.41}$$

$$E[X_{(n-1)}|X_{(n)} = x] = \frac{n-1}{n}x, \tag{D.42}$$

$$\mathrm{Var}(X_{(k)}) = \frac{k(n-k+1)}{(n+1)^2(n+2)}, \tag{D.43}$$

$$\mathrm{Cov}(X_{(k)}, X_{(r)}) = \frac{k(n-r+1)}{(n+1)^2(n+2)} \quad \text{for} \quad k < r, \tag{D.44}$$

$$\rho(X_{(1)}, X_{(n)}) = \frac{1}{n}. \tag{D.45}$$

D.5 Proofs

(R1) is obvious.

(R2):

$$\mathrm{Cov}(X, Y) := E[(X - E[X])(Y - E[Y])]$$
$$= E[XY - XE[Y] - YE[X] + E[X]E[Y]]$$
$$= E[XY] - 2E[X]E[Y] + E[X]E[Y]$$
$$= E[XY] - E[X]E[Y].$$

(R3): The proof is too long to be presented here; consult your textbook on statistics.[5]

(R4): As $E[X-\lambda]^2$ is convex in λ, all you need to do is to find that particular λ that satisfies the first-order condition for an extreme value. If you state this condition, you will see right away that the assertion holds true. Incidentally, (R4) gives you a nice interpretation of $E[X]$.

---

[4] Follows from Theorem 2.7 in David (1970).
[5] See for example DeGroot (1986, p. 213).

(R5) and (R6) follow immediately by using integration by parts together with the fact that[6]

$$\int_{-\infty}^{0} \phi(x)\,dx = \int_{0}^{+\infty} \phi(-x)\,dx.$$

(R7):

$$
\begin{aligned}
\text{Var}(\alpha X + \beta Y) &:= \text{E}[((\alpha X + \beta Y) - \text{E}[\alpha X + \beta Y])^2] \\
&= \text{E}[((\alpha X + \beta Y) - \alpha \text{E}[X] - \beta \text{E}[Y])^2] \\
&= \text{E}[(\alpha(X - \text{E}[X]) + \beta(Y - \text{E}[Y]))^2] \\
&= \text{E}[\alpha^2(X - \text{E}[X])^2 + 2\alpha\beta(X - \text{E}[X])(Y - \text{E}[Y]) \\
&\quad + \beta^2(Y - \text{E}[Y])^2] \\
&= \alpha^2 \text{E}[(X - \text{E}[X])^2] + 2\alpha\beta \text{E}[(X - \text{E}[X])(Y - \text{E}[Y])] \\
&\quad + \beta^2 \text{E}[(Y - \text{E}[Y])^2] \\
&= \alpha^2 \text{Var}(X) + 2\alpha\beta \text{Cov}(X, Y) + \beta^2 \text{Var}(Y).
\end{aligned}
$$

(R8):

$$
\begin{aligned}
\text{Cov}(X, Y) &:= \text{E}[(X - \text{E}[X])(Y - \text{E}[Y])] \\
&= \text{E}[X(Y - \text{E}[Y]) - \text{E}[X](Y - \text{E}[Y])] \\
&= \text{E}[X(Y - \text{E}[Y])] - \text{E}[X](\text{E}[Y] - \text{E}[Y]) \\
&= \text{E}[X(Y - \text{E}[Y])].
\end{aligned}
$$

The proof of the other form is analogous and hence omitted.

(R9): Apply Schwartz's inequality (R3) to the random variables $X - \text{E}[X]$ and $Y - \text{E}[Y]$, and the assertion follows immediately.

(R10) follows immediately from (R9) combined with the definition of the correlation ρ.

(R11): In the case of two random variables the assertion follows immediately by the fact that the variance cannot be negative and by rule (R9). Unfortunately, this line of proof cannot be generalized to more than two random variables. But there is a very simple general proof in two steps. Let X be a column vector of n random variables and $\text{E}[X]$ its expected values. In a first step, notice that the *covariance matrix* M of X is equal to the expected value of the vector product $(X - \text{E}[X])(X - \text{E}[X])^T$:

$$M := \text{E}[(X - \text{E}[X])(X - \text{E}[X])^T].$$

---

[6] Prove this by using the *substitution rule*: $\int_{\phi(\alpha)}^{\phi(\beta)} dF(x) = \int_{\alpha}^{\beta} f(\phi(x))\phi'(x)\,dx.$

Now consider any n-dimensional, real-valued vector $\xi \neq 0$ and the quadratic form $\xi^T M \xi$. As one can see easily,

$$
\begin{aligned}
\xi^T M \xi &= \xi^T \mathrm{E}[(X - \mathrm{E}[X])(X - \mathrm{E}[X])^T]\xi \\
&= \mathrm{E}[\xi^T (X - \mathrm{E}[X])(X - \mathrm{E}[X])^T \xi] \\
&= \mathrm{E}[(X - \mathrm{E}[X])^T \xi]^2, \quad \text{since} \quad (X - \mathrm{E}[X])^T \xi = \xi^T (X - \mathrm{E}[X]) \\
&\geq 0.
\end{aligned}
$$

Therefore, M is positive semidefinite.

(R12) follows immediately from (R4).

(R13): Since U is C^1 and concave, it follows that (see Proposition C.3 in Appendix C):

$$
\forall x \in D, \quad \forall \tilde{x} \in D, \quad U(x) \leq U(\tilde{x}) + U'(\tilde{x})(x - \tilde{x}).
$$

Since $\mathrm{E}[X] \in D$, due to the convexity of D, this inequality must also hold true for $\tilde{x} = \mathrm{E}[X]$. Therefore, one has

$$
U(X) \leq U(\mathrm{E}[X]) + U'(\mathrm{E}[X])(X - \mathrm{E}[X]).
$$

Take the expected value on both sides, and it follows that

$$
\mathrm{E}[U(X)] \leq U(\mathrm{E}[X]),
$$

as asserted.

(R14): To simplify the notation, let $\mu := \mathrm{E}[X]$ and $\sigma^2 := \mathrm{Var}(X)$.

Substitute the assumed normal distribution of X, and one obtains after a few rearrangements

$$
\begin{aligned}
\mathrm{E}[-e^{-rX}] &= -\int_{-\infty}^{+\infty} e^{-rx} \phi\left(\frac{x - \mu}{\sigma}\right) dx \\
&= -\int_{-\infty}^{+\infty} e^{-rx} \frac{1}{\sqrt{2\pi}\sigma} e^{-(x-\mu)^2/2\sigma^2} dx \\
&= -e^{r^2\sigma^2/2} e^{-\mu r} \int_{-\infty}^{+\infty} \frac{1}{\sqrt{2\pi}\sigma} e^{-[x-(\mu - r\sigma^2)]^2/2\sigma^2} dx.
\end{aligned}
$$

Obviously, the integrand is itself the density function of a normally distributed random variable with variance σ^2 and mean $\mu - r\sigma^2$. Therefore, the integral must be equal to 1, and one obtains

$$
\mathrm{E}[-e^{-rX}] = -e^{r^2\sigma^2/2} e^{-\mu r} = -e^{-r(\mu - (r/2)\sigma^2)},
$$

as asserted.

The inverse of $u(x) = -e^{-rx}$ is

$$
u^{-1}(z) = -\frac{1}{r} \ln(-z).
$$

By definition of the certainty equivalent $\hat{x}$ together with (D.24) one obtains

$$\hat{x} = u^{-1}\,(\mathrm{E}\,[u(X)])$$

$$= -\frac{1}{r}\ln\left(e^{-r(\mu - r\sigma^2/2)}\right)$$

$$= \mu - \frac{r}{2}\sigma^2.$$

(R15): Suppose $r'(x) > 0$. Then the cdf of Y is

$$G(y) := \Pr\{Y \le y\}$$

$$= \Pr\{r(X) \le y\}$$

$$= \Pr\{X \le s(y)\}, \qquad s := r^{-1}$$

$$= F(s(y)).$$

Therefore $g(y) := G'(y) = f(s(y))s'(y)$.

If $r'(x) < 0$, the third inequality is reversed; hence, $G(y) = \Pr\{X > s(y)\} = 1 - F(s(y))$ and $g(y) = -f(s(y))s'(y)$. Putting both cases together proves $g(y) = f(s(y))|s'(y)|$.

The proof of the generalization of this rule to vectors of random variables (D.29) is omitted.

(R16): Note that $\det(A^{-1}) = 1/\det(A)$. Therefore, (R16) follows immediately from (R15).

In order to prove the formula for the difference between two iid and normally distributed random variables $Y := X_1 - X_2$, with support $(-\frac{1}{2}, +\frac{1}{2})$, stated in (D.34), define $Y := X_1 - X_2$, $Z := X_2$. Then

$$\begin{bmatrix} Y \\ Z \end{bmatrix} = \begin{bmatrix} 1 & -1 \\ 0 & 1 \end{bmatrix}\begin{bmatrix} X_1 \\ X_2 \end{bmatrix}, \qquad \text{or equivalently} \qquad \begin{bmatrix} X_1 \\ X_2 \end{bmatrix} = \begin{bmatrix} 1 & 1 \\ 0 & 1 \end{bmatrix}\begin{bmatrix} Y \\ Z \end{bmatrix}.$$

Therefore, by (D.29) the joint pdf of Y and Z is

$$g_0(y, z) = f(y + z)f(z).$$

Integrate in order to obtain the marginal distribution

$$g(y) := \int_{-\infty}^{+\infty} f(y + z)f(z)\,dz.$$

Finally, use the distribution assumption. Note: $f(\cdot)$ either is equal to 1 or vanishes. For $y \le 0$ the integrand does not vanish iff $z \in [-\frac{1}{2} - y, \frac{1}{2}]$, and if $y \ge 0$ the integrand does not vanish if and only if $z \in [-\frac{1}{2}, \frac{1}{2} - y]$. Hence,

$$g(y) = \begin{cases} \int_{-\frac{1}{2}-y}^{\frac{1}{2}} dz & \text{for } y \in [-1, 0], \\ \int_{-\frac{1}{2}}^{\frac{1}{2}-y} dz & \text{for } y \in [0, 1], \\ 0 & \text{otherwise} \end{cases}$$

$$= \begin{cases} 1 + y & \text{for } y \in (-1, 0], \\ 1 - y & \text{for } y \in [0, 1), \\ 0 & \text{otherwise.} \end{cases}$$

The assertion concerning the normal distribution follows immediately from the well-known fact that every linear combination of normally distributed random variables is again normally distributed and that $\sigma^2(X_1 - X_2) = 2\sigma^2$, by (R1).

(R17)–(R19): In order to compute $F_{(k)}$, one needs to determine the probability of the event that $X_{(k)} \leq x$. This event occurs if and only if in a sample of size n, the kth smallest observation is not greater than x, that is, if *at least k* observations are below x. Therefore,

$$F_{(k)}(x) = \Pr\left\{X_{(k)} \leq x\right\}$$

$$= \Pr\{\text{at least } k \text{ among } n \text{ random variables } X_i \text{ are } \leq x\}$$

$$= \binom{n}{k} F(x)^k [1 - F(x)]^{n-k} + \binom{n}{k+1} F(x)^{k+1} [1 - F(x)]^{n-k-1}$$

$$+ \cdots + \binom{n}{n-1} F(x)^{n-1} [1 - F(x)] + F(x)^n$$

$$= \sum_{j=k}^{n} \binom{n}{j} F(x)^j [1 - F(x)]^{n-j}.$$

Using partial integration one can confirm (D.37).[7] Differentiating (D.37) gives (D.38), and (R19) follows immediately.

---

[7] See Fisz (1963, p. 439, equations (10.3.7), (103.8)) or Kendall and Stuart (1977, pp. 268, 348).

Bibliography

Adams, W. and Yellen, J. (1976). Commodity bundling and the burden of monopoly. *Quarterly Journal of Economics*, 90:475–498.

Admati, A. and Perry, M. (1987). Strategic delay in bargaining. *Review of Economic Studies*, 54:345–364.

Adolph, B. and Wolfstetter, E. (1991). Wage indexation, informational externalities, and monetary policy. *Oxford Economic Papers*, 43:368–390.

Akerlof, G. (1970). The market for lemons, qualitative uncertainty, and the market mechanism. *Quarterly Journal of Economics*, 84:488–500.

Allen, B. and Hellwig, M. (1986). Bertrand–Edgeworth oligopoly in large markets. *Review of Economic Studies*, 53:175–204.

Alvi, E. (1997). First-order approach to principal–agent problems: A generalization. *Geneva Papers on Risk and Insurance*, 22:59–65.

Amiel, K. and Cowell, F. A. (1997). Inequality, welfare and monotonicity. Working paper, no. 29, LSE, Distributional Analysis Research Program.

Anderson, P., de Palma, A., and Thisse, J.-F. (1992). *Discrete Choice Theory of Product Differentiation*. MIT Press.

Antle, R. and Smith, A. (1986). An empirical investigation of the relative performance evaluation of corporate executives. *Journal of Accounting Research*, 24:1–39.

Anton, J. and Yao, D. (1989). Split awards, procurement, and innovation. *Rand Journal of Economics*, 20:538–552.

Anton, J. and Yao, D. (1992). Coordination in split award auctions. *Quarterly Journal of Economics*, 105:681–701.

Arrow, K. J. (1962). Economic welfare and the allocation of resources for inventions. In Nelson, R., editor, *The Rate and Direction of Inventive Activity*. Princeton University Press.

Arrow, K. J. (1963). *Social Choice and Individual Values*. Wiley, New York, 2nd edition.

Arthur, B. (1989). Competing technologies, increasing returns, and lock-in by historical events. *Economic Journal*, 99:116–131.

Ashenfelter, O. (1989). How auctions work for wine and art. *Journal of Economic Perspectives*, 3:23–36.

Ashenfelter, O. and Genovese, D. (1992). Testing for price anomalies in real-estate auctions. *American Economic Review (Papers and Proceedings)*, 80:501–505.

Atkinson, A. B. (1972). On the measurement of inequality. *Journal of Economic Theory*, 2:244–263.

Averch, H. and Johnson, L. (1962). Behaviour of the firm under regulatory constraint. *American Economic Review*, 52:1052–1069.

Bagnoli, M. and Bergstrom, T. (1989). Log-concave probability and its applications. Working paper, University of Michigan.

Bagnoli, M., Salant, S. W., and Swierzbinski, J. E. (1989). Durable-goods monopoly with discrete demand. *Journal of Political Economy*, 97:1459–1478.

Bagwell, K. (1995). Commitment and observability in games. *Games and Economic Behavior*, 8:271–280.

Baron, D. and Myerson, R. (1982). Regulating a monopolist with unknown cost. *Econometrica*, 50:911–930.

Bartle, R. G. (1976). *Elements of Real Analysis*. Wiley.

Baye, M., Kovenock, D., and de Vries, C. (1993). Rigging the lobbying process: An application of all-pay auctions. *American Economic Review*, 83:289–294.

Baye, M. R., Tian, G., and Zhou, J. (1993). Characterizations of the existence of equilibria in games with discontinuous and non-quasiconcave payoffs. *Review of Economic Studies*, 60:935–948.

Bazerman, M. H. and Samuelson, W. F. (1983). I won the auction but don't want the prize. *Journal of Conflict Resolution*, 27:618–634.

Beckmann, M. and Hochstädter, D. (1965). Edgeworth–Bertrand duopoly revisited. *Operations Research Verfahren*, 3:55–68.

Bergstrom, T. and Bagnoli, M. (1993). Courtship as a waiting game. *Journal of Political Economy*, 101:185–202.

Bergstrom, T. C. and Varian, H. (1985a). Two remarks on Cournot equilibria. *Economics Letters*, 19:5–8.

Bergstrom, T. C. and Varian, H. (1985b). When are Nash equilibria independent of agents' characteristics. *Review of Economic Studies*, 52:715–718.

Bernhardt, D. and Scoones, D. (1994). A note on sequential auctions. *American Economic Review*, 84:653–657.

Bertrand, J. (1883). Review of Walras' 'Théorie Mathématique de la Richesse Sociale' and of Cournot's 'Recherches sur les Principes Mathématiques de la Théorie des Richesses.' *Journal des Savants*, pages 499–508.

Bester, H. (1985). Screening vs. rationing in credit markets with imperfect information. *American Economic Review*, 75:850–855.

Bhagat, S., Shleifer, A., and Vishny, R. W. (1990). Hostile takeovers in the 1980s: the return to corporate specialization. *Brookings Papers on Economic Activity*, Special Issue on Microeconomics:1–84.

Bikhchandani, S. and Huang, C.-F. (1989). Auctions with resale markets: An exploratory model of Treasury bill markets. *Journal of Financial Studies*, 2:311–339.

Bikhchandani, S. and Huang, C.-F. (1993). The economics of treasury security markets. *Journal of Economic Perspectives*, 7:117–134.

Binmore, K. (1992). *Fun and Games. A Text on Game Theory*. D. C. Heath.

Boyes, W. J. (1976). An empirical examination of the Averch–Johnson effect. *Economic Inquiry*, 14:25–35.

Brady, N. F., Breeden, R. C., and Greenspan, A. (1992). *Joint Report on the Government Securities Market*. U.S. Government Printing Office.

Brander, J. A. and Lewis, T. R. (1986). Oligopoly and financial structure: the limited liability effect. *American Economic Review*, 76:956–970.

Brander, J. A. and Spencer, B. (1983). Strategic commitment with R&D: The symmetric case. *Bell Journal of Economics*, 14:225–235.

Breen, W. and Savage, J. (1968). Portfolio distributions and tests of security selection models. *Journal of Finance*, 23:805–819.

Brown, M., Chiang, S., Ghosh, S., and Wolfstetter, E. (1986). A new class of sufficient conditions for the first-order approach to the principal–agent problem. *Economics Letters*, 21:1–6.

Brown, M. and Wolfstetter, E. (1985). Under- and overemployment in optimal layoff contracts. *Journal of Economics*, 45:101–114.

Brown, M. and Wolfstetter, E. (1989). Tripartite income–employment contracts and coalition incentive compatibility. *Rand Journal of Economics*, 20:291–307.

Bulow, J. (1982). Durable goods monopolists. *Journal of Political Economy*, 90:314–332.

Cagan, P. (1956). The monetary dynamics of hyperinflation. In Friedman, M., editor, *Studies in the Quantity Theory of Money*, pages 25–117. University of Chicago Press.

Capen, E. C., Clapp, R. V., and Campbell, W. M. (1971). Competitive bidding in high-risk situations. *Journal of Petroleum Technology*, 23:641–653.

Carlton, D. W. and Perloff, J. M. (1990). *Modern Industrial Organization*. Harper-Collins.

Cassady, R. (1967). *Auctions and Auctioneering*. University of California Press.

Cassidy, J. (1998). The force of an idea: What's really behind the case against Bill Gates. *The New Yorker*, January 12, pages 32–37.

Che, Y.-K. (1993). Design competition through multidimensional auctions. *Rand Journal of Economics*, 4:669–680.

Cho, I. K. and Kreps, D. (1987). Signaling games and stable equilibria. *Quarterly Journal of Economics*, 102:179–221.

Choi, J.-P. (1994). Irreversible choice of uncertain technologies with network externalities. *Rand Journal of Economics*, 25:382–401.

Clarke, E. H. (1971). Multipart pricing of public goods. *Public Choice*, 2:19–33.

Coase, R. (1972). Durability and monopoly. *Journal of Law and Economics*, 15:143–149.

Conlisk, J., Gerstner, E., and Sobel, J. (1984). Cyclic pricing by a durable goods monopolist. *Quarterly Journal of Economics*, 99:489–505.

Cournot, A. A. (1838). *Principes Mathématiques de la Théorie des Richesses*. Paris.

Courville, J. (1974). Regulation and efficiency in the electric utility industry. *Bell Journal of Economics*, 5:53–74.

Cramton, P. (1998). Ascending auctions. *European Economic Review*, 42:745–756.

Cramton, P. C. (1995). Money out of thin air: the nationwide narrowband PCS auction. *Journal of Economics and Management Strategy*, 4:267–343.

Crawford, V. and Sobel, J. (1982). Strategic information transmission. *Econometrica*, 50:1431–1451.

Crémer, J. (1995). Arm's length relationships. *Quarterly Journal of Economics*, 110:275–295.

Dalton, H. (1920). The measurement of the inequality of incomes. *Economic Journal*, 30:348–361.

Dasgupta, P. and Maskin, E. (1986). The existence of equilibrium in discontinuous economic games, I and II. *Review of Economic Studies*, 53:1–26, 27–41.

d'Aspremont, C. and Gérard-Varet, L. A. (1979). On Bayesian incentive compatible mechanisms. In Laffont, J.-J., editor, *Aggregation and Revelation of Preferences*, pages 269–288. North-Holland.

David, H. A. (1970). *Order Statistics*. Wiley Series in Probability and Mathematical Statistics. Wiley.

Davidson, C. and Deneckere, R. (1986). Long-term competition in capacity, short-run competition in price, and the Cournot model. *Rand Journal of Economics*, 17:404–415.

Davidson, C. and Deneckere, R. (1990). Excess capacity and collusion. *International Economic Review*, 31:521–542.

Davis, G. K. (1989). Income and substitution effects for mean-preserving spreads. *International Economic Review*, 30:131–136.

Debreu, G. (1952). A social equilibrium existence theorem. *Proceedings of the National Academy of Sciences, USA*, pages 886–893.

Dechert, W. D. (1984). Has the Averch–Johnson effect been theoretically justified? *Journal of Economic Dynamics and Control*, 8:1–17.

DeGroot, M. (1986). *Probability and Statistics*. Addison-Wesley.

Demougin, D. and Fluet, C. (1998). Mechanism sufficient statistic in the risk-neutral agency problem. *Journal of Institutional and Theoretical Economics*, 154:622–639.

Demougin, D. and Fluet, C. (1999). Monitoring vs. incentives: Substitutes or complements? *European Economic Review*, forthcoming.

Deneckere, R. and Davidson, C. (1985). Incentives to form coalitions with Bertrand competition. *Rand Journal of Economics*, 16:473–486.

Dessauer, J. P. (1981). *Book Publishing*. Bowker, New York.

Dittmann, I. (1997). On agency, collusion, and optimal monitoring. Discussion paper, Universität Dortmund.

Dixit, A. (1980). The role of investment in entry deterrence. *Bell Journal of Economics*, 90:95–106.

Dixit, A. and Shapiro, C. (1986). Entry dynamics with mixed strategies. In Thomas, L. G., editor, *The Economics of Strategic Planning*, pages 63–79. Lexington Books, Lexington, MA.

Dixon, H. (1984). The existence of mixed-strategy equilibria in a price setting oligopoly with convex costs. *Economics Letters*, 16:205–212.

Dowrick, S. (1986). von Stackelberg and Cournot duopoly: Choosing roles. *Rand Journal of Economics*, 17:251–260.

Dudey, M. (1992). Dynamic Edgeworth–Bertrand competition. *Quarterly Journal of Economics*, 107:1461–1477.

Dudey, M. (1995). On the foundations of dynamic monopoly theory: Comment. *Journal of Political Economy*, 103:893–902.

Dyer, D., Kagel, J., and Levin, D. (1989). Resolving uncertainty about the number of bidders in independent private-value auctions: An experimental analysis. *Rand Journal of Economics*, 20:268 ff.

Edgeworth, F. Y. (1925). The pure theory of monopoly. In Edgeworth, F. Y., editor, *Papers Relating to Monopoly*, volume 1. Macmillan.

Eeckhoudt, L., Gollier, C., and Schlesinger, H. (1991). Increases in risk and deductibe insurance. *Journal of Economic Theory*, 551:435–440.

Elberfeld, W. and Wolfstetter, E. (1999). A dynamic model of Bertrand competition with entry. *International Journal of Industrial Organization*, 17 (forthcoming).

El-Hodiri, M. and Takayama, A. T. (1973). Behavior of the firm under regulatory constraint. *American Economic Review*, 63:235–237.

Emons, W. (1988). Warranties, moral hazard, and the lemons problem. *Journal of Economic Theory*, 46:16–33.

Emons, W. (1989). The theory of warranty contracts. *Journal of Economic Surveys*, 3:43–57.

Engelbrecht-Wiggans, R. (1993). Optimal auctions revisited. *Games and Economic Behavior*, 5:227–239.

Engelbrecht-Wiggans, R. (1994). Auctions with price-proportional benefits to bidders. *Games and Economic Behavior*, 6:339–346.

Farrell, J. (1987). Cheap talk, coordination, and entry. *Rand Journal of Economics*, 18:34–39.

Farrell, J. and Saloner, G. (1986). Installed base and compatibility: Innovation, product preannouncement, and predation. *American Economic Review*, 76:940–955.

Fershtman, C. and Judd, K. L. (1987). Equilibrium incentives in oligopoly. *American Economic Review*, 77:927–940.

Fishburn, P. C. and Porter, L. B. (1976). Optimal portfolios with one safe and one risky asset. *Management Science*, 22:1064–1073.

Fishburn, P. C. and Vickson, R. G. (1978). Theoretical foundations of stochastic dominance. In Whitemore, G. A. and Findlay, M. C., editors, *Stochastic Dominance*, pages 39–113. Lexington Books, Lexington, MA.

Fishman, A. (1990). Entry deterrence in a finitely lived industry. *Rand Journal of Economics*, 21:63–71.

Fishman, M. J. (1988). A theory of preemptive takeover bidding. *Rand Journal of Economics*, 19:88–101.

Fisz, M. (1963). *Probability Theory and Mathematical Statistics*. Wiley.

Friedman, D. and Rust, J., editors (1993). *The Double Auction Market*. Addison-Wesley.

Friedman, J. W. (1983). *Oligopoly Theory*. Cambridge University Press.

Friedman, J. W. (1986). *Game Theory with Applications to Economics*. Oxford University Press.

Friedman, M. (1964). Comment on 'Collusion in the auction market for treasury bills.' *Journal of Political Economy*, 72:513–514.

Fudenberg, D. and Levine, D. (1992). Maintaining a reputation when strategies are imperfectly observable. *Review of Economic Studies*, 59:561–580.

Fudenberg, D. and Tirole, J. (1986). A theory of exit in duopoly. *Econometrica*, 54:943–960.

Fudenberg, D. and Tirole, J. (1990). Moral hazard and renegotiation in agency contracts. *Econometrica*, 58:1279–1319.

Fudenberg, D. and Tirole, J. (1991). *Game Theory*. MIT Press.

Gabszewicz, J. J. and Thisse, J.-F. (1986). Price and quantity competition in duopoly. In Gabszewicz, J. J., Thisse, J.-F., Fujita, M., and Schweizer, U., editors, *Location Theory*. Harwood Publishers.

Gal-Or, E. (1990). Excessive retailing at the Bertrand equilibria. *Canadian Journal of Economics*, 23:294–304.

Galbraith, J. K. (1988). From stupidity to cupidity. *New York Review of Books*, 25:12–15.

Gale, D. and Shapley, L. S. (1962). College admission and the stability of marriage. *American Mathematical Monthly*, 69:9–15.

Gelman, J. R. and Salop, S. C. (1983). Judo economics: Capacity limitation and coupon competition. *Bell Journal of Economics*, 14:315–325.

Ghemawat, P. and Nalebuff, B. (1985). Exit. *Rand Journal of Economics*, 16:184–194.

Ghemawat, P. and Nalebuff, B. (1990). The devolution of declining industries. *Quarterly Journal of Economics*, 105:167–186.

Gilbert, R. and Newbery, D. (1982). Preemptive patenting and the persistence of monopoly. *American Economic Review*, 74:238–242.

Glicksberg, I. L. (1952). A further generalization of the Kakutani fixed point theorem with application to Nash equilibrium points. *Proceedings of the American Mathematical Society*, 38:170–174.

Glosten, L. and Milgrom, P. (1985). Bid, ask, and transaction prices in a specialist market with heterogeneously informed traders. *Journal of Financial Economics*, 13:71–100.

Goldstein, H. (1962). The Friedman proposal for auctioning Treasury bills. *Journal of Political Economy*, 70:386–392.

Grafen, A. (1990). Biological signals as handicaps. *Journal of Theoretical Biology*, 144:517–546.

Graham, D. A. and Marshall, R. C. (1987). Collusive bidder behavior at single-object second-price and English auctions. *Journal of Political Economy*, 95:1217–1239.

Green, E. J. and Porter, R. H. (1984). Noncooperative collusion under imperfect price information. *Econometrica*, 52:87–100.

Green, J. and Laffont, J.-J. (1979). *Incentives in Public Decision Making*. North-Holland.

Green, J. R. and Stokey, N. L. (1983). A comparison of tournaments and contracts. *Journal of Political Economy*, 91:349–364.

Grossman, S. (1981). The role of warranties and private disclosure about product quality. *Journal of Law and Economics*, 24:461–483.

Grossman, S. J. and Hart, O. D. (1983). An analysis of the principal–agent problem. *Econometrica*, 51:7–45.

Groves, T. (1973). Incentives in teams. *Econometrica*, 41:617–613.

Guesnerie, R. and Laffont, J.-J. (1986). Using cost information to regulate firms. *Journal of Political Economy*, 94:614–641.

Gul, F., Sonnenschein, H., and Wilson, R. (1986). Foundations of dynamic monopoly and the Coase conjecture. *Journal of Economic Theory*, 39:248–254.

Hadar, J. and Russell, W. R. (1969). Rules for ordering uncertain prospects. *American Economic Review*, 59:25–34.

Hadar, J. and Russell, W. R. (1971). Stochastic dominance and diversification. *Journal of Economic Theory*, 3:288–305.

Hadar, J. and Russell, W. R. (1982). Applications in economic theory and analysis. In Whitmore, G. A. and Findlay, M. C., editors, *Stochastic Dominance*, pages 295–333. Lexington Books, Lexington, MA.

Hadar, J. and Seo, T. K. (1990a). The effects of shifts in a return distribution on optimal portfolios. *International Economics Review*, 31:721–736.

Hadar, J. and Seo, T. K. (1990b). Ross' measure of risk aversion and portfolio selection. *Journal of Risk and Uncertainty*, 3:93–99.

Hansen, R. G. (1988). Auctions with endogenous quantity. *Rand Journal of Economics*, 19:44–58.

Harris, M. and Raviv, A. (1979). Optimal incentive contracts with imperfect information. *Journal of Economic Theory*, 20:231–259.

Harris, M. and Raviv, A. (1981). A theory of monopoly pricing schemes with demand uncertainty. *American Economic Review*, 71:347–365.

Harris, M. and Raviv, A. (1989). Financial contracting theory. In Laffont, J.-J., editor, *Advances in Economic Theory: Sixth World Congress of the Econometric Society, Vol. II*, pages 64–150. Cambridge University Press.

Harsanyi, J. C. (1976). *Essays on Ethics, Social Behavior, and Scientific Explanations*. Reidel.

Harstad, R. M. and Levin, D. (1985). A class of dominance solvable common-value auctions. *Review of Economic Studies*, 52:525–528.

Hart, O. and Holmstrom, B. (1987). The theory of contracts. In Bewley, T. F., editor, *Advances in Economic Theory*. Cambridge University Press.

Hellwig, M. (1987). Some recent developments in the theory of competition in markets with adverse selection. *European Economic Review*, 31:319–325.

Helpman, E. and Krugman, P., editors (1989). *Trade Policy and Market Structure*. MIT Press.

Hirshleifer, J. (1971). The private and social value of innovation and the reward to inventive activity. *American Economic Review*, 61:561–574.

Hirshleifer, J. and Riley, J. (1992). *The Analytics of Uncertainty and Information*. Cambridge University Press.

Holmstrom, B. (1979). Moral hazard and observability. *Bell Journal of Economics*, 10:74–91.

Holmstrom, B. (1982). Moral hazard in teams. *Bell Journal of Economics*, 13:324–340.

Holmstrom, B. and Milgrom, P. (1987). Aggregation and linearity in the provision of intertemporal incentives. *Econometrica*, 55:303–328.

Holmstrom, B. and Milgrom, P. (1990). Regulating trade among agents. *Journal of Law, Economics, and Organization*, 7:125–152.

Holmstrom, B. and Milgrom, P. (1991). Multi-task principal agent analyses. *Journal of Institutional and Theoretical Economics*, 147:24–52.

Hotelling, H. (1929). Stability in competition. *Economic Journal*, 39:41–57.

Hylland, A. and Zeckhauser, R. (1979). The efficient allocation of individuals to positions. *Journal of Political Economy*, 87:293–314.

Innes, R. (1990). Limited liability and incentive contracting with ex ante choices. *Journal of Economic Theory*, 52:45–67.

Jeitschko, T. (1998). Learning in sequential auctions. *Southern Economic Journal*, 65:98–112.

Jeitschko, T. and Wolfstetter, E. (1998). Scale economies and the dynamics of recurring auctions. Discussion paper, Humboldt-Universität zu Berlin.

Jewitt, I. (1988). Justifying the first-order approach to principal–agent problems. *Econometrica*, 56:1177–1190.

Jewitt, J. (1991). Applications of likelihood ratio orderings in economics. In Misler, K. and Scarsini, M., editors, *Stochastic Orders and Decisions under Risk*, volume 19. Institute of Mathematical Statistics Lecture Notes.

Kagel, J. (1995). Auctions: A survey of experimental research. In Kagel, J. and Roth, A., editors, *The Handbook of Experimental Economics*, pages 501–585. Princeton University Press.

Kagel, J., Harstad, R. M., and Levin, D. (1987). Information impact and allocation rules in auctions with affiliated private values: A laboratory study. *Econometrica*, 55:1275–1304.

Kagel, J. H. and Levin, D. (1986). The winner's curse and public information in common value auctions. *American Economic Review*, 76:894–920.

Kagel, J. H. and Levin, D. (1993). Independent private value auctions: Bidder behavior in first-, second-, and third-price auctions with varying numbers of bidders. *Economic Journal*, 103:868–879.

Kahn, A. E. (1971). *The Economics of Regulation: Principles and Institutions*, volume II. Wiley.

Kahn, C. M. (1986). The durable goods monopolist and consistency with increasing costs. *Econometrica*, 54:275–294.

Kamien, M. I. and Schwartz, N. L. (1991). *Dynamic Optimization: The Calculus of Variations and Optimal Control in Economics and Management*. North-Holland, 2nd edition.

Katz, M. L. and Shapiro, C. (1985). Network externalities, competition, and compatibility. *American Economic Review*, 75:424–440.

Katz, M. L. and Shapiro, C. (1992). Product introduction with network externalities. *Journal of Industrial Econmomics*, 40:55–83.

Kendall, S. M. and Stuart, A. (1977). *The Advanced Theory of Statistics*, volume I. Charles Griffin.

Kihlstrom, R. and Laffont, J.-J. (1979). A general equilibrium entrepreneurial theory of firm formation based on risk aversion. *Journal of Political Economy*, 87:719–748.

Kihlstrom, R. E. and Mirman, L. J. (1974). Risk aversion with many commodities. *Journal of Economic Theory*, 8:361–388.

Klemperer, P. (1989). Price wars caused by switching costs. *Review of Economic Studies*, 56:405–420.

Klemperer, P. (1998). Auctions with almost common values: The "wallet game" and its applications. *European Economic Review*, 42:757–769.

Klevorick, A. (1966). Graduated fair return: A regulatory proposal. *American Economic Review*, 56:477–484.

Kofman, F. and Lawarrée, J. (1993). Collusion in hierarchical agency. *Econometrica*, 61:629–656.

Kofman, F. and Lawarrée, J. (1996). On the optimality of allowing collusion. *Journal of Public Economics*, 61:383–407.

Kolstad, C. D. and Mathiesen, L. (1987). Necessary and sufficient conditions for uniqueness of a Cournot equilibrium. *Review of Economic Studies*, 54:681–690.

Kreps, D. (1990). *A Course in Microeconomic Theory*. Princeton University Press.

Kreps, D. and Wilson, R. (1982). Sequential equilibria. *Econometrica*, 50:863–94.

Kreps, D. M. and Scheinkman, J. A. (1983). Quantity precommitment and Bertrand competition yield Cournot outcomes. *Bell Journal of Economics*, 14:326–337.

Krishna, V. and Perry, M. (1998). Efficient mechanism design. Discussion paper, Center for Rationality, Hebrew University, Jerusalem.

Kühn, K.-U. (1998). Intertemporal price discrimination in frictionless durable goods monopolies. *The Journal of Industrial Economics*, 46:101–114.

Laffont, J.-J. (1990). *The Economics of Uncertainty*. MIT Press.

Laffont, J.-J. (1997). Game theory and empirical economics: The case of auction data. *European Economic Review*, 41:1–36.

Laffont, J.-J. and Martimort, D. (1997). Collusion under asymmetric information. *Econometrica*, 65:875–911.

Laffont, J.-J. and Robert, J. (1996). Optimal auction with financially constrained buyers. *Economics Letters*, 52:181–186.

Laffont, J.-J. and Tirole, J. (1987). Auctioning incentive contracts. *Journal of Political Economy*, 95:921–937.

Laffont, J.-J. and Tirole, J. (1988). The dynamics of incentive contracts. *Econometrica*, 56:1153–1176.

Laffont, J.-J. and Tirole, J. (1990). Optimal bypass and cream skimming. *American Economic Review*, 80:1042–1061.

Laffont, J. J. and Tirole, J. (1993). *A Theory of Incentives in Procurement and Regulation.* MIT Press.

Landsberger, M. and Meilijson, I. (1990a). Demand for risky financial assets. *Journal of Economic Theory*, 50:204–213.

Landsberger, M. and Meilijson, I. (1990b). A tale of two tails: An alternative characterization of comparative risk. *Journal of Risk and Uncertainty*, 3:65–82.

Landsberger, M. and Meilijson, I. (1999). A general model of insurance under adverse selection. *Economic Theory*, 14 (forthcoming).

Landsberger, M., Rubinstein, J., Wolfstetter, E., and Zamir, S. (1998). First-price auctions when the ranking of valuations is common knowledge. Discussion paper, Center for Rationality, Hebrew University, Jerusalem.

Lazear, E. P. (1995a). Performance pay and productivity. Discussion paper, Hoover Institution and Stanford Graduate School of Business.

Lazear, E. P. (1995b). *Personnel Economics.* MIT Press.

Lazear, E. P. and Rosen, S. (1981). Rank-order tournaments as optimum labor contracts. *Journal of Political Economy*, 89:841–864.

Legros, P. and Matthews, S. A. (1993). Efficient and nearly efficient partnerships. *Review of Economic Studies*, 65:599–611.

Levin, D. (1985). Taxation within Cournot oligopoly. *Journal of Public Economics*, 27:281–290.

Levin, D. and Smith, J. L. (1994). Equilibrium in auctions with entry. *American Economic Review*, 84:585–599.

Levine, D. K. and Pesendorfer, W. (1995). When are agents negligible? *American Economic Review*, 85:1160–1170.

Levitan, R. and Shubik, M. (1972). Price duopoly and capacity constraints. *International Economic Review*, 13:111–122.

Li, H. and Rosen, S. (1998). Unraveling in matching markets. *American Economic Review*, 88:371–387.

Lieberman, M. B. (1990). Exit from declining industries: 'Shakeout' or 'stakeout'? *Rand Journal of Economics*, 21:538–554.

Lindahl, E. (1919). Just taxation – a positive solution. In Musgrave, R. and Peacock, A., editors, *Classics in the Theory of Public Finance.* Macmillan, London.

Loeb, M. and Magat, W. (1979). A decentralized method for utility regulation. *The Journal of Law and Economics*, 23:399–401.

Lorenz, M. O. (1905). Methods for measuring concentration of wealth. *Journal of the American Statistical Association*, 9:209–219.

Ma, C.-T. A. (1991). Adverse selection in dynamic moral hazard. *Quarterly Journal of Economics*, 105:255–275.

Ma, C.-T. A. (1994). Renegotiation and optimality in agency contracts. *Review of Economic Studies*, 61:109–130.

Mandelbrot, B. (1963). The variation of certain speculative stock prices. *Journal of Business*, 36:394–419.

Mankiw, N. G. and Whinston, M. D. (1986). Free entry and social inefficiency. *Rand Journal of Economics*, 17:48–58.

Martin, S. (1993). *Advanced Industrial Economics.* Blackwell.

Mas-Colell, A., Whinston, M., and Green, J. (1995). *Microeconomic Theory.* Oxford University Press.

Maskin, E. and Riley, J. G. (1984a). Monopoly with incomplete information. *Rand Journal of Economics*, 15:171–196.

Maskin, E. and Riley, J. G. (1984b). Optimal auctions with risk averse buyers. *Econometrica*, 52:1473–1518.

Maskin, E. and Riley, J. G. (1985). Auction theory with private values. *American Economic Review, Papers and Proceedings*, 75:150–155.

Maskin, E. and Riley, J. G. (1989). Optimal multi-unit auctions. In Hahn, F., editor, *The Economics of Missing Markets, Information, and Games*, pages 312–335. Clarendon Press.

Maskin, E. and Riley, J. G. (1996). Asymmetric auctions. Working paper, Harvard University.

Maskin, E. and Tirole, J. (1988). A theory of dynamic oligopoly, I and II. *Econometrica*, 56:549–570, 571–600.

Maskin, E. and Tirole, J. (1992). The principal–agent relationship with an informed principal II. *Econometrica*, 60:1–42.

Matthews, S. (1983). Selling to risk averse buyers with unobservable tastes. *Journal of Economic Theory*, 30:370–400.

Matthews, S. (1995a). Renegotiation of sales contracts. *Econometrica*, 63:567–590.

Matthews, S. (1995b). A technical primer on auction theory. Working paper, Northwestern University.

McAfee, R. and McMillan, J. (1987a). Auctions and bidding. *Journal of Economic Literature*, 25:699–738.

McAfee, R. and McMillan, J. (1987b). Auctions with a stochastic number of bidders. *Journal of Economic Theory*, 43:1–19.

McAfee, R. and McMillan, J. (1987c). Auctions with entry. *Economics Letters*, 23:343–347.

McAfee, R. and McMillan, J. (1992). Bidding rings. *American Economic Review*, 82:579–599.

McAfee, R., McMillan, J., and Whinston, M. (1989). Multiproduct monopoly, commodity bundling and the correlation of values. *Quarterly Journal of Economics*, 103:371–383.

McAfee, R. P. and Vincent, D. (1993). The declining price anomaly. *Journal of Economic Theory*, 60:191–212.

McCabe, K., Rassenti, S., and Smith, V. (1989). Designing "smart" computer-assisted markets: An experimental auction for gas networks. *Journal of Political Economy*, 99:259–283.

McGuire, T. and Riordan, M. (1994). Introduction: The industrial organization of health care. *Journal of Economics & Management Strategy*, 3:1–6.

McMillan, J. (1994). Selling spectrum rights. *Journal of Economic Perspectives*, 8:145–162.

Menezes, C. F. and Hanson, D. L. (1970). On the theory of risk aversion. *International Economic Review*, 11:481–487.

Meyer, J. (1989). Stochastic dominance and transformations of random variables. In Fomby, T. B. and Seo, T. K., editors, *Studies in the Economics of Uncertainty: In Honor of Josef Hadar*, pages 45–57. Springer-Verlag, New York.

Meyer, J. and Ormiston, M. B. (1983). The comparative statics of cumulative distribution function changes for the class of risk averse agents. *Journal of Economic Theory*, 31:153–169.

Milde, H. and Riley, J. (1998). Signaling in credit markets. *Quarterly Journal of Economics*, 103:101–130.

Milgrom, P. (1989). Auctions and bidding: A primer. *Journal of Economic Perspectives*, 3:3–22.

Milgrom, P. (1997). Putting auction theory to work: The simultaneous ascending auction. Technical report, Stanford University, Department of Economics.

Milgrom, P. (1998). *Auction Theory for Privatization*. Cambridge University Press.

Milgrom, P. and Roberts, J. (1982). Limit pricing and entry under incomplete information: A general equilibrium analysis. *Econometrica*, 50:443–459.

Milgrom, P. and Roberts, J. (1992). *Economics, Organization and Management*. Prentice Hall.

Milgrom, P. and Weber, R. J. (1982). A theory of auctions and competitive bidding. *Econometrica*, 50:1089–1122.

Mirrlees, J. (1975). The theory of moral hazard under unobservable behavior. Mimeo., Nuffield College, Oxford.

Miyazaki, H. (1977). The rat race and internal labor markets. *Bell Journal of Economics*, 8:394–418.

Myerson, R. B. (1979). Incentive compatibility and the bargaining problem. *Econometrica*, 47:61–73.

Myerson, R. B. (1981). Optimal auction design. *Mathematics of Operations Research*, 6:58–73.

Myerson, R. B. (1991). *Game Theory*. Harvard University Press.

Nalebuff, B. J. and Stiglitz, J. E. (1983). Prizes and incentives: Towards a general theory of compensation and competition. *Bell Journal of Economics*, 14:21–43.

Nash, J. (1950a). The bargaining problem. *Econometrica*, 18:155–162.

Nash, J. (1950b). Equilibrium points in n-person games. *Proceedings of the National Academy of Sciences, USA*, 36:48–49.

Nautz, D. (1997). How auctions reveal information – a case study on German REPO rates. *Journal of Money, Credit, and Banking*, 29:17–25.

Nautz, D. and Wolfstetter, E. (1997). Bid shading and risk aversion in multi-unit auctions with many bidders. *Economics Letters*, 56:195–200.

Nermuth, M. (1982). *Information Structures in Economics*. Springer-Verlag.

Newbery, D. (1970). A theorem on the measurement of inequality. *Journal of Economic Theory*, 2:264–266.

Novshek, W. (1984). Finding all n-firm Cournot equilibria. *International Economic Review*, 25:61–70.

Novshek, W. (1985). On the existence of Cournot equilibrium. *Review of Economic Studies*, 52:85–98.

Ormiston, M. B. (1992). First and second degree transformations and comparative statics under uncertainty. *International Economic Review*, 33:33–44.

Osborne, M. J. and Pitchik, C. (1987). Cartels, profits, and excess capacity. *International Economic Review*, 28:413–428.

Osborne, M. J. and Rubinstein, A. (1990). *Bargaining and Markets*. Academic Press.

Park, E. S. (1995). Incentive contracting under limited liability. *Journal of Economics and Management Strategy*, 4:477–490.

Perry, M., Wolfstetter, E., and Zamir, S. (1998). A sealed-bid auction that matches the English auction. Discussion paper, Center for Rationality, Hebrew University, Jerusalem.

Phlips, L. (1983). *The Economics of Price Discrimination*. Cambridge University Press.

Phlips, L. (1988). *The Economics of Imperfect Information*. Cambridge University Press.

Phlips, L. (1995). *Competition Policy: A Game-Theoretic Perspective*. Cambridge University Press.

Pierre, D. A. (1969). *Optimization Theory with Applications*. Wiley.

Pigou, A. C. (1920). *The Economics of Welfare*. Cambridge University Press.

Plant, A. (1934). The economic theory concerning patents. *Economica*, 1:30–51.

Plum, M. (1992). Characterization and computation of Nash-equilibria for auctions with incomplete information. *International Journal of Game Theory*, 20:393–418.

Posner, R. (1975). The social cost of monopoly and regulation. *Journal of Political Economy*, 83:807–827.

Pratt, J. W. (1964). Risk aversion in the small and the large. *Econometrica*, 32:122–136.

Pratt, J. W. (1989). Utility functions, interest rates, and the demand for bonds. In Fomby, T. B. and Seo, T. K., editors, *Studies in the Economics of Uncertainty: In Honor of Josef Hadar*, pages 225–231. Springer-Verlag, New York.

Prinz, A. and Wolfstetter, E. (1991). Unsichere Rente: Wie reagieren Arbeitsangebot und Ersparnis? *Jahrbücher für Nationalökonomie und Statistik*, 208:140–152.

Rahi, R. (1996). Adverse selection and security design. *Review of Economic Studies*, 63:287–300.

Rassenti, S. J., Smith, V. L., and Bulfin, R. L. (1982). A combinatorial auction mechanism for airport time slot allocation. *Bell Journal of Economics*, 13:402–417.

Ravenscraft, D. J. and Scherer, F. M. (1989). The profitability of mergers. *International Journal of Industrial Organization*, 7:101–116.

Riley, J. G. (1987). Credit rationing: A further remark. *American Economic Review*, 77:224–227.

Riley, J. G. (1989). Expected revenue from open and sealed bid auctions. *Journal of Economic Perspectives*, 3:41–50.

Riley, J. G. and Samuelson, W. F. (1981). Optimal auctions. *American Economic Review*, 71:381–392.

Riordan, M. H. and Sappington, D. E. (1987). Awarding monopoly franchises. *American Economic Review*, 77:375–387.

Roberts, K. and Sonnenschein, H. (1976). On the existence of Cournot equilibrium without concave profit functions. *Journal of Economic Theory*, 13:112–117.

Robinson, J. (1933). *The Economics of Imperfect Competition*. Macmillan.

Robinson, M. (1985). Collusion and the choice of auction. *Rand Journal of Economics*, 16:141–145.

Rogerson, W. P. (1985a). The first-order approach to principal–agent problems. *Econometrica*, 53:1357–1368.

Rogerson, W. P. (1985b). Repeated moral hazard. *Econometrica*, 53:69–76.

Roll, R. (1986). The hubris hypothesis of corporate takeovers. *Journal of Business*, 59:197–216.

Ross, S. A. (1981). Some stronger measures of risk aversion in the small and the large with applications. *Econometrica*, 49:621–638.

Ross, S. M. (1983). *Stochastic Processes*. Wiley.

Roth, A. (1984). The evolution of the labor market for medical interns and residents: A case study in game theory. *Journal of Political Economy*, 92:991–1016.

Roth, A. (1989). Two-sided matching with incomplete information about others' preferences. *Games and Economic Behavior*, 1:191–209.

Roth, A. (1991). A natural experiment in the organization of entry-level labor markets: Regional markets for new physicians and surgeons in the United Kingdom. *American Economic Review*, 81:415–440.

Roth, A. and Sotomayor, M. (1990). *Two-Sided Matching: A Study in Game-Theoretic Modeling and Analysis*. Cambridge University Press.

Roth, A. E. and Xing, X. (1994). Jumping the gun: Imperfections and institutions related to the timing of market transactions. *American Economic Review*, 84:992–1044.

Rothschild, M. and Stiglitz, J. E. (1970). Increasing risk I: A definition. *Journal of Economic Theory*, 2:225–243.

Rothschild, M. and Stiglitz, J. E. (1971). Increasing risk II: Its economic consequences. *Journal of Economic Theory*, 3:66–84.

Rothschild, M. and Stiglitz, J. E. (1976). Equilibrium in competitive insurance markets: An essay on the economics of imperfect information. *Quarterly Journal of Economics*, 90:629–650.

Rubinstein, A. (1982). Perfect equilibrium in a bargaining game. *Econometrica*, 50:97–109.

Ruffin, R. J. (1971). Cournot oligopoly and competitive behavior. *Review of Economic Studies*, 38:493–502.

Salant, W., Switzer, S., and Reynolds, R. J. (1983). Losses from horizontal merger: The effects of an exogenous change in industry structure on Cournot–Nash equilibrium. *Quarterly Journal of Economics*, 98:185–199.

Samuelson, P. A. (1954). The pure theory of public expenditure. *The Review of Economics and Statistics*, 64:387–389.

Sandmo, A. (1971). On the theory of the competitive firm under price uncertainty. *American Economic Review*, 61:65–73.

Sappington, D. (1980). Strategic firm behavior under a dynamic regulatory adjustment process. *Bell Journal of Economics*, 11:360–372.

Sappington, D. (1983). Limited liability contracts between principal and agent. *Journal of Economic Theory*, 29:1–21.

Sappington, D. (1991). Incentives in principal–agent relationships. *Journal of Economic Perspectives*, 5:45–66.

Sappington, D. and Sibley, D. (1988). Regulating without cost information: The incremental surplus subsidy scheme. *International Economic Review*, 29:297–306.

Sappington, D. and Sibley, D. (1990). Regulating without cost information: Further information. *International Economic Review*, 31:1027–1029.

Scherer, F. M. (1980). *Industrial Market Structure and Economic Performance*. Rand McNally.

Schmidt, K. and Schnitzer, M. (1997). Methods of privatization: Auctions, bargaining and give-aways. In Giersch, H., editor, *Privatization at the End of the Century*, pages 97–134. Springer–Verlag.

Schumpeter, J. A. (1975). *Capitalism, Socialism and Democracy*. Harper & Row.

Schwermer, S. (1995). Regulating oligopolistic industries: A generalized incentive scheme. *Journal of Regulatory Economics*, 6:97–108.

Scott, J. and Wolf, C. (1979). The efficient diversification of bids in Treasury bill auctions. *Review of Economics and Statistics*, 60:280–287.

Selten, R. (1970). *Preispolitik der Mehrproduktunternehmung in der Statischen Theorie*. Springer–Verlag.

Selten, R. (1973). A simple model of imperfect competition where four are few and six are many. *International Journal of Game Theory*, pages 141–201.

Selten, R. (1984). Are cartel laws bad for business? In Hauptman, H., Krelle, W., and Mosler, K. C., editors, *Operations Research and Economic Theory*. Springer–Verlag.

Sen, A. (1972). *On Economic Inequality*. Oxford University Press.

Shapley, L. S. and Shubik, M. (1972). The assignment game I: The core. *International Journal of Game Theory*, 1:111–130.

Sharpe, W. F. (1970). *Portfolio Theory and Capital Markets*. McGraw-Hill.

Shavell, S. (1979). Risk sharing and incentives in the principal and agent relationship. *Bell Journal of Economics*, 10:55–73.

Sheshinski, E. (1976). Price, quality and quantity regulation in monopoly situations. *Economica*, 143:127–137.

Shubik, M. (1983). Auctions, bidding, and markets: An historical sketch. In Engelbrecht-Wiggans, R., Shubik, M., and Stark, J., editors, *Auctions, Bidding, and Contracting*, pages 165–191. New York University Press, New York.

Shy, O. (1995). *Industrial Organization. Theory and Applications*. MIT Press.

Simon, L. K. (1987). Games with discontinuous payoffs. *Review of Economic Studies*, 54:569–597.

Singh, N. and Vives, X. (1984). Price and quantity competition in a differentiated duopoly. *Rand Journal of Economics*, 15:546–554.

Slade, M. E. (1989). Price wars in price-setting supergames. *Economica*, 56:295–310.

Sonnenschein, H. (1968). The dual of duopoly is complementary monopoly: Or, two of Cournot's theories are one. *Journal of Political Economy*, 76:316–318.

Spence, M. (1973). Job market signaling. *Quarterly Journal of Economics*, 87:355–374.

Spence, M. (1975). Monopoly, quality, and regulation. *Bell Journal of Economics*, 6:417–429.

Spindt, P. A. and Stolz, R. W. (1989). The expected stop-out price in a discriminatory auction. *Economics Letters*, 31:133–137.

Ståhl, I. (1972). *Bargaining Theory*. EFI, The Economic Research Institute, Stockholm.

Staudinger, H. (1982). *Wirtschaftspolitik im Weimarer Staat*. Verlag Neue Gesellschaft, Bonn.

Stefos, T. (1990). Regulating without cost information: A comment. *International Economic Review*, 31:1021–1029.

Stewart, G. (1989). Profit-sharing in Cournot oligopoly. *Economics Letters*, 31:221–224.

Stigler, G. J. (1971). The theory of economic regulation. *Bell Journal of Economics*, 2:3–21.

Stiglitz, J. E. and Weiss, A. (1981). Credit rationing in credit markets with imperfect information. *American Economic Review*, 71:393–410.

Stokey, N. (1979). Intertemporal price discrimination. *Quarterly Journal of Economics*, 93:355–371.

Stokey, N. (1981). Rational expectations and durable goods pricing. *Bell Journal of Economics*, 12:112–128.

Stole, L. (1995). Nonlinear pricing and oligopoly. *Journal of Economics and Management Strategy*, 4:529–562.

Stolper, G. (1964). *Deutsche Wirtschaft Seit 1870*. Mohr Siebeck.

Sutton, J. (1986). Non-cooperative bargaining theory: An introduction. *Review of Economic Studies*, 53:709–724.

Szidarovszky, F. and Yakowitz, S. (1977). A new proof of the existence and uniqueness of the Cournot equilibrium. *International Economic Review*, 18:787–789.

Tan, G. (1992). Entry and R & D in procurement contracting. *Journal of Economic Theory*, 22:41–60.

Temin, P. (1976). *Did Monetary Forces Cause the Great Depression?* Norton.

Tirole, J. (1986). Hierarchies and bureaucracies. *Journal of Law, Economics, and Organization*, 2:181–214.

Tirole, J. (1989). *The Theory of Industrial Organization*. MIT Press.

Van Damme, E. (1987). *Stability and Perfection of Nash Equilibria*. Springer-Verlag.

Varian, H. (1989). Price discrimination. In Schmalensee, R. and Willig, R. D., editors, *Handbook of Industrial Organization*, volume 1, pages 597–648. Elsevier Science.

Varian, H. R. (1992). *Microeconomic Analysis*. W. W. Norton, 3rd. edition.

Verboven, F. (1996). International price discrimination in the European car market. *Rand Journal of Economics*, 27:240–268.

Vickers, J. (1985). Delegation and the theory of the firm. *Economic Journal, Supplement*, 95:138–147.

Vickrey, W. (1961). Counterspeculation, auctions, and competitive sealed tenders. *Journal of Finance*, 16:8–37.

Vives, X. (1986). Rationing and Bertrand–Edgeworth equilibria in large markets. *Economics Letters*, 27:113–116.

Vogelsang, I. (1989). Two part tariffs as a regulatory constraint. *Journal of Public Economics*, 39:45–66.

Vogelsang, I. and Finsinger, J. (1979). A regulatory adjustment process for optimal pricing by multiproduct monopoly firms. *Bell Journal of Economics and Management Science*, 10:157–161.

von der Fehr, N. and Kühn, K.-U. (1995). Coase vs. PacMan: Who eats whom in the durable goods monopoly? *Journal of Political Economy*, 103:785–812.

von Neumann, J. and Morgenstern, O. (1944). *Theory of Games and Economic Behavior*. Princeton University Press.

von Stackelberg, H. (1934). *Marktform und Gleichgewicht*. Springer–Verlag.

Wadhwani, S. (1988). Profit sharing as a cure for unemployment: Some doubts. *International Journal of Industrial Organization*, 6:483–511.

Weber, R. J. (1983). Multiple-object auctions. In Engelbrecht-Wiggans, R., Shubik, M., and Stark, J., editors, *Auctions, Bidding, and Contracting*, pages 165–191. New York University Press, New York.

Weiss, A. (1983). A sorting-cum-learning model of education. *Journal of Political Economy*, 91:420–442.

Weitzman, M. L. (1984). *The Share Economy*. Harvard University Press.

Whinston, M. D. (1988). Exit with multiplant firms. *Rand Journal of Economics*, 19:568–588.

White, M. (1997). *Isaac Newton: The Last Sorcerer*. Addison–Wesley.

Whitmore, G. A. (1970). Third-degree stochastic dominance. *American Economic Review*, 60:457–459.

Whitmore, G. A. and Findlay, M. C., editors (1982). *Stochastic Dominance*. Lexington Books, Lexington, MA.

Wilson, C. (1977a). A model of insurance markets with incomplete information. *Journal of Economic Theory*, 16:167–207.

Wilson, C. (1980). The nature of equilibrium in the markets with adverse selection. *Bell Journal of Economics*, 11:108–130.

Wilson, R. (1992). Strategic analysis of auctions. In Aumann, R. and Hart, S., editors, *Handbook of Game Theory*, volume I, pages 227–280. Elsevier Science.

Wilson, R. B. (1977b). A bidding model of perfect competition. *Review of Economic Studies*, 44:511–518.

Wilson, R. B. (1993). *Nonlinear Pricing*. Oxford University Press.

Wolfstetter, E. (1996). Auctions: An introduction. *Journal of Economic Surveys*, 10:367–421.

Wolfstetter, E. (1998). Third- and lower-price auctions and corruption. Discussion paper, SFB 373, Humboldt-Universität zu Berlin.

Wright, B. D. (1983). The economics of invention incentives: Patents, prizes, and research contracts. *American Economic Review*, 73:691–707.

Yitzhaki, S. (1982). Stochastic dominance, mean variance, and Gini's mean difference. *American Economic Review*, 72:178–185.

Zhou, L. (1990). On a conjecture by Gale about one-sided matching problems. *Journal of Economic Theory*, 52:123–135.

Index

Adams, 51
Admati, 277
Adolph, 164
adverse selection, 244
   labor market, 245
   market for lemons, 244
   positive selection, 248
   rationing, 251
affiliated-value model, 205
affiliated values, 230
affiliation, 230
age of deregulation, 52
Akerlof, 244
all-pay auction, 193
Allen, 124
Alvi, 300
Amiel, 164
Anderson, 132
Antle, 302
Anton, 208
arbitrage, 26
Arrow, 17, 164, 165
Arrow–Hurwicz–Uzawa, 322
Arrow–Pratt measure, 165
Arthur, 51
Ashenfelter, 209
Atkinson, 159, 164
auction ring, 209
auctioneer, 68
auctions, 155
   adverse-selection bias, 225
   affiliated-value model, 205
   affiliated values, 230
   all-pay auction, 193
   asymmetric auction, 207
   asymmetric equilibria, 226
   auctions and oligopoly, 235
   benefit of English auction, 233
   biased estimator, 232
   collusion, 209, 210, 235
   common-value auction, 225
   declining-price anomaly, 209
   direct auction, 215
   Dutch auction, 155, 186, 188
   electric power auction, 238
   English auction, 155, 186, 190, 233
   first-price auction, 188
   linkage principle, 232
   lower-price auction, 192

   mechanism design, 214
   multiunit auction, 207, 208
   natural-gas auction, 238
   numbers uncertainty, 204
   optimal auction, 211, 212, 222
   phantom bids, 204
   pre-auction, 210
   price discrimination, 217
   priority level, 216
   private-value model, 186
   repeated auction, 208
   REPO auction, 240
   revelation principle, 214
   revenue equivalence, 187
   second-price auction, 190, 230
   selection bias, 226, 231
   sequential auctions, 208
   spectrum auctions, 235
   split-award auction, 208
   third-price auction, 192
   Treasury-bill auction, 239
   Vickrey auction, 230, 231
   wallet auction, 225
   winner's curse, 226
Averch, 53, 63
Averch–Johnson effect, 53, 55

Bagnoli, 181, 216
Bagwell, 85
bargaining, 43
   Nash bargaining solution, 48
Baron, 64
Bartle, 266
Bazerman, 225
Beckmann, 122
Bellman, 61
Bergstrom, 96, 97, 181, 216
Bernhardt, 209
Bertrand, 67
Bertrand competition, 67, 69, 72, 116, 125
   accommodating price, 119
   capacity constraints, 117
   cyclical prices, 121
   efficient rationing, 123
   parallel rationing, 122
   random rationing, 117, 122
   random sales, 121
   reaction mapping, 73
   residual demand price, 118

Bertrand paradox, 116
Bester, 258
Bhagat, 229
binary signals, 294
Binmore, 218
bonus contract, 291, 293
Boyes, 64
Brander, 79
Breen, 135
Brown, 281, 299, 300
Bulow, 41
bunching, 32
bundling, 49

Cagan, 9
Campbell, 229
Capen, 229
Carlton, 20
cartel, 98
    Antitrust Office, 99
    disguised agreement, 100
    instability problem, 99
cartel law, 111
Cassady, 187
Cassidy, 49
caveat emptor, 244
CDFC, 286, 292
Che, 239
Chiang, 300
Cho, 273
Choi, 51
Clapp, 229
Clarke, 202
Clarke mechanism, 202
Clarke–Groves mechanism, 202
club good, 35
Coase, 42
Coase conjecture, 42
collusion, 102, 131, 209
commitment and observability, 85, 222
commitment mechanism, 79, 84
commitment power, 26
common shock, 307
common-value auction, 225
comparative statics
    FSD transformation, 146, 147
    SSD transformation, 146, 148
competition for the market, 16
concavity
    pseudoconcavity, 241
Conlisk, 42
constraint qualification, 317
contracts
    bonus contract, 291
convexifiable quasiconvex program, 336
convexification, 336
convexity, 324
    composite function, 333
    convex function, 325
    convex set, 324
    global extreme value, 328
    quasiconvexity, 329
    strongly convex function, 327
convexity of distribution function
        condition, 286, 292
cooperative, 337
copy protection, 8

correlation, 340, 341
cost minimization, 55
cost-push inflation, 8
costs
    quasifixed, 12
    reversible, 12
    sunk, 12
coupons, 123
Cournot, 67, 77
Cournot competition, 67, 68, 70, 89, 125
    deterrence point, 70
    incentive constraints, 28
    isoprofit curve, 70
    monopoly point, 70
    participation constraint, 28
    price competition subgame, 126
    rate-of-return constraint, 53
Cournot monopoly, 4, 5, 216
Cournot oligopoly
    corrective tax, 105
    entry, 107, 153
    equilibrium, 125
    equilibrium size, 108
    exit, 111
    exit game, 114
    mixed entry strategies, 110
    welfare loss of, 104
Cournot point, 5, 11, 12
    without concavity, 13
Courville, 64
covariance, 340, 341
Cowell, 164
Crawford, 277
credit market, 258
Crémer, 299

d'Aspremont, 202
Dalton, 158
Dasgupta, 122, 128, 266
Davidson, 103, 131
Davis, 164
de Palma, 132
Debreu, 95
Dechert, 64
delegation to managers, 79
demand for money, 10
Demougin, 289
Deneckere, 103, 131
Department of Justice, 49
Dessauer, 229
digression, 317
directional derivative, 312
Dittmann, 299
diversification, 156
Dixit, 79, 110, 111, 114, 164
Dixon, 122
Dowrick, 77
Dudey, 43, 51, 124
duopoly, 68
durable good, 37
Dutch auction, 155, 186, 188
dynamic program, 61

Edgeworth, 67, 121
education game, 268
Eeckhoudt, 164
El-Hodiri, 63

Elberfeld, 222
electric power auction, 238
Emons, 277
Engelbrecht-Wiggans, 211
English auction, 155, 186, 190, 233
equilibrium
    intuitive criterion, 273
    noncooperative Nash e., 66
    pooling, 270, 275
    separating, 270
    sequential, 268
    unique subgame-perfect e., 75
exclusion, 32
expectations
    self-destroying, 66
    self-fulfilling, 66
expected value, 339, 340

Farrell, 51, 277
feasible direction vector, 321
Federal Communications Commission, 235
Fehr, 51
Fershtman, 80
Findlay, 148
Finsinger, 59
first-order approach problem, 300
first-price auction, 188
Fishburn, 148, 150
Fishman, 115, 277
Fluet, 289
Friedman, 90, 132, 241
Fritz John condition, 322
Fudenberg, 45, 62, 89, 111, 276

Gabszewicz, 132
Gal-Or, 79
Galbraith, 80
Gale, 175
Gelman, 124
Genovese, 209
Gerstner, 42
Ghemawat, 112, 114
Ghosh, 300
Giffen good, 150, 163
Gilbert, 19
Gini coefficient, 157
Glicksberg, 90, 121
global extreme value, 328, 336
Glosten, 266
Gollier, 164
gradient, 312
Grafen, 267
Graham, 210
Green, 132, 202, 307, 308
Gresham's law, 244
Grossman, 277, 285
Groves, 202
Groves mechanism, 202
Guesnerie, 53, 64
Gul, 42
Gérard-Varet, 202

Hadar, 144, 148, 150, 156, 170
Hansen, 208
Hanson, 146, 172
Harris, 207, 299, 300
Harsanyi, 158

Harstad, 204, 206
Hart, 285, 299
hazard rate, 139, 216
Hellwig, 85, 124, 266
Helpman, 85
Hessian matrix, 312
hidden information, 26, 243
Hirshleifer, 20, 172, 308
Hochstädter, 121
Holmstrom, 164, 283, 299, 300, 308
Hotelling, 132
Hylland, 177
hyperinflation, 11

implicit-function theorem, 314
Inada conditions, 152
incentive compatibility, 290
income inequality, 157
incomplete-insurance puzzle, 167
incremental surplus subsidy, 58, 106
    with commitment, 60
    without commitment, 62
industrial organization, 65
inferior good, 153
inflation tax, 9, 11
information
    complete, 66
    perfect, 66
Innes, 289
innovation, 17
insurance market, 253
intuitive criterion, 273

Jacobian matrix, 314
Jeitschko, 209
Jensen's inequality, 342
Jewitt, 300
job market, 267
Johnson, 53, 63
Judd, 80

Kühn, 51
Kagel, 192, 204, 206
Kahn, 42, 53
Kamien, 303
Katz, 51
Kihlstrom, 172
Klemperer, 132, 225
Klevorick, 63
Kofman, 299
Kolstad, 95
Kreps, 62, 125, 128, 268, 273, 285
Krugman, 85
Kuhn, 322
Kuhn–Tucker conditions, 322

labor-managed firm, 337
labor market, 245, 258
labor supply, 152, 153
Laffont, 53, 64, 172, 193, 202, 239, 299
Lagrange, 314
Lagrangian, 303, 315
Landsberger, 163, 164, 235, 266
Lawarrée, 299
Lazear, 299, 302
leasing, 41
Legros, 308

lemons, market for, 244
Lerner index, 8
Leviathan, 95
Levin, 96, 204, 206, 222
Levine, 51, 89, 192
Levitan, 122
Lewis, 79
Lieberman, 111
likelihood ratio, 139, 286, 292
limited liability, 290
Lindahl, 35
Lindahl prices, 35
linkage principle, 232
LMF, 337
Loeb, 57
log concavity, 216
Lorenz, 159
Lorenz curve, 158
Lorenz dominance, 158, 159
lump-sum tax, 15, 58

Ma, 298
Magat, 57
Mandelbrot, 135
Mankiw, 108
Mann's proposition, 319
markup pricing, 8
markup rule, 7, 25
market for lemons, 244
Marshall, 210
Martimort, 299
Martin, 85, 101, 132
Maskin, 26, 121, 122, 128, 205, 207, 208, 260, 298
matching
  price matching, 74
  roommate problem, 177
  stable, 176
  supply matching, 72
  two-sided matching, 176
Mathiesen, 95
Matthews, 193, 298, 308
McAfee, 51, 204, 209, 211, 224
McGuire, 299
McMillan, 51, 204, 211, 224, 235
mechanism design, 214
Meilijson, 163, 164, 266
Menezes, 146, 172
merger, 102
  breakeven point of, 102
Meyer, 148
Microsoft, 49
Milde, 258
Milgrom, 206, 228, 234, 235, 266, 267, 277, 283, 299
Mirman, 172
Mirrlees, 300
MLRC, 286, 292
monitoring, 294, 295
monopoly, 3
  antitrust violations, 49
  bilateral monopoly, 43
  bundling, 49
  complementary-goods m., 77
  deadweight loss of, 14
  durable-goods monopoly, 37
  natural monopoly, 238
  operating system, 49
  price-discriminating, 22

  regulation of, 52
  rent-seeking, 16
  social loss of, 16
  strong, 4, 22
  vaporware, 49
  weak, 4
monotone-hazard-rate condition (MHRC), 139
monotone-likelihood-ratio condition (MLRC), 286, 292
Morgenstern, 67
multiunit auction, 207, 208
Miyazaki, 259
Myerson, 51, 64, 212, 214

Nalebuff, 112, 114
Nash, 49, 89
natural-gas auction, 238
Nautz, 208, 240
Netscape, 49
Neumann, von, 67
normal good, 153
Novshek, 91, 95

observability, 85, 222
oligopoly, 65
  auctions and oligopoly, 235
  collusion, 131
  excess capacity, 131
  price wars, 132
one-stage-deviation principle, 45, 61
optimal auction, 211, 212, 222
optimization
  equality-constrained, 314
  inequality-constrained, 320
  nonlinear, 311
  unconstrained, 311
order statistics, 339, 344
Ormiston, 148
Osborne, 51, 131
overcapitalization, 54, 55
overemployment, 246

Park, 289
patents, 17
Perloff, 20
Perry, 234, 277
Pesendorfer, 51
phantom bids, 204
Phlips, 50, 91, 132
Pigou, 23
Pitchik, 131
Plant, 17
Plum, 207
Poisson, 297
pooling, 255
pooling equilibrium, 270, 275
Porter, 132, 150, 163
portfolio
  diversification, 156
  selection, 149, 170
  variance-minimizing, 159
portfolio selection, 155
positive selection, 248
Posner, 16, 193
Pratt, 150, 165
Pratt's theorem, 166
price discrimination, 26

and public goods, 34
auctions, 217
bunching, 32
exclusion, 32
first-degree, 23, 36
intertemporal, 36
limits of, 26
nonlinear pricing, 265
second-degree, 24, 36, 259, 265
sorting, 32
third-degree, 24, 36, 217
time-consistent, 40
time-inconsistent, 39
two-part tariff, 23, 33
with a continuum of types, 259
without monopoly, 35
price elasticity of demand, 7
price support, 151
price uncertainty, 150
principal–agent
    multitask problem, 283
principal–agent problem, 80
    first-order approach, 300
Prinz, 164
priority level, 216
private good, 34
product quality, 21
pseudoconcavity, 196, 241
public good, 34, 202

quadratic form, 317
quantity theory of money, 10
quasiconvexity, 329

Rahi, 266
random sales, 121
rationing, 251
    efficient rationing, 123
    parallel rationing, 122
    random rationing, 117, 122
Ravenscraft, 104
Raviv, 207, 299, 300
reaction function
    backward reaction mapping, 91
    Cournot, 70, 126
    Einpassungsfunktion, 91
    inclusive, 91, 94
    Stackelberg, 76
regulation, 54
renegotiation problem, 297
repeated auction, 208
REPO auction, 240
residual demand, 71
revelation principle, 27, 214, 260, 287
revenue equivalence, 187
Reynolds, 102
Riley, 26, 172, 204–208, 212, 258, 260, 308
Riordan, 58, 299
risk aversion
    absolute, 166, 284
    decreasing absolute, 171
    relative, 166
    strong absolute, 168
    wealth-dependent, 171
Robert, 193
Roberts, 95, 108, 267, 277
Robinson, 22, 210

Rogerson, 300
roommate problem, 177
Rosen, 181, 302
Ross, 148, 167
Ross's theorem, 169
Roth, 180, 181
Rothschild, 164, 253, 258
Rubinstein, 45, 51, 235
Ruffin, 107
Russel, 148, 156
Russell, 144

Salant, 102
Salop, 124
Samuelson, 35, 212, 225
Sandmo, 164
Sappington, 57–60, 63, 289
Savage, 135
Scheinkman, 125, 128
Scherer, 25, 104, 131, 132, 211
Schlesinger, 164
Schumpeter, 17
Schwartz, 303
Schwermer, 106
Scoones, 209
Scott, 208
screening, 245, 252, 275
    credit market, 258
    insurance market, 253
    labor market, 258
    limits of, 259
    without competition, 259
second-price auction, 190, 230
selection bias, 226
self-enforcing agreement, 66
Selten, 90–92, 100, 101, 111
Sen, 164
Seo, 163, 170
separating equilibrium, 270
sequential auctions, 208
sequential equilibrium, 267
Shapiro, 51, 110, 111, 164
Shapley, 175, 181
Sharpe, 160
Shavell, 300
Sheshinski, 21
Shleifer, 229
Shubik, 181
Shy, 132
Sibley, 57, 59, 60, 63
signal precision, 294
signaling, 245, 275
    education game, 268
    job market, 268
Simon, 122, 128
Singh, 79, 132
single crossing, 27, 143
Slade, 132
Smith, 222, 302
Sobel, 42, 277
Sonnenschein, 42, 77, 95, 108
sorting, 32
Sotomayor, 180
speculation, 20
Spence, 21, 267
Spencer, 79
Spindt, 208

split-award auction, 208
Stackelberg, von, 67
Stackelberg competition, 67, 74, 79
  Bagwell's criticism, 86
  follower, 69, 74
  leader, 69, 74
  noisy Stackelberg game, 86, 88
  with commitment mechanism, 79
  without commitment mechanism, 76
Staudinger, 52
Stefos, 63
Stewart, 85
Stigler, 16
Stiglitz, 164, 252, 253, 258
stochastic dominance, 135
  applications, 149
  comparative statics, 145
  first-order, 135, 136, 223
  FSD theorem, 137
  hazard-rate, 139
  likelihood ratio, 139
  monotone-hazard-rate condition (MHRC), 139
  monotone-likelihood-ratio condition (MLRC), 139
  normal distribution, 143
  second-order, 135, 140
  single-crossing, 143, 145
  single-crossing distribution, 142
  SSD theorem, 141
  transitivity, 143
  unanimity rule, 135, 140
stochastic similarity, 230
Stokey, 42, 307, 308
Stole, 132
Stolz, 208
strategic voting, 179
Ståhl, 45
Sutton, 47
Switzer, 102
Szidarovszky, 92

Takayama, 63
take-it-or-leave-it sales plan, 23
Tan, 222
taxes
  corrective tax, 15
  deadweight loss of, 14
  inflation tax, 9, 11
  lump-sum tax, 15, 58
Temin, 8
third-price auction, 192
Thisse, 132
Tian, 266
Tirole, 45, 50, 62, 64, 85, 111, 121, 132, 239, 276, 298, 299

total-surplus subsidy, 57
tournament
  under common shocks, 307
  under risk neutrality, 304
tournament game, 304
transformations
  FSD transformation, 146, 147
  of random variables, 144
  single-crossing, 145
  SSD transformation, 146, 148
  stretching, 144
Treasury-bill auction, 239
Tucker, 322

underemployment, 246

van Damme, 273
vaporware, 49
Varian, 50, 96, 97
variance, 340, 341
Vickers, 80
Vickrey auction, 230, 231
Vickson, 148
Vincent, 209
Vishny, 229
Vives, 79, 124, 132
Vogelsang, 59, 64
von Neumann–Morgenstern utility function, 136, 165

Wadhwani, 85
wallet auction, 225
Weber, 206, 209, 228, 234
Weiss, 252, 268
Weitzman, 85
welfare ranking, 77
Whinston, 51, 108, 112
White, 244
Whitmore, 148
Wilson, 42, 51, 228, 252, 258, 268
winner's curse, 225
Wolf, 208
Wright, 20

Xing, 181

Yakowitz, 92
Yao, 208
Yellen, 51
Yitzhaki, 164

Zamir, 234, 235
Zeckhauser, 177
Zhou, 177, 266

Printed in the United Kingdom
by Lightning Source UK Ltd.
100942UKS00001B/31-40